To Ala[n]

From

Rene e Frank.

CHRISTMAS.

1977.

Recycled to
   Clive Burton

      Happy Birthday
         from Charles, Viv
            Laura e Vicky
               November 1998.

# THE SHELL BOOK
## OF
## INLAND WATERWAYS

Cover illustration: *Narrow boats at Thrupp, from a painting by*
*Antony Warren*

# THE SHELL BOOK
# OF
# INLAND WATERWAYS

Hugh McKnight

*Editorial adviser: Charles Hadfield*

## DAVID & CHARLES

NEWTON ABBOT   LONDON

NORTH POMFRET (VT) VANCOUVER

*For June and John Humphries, Clare, Evelyn, Amanda and Diana, ideal companions on many journeys when we discovered the magic of waterways in England, France and Holland.*

ISBN 0 7153 6884 2

Library of Congress Catalog Card Number 74–20470

Set in 10 on 11 pt Ehrhardt
and printed in Great Britain
by Ebenezer Baylis and Son Limited
The Trinity Press Worcester and London
for David & Charles (Holdings) Limited
South Devon House Newton Abbot Devon

Published in the United States of America
by David & Charles Inc
North Pomfret Vermont 05053 USA

Published in Canada
by Douglas David & Charles Limited
3645 McKechnie Drive West Vancouver BC

# Contents

# Introduction

TEN or twelve years ago I used to feel faintly apologetic about my interest in canals, as the very mention of them was apt to produce a slightly glazed expression on the faces of people who had not enjoyed first-hand experience of inland waterways. Canals were, it was popularly supposed, cheerless ribbons of grey water passing through a grey and decayed urban landscape. Both glue factory and gasworks featured prominently in this mental picture. As a transport medium they were hopelessly archaic ('Surely goods don't still travel by canal barge?'); and as for any amenity value . . . 'Well, if you want to spend your holidays on a canal boat, that's your affair old chap'. Kenneth Grahame says much the same in *The Wind in the Willows*: 'The reserved rustic road was presently joined by a shy little brother in the shape of a canal, which took its hand and ambled along by its side in perfect confidence, but with the same tongue-tied, uncommunicative attitude towards strangers.' The Southern Oxford Canal hasn't really changed much.

Of course the Thames has always been better known as a boating centre, and the Broads, too. And the Manchester Ship Canal still generated a sense of wonderment that ocean liners could come inland so far from the sea. But the rest was largely unknown outside the small circle of initiates: 3,000 miles of astonishingly varied navigations, ranging from vast land-bound seas to intimate little streams spanned by age-old humpbacked bridges.

I came to know something of the waterways in an unusual, rather secondhand manner. While still several years away from leaving school, I bought a junior membership of the Inland Waterways Association in 1957. This cost 7s 6d and I debated the pros and cons of such extravagance for several days before finally obtaining a postal order and sending it off with a completed application form. I was attracted by the idea of saving canals, without having much idea of what they should be saved from. While as a family we had always kept a small boat on the Thames, I knew almost nothing about canals and only vaguely suspected that it was possible to travel by water from London to North Wales or Yorkshire. The first waterborne excursion off the Thames followed that same summer when I joined company with a friend's cruiser and we penetrated

10 miles of an enchantingly different world that lay beyond Thames Lock, Weybridge. At the time we thought we were on the Basingstoke Canal, although it subsequently turned out to be the Wey Navigation.

Every quarter (or whenever they could manage to publish) I devoured the latest IWA *Bulletin* and was stirred to learn of the exploits of people whose names were then still words on a printed page. Over the next two or three years I read, learned and determined some day to travel the whole network. But for a long time the nearest approach to this was a trolley-bus ride to the Grand Union at Brentford Gauging Locks, where, almost without fail, I could expect to see row upon row of snub-nosed working narrow boats loading or unloading at the depot. I joined in several working parties when we attacked the wooded banks of the Basingstoke Canal at its weedy junction with the Wey. Then, at Easter 1960, I talked a school friend into cruising from the Thames to Bishop's Stortford and back in my motorised camping dinghy.

We left Shepperton before dawn and watched a misty sun rise as we covered 16 familiar miles down the Thames to Brentford and the mysterious Grand Union Canal. The first surprise came with meeting the Brentford lock-keeper, Harry Barlow. He was friendly, reassuring and extremely helpful. He lent me a windlass for the lock paddles (I had not realised one was required for this section), and gave me a pile of back numbers of the BW house journal. There were narrow boats working the Hanwell Flight, lighters hauled by towpath tractors, and one horsedrawn barge. It took most of the morning to clear the locks and reach the Paddington level, so constant was the traffic. The first night, cold and hungry, we pushed on to Little Venice. Next day found us on the Regent's Canal, which presented unfamiliar views of familiar places through the zoo. Then on into the unknown depths of Islington and the East End. The outboard motor became temperamental. After a fruitless attempt to diagnose a simple fault, I lifted it over the canal's high boundary wall and located a garage in the streets beyond.

We camped the second night alongside a timber yard on the Hertford Union Canal. After that came the industrial reaches of the Lee, then, as now, alive with tugs and lighters. In the cold and rather desolate landscape of the valley we encountered rough but kindly lock-keepers, helped to recover a corpse at Feilde's Weir, and savoured the rural delights of the pretty little River Stort. Returning to the tidal Thames, and by then single-handed, I followed the somewhat rash advice of a Lee lock-keeper to enter London's river via the Limehouse Cut, using coloured cycle-lamps in lieu of proper navigation lights. I soon learned that the Pool at night was no fit place for 12ft camping dinghies. A helpful police launch towed me many miles to the greater safety of the river at Chiswick.

This first real experience of canals, so full of incident, made a fanatical waterways enthusiast of me. I was fortunate to be able to live with several narrow-boat crews for short periods as they carried cargo on the Grand Union and Northern Oxford Canals, and learned more from them in a few days than I could ever have achieved in months of pleasure boating. Then there was the architecture of the waterways – the bridges, locks, aqueducts and tunnels. In due course I was fortunate to be able to earn a full-time living photographing waterways and writing about them, spending as much as fifteen weeks a year travelling on rivers and canals in England, Scotland and Ireland.

Britain's waterways have undergone far-reaching changes since the early hire-cruiser firms were established in the 1950s. A secure future for the system on grounds of amenity value has encouraged large-scale capital investment in boatyards, marinas and a range of facilities undreamed of two decades ago, with restoration projects meeting with great success in all parts of the country. Local and central government, volunteers, the armed services and prisoners are being used to bring back to life navigations that had not seen the passage of a single boat for thirty, fifty or even a hundred years. The demand is growing from boaters, anglers, towpath walkers and the millions who derive simple pleasure from watching the boats pass by on their local stretch of river or canal.

The information in this book must at times inevitably reflect personal attitudes, but I have tried to widen the range of its coverage as much as possible. Throughout, the emphasis is on the waterways themselves, although at various points I have seen fit to mention buildings or places away from the navigation but of interest to the canal or river explorer, whether travelling by water, by car or on foot. Basically it is an account of what exists today, but I have included some of the historical background. The scene is changing. Waterways described as partially derelict in 1974 could be flourishing concerns by the end of the present decade, or earlier. New marinas are being excavated and restaurants opened with startling rapidity.

There are promising new trends in the field of waterborne freight, suggesting that this original function of inland waterways could even become a major contributor to the national transport system again.

This book is divided into two main sections, comprising a series of chapters on specific subjects followed by a gazetteer.

Use of the index will be found helpful to obtain cross-references.

While designed to help your enjoyment of inland waterways, this book is not a practical manual dealing with matters like boat handling, lock operation, lists of boatyards, water points etc. I would like to acknowledge the inspiration and help received from other reference works, notably the invaluable David & Charles series, Canals of the British Isles, largely the work of Charles Hadfield.

During the long gestation of this book, I have been helped and encouraged by many people. Chief of these is Charles Hadfield, my editor, who has patiently vetted the manuscript and made many invaluable suggestions for its improvement. Any faults it possesses are nevertheless entirely my own. To my publishers David & Charles and to Shell Marketing Ltd I am most grateful, not least for commissioning the work in the first place. The charming line illustrations are by Ann Thomson. Throughout, the text is my own, except for Carolyn Barber's wide-ranging contribution on the animal and plant life of the waterways.

In researching material I would especially like to mention officers and staff of the British Waterways Board, Peter Chaplin, Alan H. Faulkner, June and John Humphries, John Liley, the Northern Ireland Tourist Board, Val and Mike Oxley, Julian Plowright and Robert Shopland. Also various friends who have accompanied me both on my own cruiser and on other boats and who never appeared to mind waiting for the light to improve for photography and gladly let me lead them up weedy backwaters in the quest for knowledge. Thanks are due additionally to my colleagues in the Inland Waterways Association and to the members of numerous local societies and boat clubs throughout England and Wales, Scotland and Ireland. I acknowledge also assistance from a number of hire-cruiser organisations, including Frank Baker of Anglo-Welsh Narrow Boats, Market Harborough; Derek Dann of Emerald Star Line Ltd, Carrick-on-Shannon; James Hoseason of Hoseason's Sunshine Holidays, Lowestoft; Gerry Perry of the Ladyline Group, Market Drayton; and Captain Lionel Munk of Maidboats Ltd, Thames Ditton.

I should greatly welcome comments on this edition from readers or suggestions for the improvement of future editions.

*Photographs not otherwise acknowledged are from the author's collection. Line illustrations on pp 32, 106, 114, 158, 172 and 204 are the work of Malcolm Couch; the remainder are by Ann Thompson.*

HUGH McKNIGHT                    *The Clock House*
1974                        *Shepperton-on-Thames*

Brindley

Jessop

Rennie

Telford

# I

# The Making of
# Our Waterways System

I T was not until the flowering of the Canal Age in the closing years of the eighteenth century and the first quarter of the nineteenth that the means had been discovered of moving huge tonnages of freight across the face of the country. This development prompted the exploitation of coal and thus the harnessing of steam to provide the necessary power for an industrial explosion. To appreciate the far-reaching impact of such a change in the British way of life, it is helpful to take a look at inland transport over the preceding centuries.

In prehistoric times natural rivers were the sole method of moving building materials within a region. The first attempt to improve natural conditions came during the Roman occupation of Britain, when rafts and barges were introduced in place of rudimentary dug-out craft hewn from tree trunks. The Romans cut several artificial navigations such as the Foss Dyke, between the Trent and the Witham at Lincoln; the Car Dyke from there to Peterborough; and the Itchen Dyke, connecting Winchester with the South Coast. For nearly a thousand years following the collapse of Roman power little more was done.

In the reign of Henry I, *c*1121, the Foss Dyke was scoured out, and in the centuries that followed a gradual awakening to the possibilities of waterway engineering produced workable navigations like the River Lee (*c*1425), the Essex Stour (*c*1504) and the Welland (*c*1571). These were able to pass small barges.

In 1566 a short length of lateral canal alongside the Exe was opened to Exeter. This featured the first pound locks in Britain and showed that an efficient means of overcoming changes in level was practicable. Pound locks in the western world are first recorded in Holland in 1373 (see p 35).

Throughout the seventeenth century various rivers were canalised, using pound locks, navigation weirs or a combination of the two. The Hampshire Avon, Upper Thames to Oxford, Wey Navigation and Great Ouse all belong to this period. Development was generally based on demands from merchants and traders, who formed companies to promote the works in the expectation of improved transport and profits from tolls.

In the 1660s Andrew Yarranton, born in 1616, evolved a plan to make the Worcestershire Stour navigable between Stourport-on-Severn and Stourbridge, with a canal from there to join the Trent. He was paid £1,300 for a finished section from Kidderminster to Stourbridge, along which quantities of coal were conveyed.

Such concerns were nationally insignificant, and brought trading benefits only to strictly localised areas. On the other hand, certain rivers like the Severn were highly prosperous in the seventeenth century. This waterway generated more traffic at that time than any other water highway in Europe with the exception of the Meuse. But few towns were fortunate in being sited within reach of navigations like these. The transport costs of coal in most areas before the Canal Age were so high that delivery was normally restricted to a radius of 12 miles from the pits. In the mid-eighteenth century, coal consumption in England did not exceed 6 million tons a year. Before road improvements pioneered by Macadam (1756–1836), packhorse carriage of coal cost 2s 6d per ton per mile. Thus, Midlands coal delivered to London bore a transport charge of £10–£15 per ton compared with 6s–7s per ton when taken by canal or railway in the later nineteenth century.

Canal building was initially slow to develop, although solutions to most of the major engineering problems had been found during the construction of Riquet's magnificent coast to coast Canal du Midi in Southern France, finished in 1681. Britain's first truly long-distance canal with locks was the Newry, running for 18½ miles between the Upper Bann and Newry Harbour on the east coast of Ulster. There were fourteen pound locks, each 44ft × 15ft 6in. Building lasted from 1729 to 1742. Next to be finished was the St Helens Canal (Sankey Brook), which entered the northern shore of the Mersey; this had ten locks, including a two-rise staircase and ran for 8 miles. It was opened in 1757, two years before work began on the most famous canal of all, the Bridgewater. This really captured the public's imagination, eventually produced a fortune for its promotor, the third Duke of Bridgewater, established James Brindley as the popular architect of the British canal system (a reputation he scarcely deserved) and began an extensive network of canals during the following 70 years.

The Duke and his land agent, John Gilbert, employed Brindley to create a waterway connecting the ducal coal mines at Worsley with Manchester. The first section was

*Detail from a drawing published in 1824*

opened in 1761 and included a daringly conceived stone aqueduct carrying the Bridgewater Canal over the River Irwell at Barton (see pp 67 and 249).

James Brindley (1716–72) set up business as a millwright at Leek, Staffordshire in 1742 and gained much experience in water engineering as a result. The adulation he attracted is evident in a letter written at Burslem in 1767 while work was in progress on the Trent and Mersey Canal at Harecastle tunnel:

> Gentlemen come to see our eighth wonder of the world – the subterraneous navigation, which is cutting by the great Mr Brindley, who handles rocks as easily as you would plum-pies, and makes the four elements subservient to his will. He has cut a mile through bogs, which he binds up, embanking them with stones which he gets out of the other parts of the navigation, besides about a quarter of a mile into the hill Yelden; on the other side of which he has a pump, which is worked by water, and a stove, the fire of which sucks through a pipe the damps that would annoy the men who are cutting towards the centre of the hill.

Two canals – the central and eastern sections of the Trent and Mersey, completed after his death, and the Bridgewater – were wholly his work. Numerous other canal companies employed him as consultant, but the detailed planning was mainly the responsibility of other men. In practice he seems to have been rather unreliable, no doubt because of the volume of commissions he accepted.

Encouraged by the success of the Bridgewater, many joint-stock companies were established under Act of Parliament to bring industrial prosperity through inland navigation. A public meeting would be held and private finance subscribed by leading personalities. As most projects were devised in isolation, a situation developed whereby canals were designed to varying gauges, from narrow routes capable of passing boats with a payload of less than 30 tons to wide-beam barge waterways. This lack of uniformity eventually led to the commercial decline of inland water transport in all but specially favoured regions. Another disadvantage of the system was a general absence of national cooperation in the matter of quoting through-tolls over the lines of several rival concerns.

After Brindley came a host of engineers, some of whom acquired a nationwide reputation and played their part in laying out the lines of waterways in all parts of the kingdom. Most celebrated is Thomas Telford (1757–1834). It was he who steered the canals through their final flowering and expansion. His greatest works are the Birmingham and Liverpool section of the Shropshire Union and the Caledonian. William Jessop (1745–1814) was a little older than Telford but often worked with him, and should correctly be given much of the credit for structures such as Pontcysyllte aqueduct. Jessop's most notable achievement is perhaps the Grand Junction Canal (now Grand Union) between London and the Midlands. John Rennie (1761–1821) numbered the Kennet and Avon and the Lancaster among his achievements; he and Jessop appear to have had a distinct dislike of narrowboat canals, most of his navigations being wide-beam barge waterways. Additionally there were many lesser known men whose works have endured. Benjamin Outram (1764–1805) designed the Peak Forest, Derby and Huddersfield Canals, Robert Mylne had a hand in the Gloucester and Sharpness Ship Canal, and James Green (1781–1849) constructed various forms of lift instead of locks on navigations in the West Country.

Experience was to prove that canals were normally of great benefit to a locality, in spite of some early doubts. Canal building was at its most intense during the 1790s, and the interconnected waterways network of England and Wales was mostly complete by the mid-1830s, leaving few important towns more than 10 miles from navigable water.

In Ireland a rural economy failed to generate heavy traffic on a system that extended from the Shannon to the northeast and to Dublin and Waterford. The ill-fated Ballinamore and Ballyconnell Canal between the headwaters of the Shannon and Lough Erne was finally finished in 1859, new works on the Shannon in 1850, and the Erne was fully navigable in 1890.

Scotland featured a network between Edinburgh and Glasgow, comprising the Forth and Clyde, Monkland and Union Canals. Two of this country's best-known surviving waterways, the Crinan and Caledonian, were designed to reduce sailing times for small ships, but, running from one coast to another, they enjoyed none of the benefits of canals forming part of a system. In Scotland there was considerable Government aid with building costs, contrary to the normal practice of private investment employed in England and Wales.

Instead of being used to update and improve rivers and canals throughout the nineteenth century, funds were directed to the more exciting and virile new railways. A long and depressing catalogue of abandonments began in 1836, when the Croydon Canal was converted into a railway. After the 1850s the most vulnerable routes fell into disuse, a process that has continued well into the period since

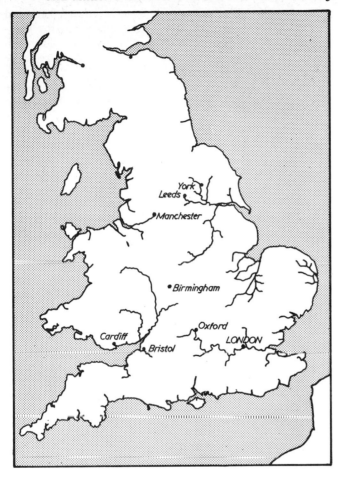

*The extent of the water-
ways system in England
and Wales in 1760*

World War II.

Some development did halt the decline, notably on routes that remained independent, such as the Aire and Calder, Weaver Navigation, Grand Union and Manchester Ship Canal. The MSC, still Britain's largest and most profitable commercial waterway, signalled the virtual end of new canal construction in Britain when it was opened in 1894. Since that date, additions have been confined to short cuts and branches.

About half of Britain's waterways were nationalised in 1948. Since the 1960s, a new role in terms of amenity development has been officially recognised. Although there is never enough public money available for the optimum

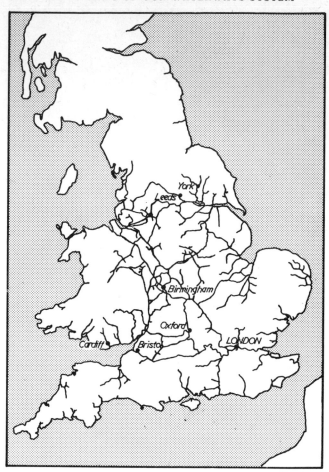

*The extent of the water-
ways system in England
and Wales in 1850*

level of maintenance to be carried out, all those routes
currently used by boats can be regarded as reasonably safe.
Several million people enjoy inland boating in Britain at
some time during the year. In certain favoured areas a
limited commercial revival is taking place (p 154), but so
far not on as ambitious a scale as throughout the rest of
Europe.

Events of the last two decades clearly show that our
waterways are entering a new age of prosperity.

Never has there been so much constructive enthusiasm
for inland navigation since men like Brindley, Telford and
Jessop mounted their horses and set out to scatter a web of
watery ribbons across Britain's fields and hillsides.

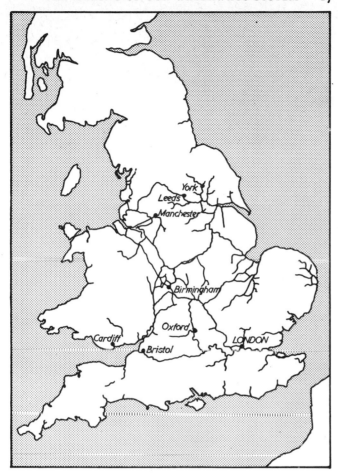

*Waterways navigable in
1975 or likely to be
within a short time*

*Napton Locks on the Oxford Canal*

# 2

# *Cuts across the Country*

TODAY we are so used to the upheaval of motorway construction, to the rapid expansion of towns and to fast efficient inland transport, that it is difficult to appreciate the impact the arrival of canals must have made on rural communities in the latter part of the eighteenth century. Most people then lived in villages or small towns, where the pattern of everyday life had changed very little for generations. Arrival of a bold new navigation, bringing boatloads of raw materials for emergent industries and permitting the transfer of manufactured goods and passengers from one part of the country to another, had a profound effect on their lives.

Once a scheme for a new navigation had been promoted, the necessary Parliamentary Acts obtained and the finance raised, work would begin on construction. In the earliest years of the canal era there were few precedents on which engineers and contractors could draw. True, experience had been gained in tunnelling from the mines and from water engineers practised in the art of building watermills, and a tradition of drainage engineering existed from the Commissions of Sewers at the time of Henry VIII and from the Dutchman Cornelius Vermuyden, who came to England around 1620 and later drained the Fens. Craftsmen carpenters, masons and bricklayers were also available for the various bridges, locks, warehouses and other structures that were necessary. But canal technology was an art in its infancy.

The notion of giant contracting concerns was still many years in the future, so that the canal engineers would divide responsibility for building the line into short sections of perhaps 15 or 20 miles each. Work would proceed at several points simultaneously, producing a consequent variation in design of buildings and equipment. Local materials close at hand were used. Thus, most original bridges over the southernmost part of the Oxford Canal are of Cotswold stone, but as you approach Banbury, red brick is used more frequently, until it has become the standard material by the time the Warwickshire border is crossed.

The first stage in canal building was a detailed survey of the ground. Local maps were not wholly reliable. Compulsory purchase powers had to be sought where agreement could not be reached with influential landowners, or estates or buildings had to be by-passed. At this juncture the canal's route could be physically pegged out on the ground. The earliest canals, such as the Trent and Mersey, Oxford, Staffs and Worcs and the original Birmingham Canal, closely followed the contours of the landscape, thereby avoiding expensive excavation. That the route was consequently rather longer was not regarded as any particular disadvantage, for it served more towns and villages between its terminal points. It was not until road and railway became rivals that canals were built for maximum speed, along the most direct line. By this stage – the 1820s and 1830s – techniques had advanced to an extent where the Birmingham and Liverpool Junction section of the Shropshire Union, the realigned Northern Oxford and the Macclesfield Canal were built so that locks were avoided wherever possible or grouped into close flights, and the fullest use was made of massive embankments and cuttings.

Once the line had been staked out, the real labour of manual digging could begin. Great gangs of men used picks and shovels, carting away the dirt in hand barrows wheeled along plankways. Sometimes horses were brought in to assist, either in hauling containers of spoil from the workings or pulling trucks along tramways. Once a reasonable length had been completed, water could be admitted and boats used to carry away earth or bring in bricks, stone and timber. The men soon earned the title of 'navigators'. The navvy remains with us to the present day, probably quite unaware of the derivation of the term. Initially, gangs were recruited from what labour was available in the locality. When the job was finished, they would return to farm work, while a few might find new employment on the canal or the trading boats. As waterway construction mushroomed towards the peak of the canal mania in the 1790s, gangs of experienced navvies moved from one work site to another. It was an incredibly tough life, even by the standards of the day. Accidents were common. There were few benefits available to those who were injured, although canal companies did from time to time make small payments to sustain workers who had become temporarily unfit.

One estimate of the size of this workforce in the 1790s suggests that about 50,000 navvies were involved in all parts of the country. Six hundred were engaged at the original Harecastle tunnel alone. It needs little imagination to understand that the impact of these gangs on small rural communities was very considerable. Farmers and smallholders lived in fear of their crops and animals being plundered. There was rape, theft, murder and endless disputes over questions of trespass and damage. By no means everyone suffered, however; for anyone with a keen sense of business opportunities there was money to be made from the canal builders. The landlord of a public house fortunate enough to be alongside the workings would find his takings multiplying overnight. The men required supplies of food and clothing, and they had many opportunities to spend what little they earned. Average rates for labourers varied from 1s to 1s 6d a day in 1770, while a skilled carpenter making lock gates might receive 11s a week. There were occasional added benefits, such as the free ale often supplied by a contractor. At times cash in small denominations was in short supply, so special tokens were issued in lieu of wages. These were accepted by local shopkeepers, inns and other traders and would be redeemed by the canal company for real money.

Money was a major preoccupation at all levels of the canal industry. The company paid its contractors at an agreed rate – so much per yard for tunnelling, for building a given number of bridges or locks, or for completing a specified length of channel. Out of this sum workmen's wages had to be found, tools and equipment bought and transport costs on building materials paid. Small wonder, therefore, that the standard gauge of the English canals of the Midlands was based on the 30-ton narrow boat, and locks, bridge holes, tunnels and aqueducts were built to fit these craft of 7ft beam. The great majority of British navigations were born of private enterprise. Exceptions were the Government-financed Caledonian Canal, Weaver Navigation (Cheshire County) and most waterways in Ireland. Canal and river construction work on the Continent was generally undertaken directly by the State, with the result that locks of bigger capacity enabled profitable transport operations to continue far beyond the period at which many of our own navigations fell into commercial decline. Some British companies and their engineers did appreciate the advantages of barge canals – notably men like Jessop (Grand Junction Canal) and Rennie (Kennet and Avon) – but most of our waterways were designed to a narrow shallow profile.

After digging the canal bed, it had to be lined with loam and clay that had been worked together to form a watertight 'puddle' or seal. This was spread over the flat bottom and sloping sides of the workings, 18in to 3ft thick, depending on the nature of the terrain. Reputedly it was worked into position by the feet of the navvies. There are also accounts of herds of cattle or sheep being driven along the bed to consolidate the lining. Sometimes the banks were protected from erosion by slabs of rock or retaining walls in brick or stone. Most commonly such methods seen today result from

*A detail from an early nineteenth-century engraving showing the design and construction of a typical cast-iron aqueduct*

later improvements or mark the site of particularly unstable lengths, such as approaches to aqueducts or embankments.

In addition to the constructional work considerable sums of money had to be spent on rebuilding roads whose courses were diverted or interrupted by the coming of the canal. Every small stream or river that could not be fed into the new watercourse had to be enclosed in a culvert or spanned by an aqueduct. Public rights of way along footpaths had to be maintained. In the Grand Union village of Cosgrove the canal is raised on a low embankment that is pierced by a narrow pedestrian tunnel. Farmers whose fields were bisected by the navigation would need accommodation bridges to enable stock to be transferred from one side to the other. A multitude of finishing touches included planting of boundary hedges, erection of stone or iron markers indicating the extent of company property, building of safety fences or railings, marking the miles, bridges and locks with appropriate plates in numerical sequence and protecting the angles of bridges, lock approaches and buildings with iron guards against towline abrasion.

Almost every canal in Britain was designed with a horse towpath. In a few isolated instances, such as parts of the Birmingham Canals where traffic was exceptionally heavy, this was duplicated on each side of the channel. Broken rubble, small stones or bricks, chalk or flints were compacted into its surface, which was then dressed with earth or gravel.

Originally most river navigations were without towpaths or haling ways, for barges moved under sail in favourable winds or were pulled by gangs of 'bow hauliers' – men heaving on ropes and making their way along the waterline as best they could. Obviously this was unsatisfactory, so paths were added in due course where needed. This improvement attracted some opposition on navigations where barges had passed toll-free. On the Severn four towing-path companies were established towards the end of the eighteenth century. Various additions were made to the 24 miles between Bewdley and Coalbrookdale, with charges varying between 6d and 1s per horse per mile. Where the path changed from one bank of the river to the other, horse ferries were used. On canalised rivers such as the Thames, Wey and Soar, wooden trestle bridges were built to carry the path over side streams or where, for example, a weir channel rejoined the navigation at the lower end of a lock cut. With the introduction of steam tugs and subsequently self-powered barges, a number of the river paths fell into disrepair, a trend that was hastened on the Thames in the 1930s and 1950s by discontinuation of ferry services. This was an unfortunate tendency, for many delightful long-distance riverside walks

are now no longer available. Most canal towpaths, inciden-
tally, while not specifically designated as rights of way,
provide excellent traffic-free footpaths. Canal towpaths are
generally divided from the adjoining fields or premises by
walls, fences or hedges. On rivers this was rarely the case,
and fences would cross the path at intervals, extending a short
way out into the navigation. Sometimes there were gates to
allow boat horses to pass; towing animals working over
many waterways in the Fens and Eastern counties were
trained to jump over stiles up to 2ft 7in high, not infrequently suffering injury.

When you think of cuttings and embankments, canals
with which Thomas Telford was associated immediately
come to mind. He was a master of bold construction techniques, as evidenced by the Shropshire Union. The difficulties
of stabilising Shelmore Embankment near Norbury Junction
doubtless contributed to his death in 1834, just six months
before the 5½-year work was completed and the first boat
could pass northwards from Autherley to join the old
Chester Canal at Nantwich. Reinforced concrete retaining
walls not being known, hundreds of thousands of tons of
marl and soil that had mostly been excavated from the soaring Grub Street cutting to the north were tipped to form
embankments. Specially selected grasses were planted to
bind the mountain of soil together. Such works, once successfully finished, have stood the test of time well, although
vigilance is always necessary to spot a potential weakness
that can grow into a major breach. Probably the outstanding
canal embankment in Britain is the one that carries the
Leeds and Liverpool for half a mile through Burnley at
rooftop level. Other notable cuttings include those on the
southern Shropshire Union (Woodseaves is a mile long and
rises to a depth of 90ft), and Galton cutting on the Birmingham main line of the BCN at Smethwick, 70ft deep and
spanned by the elegant iron Galton Bridge of 1829.

Dramatic feats of engineering apart, the average British
canal looks much more a natural river than anything designed by man from raw earth. Even in the heart of towns,
the dark sluggish water has become an integral element of
the landscape, fringed by mature trees, wildflowers and an
assortment of small creatures. To appreciate how these
peaceful byways must first have looked, you must travel on
the great barge routes of Holland, France and Germany
that have been built or enlarged since the last war. As carriers
of freight they are superbly efficient, but for peaceful holiday
cruising most people would prefer the intimate scale of the
reedy Barrow Navigation, the shady beauty of the River Ure
or the wide expanses of the Caledonian Canal.

*Stretham pumping engine on the Old West River section of the Great Ouse*

# 3
# *Water Supply*

THE subject that will least occupy the mind of canal boater, towpath walker and even the angler, is where the water comes from. It is only in times of prolonged drought or when a section of bank collapses, that the vital question of water supply suggests itself. But, both to the original engineers and to the present-day maintenance staffs, the stabilising of levels requires constant effort and vigilance.

River navigations in Britain rarely suffer from a lack of water, for with well-planned weirs it is virtually unknown for such waterways to run so dry in summer as to prevent the passage of boats. But should works fall into disrepair and the weirs become broken down, shallows soon appear, and once flourishing rivers can revert to their original state, useless for boats larger than canoes. The mighty River Wye was once navigable for substantial barges upstream from the Severn to Hay, a distance of almost 100 miles. But for a century or longer, except for a few short sections, only craft that can be manhandled over obstacles and through rapids can travel any distance. Much the same applied until very recent times to the Upper Avon from Evesham to Stratford, but here the situation has been reversed by rebuilding locks and weirs.

The rivers of Scotland, being in the main fast-flowing down steep gradients over boulder-strewn beds, prevented any efforts to bring inland navigation to all but the lowest reaches, except for those canals that were constructed as coast links or to serve specific local needs. One exception is the linking of the Forth and Clyde, Union and Monkland Canals.

The British climate, with plentiful rainfall, does however result in not infrequent flooding of natural watercourses. Navigations whose rise and fall can vary very considerably from one day to another include the Trent, Thames and Nene. Warning notices can appear in almost any month on Thames locks advising pleasure craft to exercise care in passing weirs. The Nene was fitted in the 1930s with guillotine gates at the lower ends of its locks so that it could dispel surplus water as rapidly as possible. Canals, properly engineered and cared for, offer more reliable year-round navigation than do rivers.

Apart from navigation considerations, British rivers are

very important suppliers of water to industry and the domestic user. As the demand for water increases annually, water conservation will become more and more important. In future we can expect a greater degree of interdependence between water-based recreation and water supply; the trend now is for both functions to be managed by the same broad group of authorities.

It is also essential to reduce the pollution that has grown with 200 years of industrial development. Expensive though it may be, unpurified sewage, factory waste and chemical contamination from all kinds of sources must be checked, if the water of our rivers is to be fit for domestic use and the natural wild life of the countryside conserved for everyone to enjoy. At last this has been grasped to the extent that rivers until recently so dirty that no fish, animal or plant life could exist have again begun to support a flora and fauna.

Some canals have a constant and reliable water supply. The Welsh section of the Shropshire Union (Llangollen Canal) is fed for its 46 miles by the bountiful River Dee, dammed at Llantysilio, and partly diverted through a valve house at the canal head. The waterway acts as a carrier of about 6 million gallons a day, much of which is stored in reservoirs at Hurleston for domestic use. The main line of the Shropshire Union from Nantwich to the Manchester Ship Canal junction at Ellesmere Port also relies on the Llangollen for water supplies; so did the eastern part of the Montgomeryshire Canal until its closure, and will once more in the likely event of its reopening. Following the course of natural lochs for most of its length, the Caledonian enjoys limitless water supplies in each direction from the summit at Loch Oich.

Another reliable system is used by canals that follow the line of natural rivers and take their water supplies at periodic junctions made on the level. Such lateral canals are normally possible only in the lower reaches of navigations; the principle obviously cannot be used where a watershed is crossed at the canal's summit. Good examples are the Southern Oxford Canal, accompanied for most of its route from near Banbury to the Thames by the River Cherwell, with level crossings at Aynho Weir Lock and for a considerable distance north of Shipton Weir Lock. Again, on the southern end of the Trent and Mersey, the Trent acts as a direct feeder, its course being the navigation channel for several hundred yards downhill of Alrewas. The Wey Navigation between Ripley and Weybridge Town Lock is similarly a lateral canal, fed by the River Wey above Walsham Gates, a flood lock. Similarly, the Grand Union's Leicester section only gradually changes from a lateral canal to a river navigation as it follows the line of the River Soar. The same is true

of the Sheffield and South Yorkshire Navigation's association
with the River Don.

Ideally, the summit of a canal is fed by constant supplies
from streams or small rivers, many of which have been per-
suaded to flow into a catchment reservoir. Sluices linked
directly with the canal, or with a feeder where the reservoir
is remote from the navigation, allow water to be run off into
the canal as necessary. The summit reservoirs of the Leeds
and Liverpool at Foulridge and Barrowford, those of the
Grand Union at Tring, or those near the top of the Worcester
and Birmingham's Tardebigge Flight are all good examples.
Additionally there are sometimes storage reservoirs of rainfall
which can be held for later use during the droughts of
summer and autumn. These artificial lakes were constructed
in a similar way to a canal bed, the bottom and sides being
protected by 'puddle'; elsewhere banks are lined with brick
or stone. The Welsh Harp, fed by the River Brent near
Wembley, is an important water supplier for the lower Grand
Union and Paddington Arm. Like an increasing number of
canal reservoirs, it is extensively used for sailing and other
boating activities. The Caldon Canal's main feeder, Lake
Rudyard, is similarly serving a dual purpose. Some of the
best coarse fishing is to be had in canal reservoirs. Many are
also important breeding grounds for a wide range of waterfowl, one example being at Marsworth in Hertfordshire.

These flooded valleys or areas of impounded water are often
situated in isolated localities, distant from towns, villages or
even surfaced roads. The job of maintaining levels, drawing
off supplies to the canal and tending the banks is a lonely but
responsible one. The greatest efforts coincide with the worst
of winter's rain and melting snow. Contracts to supply water
to countless factories, power stations and other industrial
plants involve skilful checking of gauges, drawing of paddles
and conservation. Poor water supplies contributed to the
death of the Thames and Severn Canal; others would have
followed for the same reason had not additional reservoirs
been constructed to meet the need. Commercial traffic was
often held up on the upper sections of canals for lack of
water towards the end of a dry summer. Growth of pleasure
boating in recent years has brought about the same danger,
particularly on the summits of the Leeds and Liverpool and
Southern Oxford Canals. For economising water in working
locks see pp 41–2.

If a flood season is causing dangerous rises in water levels,
flood paddles can be opened to release the surplus into a
convenient stream or river. Water can be passed to a lower
section of the canal by drawing paddles at each end of the
locks, or relying on bypass weirs alongside many lock

chambers. To prevent breaking of banks, overspill automatic weirs are often built. These simple devices comprise a section of concrete bank below the top of the retaining banks, frequently with stop plank grooves, enabling the level at which these weirs function to be altered. The danger of breached banks applies most particularly to embankments and aqueducts. Stop planks can be inserted at narrows at each end of such structures, so that they can be isolated from the rest of the canal in the event of trouble. Stop planks can be handled by a couple of maintenance men where the canal width is a little over 7ft, but on broad waterways lifting apparatus is required. Another safety device was the stop gate, much like a single lock gate across the navigation, which was closed (in theory) by any undue flow of water, although from the appearance of those that remain, it is doubtful if they would respond without help in an emergency. Examples occur on the Shropshire Union by Nantwich Basin, and on the Worcester and Birmingham near Edgbaston. The long level of the Bridgewater Canal from Leigh to Manchester is protected at regular intervals by complete gates lying on the bank but attached to a small manually operated iron and timber crane of a design almost as old as the canal itself.

If prompt action is not taken to isolate the length, a small hole is rapidly torn into a great crater through which huge coping stones, tons of sludge and possibly millions of gallons of water rush. The best preventive measure that can be taken is strong bank protection in timber, asbestos, rock, brick or interlocking steel piles. Concrete piles with a continuous run of concrete capping were widely used on the Grand Union system from the 1930s to the 1950s.

While every care is taken to avoid the collapse of canal banks, serious breaches do take place from time to time, requiring closure of the navigation until repairs have been completed. One such accident took place in September 1945, when the Welsh section of the Shropshire Union Canal was breached at Sun Bank Halt, two miles from Llangollen. Hundreds of tons of water poured down the valley side, tearing a 40yd crater 50ft deep in the Ruabon–Barmouth branch of the Great Western Railway. A mail and newspaper train composed of sixteen wagons and two vans was thrown from the unsupported rails, burst into flames and burned furiously for seven hours.

Canals are an important part of the drainage system for the areas through which they pass. Today this can present disadvantages, among them contaminated supplies from factory and sewerage outfalls, and pollution resulting from surface drainage of main roads and the streets of our cities. The old canal companies sometimes seemed to care very little about

*High Peak steam pumping station, now restored to working order, lifts water from the River Derwent to feed an isolated 5-mile section of the Cromford Canal*

the quality of water entering the system as long as boats could float in it! One class of artificial inland navigation, designed not so much for the passage of boats as for land drainage, can be found in the flat eastern part of England, especially in the Fens of East Anglia. Most of the complex Middle Level Navigations resulted from land drainage schemes, like the Witham Navigable Drains near Boston, built for flood prevention and improvement of potential agricultural land. Characteristic of these watercourses are their high banks, dead straight routes for mile after mile and luxuriant weed in summer. For lovers of flat bracing scenery, they do offer interesting cruising, and some of the navigable drains provide most useful links in the national network; but they do not offer the charm or interest of locks, bridges, tunnels and aqueducts.

*Towering over the River Yare is the Berney Arms mill with 24ft scoopwheel at its base*

The Dutch played an important part in the draining of the Fenlands of East Anglia, bringing with them water-pumping techniques common in the Low Countries. The first windmills adapted from grinding corn to pumping water appeared in Holland in the fourteenth century and it seems likely that they were tried in the English Fenlands from the middle of the fifteenth century. Fierce disputes sometimes resulted from these 'engines' or windmills draining one parcel of land by transferring water to that of a neighbour!

The typical Fen windmill was built of timber throughout and normally had four sails. Until about 1772 the sails were covered with canvas, which could not be adjusted without stopping the mill. Later a spring sail with shutters was introduced, enabling changes in wind direction and pressure to be allowed for while the machinery was still in motion. A brick trough outside the main mill structure housed a large scoop wheel protected by a wooden cover, and this wheel pumped the water. The scoop could lift through a height roughly equivalent to one-fifth of its diameter. In practice the lift was about 4ft, with the largest recorded scoop wheel being 25ft across. The mills provided housing for the keeper and his family, and in the early nineteenth century cost rather more than £1,000 to build. The best of them could pump 2,000cu ft of water per minute and drain about 1,000 acres of land. But they could not cope with severe flood water or operate over the change of levels that steam-driven engines dealt with. Gradually they declined, being replaced first by steam and then diesel pumps. The last surviving Fen drainage windmill, built for use at Adventurer's Fen, has been preserved at the nearby Wicken Fen, a National Trust Nature Reserve, where the pattern of vegetation and wild life re-creates the appearance of the Fens before their large-scale reclamation for agriculture. This mill is periodically used for pumping water *into* the dykes to prevent the Reserve from drying out; its modern use is thus a reversal of the original plan. Wicken Fen lies a short distance to the east of the River Cam at Upware.

Another, considerably more impressive, pumping mill stands on the banks of the River Yare at Berney Arms, Reedham, Norfolk. Now maintained by the Department of the Environment, it dates from about 1870. The main structure is of tarred brick, with a revolving top that automatically turns to direct the sails into the eye of the wind.

Wind power was rarely used to supply canals with water. One exception was a six-sailed pump used on the Thames and Severn Canal in its earliest days to lift water from a well at Thames Head. But it seems to have been replaced in 1791 by a Watt single-acting steam engine.

The engineer Rennie built a water-driven pump to feed the Kennet and Avon Canal at Claverton. It was planned to augment supplies to the 9-mile pound east of Bath locks, whose existing feeders already included the Wilts and Berks and Somerset Coal Canals, Crofton pumping station and a gravity feed at Seend. When first put to work in 1813, the Claverton pump was capable of delivering 100,000 gallons per hour from the River Avon 53ft below. A breast-shot wheel, 25ft wide and over 19ft in diameter, was supported on bearings at each end; later modifications were made to reduce the great weight on the bearings, so that now what are virtually two wheels on a common shaft can be seen. A leat from the Avon (once supplying a grist mill on the same site) leads water to a sluice and paddle gear. Beginning in 1969, volunteers from Bath University of Technology and members of the Kennet and Avon Canal Trust have restored the Claverton pump, which can now be seen operating at certain weekends. The public are welcome to visit this lovely building in yellow Bath stone in its magnificent Avon Valley setting.

The steam-driven water pump was the most common solution to the problem of conveying water to a canal summit where gravity supplies were not available. One of the best remaining examples, like Claverton, is also on the Kennet and Avon, at Crofton to the west of Bruce tunnel. There are two Boulton & Watt beam engines, one of them dating from 1801 and thus the oldest operational engine of its type in the world. The other was installed in 1810. When first operated, the engines used Watt's patented condensing cycle and were self-acting; the steam was generated in three boilers, two of them always in use and the other acting as standby. In 1844 two Cornish boilers were installed, but these were replaced in 1890 by the present pair of ex-GWR boilers, which are thought to have been removed from a pumping station on the Severn railway tunnel. No 1 pump continued to operate until April 1958, when an electric pump took over.

Aware of the great historical importance of the building and its steam machinery, members of the Kennet and Avon Canal Trust acquired Crofton from the British Waterways Board and used voluntary labour and expertise to recondition the engines. Since 1970 first one and later both may be seen at work during certain weekends throughout the year. The plume of smoke rising from the tall chimney and slow deep thud of the engines, bright in polished brass and iron, makes Crofton a thrilling place to visit. Considerable amounts of money have been raised from admission charges, and these sums are to be devoted to the canal's restoration.

Crofton's supplies are lifted 40ft from Wilton Water, a natural reservoir fed by a small river and with a capacity of about 4½ million gallons.

An ornamental chimney halfway up the Widcombe Flight and a derelict pumphouse near the junction with the River Avon are relics of another two steam pumps on this canal.

Other steam pumps still at work include Stretham Engine on the Old West River section of the Great Ouse, several miles from the Cam junction, and Leawood Mill pumping station on an isolated length of the Cromford Canal, where volunteer restoration began in 1972. Elsewhere, tall chimneys alongside ruined engine houses bear witness to vanished steam pumps: several are scattered throughout the Birmingham Canal Navigations and one on the Coventry Canal at Hawkesbury. (The Hawkesbury engine is preserved in Dartmouth.) Diesel or electric machinery can be used purely when required at short notice and calls for rather less maintenance. The Grand Union Canal's Wendover Arm at Tringford and the Sheffield and South Yorkshire Navigation's highest level, Sheffield Basin to Tinsley Top Lock, are fed by diesel pumps. Lonely diesel plants scattered throughout Fen waterways receive fuel supplies in certain instances from a small tanker barge, *Shellfen*, based at Ely.

The most unfortunate water supply story is the history of the Cong Canal, County Mayo, Western Ireland. The 3-mile navigation designed to link Lough Corrib with Lough Mask was five years in the building during the 1850s. Four stone-walled locks, commodious quays and other works were completed, but when the water was admitted to the channel at one end, it escaped through rock fissures long before the other end had even become damp! In those days before modern sealing techniques utilising polythene sheeting were available, every effort to make the canal watertight met with failure. The Cong Canal remains to this day substantially intact, a memorial to the unfortunate engineer whose navigation never saw the passage of even one boat.

*Bratch Locks, Staffordshire & Worcestershire Canal*

# 4
# Locks and Lifts

WITHOUT some means of overcoming changes in level, few natural rivers in Britain would be navigable much beyond their tidal reaches, while a network of canals such as we know today would be unthinkable. The technology of waterway construction in its earliest phases relies heavily on the use of contour canals to avoid hills (eg the Southern Oxford summit and the Leeds and Liverpool west of Gargrave) but this solution adds costly mileage to the route and only answers certain problems. Cuttings, embankments, tunnels and aqueducts are all alternative methods of overcoming obstacles presented by the face of the landscape. But the most ingenious, widespread and (to our eyes) obvious answer is the lock.

There is a wealth of variety in lock design. The chambers themselves, their gates, paddle machinery, walkways, side weirs, footbridges and name or number plates are a rich architectural heritage resulting from the work of dozens of local designers and contractors, working for scores of individual navigation companies over a span of more than four centuries.

## FLASH LOCKS

Early British river navigations were frequently obstructed by weirs either built to provide a head of water for milling purposes or to trap fish in nets or baskets. Both activities interfered seriously with movement of boats, and the conflicting interests caused endless bad feeling and disputes. One partial solution was to construct a movable section in the weir formed of small wooden flats (known as 'rimers' and 'paddles') on a framework, and another was to arrange an opening gate or door through which traffic could pass when river levels had sufficiently built up or decreased. These methods had many obvious disadvantages, for long delays would occur while the level over several miles of river changed, often interfering with the flow to mill wheels, and downhill boats would in effect shoot the rapids at considerable danger to themselves and the weir structure, while those heading upstream would have to be winched up a strong current. A survival of the technique, although installed for different reasons, can be seen in the hand-operated winches placed on each side of the West Stockwith Lock (where the Chesterfield Canal joins the tidal Trent); these were intended to assist sailing keels and other unmotorised barges to leave the river when there was a strong flow.

More sophisticated flash-lock designs gradually evolved under such names as navigation weirs (Thames), water gates (Warwickshire Avon), staunches (East Anglia) and half locks. Those on the River Nene and Fenland tributaries of the Great Ouse, dating in some instances from the early seventeenth century, used guillotine gates set in a wooden frame and operated by various methods, including huge spoked wheels driving a chain connected with toothed drums. The reach of river affected by Orton Staunch on the Nene above Peterborough was 3 miles, which resulted in frequent delays of a day and occasionally as much as a week, unless boats moved in convoy.

Until about the mid-nineteenth century Fen lighters would carry their own staunching tackle to overcome shallows on the Nene between Wisbech and Peterborough: thus temporary weirs using an empty boat, stakes and canvas sheets trodden into the river bed would raise the water level. It is believed that the Romans penetrated the Lee and other waterways in a similar manner by constructing dams with materials gathered locally.

Nene staunches remained shakily in use until the extensive lock-building scheme of 1936-41. The last on the Thames, Hart's, lasted until 1937, and on the Lower Avon the Cropthorne water gate was not removed until restoration of the navigation towards Evesham in 1961. While in no way underestimating the great achievement of reopening the Avon, it seems unfortunate that some method of preserving Britain's last flash lock could not have been found – but most improvements have their price. To this day a close relative of the breed can be found below Thames Lock on the Wey Navigation at Weybridge. Here a single wide-beam wooden gate is positioned across the navigation 100yd downstream of the lock, and it can be closed to raise the water level over the shallow bottom cill when boats drawing more than 3ft work through. It was habitually used for the passage of loaded grain barges until 1969. Another of these double river locks can be found on the Yorkshire Derwent at Stamford Bridge, where the stone-lined approach and chamber is distinctly banana-shaped.

Visible remains of flash locks can be seen on the long derelict River Nar in Norfolk, the River Lark, the River Parrett (Thorney half lock), the Great Ouse (Castle Mills Staunch, one of the most complete examples), the Nene and the Little Ouse. A most useful guide to flash locks and their remains appears in *Industrial Archaeology*, Vol 6, No 3, August 1969 (David & Charles).

## POUND LOCKS

If two flash locks were built within a very short distance, the intervening stretch of river would in effect become a lock chamber. This was certainly the case at Sutton Courtenay on the Upper Thames, mentioned in sixteenth-century documents and replaced in 1809 by the present Culham Lock. Thus, the conventional lock may easily have evolved almost by accident. First use of the pound lock is generally attributed to Chiao Wei-Yo, who was responsible for a section of China's Grand Canal. About AD 983 a 250ft-long lock with guillotine gates at each end was opened near Husi-yin. In Europe a flash lock could be seen in Holland in 1065, while the first pound lock, built in 1373 on the River Lek in Vreeswijk, had vertically rising gates. The earliest known lock of the familiar pattern, with mitre gates, was designed by the Duke of Milan's engineer, none other than the versatile Leonardo da Vinci, in the later fifteenth century. Britain's oldest pound lock was built on the Exeter Canal in the 1560s, probably with guillotine gates. During the next century many rivers, including the Thames, Wey, Lee, Welland and Medway, were improved with locks. By the coming of the Canal Age, from about 1760, the concept of the lock was well tried.

Almost every possible material has been employed for constructing lock chambers – stone, brick, wood, and more recently concrete and steel piling. Much would depend on local circumstances and supplies. Unstable sand on the Shropshire Union at Beeston necessitated the use of iron plates throughout, and further north on the same canal the Northgate staircase is hewn out of solid rock. On river navigations well supplied with water the sides of the chamber were sometimes partly or completely made of sloping grass banks, normally with a row of timber posts to prevent descending craft being stranded on the sides. This variety has survived on both the Wey and Kennet Navigations.

Although the working of a lock is easily understood, an outline of the principles involved should be given. Gates enclose each end of the chamber, in which the water level can be adjusted to equalise that above or below the lock. This is achieved by paddles, otherwise known as sluices, slats and eyes (Fens), cloughs (Leeds and Liverpool and north-east waterways), ranters, flashers and racks (Ireland). Like the domestic bath, these are 'taps' to admit water at the upper end, while the bottom end paddles are equivalent to the drain plug.

Gates are mostly heavily built in wood – oak or greenheart
are the usual choices – but iron, steel and even reinforced
concrete gates can also be found. Because of slight variations
in lock widths even in the same locality, mass production of
gates is not really possible. Replacements are normally
measured up individually and the butting wooden uprights
forming the seal planed off on the site. The normal arrangement on broad canals and rivers is a pair of mitre gates at
each end of the lock, those at the head being much shorter
than those at the tail and closing against a wooden, stone or
concrete cill. The theoretical maximum draught for boats
using the waterway is normally governed by the depth of this
cill below the surface. On narrow-boat canals the reduced
size of the gates and their consequent easier handling often
resulted in single gates at the top, with a pair at the tail. On
the Oxford Canal south of Banbury, however, and at the
Hawkesbury Junction stop lock near Coventry, where there
is a minimal rise and fall, single gates are fitted at each end.

Originally all gates were operated manually, a factor that
played a part in determining the depth of the lock. Gates are
fitted with long projecting balance beams whose length
provides adequate leverage for the gates to be operated by a
man applying his seat to the beam and walking backwards.
A curved path following the travelling course of the beam and
set at intervals with brick or stone projections gives a grip
for the feet and prevents this part of the lockside becoming a
muddy and slippery hazard. In order to close an open gate
an iron or steel hand-hold is frequently attached to the end of
the beam. Sometimes the building of a bridge over the canal
very near the gates prevents a balance beam of normal length
being used, in which case a right-angled extension arm is
adopted (New Haw Lock, River Wey Navigation, or Blackburn locks on the Leeds and Liverpool). At the Big Lock,
Middlewich, Trent and Mersey Canal, the problem is overcome by using a winch and chain.

Most locks on the Stort Navigation lacked balance beams
altogether until recent years, a much less satisfactory system
of chains being used instead. Towards the end of the last

*Easily the most wide-
spread method of open-
ing lock gates is via the
balance beam, against
which the operator
places the weight of his
body. This example on
the narrow beam Trent
& Mersey Canal near
Great Haywood, is fitted
with a long iron rod so
that the gate paddle can
be worked from the
extreme end*

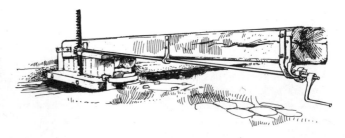

century modernisation of many Thames locks saw replacement of beams by free-standing consoles on the bank, with a vertical spoked metal wheel driving chains hidden from view in a covered channel. The majority have now vanished with mechanisation of locks down river from Oxford. The principle finds widespread use on many other rivers and broad canals. On the Caledonian elegant horizontal capstans in cast iron were turned by applying pressure to wooden spikes inserted in slots, enabling more than one keeper to help at a time. Again, mechanisation of all locks, completed in 1969, has made these devices redundant, although a number are preserved for their decorative and historic value. Much the same kind of apparatus can be found on the Sheffield and South Yorkshire Navigation at Doncaster Lock. The large locks on Ireland's Shannon Navigation, built during the depression of the mid-nineteenth century, employ vast hand-windlass-operated drums to work the gates, with seemingly hundreds of yards of heavy gauge chain to add to the total weight.

A number of trade tricks have been used at different times to speed lock operation – some officially condoned, others heavily frowned upon. A lone keeper working both gates of a wide lock may use a hooked pole to pull the far gate shut (uppermost reaches of the Thames) or work a system of pulleys and ropes to achieve the same end. Working boats on a narrow canal if descending in a lock would take a turn round the 'strapping post' of the top gate, effectively applying brakes to the boat (especially necessary with horse-drawn craft) as well as making the boat's momentum close the gate behind it. When travelling uphill, the boats' bows could be used to 'breast' or 'stem' the gates with help from horse or engine; once in the lock, a flush of water from the top paddles would help slam the lower gates closed, and on arrival at the upper level the gates would be breasted open again. The technique hardly improves the condition of worn wooden gates, even if thick rope fenders are used on the boats.

Electric or hydraulic apparatus has become quite common. Hydraulic rams were selected to open and close Manchester Ship Canal lock gates, each one of which on the largest 80ft wide locks comprises about 230 tons of timber with another 20 tons of ironwork. Rollers on granite paths assist movement of the gates under water. Power was originally supplied from steam-engine houses. With modern engineering technology, there is scarcely any limit to the size of locks now feasible, and on European waterways modern chambers can accommodate several 1,350 ton barges simultaneously. Power-operated locks, apart from the Thames, are mostly to be found on commercial routes, including the Aire and Calder

Navigation, Severn, Weaver, Trent, lower Lee, Grand Union at Brentford, and Caledonian. Sometimes the control panels are located by the gates at each end of the lock, and sometimes all operations are carried out in a central cabin.

Vertically rising guillotine gates, fitted into a high wooden or, more commonly, a steel framework, are initially more expensive to build than mitre gates, but avoid the need to fit paddles or sluice culverts. In most instances, guillotines have been selected for river navigations prone to rapid flooding; if such gates are installed at each end of the chamber, it is a simple matter to lift each gate simultaneously and allow water to flow unimpeded through the lock. All thirty-eight of the Nene's modern locks from Northampton to the Wash are fitted with upper mitre gates which can be chained open, and guillotines at the tail. Other guillotines are to be seen on the Great Ouse and the Yorkshire Derwent at Sutton. Their use on canals was rare. A particularly fine pair of guillotines hang above the chamber of King's Norton stop lock on the Northern Stratford Canal, dating from the 1790s. As the purpose of this device was to prevent loss of water from the Stratford Canal to the Worcester and Birmingham or *vice versa*, four sets of conventional mitre gates would have been necessary, enabling the lock to face either up or down hill, depending on which canal contained the higher level of water.

Guillotines were built on the Shrewsbury Canal in the late 1790s, and such structures can still be found at Hadley Park near Wellington. A modern guillotine lock designed to combat subsidence from mining can be seen on the Trent and Mersey Canal at Thurlwood (see p 425).

In almost every case lock chambers are rectangular. The few exceptions make an interesting study. On the Lower Avon, Wyre and Pershore Locks are shaped in plan like a diamond and possibly are derived from turf-sided chambers like those of the Wey and Kennet. Diamond locks occur on the Southern Oxford at Shipton and Aynho Weirs. In each case the weir locks are situated immediately below a level crossing of the River Cherwell. Geldeston Lock at the present navigation limit of the Broadland River Waveney has oval sides. Lock chambers on Lincolnshire's Louth Navigation are formed by a series of elliptical bays.

A sudden change in canal levels necessitated construction of either an exceptionally deep lock or, much more commonly, a series (or flight) with short intervening pounds between. There are countless instances throughout Britain. Longest flight of all is on the descent towards the Severn of the Worcester and Birmingham Canal at Tardebigge, with thirty locks. Another memorable series is the twenty-nine of the Caen Hill flight at Devizes on the Kennet and Avon, where the gates with their outstretched balance beams form a pattern like the backbone of some huge reptile. Great numbers of locks should not be thought of by the pleasure boatman with undue terror or alarm. Crews of working boats regarded them philosophically, relying on a routine whereby everyone had a set task aimed at moving the boat forward with minimum fuss or use of energy. One of the boat's crew travelled ahead, usually by bicycle, to set the next lock – hence the expression 'lock wheeling', which can also be carried out on foot! One of the joys of canal cruising is the satisfaction of efficiently preparing a way for the boat, pausing in the peace of either city centre or remote countryside while the chamber fills or empties, making all ready as the boat approaches, and then moving on to the next lock to repeat the process. The average British narrow canal lock contains 25,000–30,000 gallons of water, and its wide-beam counterpart some 55,000–60,000 gallons. To be able legitimately to release all this water again and again for the price of a cruising licence is remarkably good value!

Bratch Locks on the Staffs and Worcester Canal near Wolverhampton represent a stage in the evolution of the lock, for the intervening pounds are only a few feet long, while each chamber is equipped with its own individual top and bottom gates. The two locks at nearby Botterham share gates at the centre, common to each chamber, so economising on building costs, water and effort in operation. This is a 'staircase' or 'riser'. The best-known staircases are the Bingley Five Rise (Leeds and Liverpool Canal) with a total lift of 59ft; the two sets of five locks on the Leicester Section at Foxton, where a midway pound allows traffic moving in different directions to pass, and the rise is 75ft; three chambers at Northgate, Chester; and the Caledonian Canal's magnificent staircases at Banavie, Fort Augustus and Muirtown, comprising eight, five and four chambers respectively. The stonework is particularly fine. Telford had intended to build turf-sided locks throughout, as there was a plentiful water supply, but on grounds of subsequent maintenance costs and operating times it is fortunate that this plan was changed. Spectacular risers like those mentioned are rather exceptional, but two-rise locks are by no means infrequent, as at the top of the Aylesbury Arm, on the Grand Canal and Barrow Navigation in Ireland, the Grand Union at Bascote, the eastern end of the Leeds and Liverpool, the Caldon Canal at Etruria, the Gower Branch of the Birmingham Canals and many other places.

*Grand Union Canal gate paddles, supported on wooden posts, and showing the boatman's own windlass in position*

Locks placed at the tidal limit of navigations sometimes display peculiarities, apart from the obvious distinction that they can generally be worked only for a period either side of

A totally enclosed ground paddle to be seen throughout the enlarged locks of the 1930s on the northern Grand Union between Napton Junction and Knowle. Many have been adapted to display a raised indicator when open, their position thus being obvious from a distance. Otherwise inspection of a small peephole in the casing is necessary

A pear-shaped counter balance weight is found on this unusual variety on several disused locks on the Bridgwater & Taunton Canal

high water. The ship lock connecting the Thames with Lime-house Basin on the Regent's Canal is only available to craft for a certain time up to Thames high water, for if the river tide has begun to ebb, working of the lock will entail draining water from the basin. Advance warning to the keeper of your intended arrival is one way to avoid waiting overlong in a bouncy tideway. Duplicated sets of gates with pairs facing each way allow the lock to work in an uphill direction even though its normal function is downhill; the change can be brought about by abnormal water levels in the river above. An example is Denver Sluice on the Great Ouse below Ely. The nearby sluice linking the tidal Ouse with the Old Bedford River can only be used for a few minutes when the tide makes a level, or once in 24 hours if high water happens to fall in the middle of the night. Richmond Lock on the Thames is a curiosity known as a half-tide lock. Boats pass through the lock in the normal way when the tide is low on the down-river side. A series of guillotine sluices alongside are lowered at each tide to stop all water draining from the waterway as far as the first proper lock at Teddington, but for a period either side of high water at Richmond, the sluices are raised, allowing unimpeded passage of craft.

The sea locks on the Manchester Ship Canal at Eastham were built with an additional set of doors able to face outwards in the event of unusually fierce or high tides in the Mersey estuary. When a boat is worked between the Grand Union Canal and the tidal Thames at Brentford, the duplicated pair of mechanised Thames locks near the junction are generally left open at each end for a short time at high water, resulting in the canal becoming tidal as far as Brentford Gauging Locks with temporary insufficient headroom under Brentford High Street bridge. Flood control on rivers sometimes employs occasional or flood locks, which are used only when there is plenty of 'fresh' in the waterway. In summer they will be found opened at each end. The Soar Navigation and River Don sections of the Sheffield and South Yorkshire at Rotherham also use this device. Flood-gates (not locks) are used to isolate some Calder and Hebble Navigation canal cuts from river sections.

Practically every waterway features its own special type of paddle or sluice gear, resulting in a rich variety of machinery. Two basic paddle classifications exist: the ground paddle set on the lockside, where it comprises a wooden door acting as a shutter over an aperture at the end of a culvert leading into the lock chamber; and the gate paddle, which is an underwater shutter in the lock gates. Simple metal rods drive gears to raise the paddle when a windlass (lock handle) is attached to the spindle. Some kind of catch or pawl of various designs holds the paddle in the open position. Recommended procedure for closing is to wind the paddle up still further, remove the pawl and carefully wind down again. Some designs are intended to drop when the pawl is knocked off, allowing the paddle to fall under its own weight. Normally, although this creates a pleasing rattling noise, it can result in damage to the gear and angers the maintenance authorities. Working methods long in use by professional boatmen are not always best adopted by pleasure craft.

Counterbalance weights are sometimes used to ease the labour of paddle work. At their most endearing these take the form of pear-shaped lumps of stone, or metal weights hung on a chain passing over a cast-iron pulley wheel (Bridgwater and Taunton Canal). The windlass is the 'key' to the greater part of Britain's canal and river system, those with both 1in and 1¼in eyes serving to work most locks. They must be considered essential in every inland cruiser's standard equipment. A larger windlass is required for some of the Leeds and Liverpool Canal paddles, and a special small key is necessary to unlock anti-vandal chains.

When working small boats uphill through wide locks, first open the top ground paddles, beginning with that on the same side as the boat is moored; this will help pin the boat against the lock wall. Beware of raising gate-paddles too early, as the rush of water can swamp an open forward cockpit. Rather than learn lock-working technique from written accounts, watch an expert or, even better, take one with you on your first trip. Never be afraid to ask questions and above all think before acting. So much of lock operation is commonsense, yet all too frequently people tackle the subject with a thoughtless bravado. Think first, then act, and take pride in correctness and economy of effort. The lock should never be seen as a machine of terror!

To avoid detailed descriptions of the many types of paddle gear, a representative selection of designs is illustrated here. In your canal and river travels look out for 'new' patterns, like the low-geared enclosed types introduced experimentally in the early 1970s (Hurleston Locks on the Llangollen Canal, Kennet and Avon near Newbury, Atherstone Locks on the Coventry Canal and elsewhere). Discover hybrid oddities like redundant Thames paddle gear in the form of spoked wheels, placed on their sides to wind gates open (Upper Avon at Stratford, where all sorts of innovations and bright ideas characterise the cost-saving navigation works).

As water is the most precious commodity of a canal, several methods to save supplies for lockage, particularly in times of drought, have been used over the years. First, the side pond is an ingenious device for saving almost half the quantity of

*Once very common on river navigations, there appears to remain only one example of this simple wooden sluice rod: this is at the shallow rise Worsfold Gates Lock on the Wey Navigation. A steel pin is passed through a hole in the paddle bar, thus holding it in the required position. In the middle of the last century, crowbars were used to lever such paddles open*

*This cast-iron ground paddle on the Weaver Navigation has a pleasing simplicity*

*Until mechanisation of all Thames locks downstream of Oxford (begun in 1958 and now completed) spoked wheels were mounted on the gates. Indicator rods, painted red or white, showed whether the sluice was raised or lowered. This type survives on the uppermost locks of the navigation, while some have been adapted to open gates on the Upper Avon, in this case placed sideways*

*Detail of a toothed segment arrangement, part of the gate paddle gear of a lock at Blackburn, Leeds & Liverpool Canal. In this case a wooden shutter moves sideways across the paddle aperture in the gate*

water that would otherwise pass downhill from a canal summit each time a lock is operated. Alongside the lock chamber a stone-, brick- or concrete-lined pond is connected with the lock via a culvert and paddle. When descending in the lock, the side-pond paddle is first opened or 'drawn', allowing half the contents of the full lock to flow into the pond. That paddle is closed when the levels of lock and pond become equal, and the remainder of the lock water escapes through the lower lock paddles. When the lock is next filled, the side-pond paddle is first drawn, draining the pond, at which point normal lock working takes over.

Now silted up and little used, side ponds remain throughout the Grand Union at points where water supplies are prone to shortages (Marsworth, Soulbury, Stoke Bruerne), and at other locations as well. Where locks are duplicated, side by side, one chamber frequently was able to act as a side pond for the other, with an interconnecting paddle (Hillmorton Locks, Oxford Canal; Regent's Canal; the Cheshire Locks of the Trent and Mersey Canal). In times of water shortage canals still practise 'waiting turns' at locks, whereby a boat passing uphill must be followed by a boat passing downhill, or *vice versa*. In days of heavy commercial traffic the Grand Union Canal main line would be kept open by draining water supplies from the higher level of the less frequented Leicester section at Norton Junction. In recent years increasingly frequent pleasure-boat use of flights leading to canal summits has led to complete closure of a waterway by late summer, when reservoir reserves become exhausted (Southern Oxford summit level, Foulridge summit on the Leeds and Liverpool). This can never occur on river-fed summits such as the Llangollen or the Caledonian Canal. One partial but expensive answer is to pump water back to the summit. The long-term solution involves proper maintenance and extension of silted reservoirs.

Closely associated with locks are weirs, which form a barrier across the navigation. On the best-engineered river navigations the weir is often remote from the lock chamber, with an artificial canal cut constructed for the navigation channel. On 15 miles of Wey Navigation from the Thames to Guildford, 7 miles are formed by artificial cuts. Thus, even in times of flood, there is little danger of boats being drawn over the weir sluices. But many locks are situated at one end of an unguarded weir (Warwickshire Avon, River Barrow, River Don). Floating booms or rows of protective piles standing above the weir will lessen the danger. Nevertheless, at certain times movement of craft is ill-advised.

Canal weirs serve a rather different purpose. Rather than have surplus water cascading over lock gates (Sheffield and

South Yorkshire or River Nene, where paddles and guillotines must sometimes be left partly open), it is preferable for a small side weir to bypass the lock. When water in the upper pound reaches its normal full level, any excess automatically flows over the weir to top up levels below. In their original form most such canal weirs are enclosed culverts with entrances and exits scarcely visible. One disadvantage of the enclosed culvert is a tendency for branches and fallen masonry to block the passage. No maintenance worker relishes the prospect of crawling down the dark wet pipe to clear the obstruction. Inspection hatches and iron bars over the entry are two cures. Some of the most attractive canal structures include completely circular weirs, several feet in diameter, quite open or protected with a lobster-pot-like iron cage, as on the Staffs and Worcs Canal at Stewponey and elsewhere. The shape of both weir and cage varies from circular to crescent and rectangular. Nowadays open cascades are generally chosen for their easier construction and maintenance. These can either take the form of smooth water slopes (Llangollen Canal) or stepped waterfalls (Trent and Mersey at Middlewich). As the force of water escaping at the lower end can be considerable, care is necessary to avoid boats of light construction being slammed hard against the lock entrance. Niagara-like sheer drops, equal to the height of the lock, can be seen at Lapworth Locks, Stratford Canal, or spectacularly on the Delph Locks, Dudley Canal. A rather similar type of bypass weir may be found on the Warwick section of the Grand Union. Original narrow lock chambers, replaced by more modern wide ones in the 1930s, have in most cases been converted to weirs; many provide watery graveyards for single narrow boats used for carriage of construction materials at the time of the modernisation.

The smallest British lock still in use is the skiff lock on the Thames at Teddington, a mere 49ft 6in long × 5ft 10in wide, its rise and fall depending on the state of the tide. Tub-boat locks on the derelict Old Shropshire section of the Shrewsbury Canal are 6ft 2in wide. The deepest narrow lock that appears to have been built was on the disused Glamorganshire Canal at Aberfan; this had a fall of 14ft 6in, but as the width was 8ft 9in, the narrow-lock depth record should more properly be awarded to the Worcester and Birmingham's top lock at Tardebigge, just 6in shallower. The only reason for this great height is that a boat lift was originally working on the site. The longest waterway lock in Britain is Teddington barge lock at 650ft, with a width of 24ft 9in; if the intermediate pair of gates is used, the length is reduced to 279ft. But Eastham large lock on the Manchester Ship Canal is the biggest, at 600ft × 80ft. The deepest in these islands is

*A selection of the wealth of lock or wharf bollards by which boats are moored: Wood and iron protective strips at the disused Toll End Locks, Birmingham Canal Navigations*

*Heavily gnarled through rope wear, on the Coventry Canal at Glascote locks*

*Heavily gnarled through rope wear, on the Coventry Canal at Glascote locks*

easily the double-chambered Ardnacrusha Power Station Lock below Killaloe, River Shannon, with a frightening total fall of 100ft. The only means of getting ashore at the bottom end when arriving from the estuary is to clamber up 60ft of vertical ladder! One chamber is situated inside the power station building itself.

Other oddly placed locks were used in connection with inclined planes on the 46-mile underground coalmine canals at Worsley. They began operating in 1797, but are long since disused. There is a working Rochdale Canal lock under the basement of Manchester's Rodwell Tower office block, a dark hole by any standards, while motorway building in the Birmingham area has roofed in several BCN locks. One of the Farmer's Bridge locks of the Birmingham and Fazeley Canal opens out into a vast brick cavern beneath the tracks of the now closed Snow Hill station. A lofty frame for one of the Northampton Arm locks is provided by a huge M1 motorway arch.

There are a number of seemingly insignificant items of apparatus whose collective presence provides locks with much of their interest and character. All assist efficient operation in some way. Immediately above the head gates and below the tail it is normal to find grooves in the masonry, which enable a temporary dam of wooden stop planks to be quickly dropped into position if the lock is drained for maintenance or fitting new gates. A reasonably watertight seal can be quickly made by dropping ashes into the water to fill the joints between each plank. Stop planks with metal lifting-handles at each end may be stored in readiness at the lockside on open wooden racks protected from the weather by a sheet-metal or wooden roof. On the Shropshire Union Canal, however, a more permanent enclosed concrete housing is common, while on parts of the Trent and Mersey a cavity in the wall of a nearby bridge acts as a store. Wherever keepers or maintenance gangers occupy a cottage on site, several useful tools can often be seen resting on a rack, including a long wooden shaft and a keb, similar to a very long garden fork with the prongs bent at a right angle. They are invaluable for recovering windlasses dropped in the water (although a powerful magnet tied to a length of rope is more satisfactory) and for removing bricks, wood or other debris interfering with the proper functioning of gates and paddles.

Bollards intended for applying brakes to boats entering the lock, as well as for controlling them as the water rushes in, are usually found by the chamber both at the head and the tail. The wear from several generations of grit-covered ropes can cut deep grooves into bollards made of wood, stone and even iron, creating gnarled accidental sculpture. Wooden

*An unusually large and pleasing bollard whose wooden core is edged with cast iron, Shannon Harbour on the Grand Canal*

bollards by Thames locks soon attain a high degree of polish. Sizes vary considerably, from the small iron mushroom shapes dating from the late nineteenth century to the 1930s on the Grand Union system, and the chunky roughly hewn tree trunks of the Southern Oxford, to massive cast-iron posts sometimes bearing dates of installation, as on the Shannon locks, and the ship-sized bollards of docks or large commercial waterways. The Forth and Clyde uses swivelling hooks instead, and in recent years a somewhat crumble-prone version of reinforced concrete bollard has appeared on the more popular cruising canals.

*A modern steel mooring post at a Thames lock*

Hauling of unpowered boats either by tug or horse has left a varied collection of metal fittings on locks. Capstans at Brentford Gauging locks can propel dumb barges several hundred yards in a somewhat erratic fashion, rather like rail wagons in a marshalling yard. Many of the upper gates on the Sheffield and South Yorkshire are fitted with massive cast-iron fairleads to guide towropes and prevent them becoming fouled on rails. On the narrow canal system rusted pulleys sprout from stone copings to provide either a purchase or guide for horse-boat lines (top lock of the Aston flight, Birmingham and Fazeley Canal). Sometimes their use is obscure but can generally be explained by lock-keepers or retired boatmen. It will be noticed that lock handrails, bridge parapets and similar canal fittings are generally streamlined to allow towing ropes to pass easily without becoming caught. But the slightest flaw or join in ironwork, or an angle where rubbing was acute, has become deeply grooved over years of use.

*Widely adopted throughout the Grand Union system: cast iron set in concrete*

Different waterways display their own method of enabling working boatmen (and now people on pleasure craft) to get ashore to attend to gates and paddles. Many river navigations, but by no means all, are equipped with concrete or wooden stages at the lock's head and tail. An additional help will be ladders recessed into the walls of the chamber. The athletic will frequently be able to scramble ashore by climbing up the wooden cross-members of the gates; indeed, on the Leeds and Liverpool Canal, metal rungs are added for just this purpose. On canals there are normally fewer problems, for either the towpath is easily accessible above and below, or stone or brick steps are provided in the wing walls at the lower end. Sometimes the single-hander will find it difficult to climb from a small boat in a deep lock, and have to resort to hauling it in with ropes. The real difficulties arise, however, when flicking the ropes underneath fixed footbridges and catching the flying ends the other side (Foxton staircase, Leicester section), or, worse, working a boat through a downhill lock only to find that a road bridge below has no towpath (Nell

*Giant-sized iron ring and shackle for ships in Sharpness Docks, Gloucester & Sharpness Canal*

Bridge, Southern Oxford Canal). One solution here is to 'flush' the boat through the bridge by raising the upper paddles, then quickly closing them, running across the busy road and hopefully boarding the boat at the other side. Lone canal travel certainly teaches resourcefulness!

In the days of commercial use fierce disputes would quite often arise as to which boat had right of way through a lock. In an attempt to overcome these time-wasting arguments, stone or cast-iron plates were erected a short way either side of the lock and either marked with 'lock distance', '100 yards', or some similar legend. The boat passing this point first was to be given right of way. But unless the men could read, and often they were illiterate, or a company man was on hand to arbitrate, the question would be settled in a more basic manner.

Other lock signs to be found are numbers (chunky iron plates on the Kennet and Avon, or large cut-outs on the Crinan Canal), each denoting progress along the waterway; nameplates, usually a more modern introduction, either in metal (nationalised routes), or carved in the wood of the balance-beam (Birmingham Canal Navigations), or commemorating the original building or major repairs of the structure (Shannon Navigation, Thames, Beeston Iron Lock [a date], the Grand Union system [rebuilding dates]); and general observations as to what is or is not allowed. The populated Thames perhaps leads in the range of signs in this last category, one of the most frequent being that users should 'take navigation works as they find them'.

Whatever is written about locks, and no matter how many exceptions to rules are cited, some obscure lock somewhere will contradict the most closely researched study. This is part of the fascination of British locks. Much the same can be said for inland waterways in general.

## LIFTS

At the end of the nineteenth century it was calculated that there was one lock to every 1·37 miles of waterway then available in the British Isles. The canal lock is wasteful of time and water, and so, for almost as long as engineers have been concerned with inland navigation, an alternative device for overcoming changes in level has been sought. Few examples remain in working order on our waterways, but the needs of enlarged barge canals in Europe have resulted in many remarkable applications of inclined planes and lifts in recent years.

In its simplest form the inclined plane is a dry slope up which boats can be hauled between levels. Obviously, without the application of power, this system is only of use for

*A sign cast in concrete on the Grand Union Canal at Harefield*

small craft over gentle gradients. It survives on the Thames in the form of boat-rollers for dinghies, punts or skiffs to avoid the nearby lock, at Teddington, Molesey, Sunbury, Boveney and Iffley Locks. Concrete tracks are fitted with steel rollers at intervals, plus a tipping cradle at the apex of the slope. A design from the late 1960s will be found at the tidal barrier on the Essex River Stour at Cattawade Bridge and another on the Chelmer and Blackwater Navigation at Chelmsford. When Thames boating was all the rage in the Maidenhead area before World War I, the amazing congestion at Boulter's Lock, familiar from old photographs, was partly alleviated by the erection of rollers operating on the same principle as an escalator. Wooden chocks on an endless belt of slats kept small boats in position while their occupants remained seated. This 'boat conveyor' was built in 1909 and seems to have been powered electrically. Now long disused, the site on Ray Mill island is accessible to the public.

*An example of a sign from the Calder & Hebble Navigation*

Long before such simple inclined planes were introduced, many experiments were made with more sophisticated (and sometimes equally successful) equipment, intended for use by commercial craft. Both vertical lifts and slopes were used, but they were only suitable in locations where the land rose quickly over a short distance. The first application in Britain was between 1768 and 1773 on Ulster's Tyrone Canal, where three wooden ramps fitted with rollers enabled 1-ton boats to be hauled up and down. Subsequent improvements elsewhere saw the introduction of water-filled tanks set on rails, in which larger craft travelled; power was provided by counterbalance, downhill loaded boats pulling empty uphill ones, with water providing any necessary additional weight.

*Small craft by-passing Boulter's Lock, Upper Thames, by means of an electrically driven 'escalator', in service for a number of years after 1909*

During the late eighteenth and early nineteenth centuries further examples of the plane were constructed on the Shropshire, South Wales, Devon, Somerset and Cornish Canals. The Trench plane on the Shrewsbury relied on a steam winding-engine hauling tub-boats set on flat rail-mounted trolleys. The vertical rise was 75ft and it ceased working in 1921. For 25 years up to 1822 a double-track underground plane using locks at the head overcame a change in levels of 105ft in the Worsley coalmine canals connected with the Bridgewater. A water wheel provided the motive power at Morwellham plane, one of two on the Tavistock Canal, where goods were transhipped into containers for a 237ft vertical change in levels. Elsewhere 15-ton capacity buckets rising and falling in wells were tried to move craft. A more up-to-date scheme was adopted on Scotland's Monkland Canal at Blackhill, Glasgow, between 1850 and about 1887. A vertical rise of 96ft was overcome by building twin railways on a 1,040ft incline up which boats were transported in caissons run by a pair of steam engines. This device inspired both Foxton and the massive Ronquières and Arzviller inclines in Belgium and France respectively. Perhaps the most curious use of planes, which remained in use for much of the last century, was found on the Bude Canal. Small tub-boats were fitted with wheels so that they could take to the rails, with power variously supplied by water wheels, steam engines and well buckets. One of these strange craft is preserved in Exeter's Maritime Museum.

Two lifts in Britain became well known. One, the Foxton Incline, had a career of a few years only at the beginning of the century, whereas the Anderton Vertical Lift was built in 1875 and continues to link the Weaver with the Trent and Mersey Canal. We shall look at both in some detail.

The Grand Junction Canal Company had by 1897 acquired the several canals that comprised the Leicester section, giving them control of the route from their London–Braunston main line right the way through to the Trent and the Erewash Canal. Except for seven locks in the Watford flight and another ten in two staircases at Foxton, the new line was broad-beam throughout. The leading carriers were anxious to use 14ft beam craft, so it was agreed that the Foxton Locks would be replaced by an inclined plane. After a large-scale model had been successfully tested at the company's Bulbourne yard, their engineer, Gordon Cale Thomas, designed a plane to overcome the 75ft rise and fall. It consisted of a concrete ramp on which twin tanks or caissons each travelled on eight rails arranged in four pairs. Approach canals and basins were built at the top and bottom. Each tank measured 80ft × 15ft × 5ft deep and could thus accommodate a standard pair of narrow boats afloat for the ride. Vertical guillotine gates on the caissons provided a watertight seal. Steam power harnessed to huge winding drums in the engine house hauled on steel-wire ropes, although this was required only to overcome friction from the wheels and machinery. As one tank ascended, the other descended, the device being nearly counterbalanced. Construction began early in 1898 and proceeded so well that the first boats were able to use the incline on 10 July 1900. The entire operation for two pairs of boats lasted only 12 minutes, compared with $1\frac{1}{4}$ hours for a single boat to negotiate the old locks. During a normal 12-hour working day some 6,000 tons of cargo could be exchanged between upper and lower levels, allowing for 15-minute intervals between each journey. Including the cost of the land, the project had cost £39,224.

Some initial troubles were experienced with stress on the track under the great weight of the tanks. Anticipated traffic increases failed to materialise and the company's opinion of the device can be determined from their decision to rebuild the Watford locks to narrow beam between 1901 and 1902. A head of steam had constantly to be maintained at Foxton in expectation of traffic, and daily running costs in 1901 were put at £1 4s 6d. In 1908 the Foxton Locks were repaired for night use when the incline was shut down, and two years later all boats were directed through the flight. There was some limited use of the incline in 1912, the last year of its operation. Had electric power then been readily available, the outcome might have been very different, and perhaps the Foxton Incline would be operating still. The machinery was dismantled in 1926 and sold two years later for a mere £250. Now the ten locks are in summer as busy as they can ever have been, as pleasure cruisers struggle up and down the hill. The site of the incline, but for some remains of the concrete tracks and the basins at each end, has reverted to nature.

A series of seven vertical lifts on Devon's Grand Western Canal worked well for about 30 years from 1838, but with this exception all other applications of the system had been experimental failures. The trustees of the Weaver Navigation, with the encouragement of trading interests, determined to link their waterway with the Trent and Mersey Canal, which ran past the river at Anderton but 50ft 4in higher. The resulting Anderton Lift was primarily designed by the trustees' engineer, Leader Williams, who subsequently moved to the Bridgewater Canal and was responsible for the unique Barton Swing Aqueduct. At Anderton a massive iron framework was built to contain a pair of water-filled tanks of wrought iron, fitted at each end with watertight guillotine gates and each capable of holding a narrow boat pair or a single Bridgewater Canal type barge. A wrought-iron aqueduct 162ft 6in long connected the upper level of the lift with the canal via a small basin. In its original form the lift had a complicated system of applying hydraulic power in which a steam engine supplying a hydraulic accumulator allowed downward movement of one

*Britain's only surviving vertical boat lift at Anderton, seen from the Weaver*

caisson while the other travelled to the top level. The tanks would also run independently, but this took a much greater time. The lift opened in 1875 and certainly improved trading conditions between the two waterways, even if tonnage figures did not increase. One of the presses burst in 1882, causing a caisson containing a boat to fall 50ft, though quite gently, with no substantial damage. Modifications were consequently ordered. Transhipment of salt from canal craft to river barges continued via a row of chutes by the side of the lift.

Electricity replaced steam in operating the whole structure in 1903, and by 1908 counterbalance weights had replaced the hydraulic system. A charge is made for its use, for its maintenance is expensive, but this is more than compensated for by the excitement of taking a boat between the two waterways.

A keeper is in charge of the control cabin, a place of brass dials and levers like an old-fashioned railway signal-box. Those with a strong nerve and head for heights should (with permission) climb to the top of the structure to watch the winding wheels spin round as the tanks rise and fall independently of each other far below. As an example of the inventiveness of Victorian engineering, the Anderton Lift has no rivals in Britain, and it provided the necessary inspiration for similar devices in France, Belgium, Canada and Germany. It holds an undisputed place among the Seven Wonders of the British waterways.

*This brick roving bridge transfers the towpath across the Leicester
Section at the bottom of Foxton Locks*

# 5
# *Bridges*

In common with other forms of waterway engineering and architecture, the canal and river bridges of Britain present an endless variety of pattern and design. While many existing river bridges date from an era starting in medieval times the great majority of canal structures are the product of the eighty years between 1760 and 1840. Canal bridges built within this short space of time display a wealth of individuality, structures rarely being exactly alike, even on the same length of navigation.

Architectural responsibility was in some cases that of the canal engineers – men like Brindley, Rennie and Telford – but in many instances works of this nature would be subcontracted, section by section, to local craftsmen builders. Thus quite startling changes in style can be noticed within a short distance. Today we are used to civil engineering contractors being placed in charge of new motorway construction. No single man's name can be associated with motorway works: whether we applaud or deplore the stark simplicity of these new structures and flyovers, they are bound to display an anonymity in direct contrast to the friendly style of their canal counterparts. Functional though canal bridges are, they are also frequently beautiful.

### RIVER BRIDGES

Many of the most famous ancient bridges in Britain cross navigable waters. Because of its historical importance, with London, the seat of Government, and such leading towns as Oxford and Windsor on its banks, the Thames provides examples of many types of bridge from medieval days to present times. By looking at them in some detail we can build up a general picture relevant to other rivers as well.

In medieval England bridge building and maintenance was often an occupation undertaken by religious communities. The Church was in a strong position to raise the necessary finances, and had the architects and builders capable of this form of engineering. The best remaining example of a bridge built under these conditions is that at Abingdon, downstream of Oxford. Here the Guild of the Holy Cross in 1446 organised construction of both Abingdon and Culham Bridges, the latter over the Swift Ditch, then the navigation channel, which bypassed the present route through Abingdon itself and had one of the three earliest pound locks on the river. Abingdon is a long solid structure of yellow-grey stone, its many arches, of differing widths and heights, divided by massive cutwaters and offering a considerable obstacle to the flow of the river. In spite of frequent rebuilding, Abingdon Bridge retains much of its essentially fifteenth-century character.

Earlier still is Radcot Bridge, in the wilds between Oxford and Lechlade. It is composed of triple-ribbed arches, the central one, designed for navigation, being rounded and its neighbours Gothic-pointed. Undoubtedly the oldest bridge on the Thames, this fourteenth-century crossing should not be confused with the much later single span on the present Radcot navigation channel. Similar in age and appearance is the Medway's weathered East Farleigh Bridge, in a splendid setting of oasthouses and orchards with lock and weir immediately downstream. Newbridge over the Thames is second in age only to Radcot, and spans the navigation about 7 miles downstream. Its six pointed stone arches, two of them still ribbed, are particularly well preserved.

A notable sixteenth-century structure is Stopham Bridge over the Sussex River Arun. Like others of its age, this replacement of a wooden crossing displays seven rounded arches divided by massive cutwaters. The central arch is considerably higher than those on each side to enable craft to pass beneath. The well-known Clopton Bridge, crossing the Avon in Stratford, was financed by Sir Hugh Clopton in 1480, and occupies the site of an early ford. Originally 1,000ft in length, it is now reduced to 500ft. St Neots Bridge, linking Huntingdonshire and Bedfordshire over the Great Ouse, was completed towards the end of the sixteenth century. Also on the Great Ouse, St Ives Bridge is fifteenth-century, and incorporates a chapel consecrated in 1426, a reminder of one-time connections with the Church. Only three similar chapel bridges remain – at Wakefield and Rotherham in Yorkshire, and at Bradford-on-Avon.

Packhorse transport has left its mark in the form of specially narrow bridges. Of these, a good example is Essex or Shugborough Bridge over the infant Trent where the Trent and Mersey Canal runs beside it at Great Haywood Junction, Staffordshire. It is thought that it was erected at the instigation of Queen Elizabeth's Earl of Essex as a convenient crossing of the river en route to the hunting grounds of Cannock Chase. There are fourteen arches in a length of 100ft, with a series of pedestrian refuges built on top of the triangular cutwaters.

Although the best-known housed bridge of all – Old London Bridge – is now gone and its 1831 John Rennie replacement has been moved piecemeal to the United States, two smaller but similar bridges remain supporting a street of buildings. High Bridge, Lincoln, across the navigable River Witham, dates back to 1145, although the present half-timbered houses over the single-beamed arch were constructed about 1540. Bath's stone Pulteney Bridge was begun in 1769 after navigation works had reached the city. While a fine view of the river is obtainable from windows in the Robert Adam properties above the three regular curved arches, it is quite possible to walk down the street on the centre of the bridge without realising that the Avon flows beneath.

Many of the finest river bridges, especially in the south of England, display classical features of the eighteenth-century era of good taste. Larger arch spans were possible by this time with an improvement in engineering knowledge. Indeed, with a frequently growing trade in waterborne craft, this was necessary to avoid undue obstruction of navigable waterways. The Thames is especially rich in examples of this period, the two finest being perhaps Richmond and Chertsey Bridges, designed during the 1780s by James Paine. Both have five wet arches of grey stone, increasing in size to the central navigation arch, and two additional dry-land arches increase the apparent width of Chertsey. Elegant stone balustrades are characteristic. Substantial widening of the carriageway of Richmond Bridge was undertaken in 1929 with great sympathy, ensuring that its original proportions and appearance were unchanged. Henley and Maidenhead, the former still bearing a massive cast-iron plate warning the drivers of traction engines that only one truck at a time may be driven across, were completed respectively in 1786 (William Hayward) and 1772 (Sir Robert Taylor).

*The canal age coincided with a growing use of cast iron in architecture and engineering. Factory Bridge was built over the main line of the Birmingham Canal Navigations at Tipton and bears the date 1825. It has now been moved from its original site for preservation at the near-by Black Country Museum at the approach to Dudley Canal tunnel*

Similar in age, and unusually for this area and period, Sonning Bridge is built completely of warm-red weathered brick and is a considerable attraction in this prosperous village below Reading.

Possibly the loveliest classical Thames bridge of all is Swinford Toll Bridge, at Eynsham, a little above Oxford. It is composed of three symmetrical wet arches flanked on each side by three dry ones of progressively diminishing height. The bicentenary of its completion was celebrated in 1969, at which time tolls were still charged. Pressure of increased road transport during this century has gradually resulted in the transfer of privately maintained toll-bridges to local highway authorities, but a few remain open only on payment of dues. Until recently the charge for crossing Swinford Bridge was based on an old penny a wheel, so that a saloon car with a spare wheel could cross for 5d.

John Gwynn of Shrewsbury is noted for his elegant eighteenth-century bridge over the Severn at Atcham, still in its original form and bypassed by a modern concrete road bridge. He also built the English Bridge at Shrewsbury, and Worcester Bridge, both of which have unfortunately suffered from twentieth-century reconstruction.

The use of iron, with the arrival of the Industrial Revolution, which was in turn followed by steel and reinforced concrete, changed the entire concept of bridge building in Britain. The earliest examples frequently retain a considerable attraction of design. As construction techniques grew bolder, some quite original forms became possible, such as vast single spans and suspension bridges. The Iron Bridge over the once navigable Severn at Coalbrookdale, apart from its stone support piers on each bank of the river, is composed completely of iron. Erected in 1779 by Abraham Darby II and John Wilkinson, it was the first bridge of its type in the world. The nearby Dale ironworks of Abraham Darby, the first to succeed in smelting iron ore with coke rather than charcoal, had expanded by the middle nineteenth century into the biggest foundry then known. Five nearly semi-circular iron ribs support the bridge's carriageway at a height of 50ft, with a clear span of just over 100ft. In all some $387\frac{1}{2}$ tons of iron, including the $2\frac{1}{2}$in thick plates for the roadway, were floated down river from the foundry and raised into position without interrupting commercial freight on the navigation. Especially notable are the delicate decoration of the main structure and the fine railings of the balustrade. Iron was often used to highly decorative effect during Victorian times.

Thomas Telford made frequent use of iron, including memorable designs for Waterloo Bridge, Bettws-y-Coed

(1815), and the Conway Suspension Bridge (1826). This new material was used with great success in combination with the suspension principle on his Menai Bridge, probably his most remarkable achievement. While capable of far greater spans and completion at considerably reduced cost than fixed stone bridges, the suspension bridge is peculiarly vulnerable to oscillation caused by heavy loads or high winds. More than once dramatic collapses have taken place within a short time of the opening.

William Tierney Clark (1783–1852) followed in the tradition of Telford in producing Hammersmith Suspension Bridge over the Thames, upstream of London, in 1827; it was replaced by a similar structure sixty years later. He also built Marlow Suspension Bridge between Windsor and Henley, a lovely work in a perfect setting by the neo-Gothic spire of All Saints Church and the broad sweep of Marlow weir. It is supported by massive arched gateways and was opened in 1832. Repeated threats of demolition have finally been thwarted and recent reinforcement now allows a one-way flow of road traffic controlled by lights. In London R. M. Ordish's Albert Suspension Bridge of 1873 combined cantilever and suspension principles.

After the success of Telford's Menai Bridge, he was concerned with selecting designs for spanning the Avon Gorge just below the Port of Bristol. A scheme by 25-year-old Isambard Kingdom Brunel was eventually chosen, and the foundation stone of the Clifton Suspension Bridge was laid in 1836. Financial difficulties prevented its completion until 1864, five years after Brunel's untimely death. Severe yet elegant, the Clifton Bridge is one of the most impressively situated in Britain, 245ft above the river. It makes a magnificent spectacle when viewed by night from the Bristol City Docks, hanging illuminated and seemingly unsupported in mid air.

Although the early railways represented a major threat to inland waterway prosperity, their close physical connection in many cases with the canals, the fact that their building continued in bolder terms the engineering tradition of the waterways, and the frequent common ownership of railway and canal concerns, make railway bridges worthy of consideration in this chapter. They are especially notable where the railways crossed the navigations, often enhancing the landscape at those points. I. K. Brunel arrived on the scene at the right time to become one of the great railway builders. When still only 27 years old, he was appointed engineer to the Great Western Railway, and it is from this period that his most memorable work results. Three of his monumental red-brick bridges still cross the Thames at Moulsford,

*A section of cast-iron bridge parapet, seen on a span over the Birmingham Canal Navigations main line*

Basildon and Maidenhead. Moulsford, dating from the late 1830s, is notable for its curiously slanting courses of brickwork; subsequently it was considerably widened, with a small gap between the new work and the old. Maidenhead Railway Bridge boasts the widest and flattest pure brick spans in the world.

The Railway Age was responsible for the most intense period of bridge building that Britain has ever known. Between 1830 and 1860 about 25,000 railway bridges of all types were erected. Once all-important canal navigations became outdated narrow ribbons of silver water by comparison with the shining rails of the new tracks. Sometimes the canals were made to burrow beneath the lines: on the Trent and Mersey Canal in Stoke a railway crosses at the lower level of a lock, its bridge parapet only slightly higher than the bottom lock gates; and on the Birmingham and Fazeley Canal one of the Farmer's Bridge Locks is situated inside a vast cavern beneath the platforms of the now closed Snow Hill Station near the centre of Birmingham. Generally, however, the finest railway bridges – Forth, Britannia and Conway tubular bridges – leap over tidal estuaries and do not concern us here.

## CANAL BRIDGES

In connection with canals themselves, we have an enormous variety of bridges. General lack of modernisation of the waterways since their original completion has resulted in a unique survival of bridge forms frequently unchanged from their initial state. Two basic types are to be found – the fixed bridge and the movable. With smaller building costs but increased maintenance expenses in years to come, the latter type was sometimes chosen for farm access or pedestrians, although early economy was subsequently to be regretted with continuing repair bills and delays to traffic, both road and water. Some navigations frequented by masted ships, among them the Weaver, Forth and Clyde and Gloucester and Sharpness Ship Canal, obviously avoided high spans, and instead used swing bridges of different kinds. Elsewhere difficulties such as finding space for road approaches to fixed bridges, or where the bridge was added at a later date, resulted in the construction of movable bridges.

### Fixed canal bridges

By far the most common type in Britain is the single-arched bridge, often humpbacked, carrying minor roads or providing agricultural access over the navigation. Generally intended for traffic loads commensurate with the horse-and-cart era, these structures are capable of supporting much greater weights, as tests have shown. However, following the 1968 Transport Act, a far-reaching 'Bridgeguard' operation to strengthen or replace many such spans has been put into effect; its implications are likely to be evident for many years to come, causing much inconvenience to the waterborne traveller and to the re-routed heavy-vehicle driver.

Depending on availability, the humpbacked canal bridge may be built of various materials: stone, especially in the north of England and the Cotswolds; red brick in the South and Midlands; a characteristic Birmingham 'blue brick' in that area; wood, for initial cheapness, especially for pedestrian traffic only; and cast iron, particularly in industrial regions such as the intricate Birmingham Canal Navigations system. More recent replacements or additions have been built in steel, aluminium and reinforced concrete.

The simple brick or stone bridge would generally be provided with hollow abutments filled with earth or rubble. On the majority of canals a horse towpath is carried under the arch, a practice which soon resulted in serious wear as a constant succession of boat lines cut into the structure. In time cast-iron protection plates were added to the bridge sides, and these became deeply engraved with sharp edged grooves. Some canal companies whitewashed the curve of the bridge arches, and marked the navigable centre of the bridge hole with a vertical stripe, invaluable to the steerers of dimly lit night boats. This feature is still to be found, notably on the Leeds and Liverpool Canal.

In some instances the narrowness of the bridge hole did not allow for inclusion of a towpath, especially where the bridge crossed the tail or bottom end of a lock. In this case an uphill-bound horse would be unhitched and walked on to the lockside, while the boat was carried into the chamber under its own momentum (Trent and Mersey Canal or Irish Grand Canal). Sometimes a narrow arch or small tunnel was taken through the bridge abutments for the benefit of the horse, as at Possett Bridge, Marple, Lower Peak Forest Canal, and at Gailey Lock, Staffs and Worcs Canal. The sloping floor of this passage was paved with projecting courses of brick or stone at intervals to provide a foothold.

Where opposition to construction of a waterway, with its consequent heavy traffic and infringement of privacy, was declared by a landowner, pacification was sometimes achieved by the company by designing the canal in a sweeping curve (Cassiobury Park, Watford, Grand Union Canal); in this way the navigation would take on the appearance more of a natural river than an artificial cut. The vogue for ornamental canals or lakes to be found at many of the great country

*Part of a bridge parapet in cast iron in the centre of Leicester, Grand Union Canal*

houses, including Hampton Court and Blenheim Palace, resulted in a number of decorated canal bridges carrying balustrades or statues, as in Cassiobury Park or Avenue Bridge, Chillington, over the Shropshire Union near Brewood. The latter carries the drive of a private residence. In Cosgrove village, north of Wolverton, there is a particularly fine bridge over the Grand Union, with wide Gothic-pointed arch and encrustation of delicate carving on the honey-coloured local stonework.

Provision of twin navigation arches can be found downhill of duplicate locks, such as the Cheshire Locks north of the Potteries on the Trent and Mersey Canal. This shows that the former heavy boat traffic necessitated a doubling of locking capacity. Elsewhere double arches may offer a clue as to the existence of duplicate locks of which one has long vanished. The bridge below Stoke Bruerne Top Lock, Northamptonshire, and several in the Slapton area of the Grand Union in Buckinghamshire are of this practice.

A simple but ingenious device, enabling the boat's towing-line to negotiate a towpath-less bridge without casting off, is the split bridge. Here twin arms are cantilevered from the bridge abutments, leaving a central gap through which the rope can pass. The southern section of the Stratford-upon-Avon Canal retains a number of accommodation bridges of this kind, composed of brick and cast iron, and also split footbridges over the tail of some locks. Others are to be found on the Staffs and Worcs, Trent and Mersey and Caldon Canals, with a good one at Spon Lane Locks, Smethwick, Birmingham Canal Navigations. As an alternative to the centrally split bridge, a small number of single-armed cantilevered footways exist at the lower end of narrow locks. Here the span reaches the opposite side of the lock, but stands 2–3in proud of it, again allowing a boat-line to be passed through the space. Lock 33, Stoke Prior, Worcester and Birmingham Canal, and one of the Birmingham and Fazeley Canal's Aston Locks display this curiosity.

Where the towpath changed from one side of the waterway to the other, the canal builders frequently built a turnover or roving bridge to carry the horse and towline over. Easier to understand in pictorial terms than to describe, this type of bridge makes the horse cross the canal to the opposite bank, where it then passes under the bridge, having joined the new length of path. Thus any necessity for unhitching the towline was avoided. Not unexpectedly, such bridges are sometimes locally known as 'snake bridges'. One of the most elegant is Capt Clark's Bridge, Hyde, on the Lower Peak Forest Canal. The Leeds and Liverpool, Grand Union and the Macclesfield use these.

Some canal bridges are erected purely for the convenience of the boatman. Small wooden-decked platforms may be provided to cross the tail of locks as an alternative to the walkways on the gates. Foxton Flight, Grand Union Canal Leicester section, has such simple crossings with handrails. They can, however, represent a considerable inconvenience to boat-lines, especially if craft are being hauled from one chamber to the next instead of using the power of the engine. The technique of flicking the rope under the bridge and trapping it under foot when it arrives on the other side is worth borrowing from the working-boat people. In recent years several places now much frequented by pleasure-boat parties have been fitted with concreted wooden plank crossings at the lower end of locks. Similarly unsophisticated pedestrian bridges can be found crossing navigation channels: near Napton on the Southern Oxford Canal, for instance, steep steps lead up to a perilous-seeming single wooden beam over the water, with side-rails. The higher reaches of the Thames are spanned by two quite delightful wooden erections – Old Man's and Tenfoot Bridges – both painted in Thames Water Authority black and grey and illustrating the good-looking functional tradition of TWA installations.

River navigations are sometimes equipped with pedestrian crossings following a rather indirect course, first over the lock gates and then across the adjacent weir on a decked platform built over the control sluices. Where a public right of way exists, the whole structure is generally more elaborate and better equipped with guard-rails. The visual effect of the snaking path can be attractive as at Marsh and Hambledon Locks on the Thames. Those at Shepperton and Penton Hook are in part protected by beamed roofs, in the style of the famous bridge on Switzerland's Lake Lucerne. Similar simple wooden bridges carry the towpaths of many river navigations across the mouths of small tributaries, as above Thames Lock, Weybridge, or across the lower end of weir streams, as below Stoke Lock, Guildford, on the River Wey.

Canal bridges are a continual interest. After passing under a series of pleasant but unremarkable bridges one may see ahead a real gem, worthy of special attention. It may be Brindley's exceptionally wide span at Great Haywood Junction in Staffordshire, its slightly pointed arch of brick making a frame for the mellow red warehouses behind. Bridges can vary also in height: those linking the sides of deep cuttings on the Shropshire Union soar up to four times the height of normal bridges on this waterway. Wherever a canal winds along a hillside, a cliff on one bank and a sheer drop on the other may well produce weirdly angled parapets to bridges at

*Completely without decoration, but very charming nevertheless: a lock footbridge on the Montgomeryshire Canal at Welsh Frankton*

45 degrees to the water. Subtle curves of brick or stone flanking walls can provide constant pleasure, as can details like bull-nosed coping bricks, courses of stone in brickwork or *vice versa*, or the shadows cast by pierced ironwork on the bridge decking.

Later canals, following a line of embankments and cuttings, boast some of the boldest bridges. The Tame Valley Canal on the central part of the Birmingham network, and the Birmingham Main Line itself, both possess grand structures striding through space like railway viaducts. Telford's Galton Bridge spans the BCN Main Line near Birmingham for 150ft at a height of 75ft but road construction works completed in 1974 have sadly destroyed the visual impact, and the canal is now tunnelled through this part of the former cutting.

Some of the most satisfying styles are achieved in the cast-iron bridges produced between 1800 and 1840. One of the best known foundries was the Horseley Iron Works, whose named and dated products grace the BCN and are characteristic of the 1830s improvement of the Northern Oxford Canal. They show a lightness of design unexpected with such heavy material. At Braunston Junction, where the Oxford Canal makes a triple intersection with the Grand Union, a particularly well placed pair can be found, and another arches over the hairpin turn where the Oxford and Coventry Canals unite at Hawkesbury. There is a wealth of intricate detail in the ironwork. Similar bridges have become sought after by town planners, and one was removed from an arm of the Oxford Canal and placed as a feature in a central Coventry landscaping scheme.

### Movable canal bridges

To discover a Shropshire Union bascule bridge in the Cheshire countryside comes as a slight shock. Yet the Welsh section to Llangollen boasts a number, very Dutch in design

*Farm crossings or minor roads are carried over the Southern Oxford Canal by a series of attractive little draw-bridges which rise on a toothed segment of cast iron*

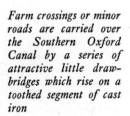

and maintained in good order. They present no great hazard to the pleasure boatman, who normally seizes a dangling rope or chain suspended from the horizontal beams 12ft above him, lifts his weight off the ground and watches the road platform gently rise away from the water. In a few cases these bridges lack the necessary chain, and one at Pontcysyllte bears the instruction: 'Cast a rope over the beam to open bridge.'

The drawbridges of the Southern Oxford Canal are stumpy weathered devices originally made of wood that has now sometimes been replaced by a lightweight alloy. These bridges have no overhead frame, but rely for counterbalance on the weight of the giant arms. A large number, providing farm access only, remain permanently open during the summer, and those that need to be opened can present problems. But for all their potential difficulties, the Oxford Canal drawbridges are a feature without which that delightful waterway would be unthinkable. The working parts of the Oxford Canal rolling bridges are a simple arrangement of interlocking teeth moving in an arc, both on the bridge and on its base.

Regional variations of the manual lift bridge may be seen on the Caldon Canal, and at Rickmansworth on the River Chess, beyond its entrance lock from the Grand Union at Batchworth. The Northampton, Welford and derelict Buckingham Arms of the Grand Union also have drawbridges. The type is more often to be found on narrow canals, for the effort required to raise a broad beam span is very considerable. Needless to say, there are some exceptions to this general rule.

Several examples on the Northern Stratford Canal make use of a winding-drum and cable operated by a lock windlass. These devices have the great advantage of being fixable in the open position before the boat ventures beneath. A 1954 addition to the Basingstoke Canal at North Warnborough is a lifting bridge with the unusually wide span of 17ft. It is operated hydraulically by a hand lever that must be moved back and forth two hundred times.

The Barrow Line in Southern Ireland possesses a really elegant drawbridge at Monasterevan, surmounted by a grooved winding wheel and having long and slender balance beams. A simpler version can be seen on the same navigation at Lodge Lock, Bagenalstown.

Among waterways where manually operated swing bridges are still in use are the Leeds and Liverpool, Upper Peak Forest, Lancaster, Macclesfield, Grand Union and Kennet and Avon. These bridges normally take the form of a wooden deck with hand-rails, and may be for local farm use or may

*The Barrow Navigation at Monasterevan is noted for this very substantial bascule bridge. Operated by the canal staff, with two men applying themselves to a heavy windlass, it causes considerable delays to road traffic should a boat wish to pass through*

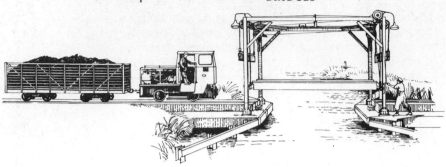

*Turf cut from the bog-*
*lands around Ireland's*
*Grand Canal is used as*
*the prime fuel for the*
*country's power stations.*
*Special diesel-hauled*
*light railways cross the*
*waterway at several*
*points; a section of*
*track is manually raised*
*for the passage of craft,*
*either as shown here or*
*in the form of a single*
*leaf bascule*

carry minor public roads. Pivoted on a turntable set on one
bank, those in regular use (and with the required greasing)
offer little resistance. Remains of a swing bridge on the
Caldon Canal at Endon Basin show a type that pivoted on a
turntable set in the middle of the waterway, leaving a narrow
channel for boats on each side. At former gauging points like
Worcester Bar, Birmingham, and Brinklow on the Northern
Oxford the simplest of swinging plank contrivances allow
pedestrian access. A singular combination of swing bridge
with fixed overhead footway can be seen near Fazeley on the
Birmingham and Fazeley Canal. On either side of it, whitewashed brick castellated towers conceal a spiral stairway to
the upper level.

As an alternative to merely pushing on the handrails of
the bridge, the swing span taking a minor road over the
Grand Union beside the Three Horseshoes, Winkwell,
Hertfordshire, is controlled by a low-geared wheel attached
to a cable drum. More than one fast-approaching car has
plunged into the gap as a boat passed through!

All bridges were made to open on the Gloucester and
Sharpness Ship Canal. These are attended by keepers, and
are worked manually or are power-operated.

Large hydraulic swing or lift bridges are a familiar part of
most extensive coastal dock systems like London or Liverpool.
Some of the biggest in Britain can be seen on the Manchester
Ship Canal, the Weaver and the North East network – Aire
and Calder, and Sheffield and South Yorkshire. These are
opened by arrangement or between certain specified hours.
Trafford Road Swing Bridge over the Manchester Ship
Canal, completed in 1894 with a span of 75ft and a total
weight of 1,800 tons, is mounted on a roller circle 49ft 6in in
diameter, with sixty-four rollers.

*Swing bridges are en-*
*countered occasionally*
*on many canals, but*
*more frequently on the*
*Macclesfield, Peak*
*Forest, Lancaster and*
*Leeds & Liverpool.*
*That illustrated crosses*
*the L&L near Bingley*

### New canal bridges

Demands for new or improved roads have in the present
century brought considerable changes to the canals. Before
World War II local or county highway authorities replaced a

number of original canal bridges by rather unattractive utilitarian structures. Such improvements may necessitate removal of the old bridge altogether, or it may well be incorporated into the new one, as at Nell Bridge, near Banbury, Oxford Canal.

With much of the Department of the Environment's efforts now directed towards motorway construction, the face of our canals is changing dramatically in some areas. Since completion of the southern section of the M1, one of the narrow locks on the Northampton Arm has been protected by a vast concrete umbrella. The M5 and M6 have opened miles of hitherto secret Birmingham canals to public view. An elevated viaduct on the Old Main Line at Oldbury is firmly planted in the canal itself, while the multi-level Spaghetti Junction intersection has brought new grandeur (or desolation, depending on your appreciation of such modern exploits of civil engineering) to the canals of Salford Junction. The northern and most beautiful reaches of the Lancaster Canal are now isolated above Tewitfield Locks because of the difference in costs between culverting and bridging with the arrival of the M6. The remoteness of one of the loveliest stretches of canal in Britain, the Oxford near Shipton and its neighbour the River Cherwell, are threatened by road plans. The Weaver and Thames alike have had new arches thrown across their waters. But, rest assured, two hundred years from now some writer will nostalgically revel in the sad beauty of creeper-clad crumbling motorway structures, lamenting the passing of late twentieth-century architectural taste! Allow sufficient time to elapse to spread a patina of age, and almost any construction becomes picturesque.

*Fixed and swing bridges occur together in this pleasant crossing of the Birmingham & Fazeley Canal at Drayton Manor. Spiral steps in the embattled turrets provide access to the upper footbridge*

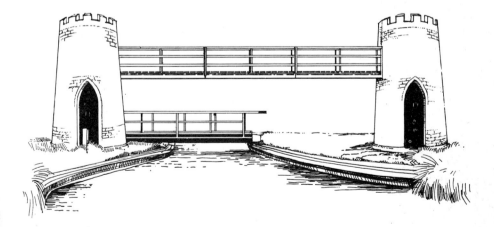

*The Pontcysyllte Aqueduct carries the Llangollen Canal high over the River Dee in North Wales*

# 6

# *Aqueducts*

OF all canal structures, there are none to match the impressiveness of our biggest aqueducts, great bridges of water carrying boats over river valleys, roads, railways and even other canals. To the waterway traveller all but the grandest aqueducts can quite easily pass unnoticed, for a slight narrowing of the channel with brick- or stone-lined banks approached at each end by an embankment may be the only telltales. But to arrive by boat at the mighty Pontcysyllte, where the impression of being suspended at a great height above the River Dee is very real, or to cruise at high level *over* the Manchester Ship Canal at Barton, are truly memorable experiences. At the risk of underlining the obvious it must be emphasised that the canal – water, boats and all – is carried by the aqueduct, presenting an intriguing prospect of large craft chugging over motorways, inter-city express trains or busy shopping streets. There really are people living in Burnley unaware that the bridge high above a main road is in fact a water-filled tank containing the surviving trans-Pennine canal.

Britain's first navigation aqueduct was so daring a project that the scheme met with popular ridicule, but laughter changed to admiration and astonishment as James Brindley's Barton aqueduct was successfully completed to unite two sections of the Bridgewater Canal on either side of the River Irwell near Manchester. It was truly a 'bridge of water'. It is now difficult to realise how revolutionary was Brindley's three-arched stone bridge totalling, with its approaches, about 600ft in length. There was sufficient clearance for sailing barges to pass beneath on the river, some 39ft below. As the navigation channel over the top was 18ft wide and 4½ft deep, it can be appreciated that this was a sizeable structure, massively built to bear the great weight of water and puddled clay laid in the masonry trough to prevent leakage. This old Barton aqueduct lasted in good condition from its opening in 1761 until 1893, when the bed of the Irwell was transformed at this point into the Manchester Ship Canal and the Bridgewater was provided with a unique swinging-span aqueduct.

No significant advance in aqueduct design followed old

Barton for over thirty years. The immense weight of water
and clay required foundations of elephantine proportions.
This largely accounts for the generally squat appearance of
early aqueducts, which were frequently just stone embankments with a succession of culverts to allow water to flow
along the river bed.

Almost every artificial waterway includes different types
of aqueduct, ranging from the succession of low arches of
Brindley's Dove aqueduct on the Trent and Mersey Canal,
near Burton, to the elliptical footpath tunnel that connects
two sections of the Grand Union village of Cosgrove, but so
secretly that without local knowledge you would scarcely
suspect its presence under the canal.

Two outstanding aqueducts, displaying features that
blend the best of Canal Era engineering with classical
eighteenth-century architecture, are Dundas and Avoncliffe,
both carrying the Kennet and Avon Canal over the upper
reaches of the Bristol Avon. Designed by Rennie, who lavishly
borrowed the Georgian style of Bath to decorate this canal,
the most visually sophisticated of all, neither would look out
of place spanning the lake at Blenheim Palace or gracing the
landscaped gardens of Stourhead. One of the most beautifully
situated is the Brynich aqueduct, set among the hills near
Brecon, where it transfers the Brecon and Abergavenny
Canal from one bank of the rocky River Usk to the other.

All the conventional aqueducts of earlier design were
equipped with towpaths, established on the masonry or on
earth banking by the water. Later varieties would either
include a path alongside and rather below water level
(Bearley on the Southern Stratford and Longdon-on-Tern,
Shrewsbury Canal), or more satisfactorily projecting over
the water, so that even if the channel was reduced to little
more than the beam of a narrow boat, there would be no
excessive drag on hulls (Pontcysyllte). The 'cork in a bottle'
effect is especially noticeable where French 340-ton péniches
on the Loire Lateral Canal must navigate a long aqueduct
over the River Allier immediately at the head of the two-lock
Guétin staircase. Each uphill barge must be completely
clear of the aqueduct before the locks can be refilled for their
next use, or it will be relentlessly drawn back on to the
upper gates.

A breakthrough in aqueduct technology came with the
use of cast-iron troughs, making the old-fashioned lining of
puddled clay unnecessary. This in turn allowed the building
of much taller structures on slender supports and at a
proportionately reduced cost. Benjamin Outram's single-
span Derby Canal aqueduct at the Holmes, now demolished,
was the first in Britain to adopt the new technique, being

opened in February 1795. But it was followed the next month by Thomas Telford's more significant Longdon-on-Tern crossing, which was regarded by its engineer as a successful trial for Pontcysyllte and many other lesser structures that were conceived over the next thirty-five years. Longdon consists of a narrow beam cast-iron trough linking embankments on each side of the river and mounted on a seemingly fragile framework of iron uprights. The stone abutments are a relic of Josiah Clowes' original masonry structure, which was washed away. Plates on the sides of the trough are connected with diagonal joints. Now nearby portions of the long-closed Shrewsbury Canal have been bulldozed into oblivion, while the dry bed of the aqueduct serves as a river bridge for farm vehicles. It is planned to re-erect the structure as part of the Ironbridge Gorge Museum Trust's open-air industrial complex at Blist's Hill, Coalport, not far from Ketley, where the original castings were made.

Use of iron became widespread for later aqueducts, and there are many good examples still in use throughout navigations of the early nineteenth century. The Shropshire Union main line has two, one over the A5 at Stretton and the other near the centre of Nantwich (A51). It is greatly to the credit of their builders that almost 150 years after completion they represent little more danger to the roads they cross than does any dry bridge. Functional elegance characterises the detail of these Telford designs, with their intricate iron railings, and carved stone pillars at each corner.

Another Telford aqueduct, carrying the Welsh Canal over the River Ceiriog at Chirk, is something of a hybrid, though a rather splendid one. The main structure consists of a conventional stone bridge 70ft high and 600ft long, with ten arches, but the bottom of the trough was formed by iron plates with hollow spandrels to the arches. In this way weight was reduced, and in the event of any leakage, water could escape without placing great strains on the masonry. Having spent the beginning of his working life as a stone mason, it seems that Telford had not gained sufficient confidence in the use of iron to provide Chirk with a trough similar to that at Longdon. It was opened in 1801 and to this day remains chunky, impressive and altogether unlikely as it strides across the narrow valley among the treetops. The illusion of unreality is increased by the canal almost immediately diving into Chirk tunnel. The scale of the aqueduct is rather reduced by an even taller railway viaduct almost alongside, though this does provide an excellent (but slightly hazardous) vantage point from which to photograph boats crossing the river.

When Chirk was completed, Pontcysyllte, crossing the Dee

3 miles away, had been under construction for six years and would not be ready for use until November 1805. There had been a contract for a normal stone aqueduct over the fast flowing Dee, but, because of the considerable difference in levels between canal and river, a series of locks on each side, lowering the height of the crossing to about 75ft, had been proposed. Between them the engineer William Jessop and Thomas Telford decided in 1795 on a 1,007ft iron trough standing on a series of slender stone piers, each solid at the base but hollow from about 70ft upwards. Despite the part he played in the project, Jessop received little credit for it in later years. Indeed, when Telford wrote publicly of the work long afterwards, he appeared to accord himself sole responsibility! Local materials were used exclusively, stone being quarried nearby, and before long the nineteen arches, each with a 45ft span, began to rise from the rocky bed of the Dee. Working conditions must have been alarming, what with the dangerously flowing river (it falls more than 120ft in the 5 miles between Llangollen and Pontcysyllte), the difficulty in placing dams around the foundation sites, and the problems associated with setting large blocks of stone in position more than 100ft in the air! A mixture of ox blood, water and lime was used as a mortar for the stonework joints.

In the village of Fron, south of the Dee, a great approach embankment had to be created to bring the canal to a level corresponding with its position on the opposite side of the river. The many-flanged iron plates that were to comprise the trough were conveniently cast at the Plaskynaston Foundry, within view of the aqueduct. They were bolted together and the joints made watertight with Welsh flannel and lead dipped in boiling sugar! In November 1805 8,000 people witnessed the opening ceremony. Pontcysyllte had cost £47,000, with labourers receiving 8s to 12s per week.

Whatever words are used to describe the finest aqueduct in Britain, and almost certainly the most spectacular aerial navigation in the world, to encounter Pontcysyllte for the first time is an experience that invariably exceeds all expectations. Local residents use the towpath, which is protected by iron railings, as a regular walk, and never quite lose a sense of Welsh pride in the magnificent view down the valley or the remarkable structure itself. The towpath is a place noted for strange encounters, such as one with the man whose forebears toiled as masons and labourers during the aqueduct's construction. For the promise of a small fee he will draw from an inner pocket a neatly duplicated brief history, and he needs surprisingly little persuasion to pose against the sky for a photograph, or even to speak a handful of well-chosen words into a portable recorder. Pontcysyllte attracts sightseers as well as boating holidaymakers, and the more astute locals are not slow to grasp a fair opportunity. But there was no wish for financial gain in the utterly credible words of the gentleman who told of his seeing a figure dressed in a crinoline approach him by moonlight along the aqueduct towpath, only to disappear completely 10ft away. Canals are always ideal locations for hauntings and few sites are better suited than the Pontcysyllte towpath.

A sheer drop of up to 121ft confronts the boatman standing in his cockpit. If you do suffer from heights, concentrate your gaze on the protected towpath side or get someone else to steer. This is the nearest you will probably come to knowing what it is like to work as a steeplejack.

Scottish canals possess four remarkable, but little known, aqueducts whose scale closely rivals that of Pontcysyllte. Three occur on the Union Canal between Falkirk and Edinburgh, crossing the Rivers Almond, Avon and Water of Leith at Slateford. Designed by Hugh Baird, they were close copies of Chirk. Soon after completion in 1822, the Slateford Aqueduct was described as 'superior perhaps to any aqueduct in the kingdom'. The Avon reaches a height of 86ft, with twelve arches spread over a length of 810ft. Almond is 76ft high and 420ft long, with five arches, while Slateford is 75ft high, its eight arches spanning a distance of 500ft. The other major aqueduct in Scotland carries the Forth and Clyde Canal over the River Kelvin in Glasgow; this comprises four arches of massive stone blocks and is 70ft high by 400ft long. It was constructed by William Gibb and John Moir of Falkirk, working under the supervision of the great engineer Robert Whitworth, who assumed general responsibility for the whole canal. The Kelvin Aqueduct was completed in 1790 and was one of the boldest such structures then existing.

All aqueducts, but particularly iron ones, are vulnerable in very cold weather. If at all possible, thick ice must not be allowed to form in the trough, where expansion could cause cracking, with serious consequences. For this reason and also to facilitate regular maintenance, the bed of most aqueducts can be isolated from the rest of the canal by shutting gates or inserting stop planks. A series of plugs can then be drawn to release the water. On Pontcysyllte a lever under the towpath achieves this result, causing a thunderous cascade of water to pour into the Dee far below. Windlass-operated paddles may be seen on the Union Canal's Almond Aqueduct, and, as there is a slight leak, the air below is filled with a constant fine spray. The Brecon Canal's Brynich Aqueduct is emptied by pulling a drain plug situated on the bottom of the nearby canal; this plug is drawn by attaching a chain to a wooden winch by the towpath and winding.

*Two examples of aqueduct railings in cast iron to be found on the Birmingham Canal Navigations*

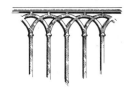

*Detail of the ironwork of the Pontcysyllte Aqueduct*

Brick is a material found less frequently on larger aqueducts than stone. One brick example is the canal 'flyover' on the Trent and Mersey's Caldon branch at Hazlehurst. Here the line to Leek was rebuilt in 1841 to cross the lower level of the Caldon, a move made necessary by railway construction works. Similar alterations to canals involving aqueducts occurred regularly as railway networks expanded. The most unusual triple intersection is that of railway, Grand Union Canal and roadway above, just north of Hanwell Locks in Middlesex. One line of canal might have to cross another (Smethwick, on the Birmingham Canal Navigations, or at Oldbury on the same system, where the Old Main Line spans the New Main Line), or a major road might be planned to pass through a canal embankment. In the present century road improvements of this type include a rather ugly reinforced concrete aqueduct, typical of the 1930s, taking the Paddington Arm over the busy North Circular Road west of London. It survived bombing during 1939–45 only to burst on to the roadway at Easter 1962. Repairs lasted several weeks. Considering the loads they bear, it is surprising that such accidents have not happened on aqueducts more often. Generally, when trouble does occur, it will be to the approach embankment. That leading to an original stone-arched crossing of the Great Ouse at Wolverton, Bucks, failed only months after completion, and Grand Union Canal traffic was forced to use locks down to the river and up the other side until the present iron 'trunk' aqueduct was opened in 1811. More recently, in August 1971, a serious collapse took place on the Bridgewater Canal's Bollin embankment near Lymm, carrying away part of the stone aqueduct arch and closing the canal to through navigation for more than eighteen months.

New aqueducts utilising the engineering possibilities presented by steel and reinforced concrete are to be found where the Tame Valley Canal passes over the M5 motorway at West Bromwich and at Dudley Port, also on the BCN. Here the Telford-built Ryland aqueduct was replaced in 1968 by a new span to provide a wider roadway beneath.

One of Britain's least known but most interesting aqueducts is the Stanley Ferry, near Wakefield in Yorkshire, on the improved line of the Aire and Calder Navigation. This appears to have been designed by George Leather, with a degree of intervention from the ubiquitous Telford. A single iron span decorated on the sides with a mass of thin upright columns crosses the Calder. Much of the load is carried by a pair of latticed ironwork arches curving over the river and connected with the trough by numerous metal cables. The resulting effect is similar to that of a suspension bridge. Still on waterways of the North East, the New Junction Canal of

1905, linking the Sheffield and South Yorkshire with the Aire and Calder via Sykehouse, possesses a series of four modern aqueducts. Several have guillotine gates mounted at each end.

Aqueducts are rarely substantially bigger than the beam of the commercial traffic for which the canal was intended. It is always wise, therefore, to hold back if another boat is about to make the crossing. Fortunately all were built quite straight, so there should be no problems of visibility.

The Barton Swing Aqueduct is unique. Whether the way ahead is clear or not, you will certainly want to stop and marvel at this expression of late Victorian engineering. The structure is just one of a series of opening bridges over the Manchester Ship Canal, a waterway that brought canal building in Britain to its peak and virtually its completion in 1894. Brindley's old Barton Aqueduct had carried the Bridgewater Canal over the Irwell for 130 years, but as the line of the river was to be absorbed into the channel of the Ship Canal, with its intended air draught of 75ft, the old crossing had to be removed. One early plan was to build a high-level fixed aqueduct approached at each end by vertical lifts similar to that at Anderton. But this was rejected on account of the serious delays that would have been experienced by the then very heavy Bridgewater traffic. Sir Edward Leader Williams was charged with the task of designing a trough of wrought-iron plates and angles, pivoted at the centre on an island in the middle of the Ship Canal. The tank, 234ft long with a navigation width of 19ft and 7ft depth of water, had to be swung full, as to drain it and refill again would have been costly in supplies and wasteful of time.

When a ship is expected to pass by, gates are closed to seal off the Bridgewater Canal at each end, and a further pair of gates attached to the opening span isolate water in the aqueduct. Wedges and rubber seals make these gates almost completely watertight and the small quantity of water between the approaches and the aqueduct is drained off. The structure can then be moved on its central circular roller-path until it lies at right-angles to the Ship Canal. Hydraulic machinery works the gates and swings the span, which weighs, with its water, 1,600 tons. A control cabin with keeper is situated at the northern end, a comfortable little establishment bright with brass controls, dials and levers. Trouble-free operation greatly depends on the aqueduct swinging in a perfect horizontal plane. One cause of anxiety to the occupants of one steamer on the Ship Canal was the fact that the aqueduct had been swung while containing a barge at one end. They feared that the 'extra weight' would unbalance the span!

*Chirk Tunnel, Llangollen Canal*

# 7
# Tunnels

THE briefest association with British canals demonstrates that oddities are commonplace. At Burnley you can cruise for many hundreds of yards above the town centre at chimneypot level, your boat hangs alarmingly in space as you ride the Anderton Vertical Lift or soar above a river valley on an aqueduct, and flights of locks lift you far above the levels where you would normally expect to travel by water; but nothing quite equals the totally unreal sensation of diving underground as you enter a canal tunnel. Long before the portal is reached, you can sense its approach. Ahead, a range of hills seems to bar the way. For as long as it is able, the canal twists and turns in its attempt to stay in the open. Finally the last bend is rounded and at the end of an ever-deepening wooded cutting a small black hole seems to block the route. As you approach, it appears that here is a railway tunnel that somehow has been flooded. More than perhaps any other feature of canal construction the tunnel is a reminder of the advances made in waterway engineering, for if Britain's network of inland navigations had been laid down in the later twentieth century rather than in the eighteenth and early nineteenth, it is certain that few if any tunnels would have been found necessary. Where all excavation had to be achieved with hand tools and the most elementary explosive techniques, however, it was generally more prudent to tunnel through a hillside than lift the top off, so creating a cutting. Later, problems of restricted craft movement or costly maintenance necessitated the complete removal of some tunnel roofs. Fenny Compton Tunnel on the Southern Oxford and Armitage on the Trent and Mersey are examples.

At present there are about 21·8 miles of navigable tunnel in England, Wales and Scotland. A further 11·4 miles have been closed to traffic during the last century or so. When the mileages of tunnels long derelict or converted at an early date into railways (Strood, on the Thames and Medway Canal was 3,946yd long) are added to these figures, we have a total distance of underground canal in Britain of about 42 miles. That is almost certainly greater than the total combined length of all other canal tunnels in the world. To make this statistic even more impressive, a further 46 miles of underground canal burrowed into the coalmines at Worsley. A substantial portion remains connected with the Bridgewater Canal, although not available for navigation.

Tunnel construction was an activity that produced endless worry for the engineers, sometimes dreadful working conditions for the gangs of navvies and often financial crises for the promoters, as the estimates of cost and completion date were rarely accurate. Such tunnelling experience as existed in the early years of canal building came from the mines. It was a rather imprecise science, composed of a mixture of judgement and luck. Mistakes were made, bores being driven crooked and attempts to cut through unstable soil or rock having to be abandoned. Cowley Tunnel on the Shropshire Union was designed to be 690yd long, but a series of collapses during building resulted in a mere 81yd of it being underground, the rest forming a rock-sided cutting.

Having determined that either a change of route or succession of locks was out of the question on grounds of expense or hindrance to navigation, the engineers would first drive a line of stakes over the hilltop in an attempt to mark out the completely straight course of the tunnel. Then, at intervals of about 150yd, brick-lined shafts were sunk from the hilltop down to the canal level. These 'wells' were important in providing ventilation down to the workings, which was sometimes improved by the erection of sails to deflect the wind, so causing a down-draught. The wells also allowed spoil from the diggings to be hauled to the surface and were later useful as ventilation shafts when the tunnel was in operation. Below the tunnel level itself a drainage culvert was normally constructed to carry away the inevitable spring water that would otherwise flood the working faces. When the shafts had reached their required depth, the staked-out line over the hill was carefully repeated, with a string stretched parallel over the mouth of the bores. A pair of plumb lines was then suspended down the hole and dropped into bowls of either mercury or water to keep them steady. These then gave an accurate direction in which the excavation should begin.

Blisworth Tunnel, at 3,056yd, was dug from no fewer than nineteen shafts, with the result that there were forty working faces, including the portals at each end. Soil and other debris was hauled up the shafts by horse-powered gins or steam-driven winches. 'Fire' or steam engines were also brought in to keep the workings dry. Sometimes the spoil could be used in the building of embankments elsewhere along the line, but more often it was left on the surface in heaps that remain to this day as grass-grown hillocks. At some of the later tunnels, eg Islington on the Regent's Canal, a horse-drawn railway track was laid along the invert of the tunnel, enabling excavated material to be hauled out as soon as the central portions had been connected with one or other of the tunnel ends.

The first three major tunnels built on British canals were Preston Brook, Saltersford and Barnton on the northern end of the Trent and Mersey. Although only 1,239, 424 and 572yd respectively, none of them is particularly straight, and they all demand a degree of concentration when navigating. The lining of the tunnels was normally of brick, erected over a wooden framework with clay rammed into the space between brickwork and the sides of the bore. Yard by yard the tunnellers progressed, the excavating gangs working ahead of the bricklayers, spending long hours in atrocious conditions with tallow candles penetrating the darkness. Accidents certainly happened as men were lowered down the shafts or as sections of the roof collapsed without warning. The work produced men with specialised skills who would move from one tunnel site to another. Doubtless they were more handsomely paid than their counterparts toiling on sections of the waterway out in the open.

One of the deepest tunnels was Morwellham on the now derelict Tavistock Canal. Near the centre it is 460ft below the surface. The Thames and Severn Canal's Sapperton Tunnel, 3,808yd long, reaches 340ft. below the highest point of the hill. At 5,698yd, Standedge on the Huddersfield Narrow Canal was the longest tunnel opened to traffic. Although the canal is now closed, occasional inspection trips are made by boat. Had a plan been carried out to connect the Manchester, Bolton and Bury Canal with the River Calder, this would have demanded a tunnel no less than five miles long.

Initially the problems of tunnel construction were so great that the bore was normally only slightly wider than the maximum beam allowed by bridge holes and lock chambers. The first Harecastle Tunnel, north of the Potteries, was 2,897yd and took 11 years to complete, from 1766 to 1777. When delays to traffic and the great inconvenience of one-way working compelled the company to call in Telford to design an additional tunnel running parallel, the new work was finished in just 3 years, from 1824 to 1827. Moreover Telford's bore boasted a towpath for the boat horses, thus obviating any need for 'legging' or poling the then unpowered cargo craft.

Until the advent of steam tugs, self-propelled boats or towpaths, craft were worked through tunnels either by shafting against the roof or sides or more normally by 'legging'. This entailed fixing a pair of special projecting boards or 'wings' on each side of the fore-end of the boat so that the crew, lying on their backs and gripping these 'wings' with their hands, could painfully push their boat through the tunnel by moving their feet along the walls. Needless to say, it was a dangerous as well as a tiring task. In the darkness only pierced by the light of a single candle it was easy for a legger to miss his footing, fall into the icy water and perhaps be crushed between the boat and the tunnel wall. When, during the last decades of the nineteenth century, there was a rash of canal novels for young readers, inclusion of a passage describing the dangers of legging was *de rigueur*. In L. T. Meade's *Water Gipsies*, a young boy named Rag is deputed to leg with his father for the first time:

> Was there ever a board so insecure as the one on which he now lay? Would it give way? Yes, he *felt* it loose; his hands relaxed their frantic clutch; his knees were powerless; he fell over – he was in the water.
>
> Yes, Rag fell into the awful lonely water that lay without current or motion in the black tunnel. It closed over his legs, his back, his head; then a hand, strong and powerful, clasped his rough, unkempt hair, and someone, or some people, dragged him again into the boat. Verily, he was delivered from the very jaws of death.

Half-drowned, Rag collapses in a deep sleep in the cabin, only to be woken shortly afterwards with a request to save his baby brother from being whipped for fainting on the towpath while trudging behind the horse. Powerful stuff, this boatmen's improvement propaganda! Yet doubtless there was more than a grain of truth in these sensational accounts. Professional leggers were employed on the Grand Union Canal at Blisworth Tunnel, where they were issued with brass armbands by the company to denote their official status. These registered leggers worked in northbound and southbound gangs, were paid 1s 6d a trip and were housed in huts next to Stoke Bruerne's 'Boat Inn' and opposite Blisworth Mill. Before the leggers were organised on this regular basis in 1827, the boat crews suffered from the over-zealous attentions of freelances, who were noted for their persuasive tactics to gain employment in much the same way as pleasure craft to this day may experience difficulty in not taking on the casual 'hufflers' who lurk around the heavy Wigan locks, demanding a substantial fee for help with gates and paddles. When in 1871 the Grand Junction Canal Co introduced steam tugs at Blisworth and Braunston tunnels, the leggers were pensioned off or found alternative work. One man, 75 years old, was given 5s a week pension in recognition of the 44 years he had spent on his back in the darkness. An

experiment had taken place the previous year in hauling boats
through Braunston by steam-driven wire cable, but this did
not meet with success.

The steam tugs lasted until 1934, by which time most
boats were self-propelled, and the remaining horsedrawn
craft had to rely on taking a tow from diesel boats. At the
turn of the century steam tugs were in regular service at
Blisworth and Braunston; at Foulridge and Gannow on the
Leeds and Liverpool Canal; at Westhill, Shortwood and
Tardebigge on the Worcester and Birmingham; and at
Islington on the Regent's Canal. The Leeds and Liverpool
craft were double-ended to avoid having to turn round at the
end of each trip. At Saltersford, Preston Brook and Barnton
(Trent and Mersey Canal) projecting wheels were attached
to the steam tugs to act as fenders against the tunnel walls.
A steam tunnel tug had been provided at Islington Tunnel
(Regent's Canal) by 1826. It was described many years later as
a kind of 'railway engine mounted on a platform, and drawn
along by means of a steel hawser, which winds itself round
two huge drums placed on the engine platform at a distance
of about eight feet apart'. About 1900 a new coke-fired steam
engine, working on a similar principle, was installed. Probably
the ugliest boat ever seen on British canals, it looked like a

*A working narrow boat
nears the northern por-
tal of the 2,042yd
Braunston Tunnel,
Grand Union Canal*

corrugated iron shed enveloped in clouds of steam. A reporter from the *Daily Chronicle* arrived armed with a gas-mask before embarking for a trip through the 960yd tunnel in 1929:

> Charon hailed me from the steam tug, as it lay at the entrance of the tunnel in Graham Street, City Road. 'Come aboard, sir, an' I'll take you through the Gates of 'Ell.' Then he saw my gas mask. He eyed me scornfully. 'Wot you want that for?' he said, scathingly. 'When you feel the smoke gripping you, dip your handkerchief in the canal and bury your face in it.' I looked at the canal. A dead cat floated by . . . I preferred my gas mask.

This venerable relic negotiated Islington in 35 minutes with nine loaded barges in tow. It was replaced about 1930 by diesel tugs.

The question of ventilation in tunnels filled with the steam and gases of coal-burning tugs was vital. A number of fatal accidents are recorded when boat crews were overcome by fumes. At Blisworth several of the old shafts remaining from the construction work were opened up. Often a line of fat brick chimneys marks the course of a canal below the ground, and nowhere does such a chimney make its presence so much felt as in the front garden of a small house at Coombeswood. This reminder of the Dudley Canal's Gosty Hill Tunnel squats in daylight-defying monstrousness a couple of feet from the occupant's front windows. You can only wonder at the insensitivity of the man responsible for building the house in such a location. When Brindley's Harecastle Tunnel had subsided to the extent that boats could no longer work through it, in the early 1900s, all traffic was diverted to the one-way Telford bore. Here, too, subsidence had taken place, and the thoughtfully provided towpath was partly under water. In such a confined place, where the headroom is sometimes reduced to a bare 6ft, steam haulage was out of the question. The problem was solved in 1914 by the introduction of an electric tug, which pulled itself along on a cable that fell away to the canal bottom. For the first 6 years the power was supplied from a bank of batteries carried aboard a 'tender' boat, one such tender being in use while the other was being charged. All boats were made to use the tow, whether powered or not, until 1954, when ventilation fans were fitted at the southern portal.

At shorter tunnels lacking a towpath, chains were sometimes fixed to the walls so that the boats could be pulled through by their crews. Elsewhere notches in the brick or stone provided a hold for poling with shafts. The horse, meanwhile, would

*An unusual garden ornament: this ventilation shaft whose top is well-protected against any hazard of missiles being thrown onto passing boats, is a constant reminder of the Dudley Canal where it passes through Gosty Hill Tunnel*

be walked over the top, whether along a sylvan path, as at
Savernake on the Kennet and Avon, or along the now rather
overgrown path at Braunston, or through the London streets
at Maida Hill and Islington. North of the Grand Union's
Hatton Locks, Shrewley Tunnel (433yd) is equipped with a
special horse tunnel, taking the towpath up a sharp gradient
to the top of the hill.

One-way tunnels over about 500yd in length normally
operated to a set timetable enforced by keepers at each end in
contact at a later date by telephone. Electric signals were
finally fitted at several places, including Foulridge, so
ensuring that boats did not meet underground. Today there
are few tunnels where pleasure craft run the risk of meeting
approaching boats and find that they are unable to pass.
Dudley and Harecastle do, however, come into this category,
and can only be used according to a timetable. When the
3,172yd Dudley Tunnel was reopened to traffic at Easter
1973 after rather more than 10 years' disuse as a through
route, a strict timetable was imposed, together with a ban on
the use of engines whose fumes could cause a hazard. In
addition to being the most exciting canal tunnel still open,
Dudley is the longest. It consists of a short bore from the
Tipton end, which soon opens out into a deep tree-covered
bowl – the Castle Mill Basin. Various limestone workings
were connected by shorter canal tunnels, including one of
1,227yd to the Wren's Nest Basin, linked with the surface via
a spiral staircase of 240 steps. The main section of navigation
tunnel remaining open is 2,942yd from Castle Mill Basin to
the top of the Park Head Locks. It passes through two
natural caverns en route, where it is possible to land and
scramble over large boulders. For passenger tripping boats
the tunnel provides one of the most memorable canal
journeys in Britain.

Construction work on the M23 motorway at Merstham in
Surrey in 1972 revealed an embarrassing complex of many
miles of tunnels, nine huge caverns, three ponds and a 44-
acre underground lake under the line of the new road. There
is a collection of stone-mining machinery and the rotting
remains of some twenty-eight canal boats. All are relics of the
quarrying activities of the first Baron Hyton at the end of the
eighteenth century. Little else is known about this strange
survival.

Much more fully documented are the 46 miles of underground coalmine waterways built to serve the Bridgewater
Canal at Worsley. Coal had been taken here since the
fourteenth century, first by working the surface and from
about 1600 by sinking shafts. But after that time few improvements had been made, and in any event the high cost of

transport to the Manchester market did not encourage
development. Then John Gilbert, having been called in by
the Duke to inspect the mines, suggested the construction of
a canal connecting with Manchester. The Duke was most
enthusiastic and eventually work on the canal began under
Brindley's supervision in July 1759.

Twin entrance tunnels 30yd apart were excavated in the
rock face at Worsley Delph, one for loaded boats being about
6ft 6in wide and the other for empties, about 8ft wide. There
was a water depth of about 4ft and headroom of 3ft 6in to
4ft. The parallel canals converged after 500yd and continued
for a long distance to Dixon Green, with large numbers of
subsidiary lines leaving the main line at right-angles. Almost
2 miles of canal, known as the Upper Level, was 35yd above
the main system. An inclined plane 151yd long allowed
simultaneous transfer of boats in each direction, the craft
travelling on cradles and the weight of descending containers
pulling loaded ones up. Boats were placed on the cradles by
draining the water from the locks, as at Ketley, Shropshire,
an ingenious system. Craft were of the type known as
'starvationers', crude double-ended containers with massive
ribs, and capable of loading 5–12 tons. They were hauled with
ropes or legged along the tunnel roof by boys. The last coal
was carried by water in the mines in 1887, but the network
still performs a useful drainage function for other workings
in the area.

The rabbit burrows of Harecastle or Dudley Tunnels are
confined spaces compared with the last canal tunnel built in
Britain, on the BCN at Netherton, duplicating the Dudley
route, which had long been a bottleneck. Started on the last
day of 1855, Netherton is 3,027yd long, with a water level
width of 27ft, including the twin towpaths. From the bottom
of the invert to the roof the height is 22ft 9in. The canal was
opened to traffic in August 1858 and was lit by gas (later this
was replaced by electricity, but there is now no illumina-
tion). The exceptionally heavy traffic of the BCN continued
well into the twentieth century, demanding 24-hour working
on certain sections. One flight of locks equipped with gas
lamps was Farmer's Bridge, so the luxury of lighting at
Netherton was quite in keeping with local practice. Today
many of the bigger and most modern Continental canal locks
work right round the clock in the glare of floodlights.

As would be expected from their gloomy atmosphere,
many tunnels are haunted, according to the verbal tradition
of the canals. Several tunnels claim the ghost of one Kit
Crewbucket. As long ago as the 1880s novelist L. T. Meade
pointed out how 'Kitcrew' was a canal term for Kidsgrove at
the northern end of the Harecastle Tunnels, and 'buggut' was

a slang term for a ghost. According to this writer, whose other facts on canal life were well researched, two men had murdered a woman and disposed of the body in the tunnel. Since then she had returned in the form of a white horse or as a headless female whose appearance signalled impending disaster, sudden death or even murder. In his *The Inland Waterways of England* L. T. C. Rolt mentions that 'several old boaters claim seriously to have seen this spectre and that its effect was singularly disturbing'. The baldness of the printed word tends to pile ridicule on these stories . . . your reactions may be rather different if you find yourself navigating the claustrophobic depths of Harecastle on your own. The Kit Crewbucket phantom associated with Crick Tunnel on the Grand Union's Leicester section is reputed to be of a more benevolent disposition!

*At the upper level, a towpath tunnel for boat horses makes this bore on the Grand Union Canal in Warwickshire quite unique*

Several decades ago a murder victim was dropped down one of the ventilation shafts of the disused Berwick Tunnel on the Shrewsbury Canal. This action resulted in the chimney being sealed up, to deter any similar attempt. A particularly nasty murder case of very recent years allegedly involved the carriage of a corpse in a pleasure boat for several days up the Trent and Mersey through Harecastle, until it was buried at a point on the canal bank some miles north of there. The police were unable to gather sufficient positive evidence to bring a case to court. If only the tunnel could tell . . .

Canal tunnels vary greatly in their portal designs. The majority are merely brick- or stone-faced holes in hillsides, and one can imagine the builders being so pleased to have completed the job that ornamentation did not greatly concern them. Elsewhere the canal was seen as a wonderful new transport medium that would enrich the lives of the people it served. Where the tunnel marked a summit level between the river valleys linked by the new navigation, some suitable symbolic flourish might be selected. For instance, at Sapperton Tunnel, 3,808yd, now derelict and partly blocked by roof falls, the uniting of the waters of Thames and Severn is commemorated in the grand manner. The east portal is a classical affair in Cotswold stone with a pair of Tuscan Doric columns, and alcoves at each side of the entrance obviously designed for statues (Isis and Sabrina?); and, although generally more plain, the west portal displays a castellated stone top. Over on the Kennet and Avon Canal, Bruce Tunnel at Savernake is embellished at its eastern end with a monumental inscribed stone tablet.

Chains are still attached to the walls of Bruce Tunnel to enable boats to be hauled through. The 502yd bore has the largest cross-section of any canal tunnel in Britain after Netherton.

Considering that it was completed long before Stratford had been elevated to its position as one of Britain's leading tourist attractions, Brandwood Tunnel on the Stratford Canal at King's Norton is surprisingly decorated with a circular stone plaque bearing Shakespeare's head between laurel sprays. This appropriate design near the beginning of the canal route into the Shakespeare Country was repeated on the company seal. Portals are often enlivened by a cluster of noticeboards dating from various stages of canal ownership in the present century. Name, distance and bridge number plates may be accompanied by warnings that the tunnel is closed to canoeists. At the narrow beam Curdworth Tunnel (Birmingham and Fazeley) the navigator is curiously requested to keep to the right. In faded lettering on a wooden

board at the Coombeswood steelworks end of Gosty Hill
Tunnel (Dudley Canal) appear the following instructions:
'Birmingham Canal Navigations. Notice. Private Motor
Tugs and Motor Boats must enter this end of the tunnel only
during the period of ten minutes before or ten minutes after
the Company's Tug has entered and the drivers must inform
the Company's driver of their intention to precede or follow
him.' No translation is available of the strange collection of
mason's marks and symbols carved in the blocks of stone at
the mouth of Burnley's Gannow Tunnel. Similar hieroglyphics can be seen on Rennie's classical Dundas Aqueduct
near Bath.

Some people can derive great satisfaction from the exploration of disused tunnels, an activity that combines boating
with potholing and is not without an element of danger where
structures have long since ceased to be properly maintained.
Greywell (Basingstoke Canal) and Sapperton are both blocked
by roof falls and Standedge, the longest through tunnel ever
built, has been barred at each end since 1951 by metal gates.
More than 3 miles in length, parts of it lie more than 600ft
below the surface. Every second year a boat passes through
to make an inspection, for the tunnel still serves as an
essential drainage channel for railway tunnels and as a
watercourse for the canal itself. There are four passing points
in the form of broad caverns, one of which retains its original
mooring rings. Benjamin Outram estimated in 1793 that the
tunnel could be cut in 5 years; it proved a more complicated
task than that, however. Standedge was finally opened to
traffic in March 1811, 17 years after work had begun. At a
total figure of about £160,000, it was second only to the much
later Netherton in expense. For much of its length Standedge is of unlined rock, rough-blasted and displaying a
rainbow assortment of subtle colours. Adits connect with the
railway and when the line was worked by steam locomotives
smoke and exhausts belched into the canal tunnel. It is an
exciting place that could have a popular and profitable future
with public tripping boats. For the present it remains
effectively sealed even to the most determined would-be
explorer.

The navigator of a modern pleasure cruiser equipped with
powerful lights will find little cause for alarm at the prospect
of working through even the longest tunnels. Features of
interest will be periodical distance markers, usually in cast
iron, the cascades of icy water that pour from roof or walls
and the curious sensation of seeming to float on air at a point
where the arch and its reflection meet at water level.

# 8
# *Buildings and Design*

A CHARMINGLY varied selection of buildings served the needs of the old navigation companies. Those constructed within the Canal Era (*c*1760–*c*1840) provide us with a rich cross-section of British domestic and industrial architecture in which individuality flourished, and functional simplicity did not rule out good taste in design. In many cases age has only accentuated their beauty. It would be extremely difficult to recall a single ugly canal building from the last century or earlier. Some replacements or additions of our own times are good, but often they are characterless and 'cheap' by comparison.

86

*Hartshill maintenance yard on the Coventry Canal*

### LOCK AND BRIDGE COTTAGES

Armies of widely scattered staff were needed to operate the waterways at the height of their commercial prosperity. Most individual locks or flights were cared for by a keeper, who might also keep records of traffic and help with maintenance. The man and his family were housed in cottages built in local materials and styles, offering accommodation often much superior to that of contemporary farm workers. It was nothing elaborate: a living room and kitchen, two or three bedrooms, an earth closet at the back, outhouses so that the family could keep a pig and perhaps a cow, and a small vegetable garden surrounded by a low wall of brick or stone or a wooden paling fence. In rural areas there was a plentiful supply of timber for the fires, or coal could easily be obtained from passing boats; it was an unresourceful canal employee or boatman who had to pay for his fuel. Decades ago, boats were working to and fro in all hours of daylight and often far into the night. There was easy transport by canal to the nearest villages and towns, and all news and supplies came to the cottages by water. Several generations of the same family

sometimes lived in one cottage, the keeper's job being handed from father to son. The system survives in places to this day, most noticeably on the canals of Southern Ireland. The family name might become synonymous with the lock. There were Tarvers once at Tarver's Lock Cottage near Banbury on the Southern Oxford Canal.

These little houses are delightfully homely. They were usually erected by local builders under contract to provide perhaps three or four along a specified stretch of waterway. Thus, within a given area, cottages will often be basically similar but differ in detail. Some idea of the difference in styles can be gauged from the illustrations.

Five of the structures along the Thames and Severn Canal, all dating from 1799, were built on a completely circular plan, using stone rendered with plaster and stucco. They are called Round Houses. No one knows why this shape was selected, though it is well suited to its purpose. Arranged on three floors, the houses' ground floor was intended as stable and store, with access only to the outside. A flight of outside steps led directly in to the 16ft 10in diameter living room with cooking range on the first floor, while an internal staircase between inner and outer walls provided an ascent to the single bedroom above. Two of this pattern, including that near Stroud, have a conical pointed tiled roof, but the others have a raised parapet concealing an inverted lead-covered cone for the collection and storage of drinking water. In spite of their charming appearance, the lack of accommodation and difficulty of furnishing the circular rooms made them unpopular with the lock-keepers and watchmen, and in later years alterations and additions were made. Two similar round houses were built on the Staffs and Worcs Canal, one still standing by the busy A5 road at Gailey Lock in mellow orange brick, with a castellated roof and square wooden-framed windows, and the other, near Stourton Junction, now in ruins.

Another rare type of house may be seen on the Southern Stratford Canal between Preston Baggot and Lapworth. There are six of them, all single storey, with an arched barrel-vault roof.

On the Thames two early cottages in Regency style stand by Penton Hook Lock, Staines, and midway along the lock cut at Sunbury. They are dated 1814 and 1812 respectively and bear the shield of the City of London Corporation, which controlled the lower river before the establishment of the Thames Conservancy in 1866. The TC (itself replaced in 1974 by the Thames Water Authority) was notable for the architectural quality of its houses. Almost all of them are pleasing buildings, often using materials or colour washes

*Cotswold stone keeper's cottage on the Upper Thames*

over new brickwork that would make them difficult to date accurately but for the Conservancy arms and year of construction, which normally appear over the main door. Many replacement cottages of the 1950s and 1960s are excellent adaptations of Georgian styles.

Scattered throughout the 100-mile length of the Birmingham Canal Navigations are lock-keepers' and lengthsmens' cottages built singly or in small terraces, each bearing a cast-iron numberplate relating to the company's properties rather than to adjoining buildings or streets. Mostly they are rather flat-fronted severe little dwellings of blackened red or blue brick, with a concrete yard surrounded by a low wall. They respond well to face-lifting schemes such as those at Birmingham's Gas Street Basin or nearby Farmer's Bridge, where pastel colour washes have given some life to rather dull elevations. Most that survive were constructed during the first half of the nineteenth century.

Scotland's Forth and Clyde Canal, and the Grand Canal and Barrow Navigation of Southern Ireland, show that company employees were allowed rather greater latitude than was normal among canal employees by being permitted to run small farms, sufficient for the needs of the keeper's family with additional produce to sell to passing traders. The

*Brick Lock, River Stort, is enhanced by this most appealing keeper's cottage in the early nineteenth-century Gothic style*

cottages are often more extensive, with a range of out-buildings, and stabling for the use of boat horses. All three waterways possess elegantly designed stone houses, with circular decorative motifs.

The beginnings of railway influence in canal architecture are found on the last major canal to be built – Telford's Shropshire Union and its various branches. The main line retains many examples of shallow-roofed wide-eaved houses and bungalows. Notable is the house at the top of Grindley Brook Locks on the Welsh section, a solid square edifice with broad central bay and overhanging slated and curved verandah. Perhaps this was intended for use by one of the company's agents. Russel Terrace, alongside Bridgwater Dock on the Bridgwater and Taunton Canal in Somerset, has a row of houses of Georgian style, constructed about 1841; seven are small cottages, but at each end is a much grander double-fronted villa.

Where canal profits were dwindling in the face of railway competition, few new houses were built, as staff was reduced. But new buildings were provided on waterways that continued to expand and flourish. The Lee Conservancy completed an extensive programme of cottage construction during the final years of the last century and the beginning of the present. Locks at Enfield, Hertford and Dobb's Weir all display a pleasing form of house with little gables and contrasting courses of brick. On the adjoining Stort Navigation, several pretty little buildings in eighteenth-century Gothic are reminders of Sir George Duckett's years of control.

Another thriving concern was the Grand Union system, which, after the amalgamations of 1929, controlled the longest inland waterway route in Britain – London to Birmingham, with many miles of branches in addition. It is still possible to discover original cottages little changed since the opening of the waterway. One is the castellated Gothic dwelling on the Regent's Canal in Camden Town, London, and another is a late eighteenth-century red brick building near the bottom of Hatton Locks, Warwick, which was left standing after the rebuilding and widening scheme of the 1930s. But generally throughout the company's lines houses date from the early years of the present century (Soulbury, Stoke Hammond, Marsworth middle and bottom locks, and Ivinghoe), or the period between the wars. Some of the least likeable types arrived after nationalisation; doubtless they are more comfortable than the buildings they replaced but they add little to our canal heritage. Norton Junction and Thames Locks, Brentford, are two of this breed. On the lower Lee, Aire and Calder, Sheffield and South Yorkshire and most other places where lock widening or improvement for increased freight capacity has taken place in the last 25 years the same ugly brick structures with metal window frames all bear testimony to a brief period when commercial considerations signified utility, and the amenity value of waterways was scarcely recognised. Thankfully, attitudes have changed considerably. During the first 3 years of the 1970s alone the British Waterways Board had introduced or prepared about eighty individual schemes to improve the visual appearance of its properties under architect/planner Peter White. Distinctive and sympathetic colours were selected for the buildings of various waterways, while owners of private property were encouraged to cooperate in improvements.

Waterways equipped with the larger opening bridges worked by keepers have bridge-keepers' cottages. In each case the cottages normally were built in much the same style as neighbouring lock houses – stone-built on the Crinan, of modern brick on the Aire and Calder, and late Victorian on the Weaver. But it is on the Gloucester and Sharpness that

*The Gloucester & Sharpness Canal is notable for its series of classical Regency bridgeman's cottages, each with pedimented portico on Doric columns*

they excel, for from one end to the other the company provided exquisite little Regency temples with Grecian porticoes, all differing in detail.

Another form of canalside building is the single-roomed hut, still to be found at many locks and often more substantially constructed than might have at first seemed necessary. These were daytime refuges for the keepers, somewhere to shelter from rain or brew tea over the open fire, to store a windlass in safety, perhaps to sleep if night work was required. At their most unprepossessing they are formed of rough wooden planks and sheet iron (Sheffield and South Yorkshire) or of precast concrete slabs (Hanwell Flight, Grand Union). The most charming include superb circular designs in brick and stone whose wooden doors are bowed to maintain the exact lines of the wall (Shropshire Union, Beeston to Chester); and neat brick and slate erections not unlike the privies at the bottom of many cottage garden paths.

Equally interesting, and often little larger, are toll-collection booths. One well-known booth, a perfect eighteenth-century octagonal, stands at the top of the Bratch Locks, Staff and Worcs Canal. The BCN system was (until very recent years) almost littered with them, at every major check point or junction; often they were situated on islands so that boats had no opportunity to slip by without their cargo being gauged and the appropriate toll collected. But, with their lack of use, all but one have been destroyed. The survivor stood on the Old Main Line in Tipton, but was scheduled for removal and preservation at the nearby Black Country Museum.

It proved difficult to let or sell these little canalside buildings in the 1950s and '60s. They lacked public services, were isolated and subject to vandalism. When finally the general public became prepared to buy long leases on canal cottages, demand swiftly exceeded supply, and it was not unusual for someone to spend several thousand pounds of their own money on improvements to such State property.

### WAREHOUSES, BASINS AND WHARVES

The architecture of water transport on the grand scale is to be found in the buildings where goods were stockpiled, transhipped between boat or barge and ship, or unloaded from canal and river craft on to horse-drawn waggons for distribution in the immediate locality. Mostly these warehouses were provided by the canal company as a service to independent carriers, and were an important source of company revenue. Ironically, a good many like those in Birmingham or throughout the Leeds and Liverpool con-

*Cottage at Johnson's Hillock Locks, Leeds & Liverpool Canal*

tinued to bring in a good profit years after all water freight had ceased, but in most cases structures designed for use with manual cranes, and with approach gateways suitable for horse transport but not 30-ton lorries, do not possess any obvious role in the later twentieth century. Some have fortunately found a new lease of life as boatbuilding yards and hire-cruiser companies' headquarters. Elsewhere they have remained empty and decaying for more than a decade – 'ripe for redevelopment' in city centres (Sheffield), or swept by unexplained fires (Ellesmere Port and the Ashton Warehouse, Dukinfield, Manchester), or quietly crumbling, as in the case of the beautiful Georgian stone buildings of Shannon Harbour on the Grand Canal.

Many warehouses are built on a truly monumental scale, quite apart from those off the Thames in London or along the Manchester Ship Canal, which belong more to the world of shipping and dockland than to inland waterways. The best of a wide selection in the village of Shardlow, where the Trent and Mersey joins the Trent, is a three-tiered complex of rusty brick whose walls are pierced by semicircular iron-framed windows. Another nearby has a broad archway, now silted up, which allowed boats to be unloaded beneath the first floor. Gabled gantries, little iron hand cranes, more sophisticated steam-powered loading apparatus, rusting disused gas lamps, grass-grown cobbles, clerks' offices, wharfingers' cottages and the more stylish residences for managers and agents, are all elements of the mostly forgotten complexes where the lifeblood of canal traffic originated or ended its water journey. Dense clusters of boats necessitated wide basins to avoid congestion on the navigation itself. Every canal terminus and many points en route were so equipped. In city centres like Birmingham and Oxford these basins were converted into car parks, built over or otherwise obliterated. Newbury, Banbury, and Manchester have had good reason to regret this policy. Having lost one basin to a bus park in the early 1960s, Banbury has excavated another as pleasure craft moorings. Holiday cruisers fill basins at Aylesbury, Market Harborough, Great Haywood and Stourport. The need for new non-linear moorings has become so acute that large-scale excavations have been made at Long Buckby and Market Drayton, with many more undoubtedly to follow.

One outstanding example of canal and rail cooperation is to be found in the extensive interchange basins of the BCN, among which were Withymoor, Hockley Port and Bloomfield Basin, Tipton. One of the best surviving – but for how much longer? – can be found at Coombeswood, Dudley Canal No 2 line: neat wharves served by travelling cranes allowed for the

*Acute canal bends are occasionally marked by vertical wooden rollers to act as guides for boats' towlines. This is on the Leeds & Liverpool Canal near Gargrave*

transfer of steel tubes and other goods between narrow boats and railway trucks all under the cover of a huge canopy. The system has lain derelict since the mid-1960s.

The Grand Union Company worked an excellent system of warehouses, some of them quite small, spaced out at suitable intervals over their empire from the East Midlands to London and the Thames. Some, like those at Brentford, still play a significant part in the storage of goods, some of which arrive by water but most by road transport.

### MAINTENANCE YARDS AND COMPANY HEADQUARTERS

Prestige buildings were just as important to the flourishing navigation company as are the towers of concrete and glass of today's commercial giants. The administrative offices of a canal company were usually to be found on the canal bank in the most important town served by the waterway. Thus the BCN Co occupied a splendid Georgian block in Birmingham, facing one end of Paradise Street, and flanked on each side by gateways that led to a pair of basins directly linked with Gas Street Basin. The headquarters was replaced about 1911 by another on the same site. All has since vanished, together with the nearby Baskerville Basins and the Newhall Branch Canal. Spread throughout the BCN was a series of maintenance yards, where new equipment from lock gates to paddles and bollards were built, boats were repaired and the day to day organisation of keeping the various routes in good running order was planned. Some yards are quite small, like that at Icknield Port, which is hidden from view up a loop line between Birmingham and Winson Green. Others, such as Sneyd on the Walsall section, comprise a comprehensive range of low buildings housing workshops for the different canal trades.

A combination of yard and company offices is not infrequent, as at Ellesmere on the Llangollen Canal (*see* p 336). The Coventry Canal's elaborate Hartshill Depot can show an irregular series of rounded windows, arches and covered drydock, all surmounted by a clocktower that is almost Chinese. By comparison, the Northwich yards and offices of the former Weaver Co are on a scale suited to barges instead of narrow boats. Wide covered slipways allow several craft to be built or repaired simultaneously. Again there is a clocktower, this time an elegant free-standing design, topped by a little cupola.

The fascination of maintenance yards is in seeing trades little changed in several generations being carried out with skill. In spite of modern power tools, there really is no way to improve on the manufacture of a pair of wooden lock gates, and although gas torches have replaced the old-style bellows

and fire of the forge, techniques of metalwork remain unchanged.

The equipment found in river maintenance yards tends to assume larger proportions than that in the canal counterparts. Locks are larger and require bigger gates, with lifting cranes of greater capacity. With weirs to build and look after, the work barges themselves are bigger with powerful tugs to accompany them. Thus, repair centres on the Severn at Worcester, the Trent, or the Thames (at Sunbury, Reading or Oxford) deal in more massive beams of timber and a heavier gauge of steel piling than canal yards, but the job done is essentially the same.

*Norbury maintenance yard, Shropshire Union Canal, has been carefully repainted under a scheme introduced by the British Waterways Board in the early 1970s to make architectural improvements to some of their canal properties*

### WATERWAYS FURNITURE

It is always a source of surprise that there can be so many different ways of saying 'Private. Keep Out'. Lacking in uniformity in every respect, the choice of words and style of typography selected for canal and river noticeboards is a subject worthy of close scrutiny. The examples illustrated range over 200 years and display prevailing fashions of lettering. They also indicate that there has always been a need to warn, inform or prohibit. The prohibitions generally applied more to an earlier era than the present day, for the last place the general public was made welcome was an urban towpath and bystanders on locksides were a bother and nuisance to traffic passing through. This has now changed out of all recognition, for even if no public right exists to use the towpath, you are normally welcomed or at the very least tolerated.

Bridge number and name plates are usually cast in iron. The fact that many numbers are missing might be explained by visits to the houses of certain waterways enthusiasts bent on creating their own private museums. Names alone are widely found around the BCN; names and numbers together appear on bridges of the Staffs and Worcs Canal. Originally they would have been cast in the canal companies' own forges, but modern replacements are by specialist firms. An alternative and more durable method of numbering bridges was to build a carved stone into the arch (parts of the Shropshire Union and Trent and Mersey). Distance markers are common on some routes, rare on others. These are most frequently cast in iron and usually refer to the terminal points of the waterway. Another related marker is the boundary post, indicating the limits of land in company ownership. The Union, Ellesmere and Coventry Canals all retain examples in stone, and iron posts will be found on the Shropshire Union, Grand Union, and Brecon and Abergavenny Canals. In this last instance Great Western Railway ownership has left a substantial number of little circular plaques mounted on top of sections of railway line fixed vertically in the ground. Signposts showing the direction to be taken at junctions normally date from recent times, when widespread pleasure cruising brought to the water navigators who might be unfamiliar with the route. A selection of earlier carved wooden finger-boards survives on the BCN.

Good design is typical of many smaller items of waterways equipment, ranging in scope from mooring rings and bollards to the cast-iron railings of bridge and aqueduct parapets. In each case there is a complete absence of mass production, at least to the extent that the fittings of one waterway tend to differ from those found elsewhere.

*Leeds & Liverpool Canal mileposts*

*Lancaster Canal mile-post*

*Grand Union, Leicester Section milepost*

*Trent & Mersey Canal milepost*

*Thames & Severn Canal milepost*

*The Swan Inn at Fradley, junction of the Trent & Mersey and
Coventry Canals*

# 9
# Public Houses

In their traditional form, serving the needs of the working boatmen, the waterway inns were among the few places where the world of the rivers and canals had brief contact with life 'on the land'. The pub was an important facet of the boat people's social life, a place to moor for the night, drink with friends, play simple games in the bar, or enjoy their own form of musical entertainment and dancing. The narrow-boat families especially had little time or inclination for town entertainment, and regarded places even a short distance from the navigation with suspicion and mistrust. But in these waterside pubs everyone spoke the language of the 'cut', and there were no eyebrows raised at the widespread illiteracy of the boat people, or their lack of knowledge of non-waterways matters, which elsewhere would be taken as a sign of stupidity.

More than a mere centre of relaxation, the canal pub was an important commercial centre, rather in the manner of the London coffee houses of an earlier period. The self-employed 'Number One' boaters knew that here they could contact a local tradesman who wanted a load of timber or mixed goods carried. Through the grapevine (which still exists today), it was a simple matter to pass on information to a carrier looking for a load. Another method used by farmers or canalside manufacturers was to erect a notice or other recognisable sign on the bank so that passing craft could learn of '20 tons of coal wanted from Cannock' or '40 tons of bricks to be delivered to Stafford'. The publican would run an unofficial news exchange for the boaters, perhaps reading them messages if they were unable to do so themselves, or operate a kind of employment agency, telling the captain of a boat known to be shorthanded that a lad now unloading craft several miles down the canal was available.

Visiting canal pubs, which now rely as much on passing road trade as the influx of summer holidaymakers in boats, will convey little of their former atmosphere. Having devoted his life to the improvement of the conditions of the working classes, among them the canal boat families, George Smith of Coalville recorded some of the vanished flavour, even if it is biased by the writer's moral attitudes. Mr Smith, round

about 1880, made a tour studying conditions along the
Grand Union near London:

> Not far from Bull's Bridge I came upon a public house
> called the Black Boat, a canal boatman's public house . . .
> Here I saw a lot of boatmen, boatwomen, and children
> who might not have been washed in their lives. One of
> the men showed me into what I thought to be the stable
> under the upper room. In going in I was met by a coarse,
> bloated, vulgar, dirty-looking boatwoman, whose face
> seemed to be almost the colour of a piece of raw beef a
> week old . . . Finding my way into a kind of horse-boxy
> looking place, I began to take stock of the surroundings.
> The fireplace consisted of a few iron bars and bricks . . .
> a boatman engaged upon a 'flour boat' would leave a white
> mark upon the 'settle' where he had been sitting to enjoy
> his 'fourpenny'; a boatman engaged in the coal trade
> would leave his black mark; and in like manner those
> engaged in the London sewage and Birmingham gas-tar
> business. Some of this 'fourpenny' I once tasted, and to
> me it was something like a decoction of saltpetre, vinegar,
> treacle, and mint. There were several poor boat children
> in the place who seemed to enjoy the 'fourpenny' quite as
> well as either the men or women. Of course the little boat
> children had not legs long enough to cause them to leave
> impress upon the 'settle', consequently their tiny marks
> were left upon the floor as they toddled and paddled about.

We can be reasonably certain that many nineteenth-
century canal pubs resembled the Black Boat.

The canal pub has several origins. First, there are the
buildings predating the coming of the navigation, normally
serving a village or small town through which the waterway
was built, with added stabling or a new doorway on to the towpath. In a few cases the canal companies themselves built
taverns, operating them for a number of years but quite
soon selling out to a local man or brewery. Glenfuir House,
standing near both the Forth and Clyde and the Edinburgh
and Glasgow Union Canals, which had become company
property when its estate was required for the waterway, was
let to an innkeeper in the 1820s and its library converted into
a bar. Then there were the company hotels of the Grand
Canal in Ireland, and the great Tontine at Stourport, built
by the Staffs & Worcs Canal Company.

Many more canal pubs were purpose-built by men with a
nose for commercial profit. Sites selected were either at
flights of locks or in villages where traffic delays assured
regular patronage, or at the regular intervals along a water-

way corresponding with the normal daily distance that could be managed by the boat horses. One can imagine the relief with which boat crews toiled up the twenty-three locks at Wigan, where their reward on arrival at the top was the opportunity of visiting any one of the taverns sited by each of the upper three chambers.

Country inns often combined their catering service for boaters with running a small farm. The two functions would sometimes be housed in the same building, as at the Bluebell, Waring's Green, on the Northern Stratford. Similarly, the Bull and Butcher, near Napton Bottom Lock on the Southern Oxford, is a small farmhouse once popular with the narrow boats.

Steam and then diesel traction, coupled with a decline in boat traffic generally, brought many canal pubs to an end during the period after World War I. A good example may be found at Long Buckby, on the Grand Union Canal, where a flight of six locks lifts the waterway to Norton Junction, which once had seven inns; the only survivor is the New Inn alongside the top lock, which losts its licence for a time but was reopened in 1971.

It comes as a surprise, therefore, occasionally to discover lost little inns that have survived the lean years of dwindling or non-existent freight traffic and begun to thrive again, during the summer months at least, as pleasure cruising increases year by year. It seems almost wrong to publicise these establishments and so build up their custom, for the temptation to replace boarded floors with wall-to-wall carpet, and oak settles with mock leather armchairs, is one that few private owners or breweries seem able to resist if they consider that they will thus be able to increase profits. But without the added trade the more remote waterway pubs will eventually die. One of the most unlikely is a tumble-down cottage set back among shrubs from the derelict Geldeston Lock, at the head of the River Waveney. A faded sign over the door proclaims (somewhat incorrectly) 'The Locks'; indeed this was once the lock-keeper's cottage. Very difficult road access means that most customers come by cruiser, and the inn is open only during the boating season. Also on the Broads, the Berney Arms on the Yare near Reedham has no road access at all, and so shuts down for the winter. But when hire cruisers are out in their hundreds, few pass without mooring up to visit the inn and inspect the great windmill nearby. The tiny Anchor Inn at Bridge 42, High Offley, on the Shropshire Union main line, only opens its doors on Friday evenings and at weekends; but a changeless atmosphere lingers.

River navigation taverns generally stand by bridge cros-

*Lettering intended to last: carved red sandstone above a pub doorway at Middlewich, Trent & Mersey Canal*

sings, at ferry points or alongside the now deserted commercial wharves or village centres. Waterways like the Thames
and the Broadland rivers, with their tradition of pleasure
cruising, have encouraged pubs whose cases of glassy-eyed
stuffed fish or yacht club burgees point to a long association
with leisure activities. Many of the houses visited by Jerome
in his *Three Men in a Boat* still bear the same names, but
otherwise would scarcely be recognisable, having been subjected to nearly a century of enlargement, rebuilding and
'improvement' in catering for the waterborne holidaymaker.
The Thames displays some of the most fashionable waterside
pubs in the country, and if your taste is for High Offley's
Anchor, you may not appreciate the immaculate lawns of
Marlow's Compleat Angler or the smart terraces of Skindle's
at Maidenhead. But there are houses on the river to cater for
most types, and in the wilder reaches upstream of Oxford
the Swan at Radcot or the Trout by Tadpole Bridge are
typical of the less assuming and unspoiled Thames pubs.

The names of waterways pubs are as varied as those of
pubs anywhere, generously sprinkled with Barges, Ships,
Weirs, Swans and Anchors. The maritime tradition is
stronger on river navigations. Canal pub names draw inspiration more from the waterways themselves or the
surrounding countryside. The Navigation is common, with
scores of Grand Junction Arms, Leeds and Liverpool,
Egerton Arms, Bridgewater Arms, and others that recall
canal promoters or companies. Situations near a prominent
landmark result in the Aqueduct, the Three Locks, the Big
Lock, King's Lock, the Tunnel House, the Ferry Boat or
simply the Bridge. There is the Eight Locks at Walsall on
the BCN. The Paddington Packet Boat at Cowley on the
Grand Union recalls the former passenger transport service
that connected rural Middlesex with countryside a mile
from London's Marble Arch. Thrupp's renamed Jolly
Boatman on the Oxford will no doubt continue to be referred
to for many years as the Britannia. The London Apprentice
on the Thames at Isleworth reminds one of the young men
from the City livery companies who would row upriver and
pause here for refreshment. The Jolly Fisherman, Pike and
Eel, and Fisherman's Rest, are places that live up to their
names during the short winter days, when few pleasure
boats are about and the bars are cluttered with keep nets,
rods, bait boxes and large green umbrellas.

A new interest in the waterways (especially canals) has
prompted the breweries to revamp some of their pubs in
accord with canal and boat themes. The new decor varies
from the importation of a few decorated narrow-boat utensils,
and a collection of framed prints over the chimney piece,

to walls covered from floor to ceiling with huge enlargements of historical photographs, and bars shaped like boat cabins. Thus, the Globe Inn at Weedon (Grand Union Canal) became the Narrow Boat, the Drawbridge Stores on the Northern Stratford reappeared as the Boatman's Rest, and the Paddington Arm's Grand Junction Arms at Willesden emerged resplendent with the same name but with all the trimmings of roses and castles, lace-edged plates and a three dimensional mock-up of a section of working boat.

The new style is best represented to date by Birmingham's Longboat Inn, a fine modern building yet in the architectural idiom of the canal era. It is the central feature in the Farmer's Bridge redevelopment that commemorated the bicentenary of the BCN in 1969. Here the bars overlook boats on moorings and the flight of Birmingham and Fazeley locks. Canal motifs appear in mosaic, etched in the glass of windows and supported by a good collection of genuine relics, including cast-iron distance markers and apparatus for lifting sunken craft. Life-sized butty boat rudders divide bars into a series of drinking areas, and huge black and white murals bring alive the old-time working spirit of the canals. Outside, a narrow boat floating in a small dock serves as an additional bar, with beer piped aboard. All this is a far cry from the old-fashioned thatched alehouse, but it is nevertheless a welcome addition to the new canal scene and must inevitably interest the many casual visitors.

*The Two Boats Inn, Long Itchington, on the Warwick section of the Grand Union Canal*

Just what kind of reception and service you can anticipate on entering a waterside inn depends very much on its location. If there is a thriving marina or sailing club alongside, the talk will be of outboard ratings and race handicaps. But find a house in a more remote setting and you will encounter conversation that might range from the current price of pigs to the prospects for a rebirth of commercial traffic along the waterway outside. Some towns and villages are traditional gathering places for one-time boatmen, people with deeply lined faces, a scarf drawn tightly round the neck in the manner of a cravat and a rich accent that might be an amalgam of London, Birmingham and the Potteries but not exactly like any of them, who, with appropriate encouragement and understanding, will discourse at length on how things were once on the Cut, with the inevitable conclusion that the old days were better.

Like pubs anywhere, facilities are variable. Beer and other drinks are much the same throughout Britain, but whether you also find a snack service or complete meals that will satisfy an appetite fed on something as stimulating as a twenty-one lock flight in steady drizzle will often be a matter for local discovery and investigation. Where there are people in boats, you can be moderately sure that their inner requirements will be catered for to some extent, even if the fare offered does not rise much above the cold pie/pickles/crisps level. Hotels in the larger towns and cities, and those along the Broadland rivers and (especially) the Thames offer meals as good as you can expect to find anywhere, though you would do well to book a table in advance. In the absence of a Good Food Guide to the canals you should trust to luck, personal recommendation and the sixth sense that some people have for nosing out the gastronomic bargain.

Although not public houses in the normal meaning of the word, there are a few rather special waterway restaurants and floating eating establishments. London's Regent's Canal has the Barque & Bite, whose Regent's Park premises are a converted double-decker Thames lighter. At the junction of Manchester's Rochdale and Ashton Canals is the City Barges Restaurant, whose atmosphere aboard a pair of short boats is more canal-orientated. Or take a trip on the Oxford Canal cruising restaurants starting at Braunston or Rugby. The number of passengers in each case is confined to a maximum of twelve, there is every personal attention, the food is excellent and nothing aids the digestion more than a slowly unfolding panorama of rural scenery beyond the picture windows as you glide along the waterway. Book in advance.

Many pubs reveal fascinating 'characters' behind the bar. Others feature singing that is sometimes a re-creation of the boat people's own banjo- and melodion-accompanied entertainment. Some have their own local games, such as Northamptonshire skittles, where wooden 'cheeses' are thrown into a net; or display the curious polyphons or other forms of late-Victorian mechanical music machines so preferable to the high-powered jukebox.

Architecturally the waterways pubs are as varied as the buildings of Britain – thatch and weatherboarding along the East Anglian rivers, stone from the Cotswolds to the far north, blue brick in the industrial Midlands, and black and white in the area around Cheshire. Canal and river pubs are as attractive and as different as motorway service stations are dreary and alike.

There is nothing quite so satisfying as a day's cruising along a waterway in late autumn or winter, when there is a sharpness in the air and maybe towards dusk a thin skin of ice forming on the water. In the gathering darkness you moor to a little wharf like that at Platt Lane on the Llangollen Canal near the peat bogs. A few hundred yards away in the village centre, the Waggoners beckons with a blazing coal fire in the grate and thick curtains drawn against the dark night. Such pleasures are the antithesis of the brash seafront at Great Yarmouth, which acts as a powerful magnet for so many Broadland holidaymakers, but if you are in tune with the pervading spirit of rivers and canals in the British Isles, you will be well suited by the little pubs that have served water travellers for so long.

In Ireland the bars invariably seem to be more a part of the waterside villages than purpose-designed to serve the needs of boatmen. Visually they normally lack the picturesque charm of their English counterparts, and in the few larger towns may seem positively utilitarian, with tiled interiors suggesting a public convenience rather than a centre for convivial entertainment and relaxation. These outward appearances are highly misleading, for it would be difficult anywhere else to chance upon such riotous evenings as can be spent in the Irish bar. Some offer home-made attractions, such as the performance of ballads, and most in country districts can be relied on to remain open long after licensing hours, provided there are customers waiting to be served. Almost always the village bar is combined with a general shop, offering the chance of buying meat, potatoes and other supplies while joining the proprietor in a glass of porter. The well-known welcome accorded to British or other 'foreign' tourists is not a mythical concoction of the Irish Tourist Board, and the friendly Irish fulfil their reputation to the extent that at times it is almost impossible to part and return to your berth or continue with the day's cruise!

*Hulme Locks, Bridgewater Canal*

# 10

# Towns and Villages

THE docks, warehouses, boatbuilding and repair yards, shops, pubs and houses for the waterway population, together created new communities that grew up in the wake of the first commercial craft trading on navigations. Many of Britain's most ancient cities and towns owe their existence to navigable rivers. London, Lincoln, Oxford, Ely, Glasgow, Dublin, Bristol, Gloucester, Manchester and Leeds are all places that were able to develop as a direct result of good inland waterway communication. But for present purposes we shall consider towns and villages whose origins are far more recent and can be traced directly to the coming of the Canal Age.

One of the most obvious and complete examples can be found in Stourport, where the Staffs and Worcs Canal joins the Severn. Until the canal was nearing completion, Lower Mitton was a tiny hamlet on the banks of the river. Then a busy commercial centre grew, where cargoes could be exchanged between the trows and wide-beam barges of the Severn and the narrow canal boats. For this purpose a pair of basins where craft could lie safe from the flood waters of the Severn was in use by 1771. The new town of Stourport soon started flourishing and a succession of industries were attracted by the benefits offered by modern efficient transport and storage. An account of the early years of Stourport mentions that 'Houses, warehouses and inns . . . sprang up as if by magic, the magic which wealth-creating industry usually gives; and iron foundries, vinegar works, tan-yards, spinning mills, carpet manufactories, and boat-building establishments were added.' Stourport gained a reputation as the object of fashionable excursions, with picnics on the river.

Today, the elegant Georgian warehouses and terraces of cottages, the duplicated series of locks and evidence of former activity still survive. The canal company, as instigator of these changes, was a leading employer of labour in the district, and, with most people closely connected with the business of the waterway, a close-knit community developed. The situation remained unchanged for upwards of sixty years, Stourport remaining essentially a canal town until water transport began to decline. With a present population of almost 14,000, Stourport has been expanding for more than a century and has spread far beyond the immediate neighbourhood of the canal. The boat basins are now peaceful moorings for inland and coastal pleasure craft. After a certain amount of thoughtless and unnecessary demolition of waterside buildings following World War II, the town has come to appreciate and accept its new role as an outstanding relic of canal history and architecture.

Stourport is an example of a place that grew out of its canal and in turn outgrew its canal. Different circumstances were at work at Shannon Harbour, where the Grand Canal from Dublin joins the River Shannon. In its early days the Harbour expanded on very similar lines to Stourport. Stone warehouses, a street of little houses, a boatyard, and a great canal hotel serving as an overnight staging point for packet-boat passengers, were all elements that promised to grow into a major town. The canal company provided a school, and an elegant Georgian house for the navigation manager. But as passenger traffic fell away, the Harbour degenerated into an overnight halt for the freight barges. Now, amid the rural beauty of the area, much appreciated by tourists from abroad, Shannon Harbour remains a little ghost town. Thick boughs of ivy festoon the gaping windows of the ruined hotel, and an ancient wooden barge rests waterlogged alongside the grass-grown quay. In the little Post Office/general store, pipe tobacco is freshly cut from a hard block on an ancient machine like a tiny bacon slicer. Milk sold over the counter has come direct from the farm without passing through some vast dairy complex miles away. The lock-keeper spends most of his day in the fields or caring for his cows.

Richmond Harbour at the junction of the derelict Royal Canal and the Shannon near Termonbarry Lock, might also have grown into a prosperous town had the promise of its early days been fulfilled. A solid row of grey stone canal buildings stands along one side of a large terminal basin, almost unchanged from the birth of the waterway in 1817. The last boat passed through the waterway from end to end in 1955 and the Royal was officially closed in 1961. From that time Richmond Harbour has found a new role in providing good sheltered moorings for holiday cruisers on the Shannon. Two access locks were repaired in 1970, a barge drydock put back into commission and an architectural facelifting scheme completed as part of a 'tidy towns' campaign.

Greatest interest normally remains in places where some particular feature of the waterway encouraged the establishment of services catering for the passing commercial traffic.

It might be the junction of two important routes (Fradley, where the line to Coventry joins the Trent and Mersey), or a dock where seagoing ships could exchange cargoes with inland craft (Sharpness and Bridgwater in Somerset). In the case of Stoke Bruerne, the Grand Union Canal is bounded to the north by the 3,056yd Blisworth Tunnel and to the south by a flight of seven locks. As a popular centre for day excursions on account of the excellent Waterways Museum and also because it is a charming little village in its own right, the origins and growth of Stoke Bruerne merit consideration in some detail.

Stoke is a particularly good example of a place whose main thoroughfare is the canal itself. Single rows of buildings on both sides of the navigation face each other above the top lock, most of them directly connected with running the waterway and their origins still traceable without difficulty. When the canal arrived, the village street was diverted to cross the navigation by a new single-arched stone bridge below the top lock. All seven locks in the flight to Stoke Bruerne were duplicated in 1835, when the existing top lock was added and an extension of the bridge constructed, resulting in the double arch that is there today. Not very many years later the original lock chamber was converted into a side pond and finally, in the early 1960s, was excavated to accommodate a restored narrow boat, the *Northwich*, which was positioned on an old boat-weighing machine taken from the Glamorganshire Canal in South Wales.

An old beerhouse alongside the first lock remains as the stone and thatched Boat. By the Boat Inn stood a lock-keeper's house, with a dairy and slaughterhouse owned by the publican. Stables for the boat horses occupied what are now tearooms. A little further along the canal towards the tunnel was a wharfinger's office (now a small canal souvenir shop) and his house. Across the water the group of brick and stone buildings is dominated by a large corn-mill, which used to be powered by a beam engine mounted in an extension alongside. This is now the Waterways Museum. The new Museum shop, built in 1970, stands on the site of the engine house. Mill workers lived in a series of small terraced houses overlooking the canal and now in private occupation. An attractive red brick double-fronted Georgian house by the top lock was for many years a post office and shop.

Near the south portal of the tunnel stood further stables, as well as a small workshop for the maintenance of the tunnel steam tugs operated by the canal company until they were discontinued in 1934.

Since the Museum was opened in 1963, Stoke Bruerne has inevitably become rather commercialised. Reedy canal banks have given way to utilitarian concrete piling. The towpath is neatly gravelled and moorings for pleasure craft in transit are packed to capacity in summer. Upwards of 70,000 paying visitors come to the Museum each year, in small groups and by the coachload. There are short public cruises available on the canal between the top lock and the tunnel mouth. But in spite of the continual influx of people from outside, Stoke Bruerne largely contrives to retain the character of a nineteenth-century rural canal village.

A rather different pattern of development will be found 20 miles north of Stoke Bruerne, at Braunston. Here the arrival of the Grand Union and Oxford Canals encouraged growth of a settlement immediately around the waterways and still quite distinct from the old Braunston, which lies a short distance away along the top of a ridge. In its most commercially flourishing times a succession of canal pubs was established between the top of the flight of six locks and Braunston Junction. Of these, only the Nelson and ·the Victorian Rose and Castle now retain their licences. Near the bottom lock stood an engine house dating from 1805, which lifted water supplies from a series of three reservoirs that now serve as a pleasure-boat marina.

Over the years the function of the basins and boat docks at Braunston has changed. Until 1847, Pickford's operated a station on the stub of the old Oxford Canal that remained after the improvements of the line to Hawkesbury in the 1830s. This station was taken over by Fellows, Morton & Clayton. Another carrier and boatbuilder on the site was the Samuel Barlow Coal Co. For many years wooden boats were launched from a slipway (the last was *Hazel* in 1958), and traditional building crafts carried out in the drydocks.

The Grand Union remained quite a busy commercial waterway until the early 1960s, so Braunston never declined as a canal village like so many others. By the time the working narrow boats had begun to be a rarity, pleasure cruisers were well established. Blue Line Cruisers Ltd took over the last pairs of Barlow working boats about 1963 and transformed the reedy reservoirs and mouldering transhipment shed and docks into a thriving marina, which was to serve as a model development. The firm sold out to the Ladyline Group in 1970, by which date Braunston was firmly placed as a leading centre for canal boating in Britain. Its situation at the junction of the Northern and Southern Oxford Canals, within 5 miles of the Northern Grand Union and just six locks and a tunnel from the Leicester Section, is excellent for holiday boat hiring. The canal provides the largest source of employment in the immediate district, for, in addition to Ladyline, former side-slips and a drydock above and below the bottom lock are now the birthplace of traditional steel-hulled narrow boats for leisure travel. Although it is a leading pleasure-craft Mecca, Braunston remains an excellent centre of canal-boat tradition.

Growth and development continue. No longer a backwater known only to canal people, the village has been enlarged by the building of new houses for commuters from Daventry, Rugby and the surrounding district. The Rose and Castle Inn near the junction has been treated to a large waterside restaurant whose design is loosely based on a nineteenth-century Oxford college barge. The service provided is a useful one. Or you can sample the cruising Lace Plate Restaurant, an intimate and characterful enterprise aboard a new narrow boat. It operates throughout the year under the personal supervision of proprietors whose family connections with the canal and long-standing association with the whole-sale butchery trade ensure a successful meal.

Lying due north of the canal, up a grassy slope, Braunston village is strung out along a single street of yellow stone and red brick shops and houses. The tower of a long disused windmill stands near the great spire of the Victorian church. Names on tombstones in the graveyard recall the narrow-boat families who regarded (and still regard) Braunston as their home village.

A canal terminus marking the junction with a river estuary or the open sea is often a fascinating development, combining elements drawn from coastal as well as inland traditions. One such place is Bridgwater Dock, Somerset, where the Bridgwater and Taunton Canal meets the River Parrett. The Dock was added to the canal some years after the completion of the latter, to enable ships to lie safely away from the rise and fall of the Parrett. It was opened early in 1841 and spent most of its active life in railway ownership. The Dock is composed of two basins, that nearer the river being fitted with more than forty sluices round its perimeter to control the water levels. A pair of gates admitting craft up to 42ft in beam connects the tidal basin with the river, while a conventional barge lock 54ft × 13ft lies alongside. A further pair of gates divides the two basins with a double-leaf bascule bridge. At the height of its prosperity in 1873 Bridgwater ranked fifth among Britain's ports for the importation of coal and culm. Old photographs of the later nineteenth century show large numbers of schooners and sailing barges filling the 200ft width of the basins, making it possible to walk from one side to the other across their decks. Along one side of the stone-walled tidal basin is Russel Place, a late Georgian-style terrace from the mid-nine-teenth century consisting of seven cottages for dock workers sandwiched between larger properties at each end intended for higher-grade dock staff. The buildings have brick walls and tiled roofs, and the doors and window frames are attractively painted in a range of pastel colours.

Bridgwater Dock was closed by British Rail in 1971 and the entrance from the river sealed off with steel-piled dams. Its future use is still undecided, but there are lessons to be learned from the rehabilitation of similar sites, including the nearby terminus of the Exeter Canal, where a maritime museum has been so successfully established in a warehouse complex.

Scotland's three coast-to-coast canals provide further examples of self-contained waterway villages at each of their terminals. Crinan, at the north-west end of the superb Crinan Canal, occupies what must be the most beautiful situation of any canal basin in Britain. It is perched above the seashore against a backdrop of wooded hills, and has views over the Sound of Jura towards the Western Isles. The sunsets at Loch Crinan are truly memorable. As Crinan is a small and slightly exclusive centre for offshore sailing craft that moor on the canal, its facilities are restricted to a boat repair yard, quality hotel and small post office with general store. Alongside the sea lock stand a keeper's cottage and small lighthouse, the latter one of a surprisingly large collection scattered throughout the British waterways. Most valuable of all is the utter silence of the place, far from main roads and the flight paths of aircraft. The other end of the Crinan Canal is at Ardrishaig on Loch Gilp, a far more bustling settlement directly on the A83 between Inveraray and Campbeltown. A long stone training-wall jutting out into the wide expanse of the loch to guard the entrance lock terminates in another stumpy lighthouse. Several more locks lift the canal high above the sea, the intermediate pounds filled with moored pleasure cruisers. Ardrishaig seems much more of a small seaport than a canal terminus.

Both ends of the great Caledonian Canal are equipped with commercial shipping wharves still dealing with substantial quantities of freight. At Corpach on the west coast, near Fort William and virtually in the shadow of Ben Nevis, there are modern berthing facilities, cranes and storage areas. Three locks lift the waterway from the sea before one reaches that most impressive staircase of eight at Banavie. Moving to the eastern end of the Caledonian, the Clachnaharry terminus near Inverness, like Corpach, has a lighthouse, clusters of herring boats and local BWB offices.

The River Weaver Navigation had a long history of commercial success and development that has left its mark at Weston Point (junction with the Manchester Ship Canal) and upriver at Northwich. Weston Point continues to expand as a cargo-handling centre under the control of the British Waterways Board, a record 460,500 tonnes of goods passing through in 1973. The complex of basins and warehouses includes a church built in 1841 for the betterment of dock workers and barge people alike. The Weaver trustees considered that surplus revenue from their commercial operation should be diverted to such endeavours. Further churches were erected soon afterwards at Northwich and Winsford, the head of navigation, together with schools. All the running costs, including teachers' and clergymen's salaries, were found by the trustees. This arrangement continued until the present century, when the schools were transferred to the Church authorities in 1905, and the churches in 1929.

Northwich, now headquarters of the NW Area Engineer of the British Waterways Board, originated centuries ago as a leading centre for the salt industry. On both banks of the river are long-established waterway facilities, including barge building and repair yards, and a maintenance depot with offices and elegant free-standing clocktower.

Even where a canal has long since been closed to traffic or has become hidden in a welter of later development, the names of streets will often give a lead to its whereabouts. There are Canal Rows, Terraces and Streets, Wharf Lanes and Navigation Roads. Similarly, a waterway may be remembered in the names of public houses.

Pleasure boating, either long-established or of recent origin, has quite often come to dominate the commercial life of waterway towns and villages. Consider how Broadland centres like Wroxham, Potter Heigham and Reedham rely on the summer cruiser traffic. Shops and supermarkets are stocked for the holidaymakers who flock to pubs and restaurants. Building and operating hire cruisers represents a major use of local labour.

One great canal town was Ellesmere Port (see Shropshire Union Canal, p 398). The demolition of its most memorable features, the Telford warehouses, has left little convincing evidence of the former scene of activity. So often subsequent industrial expansion (encouraged by the prosperity introduced by the canal) has demanded that redundant buildings be replaced by more profitable developments. Thus, the once less successful rural canal villages have a far greater chance of survival substantially in their original form, for it is these unspoilt areas that attract boating facilities, restaurants and other facets of the new leisure industry.

*Sheerlegs in use to lift out the old lock gates during maintenance work at Three Locks, Soulbury, on the Grand Union Canal*

# 11

# Operation and
# Maintenance

KEEPING either a navigable river or a canal in commission
requires constant attention. Much of the work is unspectacular, consisting in part in merely watching for danger signs,
recognising those signs when they appear and taking remedial
action in time. Water, whether in natural or artificial channels,
is for ever wearing away, seeking means of escape, under-
mining and rotting. Yet with due care a wooden lock gate
can last for forty years or longer. Many of the stone lock
chambers now in use are substantially unchanged since they
were constructed towards the end of the eighteenth century.
There are canal cuts on river navigations upwards of three
hundred years old. But everything remains in a workable
state only as the result of regular maintenance.

Unlike most other transport forms, waterways are positively
improved by use but rapidly decline without traffic: then
silting and choking weed growth occur as channels revert to
their natural state. Very few rivers in Britain would remain
navigable for long if the weirs and locks collapsed. Consider
the Wye, once usable for nearly a hundred miles from the
Severn to Hay, and now mostly fit only for experienced
white water canoeists; or the Warwickshire Avon between
Evesham and Stratford its century of dereliction until
complete restoration in 1974.

Maintenance is organised in different ways, according to
the type of waterway. Former canal company practice is
generally continued on the routes of the British Waterways
Board. A chain of maintenance yards serve each navigation,
some quite small concerns able to deal with day-to-day
routine matters, others much larger and equipped with
workshops where workboats can be slipped for repair or
new craft built. At the larger depots lock gates are constructed,
normally in timber, using methods that have not changed
materially for 200 years. Considerable skills are required for
this work, which involves the handling and shaping of massive
oak frames that must be built to fit accurately the particular
lock for which they are intended. Other tasks include casting

of concrete bank protection piles and bollards, making new lock paddle gear and other fittings, painting signs and producing a range of metalwork required for locks, moving bridges and other structures. Throughout Britain a sizeable workforce is employed, some men being permanently attached to the yards, while others move between one waterway work site and another.

Whether employed by a small private navigation company, one of the Regional Water Authorities, or the BWB, whose Area Engineers' Departments are each divided into smaller sections, the man on canal or river maintenance will be one of a small gang. Throughout the year there are always more tasks to keep the gangs busy than they can ever expect to complete fully, for on some canals there is a long-standing backlog of maintenance. To bring the existing waterways network back to its original specification and condition would cost many millions of pounds, and for many decades this kind of finance has not been available. Therefore, the jobs tackled tend to reflect the most pressing needs. Productivity varies between gangs, since they often work with little supervision. If a Section Inspector is keen and is able to communicate his enthusiasm to his men, much more can be achieved than where there is no real incentive.

In some respects maintenance men lead an enviable life. Normally working in pleasant rural surroundings and operating from a boat that carries their tools and equipment, they are mostly contemplative types like the typical agricultural labourer. A good many have been recruited from boating families whose entire life centres on the Cut. They often live in canal properties once occupied by lock-keepers, travelling a short distance by car or bicycle to the work site. There are overgrown hedges to be trimmed back, towpaths and banks to be made good, locks, buildings and bridges to be repaired and painted, silt to be dredged, and new facilities such as water points, moorings and sewage disposal points to be installed.

Another type of canal worker is the solitary lengthsman, frequently living in an isolated cottage. His tasks combine the functions of lock-keeper, weir attendant and bank ranger. He must maintain correct levels in the canal, either taking water from the higher pound or running off any surplus. He will be seen cutting reeds, treading puddle clay into weak sections of bank, or burning the debris that tends to accumulate by lock gates. In former years canal companies were able to keep a large staff on these duties, but with increased wages in other jobs and the demand for better working conditions, fewer men can be employed.

While the majority of canal locks are no longer manned,

keepers will be found at the busier flights, where pleasure-boat traffic is brisk. Similarly many rivers and commercial waterways have full-time lock-keepers. Mechanised locks like those on the Aire and Calder, Severn, Thames, and Trent are permanently manned. It is easy to appreciate that a Thames keeper has little free time during the summer cruising season, but it should not necessarily be assumed that this hectic activity has its compensations during the quiet winter months. The threat of floods, particularly in times of heavy rain, or the thaw that follows a snowfall, necessitates constant adjustment of weir sluices, while the keeper must still remain on duty to attend to any boats that wish to pass the lock.

The most obvious river maintenance is concentrated on preventing banks being washed into the navigation channel, and removing the silt and mud that does collect there. Lock cuts, areas of strong water flow around weirs, the outsides of bends, and regions near bridge supports must be guarded from erosion. The most common method (but also the most expensive) is to drive sheets of interlocking steel piling deep into the bed of the waterway, and at regular intervals connect tie bars to large blocks of concrete buried in the banks; the space reclaimed should then be backfilled with material dredged from the navigation. The scale of equipment brought in for such an operation varies with the required strength of the protective works. The larger rivers normally use massive campshedding driven into position by a compressor-powered piling hammer usually mounted on board a barge. Additional strength and permanence is provided by linking each steel sheet with horizontal members, old railway lines or motorway crash barrier guards often being used effectively for this purpose. Finally, a concrete capping along the top and treatment with a rust-preventing paint or tar provides a sound finish. Work of this kind is best considered as a branch of heavy engineering, only to be carried out by independent contractors or the larger navigation or water authorities.

Canals initially intended for slow-moving horse-drawn traffic were in most cases cut with puddled earth banks. Reeds and other aquatic grasses were sometimes planted to bind the raw banks together. The advent of powered boats, and particularly the growth of pleasure cruising, has resulted in the acute problem of crumbling banks. Not only does the towpath become unwalkable, hampering access to certain sections of the canal, but the debris eroded from the sides is deposited evenly over the channel, obscuring its original profile and bringing the bottom a good deal nearer the top than was ever intended. Even banks that were long ago protected by loose stone walls, slabs of rock or courses of brick have suffered from the wash created by powered boats. In addition to light steel campshedding, other materials in common use include driven concrete piles, suitably linked, tied and backfilled; corrugated asbestos sheet, a material that is easy to handle but tends to fracture on heavy impact; timber piles, whose disadvantage is that they tend to rot at water level; and gabions. The gabion is a fairly new introduction, which compares very favourably in cost and durability with steel piling and is often preferable aesthetically. Gabions consist of steel mesh cages assembled on site, and filled with broken rock, shingle or any other suitable material available locally. The steel is well-protected against corrosion, ensuring a long life, while the cages rapidly lose their hard outline as plants became established in the crevices. Waterways treated in this way include the Great Ouse and the Thames.

Timber bank protection remains popular on Broadland rivers, particularly along private frontages. It is surprising that the contractors concerned do not seem to have explored the possibilities of more durable materials. Small-scale work, whether in steel, timber, asbestos or concrete, is generally driven by a piling frame mounted in a work flat. Power for the hammer is still sometimes supplied by the simple expedient of hauling it manually to the top of the frame by rope and pulley, though the normal method is to take a drive off a small diesel engine.

The approaches to river locks as well as bridge piers are often protected by large wooden piles, which are most evident on the Upper Thames, providing an interesting challenge to inexpert pleasure-boat crews that attempt to moor up while waiting for locks. Then there are public quays, equipped with ladders and bollards (York, Gloucester, Nottingham), all requiring periodic attention.

Most artificial canals are expected to have a channel that is deepest at its centre. Hazards like shallows, wrecks or other obstacles should be regarded as temporary. Warning markers usually take the form of white-topped lengths of timber driven into the water or makeshift red or green flags. However, on natural watercourses the navigation channel may require to be clearly and permanently indicated. Large rivers, including the Severn, Trent, Thames and Soar, display noticeboards pointing out weirs, lock cut entrances or the correct side of an island for boats to pass. Additionally, various buoys are anchored to the river bed, their shape and colours showing whether craft should pass to port or starboard. As one waterway tends to observe different buoy conventions from another, it would be misleading to describe

*Volunteers using a hired excavator to clear a derelict chamber of one of the Ladywood Locks, Droitwich Canal, Worcestershire*

their patterns and uses here. But it is best to appreciate that codes used by coastal authorities may not apply upriver. Inland lakes like Breydon Water (Broads), Loughs Derg and Ree (Shannon) and the Upper and Lower Erne (Ulster), could be treacherous as cruising grounds were it not for the extensive system of buoys. Until you have experienced Irish waters it may be difficult to believe that binoculars, proper charts and good visibility are essential. Even in favourable conditions it is sometimes only just possible to locate the next buoy in a series.

Fixed navigation markers occasionally take the form of small lighthouses (Crinan and Caledonian Canals, Lough Corrib, and Ellesmere Port on the Shropshire Union). Illuminated buoys occur mainly in estuaries, or upriver where dredgers with long mooring cables extending to the banks may unexpectedly be encountered. Equipment of this kind all requires regular servicing. In severe weather it is not unknown for lake buoys to break adrift or 'drag anchor'. Rivers liable to flooding (Severn, Trent and Shannon) indicate the fact with tall posts that stand on what is normally dry land but whose real use will not be evident until the river banks become submerged. A related version on the Shannon consists of piles of boulders stacked on shallows, the resulting cairn being topped with a painted metal diamond or rectangle.

The design of dredging equipment over the years has displayed remarkable ingenuity. The earliest boats were spoon dredgers worked by manpower and, surprisingly, a few survive. A substantial wooden punt was fitted with a short crane on which was slung a large scoop or spoon with a long handle. This was lowered into the water, pushed into the mud and lifted by means of the crane so that the contents could be tipped into a mud hopper moored alongside. The spoon dredgers most recently in regular use were those on the Birmingham Canal Navigations, which were installed in conventional 70ft joey narrow boats. A gang of three men was able to shift 25–30 tons of silt in a day, and provided that another team was at hand to haul away the loaded hoppers to a suitable disposal point, such methods were not inefficient. Towards the end of the nineteenth century, steam power was harnessed to spoon dredgers. Soon afterwards, steam-driven grab dredgers, both land-based and mounted on barges, and devices using an endless chain of buckets that discharged silt into a barge alongside, found widespread favour.

Today dredging is undertaken by mobile bank cranes, floating grabs and (where there is no danger of dredging too deeply and so disturbing the watertight puddling of the canal bed) the bucket-chain method. If the canal has first been drained, small excavating vehicles can drive along the canal bed, through bridge holes and even into narrow locks, and effectively deal with solid refuse as well as liquid mud, depositing it on the banks for subsequent removal by small dumper and lorry. This is a field in which volunteer waterways restorationists excel. Several dozen organisations in most parts of Britain regularly hold working parties whose tasks are usually reopening derelict routes rather than helping the navigation authorities with routine maintenance. Between them, these amateurs have, during the 1960s and 1970s, accumulated a fund of expertise. Reserves of mechanical equipment and force of numbers resulted in almost 1,000 unpaid volunteers completing clearance work on the Ashton and Peak Forest Canals during a weekend in March 1972. This was valued at about £20,000.

Dredging and bank protection do not generally interfere with the passage of craft. Repairs to locks, aqueducts, bridges, and tunnels, and the necessity to bury gas mains, sewers or other services under the canal, may call for a stoppage. When commercial traffic was widespread, these closures were planned for summer holiday periods – Easter, Whitsun and August. The reasoning was that boatmen could take a well-earned rest while repairs were carried out in the long hours of daylight. Large forces of maintenance workers permitted simultaneous closures at a number of places along one canal. These arrangements are not now suited to pleasure cruising routes. Scheduled stoppages are therefore planned well in advance during the period November–March. Lists are published and consultations arranged with boat clubs and other users so that inconvenience can where possible be avoided. But difficulties do arise from work that takes longer to complete than expected, or where an emergency gate failure or bank collapse demands instant closure without advance warning. Major works like the relining of a tunnel, enlargement or mechanisation of a lock or substantial repairs to structures like Barton Swing Aqueduct or the Anderton Lift, may involve a closure lasting many weeks.

The most familiar stoppage will be that at a lock. Several days before the starting date an assortment of boats will begin to arrive from the maintenance depot – barges or narrow boats equipped as workshops, some bearing new gates, and others loaded with bricks and cement. At major river lock improvements, massive lifting gear for hauling out old gates will be mounted on pontoons hauled by a tug. Once the stoppage has been effected, the working day far outstrips the hours of winter daylight.

First, water must be drained from the site. Generally, grooves for forming a dam of stop planks are to be found at the head of the lock, and, ideally, a short length of canal will be drained off, particularly where locks are close to each other. In the case of a single isolated lock another set of stop planks must be fitted at the tail, and a mobile diesel pump used to clear water from the chamber and keep it reasonably dry while work is in progress. An alternative is to drive a temporary cofferdam across the waterway.

The scene of a stoppage is a place of mud, noise and controlled chaos. Perhaps a three-pronged sheerlegs has been erected over the chamber, so that gates can be taken out and replacements slung into place. Coordination and teamwork are very necessary when shifting heavy components. Whatever the chief cause of the stoppage, every opportunity will be taken to fit in other more routine tasks that can only be tackled with the lock dewatered. Crumbling brickwork may be cut back and replaced, or alternatively sprayed with gunite (a form of concrete resurfacing). Ground paddle tunnels will be cleared of any obstacles, and refuse removed from the lock floor. Tar on gates may still be wet when the water is reintroduced and the first of the waiting boats allowed to pass through. For some weeks after the men and equipment have gone, muddied grass and telltale patches of diesel oil and cement on the ground will serve as a reminder of the activity.

A visit to the scene of a scheduled lock closure is the best way of seeing a variety of maintenance craft. They have often been adapted from the conventional cargo boats of the district: thus narrow boats are used on narrow canals, short boats on the Leeds and Liverpool, steel lighters on the Upper Thames and wide-beam barges on the waterways of the Irish Republic. In addition there is the humble work flat, rectangular and with low freeboard, bow-hauled from the towpath or pulled by tug, and often fitted with a small hut-like cabin where tools can be stored and the workmen boil a kettle. Ancient variations of the work flat are to be found on the River Stort. Timber-built and more than a hundred years old, they were once owned by the Royal Powder Mills at Waltham Abbey. Their cabins are barrel-shaped, rather like certain types of traditional horse van.

The Waterways Museum at Stoke Bruerne preserves a set of brushes whose shape matches the profile of nearby Blisworth Tunnel. In the days of steam tunnel tugs these brushes were mounted on a small boat and swept accumulated soot from the roof as it was pulled along.

Few climatic conditions are likely to interfere with waterway traffic, although drought, floods and fog produce problems. The greatest threat to canal boats is ice. If it is allowed to freeze to more than 2–3in, it brings craft to a halt. In the old days this delayed urgent consignments of goods, with consequent loss of tolls to the navigation companies, so at the start of a cold spell, ice breakers were brought out of the maintenance yards. Mostly these were narrow boats of iron or thickly sheathed timber hulls, whose rounded underwater shape enabled them to be violently rocked from side to side by a gang of men gripping a taut rope or rail down the centre. Teams of horses would be hitched to this strange vessel, as many as a dozen animals being used if really thick

*Ice breaking on the Birmingham Canal Navigations in 1954; the heavily-built timber vessel is sheathed with plates of rolled iron and drawn by several horses (Wolverhampton Express & Star)*

ice was encountered. With the crashing of splintering ice, the shouts of the men and the white breath of the straining horses, the arrival of the iceboat was an awe-inspiring sight. There are tales of boats being rocked so far that they turned turtle or were pulled under the ice itself. Steam-powered ice breakers (used on the Leeds and Liverpool Canal until the 1940s) and diesel boats largely superseded these craft. With a general decline in freight traffic on routes most prone to

freezing, iceboats are now rarely used. One extant example is the Caledonian Canal's powerful tug-cum-ice-breaker *Scott II*, which clears a channel on the canal lengths to allow fishing craft to get through the ice. In summer she serves as a passenger vessel on Loch Ness.

Thick ice can quickly tear into the planking of a timber-built boat, hence the metal sheathing to the fore end and waterline of most wooden narrow boats. A steel hull accepts the challenge more readily, although the strain resulting from continual travelling through a frozen canal can be responsible for an overheated engine or damaged gear-box.

Little humpbacked accommodation bridges in stone or brick, which were intended for nothing heavier than a horse-drawn waggon, receive brutal treatment from constant road traffic, including lorries, when repair work is in hand nearby. Sometimes the old bridges are demolished and bare utilitarian concrete ones erected instead. Sometimes the structure is strengthened to increase its load-bearing capacity. This can either be achieved by inserting steel girders beneath the arch, an ugly method that can also severely interfere with headroom for boats; or removing the road surface as far as the top side of the arch, adding strengthening members so that loads are not in fact carried on the original bridge at all, and then replacing the surface when the job is finished. This expedient has been successfully carried out at Stoke Bruerne's double-arched bridge and at the Gothic bridge, also over the Grand Union Canal, some miles south at Cosgrove. Responsibility for bridge reinforcement lies not with the waterways authorities but with local or county highway authorities. Ironically, during Government tests held in 1936 to determine the strength of a typical 150-year-old brick bridge over the Northern Stratford Canal at Yardley Wood, it was found necessary to apply a weight of $127\frac{1}{2}$ tons for almost three-quarters of an hour before the arch finally collapsed.

Some quite small navigations have remained independent first of the railway companies and later of Government control. Their resources may be few, but normally by ingenuity, cunning and a degree of good luck, they manage to stay in business. Take the Wey Navigation in Surrey as one example. Until its transfer to the National Trust in 1963, this charming canalised river was lovingly watched over by its owner, Harry Stevens. Brought up in the old traditions of waterway maintenance (his family connections with the Wey reach back to the early nineteenth century) Mr Stevens preferred horse barges to motorised lighters, and kept his canal free of the latter. He was not over-fond of motorised craft of any type, relied on timber bank protection

(and that only where strictly necessary), and retained several
of the ancient wooden-framed turf-sided locks that had seen
no changes since the mid-seventeenth century. Old-fashioned
and rather inefficient, admittedly, but we have the doggedness
and generosity of Harry Stevens to thank for ensuring that
the waterway he so loved is now preserved for the nation,
though under National Trust control some innovations
have been allowed. Then there is the Lower Avon Navigation, rebuilt and operated by volunteers using the labour of
contractors only for the bigger jobs.

Weed control is a problem that only becomes severe
where there is little movement of boats. The well-used canal
or river is constantly stirred and agitated, with the result
that aquatic plants do not become established. But if weed is
allowed to accumulate, pleasure craft are discouraged, the
plants improve their hold, and boating becomes anything
but a pleasure. During the early 1950s parts of the now hectic
Llangollen Canal were so infested with blanket weed that
conventional screw propellers were useless. Even now, after
long warm summers, sections of the Nene, Middle Level
Navigations, Bridgwater and Taunton and other less used
waterways can become almost impassable. Weed can be
discouraged either by working blades under water from
each bank or using self-propelled weed boats fitted with
powered scythes. A floating boom traps the cut weed, which
can then be fed into a conveyor and cast on to the banks to
rot. Experiments with chemicals that are non-toxic to fish
and other forms of animal life have been tried with some
success, particularly on the Chesterfield Canal, but this
method is both expensive and ephemeral. The best control
is constant traffic.

One danger facing canals in some areas is subsidence
caused either by salt mining or coalmining operations. It
seems patently unjust that the navigation authorities must
share at least a proportion of the costs of remedial works,
even though they do not stand to benefit in any way from
the underground excavations. Arrangements have been made
in some instances for British Waterways to 'buy support'
from the National Coal Board. Expressed in another way,
this amounts to payments being made to the NCB to prevent
them from mining under the canal. Long portions of the
Trent and Mersey Canal north of the Potteries have subsided
into salt workings, resulting in the canal banks being raised
again and again above the surrounding countryside. This also
entails lifting the decks of bridges so that sufficient clearance
for boats is maintained. The old Two Lock Line of the
BCN near Dudley had to be abandoned because of severe
subsidence as did the top end of the Cannock Extension

Canal from Hednesford Basin to Norton Canes. Another badly affected route is the Leigh Branch of the Leeds and Liverpool Canal near Wigan.

The wealth of beautiful buildings, bridges and other structures that comprise the heritage of Britain's waterways can easily be spoiled by insensitive treatment. Badly sited noticeboards and hoardings, ugly new lavatories and disposal points, and a careless choice of colour washes for mellow brick and stonework must inevitably degrade the canal scene. The over-zealous efforts of maintenance gangs have produced their toll of visual blunders in a number of places. But it is increasingly being appreciated that what might have to be cheap and functional can also be attractive, or at least complement its surroundings. Now that it is very conscious of its role in keeping a great amenity intact, the British Waterways Board has established architectural standards for all its navigations.

Credit here belongs to BWB's Architect/Planner Peter White, whose reputation for sympathetic treatment of the urban canal scene was established through the Farmer's Bridge scheme while he was still employed by the Birmingham City Architect's Department. Mr White's *Waterway Environment Handbook* is a fully illustrated directory of guidelines to area engineers and local section inspectors on what colours are best for their lock cottages, bridges and fuel tanks, what kind of shrubs and trees best suit different locations, what new uses may be found for redundant buildings like lock lobbies or small stables, and scores of similar matters. The increasing involvement of local authorities, breweries, boatyards and other developers in making fuller use of waterside sites, especially in towns, is recognised in sections of the *Handbook* aimed specifically at these concerns. The period of haphazard creation of new marinas, boat clubs and similar facilities has now passed. In future new developments will be carefully considered by the Board in a national context and designed to avoid saturation of the more popular areas. Ideas like these are always laudable but are seldom put into practice. The difference with BWB's Waterway Environment policy is that maintenance staff at local level will be compelled to comply with the recommendations. Already our rivers and canals are showing distinct benefits.

*Traditional canal narrow boats at work*

# 12

# *Working Boats*

ON the majority of Britain's rivers and canals commercial traffic has long been declining. Since World War II, practically all smaller craft with a carrying capacity of between 25 and 100 tons have disappeared. Since canal boats had changed little for upwards of 150 years, it is in some ways remarkable that they should have survived so long. What other transport form could make a similar claim?

Fortunately for the waterways enthusiast, the great majority of canal and river craft live on in some guise, whether trading, preserved by trusts or museums, or enjoying a new lease of life as pleasure boats. Freight craft more fitted to late-twentieth century conditions and economics are described in Chapter 13. This present chapter should be regarded more as an historical account than a guide as to what you might expect to encounter during a cruise.

It is a grey winter day, with occasional flurries of snow and a skin of ice forming where the surface of the canal is sheltered by a ragged hedge. The Midlands countryside is silent but for a muffled sound of traffic from the motorway several fields away. Then a new noise is heard on the cold air, perhaps the engine of a farm tractor taking hay to stack. But no, as the sound comes closer it assumes a rhythmic *tunc, tunc, tunc* . . . there is an urgency about it. Suddenly it increases in volume and faint puffs of thin blue smoke rise in quick succession by the bridge just out of sight round the bend. A narrow-boat pair is coming!

First we see the blunt black fore-end of the motor, with barely 12in freeboard, pushing a wall of water ahead, ripples feathering out to the canalsides and sucking water away from the banks. Slivers of broken ice tinkle against each other. Dead brown reeds bend in the wash. There is a splash of bright colour on the cratch, a round fat rope fender and a single electric headlamp. Then a long wedge of black sheeting comes into view, neatly roped in position over some unknown cargo, and at the end of this seemingly endless hold a square cabin, gleaming with colours of ornate lettering and decorative panels. We see a furiously smoking chimney, shiningly brass-bound, and rose-painted water cans alongside on the roof. There is an old bicycle lying against the cabin end. A grim-faced man, in black shapeless felt hat, brown coat collar pulled up, stands inside the cabin doorway, staring intently ahead, one arm reaching behind him to the long brass tiller. He glances towards us, silent, then looks away down the canal. Water gurgles under the boat's counter where tiny icicles hang from a mass of plaited rope fenders. Engine noise increases as the open engine-room doors pass by, ten feet from where we stand. A big white mug rests on the roof in front of the steerer. A long taut dripping rope, perhaps 70ft of it, follows the motor, and round the bend we see another narrow boat, loaded deep and painted in the style of the first. As the motor glides away, its butty draws alongside us, silent but for the sluicing water, the crumpling ice and the laughter of some children hidden from view in the cabin, also topped by a brass-bound smoking chimney. A stout red-faced woman in an old tweed coat and head scarf nods in our direction, saying nothing, then averts her eyes, leaves the great curved wooden tiller for a moment and bends to attend to something inside the cabin.

The colours, shape and mystery that surround these craft, the quiet confidence of the rather drab-looking people working them, make us gaze after them down the waterway. Already the motor's *tunc, tunc, tunc* has grown faint, the water become still again. For a brief time we have intruded on another world, another set of lives. What were these boats carrying? Where did they load? Where are they bound for? The canal has ceased to be a narrow strip of muddy water; to us it is now a highway with the interest of any commercial harbour or shipping lane.

When the British Waterways Board took over responsibility late in 1962, it was clear that most canals, especially those used by narrow boats, were much too small for economic working under modern conditions. On the other hand they had a bright future for cruising and other amenity activities. The Board planned its work from the beginning on this assumption, and the result was a new classification of waterways into cruising and commercial categories under the 1968 Transport Act.

During the 1950s and early 1960s freight was carried on many routes now used by pleasure craft alone, but during the last decade one regular traffic after another has left the water. There is now little working-boat activity on the 'amenity' network. Some local canals were constructed to meet a local transport need, but with changes in the area's industry, that need was gone. Other canal companies sold out to the railways or were forced to merge, and for them a century of

half-hearted traffic operation and lack of modernisation
followed. But others remained independent, maintaining and
renewing the track and facilities. They worked in successful
competition with the railways, for frequently rates for
waterside to waterside carriage of bulk goods were more
favourable than either road or rail. Some companies operated
at a profit until nationalisation in 1948. The following
factors, however, combined to kill much commercial canal
traffic:

1 Lack of modernisation of waterways and boats.
2 Poor handling methods. As late as the 1960s, loads like
  timber and coal were being moved plank by plank or
  by the shovelful.
3 Small cargo capacity of the boats.
4 Low pay and hard working conditions for boat families.
  Many boat people were so dedicated to the life that they
  were prepared to tolerate hardships.
5 Change in industrial needs. Coal and wheat, two main
  Grand Union narrow-boat traffics, disappeared because
  of the decline of coal as a fuel and the use of docks
  unsuited to canal traffic for berthing of grain ships.
6 The door-to-door service, cheap operating cost, and
  increased speed and size of the motor lorry.

Almost all the types of inland vessel described here could
be seen at work well into the twentieth century, many until
after World War II.

### ON EARLY NAVIGATIONS

Before the coming of the Canal Age (c1760–c1840) commercial craft on the rivers were small local boats designed for
a range of duties from fishing, ferrying, and passenger-
carrying to movement of goods. Alternatively, barges could
be seen, especially in the lower reaches, of the same type as
those navigating inshore coastal waters. Sometimes they
would be scaled-down versions with minimum draught, able
to negotiate the indifferent conditions then met with on many
river highways. A number of these regional craft survived
until modern times. Some canals were specially constructed
to accept them – the Humber waterways for keels, the
Stroudwater Canal for trows – or the design of canal boats
can be directly traced back to vessels long established in that
region.

Relics recovered from Thames mud or peat bogs in Ireland
and Shropshire indicate extensive use of primitive dug-out
canoes from prehistoric to medieval times. The Severn, the
Shannon and other Irish rivers, the Irish lakes, and the

E

rivers of North and Mid-Wales, were navigated well into the present century by that most rudimentary but practical boat, the coracle, which was possibly in use over a thousand years ago. Varying in size and shape from one place to another, these basin-like craft were mainly used in net fishing. Consisting of a frame of woven withies on which a tarred hide is stretched, they reach a beautiful and sophisticated form in the Irish curragh, a long dinghy for two to four pairs of oars and even equipped with a lug sail, still used in the west of Ireland.

Sails, sweeps (large oars relying on tidal flow) and bow-hauling by gangs of notoriously rough individuals were the normal methods of barge propulsion on rivers well into the eighteenth century. The construction of horse towpaths roughly coincided in most instances with the development of the canal system. Some waterways, like the Warwickshire Avon between Stratford and Tewkesbury, never received such paths, bow-hauling continuing until the introduction of steam tugs about 1860.

Some boats working inland before the days of the canals were of considerable proportions. The West Country barges of the Upper Thames, for instance, could reach Oxford with 90 tons in the early eighteenth century. But depending on prevailing conditions of flood or drought the journey from London might take several weeks. On the Severn trows under sail or hauled by gangs on the banks loaded up to 80 tons. Yet at the other end of the scale flat-bottomed craft working the River Wye to Hereford at this time carried a single ton on a 12in draught. Compared with the available alternatives – waggons on indifferent roads, or packhorses – even little boats like these served a useful purpose.

One of the earliest boats specifically designed for canal use was the 'starvationer', a crude open wooden vessel, pointed at each end with massive knees, intended for working the underground canals at Worsley on the Bridgewater. Manchester Museum and Monks Hall Museum, Eccles, Lancs, both have preserved examples. Trains of box-like tub-boats carrying between 4 and 8 tons each were in regular use on West Country waterways – the Grand Western, Chard, Torrington and Bude Canals, and the Shrewsbury and Shropshire Canals – where installation of inclined planes rather than locks precluded large craft.

### NARROW BOATS

Exactly what reason determined the choice of the narrow canal gauge is obscure, but it is logical to suppose that locks to the order of 72ft by 7ft 2in were found to be the most economical in terms of building cost and use of water.

*A Braunston boat woman*

Further, the boats which exactly fitted these structures would travel well on a canal of narrow cross-section, and, horsedrawn, would take loads up to 30 tons, an appreciable amount by the standards of 200 years ago. Once the canals of the Cross, chiefly engineered by Brindley, had linked Thames, Trent, Mersey and Severn via the Birmingham area, mainly using narrow locks throughout, the pattern had been established for the majority of Midland canals. Away from this region the canal companies failed to adopt any uniform system, building lines in direct competition with each other and producing a dreadfully complicated mass of gauges. Of three trans-Pennine routes, the Rochdale accommodated both wide barges and narrow boats, the Huddersfield narrow boats alone, and the Leeds and Liverpool short wide boats.

The first reliable illustrations of craft closely resembling the narrow boat we know today date from the first quarter of the nineteenth century, although it is probable that in many respects similar boats were in use from the opening of the narrow canals. Until iron provided an alternative from about 1870, they were normally built with oak sides and elm bottoms, with iron knees or ribs. To prevent 'spread' of the sides, a system of movable cross-members, either rigid timber or tensioned chains, connected the top plank of the hull across the hold. From the time when long-distance narrow boats became the permanent homes of the boating families who worked them, and cabin accommodation as we now know it became standard, the characteristics of the horsedrawn narrow boat changed little. Thus, in the unpowered craft still at work on English canals there is a design survival of more than 140 years.

According to one well-known narrow boat dock owner, there are at least 394 distinct varieties of these craft. The enthusiast delights in locating various types, although the casual observer may nowadays be hard-pressed to discover more than two dozen designs among working or pleasure craft. There is space here to describe general characteristics only. It is logical to look first at the horsedrawn boat, still in use as an unpowered 'butty' when working as one of a pair with a motor.

Hung on iron pintles at the stern is a massive wooden rudder, the 'Ram's Head', of similar design to that on a Mersey sailing flat. Gently raked backwards, in line with the pointed stern, the rudder has a square socket into which the tiller, or '(h)'elum', fits. Formed in a graceful curve, this is reversed in the socket when the boat is moored up, leaving clear access to the stern well and cabin. On the tiny triangular stern deck is an iron T stud, which is used for making the boat fast to another when breasted up, forming part of a tow or mooring. A small cupboard beneath the deck opens into the well a few feet astern of the little cabin, which extends the full width of the boat and has a pair of doors. Above them is an opening hatch in the roof, known as the 'slide'.

Cabin layout today does not vary between one boat and another, and from pictorial evidence is unchanged from the 1880s, and probably rather earlier. To the left stands a coal-fired range, for heating and cooking; during the last century a tall bottle-shaped fire was used instead, and the type survives on some Birmingham Canal dayboats. The detachable chimney stands in a socket on the roof, secured against knocks from low bridges or overhanging branches with a brass chain. Beyond the range a food cupboard, whose door is hinged at the lower edge to form a table when open, is practically the only mobile fitting. Facing this on the right of the boat is a small seat or child's side bed. Small cupboards, drawers and shelves, a 'soap hole', a ticket drawer for toll documents, and a coal-box (doubling as a step into the living quarters) all have their traditional positions. At the forward end of this minuscule dwelling a folding double bed extends across the boat, blocking access to the hold, which has a narrow central door that is usually fitted at the top with a hinged window. Between food store and stove, a bracketed brass oil-lamp provides light, though electricity is often used in more modern craft. The length of a cabin on such a family boat varied, but was normally 10 to 12ft overall. Plumbing used to be limited to wooden barrels, and painted metal cans were used for many years for water; they were placed on the roof in front of the chimney. Other needs are served by dippers (a bowl with a straight handle at the side) and a bucket.

The undecked hold is covered by tarpaulins erected over a wooden framework of upright stands and top planks. The upright nearest the fore end is stouter than the others and is fitted with a towing hook. The planks are secured to a wooden cabin block on the roof at one end and to a flattened triangle of timber, the 'cratch', at the other. The foredeck is thus divided from the cargo space. Top cloths stretched over each side of the framework overlap side cloths secured to the gunwales, and all this sheeting is tied down with ropes. Non-perishable cargoes like coal or stone generally had no need to be sheeted unless it was essential to keep them dry.

The small foredeck may be a store for ropes, horse feed, tackle etc, and in former years sometimes had a tiny bow cabin providing additional accommodation. Bow shapes vary from an almost upright bluff stem to an elegant undercut streamlined design, offering less water resistance but reducing cargo capacity. Hulls ranged from the fine round-sided Shropshire Union fly-boats to the box-like shape of Severn boats, whose sides were at right-angles to the flat bottom.

While the first successful inland steam-powered boat in Britain was Symington's *Charlotte Dundas* on the Forth and Clyde Canal in 1801, fears about the damaging effects of wash on banks and a reduction in loading capacity delayed installation of engines in narrow boats until the 1860s. Narrow-beam steam tugs had, however, been in use for a number of years, especially on levels with few locks. Fellows, Morton and Clayton operated the largest fleet of about thirty steam narrow boats from the mid-1870s until after World War I, but four-legged horsepower remained largely unchallenged. Further, the boilers and coal required space that could otherwise be devoted to more cargo.

Towards the end of the nineteenth century increased interest in canal transport led to many experiments in boat traction. The search for a reliable and compact engine resulted in the wide adoption of the semi-diesel – Gardiners and Bolinders – from about 1911. Rated at 9–12hp, these units met with universal approval, and survivals of the type may still be found in use today. Horse boats could be modified by replacing the pointed stern with a rounded counter, but in due course purpose-built 'motors' were launched. These were equipped with a slender metal tiller, slightly smaller stern cabin and beyond that an engine room with exhaust outlet (strangely but invariably) blowing through the roof and into the steerer's face! A narrow catwalk was provided on each gunwale. When fitted with an engine, the draught of a narrow boat varies little between loaded and empty, for, when unladen, the bow towers out of the water, while the weight of machinery puts the stern well down. In other respects the construction of a 'motor' is little different from its unpowered butty.

Pairs of boats were built in large numbers throughout the first three decades of this century for 'Number One' (owner-operator) use, and for smaller companies, such as Anderton Carrying, Severn and Canal, Ovaltine, Samuel Barlow, and Midland and Coast, or giants like the legendary Fellows, Morton and Clayton and the Grand Union Canal Carrying Co, formed in the early 1930s. Theoretically increased capacity and a really businesslike approach to operations never produced the deserved profits. On nationalisation in 1948 the Government became responsible for the FMC and GUCCC fleets, then about 460 craft. Gradually they dwindled in number as they were sold for conversion to pleasure boats or to other carriers, until they were officially 'phased out' in 1964. (Until 1972 British Waterways continued quietly to

*A weird experimental outboard engine, tested about 1917 on the Birmingham Canals as a means of easily converting horse-drawn narrow boats to mechanical traction*

operate three pairs out of Brentford.) Private carriers who ceased operations during the 1950s and 1960s outnumbered the small wave of enthusiast-financed companies, which met with varying degrees of success. For a complex variety of causes narrow boats have rarely been economic since World War II, during which time they materially assisted with national transport. If you include proper depreciation figures, so that replacement craft could have been purchased at current building prices and the boatmen paid fully competitive wages, it is doubtful whether narrow boats have been truly economic since about 1880. No new carrying boats have been built since about 1960, when surprisingly British Transport Waterways commissioned a small number of a revolutionary but rather impractical design. These were fitted with blue glass-fibre hatch covers, and several of the motors used a novel inboard-outboard Harbourmaster drive unit.

No form of British canal vessel has a more enthusiastic following than the narrow boat, and this enthusiasm increases in intensity as the numbers of craft dwindle. Perhaps the most obviously attractive aspect of the narrow boat is its strange and colourful decoration, one of the few surviving folk arts in Britain. No conclusive evidence is available as to its origins, but any suggestion that there are old links between the boat people and gipsies meets with universal disapproval among boat families. It seems likely that the roses, castles, decorative ropework, shaded lettering and various other motifs date back to the time when families took to living abroad permanently during the 1830s and 1840s. The earliest known recorded evidence of painted decoration appears in an 1858 edition of *Household Words*, a family magazine edited by Charles Dickens:

> The two sides of the cabin, seen from the bank, and the towing path, present a couple of landscapes, in which there is a lake, a castle, a sailing boat, and a range of mountains painted after the style of the great teaboard school of art. If the *Stourport* cannot match many of its companions in the freshness of its cabin decorations, it can eclipse every other barge upon the canal in the brilliancy of a new two gallon water-can, shipped from a bank-side painter's yard, at an early period of the journey. It displayed no fewer than six dazzling and fanciful composition landscapes, several gaudy wreaths of flowers, and the name of its proud proprietors, Thomas Randle, running round the centre upon a background of blinding yellow.

More than a century later, this description is still applicable.

Decoration was normally applied when a boat received its regular docking, when lettering and paintings were added with an amazingly rapid skill. 'Coachbuilder's' work of this type was considered superior to that practised by boatmen themselves, although a number of self-taught artists were extremely proficient. While conforming to a general pattern of layout and conventions, narrow-boat painting varied in style from one area to another.

The most elaborate decoration was to be seen on boats belonging to Number Ones or the small companies, for here the full glory of roses, hearts and castles was displayed beside gleaming brass knobs, chimney rings and fittings. These boats were also noted for their distinctive brown Measham pottery, with its appliqué flowers and fruit and messages like 'A Present to Arthur Hanbridge' or 'Forget-me-not', and clusters of Victorian and Edwardian 'lace-edged' plates, originally seaside souvenirs which the boat people made very much their own. In the crowded cabins these plates vied for positions with framed family photographs and cabin lace – little curtains and hangings worked to traditional crochet designs. Even boat horses would be dressed with brasses and coloured harness beads, and fed from a flower-painted bowl. It should be remembered, however, that, at the height of canal-carrying prosperity, for every smartly turned out boat there were probably several with faded chipped paintwork, austere cabins and worn sad horses. Nowhere was this more evident than on the Black Country canals until the 1940s and early 1950s. For all the apparent gaiety of the best narrow boats, the life was undoubtedly a hard one, and the highest standards were not always maintained.

Few examples of narrow-boat art survive from the last century, for the decorated surfaces received hard wear and a freshly painted panel was always preferred to a weathered one. The finest collection, including some exhibits seventy or eighty years old, is housed in the British Waterways' museum on the Grand Union Canal at Stoke Bruerne, Northants.

The slow decline of narrow-boat carrying forced families to find employment 'on the land', and the traditions of this hardworking but proud race will in time become extinct. Many of them retain close ties with the canals, living in waterside villages and towns like Hawkesbury, Thrupp, Middlewich and Braunston, where several generations of their families are buried in the churchyards. Some of the more fortunate ones can be found in British Waterways maintenance teams. There is a good chance that the owner of

*For many years a school for narrow boat children was established in an old barge on the Grand Union Canal at Bull's Bridge*

the weatherbeaten face at the tiller of a tug towing a boatload of new lock gates down the Trent and Mersey was born in a boat cabin like his father and grandfather before him. In the evenings he will join the old men in a canalside pub. Retired boaters will be seen on the towpath at most boat rallies, discussing the elaborate converted narrow boats which they remember vividly from trading days.

### WIDE BOATS

Craft whose beam lies between that of a narrow boat and the 14ft or more of a barge are usually known as wide boats. Construction and decoration were in narrow-boat style, over which the wide boat had a theoretical superiority in being able to carry a tonnage equivalent to that of a narrow-boat pair. Although it was seen on London waterways, the Thames, Wey, Kennet and Avon, and especially the Grand Union south of Blisworth Tunnel, the wide boat never achieved the extensive use envisaged by the builders of these broad-beam routes. Compared with the narrow boat, however, living accommodation must have seemed palatial. The enlargement of the Grand Union to nominal wide beam between Braunston and Birmingham before World War II prompted the GUCCC to build the prototype diesel wide boat *Progress*, launched at Tring, while FMC introduced a similar craft, built at Uxbridge and named *Pioneer*. Both had a capacity of about 60 tons. But insufficient widening of the canal's channel, the need for one-way working of the tunnels, and less profitable returns on the considerable narrow-boat fleet investment of this time, helped to scotch further experiments in this direction. After a number of years in maintenance work, *Progress* was recovered from the canal bottom and converted for residential use. Several other wide boats can be seen, at Paddington and Rickmansworth, also serving as houseboats. The breed was beaten by the physical drawbacks of the track on which it was designed to run.

### BARGES

The term 'barge', where correctly applied, includes many local types. Generally boats in this category were designed for fairly exclusive use on a particular canal or group of navigations. Many were inland derivatives of sailing craft, like the horsedrawn or diesel-powered Calder and Hebble barges, constructed on the same lines as Humber keels. Massive wooden vessels, one of the last fleets to operate was that of the Calder Carrying Co, whose Mirfield, Yorkshire, yard was the scene of many spectacular sideways launchings.

For enthusiasts with an eye for rugged workmanlike boats, there is a very special appeal in the bluff-bowed barges of Southern Ireland's waterway network – the Grand Canal, Barrow Line, Shannon and River Suir. Here the need was for a self-propelled boat small enough to fit canal locks while also sufficiently seaworthy to cross the great Shannon lakes, Derg and Ree, and negotiate the tricky tidal estuaries of Barrow and Suir. Unpowered wooden (and from about 1870 iron and steel) craft, horsedrawn on the canals and towed elsewhere by steam tug, began to be modified in 1911 by the installation of 16hp Bolinder semi-diesels, which produced a characteristic 'chuffing' exhaust note. About thirty such conversions were undertaken by the Grand Canal Co, which

*A towpath tractor hauls a dumb lighter into one of the Hanwell Locks, Brentford section of the Grand Union Canal*

*A Bolinder-powered maintenance barge on Ireland's Grand Canal*

abandoned the earlier practice of naming boats, providing instead a number with the suffix 'M', denoting motorisation. Private operators' craft (hack boats) were numbered with the suffix 'B' for bye-trader. It was not unusual for a company boat to be hired by a private trader. In 1925 the first GCC modern steel barges were put in hand at Dublin's Ringsend Dockyard Co; others were later made by Vickers (Ireland) Ltd. Forty-nine of them had come into service by 1939. The World War II fuel crisis prompted construction of some twenty-nine Government-financed wooden horseboats (G boats) to carry turf to power stations and into Dublin. These were leased to bye-traders, who paid tolls to the canal company. None now survive.

Designed as a close fit in the canal locks, the Grand Canal barges that remain today for maintenance work are of all-steel construction, with wide side decks, counter and fore-deck on the same level, and the appearance of small Continental *péniches* with an open steering position. The engine-room walls and roof project about 18in above the deck in front of the tiller. The male crew of four (in later years three) are quartered in the bows in a spacious cabin with three bunks along its walls, a peat-burning stove, a table and some cupboards. The crew consisted of a master, engineman, deckhand and 'greaser', the function of the last named being to cook and keep house – he was usually a lad, whose father might well be master. Grand Canal boatmen rarely lived aboard for more than short periods, since the longest journeys, such as Dublin to Waterford, Carrick-on-Shannon or Limerick, were timed to take only four days. 'Family' boating as in England was unknown. The hold was either decked with movable planks or roughly sheeted when bulky cargoes were carried. A wide variety of goods were transported, among them porter, logs, sugar beet, cereals and assorted general commodities.

The colour scheme of the company barges was limited to a black hull showing a registration number painted on a red ground, with a distinguishing colour for the water barrel carried on deck. Private carriers devised their own liveries for number panel and superstructure.

The undertaking was nationalised in 1950 and thereafter slowly declined. By 1958, private barges had ceased to work the Grand and in November 1959 Coras Iompair Eireann announced that boats would be withdrawn as from 1 January 1960. The last boat to trade was 51 M, which loaded a cargo of Guinness stout in Dublin for Limerick on 27 May 1960.

A number of these fine boats have been converted to pleasure use. Others are still occasionally to be seen chugging down the Grand and the Barrow on maintenance duty, bearing a number and the suffix 'E' (Engineering), their faithful and reliable Bolinders still in service.

Another distinct variety of wide-beamer, generally associated with the Leeds and Liverpool Canal but also trading on the Bridgewater and connecting wide waterways, is the short boat. Her size was determined by the capacity of the locks between Wigan and Leeds, which admitted a boat about 62ft long and 14ft 3in wide. The wooden construction was obviously derived from river barges of the Mersey and Weaver, giving a maximum load of 45 tons on a 3ft 9in draught. Crew accommodation was provided in fore and aft cabins, normally below deck level but sometimes extending as a low superstructure on the latest steel-hulled motorised types. Steam engines were fitted from about 1890, a well-known type being the 'vee'-shaped twin unit of the Leeds and Liverpool Canal Carrying Company fleet of Wigan.

*One of the massive timber-built Wey barges which continued to carry grain between London Docks and Coxes Lock Mill, Weybridge, until the service was discontinued in 1969*

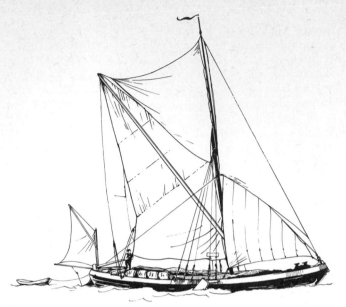

*Until after World War II, Thames sailing barges were a regular sight on London River. Those that remain are owned by preservation trusts or private individuals*

Like the narrow boats, these worked in pairs on a 'motor' and 'butty' system. The last new one was launched in 1936, but they were not finally withdrawn from service until the mid-1950s. The surviving regular short-boat traffic, engaged in coal transport to Wigan power station along the Leigh branch, was terminated in 1972. Two notable short-boat features are the square-sectioned wooden chimneys to the cabin stove (which not infrequently caught fire!) and the strange ornate decoration on bow and stern, displaying baroque scrolls, flowers and geometrical paintings more akin to the fairground than to Midland narrow boats.

There are numerous other barges, localised in origin and use, often associated with individual waterways. Few now survive in trade, although efforts to preserve examples are being made as the great current interest in things of industrial archaeological importance continues.

### SAILING CRAFT

Well into the twentieth century much of Britain's trade was conducted in sailing vessels working the coasts and estuaries, and scores of little ports now decayed were centres of small-ship building. Where inland navigations joined river estuaries, it was a natural development to find scaled-down sailing ships penetrating the countryside; thus a special pattern of shallow-draught sailing barge came to be used on the Thames, Severn, Mersey and Humber and their adjoining waterways. All have now ceased to function, but their use was widespread until quite recently. The last Thames barge working under sail alone, the *Cambria*, made her final voyage in 1970, and most other breeds were a part of the English landscape until after World War II.

From the creeks and rivers of the East Coast, past the Thames and the Medway and round the North Foreland to the South Coast of Sussex and Hampshire, Thames barges, glorious under their red-brown canvas, traded by wind and tide. They were flat-bottomed, with leeboards in place of keels, but their two or three-men crews were notoriously adept at handling the heavy gear and navigating difficult sandbank-strewn waters in tricky weather. But they did not always escape disaster. Documented accounts of these magnificent boats, such as Edgar March's *Spritsail Barges of Thames and Medway* (David & Charles), abound with tales of wrecks, not least during World War II, when hundreds of barges performed a vital service in bringing supplies into London under enemy attack. Skippers were also required to possess the skills of the inland boatmen, in shooting Thames and Medway bridges with gear and sails lowered and raised once more before steerage was lost. It is well realised that to relegate boats of this kind to a museum existence up some muddy backwater is the quickest way to ensure their rapid decay. Fortunately a number of concerns maintain Thames barges in working condition, providing opportunities for the individual to spend time afloat learning the skills of the old sailormen (see pp 201–2).

Like the Thames barge, the trows of the Severn evolved from square-rigged boats whose ancestry probably reaches back to the fifteenth century. During the 1840s and 1850s these were equipped with fore and aft ketch, cutter or sloop rig. Their use extended from the upper navigation limits of the Severn at Stourport to the Bristol Channel ports, along the Wye and the Stroudwater and Droitwich Canals, and even as far east as Honeystreet and Aldermaston on the Kennet and Avon, where a number of canal-sized trows were built. Distinctive characteristics were a D-shaped transom stern and an amazing longevity, especially where they were used to carry salt from Droitwich. For instance, the *William* put in 130 years of service before being wrecked in 1939! Dismasted trows were used as dumb barges on the Severn until recent times, although none now appear to remain in a state fit for preservation.

The ancestry of the Humber or Yorkshire keel is said to go back to the Vikings, and a connection with the Norse longships certainly seems likely in view of the great square mainsail, surmounted by a smaller topsail.

Early inland keels carried between 40 and 50 tons, as the waterways they worked were generally only about 3ft 6in deep. Slightly larger craft, differently rigged and called sloops,

*Another obsolete sailing barge is the Severn trow, with its distinctive D-shaped transom*

*While they no longer trade under sail, motorised Humber or Yorkshire keels can still be found in freight on waterways of the North East*

navigated the tidal sections, including Selby to Hull. These carried about 70 tons and were not unlike the billy-boys that traded down the north-east coast. As the waterways were improved to draughts of 7ft, the coastal barges were able to penetrate further inland. From 80 to 100 tons might be carried in a hull measuring 58ft by 14ft 2in beam. Often, these sloops were manned by families who spent all their lives aboard.

The keels were of massive wooden construction with vast stem post and ribs, a low wooden rail around the stern deck and a row of chunky bollards on each stern quarter. A small amount of decorative paintwork and lightly varnished upperwork relieved the black tar of the hull, while a fat round rope fender would hang over the extremely bluff bows. They possessed an ability to sail very close to the wind, while their manoeuvrability was such that in quite narrow waters they could be handled by one man alone. Throughout north-eastern navigations they were a familiar but in appearance essentially an un-British part of the waterways scene. Similar horsedrawn or motorised keels were in use on the Calder and Hebble Navigation, and in these remaining barges we can still examine constructional details of the hull. But the sailing keel has vanished in day to day commerce since 1949, though efforts are now being made to preserve one.

Sailing barges on the Mersey, Irwell and Weaver increased in use with the growth of trade in coal, salt and cotton during the second quarter of the eighteenth century, and by the early 1800s were equipped with a fore and aft rig, either single-masted or with a mizzen as well. Oak-hulled barges all had pitch pine decks, and many features subsequently adopted by the Midland canal horseboats. Particularly is this noticeable in the rudder, an enlarged version of that on the narrow boats. The Mersey flats were up to about 70ft in length on a 14ft 3in to 14ft 9in beam, and loaded about 80 tons. These dimensions allowed access to the Bridgewater, Northern Shropshire Union and St Helens Canals. The Weaver flats (or 'Number One' flats, a reference to their generally being manned by their owners) were generally 20ft longer on a 21ft beam. Drawing up to 10ft 6in of water when loaded, they could carry 250 tons. Four such vessels could pass through the Weaver locks in company. Unlike the keels and Thames barges, leeboards were never seen, and in spite of flat bottoms with curved hull sides, they appeared to remain quite stable.

By the end of the nineteenth century practically all Mersey flats had become dumb barges, relying on steam tugs or horses for haulage. Steam engines also replaced the gaff sails of the Weaver flats, of which fewer than twenty remained

*Mersey flats were once extensively distributed throughout the North West*

fully rigged by 1935. Seagoing craft in the fullest sense, the bigger flats frequently navigated the Mersey estuary and the North Wales and Lancashire coasts, and even voyaged as far south as Land's End to load granite. The advent of the steam engine and the opening of the Manchester Ship Canal in 1894 sounded the death knell of the sailing flat, but even now substantial remains of several can be seen on the Weaver above Frodsham and along the Mersey at West Bank, Widnes.

South coast navigations, among them the Sussex Ouse and the Arun, were during the nineteenth century used regularly by sailing barges of a local type. Still in use up to the 1930s was the West Country Teignmouth keel, carrying clay on the River Teign, Stover Canal and Hackney Canal in Devon. These undecked barges carried a single square sail set well forward.

The wherry of the Norfolk and Suffolk Broads is among the best known types of inland sailing cargo boat. Wherries were of oak clinker planking, and their capacity ranged from 12 to 83 tons. They set a single boomless gaff (four-sided) sail traditionally dressed with fish oil and coal tar, resulting in a vast spread of black canvas. The tall mast could be easily lowered to negotiate bridges, and the crew would propel their wherry with long poles known as 'quants' where conditions were unfavourable for sail. A white-painted quadrant on each side of the bow warned other craft by night

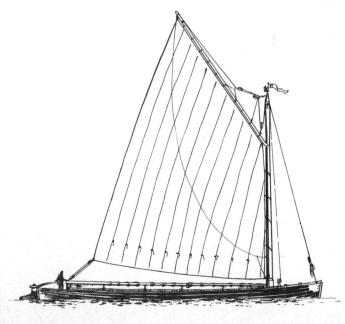

*Once a common feature of Broadland water-ways, only one Norfolk wherry is now preserved in working condition*

of the wherry's approach. The wide range of cargoes they carried throughout the Broads and to the seaport at Yarmouth included timber, agricultural produce, reeds, and building materials. Long-established as a holiday cruising region, the Broads in Victorian and Edwardian times offered on hire pleasure wherries, converted or purpose-built, which were fitted with every comfort, even a piano, with the services of an experienced boatman and a boy thrown in. One trading example of a wherry still in sailing order is the 1898-built *Albion*, preserved and operated by the Norfolk Wherry Trust.

## COMPARTMENT BOATS

The concept of using trains of small barges instead of larger single craft is as old as the British canal system. Rectangular tub-boats achieved popularity in the West Country on the Torrington and Bude Canals. During World War I 20ft long tub-boats were still at work on the Coalport Canal in Shropshire, each loading about 5 tons. As many as twenty were towed in a train by horses, the long serpent being steered by a man on the towpath pushing the leading container with a pole. A similar system of Fen lighters was once widespread on the Great Ouse and Middle Level systems, where up to five wooden barges, each about 42ft long, were coupled together with poles and chains, and hauled by horse or steam tug.

But it was on the waters of one of the most progressive companies – the Aire and Calder Navigation – that the use of compartments became most common, and indeed these 'Tom Puddings' or 'pans' remain today an important part of the carriage of coal from Yorkshire pits to waterside power stations and colliers at the Aire and Calder's own seaport of Goole. Tom Puddings are iron or steel boxes about 20ft by 16ft, loading 35 tons on a draught of 6ft. They are tightly coupled one to another with chains and are now towed by British Waterways diesel tugs, although formerly steam tugs pulled and initially pushed the trains. Loading is accomplished by shunting the boats beneath chutes set up along the waterway at convenient distances from the pit, where coal is tipped either from railway trucks or lorries direct into the boats.

On arrival at their destination, they are manoeuvred under a huge gantry, where each compartment is lifted clear of the water and inverted in a cradle, causing the coal to cascade down a conveyor into the hold of the waiting ship. The best place to view this unique apparatus is at Goole Docks. It is difficult to appreciate that this equipment has been in operation, basically unchanged, since about 1865. An enlarged application of the system has supplied Ferrybridge 'C' Power Station, also on the Aire and Calder, with fuel since 1967. The handling capacity of this device is 1,000 tons per hour. Steering long trains of compartment boats is a somewhat erratic affair, so that skippers of pleasure craft are warned to give them a wide berth, and to remember that the 'tail' of the train may swing considerably behind the tug, especially on bends.

### MOTOR BARGES

The Trent, Severn, Thames, Humber, Aire and Calder, Sheffield and South Yorkshire, and River Weaver all remain busy with commercial traffic, mostly diesel-powered barges of up to 350 tons capacity. These sturdy craft, able safely to penetrate tidal reaches whose weather conditions can become as difficult as on the open sea, are operated by both British Waterways and independent firms of carriers. The smaller types, such as the 90-ton steel barges of the North East, are directly descended from Yorkshire keels; indeed some still in service are conversions from sailing craft. Others are designed to carry specialist cargoes like bulk fuel. In some respects their operation and equipment owes more to sea-going craft than to canal boats, and there is little essential difference between them and the small coasters that frequent the Gloucester and Sharpness Ship Canal, the Caledonian Canal, the Weaver and the Humber. Few of Britain's waterways admit real ships for much distance inland, a notable exception being the Manchester Ship Canal, where vessels arrive from all parts of the world.

### TUGS

Mechanical haulage on canals was slow to be adopted. Companies feared wash damage to their banks and often sought to ban powered craft altogether. But by the 1850s the obvious advantages of towage independent of towpath and horse ferry had begun to be accepted. Dumb craft and sailing vessels need no longer be subject to wind and tiring horses. Numerous experiments with steamboats – paddle- and screw-driven – resulted in tugs like the prizewinning *Birmingham*, which in 1855 pulled a gross weight of 1,231 tons in twenty barges along $11\frac{1}{4}$ miles of the Regent's Canal, performing the task at a snail's pace in 13 hours! Tugs were especially useful on long lock-free pounds – the Paddington Level in London, the Birmingham Canals, or rivers, including the Trent and Severn – where they could haul strings of lighters and narrow boats, sometimes two dozen or more at a time. One of the finest tug fleets was the collection of elegant narrow-beam steamers operated by the Manchester Ship

Canal's Bridgewater Department, whose tall funnels and long low superstructures were common throughout the Bridgewater Canal during the first quarter of this century. Narrowboat tugs, full-length or, especially on the BCN, about 40ft overall, bore proud names, such as *Enterprise, Early Bird* or plain *Powerful*. These handy craft are now widely admired as pleasure craft conversions, and many now appear more glorious and shining in their traditional paintwork than ever they did when drawing prosaic trains of coal or gravel boats.

Many of the longer canal tunnels built without towpaths were worked by steam tugs hauling the horseboats through, and the backbreaking task of 'legging' became less frequent. As cargo boats were fitted with engines, the towage services lapsed. One of the last was an old, electrically driven vessel which ran through Harecastle new tunnel on the Trent and Mersey until after World War II.

River tugs are wide-beamed busy little boats, developing a considerable power, and whether attached to ocean liners on the Manchester Ship Canal, drawing lighters in the Thames, or perhaps taking the occasional barge down the Regent's Canal, lower Grand Union or the heavily used River Lee, they contrive to display a character that is oddly endearing. Mention should also be made here of the small towpath-based tractors found on the Brentford district of the Grand Union, on the Regent's Canal and on the Lee. These replaced some of the last remaining working canal horses in Britain during the 1950s and should be given priority of passage by pleasure traffic. To become entangled in their lines is not only dangerous but invites savage criticism from the lightermen!

### PASSENGER CRAFT

Inland waterways have for so long been regarded by the general public as a slow and outmoded transport medium that we tend to forget that for seventy years up to, and to a lesser extent after, the arrival of railway competition, packet boats for passengers were a convenient, pleasant and quick alternative to horses and coaches on frequently indifferent roads. Few navigations ignored the opportunity of deriving added revenue from this source, some operating their own boats, others leaving the service to independent owners.

One early account of scheduled services dates from 1776, when passage boats were plying on the Bridgewater Canal between Lymm, Worsley and Manchester at 1d per mile. Boats were horsedrawn and by using two animals and changing them at frequent intervals, average speeds of 3–4mph were normally achieved. The craft were of finer lines than contemporary cargo boats, and lightly built, with rounded bilges and a pointed bow. Passengers were accommodated in two or three classes, standards of comfort ranging from carpeted luxury with piped central heating to bare benches and plain wooden floors. Published descriptions of this method of travel vary from the recorded pleasure of one John Fox, who noted in his diary for 1839 that the run from Preston to Kendal on the Lancaster Canal was 'the most delightful journey that ever I made in my life', to the tedium experienced in an Anthony Trollope novel by Martin Kelly, whose journey along Ireland's Grand Canal, probably autobiographical, prompted the comment: 'I believe the misery of the canal-boat chiefly consists in a pre-conceived and erroneous idea of its capabilities. One prepares oneself for occupation ... and the mind is fatigued more by the search after, than the want of, occupation.' An excellent fictional description (but one based very closely on fact) of a journey starting on the Thames and Severn Canal by packet boat and ending in London can be found in C. S. Forester's *Hornblower and the Atropos*. This is thoroughly recommended for its re-creation of the authentic atmosphere of canal travel during the early 1800s.

Some of the first experiments in steam propulsion were conducted with packet boats on the Forth and Clyde and other Scottish canals at the beginning of the nineteenth century, and thereafter steamers ran scheduled services on scores of routes until World War I. Nowhere was this more widespread than in Ireland, where dozens of paddle and screw boats plied the Shannon and other rivers and lakes. By the 1870s inland water travel had become a matter more for pleasure than necessity, although L. T. C. Rolt records that the last regular passenger service in Britain, as opposed to pleasure excursions, was that run by the Gloucester & Berkeley Steam Packet Co until about 1935.

Salter's 'steamers' on the Thames to Oxford, though now steamers in name alone, are among the concerns in all parts of the network that continue the tradition of passenger craft into the 1970s. River trips have never waned completely in popular esteem, while the growth in similar services on the canals since the war is phenomenal. From *Jason's Trip* (started in 1951) aboard a pair of traditional narrow boats on London's Regent's Canal, to purpose-built cruisers for public rides, private parties and business conferences, in every area, the demand for instant canal exploration seems insatiable. Details of many passenger tripping firms are published in *The Canal Enthusiasts' Handbook No 2* (David & Charles) and *The Inland Waterways Guide to Holiday Hire* (IWA).

## INSPECTION BOATS

Inter-authority rivalry perhaps coupled with a tinge of arrogance resulted in the Victorian and Edwardian waterways companies maintaining directors' launches in which inspections of the navigation were made as was necessary (and sometimes merely for the sake of a well victualled excursion!). These inspection boats were the lords of the waterways, where, particularly on the canals, few other pleasure craft existed to vie with their level of luxury. In such status symbols were incorporated all the skills of the boatbuilder, joiner and upholsterer. Like the railway saloons of royalty, they reflected the lavish confidence of the Victorian age.

There was the Weaver Navigation Trustees' 60ft narrow boat *Water Witch*, and the Worcester and Birmingham's steamer *Swallow*. There was the open clinker launch *Gadfly* of the Grand Junction's Northern District Engineer, and the same concern's steam launch *Swift*, which was followed in 1928 by the still extant petrol-engined *Kingfisher*. The Trent and Mersey Canal had the *Dolly Varden*, and the Staffs and Worcs one of the most famous, the *Lady Hatherton*, which was launched in 1898 with the company's ornate monogram etched on its plate-glass windows. Leather-buttoned seats, wine bins and mahogany panelling with extensive brasswork provided a suitably opulent atmosphere

*Donola, steam-driven inspection launch of the former Thames Conservancy, during her last journey to the National Maritime Museum at Greenwich*

for horsedrawn voyages on hot summer days. The *Lady Hatherton* is now in private hands, and is fully used; she is as splendid as ever, having been equipped with a replica hull in 1965 to ensure that she will remain so. The Thames Conservancy's superb steam launch *Donola*, bought from a private owner during the 1920s when she was already something of a celebrity, carried judges on an annual inspection of lock gardens until 1969, when she was retired to the National Maritime Museum at Greenwich, to which she made her own way and where she is on permanent exhibition.

There are no modern equivalents of these beautiful vessels, for navigation authorities no longer feel the need for an outward show of riches. The British Waterways Board's chairman has a standard canal cruiser for his personal use, and while the vogue for inspections by members of the Board, various advisory bodies and local authority representatives is greater than ever in the past, suitable tripping narrow boats, launches and cabin cruisers are generally secured for the purpose. Two exceptions are BWB'S *Lady Rose of Regent's*, based in the London area, and the converted motor barge *Fair Maiden*, on South Yorkshire waterways. The Thames Water Authority's launches are trim vessels with glass-reinforced plastic hulls, as are the boats of the Metropolitan River Police that patrol the lower part of the Thames. The taste for luxury is now more often the prerogative of the private owner than of the concern to which he pays his licence money.

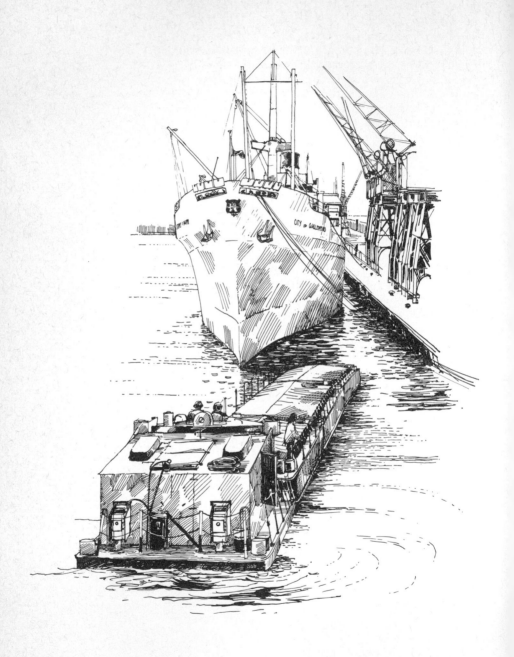

*BACAT barges being manœuvered by a push tug in Hull docks*

# 13
# Commercial Carriers

In most European countries, water transport is an expanding activity, assisted by much Government expenditure on modernisation or new construction schemes. In France, Germany and the Low Countries the trend is towards adoption of a 1,350-ton capacity or larger barge network, achieved either by enlargement of old 250- or 300-ton routes or quite often by the building of completely new sections of navigation. Some routes are being further enlarged for 9,000-ton push-tows. Although many thousands of the smaller motorised barges continue to trade, they are fast declining, with the result that smaller waterways like the beautiful Canal du Nivernais in Central France were recently faced with closure. After long delays, pleasure cruising has now begun to show, and should in the long term save such lesser canals, and even encourage their development for amenity use.

The position in Britain is in most places quite different. At the time of nationalisation in 1948 a large number of our canals, including those suitable only for 25-ton capacity working narrow boats, were commercially used. The leading bulk cargo was coal, supplemented by many other commodities, including timber, metals, liquid fuels and foodstuffs. Canal transport was only economically possible because of family-operated boats, which a father, mother and several children were prepared to spend most of their waking hours working in return for a wage that would scarcely have been adequate for a single man working a 40-hour week in some other industry.

Excluding the Manchester Ship Canal and the Irish waterways, about 14,264,000 tons were carried on British rivers and canals in 1953. Compared with the 900 million tons conveyed by road in 1952, it will be seen that water transport, although a fairly small industry, was nevertheless important. Looking back at such a recent stage in waterways history, it comes as something of a shock to realise that steam puffers were still plying the Crinan Canal with coal and timber, and that the Forth and Clyde Canal (closed in 1962) was busy with herring fishing craft and oil barges. The Grand Canal and the Barrow Navigation in Ireland carried over

160,000 tons of goods in 1947, and the whole length of the
Leeds and Liverpool Canal was regularly used by motorised
short boats, some of them newly built. Even the now peaceful
backwaters of the Southern Oxford, Staffs and Worcs and
Great Ouse then contributed to the national water freight
figures. Much has changed in two decades!

During the first five years following nationalisation cargo
totals increased quite sharply, mostly as a result of improvements in the Yorkshire area. Apart from substantial 'bonuses'
from water sales to industry, Government-controlled rivers
and canals were then considered almost solely for their
freight-carrying capacity or potential. Revenue from pleasure
boating, angling or other amenity uses was virtually non-
existent or only just starting to be regarded as a reason for
keeping a route open. Therefore, the canal that still carried
commercial traffic had a much better prospect of survival
than one that had lost its trade. Closures by Act of Parliament
had been numerous in the 1940s. Waterways that were wholly
or partly shut during or soon after World War II included
sections of the Shropshire Union Canal and the Birmingham
Canal Navigations, and also the Barnsley and Huddersfield
Canals. Among those closed after 1948 were the Manchester,
Bolton and Bury, Forth and Clyde, St Helens, Monmouthshire, Cromford, Union, and parts of the Chesterfield and
Lancaster Canals. Some of these casualties were later to be
revived and given an opportunity to flourish in a new climate
of amenity use.

Working boats and patterns of freight movement had
changed very little in half a century. With common ownership of many rivers and canals, through goods rates could at
last be quoted and small fleets combined into larger and more
economic units. Most carrying was conducted by private firms
paying tolls for the use of the route. About one-fifth of vessels
plying the nationalised waterways of Britain were operated in
1953 by the British Transport Commission, a forerunner of
the British Waterways Board. These included 199 motor
narrow boats, 315 unpowered butty narrow boats, 47
motorised barges, 697 dumb wide-beam craft and 25 tugs.
Private concerns worked large numbers of narrow boats,
while sizeable fleets of large-capacity tankers and general
merchandise barges used waters like the Severn and the Aire
and Calder. A good many large manufacturers maintained
their own transport fleets, ranging from the coal-carrying
narrow boats of Messrs Ovaltine to the steam flats and barges
of ICI Ltd on the Weaver and Bridgewater Canals.

Throughout the present century Britain's waterways have
been under constant scrutiny, with official reports being
published at regular intervals and consequent changes in

policy. Until the 1968 Transport Act, which effectively established a distinct role for both commercial and amenity waterways, the official line of thought was mainly concerned with the freight capabilities, or lack of them, of our rivers and canals. A good deal of development that took place during the 1950s was detailed in a 1961 report, *Six Years of Progress*, published by British Transport Waterways. During the years 1954–60, 132 miles of concrete or steel bank protection was erected in an effort to make navigations constructed for horse-drawn or sailing craft suitable for wash-creating powered boats. Most of this was concentrated on routes now designated as 'commercial'. Twenty-three dredgers, with forty hopper barges, were added to the national maintenance fleet in an attempt to tackle a huge backlog of work. In those six years some 8 million tons of silt were removed from navigation channels. By the end of 1962 about forty locks had been converted from manual to mechanical working, on the Trent, Severn, Aire and Calder, Weaver, lower Grand Union Canal, and Lee Navigation. BTW's traffic fleet was improved, with worn or obsolete craft being replaced. Forty steel narrow boats took the place of wooden ones, fifty new compartment boats were put into service in the Aire and Calder coal trade, with new diesel tugs replacing steamers, and some of the motorised barges of the North East were lengthened, providing 50 tons of additional cargo capacity each. Improvements were also made in the handling and storage of goods at waterside wharves and warehouses. In the six years from 1954 120,000sq ft of covered storage was added to existing facilities. These figures are included here to demonstrate that commercial traffic was not mismanaged or deliberately allowed to decline, as is sometimes supposed, though not nearly enough was spent to keep waterway development level with road expansion.

The pattern of improvements, coupled with unfortunate traffic losses, continued throughout the 1960s. British Waterways had ended most of their narrow-boat carrying within the first few years of the decade, and by 1970 virtually all the private operators had followed. The 1968 Transport Act defined the routes on which freight movement could be encouraged by the Board. Elsewhere trade had mostly fallen off, even on the once hectic tidal Thames through London, where lighter traffic to and from the docks fell sharply as shipping patterns altered. Some ports like York and Norwich, although well inland, continue to be served by small coasting vessels, but centuries of traditional barge activity has been ended on private routes like the Wey Navigation and the Chelmer and Blackwater. During the 1970s much of British inland water transport has failed to compete with the road lorry, largely because of an absence of modernisation of both craft and waterways, coupled with a lack of any national policy for truly integrated transport. Road, rail and water carriage abroad are encouraged to complement each other instead of competing.

PRESENT AND FUTURE TRAFFIC

The gloomy and troubled past of canal and river freight movement must not be allowed to overshadow the small but energetic present-day operations or the exciting new developments that may come in the years ahead. One thing is reasonably certain. Very few of the smallest canals, so much appreciated for their pleasure cruising and relaxation value, will ever see more than the smallest return to commercial traffic. If we are to have new waterways in Britain, they will be just that, and not enlarged eighteenth-century watercourses. Of course, as with most remarks that can be made about canals, there could be exceptions to the rule, but the general principle remains true.

For movement of goods by water we must therefore look to the larger river estuaries, linking towns with the coast, and to the river and canal navigations that penetrate inland from such areas. The land mass of Britain is of such a shape that no industrial region is more than a hundred miles from the sea, in sharp contrast to the European Continent. On the tenth anniversary of the British Waterways Board, early in 1973, the Board was able to report that in recent years it had increased the capacity of the Aire and Calder Navigation from 250 to 500 tons with the possibility of 700-ton vessels. The Gloucester and Sharpness Canal enabled 1,000-tonners to reach the port of Gloucester, whereas the maximum had previously been only 750 tons. The Weaver Navigation could now accommodate 650-ton craft, compared with 550-tonners previously. On the Trent a bottleneck bridge hole at Newark had been slightly enlarged in 1972 to provide 7ft draught throughout the waterway, so increasing potential barge capacity by 20 per cent to 350 tons. At present British Waterways operate 340 miles of waterways designated 'commercial', which are managed by their Freight Services Division. The FSD has responsibility for running BW's own barge fleets, together with its dock and warehousing facilities. In 1973 it achieved an operating surplus of £375,000 with a net profit of £237,000. In addition to these 340 miles there are 300 miles or so in the care of a variety of authorities. These range from the Manchester Ship Canal to the Yorkshire Ouse, and from the lower Thames, lower Trent, Humber and Medway to the Mersey from Warrington to the sea.

British Waterways has achieved considerable success with

its ship docks at Sharpness and Weston Point, which handled 628,900 and 460,500 tons respectively in 1973.

The most exciting aspect of commercial transport on Britain's rivers and canals results from the introduction of a completely new category of vessel in the barge that can be lifted aboard purpose-built ships to make the sea passage to waterways of the Continent and America. Britain's association with the Common Market has been the prime factor in encouraging this progressive move. There are three systems now under development – BACAT, LASH and SEABEE.

## BACAT

Short for Barge Aboard Catamaran: this system was initiated by BWB in association with a Danish shipbuilding firm. Ten barges, each loading up to 140 tons, are carried on the deck of a catamaran ship, together with three LASH lighters (see below) between the two hulls. BACAT barges measure 55ft by 15ft and draw 8ft 1in when fully loaded. Special push tugs (they can also pull if required) are close-coupled with trains of normally three barges, although up to nine can be dealt with simultaneously. The first BACAT containers have been operational on the Sheffield and South Yorkshire and Aire and Calder Navigations since 1971, powered by push tugs *Freight Pioneer* and *Freight Trader*. Fifty-seven of the barges were ordered to be built in Hull, while the first £2 million mother ship came into service in 1974. When this system is fully operational, it should result in the carriage of an annual 300,000 tons of cargo on waterways of the North East, moving goods from inland terminals in England to similar terminals abroad, at present Rotterdam.

Because the capacity of the Sheffield and South Yorkshire Navigation locks uphill of Doncaster is only 90 tons (they were designed for Yorkshire keel barges), the BACAT trains have at present to be broken down into four sections at each of the eight locks between Doncaster and Rotherham Depot. British Waterways have pressed for enlargement of the canal for 700-ton units to Mexborough and 400-ton units to Rotherham at a cost of about £2·4 million. In this they have the full support of local authorities, industry and private water-transport firms. An authorising Act has been passed, but late in 1974 no money had yet been made available.

## LASH

Lighter Aboard Ship, for which LASH is the abbreviation, is a similar method of loading inland barges on ships that has been developed by an American concern based in New Orleans. In 1973 some twenty-two LASH ships had been constructed or were on the stocks, some of them described

as the largest cargo liners in the world. Those currently in
service cross the Atlantic at fortnightly intervals between
New Orleans, Sheerness (Medway estuary) and Rotterdam,
each carrying seventy-three lighters stacked on deck in
several tiers. A travelling crane straddling the ship can transfer barges from water to deck or *vice versa* as they are mar-
shalled in a small 'dock' at the stern. It will be appreciated
that the turnround time of barge-carrying ships is very rapid
compared with conventional ocean-going vessels, and delays
can be kept to a minimum, provided a sufficient number of
barges are available. Each LASH lighter is 61ft 6in by
31ft 2in, with an 8ft 8in draught and capacity of about 435
tons. They can be formed into single or breasted-up trains
and propelled by push tugs or hauled by ordinary tugs. The
first LASH ship to visit Britain was *Acadia Forest* which
anchored at the mouth of the Medway off Sheerness in 1970.
It must be appreciated that LASH barges are suitable for
only the largest class of British locked waterways, although if
a fairly elementary lock enlargement programme could be
undertaken, they would be able to serve many of our inland
ports.

### SEABEE

This system, also American, began operating in 1972 when
the first ship, *Doctor Lykes*, went into service on the Gulf–
Rhine route. The barges are considerably larger than either
LASH or BACAT, being 98ft long by 35ft wide, and loading
about 850 tons. Thirty-eight of these units are carried aboard
the ship. SEABEE ships now make regular visits to the lower
Thames.

There is a growing demand in Britain for the increased use
of inland waterways freight facilities on environmental as
well as economic grounds. While even massive investment in
this transport medium cannot alone solve the ever-expanding
problem of the heavy lorry, carriage by water could make a
significant contribution to relieving urban road congestion.
British Waterways and the Greater London Council have a
plan under active consideration, whereby the lower Grand
Union Canal would be used as a freight link between the
London Docks and a point near Rickmansworth, Herts. Road
traffic would be directed to an extensive transhipment depot
near the southern end of the M1 motorway, whence goods
would continue their journey to London by water. To reduce
handling costs, some form of containerisation seems essential. Locks and bridges on the canal would require rebuilding,
to create a capacity roughly equivalent to that now being
sought for the Sheffield and South Yorkshire Navigation. It

has been suggested that the flight of locks at Hanwell, near the Grand Union's junction with the Thames at Brentford, might be replaced by a water slope, similar to an experimental one constructed in southern France at Montech. Here barges overcome the change in levels by travelling up or down the slope on a wedge-shaped pool of water that is impounded at the lower end by a moving gate. A feasibility study, jointly promoted by British Waterways and the Greater London Council, was announced in November 1973 to consider the lower Grand Union proposal. Within four or five years of the enlargement being begun, several million tons of freight could reach the metropolis by water. A barge train composed of ten units would move the same quantity of freight as that hauled by a fleet of seventy 30-ton lorries.

Water transport suffers chronically in Britain from an outdated image. Devotees of the 25- or 30-ton capacity traditional narrow boat (attractive though it may be) do not perform a useful service in helping to achieve Government acceptance of the notion that modern barge-carrying is the most civilised, economic and sensible method of moving huge quantities of freight. Looking to the future, our close ties with the nations of Europe could well result in our adopting many of their transport methods. Before the end of the century Birmingham, former centre of a web of eighteenth- and nineteenth-century waterways, could be linked to the coast via the Trent or the lower Nene in one direction and the Severn in another. A new Midlands port could be handling 1,350-ton seagoing barges. It would be unfortunate, to say the least, if we were to concentrate on new motorway construction to the virtual exclusion of alternative transport methods, and ensure that the heavy lorry destroys Britain's environment by the year 2000.

Typical of the serious consideration being given to waterway development is the work of the Inland Waterways Association's Inland Shipping Group. Members of this body possess between them a fund of experience drawn from freight-carrying activities on the rivers and canals of Europe. Already there are signs that Britain, once ahead of the world in canal transport, might again come to be regarded as a serious user of waterway freight services. But we have a great deal of lost ground to catch up.

# 14
# *Pleasure Cruising*

WE tend to think of holidays on the waterways as being a recent discovery. Considering them as a pastime for the masses, we are right, for during the 1950s they were almost unheard of. But for a select band of pioneers who chose to write about their experiences (and presumably a good many more who cruised anonymously), canal boating began well back in the nineteenth century.

The ancient river navigations have to some extent always been used for boating excursions. The sport did not really begin to take hold, however, until Victorian times. Manually propelled craft of the *Three Men in a Boat* era retained a great popularity on the Thames until after World War II, when they declined rapidly in favour of plastic runabouts and small mass-produced cruisers. Nevertheless it is quite a tribute to the craftsmanship of their builders that skiffs, punts, dinghies

*A lunchtime halt near Solihull on the northern section of the Stratford-upon-Avon Canal*

and Canadian canoes in varnished mahogany planking and with brass fittings have survived upwards of sixty years of use. Privately owned, or more commonly belonging to fleets for hire, they linger on, recalling hot summer days of picnic hampers and simpler pleasures than most waterway users now demand. The great collections at Richmond, Staines, Windsor and Oxford have dwindled, but they seem to hold their own at Godalming on the Wey, Broxbourne on the Lee and at Chester and Bedford. Updated techniques in boat building to satisfy new demands have resulted in few yards constructing these little boats. Heavy 14ft clinker fishing skiffs are still made at Williamstown on the shores of Lough Derg in Ireland, or on the Erne at Kesh, and fair imitations in glass-reinforced plastic are manufactured elsewhere.

In the last century the highlight of the summer for thousands of people was a day out on the river aboard a passenger steamer. Whether travelling down the Thames with one of Salter's majestic craft, along the Forth and Clyde Canal aboard one of the *Queens*, on Windermere, Loch Lomond or the Staffs and Worcs Canal, such a trip was an occasion of great excitement. Where purpose-designed craft were not available, church, school and charitable groups would charter any suitable working boat, fill the hold with rough benches and bottles of lemonade, and take a horde of local children up the cut. Old photographs show Humber keels, narrow boats and Fen lighters pressed into service in this way.

For the wealthy boating enthusiast of late Victorian and Edwardian times there were steam launches, sleek, nearly silent, graceful vessels, canopied or fitted with little upright cabins. The greatest number were based on the Thames. Almost a hundred small steam launches survive on British inland waters, some of them over a century old; they appear for occasional rallies and even have their own Steam Boat Association of Great Britain. To satisfy a need in some people to own a boat that is different from the run of mass-produced cruisers, new steamers fitted with replicas of Edwardian engines and boilers are now built.

Until the 1940s and early 1950s the long-distance canal cruiser was an exception. Amazingly few holidaymakers appreciated the attractions of a waterways network then even more extensive than it is now. But it should be remembered that the canals were a rough world of working-boats and barges, lumbering towpath horses, and companies that often not only did little to welcome mere pleasure trippers but in some cases actively discouraged them, going so far as to place annoying restrictions on the use of locks. Once permission to navigate and a suitable boat had been obtained, there remained the question of tolls: in 1908 the GWR Co charged launches £5 6s od for a single passage of the Kennet and Avon, while the Grand Union from Brentford to Leicester cost £3. Conversion of these rates to present values makes today's cruising licences appear bargains indeed!

A number of published accounts of early canal voyages for pleasure survive. Most of them hardly mention boatmen and commercial activity. The anonymous author of *Chester–Kendal Canal Trip, 1899* reveals that his and his companions' progress (they were taking turns to row a skiff or travel ahead by bicycle) was exactly timed. They reached journey's end at Kendal on Tuesday, 5 September, at 2.23 pm, one minute late! At one stage they booked a private train to take them to their night's lodgings. Railway companies operated a scale of fixed charges for conveying boats from one point to another. According to *Taunt's Thames Guide* (c1887), the GWR's rates where special trucks were to be attached to a train were 3d per mile for the first truck, 2d per mile for each additional truck and a minimum fee of 7s 6d and 5s respectively.

The Broads became a fashionable boating area from about 1880, with a wide range of small craft, large sailing cutters and adapted sailing wherries available for hire by the week. Jarrolds' *Handbook to the Rivers and Broads of Norfolk and Suffolk* (1891) lists a selection of wherries, 'furnished throughout with blinds, soft cushions, plenty of rugs and lighted at night by lamps ... Two men are provided by the owners to look after and sail the Yachts, and are under the direction of the party hiring the boat; they will attend to the cooking, cleaning and washing up, and to the wants of the party on board ... A piano can be provided.' There is no indication of the charter fees, but one Norwich firm could supply 'The Water Lily, 4-ton Una-rig yacht. Good sleeping accommodation in Cabin for 6 persons. £3 per week, with Man, £4.'

To travel in comfort on the canals, however, presented greater difficulties. In his The 'Flower of Gloster' (1911), E. Temple Thurston had to seek out an Oxford Canal narrow boat and skipper. This set him back £1 10s 0d a week, plus food for boatman and horse, although the writer later concluded that £1 would have been quite adequate. Mr and Mrs J. B. Dashwood recount their navigation of the Wey and Arun Canal, shortly before its demise, in a little open sailing boat drawn by a horse in The Thames to the Solent by Canal and Sea (1868). Any imaginative reader of this scarce Victorian travelogue will immediately be fired to join the volunteers who are now trying to bring this lost waterway back to life. Quite the most charming and evocative account of canal travel in the earlier years of this century is C. J. Aubertin's A Caravan Afloat (c1920), which describes the journeys of a vessel designed rather like a gangers' work flat, and moved either by horse or by bow-hauling from the towpath. Both whimsical and amusing, Aubertin's book deserves wider recognition as a canal classic.

No survey of the canal pleasure-boat pioneers would be complete without mention of D. W. Noakes, one-time mayor of Greenwich. In 1891 he presented a 'New and Original Dioramic Entertainment' at the Crystal Palace entitled 'England Bisected by Steam Launch'. This somewhat alarming suggestion was a reference to a tour of more than 600 miles aboard the steamboat Lizzie from the Thames at Brentford via the Grand Union, Stratford Canal, Worcester and Birmingham, the Severn and estuary to Avonmouth, and through the Kennet and Avon Canal back to the starting point. All this was recorded on a collection of slides, many of them hand-coloured. Even more exciting was the fact that these remarkable photographs were designed to be projected through the Noakesoscope, a unique gas-powered magic lantern containing no fewer than four brass-mounted lenses. By simultaneous projection of four slides, some equipped with handles to simulate movement, near cinematographic effects could be produced. Thus day dissolves into night, Chinese lanterns appear in clusters on the Lizzie, and the 1871

*Old style cruising on the Broads: a traditional gaff-rigged sloop of a type which is still available for hire*

Warwick Castle fire is re-created with realistic leaping flames. By 1897 D. W. Noakes had presented more than 5,000 lectures, including several at the Royal Albert Hall. His machine and his programme were demonstrated to a large audience of IWA members at the old Lyric Opera House, Hammersmith, in 1962.

While *The 'Flower of Gloster'* enjoyed a moderate success, it was not until L. T. C. Rolt's *Narrow Boat* was published in 1944 that a mass public became fully aware of the possibilities of long-distance canal travel. Shortly afterwards the Inland Waterways Association was formed, and the canals of Britain have not looked back since, at least in terms of amenity development. Self-drive motor cruisers were available on both the Thames and the Broads between the wars, but the first canal-cruiser firm was not established until 1935, near Chester. A slow growth accelerated during the late 1950s and, even more, in the 1960s, as the emergence of a more secure future for the system prompted investment. In 1971 there were nearly 55,000 pleasure craft registered on Britain's inland waterways, including 26,000 on the Thames, 10,000 on the Broads, 14,000 on the routes of the British Waterways Board, and 3,500 on the Great Ouse. Of these, 7,750 were available for hire, 2,250 of them being small unpowered boats. To these figures should be added a small but significant number of craft used on other categories of navigation, and about 270 Irish boats.

At busy summer weekends lock queues now collect on the Thames, and areas like Potter Heigham and Wroxham on the Broads are hectically congested. Even on the Shropshire Union or Llangollen Canals it may be necessary to wait up to half an hour for your turn at locks if you encounter the twice-weekly hire cruiser exodus. Conversely, pleasure cruising remains underdeveloped on most northern waterways, especially in the North East, on Scotland's Caledonian Canal, and on Ireland's Erne, Shannon and canals. Provided growth is directed in future to the more remote but often most attractive areas, there will be ample room on the waterways of Britain for many decades at the current annual increases. The reasons for the expansion are more money and leisure time, longer paid holidays, and the mass ownership of cars, which enables boating enthusiasts to reach their craft quickly, even if they are moored a long distance from home.

## BOAT TYPES AVAILABLE

Anyone considering buying a cruiser for use on inland waterways will be faced with a bewildering choice. In most cases the best course of action will be to spend several weeks aboard hire cruisers to determine the needs of you or your family before making a costly purchase. The ideal boat is rarely the first one you buy, however, and there are a few cruising devotees who change their craft with the regularity with which many of us change cars.

First, decide what you expect of the new cruiser. Do you intend to base it on a river navigation with the prospect of occasional coastal trips? If so, you require a powerful engine, wide beam and an altogether more rugged construction than is required for canals only. If your preference is for the narrow canals, your chosen vessel will in most cases be unsuitable for sea use. But do remember that parts of the inland network can only be reached by navigating sections of tidal water. If you hope to visit all parts of the connected system of England and Wales, you must choose a cruiser within the following maximum dimensions: length 46ft (with the exception of the Middle Level Navigations, this can be increased to 58ft, the limit of several NE locks and the Leeds and Liverpool Canal), beam 7ft, draught 2ft, height above water about 5ft 11in. Except for certain northern canals, an overall length of 70ft is acceptable, but sooner or later you may wish to pass through the Leeds and Liverpool, where locks are only about 62ft long. It would be misleading to suggest that a 7ft beam is an essential requirement of British inland cruisers, for there are extensive networks from the Manchester area across the Pennines to Yorkshire and up the Trent to the East Midlands capable of accommodating 14ft beamers. Similarly the Thames, Wey, Medway, Kennet and Avon (when reopened throughout), Severn, Lee and Stort, and Grand Union nearly to Birmingham, will all pass wide-beam craft. But for the bottlenecks caused by narrow locks on the Northampton Arm and the Leicester section of the Grand Union at Watford and Foxton, there would be a wide-beam link between north and south.

For the first ten or fifteen years after World War II very few pleasure craft were specifically built for cruising on the canals, and mass production certainly had not arrived. Suitable hulls of the correct dimensions were pressed into service, including large numbers of small lifeboats, landing craft, pontoons and other ex-Government apparatus that was in plentiful supply. Provided they conformed to the maximum 7ft beam, smaller river launches were also to be seen – 1930s slipper sterns, somewhat upright cruisers looking like scaled-down ocean liners, and a good many motorised dinghies, skiffs and camping punts. This was also what is now appreciated as a golden age for the acquisition of ex-working canal boats, which admirably converted into pleasure craft. In the late 1950s there were still several hundred freight narrow boats at work, many dating from the 1930s. As cargoes were lost, the carriers contracted or folded up completely. While superficially neglected, the boats could then be bought complete with serviceable engines for as little as £90 (1961 example), while unpowered steel butty boats were disposed of for less than their scrap value. A good unconverted motorboat now would command a price upwards of £3,000. Then there were ice breakers, tugs (short narrow boats), and even a few of the old company inspection craft, which could be adapted at little expense into holiday homes of great character and increasing worth. Today the only remaining boats of this type, complete with traditional decorations and fittings, are those that have been 'rescued' and restored by the new breed of weekend boatmen.

*Some of the most sought-after craft for inland use are former working boats, adapted where necessary for cruising. This 1896-built Birmingham Canal Navigations ice breaker, although originally horse-drawn, is now fitted with a hot-bulb semi diesel engine and fully traditional boatman's cabin*

Because of their greater bulk and more restricted cruising grounds, the wide-beam working boats never attracted the same devotion, and converted keels and short boats are rare except as normally static houseboats. It is worth mentioning that one Leeds and Liverpool steel-hulled motor short boat, part converted, travelled down the east coast to the Thames and later across the Channel to make an extensive exploration of French waterways, all under her own power. Several years before that a wooden Calder and Hebble motor keel successfully voyaged to Belgium and back. In each case the owners were expert navigators, a necessity when exposing such

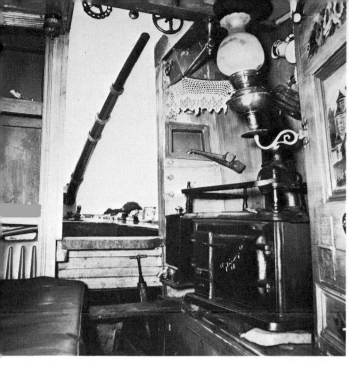

*Part of the boatman's cabin aboard the author's converted ice breaker* Parry II

flat-bottomed boats to the potential hazards of salt water.

Around the mid-1960s the demand for good ex-working boats began to outstrip the supply and it became cheaper to build new replicas. First, wood was widely used, but it was soon replaced by steel for the hulls. Styles varied from ultra-traditional with tiller steering, boatman's stern cabin and full decoration throughout, to compromises that took the best features from cargo craft and combined them with elements from conventional motor cruisers. It would be a bold writer who claimed in cold print that wheel steering is better than tiller, or that flat-bottomed hulls are preferable to a shallow V shape. Everyone must form his own judgement. Likewise with engines. Larger and heavier craft are best fitted with diesels, but should you select a conventional propeller shaft drive or opt for a hydraulic drive, enabling the engine to be mounted anywhere you like and removing alignment problems? Another alternative is the inboard/outboard drive, where steering is achieved by changing the direction of the propeller rather than using a rudder. Before reaching any conclusion, and placing an order, talk to boat owners at marinas or canal rallies and see what they think. You will normally receive less biased answers than those you will get from a boatyard salesman operating on a commission.

The above remarks apply mainly to boats at the more expensive end of the market, where price ranges are from about £2,500 to £6,000 or more, all depending on the degree to which the chosen craft is fitted out and on the equipment installed. Also to be included in this category are many designs of narrow-beam motor cruisers that are derived more from river and coastal craft. Construction materials vary from marine ply, mahogany and steel to the ubiquitous glass-reinforced plastic, and even concrete, which appears under several brand names.

It would be a pity if preoccupation with the running of an expensive waterway cruiser obscured the basic delight of canal and river travel. There are some who are just as content to be bow-hauling their camping punts, or sleeping under canvas in the lightweight tents carried aboard their canoes. As a complete change from the normal busy world, there is much to be said for a simple and uncomplicated approach to boating. For trips of short duration (two or three days), the outboard-powered inflatable, which can be packed into the boot of a small car, has much in its favour. The most isolated, far-flung or disconnected waterway is within a few hours' driving distance, and should you want to explore partially derelict navigations, then ruined locks or other obstacles can be negotiated without difficulty. The inflatable is an ideal addition for a family that already has a normal cabin cruiser.

At the lower end of the motor cruiser market, there are dozens of production craft, mostly in glass-reinforced plastic, in the 15–30ft range. These will often be intended for outboard power, with the possibility of fitting inboard engines at additional cost. Outboards are a blessing in many ways, not least for maintenance, but larger models can be atrociously thirsty on fuel. Where this is petrol/oil mixture, using 8–10 gallons a day can seriously damage your finances. On the canals the smaller outboards will propel a medium-sized cruiser as fast as you wish (or are allowed) to travel. You will not be thanked for throwing up a breaking wave on the banks in any case. Should you contemplate much river or tidal work, then you need some reserve power. If you want to avoid a costly change of boat after the first season, buy something rather larger than you or your family can sleep on at a squeeze. When the initial novelty of ownership has worn off, the luxury of a four-berth vessel is something you will long appreciate, even if there are generally just two people aboard. There are 22ft canal cruisers advertised as five-berth, but then upwards of a dozen record-breaking students have been known to occupy a telephone call-box simultaneously.

Hiring a river or canal cruiser is now an easy matter, though they may be in short supply at the height of the summer. It is possible to obtain a boat on most parts of the British and Irish networks, and even on shorter isolated lengths like the Lancaster Canal and Brecon and Abergavenny. Each area is quite different in character, and changes remarkably with the time of year. First decide where you would like to cruise, remembering that virtually every river and canal is of interest and that a holiday in Staffordshire can be every bit as enjoyable and memorable as one in the Scottish Highlands or the Border Country of North Wales. Select a cruiser firm from those that advertise in the national press, boating magazines or the various waterways annuals, and write off for a brochure. Organisation of the holiday should then become a simple matter.

There are practical handbooks available on motor-cruiser handling, the operation of locks, the acquisition of lock windlasses and licences, the avoidance of 'stemming up' (running on the mud), and on getting off the mud should you fail at the first attempt. Blow by serious blow, these books dissolve all the mystery from weed hatches, reverse steering and mooring up, though much of the fun of a first cruise comes from finding out by practical experience after receiving the short instruction period supplied by most yards. Most car drivers learn at the wheel of a car, not by reading about it all beforehand, and much the same applies to inland boating, except that mistakes rarely end in disaster. If you can drive a car, you will rapidly master boat handling, although everyone continues to learn, no matter how long they have been at it. Use the handbooks if you want to check on the experts' methods, but do not consider you have any competence until you have spent several days afloat. Old sea dogs who may know their ocean racers backwards will soon discover that the canals demand the learning of a variety of new tricks! Above all, avoid becoming so obsessed with the mechanics of boats and boat handling that you forget to enjoy the waterways themselves.

If you do not feel up to navigating a cruiser, working the locks and making a succession of decisions throughout each day, book a cabin aboard a hotel boat. Mostly these are converted narrow boats, operating singly or in pairs, equipped with double and single cabins for six to twelve passengers. An experienced crew attends to running the boat, but there are normally opportunities to help if you like. The standard of catering is generally high. Each hotel-boat company maintains a series of week-long scheduled runs ranging over most narrow-boat rivers and canals of England and North Wales. Wide-beam vessels, again converted working boats or purpose-built, operate as travelling hotels on the Shannon, Thames, Trent waterways and Leeds and Liverpool Canal. The extra beam allows more spacious accommodation for passengers. The weekly all-inclusive rates per person are roughly equivalent to the cost of hiring a four-berth self-drive cruiser in the low season.

For people requiring the most economical holiday, one

answer is to hire a camping boat. These can vary from motorised pontoons with all basic facilities under a canvas awning to single or paired narrow boats, short boats or Irish canal barges, in which the cargo space has been equipped with essential fittings and sheeted over with tarpaulins. Such camping or hostel craft are particularly suited to youth groups and young people generally; whether running their own holiday or using the services of a professional skipper, the passengers are expected to lend a hand with steering, lock operation and cooking.

Many parts of the waterways networks are served by day-tripping vessels, either operating on scheduled cruises or available for private charter for periods up to a day. These include traditional working craft, steam launches and pur-pose-built cruisers. There are few better ways of investigating an unknown section of canal or river than spending a few hours aboard one of these. Several are designed specially for lunch and dinner cruises (private charter or scheduled services), combining a trip with good food and wine. The areas where this service is available include London, Thrupp (near Oxford), Braunston, Rugby, and Loch Lomond. Most, but not all, cease to function in the winter months. Addresses of all concerns involved in cruiser or passenger boat hire may be obtained from the Association of Pleasure Craft Operators (APCO), the British Waterways Board, the Irish Tourist Board, or the Inland Waterways Association's *Inland Water-ways Guide to Holiday Hire* (annually).

### CRUISING ROUTES AND METHODS

One of the great assets of the English waterways network is that a wide range of circular journeys is possible. Some, as in the Birmingham and Black Country district, can be accomplished in a day or two, and others require ten days or a fortnight. Provided your boat is under the maximum per-mitted dimensions, the variety of runs is almost endless. In the south the Thames, Oxford and Grand Union Canals offer three distinct types of waterway – the first a broad sophis-ticated river with mechanised manned locks, the second an intimate rural charm, and the third wide-beam locks and changing scenery. This circuit is about 250 miles and would take a busy ten days or a less hurried two weeks. Much the same mixture of countryside, and canal and river, is ex-perienced on the Avon cruise from Stratford, via the North and South Stratford Canals, Worcester and Birmingham Canal, River Severn and Lower and Upper Avon Naviga-tions. Another admirable cross-section of inland waterways is the Cheshire Ring, which comprises parts of the Trent and Mersey and Bridgewater Canals, with a link to the Macclesfield, Lower Peak Forest, Ashton and Rochdale Canals. Alternatively the major parts of the Trent and Mersey and Shropshire Union Canals are conveniently linked in the north by the Middlewich Branch and in the south by a section of the Staffs and Worcs Canal. Still more extensive travels can be devised: for instance, the Leeds and Liverpool, Bridgewater, Trent and Mersey, River Trent, Sheffield and South Yorkshire, and Aire and Calder circuit would require three to four weeks, although longer could easily be spent to good advantage.

Apart from retired people, the wealthy or schoolteachers with long holidays, the private boat owner is unlikely to have more than three or four weeks in the year for extended cruising. Many of the more enthusiastic waterways devotees nevertheless contrive to clock up in excess of 1,000 canal and river miles each year. They achieve this by combining one or two long trips with a succession of weekends, moving the boat from one safe marina mooring to another and relying on the use of two cars, folding push bikes or motorcycles carried on board, or public transport, to allow them to return home at the end of each stage. At least one narrow-boat cruiser is equipped with a loading device enabling a small car to be stowed out of sight in the hold. Such methods are for people determined to obtain maximum use from both boat and waterways.

Not everyone demands this kind of aggressive and energetic boating. A good many owners seem quite content to base their vessel in one carefully chosen area – perhaps a long lock-free

*A grp Caribbean cruiser, whose wide beam makes it suitable for family holidays for up to eight people. This type is built on the Broads and utilises an inboard diesel engine mounted aft. There are two steering positions – on the cabin top or completely sheltered from the weather in the forward saloon*

pound – and rarely move more than twenty miles. Who is to say that they do not gain greater enjoyment and relaxation from their less adventurous activities? The extreme, where a boat is regarded as a kind of floating garden shed for weekend pottering and seldom moves anywhere, is altogether a different matter.

Whether aboard your own or a hired cruiser, your rate of daily progress depends on the length of daylight and frequency of locks. Obviously more time is required to navigate the 30 miles from Birmingham to the Severn at Worcester in December (fifty-eight locks) than to cover an equivalent distance in June from Napton Bottom Lock to Hawkesbury Junction via the Oxford Canal (three locks). In any event, it is a great mistake to hurry on the waterways. Only in exceptional circumstances should you plan to cruise more than a daily average of 25 miles. Often it will need to be rather less.

When there was heavy commercial traffic but few pleasure craft, stoppages for repairs were normally scheduled for Bank Holiday periods. Boat crews could enjoy a few days' enforced idleness while large gangs of maintenance men renewed lock gates, replaced paddles or tackled engineering problems posed by bridges, tunnels and aqueducts. Now the normal policy is to avoid scheduled stoppages between April and October, and take rather longer over closures during the winter months than used to be the case. On the nationalised navigations, where possible, the closure of one route for several weeks in December or February is planned with an alternative way remaining open. Lists of the coming year's closures are available from the waterways authorities in December or January. However, delays in completing work on schedule can and do occur, not to mention the unanticipated emergency breach or failure of lock gear that has no respect for the time of season when most craft are about. So first obtain up-to-date information. Some major repairs or rebuilding of structures can close a navigation for as long as six months.

It is unfortunate that the length of winter stoppages, often for the benefit of work like sewer laying or bridge building, which is of little interest to the waterways user, can seriously hamper movement in the off season. Problems presented by ice and floods apart, our rivers and canals are delightfully deserted, while the bare trees reveal views that are usually hidden by dense summer foliage. Sunrise at Christmas over a frosty countryside, or flocks of seagulls following the plough at work in an undulating expanse of freshly turned brown soil, are memories that will long be treasured. But you do need home comforts. Central heating, whether from solid fuel, diesel, gas or paraffin, makes all the difference between misery and complete well-being. Steel-hulled craft can break their way through thin ice with no greater damage than the loss of a little paint, but timber boats are easily holed as the knife-sharp edges of ice tear again and again at the same part of the hull. Should you anticipate much winter cruising, a steel hull is the answer, though metal sheathing over timber provides a partial compromise. Some hire-cruiser operators will charter craft in the off-season months, often at very much reduced rates, but do not expect to find the same range of fuelling, restaurant and other facilities that are available in spring, summer and autumn.

The once widely held interpretation of the word 'canal' as a dreary stretch of water lined by derelict factories becomes less common as local authorities and the general public learn the real truth. But just occasionally you may chance upon a waterway that actually lives up to that reputation – a dull urban stretch seeming to offer nothing either in industrial archaeological interest or in enhancing the townscape. (It is healthy that the most committed enthusiast can recognise these places.) But if you find that you still enjoy your cruising, as you almost certainly will, then you can consider that you have become one with the waterways. Even this depressing length may lead, around the next bend, or the bend that follows that, to fascinating and beautiful places. To a man living in a sad terrace on the banks, the canal may hold no magic, but to us it is the gateway to an extensive world waiting to be explored.

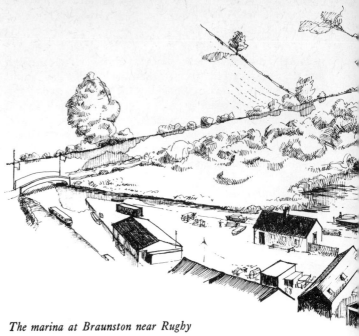

*The marina at Braunston near Rugby*

# 15
# Boatyards and Marinas

PERHAPS the ideal place to keep your own boat is on a mooring at the end of the garden. Most people, however, berth their boats at yards where there is generally a wide range of facilities. Borrowing a term from coastal sites (one that had earlier crossed the Atlantic), the larger inland yards sometimes advertise themselves as 'marinas'. In the context of narrow canals, this is singularly inappropriate, but the word seems destined to remain with us.

Many yards of the Thames, the Broads, and a handful of rivers where pleasure boating was popularised years ago, are old-established family concerns, updated in recent years perhaps but still displaying their Victorian origins in weather-boarded boat sheds that sometimes have decorated Gothic gables. The firm of J. Tims and Sons of Staines, while operating a flourishing and up-to-date hire fleet, still occupies

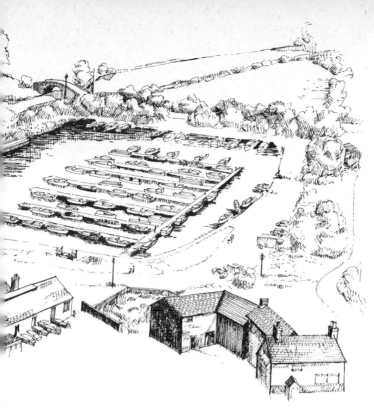

buildings that have remained substantially unaltered since the days of their 'bathing house on the eyot, ladies' and gentlemen's changing rooms' and the information, published in their advertisement of 1885, that they would attend to the housing, repair and varnishing of 'gentlemen's boats'. The Potter Heigham firm of Herbert Woods on the Thurne in Norfolk is similarly housed in timber-clad buildings grouped round a series of small basins that have been excavated as the demand for berths has increased. Until some years after World War II the old order changed little. Mass production of pleasure craft arrived only with the introduction of glass-reinforced plastic, a development that dates only to the mid-1950s. After that time premises for boatbuilding and moorings to cope with the increased boat population began to take on a new form.

Until a certain density of craft is reached in any given locality, bankside moorings spreading from the slipway, docks and other yard installations are quite adequate. But if this kind of development is allowed to expand unchecked, a degree of linear sprawl becomes evident. This is undesirable on both rivers and canals, for no one enjoys cruising up the centre of a solid line of boats. Examples can be found in a number of the more frequented areas, especially in the south-east of England. Preferable by far is the grouping of moorings

and associated facilities off the main navigation channel.
Here a compact arrangement of well-planned mooring
jetties in a landscaped and planted environment can improve
the look of the location in a way that linear moorings seldom
can.

Worked-out gravel pits are particularly suitable for marina
use. A number are to be seen along the Thames, connected
with the navigation channel by a short canal cut. One of the
best known (and probably the largest inland in Britain) is
Penton Hook Marina, which is approached via the Penton
Hook Lock weir stream near Staines. Neat rows of floating
jetties provide permanent moorings, while on shore there are
ample car parking spaces, a chandlery shop, fuelling station,
clubhouse and grassed areas. A frequent argument advanced
by people opposing creation of new marinas of this kind is
that the reach of river concerned will suffer from acute
congestion, as will the locks at each end of the pound in
question. If every boat of the several hundred based at the
marina were to be taken out on to the river simultaneously,
overcrowding would undoubtedly occur; but this is never the
case, as a substantial number of boat owners seem to want to
go cruising comparatively little each season, and many are
quite content to stay on board at their moorings, or tinker
about with their boats.

In any event, an extensive and attractively planned marina
is a pleasant place to spend a weekend afloat. One can cite the
example of Farndon Marina, connected with the Trent near
Newark, which provides ample cruising space for short trips
even before joining the river channel itself. There are a
variety of marina sites, two of the most unusual being one-
time water supply filtration beds connected with the Thames
via a flood lock (Thames Ditton), and a formerly silted and
reedy swamp, which has been dredged and piled, on the
same waterway at Walton Bridge.

The canal system was provided with pleasure craft moorings when traditional trading activities ceased, making
working-boat yards available. Often these were merely small
strips of waterside land, perhaps with a slipway or drydock
and ideal for small-scale operations. Then there are many
short arms, docks and basins, no longer required for goods
traffic. These almost always belong to the navigation
authority, and a conflict of future use can arise here in town
or city centres, where the water represents a highly valuable
asset in terms of potential building land. Places that should
long ago have been utilised to meet a demand for urban
moorings (Paddington and City Road Basins in London,
Sheffield Basin and the Rochdale Canal basin at its junction
with the Ashton Canal in Manchester) have been long and

frustratingly kept from this purpose. In most instances some kind of compromise is likely to be reached, where building development and use of the water for boating purposes complement each other. In spite of the record of delays or lost opportunities, there are many cases of short canal lengths off the main lines now put to excellent use. Basin End, Nantwich, former terminus of the Chester Canal, is an admirable marina development shared by a local cruising club and the British Waterways Board's north-west hire fleet. Disused arms of the Northern Oxford Canal that remained from its straightening programme in the 1830s have in some instances been turned into moorings, among them yards at Hillmorton, Brinklow and Rugby. A little further south one of the best canal sites in Britain for marina use can be seen at Braunston. Here a section of the old Oxford Canal previously used by a working narrow-boat carrier is linked with two large canal supply reservoirs at the same level. Moorings for several hundred craft have thus been created, with associated boat showrooms, chandlery, showers and repair facilities.

Such locations that remain undeveloped must inevitably become fewer in number, prompting construction of completely new basins specially for marina use. If these can be planned to yield high quality gravel or ballast before being laid out as moorings, the developer has an added incentive. Most of those that have so far been created were excavated solely with boats in mind. One of the first was at Market Drayton on the Shropshire Union Canal. Here Messrs Ladyline, in the later 1960s, increased the width of the canal very considerably, enabling cruisers to moor alongside jetties placed nearly at right-angles to the bank. Suitable arrangements must of course be made to ensure that canal water cannot seep away through the new workings. Marinas were constructed on the Oxford Canal at Napton Junction, Fenny Compton, and on a branch of the Llangollen Canal at Prees. The largest canal exercise of this type to date is at Whilton Marina, immediately south of Buckby Locks on the Grand Union in Northamptonshire. Here a field, bordered on one side by the canal and on the other by the railway from London's Euston Station, has been excavated and flooded to provide several acres of water space that is floodlit after dark. A development like this, otherwise excellent, does produce a degree of congestion at the adjacent Buckby Flight, even assuming that the greater proportion of craft making short trips from Whilton will head southwards along the 16-mile pound to Stoke Bruerne.

The siting and planning of marinas is a complex business. Private developers are no longer granted permission to create facilities without the navigation authority studying the immediate and long-term effects. Local authorities working under the various Planning Acts need to be satisfied over many points ranging from adequate car parking space to social and economic considerations like labour availability and the conservation of attractive landscape. New marinas and boatyards do not cater solely for the private boat owner, but increasingly play an important role in hiring out craft by the week or fortnight, an activity bringing an influx of tourists to an area and generally welcomed by local government representatives. Priority is now being given to marina schemes that (1) will encourage tourism or (2) are located near the large centres of population and are consequently likely to be enjoyed by the greatest number of people. As a rough method of siting boat moorings on the canal system, large marinas should be set at 15–20 mile intervals, and smaller bases sometimes offering no more than basic refuse-disposal facilities, water and fuelling, 5–10 miles apart. Because the inland waterways are in so many ways the antithesis of control and regulation, since we use them largely to escape from the complications that fill the normal working day, it may seem wrong to be thinking about dividing our canals into neat sections with the equivalent of regular service stations strung out along them. Consider the alternatives of unchecked ribbon development, however. When you do, the strictest of planning controls immediately become attractive.

Boatyards vary greatly in their appearance: a tidy well-maintained establishment where the staff seem genuinely interested in catering for your needs obviously deserves to succeed, whereas a scruffy group of corrugated iron buildings and collection of shabby boats tells its own story. Or so you would think. On the canals this is not always true, especially in traditional yards that have invaluable skills centred on building or repairing ex-working boats. If the firm specialises in refitting or converting narrow boats, you will expect to see rusting hulks awaiting their beauty treatment. As a canal bank in winter can be a cheerless place to fit new planking to a wooden hull, a temporary shed of canvas or plastic sheeting may have been thrown over a rough framework, so providing some kind of shelter. A yard that is all neat gravel, white paint and gay bunting is likely to be a flourishing concern, but you could possibly get better value at the other type of establishment, where sales talk is based on years of practical experience.

One of the loveliest boatyards in Britain can be found on the Brecon and Abergavenny Canal at Llanfoist. In a wooded setting high above Abergavenny, with a soaring backdrop of trees, this hire-fleet base displays lawns extending to the water's edge, and the proprietor's house and a half open stone warehouse covered by masses of rambling roses. It manages without flags, hoardings and all the other devices with which some firms hope to attract custom. Perhaps the siting of the Llanfoist yard on a waterway that mostly runs through the Brecon Beacons National Park contributes to this admirably restrained treatment.

We have already mentioned the British Waterways Board's *Waterway Environment Handbook*, which outlines a 'code of practice' for future BWB developments and contains a series of invaluable recommendations for private schemes. Covering the complete range of waterways situations and structures, it suggests that bogus 'naval'/estuary/maritime decor should be avoided at hire-cruiser bases. Instead they should blend into the canal surroundings, using appropriate colours and following canal traditions. There is still ample scope for all kinds of exciting ideas, so long as they repeat or extend the architectural balance and sensitivity of canals.

The inland marina need not be a centre of summer boating alone. The sides of a basin can sometimes provide an ideal setting for small-scale housing schemes, combined with attractions like restaurants or cafés that appeal to non-boaters as well as boaters and so help to create life and activity throughout the year. Some of the most successful enterprises operate a tripping boat, using either river launches or narrow boats. On London's Regent's Canal a remarkable centre

*Glasson Dock on the Lancashire coast is linked with a branch of the Lancaster Canal by an extensive basin where there are facilities for all types of seagoing and inland boats*

called the Camden Lock was opened in 1973 in Camden
Town at the former Dingwall's timber wharf, where there is
a small basin. Victorian stores and warehouses on three
sides have been thoughtfully converted to provide a booking
office for passenger boat *Jenny Wren*, together with about
twenty other businesses that range from the Lock, Stock and
Barrel (a licensed restaurant) to a dance hall, various craft
workshops, and picture and antique galleries. The Camden
Lock has developed into a most successful arts and entertainment centre, with open air jazz concerts, chamber music, ox
roasts and periodical exhibitions that reflect the moods and
hopes of the local community. It is a first-rate example of
how a section of urban waterway can be integrated into the
everyday life of the district through which it passes. There
is surely a lesson here for established boatyards to broaden
their scope to include land-based activities.

The Irish Tourist Board has achieved a notable success in
cooperating with local and central Government to create
facilities for boating in hire cruisers. These lie mostly along
the River Shannon, where substantial grants have been made
available to private companies to establish marinas. The
most striking development area is at Carrick on the upper
reaches of the river, where mooring quays backed up by
bank-based facilities have made dramatic improvements to
the water tourism records. Commercialism can so easily spoil
the very qualities that appeal to waterway enthusiasts, but
the series of little harbours that have been reopened or newly
built along the Shannon display perfectly the restraint in
design that it is vitally important to maintain.

One special type of marina combines inland and marine
traditions. It can be found at coastal terminal points of
canals, where canals join large rivers or indeed in the lower
reaches of river navigations themselves. Flood-free moorings
are provided for seagoing craft, together with boatyard
equipment and facilities to match. Each end of the Crinan
Canal is popular with offshore sailing boats. Bowling Harbour, the only section of the Forth and Clyde Canal currently
navigable from the Clyde, is filled with an assortment of
coastal vessels, and Stourport and Worcester Canal Basins
serve a similar function, as the world of the narrow boat here
meets the wide waters of the Severn. Naburn Marina by the
Ouse downstream of York, the little West Stockwith Basin
at the junction of the Chesterfield Canal and the tidal Trent,
Heybridge at the point where the Chelmer and Blackwater
Navigation meets the Essex coast, and Gravesend Basin, all
that remains of the Thames and Medway Canal, are all
places of interest where masts and rigging rise from broad
beam decks.

In addition to servicing boats belonging to permanent customers or casual visitors, the good boatyard should be able to deal with repairs or fitting out, whether in glass-reinforced plastic, timber or steel. Many of them sell new and secondhand craft or build their own designs. A boatyard should above all be a place where a potential customer can ask advice without feeling he is being pressurised into a sale. The boating scene retains for the most part a friendly atmosphere. Stop a boat owner about to leave his jetty and ask him what he thinks of his engine, whether he has any experience of a particular type of cruiser or indeed what level of service can be expected from the yard, and the chances are he will willingly tell you everything, and more than, you want to know.

Before taking permanent moorings (and this applies mainly to the larger marinas), first ask whether the firm encourages do-it-yourself maintenance, or whether they insist that all work to your boat is done by their own staff. Find out what the charges are for winter storage ashore, compared with remaining afloat. Above all, be sure that you are going to get on reasonably well with the owners or management, for you certainly do not want your boating enjoyment. spoiled by constant irritations. Generally, if you stick to the rules, avoid obstructing the main gate or top of the slipway with your car, refrain from constantly asking whether you can borrow tools, and buy your supplies of food or chandlery through the marina shop, you will be well treated and receive good value for the money you spend. Remember that if the nearest road access to your boat is 300 yd away and the mooring consists of a steep bank overhung by a willow tree, you should not expect to pay as much as for a private jetty with water and mains electricity laid on and a well-surfaced road alongside. Whether you prefer being one of three hundred boats arranged in neat rows or an individualist under that willow tree is a matter that you alone can decide.

An option open to the private boat owner is to join a cruising club and take advantage of non-profit-making moorings and other facilities. Here the clubhouse bar remains a focal point throughout the year, where meetings, rallies and other social events staged for members are discussed. Communal working parties may be held to construct a new slipway, erect additional jetties, or haul boats from the water for their winter refit. Not infrequently the obvious advantages of this arrangement result in long waiting lists for clubs. Details may be obtained from the Association of Waterway Cruising Clubs, whose address appears on p 208.

# *16*
# *Animal and Plant Life*

*Flag iris*

by Carolyn Barber, BSc

THERE is no more ideal time than that spent leisurely in a boat on a river or canal to take stock of the surrounding countryside. The slow pace of a boat is conducive to just sitting and looking, and it is looking a little more closely that makes it possible to recognise what suddenly made the reeds rustle, what produced the sinuous ripples in front of the boat or what the white flower is that bobs up and down on the water's surface.

## SPRING

By the end of February the trees along the water's edge are showing signs of renewed life – spring is on its way. The early blossoms of the hazel, alder and willow are suddenly very obvious. The long drooping pollen-laden lamb's tails of the hazel are dancing in the wind long before the hazel leaves appear. The slender alder tree with its small spreading branches is common along river and canal banks. Its catkins show fluffy in the spring before the hazel, and the dark green heart-shaped leaves burst after the blossoms.

The willow is the proverbial waterside tree. There are many kinds, with crosses between them, so if you are interested it is well to take a book on native trees with you. There are the weeping willow (*Salix babylonica*), pussy willow (*Salix caprea*), crack willow (*Salix fragilis*), and the white willow (*Salix alba*), of which cricket bats are made. There are two willow shrubs, the purple willow (*Salix purpurea*), and the common osier (*Salix viminalis*), whose long flexible branches are used in basket work.

The willow trees and shrubs that line the banks of rivers and canals not only provide a beautiful setting for those travelling along the waterway but are important to the local plant and animal life. Their roots bind the earthy banks together to prevent erosion, and their leaves and branches give shade from the summer's sun, and also provide food for many insects and hideaways for nesting birds.

As spring progresses into April and May, the bright yellow flag or iris and the equally gaudy marsh marigold or kingcup give an added splash of colour to the fresh green of

*Kingcup*

180

the countryside. Cowslips and meadow buttercups are growing in profusion in the watermeadows. Close to the hedges lie primroses, violets, bluebells and dandelions. The large three-cornered leaves of the cuckoo-pint or lords-and-ladies (*Arum maculatum*) are conspicuous under hedges. Be cautious of its brilliant red berries, for, though attractive, they are very poisonous. By the lock gates stand the tall white umbrella-like flower heads of the cow parsley and the red and white clovers. The hop trefoil or hop clover has similar small but yellow flowers. Nearer the water's edge you will find the water forget-me-not.

*Water forget-me-not*

A couple of flowers to look out for in the wake of the boat are the brooklime (*Veronica beccabunga*) and the water crow-foot (*Ranunculus aquatilis*). Brooklime has smooth round fleshy leaves and small deep-blue flowers. Its creeping stems may either be rooted in the bottom mud or float in the water. Water crowfoot has white buttercup-like flowers and may have two types of leaf – broad ones that float on the surface and fine thread-like ones that trail submerged, offering little resistance to the flow of the water.

Two other plants to be seen during the spring are the watercress (*Nasturtium officinale*), with small inconspicuous white flowers, which does grow wild but is also cultivated in beds in shallow rivers, and the water starwort (*Callitriche stagnalis*). This tiny nearly submerged plant would be easily overlooked except for its sheer abundance on some canals.

*Sedge warbler*

Birds are in full song and the migrants are arriving all the time. Suddenly there are swallows, martins and swifts skimming over the water for the first insects of the year. All three birds look alike, with their long wings and forked tails, but with a little practice it is possible to tell them apart. The swallow has a chestnut throat and forehead, and extremely long tail feathers. The sandmartin has a brown back and a brown band under its chin on an otherwise completely white chest. The housemartin, which also feeds over rivers and canals, is recognisable by its white rump and completely white front (no chin band) and blue-black back. The swift is quite black, back and front, except for a pale throat, and so is easy to identify.

Another spring and summer visitor to the waterside willows is the sedge warbler, a brown bird with a streaked back, pale front and reddish rump. The reed-bunting, small and brown, is with us all the year round. Another native bird is the kingfisher. A sudden blue flash across the water means it is making for its nest hole in the river bank.

*Reed bunting*

The coot, moorhen, mallard, swan, dabchick and great crested grebe are just a few more of the water birds that remain faithful to our inland waterways throughout the year.

House martin

Kingcup

Swallow

*agonfly*     *Crack willow*     *Butterbur*     *Pied wagtail*     *Mallard*

*Dabchick*

Spring is the time for courting and nest-building, laying eggs and rearing young. The coot builds its large nest almost at water level but banks it up with dead reeds. The moorhen nests on the mudbank, making the nest high as a precaution against possible water rise. The coot has a white forehead, the moorhen a red forehead. They both have large families of as many as fifteen chicks, but only a few survive to adulthood. The female mallard may build her nest in a pollarded willow several feet above the ground. As soon as the ducklings are hatched and dry, the duck leads them to the water, each one tumbling down from the nest apparently without any injury. Swans mate for life and nest in the same area year after year. The large circular nest is often quite conspicuous among the reeds, but this does not really matter, for the male swan, the cob, keeps constant guard over the female, the pen, and her clutch. Baby swans and dabchicks love to ride on their mothers' backs. When the dabchick dives for food, the youngsters bob to the water's surface like corks.

*Moorhen*

The birds are not the only animals to be busily building homes at this time of year. The water vole makes a thick-walled globular nest of reeds and grasses in a special chamber in one its many burrows in the river bank. These burrows can cause considerable damage to the banks but the vole compensates by keeping the waterways clear of weeds and rotting vegetation. The tiny silver-coated water shrew also tunnels into the bank, burrowing well in to make a small nursery lined with moss and fine roots.

Spring is the time when the frogs, toads and newts emerge from their winter sleep to lay their eggs. Frog spawn is laid in a mass, with each little black egg surrounded by a protective coat of jelly. Toad spawn is laid as a string of eggs wound by the toad around the stems of waterweeds. Unlike the frogs and toads, the female common or smooth newt lays very few eggs and only one at a time. The place to look for eggs is under the leaves of waterweeds.

The fish are active now. The little male three-spined stickleback becomes more brightly coloured, and makes his nest for the female to lay her eggs in. He is an industrious father and keeps guard over the babies until they are ready to leave home. The miller's thumb or bullhead, another small river and canal fish, now ventures into the shallow waters to get any of the spring sun's warmth.

As the days lengthen and become warmer with the approaching summer, the first butterflies appear after their long winter sleep. Bees and wasps are humming in the air and ladybirds are about. The dragonflies and mayflies are also on the wing.

*Water vole*

## SUMMER

With June the willows are in full leaf, giving shade to many a hidden creature and food to the myriads of insects now about. The watermeadows are full of flowers and blossoming grasses line the towpaths. The fronds of bracken are now uncurled and fully expanded, forming dense carpets of green. Little frond clusters of another fern, the hart's-tongue (*Phyllitis scolopendrium*), may be seen growing in cracks in the lock walls. This cannot be confused with any other British fern because its blades are quite undivided. Often growing in the shallow water at the edges of waterways are water horsetails (*Equisetum fluviatile*) easily recognisable by their tall gaunt stems and whorls of spiky branches.

*Three-spined stickleback*

The hawthorn or may shrub lining many waterways is now laden with small white blossoms. Entangled and twisted around its branches are the white trumpet-like flowers of the bindweed (convolvulus), the sweetly scented honeysuckle blossoms and the prickly pink and white dog roses.

The colour and variety of flowers is astonishing. The golden-yellow dandelion-like fleabane (*Pulicaria dysenterica*), creamy flower clusters of the meadowsweet (*Filipendula ulmaria*), the white or pinkish yarrow or milfoil (*Achillea millefolium*), the pinky-mauve jumping jack or Himalayan balsam (*Impatiens glandulifera*), the purple loosestrife (*Lythrum salicaria*), and the blue flowers of the common skullcap (*Scutellaria galericulata*), are only some that you can find.

The water also features a luxuriant growth of plants during the warm summer months. There is the tall 9ft high reed (*Phragmites communis*), with its quivering head of tiny flower spikelets, overshadowing the common bulrush (*Scirpus lacustris*), which grows to no more than 6ft. This kind of rush has dense bunches of flowers, whereas the reedmace (*Typha latifolia*), familiarly known as the bulrush, has thick brown velvety cylindrical flowers. Hidden among the rushes and reeds is the bur-reed (*Sparganium ramosum*), which grows on the muddy banks close to the water. The flowers of this small water plant, only 2ft high, are tiny balls covered with spikes.

Birds and insects alike find the platforms made by the wide leathery leaves of the waterlily very useful as a resting stage or a place from which to fish. The flowers of the yellow waterlily (*Nuphar lutea*) project a few inches above the water, whereas those of the less common white waterlily (*Nymphaea alba*) float on the water's surface.

*Bullhead*

Three other attractive white flowers that are blossoming in the water are the water soldier (*Stratiotes aloides*), the frogbit (*Hydrocharis morsus-ranae*) and the arrowhead (*Sagittaria sagittifolia*). The water soldier is particularly common in the

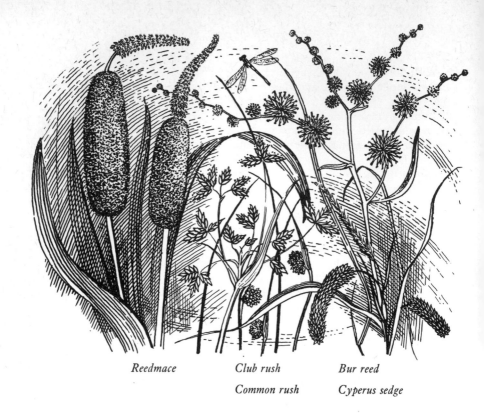

*Reedmace*       *Club rush*       *Bur reed*

               *Common rush*       *Cyperus sedge*

Broads. The frogbit is not rooted to the bottom. Its round leaves float on the surface, with its small three-petalled white flowers poking above them. The arrowhead is a common canal plant, its large arrow-shaped leaves making it quite unmistakable. The flowering stem may grow to 3ft above the water and bear several delicate three-petalled flowers. The water-plantain (*Alisma plantago-aquatica*) has small flowers growing on long stalks above the water, but they are tinged with pink and only open in the afternoons. Another common canal and river plant is the amphibious bistort (*Polygonum amphibium*), which has smooth leathery elliptical leaves and spikes of honey-scented pinky-red flowers.

The pondweeds and duckweeds are the most abundant and widely spread of all water plants. The many varieties of pondweed cannot be overlooked. They are not easy to identify because they vary so much, depending on whether they are growing in deep or shallow, fast or slow-moving, water. The commonest is probably the Canadian pondweed (*Elodea canadensis*), which was first introduced to Ireland from North America but now grows in great profusion throughout the British Isles. The common duckweed (*Lemna minor*) is, as its name implies, the commonest of several kinds of duckweed to be found throughout the British

*Horsetail*

Isles. It is a tiny floating plant with small flat round leaves little more than $\frac{1}{10}$in across and a single root, and grows so profusely as to form a green carpet over the water's surface.

*Kingfisher*

The summer months are strangely quiet of any bird song. This is because the adult birds are too busy gathering food for their demanding youngsters. There is plenty of food in and around the water at this time of the year for the insect-eating birds. A good hunting ground is a reed bed or a willow tree, where there are bound to be many caterpillars feeding on the leaves. The pied wagtail is more adventurous. With constant flicks of its tail this distinctive black and white bird walks across the lily leaves to look for water insects. It is only in summer that the many insect-eating birds will be found by the water. With the approach of winter these birds return to the fields and farms.

Throughout the year the kingfisher and heron remain close to the water. They are kept busy now looking for fish to feed their broods. The kingfisher may perch on a branch over-hanging the water and then suddenly dart and snatch its victim from the river. The tall stately heron stands solitary and motionless at the edge and then quite unexpectedly shoots its neck and powerful bill into the water and seizes its prey.

The water birds are also busy with their growing families, grey cygnets, moorhen chicks or downy mallard ducklings.

The river is the natural habitat of the otter. It will be seen only in the cleanest of waters, for it cannot tolerate pollution in any form. Few are privileged to see this playful creature, but you may see the wake that it leaves as it makes for the side, or its footprints in the mud and the slides it makes on the banks.

A sudden 'plop' in the water does not mean the otter is abroad but that the water vole is tracking down its favourite food of whirligig beetles. This delicate feeder is also partial to willow leaves and bark. The first young water voles are about now; they take readily to the water, keeping close to the safety of the bank.

In the heat of the summer sun lizards laze on walls and lock gates, though a sudden shadow passing over them brings them quickly to life again. The sinuous ripple travel-ling across the water's surface is probably made by a grass snake hunting down young frogs that are gorging themselves on flies, unaware of the approaching danger.

*Otter*

During summer the pike finds cover in thick weed beds. It is the largest of all canal and river fish, often reaching 37lb. Aptly known as the freshwater shark, it is a vicious and aggressive creature. With its yellow-green dappled torpedo-shaped body it can remain well hidden among the reeds. When hungry, it moves with speed and precision on to its prey of perch, roach, rudd, dace, minnows and sticklebacks.

The depths of the canal and river are the world of small creatures. The summer months are the best time for the jamjar naturalists, for this underwater life is now at its most exciting and prolific. A net dragged in the mud at the bottom of a shallow river might well pick up an orb-shell cockle (*Sphaerium*) or a swan mussel (*Anodonta cygnea*), a ram's horn snail, with its coiled shell, or the great pond snail, with its conical whorled shell, or even a freshwater crayfish. Canal summit levels like the Grand Union at Marsworth are a good place to look. A few alarming creatures such as the water stick-insect (*Ranatra linearis*) and the water scorpion (*Nepa cinerea*) may also find their way into the net. The larvae of many aerial animals spend their early lives in the depths, too. The caddis fly larva is one example. They make themselves protective cases of bits of stick and tiny shells to disguise themselves from enemies. This makes them easy for us to recognise!

The many different kinds of water beetle and water boatman live among the plants in the surface waters. The water spider (*Argyroneta aquatica*) is the only British spider that spends all its life under water. All are on the lookout for other creatures to eat. In fact a continual war is waged between predator and prey among these tiny animals.

Doing an endless series of pirouettes on the water's surface are whirligig beetles (*Gyrinus natator*), while long-bodied pond-skaters (*Gerris*) walk gingerly over the water on their stilt-like legs. Both are food for the swooping swallows or the hidden water vole.

Adding colour to this summer circus are the hovering dragonflies, their bodies sparkling in the sun. One of the largest and most beautiful is the 6in-long blue emperor (*Anax imperator*). It has two pairs of large powerful wings and can hover and even fly backwards. The golden-ringed dragonfly (*Cordulegaster boltoni*) has a brightly striped body in yellow and black and big green eyes. Bees, wasps, flies, gnats and butterflies are everywhere in summer but especially evident over the water, as the insect-eating birds know well. The whirring and humming of the insects' wings are in complete harmony with the continual chirring of the crickets and grasshoppers hiding in the long grasses. These summer sounds do not last long. With the beginning of September comes one of the first signs of autumn – the migrant birds are getting restless once again and are gathering together to make their long journeys.

*Pike*

*Dragonfly and nymph*

## AUTUMN

As autumn progresses, leaves turn colour, and you can

*Hart's-tongue*     *Polypody*     *Marsh fern*     *Lady fern*

gather hazel nuts and conkers, blackberries and rose hips. The 'spinner' fruits of the sycamore and the ash 'keys' fall helicopter fashion to the water, landing with a gentle splash to float away with the current. The alder catkins are just appearing but will not develop until spring.

Many of the spring and summer flowers along the water's edge are still in bloom. But the traveller's joy or old man's beard (*Clematis vitalba*) is the most conspicuous plant of autumn, with its masses of feathery seeds covering every shrub and bush. The bracken has begun to turn brittle and brown but the hart's-tongue fern stays green right through the winter.

In the water the bulrushes and bur-reeds rustle in the wind. The reedmace is still bursting its seed heads into candyfloss masses. The arrowhead and amphibious bistort flowers are still out in the water but with October they will quickly die.

Swallows, swifts and martins are gone, but the coots, moorhens, swans and herons remain by the waterside throughout the year.

By the end of October the winter sleepers are hidden away. Snakes and lizards, frogs, toads and newts, snails and butter-

*Mute swan*

*Some waterside mosses and lichens:*

| | | |
|---|---|---|
| *Leskea polycarpa* | *Marchantia* | *Placythium nigram* |
| *Calypogeia muelleriana* | *polymorpha* | *Lecanora muralis* |
| | | *Conocephalum conicum* |

flies have all found suitable winter quarters. Strangely enough, autumn is the time of year when the spiders are at their best. Their dew-laden webs are certainly much in evidence.

In the water the beetles and boatmen are still about, but not for long. Even the fish have retired to deeper waters for the cold months ahead.

### WINTER

A sky filled with racing clouds means winter has come. The trees are bare but it is possible to recognise them by the structure of their branches and stems. The holly is dotted with red berries and the parasitic mistletoe, with its sticky white berries, hangs in clusters in the branches of the poplar and apple. The green berries of the ivy will soon ripen to a dark purple. Few flowers can stand the winter cold but the flowerless plants, the mosses and lichens, are growing well. The rushes and reeds rustle in the wind, their leaves yellow and dry.

With the majority of animals enjoying their long winter slumbers, the countryside seems quite quiet. The water birds have ice to contend with and stand huddled together, their feathers fluffed out, to try and keep themselves warm. From the north come flocks of wild geese, their continual babbling sounding strangely loud in the cold quietness of winter. Tracks in the snow on the muddy banks mean that the otter is still active, however. Rabbits, foxes and weasels also leave their mark as they move stealthily across the white meadows. But it is not long before the buds will be bursting on the trees again and the bird song will break the silence. The spring visitors will arrive and a year by the waterside will have gone full circle.

*Perch*

*Ladysmock*

*Water dropwort*

*Roach*

*Monkey musk*

*Minnows*

*The Waterways Museum, Stoke Bruerne*

# 17
# Waterway Museums

MUCH of the canal and river system of these islands is an open-air museum of industrial archaeology that survives through regular use and maintenance. We may at times complain that our inland navigations have hardly been improved since they were first opened, but the network as a result does constitute a remarkable survival of an early nineteenth-century transport system, complete with engineering structures, buildings and frequently scenery that remains much as it was 150 years ago. By comparison, the railways have lost a rich architectural heritage in the wake of rationalisation and modernisation, unless they are taken over by preservation groups. We must ensure that their fullest development for amenity use does not disturb or destroy the qualities that make the waterways of Britain so uniquely attractive.

So much for the physical routes, where suitable new roles must be found for redundant warehouses and other quality buildings. There are also relics of a more fragile nature that will not last for the enjoyment of future generations unless their preservation is secured soon. First, and perhaps most important, are the boats of all types from sailing barges to every regional variety of freight carrier, from maintenance vessels to traditionally built pleasure craft. Most are still fairly familiar, for they have only recently ceased to trade or are still used in their original role in dwindling numbers. Examples of many of them remain in private ownership, from Victorian steam launches to various breeds of narrow boat, from Thames sailing barges to Leeds and Liverpool Canal short boats. Unfortunately no West Country barge (such as used to trade on the Upper Thames), or Severn trow is now available for preservation or likely to be rescued from dereliction. We can surely do better to record this facet of British life than to rely solely on scale models exhibited in museum showcases.

At the time of publication of this book, details of museum opening times etc were correct. It would be advisable, however, for the reader to check them before making a visit.

### NORTH WEST MUSEUM OF INLAND NAVIGATION

Information from Edward Paget-Tomlinson, Windy Ash, Osmotherley, Ulverston, Cumbria, LA12 7PB.

A start has been made by a charitable trust to save certain craft. During 1974 negotiations were in progress for a permanent exhibition site at Ellesmere Port. The museum intends to preserve not only boats but also their fittings and decoration, the tools and techniques of building and repair and the lore of the people who worked them. Exhibits earmarked for display so far include the Shropshire Union wooden ice breaker *Marbury*; the Mersey flat *Mossdale*; the ex-Thomas Clayton decked gas boat *Gifford* (a horse-drawn narrow boat); *Worcester*, one of the former tunnel tugs of the Worcester and Birmingham Canal, originally steam-driven; the timber-built short boat *George*; and the Norfolk sailing wherry *Lord Roberts*. Members of the public are encouraged to join the trust and so help finance its work.

### THE WATERWAYS MUSEUM

Stoke Bruerne, near Towcester, Northants. Tel: Northampton 862229. Open daily, 10.00am–12.30pm; 2.00pm–5.00pm; 6.00pm–8.00pm. Closed Christmas Day, Boxing Day and every Monday from the second Monday in October to the Monday before Good Friday, inclusive. During the period of Monday closures, the museum remains open until 5.00pm only.

This is quite the best establishment for canal relics apart from actual craft. Located above the top lock at Stoke Bruerne on the Grand Union Canal midway between Northampton and Towcester, it was set up in a disused corn-mill by the British Transport Commission and opened in 1963. Its outstanding collection of objects large and small, acquired by direct purchase and donation, is displayed on three floors. Inevitably the wealth of material owned by the museum has outstripped the available display space, and a new gallery could be added with advantage. Equally popular with school coach parties, serious students of canal history and waterway holidaymakers, Stoke Bruerne displays an astonishingly rich range of relics, from prints and photographs to boat people's clothing, boat models, steam and diesel engines, replicas of a traditional narrow-boat cabin and the Anderton Lift, company seals, painted ware, canal ropework, boatbuilding and maintenance equipment and noticeboards of all types. There is a well-stocked shop attached, with a wide range of inexpensive books and souvenirs.

### LLANGOLLEN CANAL EXHIBITION

Information from David Wain, Inland Hire Cruisers Ltd,

Rowton Bridge, Chester (Tel: Chester 35180), or from The Wharf, Llangollen (Tel: Llangollen 860702).

A completely novel type of canal display, allied to the Victorian 'panorama' show, was opened to the public at Llangollen wharf in North Wales in July 1974. Conceived by David Wain, whose family hire-cruiser business ran from 1935 to 1972, the exhibition is housed in a charming little canal warehouse. It aims to tell the story of our canals through working models and tableaux arranged in a carefully planned sequence. An added attraction for visitors who have toured the exhibition is a journey along the canal to the Pontcysyllte Aqueduct in one of three specially designed horsedrawn craft. The company hopes to establish similar shows elsewhere in the future.

While there are no museums in Britain expressly devoted to waterways other than the three just listed, many collections do contain sections with strong canal and river interest.

### EXETER MARITIME MUSEUM

The Quay, Exeter, EX2 48N. Tel: Exeter 58075. Open daily except Christmas and Boxing Days. May–October 10.00am-6.00pm. November–April 10.00am-5.00pm.

The museum is accommodated in stone warehouses at the terminus of the Exeter Ship Canal in Devon. Sponsored by the International Sailing Craft Association, it was opened in 1969. It possesses upwards of fifty vessels drawn from Britain and overseas, and its chief objective is to maintain as many of the exhibits as possible in working condition. Most of them are shown afloat and visitors may even hire traditional clinker-built skiffs and rowing dinghies, or enjoy cruises in a vintage motor launch. Ashore there is one of the curious Bude Canal tub-boats, fitted with iron wheels so that it could be hauled up and down the inclined planes on that odd waterway. An amazing steam-powered drag-dredger was brought overland from Bridgwater Dock on the Bridgwater and Taunton Canal. One of the oldest steamboats in the world, the dredger displays a brass plaque in the engine room showing that she was built in 1844, most likely to the design of Isambard Kingdom Brunel. Even in retirement she performs a useful function in clearing silt to provide berths for new arrivals. Another oddity is the appealing little *Cygnet*, shaped like a swan and built about 1860 in Exmouth as tender to a larger but similar vessel named *Swan*. Fishing boats include Teifi and Tywi coracles from Wales, and one from the Severn built by an expert craftsman still in business at Ironbridge. There is an 18ft doble from the Medway (of open clinker construction like the Thames Peter boat) and a 21ft Exe salmon boat. One of the chief features of the

*The headquarters of the Exeter Maritime Museum by the side of the Exeter Canal Basin are well suited to displaying some of the larger boats afloat*

museum is its splendid setting, flanked on one side by the canal and on the other by the River Exe.

### THE BLACK COUNTRY MUSEUM

Information from Dudley Museum and Art Gallery, St James's Road, Dudley, Worcs. Tel: Dudley 56321.

At the time of writing this ambitious project is being established as an offshoot of Dudley Museum. The intention is to gather together relics of Black Country industry, including nail and chain making, mining, heavy engineering and transport, from the last 250 years. The site, at the Tipton approach to Dudley canal tunnel, is intersected by part of Lord Ward's Canal, and suitably reflects the great importance of local canals in making industrial development possible in the Midlands. Among canal exhibits are the cast-iron Factory Bridge that until recently spanned the BCN main line below Tipton locks, one of the last brick and slate BCN octagonal toll houses, various items of canal furniture, and the locally built ice breaker *North Star*. Various examples of freight-carrying boats are also to be preserved.

### IRONBRIDGE GORGE MUSEUM AND BLISTS HILL OPEN AIR MUSEUM

Southside, Church Hill, Ironbridge, Telford, Shropshire.

Tel: 095-245 3522. Open daily, 10.00 am-6.00pm.

This is Britain's most extensive national park of industrial archaeology, covering an area of about a square mile on the north bank of the Severn between Ironbridge and Coalport Bridge. The region was of great importance as an early centre of ironworking and is dominated by the great iron bridge itself. This lacy structure is the oldest bridge of cold blast iron in the world, and was cast in 1779 by Abraham Darby's Coalbrookdale Company. Today it carries pedestrians only. The original furnaces, buildings, forges and machinery of the Ironbridge gorge are now preserved by the Museum Trust. Waterways interest is catered for by a tub-boat discovered in 1972 serving as a farm water trough at Lilleshall, and of a type launched into the Severn by John Wilkinson in the 1780s. Sections of the disused Shropshire (Coalport) Canal, including stop locks and an inclined plane, are being restored by voluntary labour. Telford's pioneer cast-iron aqueduct at Longdon-upon-Tern, built in 1796, is scheduled to be removed from the derelict Shrewsbury Canal and re-erected at the museum.

### MORWELLHAM QUAY

Morwellham, Near Tavistock, Devon. Tel: Gunnislake 766. Open: summer, 10.00am-7.00pm; winter, 10.00am-dusk.

This old port on the River Tamar was opened to the public in 1971 to display industrial relics of this exceptional river valley. Two signposted routes rather like nature trails have been laid out. One indicates a tramway tunnel and inclined planes on the way to the Tavistock Canal towpath between the top of one plane and the portal of the 2,540yd Morwell-down canal tunnel, now used as a watercourse to supply the turbines of a small power station. The other route is around the immediate quay area, with its tramways, water wheel, ore chutes and limekilns. Models and a collection of old photographs are housed in a small museum.

### CROFTON STEAM PUMPING STATION

Kennet & Avon Canal Trust, Crofton, near Great Bedwyn, Wilts. Enquiries to Nicholas Reynolds, 11 The Vineyard, Richmond, Surrey. Tel: 01-948 1577. Open every Sunday, 10.00am-6.00pm; and at various 'steaming weekends' during the summer, 10.00am-1.00pm and 2.00pm-6.00pm.

Details of the pair of restored beam engines that were designed to lift water to the Kennet and Avon Canal will be found on pp 30-1. In a beautiful rural setting between Hungerford and Marlborough, the pumping station is an ideal objective for a day excursion.

## SOUTH YORKSHIRE INDUSTRIAL MUSEUM
Cusworth Hall, Doncaster, Yorks. Tel: Doncaster 61842.
Open to the public on application to the curator.

Built in 1740 by George Platt and shortly afterwards
altered by James Paine, the house is now the home of a
remarkable collection of relics, documents and other material
relating to Yorkshire's industrial history. Inland waterways
feature prominently among the transport exhibits.

## THE SCIENCE MUSEUM
Exhibition Road, South Kensington, London, SW7. Tel:
01–589 6371. Open: Mondays–Saturdays, 10.00am–6.00pm;
Sundays, 2.30pm–6.00pm. Closed Good Friday, Christmas
and Boxing Days.

Models show a commercial narrow boat, canal cruiser,
Thames lighter and sailing barge, Norfolk wherry and
Humber keel. There is also quite a good print collection.

## NATIONAL MARITIME MUSEUM
Greenwich, London, SE10. Tel: 01–858 4422. Open:
Mondays–Saturdays, 10.00am–6.00pm; Sundays, 2.30pm–
6.00pm. Closed Christmas Eve, Christmas and Boxing Days,
and Good Friday.

While anyone interested in the craft of inland waters will
almost certainly enjoy walking round the galleries of this
outstanding shipping collection, several exhibits are of
direct canal and river appeal. One of the finest is the 53ft
Thames steam launch *Donola*, built at Teddington in 1893.
From 1920 she was owned by the Thames Conservancy and
made a tour of the waterway on an annual inspection. In 1969,
having been presented to the museum, she made her way
down river from Reading to Greenwich, with the late Sir
Francis Chichester among her passengers. There is a steam
tug from the Manchester Ship Canal, and a full-sized reconstruction of a Thames boatbuilding workshop, with a
typical waterman's clinker boat half-built and another being
repaired. Experts are on hand in the educational centre to
give instruction on small-boat building to one or two amateurs,
using traditional materials and methods. The public may
watch work in progress. The museum has a fine collection of
prints and photographs, many of them relevant to inland
shipping.

## MANCHESTER MUSEUM
Oxford Road, Manchester 13. Tel: 061–273 3333. Open:
Wednesday, 10.00am–9.00pm; other days, 10.00am–5.00pm.
Closed, Christmas Day and Good Friday.

As part of the University of Manchester, the museum has

built up a good canal collection. There is a series of 1/16 scale models, including the packet boat *Duchess Countess*, the Weaver flat *Elizabeth*, two examples of Bridgewater Canal starvationers and the canal ice breaker *North Star*. A full-sized starvationer is also shown at Manchester: 30ft long with a 3ft 8in beam, these were the crude craft with stout ribs that worked the underground canals in the Worsley mines. There are also choice items of decorated narrow-boat ware and equipment.

## GOOLE MUSEUM

Carlisle Street, Goole. Tel: Goole 3784. Open: Monday, Wednesday, Friday, 10.00am-11.30am and 2.00pm-7.00pm; Tuesday, Thursday, Saturday, 10.00am-11.30am and 2.00 pm-5.00pm.

Here is housed a collection in nine sections depicting different activities in and around Goole. One section concentrates on Goole Docks and nearby waterways, and includes paintings, boat models and photographs.

## GLOUCESTER FOLK MUSEUM

Bishop Hooper's Lodging, 99–103 Westgate Street, Gloucester. Tel: Gloucester 24131. Open on weekdays, 10.00am-5.30pm.

A group of three timber-framed buildings with exposed beams dating from about 1500 have housed the folk museum since 1935. An interesting display shows different methods of salmon fishing in the Severn with nets and boats. Additionally there is a rectangular cast-iron distance plate from the Thames and Severn Canal, a painted narrow-boat masthead lamp, and a model of a boat-weighing machine from Brimscombe Port.

## HULL MARITIME MUSEUM

Pickering Park, Hessle Road, Hull. Tel: Hull 27625. Open: weekdays, 10.00am-5.00pm; Sunday, 2.30pm-4.30pm. Closed Christmas and Boxing Days and Good Friday.

Among a primarily sea-orientated collection are models of Humber sloops and keels, steam barges and tugs. There is also a fine painting of the 1874 Humber Keel Regatta.

## BRISTOL CITY MUSEUM

Queen's Road, Bristol 8. Tel: Bristol 27256. Open on weekdays, 10.00am-5.30pm.

A well-known model of the Severn trow *Alma* and a restored 'flatner', a type of small boat used on the Somerset River Parrett, are at the time of writing the only exhibits of waterway interest.

## MARITIME MUSEUM FOR EAST ANGLIA

Marine Parade, Great Yarmouth, Norfolk. Tel: 0493 2267.
Open every day, June–September, 10.00am–8.00pm.

Craft of the Broads, with model sailing wherries take their place alongside the history of the sea and ships.

## WILLIS MUSEUM

New Street, Basingstoke, Hants. Tel: Basingstoke 5902.
Open Monday, 1.30pm–5.50pm; Tuesday–Saturday, 10.00 am–12.30pm and 1.30pm–5.30pm. Closed Bank and Public Holidays.

This is a good mixed collection, ranging over many subjects. There is some material on the history of the Basingstoke Canal.

## CITY OF LIVERPOOL MUSEUMS

William Brown Street, Liverpool L3 8EN. Tel: 051–207 0001. Open weekdays 10.00am–5.00pm; Sunday, 2.00pm–5.00pm. Closed Good Friday and Christmas Day.

The extensive collection of ship models, including some inland craft (Mersey flat etc), has been in store for many years on account of space shortage. Some of them are displayed from time to time. As a long-term project, a full-scale maritime museum may be set up near the Pier Head.

## MANCHESTER SHIP CANAL CO MUSEUM

Ship Canal House, King Street, Manchester 2. Tel: 061–832 2244. The public are normally only admitted in connection with research projects etc, on application to the public relations officer.

Exhibits deal with the promotion, construction and operation of the Manchester Ship Canal.

## CORINIUM MUSEUM

Park Street, Cirencester, Gloucestershire, GL7 2BX.
Tel: Cirencester 2248.

The museum was built in 1938 and was much extended during 1973–4; it features one of the best collections relating to Roman Britain. Recent expansion includes a display on the Thames and Severn Canal.

## BOAT PRESERVATION

Several organisations are devoted to maintaining historical waterways craft on a charitable basis. Enthusiasts are normally welcomed as members, first to support efforts with financial contributions, secondly to assist with restoration and maintenance, and thirdly to travel sometimes aboard the boats, with the aim of keeping them in working condition.

### The Narrow Boat Trust

Information from the Hon Secretary, Juliet Miller, 24 Horsell Park Close, Woking, Surrey.

The trust owns the motorboats *Alton* and *Nuneaton* and the butty *Satellite*, all of them steel craft from the former Grand Union Canal Carrying Co fleet constructed in the 1930s. Substantial restoration and refitting has been necessary and continues at the time of writing. Centre of operations is Norton Canes Dock on the Cannock Extension Canal. Where practicable, cargoes will be carried, using members as crew, thus ensuring that the craft remain mobile without the operation having to 'make a profit'. Thus the trust aims to carry on the traditions of working narrow boats.

### The Norfolk Wherry Trust

Secretary, J. R. M. Bryce, 33 Brettingham Avenue, Cringleford, Norwich, Norfolk, NOR 96D. Tel: Norwich 52183.

Formed on the Broads in 1949, the trust maintains in good working order the last sailing wherry, *Albion*, in original trading condition. There are a number of similar craft remaining in private hands that have been converted for cruising or purpose-built as pleasure yachts. The trust places a particular emphasis on teaching young people elementary sailing techniques through courses aboard *Albion*.

### The Dolphin Sailing Barge Museum Trust

Dolphin Yard, Crown Quay, Sittingbourne, Kent. Normally open, weekends, Easter–October, 10.00am-6.00pm.

Of the great fleets of Thames sailing barges whose working area ranged from the London Docks to the Medway and East Coast, a fortunate number of vessels survive either as houseboat hulks or fully rigged and converted for charter or private use. One of the best places to find a dozen or more is alongside the quay at Maldon on the tidal Blackwater in Essex. Since 1969 the Dolphin Trust has occupied a small traditional barge-building and repair yard where members may learn and practise building and sailing skills. The curator's own barge, *Nellie Parker*, is berthed there.

### The East Coast Sail Trust

Appeal Secretary, Newney Hall, Writtle, near Chelmsford, Essex, CM1 3SE.

The trust has, since 1966, operated the 150-ton 'mulie' auxiliary sailing barge *Thalatta*, which is used to provide educational cruises for young people between 12 and 18 from regions of very restricted opportunity. These activities range from teaching the rudiments of seamanship, navigation,

*Measham teapots were prized possessions of many narrow boat families. They were sold at various canal centres, including Measham on the Ashby Canal, and personal mottoes, dates and similar messages were added to the other decoration*

and local maritime history to studying marine biology and the ecology of the tidal margin. A secondary but important objective is the preservation of spritsail barges in seagoing condition for a period of at least thirty years. An appeal is in progress to provide funds to buy and maintain *Thalatta*, as well as to acquire a second sailing barge as a memorial to the first president of the Inland Waterways Association, the late Sir Alan Herbert.

### The Maritime Trust

At 53 Davies Street, London, W1Y 1FH. Tel: 01–629 5782.

This organisation, whose president is HRH The Duke of Edinburgh, exists to restore, look after and put on display the ships and equipment of interest and importance in the technical, commercial and military history of Britain. In many ways it is akin to a National Trust of ships and boats. Apart from the provision of funds to maintain many seagoing vessels, it is concerned with the following inland craft projects: (1) to raise £35,000 for the purchase, restoration and maintenance over seven years of *Cambria*, built in 1906 and the last Thames barge to trade under sail alone; (2) to assist with the construction of a museum at Bowness to house the steam launches of the Windermere Nautical Trust; and (3) to secure for restoration an example of a Humber sailing keel. Additionally, the trust is providing various regional boat museums with advice on restoration and fund raising.

### River Stour Trust

F. H. L. Frecknall (Working Party Organiser), North House, 66 Cambridge Road, Stansted, Essex. Tel: Stansted 2245.

Members of the trust discovered one of the unique wooden barges familiar from John Constable's paintings. Although it had been buried in silt for fifty years or so, it was found to be in fair condition and was refloated in 1972. Planning consent has been received from the Essex River Authority for construction of a dock on the Stour in which the barge can be housed. No fewer than fourteen similar barges were discovered in Ballington Lock cut, that selected for preservation being judged to be in the best condition. Dating from 1870–1910, the barge is 46ft 9in long overall, with a narrow central decking dividing the cargo holds. It was almost certainly decked at each end and in many ways closely resembles its near neighbour the Fenland lighter.

### Oxford College Barges Preservation Trust

C/o Barclays Old Bank, High Street, Oxford.

About the middle of the last century six London Guild barges of the type long used for ceremonial and State occasions were taken to Oxford. Here they were adapted as floating clubhouses for the University oarsmen, and in time similar craft were constructed by various colleges, displaying elaborate and fanciful carved decoration. The appropriate college coat of arms generally featured prominently in the design. Late Victorian and Edwardian additions brought the number of these magnificent 'grandstands' up to twenty-seven. But the passage of time brought its toll, although one of the original six, the Oriel barge, remained among the long procession at Christ Church Meadow until the early 1950s. Shortly before World War II, several colleges commissioned more conventional brick-built boathouses on the shore, and this process has accelerated in recent years, with the result that now only four barges survive. One more can be seen on the lawn of the Shillingford Bridge Hotel near Dorchester, while at least one other serves as a houseboat in a backwater a short way down river of Oxford.

The trust aims to secure retention of the last four, using them as a museum of rowing and Thames history. Already the Jesus barge has been rebuilt, and the superstructure of the Hertford College barge been transplanted onto a new steel hull.

*The Humber Keel and Sloop Preservation Society*
Hon Treasurer, G. Fussey, 67 Gillshill Road, Hull.

During 1974 the society was negotiating to buy the steel-hulled keel *Comrade*, still trading under power. Built in 1923 as a sailing craft, she was motorised in the 1930s. Once purchased by the society, she was to be restored and re-rigged as a square-sailed vessel.

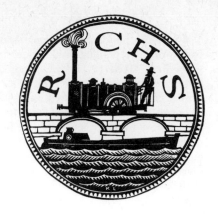

# 18

# *Associations and Boat Clubs*

VARIOUS waterways pressure groups have campaigned for the betterment of the canals and rivers of Britain since World War II, the oldest of them among the earliest amenity and environmental associations. The concept of waterway preservation using voluntary labour has been emulated since by scores of similar organisations whose interests range from railways to ancient buildings and industrial archaeology.

### THE INLAND WATERWAYS ASSOCIATION AND THE LOCAL CANAL SOCIETIES

The oldest and most influential group is the Inland Waterways Association, founded in 1946 by a quartet comprising Robert Aickman, Frank Eyre, Charles Hadfield and Tom Rolt. It would be invidious to credit any one of these men with the original idea, but there is no doubt that Rolt's classic *Narrow Boat*, published in 1944, had fired the public imagination and paved the way for a national waterways revival. The waterways of Britain were then largely the responsibility of a wide-ranging collection of private concerns, including railway companies, antiquated boards of trustees, well-organised official bodies like the Thames Conservancy, river catchment boards, and even individual and completely autonomous owners. Some waterways had long since fallen derelict and given up the fight for survival; some, like the Kennet and Avon, lingered in a state of weedy near-ruin, navigable only with supreme endurance; but others supported heavy traffic, with great fleets of narrow boats, steam tugs, horsedrawn barges and inland sailing craft. Some canal companies actually made an annual profit, even if it was small by comparison with the golden years rather more than a century earlier.

In 1946 it was possible to navigate over the Pennines by no fewer than three routes: Leeds and Liverpool, Rochdale, and Huddersfield Narrow Canals. You could visit Kendal at the northern limit of the lovely Lancaster, or make a circular trip round the Derby, Trent and Mersey, and Erewash Canals. The Stroudwater Canal was penetrable between Saul Junction and the Thames and Severn. Ireland's delectable Royal Canal linking the Shannon with Dublin was open from end to end, and sizeable yachts could move from the east to the west coast of Scotland via the magnificent Forth and Clyde. Since 1946 all these possibilities, and others too, have been taken away. Without the constant pressure exerted by the IWA and its later satellites it is quite probable that all but the largest commercial navigations would by now have followed the Wey and Arun and the Grantham into a state of reed-choked pools with lock gates falling drunkenly from their hangings.

At the end of World War II, waterways control and lack of development was sometimes so disgraceful that the nationalisation of most of the network in January 1948 under the British Transport Commission was largely welcomed. At this time inland navigations were regarded as freight carriers and suppliers of industrial water. The Commission was mainly concerned with transport, and only later began to realise the great potential amenity and recreation use of the canals. Pleasure boats were scarce, with fewer than a dozen possibilities for hiring cabin cruisers away from the Thames and Broads. Now that the future of the so-called 'amenity' waterways is assured for towpath walking, boating, angling and general relaxation, it is difficult to appreciate that the change was brought about in the space of a single generation. Largely under the leadership of Robert Aickman for its first 20 years, the IWA did much to turn the tide. This is not to imply that success was achieved everywhere, for the catalogue of waterways that have fallen into disuse since the late 1940s, few of which would ever have been allowed to close in today's more enlightened circumstances, makes dismal reading.

The early days created a pioneer spirit among the growing band of pleasure boatmen who set off into the sometimes hectic commercial melée of the Grand Union or fought with the blanket weed of the Llangollen. They used a variety of interesting craft, including converted ships' lifeboats fitted with car-engine-driven paddle-wheels, ex-Government landing craft (they were in plentiful supply), or redundant narrow boats. In 1950 this canal world converged in Market Harborough for the IWA's Festival of Boats and Arts, an annual event since held in different locations and now normally attracting more than six hundred vessels. But the IWA is not a boat owners' club. Its brief includes not only the promotion of rivers and canals for multi-functional use, including trade, recreation and water supply, but also their restoration in collaboration with other enthusiast bodies.

The first example of this policy was the acquisition of the Lower Avon Navigation from Tewkesbury to Evesham in 1951 by enthusiast Douglas Barwell. A charitable trust was formed, locks rebuilt, the channel dredged and a new and beautiful waterway appeared from the crumbling chaos that confronted the pioneers. Up to 1965 £77,862 had been raised from voluntary sources for the work; improvements still continue, supported by boat tolls and donations.

Another milestone was the rebirth of the Southern Stratford Canal, 13 miles of heavily locked rural waterway between Lapworth and the Avon. The IWA was influential in this canal's successful transfer from the British Transport Commission to the National Trust in 1961. By using voluntary, Service and prison labour, under the inspired leadership of a young Midlands architect, David Hutchings, the first boat in 25 years reached Stratford via the canal in February 1964. In July the works were officially reopened by HM Queen Elizabeth the Queen Mother. The party that accompanied these celebrations lasted almost a week. Waterways and the IWA had truly arrived.

In 1962 the British Waterways Board had been established, and for the first time about half the rivers and canals in Britain found themselves under single ownership and free from the domination of powerful road and railway interests. From then on an increasing degree of cooperation was achieved between the Board and the Association. Under the aegis of the Waterways Recovery Group, voluntary working parties restarted neglected maintenance and undertook actual restoration in many places during most weekends of the year. The IWA's position is one of independence, combining the roles of watchdog, development planner (especially through its Inland Shipping Group), and public informant. The ultimate mark of respect for the Association came in 1972 when its then chairman, John Humphries, was invited to advise the Government on their reorganisation programme for water space in Britain. In April 1974 he became chairman of the Water Space Amenity Commission (WSAC).

Membership of the IWA (now well in excess of 12,000) is open to individuals, other societies, industrial firms, boat clubs and members of the waterways trade. Details will be supplied on application to its General Office at 114 Regent's Park Road, London, NW1 8UQ (Tel: 01-586 2510/2256).

The Inland Waterways Association is organised in seven regions, each divided into a number of branches, so that all members can participate in local activities. It also works closely with the very many local societies which are usually concerned with one or a small group of canals. Many of these support restoration groups, run a varied programme of social and boating events, and generally attract the more active and concerned waterways enthusiasts. Membership of at least one such society as well as of the IWA itself is essential if you are to benefit fully from an interest in waterways while at the same time helping to promote their use and well-being. As local secretaries change, they are not listed here. Instead, consult the current edition of the *Canal Enthusiasts' Handbook*, published by David & Charles, or seek the advice of the IWA's General Office in London.

*An Inland Waterways Association National Rally of Boats in the heart of Birmingham*

## BOAT CLUBS

There is hardly an area in the British Isles not served by boat clubs whose members combine to share various facilities on a non-profit-making basis. These are usually friendly concerns catering both for experienced craft owners and novices. As distinct from certain coastal yachting establishments, there is a distinct lack of snobbery, with an equal welcome extended to the man who runs a 16ft two-berth cabin cruiser and to the owner of a large motor yacht or converted narrow boat whose value may be well in excess of £5,000. Such clubs generally have their own moorings, which are reserved for members, the site either being leased from the waterway authority or owned outright. Shore-based facilities often include a clubhouse for social meetings, a slipway or crane, and space on the bank for craft to winter out of the water. Some clubs are purely designed to further social and boating aims, but others take on the role associated with waterway societies, campaigning for improved navigation conditions, running voluntary working parties and encouraging nation-wide travel with their own rallies or attendance at those of similar clubs.

Joining a boat club confers several valuable benefits, like sharing the fund of knowledge and experience of the other members as well as taking advantage of mooring rates that are normally a fraction of those in commercial yards.

To obtain details of clubs in a particular area, consult the appropriate navigation authority or ask the Association of Waterways Cruising Clubs, whose secretary is J. Cotterill, 125 Kingsdown Road, Burntwood, Staffordshire. The AWCC, which was founded in 1965 to further cooperation between cruising clubs, provides emergency assistance, moorings etc to members when travelling, and organises inter-club rallies and competitions. It is also a useful negotiating body, committed to putting the cases of member clubs to the various authorities in the event of disputes or where improvements might be made.

There are further bodies whose activities are national rather than merely local. The Residential Boat Owners' Association, which promotes the interests of people who choose to live afloat permanently, is open to all whose craft conform to certain specified regulations. The Narrow Boat Owners' Club, which aims to keep alive the traditions of ex-working narrow boats in their original or converted form, promotes extended winter cruising, among other activities. The Steamboat Association of Great Britain fosters interest in all types of steam-driven craft, both vintage and modern.

# Selected Bibliography

Ball, E. and P. W. *Holiday Cruising on the Thames*. David & Charles, 1970.
*The Broads Book*. Link House, annually.
Burton, Anthony. *The Canal Builders*. Eyre Methuen, 1972.
*The Canals Book*. Link House, annually.
*Canal Enthusiasts' Handbook No 2*. David & Charles, 1973.
Carr, Frank. *Sailing Barges*. Conway Maritime Press, 1971.
Chaplin, Tom. *A Short History of the Narrow Boat*. Hugh McKnight Publications, 1974.
De Salis, Henry. *Bradshaw's Canals and Navigable Rivers of England and Wales (1904)*. David & Charles, 1969.
Doerflinger, Frederic. *Slow Boat through England*. Wingate, 1970.
　　　　　　　　　　*Slow Boat through Pennine Waters*. Wingate, 1971.
Edwards, L. A. *Holiday Cruising on the Broads and Fens*. David & Charles, 1972.
　　　　　　*Inland Waterways of Great Britain*. Imray, Laurie, Norie & Wilson, 5th ed, 1972.
Gagg, John. *The Canallers' Bedside Book*. David & Charles, 1973.
Gayford, Eily. *The Amateur Boatwomen: Canal Boating, 1941–5*. David & Charles, 1973.
Hadfield, Charles. *British Canals: an illustrated history*. David & Charles, 5th ed, 1974.
　　　　　　*The Canal Age*. David & Charles, 1968.
　　　　　　*Introducing Inland Waterways*. David & Charles, 1973.
Hadfield, Charles, and Streat, Michael. *Holiday Cruising on Inland Waterways*. David & Charles, 2nd ed, 1971.
Harris, Robert. *Canals and their Architecture*. Hugh Evelyn. 1969.
*Inland Waterways Guide to Holiday Hire*. Inland Waterways Association/Boat World, annually.
Lewery, A. J. *Narrow Boat Painting*. David & Charles, 1974.
Liley, John. *Journeys of the Swan*. Allen & Unwin, 1969.
McKnight, Hugh. *A Source Book of Canals, Locks and Canal Boats*. Ward Lock, 1974.
　　　　　　*Canal and River Craft in Pictures*. David & Charles, 1969.
*Nicholson's Guides to the Waterways*: 1: South East, 1971. 2: North West, 1972. 3: South West, 1973. 4: North East, 1973. 5: Midlands, 1974. British Waterways Board (paperback), David & Charles (hardback).
Ransom, P. J. G. *Holiday Cruising in Ireland*. David & Charles, 1971.
Rolt, L. T. C. *The Inland Waterways of England*. Allen & Unwin, 1970.
　　　　　　*Narrow Boat*. Eyre & Spottiswoode, 1972.
　　　　　　*Navigable Waterways*. Longmans, 1969.
　　　　　　*Green and Silver*. Allen & Unwin, 1969.
Russell, Ronald. *Lost Canals of England and Wales*. David & Charles, 1971.
　　　　　　*Waterside Pubs*. David & Charles, 1974.
Seymour, John. *Voyage into England*. David & Charles, 1966.
*The Thames Book*. Link House, annually.
Ware, Michael E. *A Canalside Camera 1845–1930*. David & Charles, 1975.

# Gazetteer

Note that m = miles throughout Gazetteer section.

## Waterways Authorities

ABOUT half the total mileage of navigations in England, Wales and Scotland are nationalised and maintained by the British Waterways Board, Melbury House, Melbury Terrace, London, NW1 6JX. Many other authorities in England and Wales were changed in 1974 with the reorganisation of water services. Up to date details may be obtained from the Inland Waterways Association, 114 Regent's Park Road, London, NW1 8UQ, or the Water Space Amenity Commission, 1 Queen Anne's Gate, London, SW1H 9BT. For Ulster and the Irish Republic, consult the appropriate Tourist Boards.

## Derelict Waterways

NUMEROUS rivers and canals in these islands that are closed for navigation are still a source of great interest to the waterways enthusiast or industrial archaeologist. This book is mainly concerned with routes that remain fully operational, and incidental mention only has been made of abandoned sections. For further details of such relics, Ronald Russell's *The Lost Canals of England and Wales*, published by David & Charles, is strongly recommended.

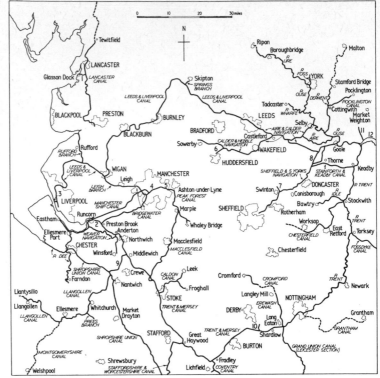

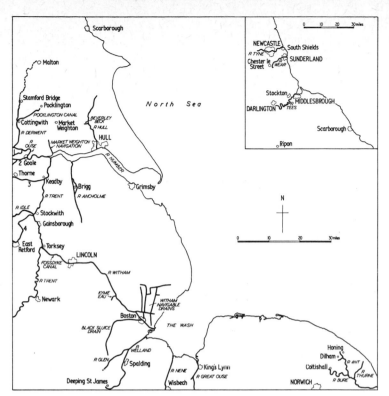

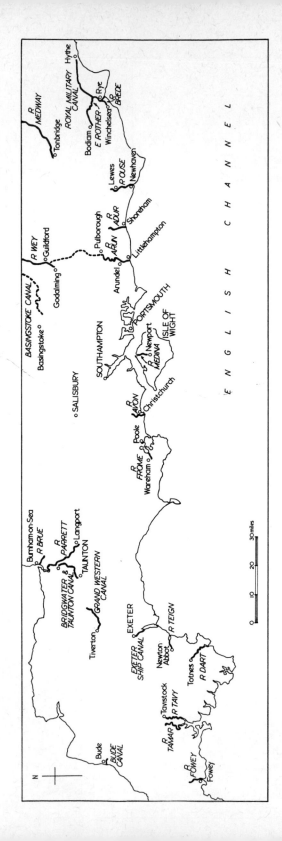

# England and Wales

### ADUR, RIVER

FROM the English Channel to Bines Bridge, via Shoreham-by-Sea, Sussex; 11m. One of the disconnected South Coast rivers, it once continued for over 3m to Baybridge, via the Baybridge Canal. This section and its 2 locks became derelict in the 1860s. Craft drawing up to 3ft, with a headroom of less than 5ft 6in, can reach Bines Bridge on a favourable tide. The river is tidal throughout, and is best navigated on a rising tide from Shoreham upstream. There is a speed limit of 5½ knots.

The river is a pleasant waterway, used for an annual Two Rivers Canoe Race, where the course also includes the Arun. A watch should be kept for shallows at low water opposite Shoreham High Street and several places between there and Beeding Bridge. The chief town, Shoreham, is more a port than a seaside resort. There are mudbanks and huge ridges of shingle where the Adur runs parallel with the sea before finally joining it. Worthing lies to the west and Brighton to the east.

### AIRE & CALDER NAVIGATION

The main line runs from Goole Docks to Castleford, where it divides into two sections, one leading to the Calder & Hebble Navigation at Wakefield and the other to Leeds, junction with the Leeds & Liverpool Canal. Goole to Leeds is 34m with 13 locks, Castleford to Wakefield 7½m with 4 locks. There is a link between Bank Dole Junction, on the main line at Knottingley, to Selby (Yorkshire Ouse) via the River Aire and Selby Canal. This extends for 11¾m with 4 locks. The New Junction Canal, connecting the A&C near Pollington with the Sheffield & South Yorkshire Navigation at Bramwith, was jointly constructed by the A&C and the S&SY and is described on p 388. Maximum craft dimensions are subject to progressive improvement in order to accommodate more economical commercial loads. At the time of going to press they are 182ft (Leeds to Goole) and 132ft (Castleford to Wakefield) × 17ft 9in × 8ft draught × 12ft headroom. Between Knottingley and Selby 78ft × 17ft 6in × 6ft draught × 8ft headroom. Locks are in most cases much larger than these limits suggest.

The Aire & Calder has long been a flourishing commercial highway and has been continually enlarged and updated. Under the influence of its resident engineer, William Hamond Bartholomew (1831–1919), who served the navigation in various capacities for the extraordinarily long period of 66 years, the A&C was one of a small group of waterways in Britain that more than held their own in the face of railway competition. The A&C is synonymous with trains of coal-carrying compartment boats (Tom Puddings) and the larger coal boat trains serving Ferrybridge C Power Station (pp 144 and 145). Coal remains a major traffic, while substantial quantities of liquid fuels and general merchandise are also carried. During an average month in 1973 private carriers' craft conveyed some 170,000 tons on the A&C. Barge capacity was increased during the 1960s and 1970s from 250 tons to 500 and is likely to grow still further to 700 tons. From this information it may be correctly inferred that the part of South Yorkshire served by the A&C is industrialised country, with power stations and coalmines. In addition to its usefulness as a cruising connection with other, more scenic waterways, the navigation's chief interest derives from its freight traffic.

*Goole*   The town owes its existence entirely to the A&C, which established a seaport on the banks of the tidal Yorkshire Ouse with the opening of the Goole Canal in 1826. Inland barges share berths with ships from many parts of the world. These include colliers which are loaded at curious Victorian hoists designed to lift and invert Tom Puddings that have travelled in close-coupled trains from inland pits. The docks transformed Goole from a village of 400 inhabitants to a town of about 20,000. Most of the original workers' estate houses of the 1830s have been demolished, but St John's church, built with A&C help in 1843–8, remains, with an elegant spire; its juxta-position with masts and funnels of ships is both memorable and unusual. Two exits provide access to the river – the great Ocean Lock used by ships, and the duplicated Victoria Locks for barges and pleasure boats. Cruisers should report their arrival to the dock master's office.

Leaving Goole en route to Leeds and Wakefield, the waterway passes first the BWB repair yard where work in progress includes maintenance to Tom Puddings on apparatus that inverts them for ease of access. Then follows another yard established in timber ponds where pleasure craft are catered for. The line of the canal continues almost completely straight for nearly 6 miles to New Bridge, with the Dutch River immediately to the south. Scenery is quite flat.

*Pollington* (9m 4f)   Reservoirs on the right face the beginning of the New Junction Canal (7m 2f), jointly built by the A&C and the Sheffield & South Yorkshire and opened as recently as 1905 (see p 388). The first change of level since Goole is at mechanised Pollington Lock, with a 7ft rise. Like others on the A&C, it is manned by keepers working on a shift system. Pollington village lies a little to the north.

*Great Heck* (11m 4f)   Because the wash from commercial traffic can be considerable, pleasure boats are advised not to moor in the main channels, where the banks are generally steel-piled. A welcome will be extended to visitors to the headquarters of the South Yorkshire Boat Club in Heck Basin, a rare centre of cruising activity for these waters and completely protected from the effects of passing vessels.

*Whitley Bridge* (13m 4f)   The next feature is the long chamber of Whitley Lock, progressively lengthened and still fitted with an intermediate set of gates. An original lock alongside is now used as a bypass weir. Whitley Bridge is a useful overnight halt on the A19, with shops, garage and railway station.

*Knottingley* (17m 2f)   The character of the navigation changes as the waterside Kellingley Colliery by Bridge 15 is approached. Here is one of several loading staiths where coal is transferred to barges. At the outskirts of industrial Knottingley the River Aire forms a V-junction with the main line and so provides navigational access to the Yorkshire Ouse at Selby (p 363). Knottingley's greatest interest to the boater is John Harker's shipyard, where craft ranging from inland tanker barges to small seagoing ships are launched. Another major activity is production of bottles and jars at the factory of Rockware Glass Ltd. Surroundings remain largely devoted to various manufacturing processes until the far side of Castleford.

*Ferrybridge* (18m 6f)   There is a tangled meeting of main roads and railways in this part of the county of Yorkshire. Pontefract, lying off the A1 to the south, is well known as a centre of confectionery, especially of sweets based on liquorice. Beyond Ferrybridge Lock the canal joins the natural River Aire and no fewer than three power stations, named Ferrybridge A, B and C, loom up. Several of the seven giant cooling towers at the C station were partly demolished by high winds soon after their completion in the mid-1960s. (They were subsequently rebuilt.) Relying mainly on waterborne coal, C power station has been supplied since 1967 with loads brought in modern Tom Pudding pans propelled in trains of three or four units by push tug. Each unit carries up to 210 tons. Operated jointly by Cawood's and Hargreaves', both long established barge firms, the giant pans are unloaded by docking them under a 'tippler' – a cradle that lifts the barges 40ft in the air and inverts them, tipping the coal down chutes. One unit is thus handled in 9 minutes, while around 1,000 tons of coal an hour can be so delivered.

*Castleford* (24m)   Moderately high banks characterise the course of the Aire to Bulholme Lock, where a broad loop of the river is bypassed by an artificial cut. There are further signs of coalmining activity, with a colliery on the waterside at Fryston. As the junction of the rivers Aire and Calder, Castleford inspired the rhyme:

> That's why the Castleford girls are so fair,
> They bathe in the Calder and dry in the Aire.

This practice can no longer be recommended, for the quality of water hereabouts is classified as grade 4 by anti-pollutionists, indicating that it is unable to support virtually any kind of life! The navigation is a leading feature of the town, with a barge carrier's depot, BWB maintenance yard, offices of the North East Area Engineer and commercial traffic toll office alongside the Flood Lock. This is one of just 3 points where freight dues are calculated on nationalised waterways in England and Wales. The others are at Bow (London area) and Anderton (North West). The Flood Lock, at a 4-way junction, has an unusually wide and slightly curved chamber. This presents a blind corner at a point particularly busy with commercial traffic, and is controlled by lights from a raised cabin. Ahead is the navigable River Calder (the Wakefield section of the A&C, see p 219), to the left a length of Calder leading to a weir near the town centre, and to the right the continuation of the main line to Leeds.

*Kippax Locks* (25m 4f)   Much of the remaining journey is through bleak surroundings with widespread mining activity and locks at regular intervals. But the waterway is deep and wide and rarely lacking in interest as coal barges, fuel carriers and other vessels surge to and fro. Near the automated Kippax Locks a new opencast mine began sending, early in 1974, up to 5,000 tons of coal each week to waterside power stations and the port of Goole. Conventional Tom Pudding boat trains are used for this purpose, and the traffic is expected to outlast its initial contract period of 5 years. Lemonroyd Lock (27m 4f) follows after Saville Colliery, where motor barges will generally be seen loading in a basin. The lock was enlarged to a length of about 220ft during 1973-4, the third time the existing structure had been increased in capacity on the present site. Similar improvements followed at neighbouring locks shortly afterwards, thus enabling 700-tonners to reach Leeds (the nineteenth-century capacity was 150 tons). An oil depot, left, above Lemonroyd, is situated alongside the Fleet Cut, where a former lock connecting with the Aire has been converted to a weir.

*Woodlesford* (28m 6f)  Close to the A642 road bridge is a convenient railway station. The village has been developed as a Leeds suburb. This is the best access point for Temple Newsam, a Carolean mansion mostly dating from *c*1630. Both house and grounds of 900 acres were acquired by Leeds Corporation in 1922 for the establishment of a museum.

*Leeds* (34m)  Desolate countryside gives way to more interesting industrialism as the city boundary is crossed between Woodlesford and Fishpond Locks (30m). There are further power stations, much commercial traffic, an unloading dock for oil tankers and British Waterways' extensive Knostrop Depot, catering for various classes of waterborne freight. Three further locks complete the journey to the city centre – Knostrop, Knostrop Flood (where the Aire is rejoined) and Leeds. Near City Station, a junction is made with the trans-Pennine Leeds & Liverpool Canal, which is now as lacking in working boats as the A&C is busy with them. With a population of more than half a million, Leeds is a flourishing city whose fortunes grew with the development of woollen and textile industries. Civic buildings are suitably grand, especially the great pillared Town Hall (1853-8).

*Aire & Calder Navigation. A motorised freight barge negotiates a lock on the New Junction Canal described on p 388*

*Wakefield section* (distances are measured from Goole)  After passing through Castleford Flood Lock (24m), the navigation continues straight ahead along the River Calder, with views of the mining village of Allerton Bywater to the north, on the banks of the Leeds line. Two locks (Fairies Hill and Altofts) are now disused, through navigation being along a parallel route via Woodnook Lock, with an exceptionally deep chamber where the rise and fall is 13ft 6in (26m). The Calder is now abandoned in favour of an artificial channel that avoids the contortions of the river. King's Road and Birkwood Locks (27m) are both situated close to the village of Altofts, a grey settlement based on the coal trade. The outstanding feature of this section is Stanley Ferry Aqueduct, carrying the canal over the Calder (27m 5f). This little known but important structure consists of an iron trough suspended between a pair of cast-iron bow-string arches. It was designed by George Leather, whose earlier plan of a six-arched bridge was rejected in view of the volume of flood water that regularly passed down the Calder. Building began in May 1837 and was completed a little over 2 years later. With a series of classical pillars on each elevation, the 8ft deep trough is 180ft long. Total weight of the aqueduct is about 1,700 tons. During 1971–2 timber fendering was replaced by rubber and other changes made to protect the ironwork from collision by barges. Nearby is the BWB maintenance yard where boats are built or repaired and heavy engineering carried out, including construction of massive new lock gates for use in the area.

A colliery, right, where modern compartment barges load coal for Ferrybridge C power station, is followed by Broadreach Flood Lock (28m 4f). Beyond this point navigation continues along the Calder into Wakefield and a junction with the Calder & Hebble Navigation (p 262). One former connection downstream of Fall Ing Lock is the Barnsley Canal; capable of passing Yorkshire keel barges, it was opened in 1804 and ran for 15m with 20 locks to join the Dearne & Dove Canal (now also closed). Acquired by the A&C in 1875, one small section of the Barnsley was closed in 1893, while the majority followed in 1953.

*Selby section* (distances are measured from Knottingley)  Now forming a link between the A&C at Knottingley and the Yorkshire Ouse in Selby, this line was the main through route from Leeds to the Humber until creation of the port of Goole and Knottingley–Goole Canal. After passing through Bank Dole Lock, Knottingley, navigation proceeds via the River Aire for 6½m. Compared with the long straight cuts of other sections of the A&C, the course of the Aire is exceptionally twisted. Apart from a small village and lock at Beal (2m 6f), there is limited interest in the surrounding countryside, which tends to hide behind flood banks. On reaching Haddlesey Flood Lock (6m 4f), the Aire leaves the navigation to run for 16¾m before it unites with the Ouse. However, this tidal route is not currently open, as Haddlesey Old Lock is derelict. Turning left therefore at Haddlesey Junction, one follows the Selby Canal. Opened in 1778, it declined in importance after the emergence of Goole, and, although in good condition, it now carries minimal commercial traffic. Until it reaches the outskirts of Selby (11m 6f) the canal lacks features of any particular note. Selby Basin is a pleasant and well-used mooring for pleasure craft, safe from the ripping tides of the Ouse just beyond, through Selby Lock. Both lock and nearby swing bridge are operated by a resident keeper. Selby achieved national importance in the early 1970s for its coalmine, which has been developed to exploit one of the richest seams in Britain. For further information on the town, turn to p 363.

## ALDE, RIVER

From the Suffolk Coast at Shingle Street (where it is called the Ore) past Orford and Aldeburgh to Snape Bridge; 21m. Only restriction is of draught, which is 10ft to Slaughden Quay, Aldeburgh, 4ft to Iken, or on a favourable tide 5ft to Snape. (A small loaded coaster reached Snape about 1967.) There is no navigation authority.

The Alde follows a most curious course in that it seems quite determined to join the sea at Aldeburgh, 8m 4f from Snape Bridge. Instead it runs like a letter S several hundred yards inland from the coast for its remaining 12m 4f past Orford Ness and Orford Beach. The entrance near Shingle Street is a particularly dangerous area on account of a shifting bar of shingle. The lower reaches are muddy and reedy. Butley Creek is navigable for about 4m to near Chillesford. Orford, with a quay on the river, is a small boating centre with a ruined church and twelfth-century castle. Aldeburgh is a former fort town, now seaside resort, developed as such from the early nineteenth century. The whole region, with its evocative marshes, has provided inspiration for composer Benjamin Britten, whose English Opera Group has held a music festival each June since 1948. Upstream the country becomes partly wooded, with a wide lagoon near Iken. The mid-nineteenth-century Snape Maltings have been converted into a famous concert hall. In 1862 a 50ft boat burial dating from about AD 635 was discovered on Church Common. The Alde retains a wild lost atmosphere, epitomising the best of unspoiled Suffolk.

## ANCHOLME, RIVER

From South Ferriby Sluice, River Humber, to Bishopbridge, Lincolnshire; 19m with 2 locks. Maximum craft dimensions are 80ft (69ft above Harlam Hill Lock) × 19ft (16ft above Harlam Hill Lock) × 6ft 6in draught from the Humber to Brigg, gradually reducing to 3ft at Harlam Hill Lock. Headroom is about 11ft. The waterway was made navigable over a period up to the 1820s, with considerable engineering work by John Rennie. As the only access is from the fast-flowing Humber, and the line of the navigation is mostly very straight with limited views over high flood banks, the Ancholme is of rather limited interest to cruising enthusiasts.

Principal working boats trading on the Ancholme were Humber keels and billy-boys. The only place of any size is Brigg, 10m from the tidal lock at Ferriby Sluice. Both old and new rivers are navigable through the town, remembered in Delius' *Brigg Fair* and not otherwise of any great note. Reasons for travelling along this waterway are twofold: (1) if you live in the area and wish to base a boat nearby for convenience, and (2) if you belong to a growing band of canal and river adventurers who cannot rest until they have penetrated every navigable creek, canal or river in the kingdom.

## ARUN, RIVER

From the South Coast at Littlehampton to Pallingham; 25½m with no locks. Maximum dimensions for craft are about 95ft × 10ft × a draught of perhaps 10ft, depending on the state of the tide. Headroom under bridges varies with the height of the tide. Sizeable cruisers can reach Arundel, beyond which the river is only suitable for smaller powered boats and dinghies. The navigation was in full operation between 1790 and about 1889 (Houghton Bridge, 15½m upstream of Littlehampton to New-bridge, start of the Wey & Arun Canal). With all locks quite derelict, the part now usable is virtually the natural course of the Arun.

This is a charming waterway, well worth exploring by small seagoing craft wishing to discover something of inland waterways and by inland boats whose owners fancy a short association with tidal waters. Since influential efforts are being made and practical work is in progress to reopen the canal link between Wey and Arun, the river could well assume a considerable importance in years to come as a heavily used route between the Upper Thames and the Solent.

*Littlehampton*  An agreeable seaside resort with the usual range of entertainments and a good sandy beach. The mouth of the river is a busy little harbour, with quays, boatyards, pleasure craft at moorings, public tripping craft and a public slipway for launching small craft. At times there is a strong current. Boats exploring the river are advised to do so on a rising tide, taking due care that there is sufficient headroom under bridges at Littlehampton, Ford, Arundel, Offham and South Stoke. Views are rather restricted over the muddy banks as far as Arundel.

*Arundel* (6m 6f)  The town is clustered around the dominating feature, Arundel Castle, home of the Duke of Norfolk. This originated as a large late eleventh-century structure built by Roger Montgomery, Earl of Shrewsbury. It was extensively re-modelled, first in the Gothic style between 1791 and 1815, and nearly a century later in a mock Windsor Castle fashion. The present Duke now lives in the park in a neo-Georgian house. Mooring for a short time is possible near the bridge (but the banks are muddy). Upstream the scenery improves as the river passes through the South Downs. A bargeman's inn once frequented by sailing craft crews, called the Black Rabbit, is pleasantly situated below a wooded chalk cliff (7m 6f).

*Houghton* (14m 4f)  The length between Arundel and Houghton is the most dramatic, with a gorge through the Downs known as the Arun Gap. Houghton resembles Cliveden on the Thames.

*Coldwaltham* (17m 7f)  Pretty villages are to be seen at Bury, with flint church and broach, and shingled spire, and Amberley, where there is a splendid castle fortress on a hillock, dating from the late fourteenth century. Former navigation works, including Waltham Lock and Hardham Tunnel, both on the Coldwaltham Cut, are bypassed by the dredged channel of the natural river. At the upper end of the cut the Western Rother Navigation (not to be confused with the Eastern, or Rye Rother) branches off towards Midhurst, 11¼m distant. There was once a short additional line to Petworth, mostly disused by 1888 and legally abandoned in 1936. There are numerous remains to be found of the 10 locks, that at Stopham being spanned by a rusty iron draw-bridge. Full details of these lost Sussex waterways are contained in P. A. L. Vine's *London's Lost Route to the Sea*, easily the most readable canal and river history yet published.

*Stopham* (22m 2f)  A short distance from Pulborough (21m), which lies close to the river and is a pleasing little town with useful adjuncts of civilisation, including a railway station. Stopham village with church, White Hart Inn and cottages, is at its best by the Arun. The bridge is easily the finest medieval river crossing in Sussex. Built in stone in 1423, its 6 pointed side arches are completely original, while the central navigation arch was enlarged in 1822.

*Pallingham* (25m 4f)   Even as far from the sea as this, the Arun is still noticeably tidal, with a rise and fall of up to 2ft, although navigation is only possible for shallow-draught craft above the limit of recent dredging at Pulborough. The first lock of the Wey & Arun Canal is situated at Pallingham in a private garden, where two chambers of equal size are visible in the form of a staircase; although wide-beam, they appear to have been fitted with single gates rather than pairs.

*Wey & Arun Junction Canal*   Further progress towards the Wey is now impossible, as the W&A has been derelict since 1871. Passing through 23 locks in the course of 18½m to Shalford on the Wey Navigation (see p 443), this is one of the most lamented inland cruising routes in Britain. During the early 1970s, however, its hitherto hope-lessly lost cause has been the subject of much activity by members of the W&A Canal Trust. Working parties are regularly staged and small sections have been returned to use. The problems confronting restoration include vanished lock sites, development on parts of the canal bed and the necessity to obtain agreement from sometimes reluctant landowners for rebuilding to start. It is too early to predict if or when the W&A will reopen, but its prospects are really quite bright. The countryside it traversed through Wisborough Green, Billingshurst, Loxwood, Sidney Wood, Cranley and Bramley is some of the best in Sussex and Surrey. Would-be pedestrian explorers should seek the advice of the Canal Trust before setting out over private land. A classic description of a voyage from the Thames to Littlehampton shortly before the demise of the W&A is J. B. Dashwood's *The Thames to the Solent by Canal and Sea*, published in 1868. Copies are extremely rare.

Small craft may be hired at Arundel, Houghton and Pulborough.

*River Arun. Stopham Bridge, several miles from the junction with the derelict Wey & Arun Canal*

## ASHBY CANAL

From the Coventry Canal at Marston Junction, Bedworth, to a terminus at Snarestone; 22m with a stop lock at Marston. Dating from an Act of 1794, the Ashby was built largely to cater for coal traffic. This cargo remained important for as long as regular narrow-boat traffic continued and even now survives with the support of 'enthusiast' carriers. Coal also resulted in the demise of the final 8m of canal to Moira, progressively closed since World War II because of subsidence problems. The waterway is now mainly rural throughout its length, and, although lacking in any outstanding engineering or architectural features, it does possess a distinct quiet charm. Maximum dimensions for craft are 72ft × 7ft × 3ft 6in draught, with a headroom of 6ft 6in.

Not forming part of a through route, nor enjoying any specific objective at its far end, such as the Llangollen or even the Erewash Canal do, the Ashby tends to be neglected by many pleasure cruisers. This neglect is totally undeserved.

*Marston Junction*   The stop lock is now open at each end, thus creating (with the Coventry Canal) one of the longest stretches of level navigation in Britain. Much of the Ashby is a haven for wildflowers and animals.

*Hinckley* (5m)   A 300-yd arm connecting with the town wharf is now given over to boat moorings. This small town is notable for the installation of a stocking frame as early as 1640, long before the centre of such activities was established in Leicester.

*Shenton* (13m)   The canal skirts the west edge of Bosworth Field, scene of King Richard III's downfall in 1485 at the hands of Henry Tudor. Ancient hawthorns still grow on Crown Hill, Stoke Golding, where traditionally Richard's crown was discovered after the battle in a thorn bush.

*Market Bosworth* (14m 7f)   The old market town, 1m east of the canal, has declined in importance since the Middle Ages. There are thatched cottages and an unexpectedly large parish church, partly fourteenth-century. The famous Hall is early eighteenth-century, with much later work.

*Shackerstone* (18m 2f)   A small aqueduct carries the canal over the River Sence. West of the unspoiled village is Gopsall Park, where Handel composed the *Messiah*. The house was demolished in 1951–2. Eastwards lies the oddly named village of Barton in the Beans.

*Snarestone* (21m)   Here is a wide-beam tunnel, 250yd long, with the small agricultural village above. Shortly beyond, past Bridge 61, a winding hole has been constructed at the new end of the waterway. In its original form the Ashby crossed the border from Leicestershire into Derbyshire and served various mines at Measham, Donisthorpe and Moira. Measham gives its name to the distinctive narrow-boat ware – teapots, jugs and other motto-bearing pottery in brown or occasionally blue, with flowers or fruit in relief. Such pots were reputedly made in neighbouring villages and sold to the boat families, with which they became prized possessions. Conflicting evidence suggests alternative centres of manufacture, including, obviously, the Potteries. Certainly there are surviving examples bearing Cornish legends, suggesting a link with the carriage of kaolin (china clay) by sea and canal from Corn-wall to Stoke-on-Trent. The oldest known teapot is reliably dated 1792, while the most recent (apart from a modern revival for canal enthusiasts) was probably made shortly after World War I.

## ASHTON CANAL

From a junction with the short remaining navigable portion of the Rochdale Canal, Manchester, to Dukinfield, junction with the Peak Forest Canal; 6¼m with 18 locks. Maximum craft dimensions are 70ft × 7ft × 3ft 3in draught × about 6ft headroom. This most useful urban canal forms part of the Cheshire Canal Ring (com-prising Ashton, Peak Forest, Macclesfield, parts of the Trent and Mersey and Bridge-water and a section of the Rochdale). Opened about 1799, it had lost its commercial traffic by 1957, and fell derelict in 1961, when the last pleasure boat made a passage with the greatest difficulty. After strenuous efforts by the IWA and Peak Forest Canal Society, clearance work began in September 1968, when 600 volunteers spent a memorable weekend in torrential rain; 500 lorry loads of junk were carted away. A similar exercise in March 1972, attended by 1,000 volunteers, signalled the start of complete restoration of this and the adjoining lower Peak Forest Canal (see p 373). Estimated cost of the work involving 13m and 34 locks was £225,000, shared between the BWB, local authorities, the IWA and the PFCS. Reopened in 1974.

*Manchester*   The Ashton leaves the Rochdale at Ducie Street Junction, near Piccadilly Station. Surroundings are densely industrial, the canal passing the backs of numerous factories. Shortly after Store Street Aqueduct the locks begin with the Ancoats flight of 3. These are followed by 4 in the Beswick flight (1m 2f), 9 in the Clayton flight, and 2 singles at Fairfield, near Droylsden. Several tracts of open waste land suggest landscaping possibilities. A start in this direction has been made by various firms whose premises border the waterway, notably the Anchor Chemical Co, which has paved and planted the surrounds of Lock 9 at Openshaw in collaboration with the BWB.

*Ashton-under-Lyne* (6m)   A level pound of almost 3m leads to Dukinfield Junc-tion, where a magnificent stone warehouse with internal boat docks and original cast-iron cranes, built in 1834, was sadly gutted by fire in 1972. The Peak Forest Canal leads away towards Marple under a really lovely slender stone towpath bridge.
   The Ashton had several important branches that once carried heavy commercial traffic. These were the Islington (2f), Stockport (4m 7f), Hollinwood (4m 5f), and Fairbottom (1m 1f). They were abandoned between 1955 and 1962.

*Huddersfield Narrow Canal*   Reached from the Ashton beyond Dukinfield Junc-tion and in a state of utter ruin, this was closed in 1944 (an exceptionally black year for canals, when emergencies resulting from the war allowed such acts to be perpetra-ted with little opposition) and ceased to be navigable soon afterwards. One of three trans-Pennine links (the Leeds & Liverpool survives alone, now that the Rochdale is also gone), the Huddersfield Narrow ran for almost 20m to join the Huddersfield Broad and thence the Calder & Hebble Navigation. It was equipped with no fewer than 74 narrow locks and Britain's longest canal tunnel at Standedge (see pp 77 and 85).

## AVON, RIVER (BRISTOL)

From the Kennet & Avon Navigation at Hanham Lock to the Bristol Channel at Avonmouth; 13m with 2 locks. The Floating Harbour (Bristol Docks) is entered via Cumberland Basin Lock. Maximum craft dimensions are 100ft × 17ft 6in × 6ft draught × 10ft headroom. Ships may use the waterway to Bristol Docks.

Once a leading seaport, Bristol is now virtually disused by ships, such commercial activity having moved to Avonmouth. This has left the problem of what to do with Bristol's docks. Considerable argument over a plan to close the docks completely, and even fill in sections of the Floating Harbour, has resulted in a compromise agreement: much of the water space will be retained for amenity use, and the passage down river from Bath through Bristol to the coast assured for pleasure traffic at least. Nonetheless, it is remarkable that a once flourishing seaport can have experienced so rapid a change in fortune.

Bristol is a magnificent city, not least for its connections with trading ships once working to all parts of the world, and for its nineteenth-century associations with Isambard Kingdom Brunel. His glorious Clifton Suspension Bridge, spanning the memorable Avon Gorge below the docks, is a never-to-be-forgotten sight when illuminated at night by strings of fairy lights (see p 57). Brunel's mid-Victorian steamship *Great Britain* is permanently berthed in the drydock where she was built and is slowly being restored to something approaching her original condition. She was towed on a raft from her resting place in the Falkland Islands and is now a leading Bristol attraction.

Tidal influences are experienced normally as far upriver as Netham Weir, Bristol. The maximum rise and fall in the river is sometimes as great as 37ft, meaning that it can vary between a muddy trickle and a brimful seaway, capable of accommodating 3,000-ton craft. At Shirehampton, upstream of Avonmouth, lies the famous Horseshoe Bend, and on the opposite shore the attractive little pilots' village of Pill. Commercial barges, including wide-beam tankers, ceased trading on the river between Bristol and Bath in the 1960s.

With the prospect of the Kennet & Avon Navigation being reopened from the Thames, probably around 1980, many inland craft will be tempted to make a passage through Bristol into the Severn Estuary and up to join the Gloucester & Sharpness Canal. It must be emphasised that while small craft and even canal narrow boats have completed this journey, the tidal Severn is treacherous water and certainly must not be regarded as suitable for novices. Those unfamiliar with the area are well advised to obtain the services of a qualified local pilot.

## AVON, SHAKESPEARE'S

From the Severn at Tewkesbury to Stratford-upon-Avon, junction with the Southern Stratford Canal; 44m with 17 locks.

For a variety of reasons the Warwickshire Avon is one of the most remarkable navigations in Britain. It was completed between 1636 and 1639 by one William Sandys of Fladbury, who spent an estimated £20,000–£40,000 of his own money. Since 1717 the Upper and Lower Avons have been under separate ownership, the dividing line being Evesham's Workman Bridge. Improvements were made at various times until, under railway control, the Upper river became impassable to commercial craft about 1873, although it achieved a moderate popularity with skiff and canoe parties willing to make a series of difficult portages. The Lower river became unnavigable upstream

H

of Pershore during World War II, and in 1949 C. D. Barwell bought the waterway for £1,500, and formed a charitable trust to restore, maintain and improve the river to Evesham, a task completed by 1965. The Lower Avon Navigation Trust established a pattern in voluntary restoration that has been emulated with success on other waterways and in many other fields also.

After the rebuilding (1961–4) of the Southern Stratford Canal under the leadership of David Hutchings, who was working for its new owner, the National Trust, surveys and lengthy negotiations began, again with Mr Hutchings, to restore the Upper Avon and so complete an extensive circular route comprising Avon, Stratford Canal, Worcester & Birmingham and Severn. The astonishing anonymous gift of £100,000 from one individual, together with a further £200,000 in large and small amounts enabled nine completely new locks and weirs to be constructed and vast quantities of rock and mud to be removed. Construction work began in May 1969 and was completed during 1974, almost exactly a century after the last craft worked upriver to Stratford. Recent history of the Avon clearly shows that, where waterways are concerned, individuals can achieve results little short of miracles. Maximum dimensions for craft are 70ft × 13ft 6in × about 4ft draught. The new locks above Evesham are all larger than those below, although present draught is restricted in places to 3ft.

*Tewkesbury*    Lies a short way up the Avon, past large grain mills still supplied by motor barges from Gloucester and through the first LANT lock, where cruising licences are issued and river guides sold. Attractive modern lock-keeper's cottage on piles (as a safeguard from flooding). Charming riverfront in the town, with picturesque buildings and backs of shops having waterside gardens. There are many ancient inns,

*Shakespeare's Avon. Borough Flour Mills at Tewkesbury: grain supplies are still brought by barge from Gloucester Docks via the Severn*

the Black Bear claiming to date from 1308, and much genuine half-timbering. The Norman nave and massive ornate tower of the Abbey are equal to the best of British church architecture. It is said that the roof was replaced in the fifteenth century after being set on fire by a monk reading by candlelight in the nearby dormitory. There are several boatyards and a large marina catering mainly for gleaming seagoing motor yachts; those on moorings above the bridge are a remarkably opulent collection. Rowing boats may be hired and a tripping launch operates. The 5-arched stone King John's bridge provides the lowest clearance of all Avon bridges. Several dinghy-sailing clubs and small cruisers tend to make the river crowded here in summer.

*Twyning* (3m) The pleasant Fleet Inn, left, becomes congested with boats in the season. Overnight and short-stay moorings can be difficult to find throughout the Lower Avon, for most of the banks are private. Sites indicated by light-blue posts or markers have been made available by LANT, but they are often inadequate.

*Bredon* (3m 6f) After the M5 motorway bridge. A 4m walk to the summit of Bredon Hill (980ft) can be made from the village or over a shorter but steeper route from Nafford Lock or Great Comberton. The Hill, part of the Cotswold chain, has the remains of an Iron Age fort and dominates the river for many miles, first to the right, then behind, then ahead, as the waterway winds towards Evesham. There is a fourteenth-century tithe barn (National Trust) 132ft long in this exceptionally pretty village.

*Strensham Lock* (6m) The red-brick Victorian keeper's cottage was bought by the Trust in 1952 for £419 and made habitable as part of the restoration programme, which cost £77,862 between 1951 and 1965. Apart from Strensham, Tewkesbury and Evesham, boat crews work all locks for themselves. The approach from downstream of Strensham into the short lock cut is slightly tricky, because vision is limited. Above, on a hill to the left, are the square tower of Lower Strensham Church and the remains of an old castle. Now follows a superb reach, quite unspoilt and recalling the best of the Upper Thames.

*Eckington Bridge* (8m) First comes Defford railway bridge, which is not un-attractive, with an iron span on large yellow-brown stone piers and a simple Victorian balustrade. Eckington Bridge, medieval in origin in weathered red sandstone, has 6 wet arches and prominent cutwaters. There are moorings for the village shortly upstream on the right. Gnarled pollarded willows and Bredon Hill, now straight ahead, create a typical nineteenth-century riverscape where little can have changed in hundreds of years.

*Nafford Lock* (9m 7f) Acute bends – the Swan's Neck – bring us to the lock, left, difficult to approach from above and below in times of strong current because of the adjacent weir. A wooden swing bridge takes a footpath over the chamber. The Elizabethan Woollas Hall, 1m distant on lower slopes of Bredon Hill, can be visited by appointment (ring Eckington 308).

*Pershore* (15m 2f) Waterside orchards, with all boat services at Sanders' boatyard (right), introduce the prosperous Georgian town, thriving on the local fruit-growing industry, especially plums. In Bridge Street stands the fine Perrott House, built in 1760 by George Perrott, the year in which he bought the Lower Avon Navigation. The much repaired 6-arched bridge is of medieval origin in mixed yellow and red sandstone with blue and red brick. The large central arch dates from after the Civil War, when it was reconstructed. A huge abbey was largely destroyed at the Dissolution of the Monasteries but the pinnacled tower and Norman arches remain in the structure of the newer church. Up the weir stream is Pershore Mill in red brick with lattice windows, to which grain was regularly carried by the small motor barge *Pisgah* until 1972. The diamond-shaped lock chamber, one of several on the Lower Avon, is probably a conversion from a turf-sided one; craft must keep to its deep central section when descending. There are good moorings for the town alongside the recreation ground. The navigation weir or flash lock survived until 1956, when it was removed on account of the lengthy process of building up a level.

*Wyre* (16m 5f)   The lockside mill is now a pleasant LANT clubhouse, although the asbestos and iron roof is an unfortunate if economical replacement. The Trust's fleet of maintenance craft is based here. Another diamond-shaped lock chamber is alongside. During summer weekends volunteers assist with working most locks. Beyond is the riverbank village of Wyre Piddle (left), with prosperous detached houses mostly with cruisers at the bottom of their gardens but, as on many other reaches, lacking in public moorings. From this point to Evesham dredging has not been completed with the same thoroughness as downstream to Tewkesbury, and care should be taken to follow the channel.

*Fladbury* (20m 4f)   Downstream of Jubilee Bridge can be seen the remains on each bank of the former flash lock, removed in 1961, the last genuine example of such a structure in Britain. Good meals are available at the Riverdale Restaurant by the modern bridge. One of the best buildings on the whole river is Fladbury Mill, with an extensive reed-bordered weir alongside the lock cut. A small cable-ferry connects with the village. A steep, heavily wooded hill after the golf course (left) overlooks orchards on the other side of the river, the B4084 to Evesham following close to the waterway.

*Chadbury* (22m)   Another well-situated mill is now a private residence, a reminder of the once intense grain-barge activity.

*Evesham* (26m 4f)   Surrounded on three sides by the river, Evesham has an extensive waterfront. The premises of Sankey Marine (24m) on the left bank are a credit to the firm, which has converted attractive old buildings and laid out the area with gravel paths and lawns in a tidy but completely uncommercial manner. This alone is good reason to use the range of facilities offered. Below a long ridge called Clarke's Hill (right) Hampton Ferry (25m 3f) operates across the river on a rope, which will be lowered to allow craft to cross on three blasts of the boat's horn.

As at Tewkesbury, the Avon here is well used, with small hire craft, waterside caravans and commendable municipal gardens, where cruisers are not only encouraged to moor but also made welcome. Tripping craft include the ex-Thames steamer *Gaiety*, brought through the Kennet & Avon and via the British Channel. Little remains of the huge abbey whose precincts run down to the river. Two churches, All Saints and St Lawrence, share both churchyard and bell tower (a magnificent example of the Perpendicular style). A good shopping centre with many old inns, Evesham is perhaps best remembered for its battle, on 4 August 1265, when Henry III's son Edward defeated Simon de Montfort and his rebel barons in an engagement lasting 3 hours and resulting in the deaths of 4,000 men.

Evesham Lock was the last to be rebuilt by LANT, in 1964, and with the start of downstream traffic from the Upper Avon a lock-keeper's house was added in 1972. Although the historical boundary between Upper and Lower rivers is Workman Bridge in the town centre, since restoration to Stratford has been completed the Bridge Inn at Offenham, about 1m upstream of Evesham, has marked the division. Tolls are collected at the inn and information on the Upper Avon Navigation Trust is available.

*George Billington Lock* (29m 1f)   The Avon now assumes a more remote and adventurous air, for only since 1970 have craft been able to navigate these reaches, for the first time in a century. There is very little commercial development and so far limited boating facilities and boatyards. Each new lock and weir has been designed with great ingenuity, combining strength with economy of materials, yet the equipment is easy to work and final touches, such as landing stages above and below, ladders in the chambers and ample bollards, tend to make navigation simpler than on many British rivers. Secondhand gates were salvaged from the Bridgewater Canal's abandoned Runcorn Flight, from the Thames Conservancy and from London's Surrey Canal, and paddle gear was supplied without charge in many cases by a Sheffield foundry. The gates of George Billington and Stratford Locks are operated by ex-Thames paddle machinery mounted sideways. For all the mixture of gear, however, these Upper Avon locks possess a distinctly pleasing functional appearance. While possession of a navigation chart and instructions from the UANT is advisable, an excellent system of signboards indicates which part of the channel has been dredged and where the lock cuts begin. George Billington Lock stands near a ford by the Fish and Anchor Inn near Harvington. Knowing that he had little time to live, Mr Billington gave his life savings of £5,000 to enable the lock to be constructed. It was built between 1 November and 15 December 1969 and a plaque marks the generosity of its donor. Another plaque on the bridge spanning the upper cut reads: 'In memory of William Smith of Evesham, 1830–1906, who fought hard for the restoration of the Upper Avon.'

*Harvington Lock* (Robert Aickman Lock, 30m 2f)   A pretty reach of river with wooded hills on the right leads to the first lock to be built by the UANT near the site of the old Harvington Upper Lock. Before work began, the only section of original lock gate remaining on the river was discovered caught by the trunk of a willow tree. A track leads to Harvington village, where the former railway station is Trust HQ. A ruined watermill and open weir are very reminiscent of Ireland's River Barrow. A broad reach now follows, its thick trees and undergrowth providing an almost tropical atmosphere.

*Marlcliffe Lock* (Inland Waterways Association Lock, 32m 4f)   A long and substantial ridge, some distance to the right at Harvington, gradually approaches the river, finally forming a steep cliff, which rises from the water. A short distance above a caravan site (left bank) at Salford Priors, offering moorings and other facilities and well-screened from the water by a high bank, can be seen the remains of the old diamond-shaped Cleeve Lock. This part of the waterway must be as remote and beautiful as on any river in Britain, and there are many occasions when, from the deck of a cruiser, it is difficult to see any signs of human activity apart from occasional field fences. Huge quantities of spoil had to be removed from the river bed to provide adequate water depth. After the junction with the River Arrow (left) as Marlcliffe Lock is approached, these problems became almost insuperable, for the exceptionally hard marl clay defeated conventional dragline methods of dredging, and the army was called in to use explosives. The lock (right bank) and approach channels have been built partly into the face of the cliff; at the upper end an overhead gantry is a sluice-gate used in connection with the weir alongside. A swing bridge spans the chamber, as at Harvington, to provide vehicle access to the weir. Although the navigation lacks a towpath throughout, it is possible to walk along the right bank to Marlcliffe village about 1m from the lock.

*Bidford-on-Avon* (33m 4f)   One of the first indications of the town is a gasholder screened by trees on the left bank, but that apart, it is a really pretty little place. It has become quite popular as a riverside resort where small craft can be launched from a public park. Shortly below the largely fifteenth-century 9-arched bridge was a former navigation weir, but all remains have been removed. The navigation arch, instead of being the largest central opening, is a smaller one on the right bank, selected as machine access was easier to lower the foundations 6ft. Work was mainly completed by prisoners from Gloucester Gaol, who constituted the major and most regular labour force for the whole restoration. After a session at the Falcon Inn, Shakespeare

*Shakespeare's Avon. The fine old stone bridge at Bidford with the Georgian White Lion Inn*

credited Bidford with the adjective 'drunken'. The Falcon is now a private residence sympathetically restored in local stone, but pubs remain in plenty, including the White Lion, said to have been founded by nine monks in return for their each having constructed one arch of the bridge. In the bar a decorative advertisement of 1888 establishes that the village was then a boating resort, with accommodation and full board at £2 per week. The main street, excellent for shopping, is composed of a delightful range of fifteenth- and sixteenth-century Cotswold stone houses, features good half-timbering, and there are later terraces of chequered brickwork. Much of the detail of mullioned windows, doorways and chimneys is very fine. Aware of the need to preserve and restore the essential character of the village, Warwickshire County Council has published an excellent illustrated booklet, *Bidford-on-Avon Design and Materials for the Locality*. Perhaps the best view is from across the river towards the haphazard jumble of gables and chimneys of cottages and shops backing on to the water. The fourth lock of the Upper Avon is at Barton, about ½ mile upstream of Bidford bridge (E. and H. Billington Lock).

*Pilgrim Lock* (35m 3f)   Originally Bidford Grange, the lock's name was changed to commemorate the Pilgrim Trust, which financed the construction costs. Unlike others on the waterway, it is built with concrete blocks, reinforced with steel bars and backfilled with concrete.

*Welford-on-Avon* (37m 1f)   The river skirts the foot of a line of hills, right, rising to 269ft, and in so doing describes a great loop. Welford lies in the peninsula thus formed. The village is one of two of that name on the Warwickshire Avon, the other being served by a branch of the Grand Union's Leicester Section many miles upstream. Like other settlements in the Shakespeare Country, there are many pretty cottages and small houses, some thatched, and an abiding rural atmosphere. At the downstream end of the river's loop is W. A. Cadbury Lock, another structure which acknowledges its donor. This was built during 1971, when layers of rock caused problems while the steel piling of the chamber was driven. The original navigation works at Welford consisted of two locks, ½m apart, the lower one with a rise of just 1ft 9in. Sections of the stonework could be seen in the river bed before restoration began.

*Binton Bridges* (38m)   A minor road between Welford and Binton is carried over the river by a long bridge consisting of two sections, each of 6 arches, leading to a central island. There is a useful public house on the south bank.

*Luddington* (39m 5f)   Formerly there were two locks, the upper one having a circular chamber 75ft in diameter. Now there is just one, whose secondhand steel piles, erected in three layers of rock, needed many hours of work with heavy pneumatic hammers before they could be driven to the required depth. Luddington itself, reached up a track left of the lock, is a straggling little village, virtually a suburb of Stratford.

*Weir Brake Lock* (41m 6f)   The last lock to be built, this is situated just below the confluence with the unnavigable River Stour. There were many problems in the course of its construction, including extensive rock slabs in the river, whose level could not be raised to its original height because of orders to the contrary from the local drainage authority. For several months at the end of 1973 a short section of earth at the entrance to the lock's approach channel was intentionally and symbolically left in position until such time as the UANT's exhausted funds were replenished from private donations. The history of the Upper Avon's 5-year reconstruction as a navigable waterway, almost without any official or Government aid, in many respects mirrored the efforts of the canal-building companies of 200 years earlier. Tactful negotiations had to be conducted with landowners for vehicle access and the use of waterside fields to dispose of dredgings, the river authority repeatedly presented difficulties in spite of the new works greatly improving drainage, and finally the borough of Stratford scarcely accorded its full official support, although the town is more than pleased with the end product and the reality of visiting boats coming up from the Severn.

*Stratford* (44m)   The approach to the town is as pleasant as is the course of the waterway from Evesham. Until late Victorian times Lucy's Lock, bearing the name of a local milling family, was a two-rise staircase. The new structure is situated immediately upstream of a disused railway bridge on the right bank. During driving of the steel-piled chamber, the very unstable surrounds threatened to push the walls inwards, and as a matter of great urgency, a series of steel portal frames, or arches, were erected above the lock. The rise and fall is 11ft 6in, twice the average lift of an Avon lock. The sides are planted with trees and landscaped as a feature of the municipal recreation ground. Opposite, across the water, is the great spire of Holy Trinity church, containing Shakespeare's tomb.

The river is alive in summer with rowing boats, swans and tripping launches. Since the reopening of the Southern Stratford Canal in 1964 (see p 406) and the official inauguration of the Upper Avon, also by Queen Elizabeth the Queen Mother, almost exactly a decade later on 1 June 1974, local craft have mingled with those from much further afield. The Shakespeare Memorial Theatre, dominating the river, is very much a part of the Stratford waterfront. Its architecture of red brick and steel window frames is unmistakably in the grand cinema tradition of the early 1930s. Past the lock providing access to the Bancroft Basin and start of the canal, the river flows beneath a brick bridge with 9 arches, built in 1823 for the Stratford–Moreton horse tramway. This is immediately followed by Sir Hugh Clopton's lovely stone road bridge (c1480), with 14 pointed arches remaining of an original 19. Navigation is possible for a further 3½m to Alveston Weir, the river becoming gradually more peaceful as the town and its tourists are left astern. Undoubtedly Stratford's waterway is at its best during a midsummer sunrise. Twelve miles beyond Alveston the river flows beneath an aqueduct of the Grand Union Canal above Warwick Castle; a most commendable dream that is by no means impossible would be to tame this length of river and construct locks or a lift to connect with the canal. Thus, a broad beam waterway route between Thames and Severn would be created. Meanwhile, the Upper Avon Navigation Trust, in the 5 years to 1974, has moved around 1 million tons of rock and silt, built 9 brand new locks and 5 weirs and added many miles of remarkably beautiful waterway to the network. To date this is the most outstanding waterway restoration feat completed in Britain by a privately supported body.

### BASINGSTOKE CANAL

From the Wey Navigation at West Byfleet to the east end of Greywell Tunnel, near North Warnborough, Hampshire; 31m with 29 locks. Maximum craft dimensions are 72ft 6in × 13ft 6in × 3ft 6in draught (the 'official' figure, but in reality it is often considerably less at present) × 7ft 6in headroom from the Wey to Fleet, and 5ft beyond. At the time of writing, the whole canal is in a state of near dereliction, and indeed has been in poor condition for much of the twentieth century. It has been owned by a succession of private concerns, among them a company in which Horatio Bottomley, MP, was prominent in the first decade of this century, and more recently the New Basingstoke Canal Co, which bought the waterway in 1949. Until the early 1950s the Basingstoke was navigable (with difficulty) to Greywell Tunnel, and indeed commercial timber traffic continued to Woking until 1949. Since that time all locks have fallen into disrepair and the channel has become badly silted.

Following an influential campaign for restoration by the Surrey & Hampshire Canal Society, the two county councils concerned have taken over their respective portions of the waterway by compulsory purchase and once more there is every prospect of the navigation being reopened as far as the collapsed Greywell Tunnel. The original line continued for a further 6¼m to Basingstoke itself.

In an area otherwise lacking in recreational water facilities, the Basingstoke when restored will be of great value, for it passes through fine country, with heathlands and pine trees.

*Woodham*  Leaving the River Wey beyond New Haw Lock, the canal passes through a flight of 6 locks. A large number of residential boats were introduced in the late 1950s and their movement involved occasional operation of the locks throughout the 1960s. Thirty craft, narrow boats and barges among them, were able to assemble for an IWA rally in Woking at Easter 1962, and several navigated as far as Goldsworth Bottom Lock, 5m from the Wey.

*Woking* (3m 7f)  An expanding town at the heart of a residential part of Surrey. The revitalised canal should become one of its most attractive features.

*Goldsworth Locks* (5m 2f)  A series of 6 locks marks the beginning of the really attractive part of the waterway. Housing development decreases and the banks are covered with a wide variety of trees and rhododendrons.

*Brookwood* (7m 3f)  Three more locks in the vicinity of Brookwood Hospital bring the canal to the 150ft contour.

*Frimley Locks* (8m 5f)  The canal's major flight begins at Pirbright, with 14 locks in just under 2m. Together they overcome a change in levels of 90ft. The scenery continues thickly wooded.

*Mytchett* (13m 2f)  A deep cutting gives the name of Deepcut to the district. After an impressive 4-arched aqueduct, rebuilt in 1900, over the London–Southampton railway, the waterway enters the north side of Mytchett Lake, which is followed in turn by a series of smaller flashes. Here the Basingstoke is perhaps at its most delightful.

*Ash* (16m)  The single lock marks the beginning of the long pound that continues to the terminus.

*Aldershot* (17m 6f)   Army land consisting largely of heathland and pine trees is
characteristic of this Hampshire section. Then comes the boundary of the Royal
Aircraft Establishment at Farnborough.

*Fleet* (21m 5f)   This end of the canal possesses a number of waterside inns at
Crookham, Grubb's Farm Bridge, Winchfield, Odiham and North Warnborough.
There are several attractive red-brick bridges near Odiham and beautiful stretches of
completely rural countryside.

*North Warnborough* (30m 1f)   Here is a curious wide-beam bascule bridge, which
replaced a swing span in 1954. Operation of the hydraulic lever-operated machinery
takes up to 45 minutes.

*Greywell Tunnel* (31m 1f)   The derelict tunnel, 1,200yd long, is approached by a
shady cutting. Restoration of the canal will cease here. Another shorter tunnel follows
in the overgrown course of the waterway, and filling in has taken place at several points.
The line of the canal becomes progressively more difficult to trace as it approaches
Basingstoke. The former terminal basin, predictably enough, is now a bus station,
recalling similar 'improvements' that have been made to other waterways, including
the Oxford Canal at Banbury and the Kennet & Avon in Newbury.

### BEVERLEY BECK

From Beverley, Yorks, to the River Hull at Grove Hill; ¾m with 1 lock. Maximum
craft dimensions are 65ft × 17ft 6in × 6ft 6in draught.

This short navigation was opened in 1731, and like other waterways in the area was
used by sailing keels. It is still a commercial route, operated by the local corporation.
The chief attribute of Beverley Beck for pleasure craft is in providing a safe mooring
off the tidal River Hull. Beverley is the capital of the East Riding, and boasts one of the
finest churches in the country – the Minster, of cathedral proportions, built between
the thirteenth and fifteenth centuries. Always an important trading centre, it has an
impressive market place, a wealth of old buildings and one of five town gates that were
originally equipped with drawbridges.

### BIRMINGHAM CANAL NAVIGATIONS

If the canal and river network of England is considered as an untidy spider's web,
its most closely woven centre is the BCN. Serving Birmingham and the Black Country
within an area bounded in the north by Wolverhampton and Cannock and extending
southwards to near Stourbridge and Birmingham itself, there were no fewer than 160m
by the mid-nineteenth century. Today about 100m remain, and the long and depressing succession of closures that have been brought about by mining subsidence and
decreasing commercial traffic is now certainly at an end. The BCN is composed of a
union of several routes, the first being the Birmingham Canal from Birmingham to
Wednesbury, opened in 1769. In an area utterly devoid of rivers that could be made
navigable, the BCN spread its web to serve coalmines and in turn attracted great con-
centrations of heavy industry along its banks. At its greatest extent there were 212
narrow locks, more than 550 private side basins serving factories, 3 exceptionally long
tunnels (Dudley, Netherton and Lappal), and numerous bridges, aqueducts, pumping
stations, railway interchange basins, maintenance yards, cottages and other structures.

*Birmingham Canal Navigations. A refurbished lock keeper's house on the Birmingham & Fazeley Canal at Farmer's Bridge, seen from the terrace of the Longboat Inn*

What now survives constitutes the most concentrated and vivid reminder of urban canal navigations in Britain.

As late as 1888 the BCN transported nearly 8 million tons of goods annually. Even in the early 1950s about 1 million tons a year remained. Much was short haul, in trains of utilitarian 'day boats', worked by men who went home ashore each night. Without its teeming traffic, the BCN is a changed place today. It is down at heel, with daisies and willowherb along the horse-less towpaths, junk obstructing the less frequently navigated bridge holes, scum and timber on the water, and abandoned working boats quietly rotting. But a wealth of ironwork, ribbed courses of brick where the towpaths rise at each lock, signposts, bollards and lamp brackets, which recall a vanished period of 24-hour working, are all there.

The BCN means lonely bonfires of oil-soaked timber and tyres blazing unattended on the cobbles of a lockside, a shaft of sunlight striking the pea-soup water deep between the fastnesses of derelict warehouses, or fresh dung from the last working narrow-boat horse to remain on English canals. Stray from the city centres, and the outlying parts of the BCN are astonishingly rural: for example, the red sandstone cuttings of the Tame Valley Canal and the Birmingham & Fazeley Canal at Curdworth.

Aesthetically attractive though it is in its near-Gothic melancholia, the BCN's future lies very much in restrained development for leisure use. Gas Street Basin and Farmer's Bridge, Birmingham, are two areas successfully revitalised to serve as a popular point of introduction for a public that otherwise would know little of the miles of tranquil waterside walks available. In Wolverhampton, up the Titford Canal, and at the Park Head approach to Dudley Tunnel, landscaping has made places of real beauty from derelict wastes. This revitalisation will undoubtedly expand and blossom, as one local authority learns lessons from its neighbour. Let us hope that not all the wild unkempt places become too municipalised and orderly.

A week's continuous cruising is offered by the BCN, with splendid opportunities for circular routes. This is the only real way of exploring Birmingham and the Black Country. John Smith, the leading waterways and countryside benefactor, wrote: 'Those who think there is nothing left to discover should go to Birmingham from any-where, by boat.' The BCN, with its numerous connections, makes that journey possible.

The BCN is mainly situated on three levels – the Walsall at 408ft, the Birmingham at 453ft, and the Wolverhampton at 473ft. The approach by canal to the West Midlands plateau is via several series of locks, including flights at Wolverhampton, Lapworth, Curdworth and Stourbridge. Rising via six locks at Oldbury, the Titford Canal reaches a height of 511ft above sea level, making it the highest navigation still open to boats in Britain. In its original complete form the network was supplied with water by 6 reservoirs and no fewer than 17 supply or recirculating pumping stations. Maximum dimensions for craft using the BCN are 71ft × 7ft × 3ft 6in draught. Headroom is normally 8ft 6in, but is reduced in places to 6ft 6in.

*The Birmingham–Wolverhampton Main Line*
This is the most direct and convenient link for craft travelling from the Northern Stratford and Worcester & Birmingham Canals to the Staffs & Worcs and Shropshire Union Canals. It begins at Gas Street Basin, Birmingham, near the City Centre. Still known as Worcester Bar, as a result of a physical stone barrier over which goods had to be transhipped until opening of a stop lock in 1815, the basin is a remarkably colour-ful and attractive stretch of urban water, surrounded by nineteenth-century canal cottages and warehouses. Numbers of narrow boats, converted and unconverted, moor here. The City Council has proposed a multi-million-pound scheme to develop part of the site, with offices, housing and leisure facilities, and these plans could not help but change the present unique character of the area. The canal dives into a bridge hole of tunnel-like proportions beneath Broad Street and the Church of the Messiah. This is the most convenient mooring for the city centre (although beware the noise from a canalside night club). During the 1960s and early 1970s Birmingham was substantially rebuilt, a process which continues. Fast roads and high-rise blocks predominate. Even residents experience difficulty in finding their way about. There are many notable public buildings from the last century and later, including the temple-like Town Hall, the classical Council House, the City Museum and Art Gallery (all nineteenth-century); the Hall of Memory and Municipal Bank (between the Wars); and New Street Station and the Bull Ring, its cylindrical Rotunda towering to 24 storeys (both from the 1960s). The atmosphere of Birmingham is exciting if rather troubled. One place of great interest to canal users is likely to be the Museum of Science & Industry in Newhall Street, where exhibits reflect much of the varied influences that have made Birmingham what it is.

The canal leaves Gas Street between cavernous brick walls with grassy towpaths. This line has twin paths for much of the route, with blue-brick banks to the canal edges, both factors recalling the former intense volume of traffic. Many overhead bridges are double-arched. Keep right when travelling towards Wolverhampton, as the left arches are frequently obstructed. The Birmingham & Fazeley Canal shortly branches to the right, leading to Farmer's Bridge and Cambrian Wharf. Opposite, left, is the Oozells Street Loop, one of many short circular lines either constructed to serve as water or traffic feeders or remaining as backwaters after improvements to reduce the length of the through route. Another loop, the Soho, soon follows on the right; while the subject of considerable volunteer clearance effort, its condition unfortunately fluctuates with the activities of local vandals.

The area, while densely urbanised at the approach to Smethwick, is fortunate in having the peaceful haven of its canal, where trees and flowers grow wild on the banks of cuttings. Three locks, right, take the traveller up to the older Wolverhampton Level, while the Main Line continues, soon to pass beneath a canal flyover in the form of an aqueduct carrying the Engine Branch 20ft above. A deep cutting now follows, spanned by Telford's superb cast-iron Galton Bridge, a lacy affair, with a span of 150ft, dating from 1829. It is scheduled as an ancient monument, but unfortunately its setting and scale are being badly disrupted by further ubiquitous new road bridges. A new Galton Tunnel, 123yd long, 16ft wide and 17ft 6in high, has filled the centre of the cutting since 1974.

Passing again beneath an aqueduct of the Old Main Line at Spon Lane (Steward Aqueduct) and the lofty M5 motorway, the waterway makes a series of junctions. In order they are Spon Lane (where three locks rise to the Wolverhampton Level); Pudding Green, right, start of the Walsall Canal; Albion, left, linking via three locks, including a 2-rise staircase, with the Old Main Line; and Dudley Port, left, turn-off for Netherton Tunnel. Just beyond the new Ryland Aqueduct in concrete has a clear span of 80ft, with road traffic headroom of about 23ft. It was built in 1967–8 at a cost of £170,000 and replaced the original Telford structure from which a large nameplate is preserved at Stoke Bruerne. Between Pudding Green and Tipton the route is wide, straight and rather dull.

At Factory Three Locks, Tipton, the canal ascends 20ft to join the Wolverhampton Level, with the Old Main Line entering left. Features of note are the centrally 'split' bridge over the tail of the bottom lock, a fine but decaying canal stable block, a boatmen's chapel (now a factory), and, at the lower end of the flight, one of a number of surviving cast-iron BCN boundary posts. The ornate iron Factory Bridge itself has been removed for preservation to the Black Country Museum nearby (see p 196).

Coseley Tunnel, Deepfields, has a generously wide bore and twin towpaths along its 360yd length. Beyond, at Anchor Bridge, is one of the last narrow-boat yards still operating on the BCN on its original site and specialising in the building and repair of wooden craft. The demise of commercial traffic has resulted in its production being geared solely to the pleasure-boat trade. Deepfields Junction, right, marks the start of the Wednesbury Oak Loop, now a 2m stub left from the first canal to Birmingham, which avoided Coseley Hill. At its terminus stands Bradley Workshops, a maintenance yard where lock gates are built and where a remarkable cradle-dock enables narrow boats to be tipped on their sides for access to the bottom when repairs are necessary.

Now approaching the outskirts of Wolverhampton, the waterway is dominated by the giant Bilston Steel Works, which has the last surviving blast furnace in the Black Country. After Horseley Fields Junction, right, the beginning of the Wyrley & Essington Canal, comes the centre of Wolverhampton. Although still heavily industrial, the area is being landscaped in a way that should make the most of this waterside situation. Wolverhampton, 'Capital of the Black Country', was first recorded in a royal charter of 985. Its impressive church of St Peter in red sandstone retains portions built in 1205, with a notable fifteenth-century tower and carved stone pulpit. Local industries, including locksmiths' work, japanning, cut steel and porcelain, are prominent in the collection housed in the municipal museum and art gallery in Lichfield Street. Like Smethwick and other towns of the West Midlands, Wolverhampton now has a large Asian population. A flight of 21 narrow locks evenly spread over almost 2m epitomises the contrasts of BCN scenery – grimily urban in the town centre and almost completely rural past the racecourse at its lower end. By the time Aldersley Junction and the Staffs & Worcs Canal is reached at the bottom of the flight, the fascinating concentration of industrial development, almost endless since Birmingham, has been replaced by woods and green banks.

### The Old Main Line

This is a useful alternative direct route between Birmingham and Wolverhampton and offering greater interest than the section of New Main Line it duplicates between Smethwick and Tipton. After its 20ft climb through the 3 duplicated Smethwick Locks, the canal reaches a left fork – the Engine Arm – which crosses the New Main Line via Telford Aqueduct, a richly decorated Gothic structure in cast iron with stone abutments. Built as a feeder, the branch terminated from 1778 at the first Boulton & Watt steam engine installed by the Birmingham Canal Co. After 120 years work on that site, the engine was transferred to Ocker Hill to lift water supplies from disused mine workings. During the 1950s it ceased operations, and is now in store at Birmingham's Museum of Science and Industry.

Passing through Oldbury – where there are some extraordinary views of the M5 motorway whose supports stand on the canal banks and even in the navigation channel for a considerable distance – the Old Main Line veers left along a flyover crossing the New, with access to the lower waterway through Spon Lane Locks, straight ahead. A junction at Oldbury, left, marks the start of the short Titford Canal, reached through a flight of six locks known as 'The Crow'. Water supplies enter the Titford from Rotton Park Reservoir. A major industrial building on the canalside is the Langley Maltings, whose future is to some degree assured by a preservation order. The line terminates amid motorway development at Titford Pool. Local authority landscaping has much improved the immediate area.

Continuing parallel with the New Main Line and connecting with it at Bradeshall Junction via Brades Locks and the short Gower Branch, the waterway makes another flyover crossing, this time spanning the Netherton Tunnel Branch, with a good view of the huge tunnel portal below on the left. In Tipton there is a junction with the Dudley Canal near the NE portal of Dudley Tunnel. The canal then terminates at Factory Junction, where the direct route to Wolverhampton continues via the New Main Line.

### Dudley Canals

There are two. The Dudley Canal Line 1, 4½m, connects the Old Main Line at Tipton with the Stourbridge Canal at the bottom of Delph Locks. This section includes the famous Dudley Tunnel. The Dudley Canal Line 2, about 5½m, runs from Park Head Junction (southern end of Dudley Tunnel) past the south portal of Netherton Tunnel at Windmill End Junction to a present terminus at Coombeswood Basin, Halesowen. Until 1917 the canal continued through Britain's fourth longest tunnel at Lappal (3,795yd) to join the Worcester & Birmingham Canal at Selly Oak. Part of the tunnel collapsed, however, and it was never rebuilt.

No 1 Line, opened in 1792, is mainly notable for the tunnel that bores under the town of Dudley and its castle, taking in en route some remarkable limestone caverns (see p 81). Since its reopening to boats in 1973, engines have been prohibited because of a possible danger from fumes. Crews must therefore resort to legging (p 77) or poling. At the Tipton approach, the Black Country Museum occupies a waterside site at the intersection with Lord Ward's Branch Canal (p 196). Dudley is one of the finest towns in the Midlands, built around the craggy hill on which stands the Norman Castle. There is a good zoo in the castle grounds. The area is of considerable geological interest, being a centre for fossils.

At the southern end of the 3,172yd narrow-beam tunnel, through which a trip boat of the Dudley Canal Trust operates at certain times, lies a broad sweep of landscaped open land and the three Park Head Locks. This area was improved for the tunnel reopening in 1973 as a joint exercise by the local authority, the BWB and volunteers. Beyond Blower's Green Lock the Two Lock Line provided a short cut between No 1 and No 2 canals until 1909, when it fell into disuse after severe subsidence problems. The locality is now quite open and pleasant, but it was subjected to much mining and other industrial activity over several centuries. The No 1 Line joins the Stourbridge Canal at the foot of Black Delph Locks, which are still known as The Nine although rebuilt as a flight of eight in 1857–8. Each boasts a rocky vertical overflow waterfall.

No 2 Line, completed in 1798, forms part of the through route from Netherton Tunnel to the Stourbridge Canal. A notable feature is the vast Round Oak Steel Works at Brierley Hill. Near Windmill End Junction, up the Bumblehole Branch, stands one of the few pleasure craft yards on the BCN. Further local-authority landscaping has

*Birmingham Canal Navigations. A working boat nears the end of the cavernous Netherton Tunnel, completed in 1858* (Bill Kennedy)

been completed or is proposed around this point. The 577yd Gosty Hill Tunnel is narrow beam and in parts has an unusually tall cross-section. There are the remains of a covered dock for the former tunnel tug at the NW end. On leaving the far end of the tunnel, the canal passes through the heart of Coombeswood Tube Works, where a large number of day boats are still used for movement of pipes within the factory. Also surviving is the Works' narrow-boat repair yard, with side slip and protective canopy mounted on wheels to provide shelter while carrying out maintenance to the fleet. The great cluster of craft offers a vivid impression of what most of the BCN was like in the days of its full commercial use. The line ends at Coombeswood Basin, a now derelict railway interchange depot, with covered quays, which remained in use until closure of the railway in the mid-1960s.

Netherton Tunnel Line, between Windmill End and the New Main Line at Dudley Port, although not technically part of the Dudley Canal, is most conveniently mentioned here. The 3,027yd tunnel was the last major canal bore to be built in Britain (opened in 1858), and it also has the biggest cross-section (see p 82).

## Birmingham & Fazeley Canal

Providing an important entry route to the BCN, it runs from Farmer's Bridge Junction, Birmingham, via Salford (Spaghetti) Junction, to Fazeley, where it meets the Coventry Canal (p 274). With a length of 15m, it has 38 locks.

At Cambrian Wharf, Birmingham, a Midlands canal showpiece was completed for the bicentenary of the Birmingham Canal in 1969. In a joint exercise between the City Architect's Department and the BWB derelict warehouses were demolished and the Longboat Inn built on their site, incorporating a strong canals theme. Several original canal cottages in Kingston Row were completely restored. One is now occupied by British Waterways as an information centre and canal shop. The stark contrast between the scale of the waterways structures and nearby municipal high-rise blocks of flats is far from happy, although the housing greatly benefits from its association with the canal. A flight of 13 locks falls away from the Birmingham Level in the first mile. Surroundings are thickly industrial, although recent redevelopment has removed some of the soaring black-brick walls that once gave an intense quality of secrecy to a route traditionally known as 'The Bottom Road'. Many bridges span the canal, most fitted with red-painted wooden doors in their parapets to enable the Fire Service to draw water. The Museum of Science & Industry, a huge tunnel-like cavern containing a lock under the platforms of the disused Snow Hill Station, and the Birmingham GPO Tower, are among the sights to be seen. At Aston Junction the mile-long Digbeth Branch forks to the right through 6 Ashted Locks and the short Curzon Street Tunnel, to connect with the Grand Union Canal at Bordesley Junction. The Birmingham & Fazeley continues, with another 11 locks in the Aston Flight extending almost to Salford Junction. This is a weird intersection, with the unnavigable River Tame at the lowest level and two canal aqueducts crossing it. Left is the Tame Valley Canal and sharp right the beginning of the Grand Union. The waterways are subjected to the constant shadow and roar of Britain's most complex motorway interchange, twisting at multiple levels overhead. Opened in 1972, it is universally known as Spaghetti Junction.

Scenery continues to be industrial, with cooling towers, a succession of factories, and the M6 motorway elevated on the right. Shortly after Salford Junction the canal is completely roofed over for 200yd by a factory supported on concrete beams. Then, right, is the Fort Dunlop Works. There are 3 locks at Minworth, the highest generally affected by a pall of smoke from the seemingly everlasting bonfire used to dispose of the piles of oily timber and refuse that collect by the upper gates. In the first pound a particularly welcome factory landscaping, using lawns and ivy, much improves the canal frontage of the Cincinnati Works. As the bottom lock is reached, urbanisation finally ceases, and for its last 8m the canal is mainly very attractive and quite unlike the popular conception of a BCN waterway.

Curdworth (9m 4f) survives intact as a small village, with its part-Norman church of St Nicholas. A shallow cutting leads up to the narrow Curdworth Tunnel, 57yd, built with towpath and curiously bearing a request that 'Boats should Keep to the Right'. Craft other than canoes would experience difficulty in deciding whether they were on either right or left! Amid fine country, disturbed at times by the closeness of a busy road, the canal descends through 11 locks. There are some pleasant groups of BCN cottages, like those at the Bottom Lock, numbered 257–60 and bearing an iron date plaque MDCCCXX. As is general practice throughout the BCN, bridges bear nameplates rather than numbers. The Dog and Doublet public house stands beside the third lock from the bottom of the flight, offering the possibility of a welcome pause for refreshment.

Drayton Bassett (14m) has a Manor Park and zoo, open daily and Sundays only in the winter. Sir Robert Peel lived there. The proximity of the Park undoubtedly explains the folly-like Gothic footbridge spanning the canal, with spiral brick stairways and a swing deck as well. There is nothing quite like it anywhere else. Arriving at Fazeley and the Coventry Canal, a place that lives under the constant strain of the roaring A5 Watling Street, the Birmingham & Fazeley completes its course at a T-junction, overlooked by a dignified red-brick double-fronted canal house.

*Tame Valley Canal*

Almost last to be built in Britain, the Tame Valley arrived in 1844 to provide an alternative to the congested Farmer's Bridge/Salford Junction section of the Birmingham & Fazeley. It is 8m 4f long, and there are 13 locks in a flight at Perry Barr. It connects Salford Junction with the Walsall Canal at Tame Valley Junction, and is joined midway by the Rushall Canal. Compared with the first 'modern' canals of 80 years earlier, the Tame Valley is of sophisticated construction, with twin towpaths, brick-lined banks and cuttings that are both deep and wide.

After an industrial start the canal is accompanied for most of the Perry Barr Locks by Perry Park. Above the Top Lock more open surroundings and a red sandstone cutting gradually give way to a mile-long embankment providing extensive views over a partly suburban area near West Bromwich. After Piercy and Spouthouse Aqueducts comes a deep sandstone cutting crossed by 2 bridges at a very considerable height. Rushall Junction, right, is dominated first by the M5 link road and then by the M6, which is itself crossed by a new concrete aqueduct, protected against the possibility of leaks by stop gates. Further aqueducts span a railway and a road. Now in West Bromwich, the Tame Valley commands a wide view from its embankment. It represents a broad strip of undeveloped land in an otherwise urban area. The final length of the waterway is straight and not particularly noteworthy through Wednesbury. It joins the Walsall Canal at Tame Valley Junction, which is dominated by the massive Ocker Hill Power Station, with four tall chimneys and three cooling towers.

## Walsall Canal

From Walsall to Ryder's Green Junction the canal is linked at its northern end via the Walsall Branch to the Wyrley & Essington, and from Ryder's Green Junction to Pudding Green Junction on the New Main Line (Birmingham Level) by a section of the Wednesbury Old Canal. Taken as a whole, this line stretches 8m 5f, with 2 flights each of 8 locks at Ryder's Green and Walsall. There are several short arms and many side basins, with a rich collection of cast-iron bridges and other canal relics. Surroundings are mainly industrial. One very useful connection was via the Toll End Locks from Tipton to near Tame Valley Junction, but this section was closed about 1960. A derelict building at Walsall Top Lock bears the stone-carved inscription 'Boatman's Rest 1900', and was one of many missions or institutes throughout the canals. It is certainly deserving of preservation.

## Wyrley & Essington Canal

One of the most rural sections of the BCN, the Wyrley & Essington provides the northern perimeter of the system. Completed in 1797, it runs from the Main Line at Horseley Fields Junction, Wolverhampton, past the Walsall Branch and the Cannock Extension to Catshill Junction and the Daw End Branch. Here it turns left to Ogley Junction, with the Anglesey Branch continuing to Chasewater reservoir. Until 1954 the W&E ran beyond Ogley to pass through 30 locks before arriving at Huddlesford, junction with the Coventry Canal. Little remains of this eastern portion but a few hundred yards at Huddlesford. Its loss was singularly unfortunate. The remaining portion is 16m 3f long and is lock-free, making it possible to reach Smethwick, Oldbury and Dudley, all on the Wolverhampton Level, without passing through a single lock.

A major traffic of the W&E was coal from the Cannock pits. Boats were gauged for toll purposes at a number of 'narrows' formed by islands in the middle of the channel. Originally many had octagonal toll-houses. One such island occurs near Horseley Fields Junction, and another at Wednesfield Junction, where the Bentley Canal falls away via 6 locks, the only part still navigable. Until about 1961 the Bentley connected with the Walsall Canal via the Anson Branch. Sneyd Junction, Short Heath, is the location of another lost canal, the Sneyd & Wyrley Bank Branch. A canal maintenance yard overlooks the very sharp bend. Beyond Birchills Junction (with the Walsall Branch) and through Little Bloxwich, one may find some of the most pleasant scenery of the entire BCN, especially at Pelsall Heath, where the Cannock Extension Canal heads due north, as straight as an arrow. The Cannock Extension appeared as late as 1858 and ran for almost 6m to Hednesford Basins. Severe subsidence from the coalmines reached a peak in July 1960, when, during a single week, the canal bed fell 21ft and the banks had to be rebuilt as the water threatened to burst over the top. At this date there was still heavy coal traffic, but 3 years later the northern portion beyond the A5 was closed completely and little now remains. A further vanished connection was the Churchbridge Canal from Rumour Hill Junction to Churchbridge and thence to the Staffs & Worcs Canal via the Hatherton Branch; this was abandoned in 1955. There are three busy yards near the present terminus of the Cannock Extension at Norton Canes, all specialising in pleasure narrow-boat building and repair. The heathland scenery is very pleasant, although it is a bleak area in winter.

The 1½m spur leaving the W&E at Ogley Junction is the Anglesey Branch, again rural and extending to the large park that surrounds Chasewater Reservoir, a noted powerboat racing lake. Coal traffic from Anglesey Basin ceased only in 1967.

## Rushall Canal and Daw End Branch

From Rushall Junction on the Tame Valley Canal to Longwood and Catshill Junctions, Wyrley & Essington Canal; 8m with 9 locks in the Rushall Flight. This section includes some pleasant semi-open country beyond a vast M6 motorway embankment at Rushall, with extensive views across the Black Country. A short arm at Longwood provides permanent pleasure-boat moorings. The Daw (pronounced 'Doe') End Branch can show some high embankments, an industrial estate at Aldridge and much evidence of mining subsidence through Walsall Wood to Catshill, where the surrounding terrain has fallen away from the now elevated waterway.

## BLYTH, RIVER

From the Suffolk Coast to Blythburgh; 5m with no locks. Promoted under an Act of 1757, it ran for a further 2m to Halesworth, with 5 locks, but these were closed to navigation in 1934. The four lower ones incorporated galley beams in their structure, like those on the Suffolk Stour. Craft using the remaining tidal section are unlimited by length and beam. Maximum draught to Blythburgh at high water is 4ft with a headroom of 6ft. The course of the river is through marshes, with a broad stretch of saltings at Blythburgh. This medieval town has a magnificent church of the Holy Trinity, mid-fifteenth century, with tower of about 1330.

## BRECON & ABERGAVENNY CANAL

Now an isolated waterway of $33\frac{1}{4}$m and 6 locks, running from Brecon to Pontymoile, junction with the derelict Monmouthshire Canal.

This is indisputably one of the most attractive cruising waterways in Britain. Throughout it lies within the Brecon Beacons National Park, closely following the valley of the River Usk. There is an utter lack of any kind of commercialism and even the boatyards are more thoughtfully planned and restrained than is usual. There are two reasons for the canal's survival in a completely rural state. First, unlike the Monmouthshire Canal to the south, which served a growingly industrial area, the Brecon ceased to be important as a freight carrier by about 1870. Second, since establishment of the National Park in 1957, stringent planning controls have been able to keep a close watch on any developments that might impair the visual beauty of the region.

The Brecon & Abergavenny was built between 1797 and 1812 to the design of Thomas Dadford, junior, also engineer of the Monmouthshire. The B&A was bought by the Monmouthshire in 1865, mainly to safeguard water supplies brought from the Usk at Brecon to feed both waterways. The two canals passed into Great Western Railway Co ownership in 1880 and were nationalised in 1948. A joint restoration programme to improve the then rather indifferent condition of the B&A was completed in 1970 by Monmouthshire and Brecon County Councils and the British Waterways Board. Nearly 7m between Talybont and Brecon were reconnected with the rest of the line by constructing a new bascule bridge and reopening Brynich Lock. (In consequence of this cooperation the canal is now sometimes known as the Monmouthshire & Brecon.)

One characteristic of the B&A is the remains of an extensive network of horsedrawn waggon ways that were connected with it and mainly used to bring stone, coal and

*Brecon &*
*Abergavenny Canal.*
*A beautifully*
*situated boatyard in*
*the woodlands at*
*Llanfoist, high*
*above Abergavenny*

iron ore from the hills to be transported by water. Various sections of track can be seen today, especially at wharves at Llanfoist, Llangynidr and Llangattock. In case the waterway should be considered rather short for a week's cruise, it should be emphasised that the surrounding countryside of the Park provides innumerable possibilities for walks, study of natural history and caving. Full details of excursions that may be made are contained in *Brecon Beacons Guide*, HMSO, 1972.

Craft dimensions are 34ft × 8ft 6in × 3ft draught (or 55ft on a beam of 7ft or less), with a headroom of 5ft 10in. The original maximum length of 64ft still applies except at a very acute bend introduced during bridge construction on the Heads of the Valleys road near Abergavenny. There are several firms offering hire cruisers, and slipways at various points enable trailed craft to be used. The towpath, of mown grass or gravel, is in an excellent state throughout, offering easily the most pleasant and trouble-free canalside walk to be found in Britain.

*Brecon*   At the terminus of the canal a large basin has been filled in and surfaced so that the original wharf buildings and warehouses now overlook a sea of tarmac, whereas a splendid cruiser base could have been laid out here! Nevertheless, there is excellent road access to the canal, which is very close to the town centre. Water supplies that feed the entire line enter the canal via a culvert from the River Usk.

Brecon's borough charter was granted in 1270. The massive church formerly attached to a Benedictine priory was given the status of a cathedral in 1923. There is a National Park information centre at 6 Glamorgan Street. Tallest of the nearby Beacons is Pen y Fan, 2,906ft, several miles to the SW. There is a fine swimming pool in

Brecon, several good hotels and game fishing on the Usk, where small boats may be hired on the Promenade. Only short sections of the rocky Usk, however, are navigable.

The canal will be found to be rather shallower throughout its length than is normal, and some difficulty may be experienced in mooring along the banks, but within these limitations the navigation is well cared for. Pleasant country begins almost immediately after Brecon Wharf, with the canal soon entering a wood. There are excellent views of the Beacons on the right. Note the unusual design of the circular iron mile plates, marking also ¼m, ½m, and ¾m intervals; many of the original series remain. Allied relics are circular boundary markers, bearing the initials of the GWR Co and mounted on short lengths of rail.

*Brynich Lock* (2m)   As with other locks on the waterway, the width is a little over 9ft. Working boats of this and associated canals in South Wales were about 60ft long × 8ft 6in in beam, being shorter and wider than the narrow boats of the English canals. The painted stone lock cottage faces a row of pretty buildings on the banks of the Usk, crossed at this point by an ancient stone bridge. Shortly the canal makes an S-bend to pass over the river via Brynich Aqueduct, which has 4 stone arches. Although not the tallest aqueduct on the B&A, it is the most impressive. At the far side a wooden roller by the towpath hedge was linked by a length of chain to a paddle in the canal bed, enabling the section to be drained if necessary. The scenery alternates between open meadows and woods, with many trees growing on the slopes of the hills on each side of the valley. A waterside residence near Bridge 158 on the B4558 (3m 2f) has an unusual stone boathouse with a slate roof, indicating that pleasure cruising is a long-established activity. As long ago as 1896 *A New Oarsman's Guide* noted that 'the 33 miles row from Pontymoyle to Brecon is of a high order of beauty, such as not many of our natural rivers can surpass'.

*Pencelli* (4m 4f)   After a low aqueduct over the River Menascin (the narrowest part of the canal, allowing a beam of just 8ft 6in), we encounter a wooden bascule bridge (no 155), whose platform almost touches the water. By Castle Bridge, no 152, are the remains of Pencelli Castle, one of four Norman strongholds granted to knights. There were others at Blaenllynfi, Tretower and Crickhowell. The canal was built through the moat of Pencelli Castle, and several original sections of walling can be seen in the yard of the farmhouse that now occupies the site. The present house has an oak door dated 1542, and a fifteenth-century refectory table, one of whose matching benches can be seen in the Brecon County Museum. Bridges 150, 149 and 148 are all wooden drawbridges, the last of them providing access to a farmyard on the right.

*Talybont* (6m 6f)   The elegant modern drawbridge, with slightly convex deck and correspondingly concave support beams, carries a surprising amount of road traffic in the centre of the village. Operated by boat crews who must first close safety gates over the road (there are warning red lights by night), the bridge is worked by moving back and forth a lever that is located under a manhole in the towpath. To provide adequate headroom for boats to pass through, well over 100 strokes are necessary, and the operation must be repeated to return the bridge to its closed position. A similar hydraulic mechanism exists at North Warnborough's lift bridge over the Basingstoke Canal, where the procedure takes as long as ¾ hour!

There are shops and public houses within a few yards of Talybont Bridge. This is perhaps the best point to leave the canal for a visit to the 365-acre Llangorse Lake, several miles NE, which is one of the most attractive inland stretches of open water in Wales and is popular among dinghy sailors, boaters, anglers and bird watchers. There are also facilities for pony trekking here and throughout the National Park. The track of the Bryn Oer tramroad, last used about 1865, crosses the canal at Bridge 143.

Now follows the 375yd Ashford Tunnel, the longest of just 6 tunnels built on South Wales canals (7m 6f). In cross-section Ashford is more oval than circular, with a lower section in the centre. As it lacked any towpath, notches in the stone-faced walls provided a grip for boats that were shafted through. A shallow bracken-bordered cutting follows at the southern end. Almost always there is a minor road accompanying the canal or 100–200yd from it, with a good bus service connecting many points. This feature can be very useful for owners of trailed craft or inflatables who may wish to recover their car from the starting point at the end of a day's cruise.

*Llangynidr* (10m)   Apart from Brynich, all the other 5 locks are grouped within a short distance between Cwm Crawnon and Llangynidr Bridge. The thickly wooded banks are purple with clusters of foxgloves in late spring and early summer. There is a BWB section office and a well-designed stone warehouse at the bottom lock (no 6). The River Usk is suitable for swimming near canal bridge 131. The waterway from this point to its southern terminus is a level pound almost 25m long, a feat that was achieved in very hilly country by making many bends and quite substantial embankments.

*Crickhowell* (15m 2f)   This little town lies about 1m NE of the canal at Llangattock Wharf, and can be seen for a long while well below the level of the waterway. Due north is the Black Mountain range, reaching a peak of 2,66oft at Waun Fawr, the Sugar Loaf. Some splendid walks are possible in the area. There is a medieval bridge of 13 stone arches over the Usk, the remains of a Norman fortress in a small park off Beaufort Street, and, several miles NW on the A479, the fourteenth- and fifteenth-century Tretower Court, the finest surviving house of its period in Wales. It possesses a magnificent gatehouse, courtyard and some superb interior timber roofwork. A furlong to the NW lies Tretower Castle, a twelfth-century fortification with a well-preserved and unique circular 'juliet' keep. It was attacked and much damaged in 1403 by Owen Glendower and subsequently abandoned in favour of the Court. Maintained by the Ministry of Works, both buildings are open to the public throughout the year. Workhouse Bridge (no 118) stands by an old workhouse still used as an old people's home. There are moorings near Bridge 115, Llangattock, for a number of cruisers, plus a slipway and the remains of several old stone limekilns on the canal bank. By following the route of an old tramway for 2,000yd to the SW from Lower Yard Bridge 114 you can reach the Craig-y-Cilau Nature Reserve, which extends from Llangattock limestone quarries. Apart from the rare plants and animals to be seen at the reserve, there is the Agen Allwedd cave, comprising more than 13m of underground passages. Four weeks' advance notice to enter the cave must be given. Information on this, and other caves in the National Park that are more freely open to the public, may be obtained from the Park offices in Brecon or Abergavenny.

After one leaves the borders of Llangattock Park, at Bridge 113, a really fine redwood tree and masses of red and purple rhododendrons take the eye. The surroundings are well wooded, with several larch plantations.

*Gilwern* (18m 6f)   An aqueduct carries the canal over the River Clydach near the centre of this little village, where there are shops and two inns. Rowing boats may be hired from G. Price at Gilwern Bridge (no 103).

*Govilon* (20m 6f)   A new bridge (no 102), carrying the spectacular Heads of the Valleys road between Abergavenny and Merthyr Tydfil, has produced a very sharp blind corner on the canal. Shortly afterwards one comes upon the extensive moorings of the Govilon Boat Club, which has most facilities, a slipway (available on request) and a canal office. There is a bus service from the village into Abergavenny, several miles to the NE; alternatively leave the canal at Llanfoist.

*Abergavenny*   Almost a mile from the canal at its nearest point, this is a flourishing market town, often described as 'The Gateway to Wales'. A good shopping centre, it has a ruined Norman Castle (open to the public) overlooking a broad reach of the fast flowing Usk.

*Llanfoist* (21m 6f)   This is perhaps the finest section of a lovely waterway, for the canal clings to a hillside with huge forest trees, and there are glimpses beyond the towpath of Abergavenny in the valley below. Remains of stop gates and much modern bank protection suggest that in the past the canal has been breached and has drained down towards the town. Beech woods and sheer rocky banks (left) covered with mosses and ferns make this one of the wildest and most natural portions of the waterway. Tod's Boathouse (hire cruisers and other services) is set around lawns on a bend of the canal where it passes closest to Llanfoist; it has a charming white-painted house, a semi-open warehouse used as a workshop, and a magnificent backdrop of trees. This is arguably the most attractively located canal boatyard in Britain. A narrow tunnel dives under the cut, providing pedestrian access between the yard and the village. The remains of a tramway can be seen at Tod's Bridge, heading up the mountain. This is the setting for Alexander Cordell's novel *Rape of the Fair Country*.

*Goytre* (27m 2f)   South from Govilon the canal appears to be rather deeper. The countryside continues to be outstandingly beautiful, with occasional Welsh cottages of whitewashed stone under grey slate roofs. Gradually the mountainous surroundings that have characterised the route since Brecon begin to be replaced by more open meadowland. At Goytre Wharf (aqueduct) the canal winds through a broad arc around the buildings of Red Line Boats (hire cruisers), grouped at the foot of a steep embankment. There is a short wharf arm and a slipway. Operating in the area is a steel-hulled tripping boat, the *Owain Glyndwr* (the visitor is apt to become confused by English and Welsh alternative spellings of people and places).
From Bridge 70, Bird's Pool, an unexpectedly broad stretch of water, the canal ceases to be spectacular, taking on the aspect of the many miles of pleasant rural waterway to be found throughout the English Midlands.

*Mamhilad* (30m 4f)   Near Bridge 60, Govera Bridge, is a huge and modern ICI nylon factory.

*Pontypool* (33m 2f)   At the outskirts of the town the waterway suddenly becomes very shallow and rather weedy. Technically the Brecon Canal ends at Pontymoile Bridge and the remaining 1¼m belongs to the Monmouthshire Canal. This is virtually blocked by the rebuilt Crown Bridge, Sebastopol, where the 'navigation' passes through an 8ft diameter pipe. There are most facilities at the junction between the two canals, together with a BWB toll-house. In view of public and local-authority interest in the amenity use of waterways in South Wales, it is extremely unfortunate that any restoration (other than short isolated portions) of the Monmouthshire Canal seems very remote.

### BREDE, RIVER

From a junction with the Eastern River Rother at Rye, Sussex, to Brede village; 7m 7f, with 1 lock fitted with gates opening in both directions from the tidal Rother. Maximum craft dimensions, imposed by the lock and adjacent bridge, are 40ft × 12ft × about 3ft draught (depending on the tide in the Rother) × about 8ft headroom. The waterway is, however, only really suitable for small craft. It passes through Winchelsea, one of the Cinque Ports, added with Rye to the original five in the late twelfth century. There are many medieval remains, including a number of cellars and three town gates.

### BRIDGEWATER CANAL

From the Castlefield Junction with the Rochdale Canal, Manchester, to Runcorn (now a dead end), the canal runs 28m with no locks. The Stretford & Leigh Branch runs from Water's Meeting, Stretford, to the Leigh Branch of the Leeds & Liverpool Canal – 10¾m with no locks. Further short branches are the Hulme Lock Branch, ⅛m with one lock, leading to the Manchester Ship Canal in Manchester; and the Preston Brook Branch, ¾m with no locks, forming a connection with the Trent & Mersey Canal. Maximum craft dimensions are 70ft by 14ft 9in by 4–5ft draught by 11ft headroom on the main line (8ft 6in, Stretford & Leigh Branch; 10ft 6in, Hulme Lock Branch).

Britain's earliest 'modern' canal and the one that inaugurated the Canal Era. The first section was opened for traffic in 1761 and various further additions were made over the next 98 years (see *The Canals of North West England* by Charles Hadfield and Gordon Biddle). It is now operated by the Bridgewater Department of the Manchester Ship Canal Co, but it is planned to transfer the canal to a charitable trust, with maintenance grants provided by the local authorities. Commercially the Bridgewater became a huge success, bringing its instigator, the third Duke, an annual income in excess of £80,000 a year in return for the capital he invested in construction of around £200,000. Regular trade continued until the early 1970s, but the future of the waterway now lies in its great amenity value. Passing through industrial centres as well as peaceful open countryside, it is increasingly popular with pleasure craft, of which large numbers are based along its course.

*Leigh*   The description provided here begins with the Stretford & Leigh Branch and then continues with the section from Manchester to Runcorn. After the lunar landscape of the Leeds & Liverpool's branch from Wigan, the Bridgewater Canal begins at a junction that would pass unnoticed but for a sign board indicating the end of the BWB jurisdiction and the first of a series of manually operated cranes set up at regular intervals. These were designed to drop 'stop gates' into grooves on each side of the waterway, enabling a section to be drained for repairs or isolated in the event of a burst.

*Worsley* (6m)   The canal passes through parkland before reaching the M62 motorway and the fascinating village of Worsley, where iron ore colours the water bright orange. Here is the entrance to the underground canal system (see p 81) created to bring the Duke's coal to the surface and thence by water transport to Manchester. Worsley Old Hall, now a restaurant, is a partly timbered building dating from the sixteenth century but extensively remodelled in the nineteenth. James Brindley lived here while working on the canal with the Duke's agent, John Gilbert. Overlooking the canal basin, with trees screening some of the nearby road traffic, is the half-timbered Packet House and former passenger-boat landing steps. Worsley Hall, built in the 1840s for the Duke's nephew, the first Earl of Ellesmere, was demolished in 1947. There is also a boatyard with drydock.

*Barton Aqueduct* (8m 4f)   After passing interesting warehouses, the canal's surroundings become more urban again as it enters the fringes of Greater Manchester. The masonry Barton Aqueduct, carrying the canal over the River Irwell, was demolished during construction of the Manchester Ship Canal in the 1890s and was replaced by the unique Barton Swing Aqueduct, conveying the Bridgewater over the MSC. There are fine views of this inland seaway (see pp 67 and 73).

*Stretford* (10m 6f)   A junction known as Water's Meeting enables craft to turn left

*Bridgewater Canal. A coal-laden short boat passes pleasure craft at Worsley, in 1965. Commercial traffic has now virtually ceased*

for Manchester and connections with the Ship Canal and Rochdale Canal, or right
for Preston Brook and Runcorn.

*Manchester* (distances are now calculated from Manchester to Runcorn)   The
commercial capital of the north-west, its prosperity derived to a large extent from the
Bridgewater Canal (now virtually disused by working boats) and the late nineteenth-
century Ship Canal, which made it an inland seaport. A point near Castleford Junction,
where the Rochdale Canal (p 380) ascends a flight of locks to join the Ashton, is the
beginning of the short Hulme Lock Branch, providing access with the MSC. With a
population in excess of 600,000, Manchester boasts many fine public buildings, among
them the Gothic Town Hall, completed in 1877, and the Free Trade Hall of 1853–6,
home of the Hallé Orchestra. The Perpendicular-style cathedral is largely fifteenth-
century. The Bridgewater Canal passes through Old Trafford and the city dock area
to join the line from Leigh at Stretford (2m 6f). Much heavy industry is evident.

*Sale* (5m 1f)   Beyond Rathbone's boatyard, with sideslips, at Longford (3m 4f),
the waterway passes the headquarters of the Watch House Cruising Club, near a
vast and crowded cemetery. The Mersey is spanned by an aqueduct (4m 3f) and at
Sale the Bridgewater crosses from Lancashire to Cheshire.

*Timperley* (6m 7f)   Convenient railway stations lie near the waterway at Sale,
Brooklands, and Timperley, where there is a boatyard offering day boats and weekly
cruisers for hire.

*Altrincham* (8m 4f)   Still industrial, but the town is pleasant, with many black and
white timbered buildings in the Market Place.

*Bollin Aqueduct, Dunham* (10m 2f)   Leaving Altrincham, the canal traverses
attractive countryside with broad views across the fields towards the Ship Canal
several miles NW. The canal is carried along substantial embankments through
Dunham Park, home of the Earl of Stamford, whose grounds are open to the public.
A serious breach occurred where the stone aqueduct crosses the River Bollin in
August 1971. Repairs cost £125,000 and were not completed for 2 years, thus severing
the through cruising route. The canal is carried in a new concrete and steel piled
channel.

*Lymm* (13m 5f)   A charming residential village, seemingly unaffected by the closeness of Warrington. There are hilly streets, a little lake near the Victorian church,
and, in a central square, a seventeenth-century cross mounted on a rocky outcrop with
replica wooden stocks. Beside the canal are some stables (a former boat-horse
'hospital'), the luxurious clubhouse and facilities of the Lymm Cruising Club (less
agreeable is the long length of wire and concrete fencing to protect members' boats)
and a marina within the Ladyline Group. Several charming private houses look out
over the water. From an embankment at Statham (15m) ocean-going cargo vessels
can be seen making their way along the nearby Ship Canal. Beyond, a long high
viaduct carries the M6 motorway over both navigations. Trees, and masses of bluebells
in spring, border the canal at Massey Hall, now a school.

*Stockton Heath* (18m 4f)   A residential suburb of Warrington, which lies to the north. It is preceded by the pretty village of Grappenhall, with cobbled paving and an interesting church of St Wilfred. The canal narrows in a wooded cutting at the approach to Walton.

*Daresbury* (22m)   Birthplace of Lewis Carroll whose father was rector of All Saints church which contains stained-glass windows depicting characters from *Alice's Adventures in Wonderland*. Daresbury Nuclear Physics Laboratory borders the waterway, its modern buildings made of materials selected to blend with the lovely surroundings and its site landscaped so as to enhance the canal. Thus, the staff canteen enjoys a magnificent view across the water to the rolling fields beyond.

*Preston Brook* (23m 3f)   Here is the junction with the short Preston Brook Branch, connecting with the Trent & Mersey Canal (see p 421). Remains of extensive warehouses indicate the former importance of the village as a transhipment centre between Midlands narrow boats and the wide-beam barges of the NW waterways. One warehouse alongside the branch has been transformed into the Neptune Club, with a good deal of bogus nautical paraphernalia. The village, dominated by the M56 motorway, is now an important pleasure-boating centre and base for hotel and tripping narrow boats operated by Inland Waterway Holiday Cruises. A new concrete aqueduct spans the Crewe–Liverpool railway.

*Runcorn* (28m 1f)   The remaining portion of the canal runs largely through parkland in the area of Norton Priory. Many changes are occurring with the spread of Runcorn New Town, but apart from numerous additional bridges, much of the waterway will remain unaffected, for it is at the centre of a designated linear park. The New Town extends almost to Daresbury and Preston Brook, and sought from 1964 to raise the population from about 30,000 to 90,000. The canal reaches an abrupt terminus, with many moored boats, at Waterloo Bridge, a double-arched structure with ornate iron railings. Beyond, portions of lock gates, paddle gear and bollards protrude from unsightly rubble – all that remains of a truly monumental flight of ten duplicated locks, of which one set was abandoned in 1949 and the other as late as 1966. They connected with the MSC, providing access to the Mersey, and with Runcorn Docks, from which the Runcorn & Weston Canal led to Weston Point. Their loss was a tragedy for industrial archaeologists as well as cruising enthusiasts. One of the last craft to make a passage was John Seymour's hired cruiser *Water Willow* in 1963. In spite of their virtual dereliction, he succeeded, giving a stirring account in his book *Voyage Into England*. Bridgewater House, an imposing Georgian mansion erected for use by the third Duke during construction of the waterway, remains amid the dereliction of the ruined locks. Here also is the Manchester Ship Canal and a broad reach of the Mersey, connected with Widnes on the north shore by a magnificent steel arched road bridge spanning a gap of 1,082ft. When completed in 1961, it was the third largest structure of its kind in the world. It replaced an early twentieth-century transporter bridge that consisted of a moving car suspended over the river by steel cables.

## BRIDGWATER & TAUNTON CANAL

From Bridgwater Dock, Somerset, former junction with the River Parrett, to

Taunton on the River Tone; 14¼m with 6 locks. Once part of an extensive system of Somerset and East Devon interconnecting navigations (these included the Parrett, Tone, Chard and Grand Western), the B&T is now quite isolated. Locks and a number of swing bridges have been inoperable since World War II. All commercial traffic had ceased by about 1907, with the exception of that in Bridgwater Dock, which was closed to shipping in 1971 and subsequently sealed off from the Parrett by concrete dams. There are various proposals to make fuller use of the waterway's amenity potential, the county council having agreed to raise fixed swing bridges to provide 3ft 6in headroom. However, until full clearance is arranged and the locks restored to working order, this beautiful navigation through charming scenery can only be used by the smallest class of portable boat. One unique feature is the pattern of lock paddle gear, where iron or stone weights are fitted as counterbalances. Theoretical maximum craft dimensions are 54ft × 13ft × 3ft draught × 8ft headroom (see comment above).

*Bridgwater*  The formerly crowded shipping dock is intact but deserted, and, instead of being a busy pleasure craft marina serving canal and seagoing craft, is now separated from the tidal Parrett (see p 372). The town is a fascinating place, where the only remains of a thirteenth-century castle is the water gate. The best parts are along the riverside quays. Much of the seventeenth- and eighteenth-century atmosphere when it flourished as an inland port survives in its fine buildings. The canal leaves the town via a stone-walled cutting, is then spanned by the M5 motorway and emerges in open country at Huntworth.

*North Newton* (7m)  Few main roads spoil the rural aspect of the waterway as it passes through small villages at Fordgate and North Newton. Four of the locks (Standard, King's, Maunsell and Higher) occur within 2m, and should be inspected for their novel paddle gear and unusual concrete balance beams. All are in generally fair condition, although weeds can cause difficulties for small boats in summer. From Higher Lock through to the Tone in Taunton there are no obstacles to navigation (apart from swing bridges), resulting in 7½m of waterway available to light craft. BWB have a small maintenance yard at Durston (8m).

*Creech St Michael* (11m 1f)  The village has recently succumbed to modern housing development, but the canal is unaffected. At this point the derelict Chard Canal, which lasted only from 1842 to 1868, began its 13½m course to Chard via 2 locks and 4 inclined planes, which restricted the size of boats to a mere 26ft × 6ft 6in.

*Taunton* (14m 2f)  A pleasing town with county museum in the castle, parts of which were built in the twelfth century. Firepool Lock, with a rise and fall of 1ft 6in, lowers the canal to the Tone alongside a weir (this appears to be quite workable). A small plaque mounted near the main river bridge bears the following inscription: '1699–1969. Conservators of the River Tone. Near this spot were the steps and landing place of the Conservators of the River Tone. From 1699–1839 the Conservators kept the river navigable between Taunton and Bridgwater. From 1839–1969 they had a statutory duty to inspect annually the Bridgwater & Taunton Canal and the section of river through the town.' About ¾m of the Tone remains navigable, and there are generally a number of small boats in use. There was once a link with the Grand Western Canal (see p 305).

(see p 305)

## BROADS, THE

This extremely popular boating region in Norfolk and Suffolk is a self-contained series of navigations based on the courses of 5 rivers – Yare, Bure, Ant, Thurne and Waveney. There are various branches, and the Broads themselves – shallow lakes of varying size. The origin of these is somewhat obscure, but undoubtedly some of them result from peat workings from the thirteenth century onwards. Navigable connections exist with the East Coast via Great Yarmouth and Lowestoft harbours. The only operable lock is Mutford, between Oulton Broad and Lowestoft harbour. Total length of the Broadland navigations is about 127m.

A succession of Acts of Parliament from the seventeenth, eighteenth and nineteenth centuries achieved improvement of the rivers for trading craft, most picturesque of which were the sailing wherries. The upper lengths of the rivers and their locks have been abandoned, although serious consideration is now being given to their reopening and even to the provision of a link between the Broads and the waterways of the Great Ouse system in the Fens.

From the latter part of the last century, Broads cruising has continued to attract many thousands of devotees, to the extent that parts of the area have now reached saturation point at the height of the season. Nowhere in Britain is there such a concentration of hire cruisers, motorised boats being very much in the majority compared with more traditional sailing craft.

### River Yare

*Great Yarmouth*  A flourishing and rather brash seaside resort occupying a long peninsula between the coast and the river estuary, it would be quite misleading to regard Yarmouth as in any way typical of the Broads. Its souvenir shops, amusement arcades, three piers, theatres and many other facilities do, however, attract many Broads boat-hirers. The harbour (out of bounds to hired craft) is a busy commercial area, and was a leading centre of the herring-fishing industry until the 1930s. Public cruises into Breydon Water and beyond begin at North Quay. With good reason, Great Yarmouth is known as the gateway to the Broads. There are fast currents in the estuary, with a tidal rise and fall of 4–5ft. These tides affect the whole Broadland navigations, although only to a very limited extent in the upper reaches of the rivers.

*Breydon Water* (3m from the mouth of the Yare)  A great tidal lake displaying acres of glistening mudflats at low water, Breydon covers 2,000 acres and is up to 4m long. The channel is clearly marked by stakes, and navigation presents few problems.

*Berney Arms* (7m 1f)  At the western end of Breydon Water and beyond the junction with the Waveney, Berney Arms is the first safe bankside mooring up from Yarmouth. There is a public house alongside the spectacular High Mill, dating from about 1870 and standing more than 70ft high. The mill is maintained by the Government and open to the public (see p 30). A careful watch should be kept not only for sailing cruisers and other pleasure craft but also for small seagoing cargo ships of several hundred tons, which trade on the Yare to Norwich. The river continues through reed-fringed marshlands, with many drainage mills and windpumps.

*Reedham* (10m 6f)  On the left bank the New Cut leads quite straight to the Waveney. Reedham has a diesel-powered chain ferry for cars and passengers, and a centuries-old heronry near the church. The railway bridge has a swinging section to allow sailing craft through.

*River Chet* (12m 3f)  At Hardley Cross, left, an obelisk marks the end of Yarmouth's navigational jurisdiction and the start of Norwich's. The tortuous Chet extends for 3½m to the village of Loddon, an eighteenth-century market town that has become an important boat-hiring base in recent years. A series of small dykes connects various villages with the Yare, and many of them, such as that leading to Hardley, are navigable.

*Cantley* (15m)  Dominated by a huge waterside sugar-beet processing works, which received supplies of beet by motorised wherry until 1962. There is also the Red House Inn and a ferry. The short Langley Dyke is navigable to the Wherry Inn. It should be realised that not all the waterways or Broads are public navigations, for some are in private ownership or set aside as nature reserves – one such is Buckenham Broad, linked to the Yare via Fleet Dyke.

*Rockland Broad* (19m 1f)  Access is through Short Dyke. The Broad is the largest stretch of open water in the valley of the Yare, although its area has contracted considerably since the early nineteenth century. Peat islands grown over with reeds form an ideal habitat for water-birds. There are free moorings, rowing boats for hire and the New Inn at Rockland St Mary staithe.

*Brundall* (21m)  The river becomes more wooded above Rockland, and like all the other Broadland navigations is scenically more attractive in its upper reaches. After passing the Coldham Hall Inn, left bank, the river slides by numerous summer bungalows crowding the waterfront. There are convenient facilities, including a railway station and several large boatyards. A maze of channels link the two lakes of Surlingham Broad. Owned by the Norfolk Naturalists Trust, this series of waterways, swamps and fenland covers 253 acres. Drainage works during the last 150 years have reduced the area of open water. The cruiser approach up a pretty tree-lined cut (speed limit 5mph) leads to the Broad itself, with another channel back to the Yare. The more overgrown parts are best explored by dinghy.

*Bramerton* (23m 2f)  Sloping wooded banks recall the Thames at Goring.

*Norwich* (28m 5f)  An extensive river maintenance yard with tugs, work boats, barges and pile-driving equipment (right bank), heralds the city outskirts. A detour is possible through Thorpe village along the original course of the Yare, but headroom under railway bridges at each end is normally reduced to 6ft. The present navigation continues via the New Cut. Plenty of municipal open space by the river is combined with gasholders and a power station. The Yare turns southwards at Trowse and shortly ceases to be navigable. Boats continue into the city centre along the River Wensum.

Mills and warehouses are still served by commercial craft. There are extensive pleasure-cruiser moorings at the City of Norwich Yacht Station, conveniently close to shops and all facilities. The river is navigable with care to New Mills, where a barrier of sluices stops any further progress. The city bridges include several of great interest. The oldest is Bishop Bridge in red brick and flint, dating from about 1340. Then comes Sir John Soane's Blackfriars Bridge of 1783, with a later cast-iron railing. An early iron structure of 1804 is Coslany Bridge, while Foundry Bridge, with decorated balustrade, was built in 1844.

Opposite the cruiser moorings is the fifteenth-century arch of the Water Gate, an important entry to the city for waterborne travellers, with the sixteenth-century Pull's Ferry House alongside. The medieval Norwich was surrounded by 2¼m of 20ft wall, with towers at intervals. Substantial parts remain, including the 50ft Cow Tower in fourteenth-century brick.

Apart from its magnificent cathedral, with a spire that is the second tallest in Britain, there are no fewer than 32 medieval churches, many of them now used for other than their original purpose. The city is full of historic buildings and quality shops. The banning of road traffic to form pedestrian precincts has been a notable success. The general market, with striped stall awnings, is open every day except Sunday. Norwich Castle was built shortly after the Norman Conquest, rebuilt in part as a prison in the late eighteenth century and is now a museum. Norwich is one of the most beautiful and historically interesting cities in the country.

*River Waveney*

*Burgh Castle* At the confluence with the Yare, SW corner of Breydon Water, Burgh was a Roman fortress of about AD 290, with massive ruined walls overlooking marshland that was formerly the estuary of the Yare. The Waveney forms the boundary between Norfolk and Suffolk for all its navigable course. There are several boatyards, restaurants and cafés.

*St Olave's* (5m 3f) Reached after a winding section through marshlands where the muddy banks and reeds dry out at low water. Just before the village is a narrow stream, left, leading to the 3-mile long Fritton Decoy, so named after the practice of catching wildfowl. Though the lake is used for local boating and angling, craft are prevented from reaching it by sluices. St Olave's consists mainly of seventeenth-century houses along a single street leading to the river bridge. Nearby are the ruins of a fourteenth-century priory, with brick vaulting. The New (or Haddiscoe) Cut, opened in 1832, enters on the right and runs quite straight to join the Yare at Reedham.

*Somerleyton* (7m 4f) Noted for its swing-span railway bridge. Two inns and moorings up a short dyke.

*Oulton Broad and Lowestoft* (12m 5f) Further marshland leads to a junction with Oulton Dyke. Here the fenlands give way to more wooded surroundings, with a number of pleasant waterside houses, some thatched, a sailing and canoeing club and various boatyards in Oulton Broad. This wide stretch of water is periodically used for powerboat racing. Until construction of Mutford Lock in 1831, the Broad and Lake Lothing were divided by a land barrier. Craft can now pass through the lock (fitted with gates facing each way and able to cater for all states of the tide) and so out into Lowestoft Harbour and the North Sea. Oulton is a major boating centre and headquarters of the leading craft-hire agency of Hoseason's, which has almost 1,000 boats available on Norfolk and Suffolk waterways. Private craft may continue through Mutford Lock into the fishing port and seaside resort of Lowestoft, whose fleet of about 100 motor trawlers are a thriving part of the scene. The Ness is the most easterly point on the English coastline.

*Burgh St Peter* (11m 5f)   Back on the Waveney, the village of Burgh St Peter occupies a ridge overlooking the river. The church is a remarkable thirteenth- and fourteenth-century structure with thatched roof and a curious 'stepped' tower of mixed brick and stone, not unlike a wedding cake. Typical Broadland facilities include grocery, boat station, dance hall and bingo, but the area is by no means as commercialised as this description might imply.

*Beccles* (18m 5f)   Pleasant but unremarkable countryside with several ruined pumping-mills precedes the charming town of Beccles, a place of well-preserved eighteenth-century houses. The bridge has somewhat restricted headroom at high water. The town rises sharply from the river bank, where gardens of private houses have their own moorings. Beccles was an island in the marsh 900 years ago, with fishing boats coming inland up an arm of the sea. Fourteenth-century St Michael's church has a 97ft stone-faced tower standing quite apart from the nave.

*Geldeston* (21m 7f)   The upper 3m of the Waveney are quite the most attractive, gently winding through meadows and in the shade of huge silver-leaved willows. Thankfully, by no means all the hire craft that visit Great Yarmouth penetrate as far as this. A navigable dyke provides water access to Geldeston. Remain on the river itself and you will soon reach Shipmeadow (or Geldeston) Lock, which is very isolated and unspoiled. The lock cottage has for many years been an inn called The Locks, famous for its candle-lit interior and eccentric landlady, 'Susan' Ellis. It was acquired by the river authority in 1973, following Miss Ellis's death, so saving it and its surroundings from commercial exploitation. The navigation works at Shipmeadow, Ellingham and Wainford Locks are now derelict, but the river was once used by wherries for another 8m to Bungay. Restoration is much discussed, but Broadland boating interests differ as to whether the average holidaymaker should (or would want to) operate rebuilt locks. For those in search of solitude, however, these reaches may be explored by light craft that can be carried round the few obstructions. About 32m upstream of Geldeston are the sources of both Waveney and Little Ouse. The prospect of linking the Broadland rivers with the Fenland waterways by canal via this route is a most tempting idea, and one that would help alleviate congestion on the Norfolk and Suffolk rivers.

## River Bure

*Great Yarmouth*   The river begins by skirting Yarmouth and acting as a barrier to its future expansion. Moorings are so popular that craft may be required to lie two or three abreast. Payment is expected, as at most other Broadland centres. The banks are muddy and the tide fast-flowing, although it is not dangerous like Yarmouth Harbour. On leaving the town one may see no fewer than nine ruined windmills simultaneously, all close to the river banks, their weathered timbers distinctly green with algal and mossy growths. In the first 3 or 4m, with muddy banks and tidal rise of up to 4ft, the Bure is not very agreeable, though it is always full of traffic. Except in areas where speed limits are indicated by signs, the habitual progress of hire craft seems to be flat out, and it is as well not to expect the kind of courtesy that is usual in other parts of the country. Two, Three, Five and Six Mile Houses all mark the distances from Yarmouth.

*Stokesby* (9m 5f)   A dramatic improvement in scenery that continues. It is now safe to moor up for the first time since leaving Yarmouth. Muck River leads to 5 connected Broads – Ormesby, Rollesby, Lily, Filby and Little. They are all most attractive, but sadly cannot be approached from the Bure.

*Acle* (11m 4f)   The small town stands at a road junction and can be reached via a dyke. Victorian and Edwardian boatyard buildings stand near the unpleasant concrete road bridge, which replaced a stone one about 1930. This was once a public execution site, and a flourishing one evidently, for wherry men complained that decomposing bodies suspended in the bridge arches hindered navigation! Note the thatched bridge inn, surmounted by a weather-vane depicting a Norfolk wherry.

*Thurne Mouth* (14m 3f)   Here the River Thurne enters on the right close by a splendid white windmill.

*St Benet's Abbey* (16m 1f)   Much loved and painted by members of the Norwich School of artists, this picturesque ruin on the bank of the Bure was founded by King

*The Broads. The White Mill at Thurne, close to the junction of the Rivers Thurne and Bure*

I

Canute before the Conquest. It is reputed to be the only religious house that escaped dissolution at the hands of Henry VIII. Within the ruins is an eighteenth-century windmill, bereft of sails.

*South Walsham Broad* (16m 6f)   Opposite the mouth of the River Ant the original course of the Bure makes a great horseshoe loop around Ward Marsh. The through navigation upriver is via an artificial channel, but the lower part of the horseshoe provides access via Fleet Dyke to South Walsham Broad, consisting of two connected lakes, the inner one of which is private.

*Ranworth* (18m 5f)   Upstream of Ant Mouth, Ranworth Dyke leads to Ranworth Broad, part of the Bure Marshes National Nature Reserve and normally closed to boats (rowing craft may enter in summer by arrangement). The adjoining Malthouse Broad is, however, accessible to motor cruisers. Four derelict sailing wherries can be seen partly submerged at the entrance to Ranworth Broad. The tall tower of St Helen's church overlooks the Broad from a small hill; within is one of the finest painted rood screens in Britain. Broadland churches are remarkable for their number, beauty and antiquity. Facilities at the staithe include the usual inn, shop and moorings.

*Horning* (21m)   A maze of channels characterise the area. Cockshoot Broad (left bank) is private, as are Decoy Broad and Woodbastwick Fen. The former is a nature reserve and may be entered in small boats with appropriate permission. By St Benedict's church, overlooking a sharp bend in the river, the preserved sailing wherry *Albion* is often moored, although it does travel widely throughout the system. There are two Hornings – Upper Street, well back from the river, and Lower Street, where one-time commercial wharves have now been much developed to cater for the pleasure-boating public. Some splendid private houses with magnificent gardens and thatched boathouses make this a particularly pleasant waterway. Many houses are served by short canals. Several inns and restaurants serve the holidaymaker. Hoveton Little Broad (right bank) is open to boats between Easter and September.

*Hoveton Great Broad* (22m 3f)   On the right bank and situated in a great bend of the river, the Broad, though privately owned, has a Nature Trail more than ½m long and open to the public during the season on weekdays and Sunday afternoons (closed Saturdays). You can see unreclaimed fen, various mosses, ferns and lichens and many varieties of wild waterfowl.

*Salhouse Broad* (22m 7f)   A very fine wooded reach above Horning passes the northern side of Salhouse Broad, with two connecting channels. This is a delightful lake, well used by sailing dinghies and one of the most attractive parts of this river.

*Wroxham* (24m 4f)   Wroxham Broad is a well-known sailing lake, covering 112 acres. The river joins at two points ½m apart. Wroxham is the 'capital' of the Broads, and it is here that the pleasure-boating habit was started in the second half of the last century. Now there are over 20 boatyards, chandleries, supermarkets (Roy's advertise themselves as the largest village store in the world), and many little dykes connecting the various moorings. At the height of summer Wroxham is exceptionally busy, and has the appearance of a seaside town. Day boats may be hired. The road bridge demands some care when navigating large craft. As many as 150 geese may be seen in the grounds of the waterside Castle Inn.

*Belaugh* (28m)   The mainly Norman church of St Peter stands high above the river amid woods.

*Coltishall* (28m 7f)   A very pretty village containing several old and mature houses near the Rising Sun Inn. Beyond are green meadows, ancient pollarded willows and the derelict Coltishall Lock (now with fixed sluices). Navigation originally extended for an extra 10m through 4 further locks to Aylsham Bridge. Small boats may be carried over a ramp at Coltishall to proceed for about another 4m to Buxton Lamas. Restoration of the derelict navigation works is both desirable and likely, although it would be difficult to predict when this might happen.

### River Thurne and Connections

*Thurne*   Close to the junction with the Bure, a short dyke, right, leads to the village. At its entrance is a beautifully preserved brick tower drainage-mill, painted white and standing on the water's edge.

*Womack Water* (1m 2f)   This elongated Broad extends for almost a mile to Ludham, whose main feature is the large church of St Catherine, partly fourteenth-century, with a very fine rood screen.

*Potter Heigham* (3m)   The approach is dominated by a rash of summer bungalows, individually agreeable, but collectively rather overpowering. They include two windmills well converted to holiday homes. Herbert Woods' boatyard, left by the bridge, incorporates mooring basins for their hire fleet and facilities for the building of large pleasure cruisers for river and sea use. The famous bridge is a medieval structure in stone with a notoriously low and narrow navigation arch that prevents the larger class of cruiser from proceeding further upstream. Hire craft should take a pilot on board to steer through the hole with inches to spare over the deck and along the sides; to maintain steerage, this manoeuvre is normally taken at full speed. The passage constitutes one of the most exciting inland waterway experiences available.

*Martham Broad* (5m 5f)   A rather overgrown lake but navigable to West Somerton, where the coast at Winterton-on-Sea is about 2m away.

*Hickling Broad*   This is the largest of the Broads, freely accessible to craft provided they remain in the marked channels (elsewhere it is very shallow). The approach from the Thurne is via Candle Dyke and Heigham Sound. A nature reserve takes up 1,300 acres, and a combination of abundant wildlife, great reed beds and totally unspoilt surroundings excellently illustrates the traditional concept of Broadland. There are two routes, one leading to Catfield Dyke and the other to splendid moorings by the Pleasure Boat Inn in the NW corner. Nature trail tours round the Broad begin at the inn. Those with limited time should be sure to include Hickling on their itinerary.

*Horsey Mere*   A narrow winding channel, Meadow Dyke, leads from the junction of Hickling Broad and Heigham Sound, and it is no wider than many narrow-boat canals. Past willows and silver birches, the navigation opens out into the triangular Horsey Mere, about 1m long. At its NE corner is a mooring staith (very narrow and often congested) overlooked by a preserved National Trust windpump. Built in 1912, the pump was restored in 1961. The Trust also owns the Mere and adjoining marshes and marrams (total of 1,732 acres), Horsey Hall and farmland. Waxham Cut, extending from the NW corner of the Mere and running for over 2m to Bridge Farm, was formerly navigable for another 2m to Lound, but is now heavily weeded. The coast is a 1m walk from Waxham Bridge. In the eighteenth century there was a flourishing trade in smuggled goods, which were landed from ships, transferred to Norfolk wherries and then taken inland to Norwich.

*River Ant*
A narrow twisting waterway that joins the Bure near South Walsham Broad.

*Ludham Bridge* (7f)   A low arch, square in cross-section, is not the same obstacle to navigation as is found at Potter Heigham. The river banks are thickly wooded beyond. One must keep an eye open for the numerous sailing cruisers that tack backwards and forwards in the very restricted channel.

*How Hill* (3m)   A thatched mansion overlooking the river, and owned by the Norfolk Education Committee, possesses outstanding water gardens. There are many agreeable moorings and much evidence of reed-cutting for thatch. This Norfolk craft is inevitably declining, with high labour costs, but the stacks of drying reed and small open boats used to transport the material are still an integral part of the river life of the Ant.

*Irstead* (4m 1f)   Here is a public staithe, thatched cottages and houses, and the little flint and stone church of St Michael, mostly in the Decorated style.

*Barton Broad* (4m 4f)   Covering about 270 acres and owned by the Norfolk Naturalists' Trust, it is an open navigation. There are numerous 'drowned' islands of reed. Old Lime Kiln Dyke runs for ½m to Neatishead (SW). Nelson learned to sail on Barton, an activity now made all the more exacting by the necessity for keeping within the marked channels. The Broad is about 2½m long. Near its northern end are moorings by the village of Barton Turf.

*Sutton Broad* (6m 2f)   Beyond Barton the Ant assumes its true river form again, soon to pass a junction on the right. This channel splits into two, forking right for the sausage-shaped Sutton Broad, which is in fact filled with reeds except for a wide stretch of navigable water extending to the Sutton Staithe Hotel (restaurant); and left, at the east end of the Broad, for Stalham Dyke, which is heavily commercialised, with boat sheds, a village of holiday chalets and many cruisers.

*Wayford Bridge* (7m 7f)   Upstream of the line to Sutton stands Huntset Mill amid trees on a bend of the Ant. In warm red brick, both preserved mill and cottage are a private residence set in a splendid garden. Wayford Bridge, surrounded by water-meadows, is a boating centre with all facilities and several boatyards.

*Dilham Dyke* (8m)  A very narrow tree-lined waterway running for 1m to Dilham village. The dyke was dredged and reopened to smaller craft in the mid-1960s after 50 years of disuse.

## North Walsham & Dilham Canal

Like other locked navigations of Broadland, the canal, owned by the North Walsham Canal Co Ltd, is largely derelict. It is, in effect, the canalised River Ant, and was opened early in the nineteenth century. The lower 3 of 4 wherry-sized locks (50ft × 12ft 4in) remained in use until 1935. Scenery along its 7¼m is mainly wooded. Medium-sized craft can reach the first lock at Honing, about 2¼m from the mouth of Dilham Dyke, and the journey can be highly recommended.

## BUDE CANAL

From Bude Sea Lock, Cornwall, to Rodd's Bridge, the canal runs 1¼m with 1 lock. This great curiosity among canals, as opened for trade in 1823, ran for 35½m, with 3 locks and 6 inclined planes equipped for tub-boats fitted with iron wheels (one such vessel can be seen in Exeter's Maritime Museum). The majority of the waterway was closed in 1891, and the part that remains navigable is really an extension of Bude Harbour. Maximum craft dimensions are 85ft × 24ft × 9ft 6in draught. Headroom is unlimited to Falcon Bridge, a swing span legally fixed since 1960, and is 3ft 6in to the present head of navigation. Chief cargo carried on the canal was sand, which was used as a fertiliser. The nearest inclined plane to Bude is Marhamchurch, just over 2m distant. Double track, the plane was 836ft long, overcame a rise of 120ft and was powered by a water wheel 50ft in diameter. A boat passed from top to bottom in about 5 minutes. Bude is now a flourishing seaside resort.

## CALDER & HEBBLE NAVIGATION

From the Aire & Calder Navigation at Wakefield to Sowerby Bridge, Yorkshire; 21½m with 39 locks. Until closure of the Rochdale Canal in 1952, navigation continued from Sowerby Bridge over the Pennines to Manchester. There are several short branches remaining open. The Horbury Branch (2 locks) is now closed, as is the 1¾m Halifax Branch, with 14 locks, which was abandoned in 1942.

Maximum craft dimensions are Wakefield to Broadcut Top Lock (3m 5f), 120ft × 17ft 6in × 6ft 6in draught × 11ft headroom; and Broadcut Top Lock to Sowerby Bridge, 57ft 6in × 14ft 2in × 5ft draught × 9ft headroom. Most traffic was in keels, horse-drawn, sailing and latterly motorised. Some commercial carrying remains. The short wide-beam locks gave rise to a suitably shortened version of the narrow boat, able to trade on the Trent & Mersey, Macclesfield, Peak Forest and Ashton Canals as well as the Calder & Hebble, which was reached via the now abandoned Huddersfield Narrow Canal, connected with the C&H via the Huddersfield Broad Canal at Cooper Bridge. One of the last carriers with these unusual craft was Seddon's, the Middlewich salt firm. Locks have paddles worked by a removable handspike in place of the normal windlass. Another interesting feature is the occurrence of flood locks and flood gates to prevent high water in the river sections entering canal cuts. While the lower part of the waterway is mainly industrial, it is not without considerable interest; above Mirfield (9m 6f) the scenery of the Calder Valley becomes most attractive.

*Wakefield*  Once a market town and the centre of the Yorkshire cloth industry,

Wakefield now looks to engineering for its prosperity. Not without a degree of charm, the city is typical of everyone's mental picture of a manufacturing district of the north-east, with mills, chimneys and warehouses in plenty. The cathedral, of blackened stone, was elevated to that status in 1888, but remains more a large parish church. The navigation rises through Fall Ing Lock as it leaves the Aire & Calder, passes the BWB Wakefield Depot and joins the Calder for the first of many river sections beyond Wakefield Flood Lock.

*Horbury* (3m 4f)   Evidence of mines in the surrounding countryside point to one of the navigation's reasons for construction. Motor barges still load coal at a chute above Broadcut Top Lock, and carry it to Thornhill power station beyond Dewsbury. Two modern intrusions are a bridge of the M1 motorway and the soaring pencil-thin Holme Moss TV mast on Emley Moor.

*Dewsbury* (7m 2f)   Navigation continues largely along artificial cuts, although the River Calder is never far away. Signs of former locks show where connections were made before improvements resulted in the present line. One such example occurs at Figure of Three Locks, where there used to be a chamber rising from the river above the present 2 locks. Part of a loop line is still navigable to Dewsbury's Savile Town Basin, ¾m long. A pair of staircase chambers, Double Locks, takes the main line past the town, a long-established industrial settlement with stone-built woollen mills.

*Mirfield* (10m)   At Greenwood Lock the steep and wooded sides of the river valley bring about an improvement in the scenery. There are plenty of facilities in the town and a BWB maintenance yard above Shepley Bridge Lock. The town was once an important centre for building keel barges.

*Cooper Bridge* (13m)   The Huddersfield Broad (or Sir John Ramsden's) Canal leaves the C&H at a sharply angled junction above a set of flood gates (see p 306). On the right side of the navigation is Kirklees Park, where ruins of a Cistercian priory are reputed to contain the grave of Robin Hood. (His mother was prioress.) It is a romantic spot with clusters of rhododendrons. Further on near the M62 motorway bridge is Kirklees Hall, built in the sixteenth and seventeenth centuries. The last point at which the course of the Calder provides the navigation channel is after Anchor Pit Flood Lock.

*Brighouse* (15m 4f)   A useful basin leads off at the upper end of a pair of locks, providing moorings almost in the market place. As well as a small boatyard here, a new marina was opened in Brighouse by Ladyline in 1974, providing much needed facilities in an area that has been slow to develop its cruising potential. The local authority has undertaken a commendable landscaping exercise of the canal banks between Anchor Bridge and Ganny Lock. The best portion of the navigation now begins, compensating in every way for the industrial regions already passed. Wooded parkland accompanies the waterway through Brookfoot, Cromwell, Park Nook and Elland Locks, with rugged hills that have long been quarried for stone.

*Halifax* (19m 4f)   Three locks at Salterhebble have replaced a staircase erected in the 1760s and wasteful of water supplies. A recent innovation was the construction of an electrically operated guillotine gate at the lower end of the bottom chamber. The lock-keeper will advise on its working. Halifax hardly impinges on the canal, for it was served by its own heavily locked branch line until 1942. A few hundred yards survive.

*Sowerby Bridge* (21m 4f)   Having now reached its summit level, the C&H enters a hilly valley and so arrives at its terminus, the Sowerby Bridge basin. All the fine stone warehouses are being preserved in a comprehensive development plan that includes boat-hire centre, canalside walk, boatbuilding facilities, waterways museum and restaurant. This is a thoroughly laudable example of a private company bringing life to a waterway whose commercial role has changed to one of amenity use. At the gateway to the Pennines Sowerby Bridge (the bridge itself is probably seventeenth-century and crosses the Calder) is industrial but not unattractive. The magnificent Rochdale Canal (p 380) has been piped through the town and any prospect of ever again being able to continue the journey by water to Manchester is inevitably remote.

## CALDON CANAL

From the main line of the Trent & Mersey Canal at Etruria, Stoke-on-Trent, to Froghall; 17½m with 17 locks. The Leek branch leaves the Caldon Canal at Hazlehurst Junction and runs for 2¾m, almost to Leek. Strictly, the Caldon Canal is a branch of the Trent & Mersey. The Caldon was completed in 1779 and the Leek branch added 23 years afterwards, part of its purpose being to carry water supplies from Rudyard reservoir, built some 4m beyond the terminus. Carriage of limestone was the major function of the waterway for many years, and a system of horsedrawn tramways was laid out to connect Froghall with quarries at Caldon Low. After 1811 a further 13¼m of canal continued navigation from Froghall to Uttoxeter, through 17 locks. When the North Staffordshire Railway bought the Trent & Mersey in 1846, the Uttoxeter extension was closed down and parts converted into a railway. A cast-iron mile post at Etruria still records the distance by water to Uttoxeter.

The Caldon was never officially abandoned, and remained navigable in part until the early 1960s. Boats continued to cruise with difficulty as far as Hazlehurst, beyond which the lines to Froghall and Leek were impassable. Considerable pressure was brought to bear by the Caldon Canal Society to restore these reaches, resulting in a rebuilding alliance being formed in 1972 by Stoke City Council, Staffordshire County Council and the BWB. With the help of volunteer workers, the waterway was re-opened to boats throughout in 1974. Maximum craft dimensions are 72ft × 7ft × 6ft 6in headroom × 3ft draught. There are few canals whose scenery undergoes such extreme changes as the Caldon, whose beginnings in the Potteries are heavily industrialised but whose surroundings along the Churnet valley towards Froghall are outstandingly beautiful.

*Etruria*   The Caldon Canal leaves the T&M main line above Etruria top lock, amid waste tips, chemical works, chimneys and grimy terraced houses. Here, unusually, is a canal that lives up to the popular misconception. After a sharp bend the route ascends the two-rise Bedford Street locks, followed in ½m by Planet lock. Surroundings improve as the waterway passes by Hanley Park, with numerous bridges. Some of the surviving brick-built bottle kilns may be seen overlooking the towpath. A welcome use of 2 specially constructed narrow boats to convey pottery between Johnson Bros' Hanley works at Bridge 8 and another factory at Milton, 3m further on,

*Caldon Canal. Dense weed growth and overhanging trees introduce an element of adventure to exploration of the branch to Leek Tunnel*

demonstrates the advantages of this transport medium in handling delicate cargoes with minimum breakages. More than 2 centuries ago, Josiah Wedgwood came to the same conclusion when he actively supported construction of the T&M.

*Foxley* (4m 3f)   The first of several heavily built drawbridges is Ivy House (no 11). Another follows in Foxley, junction with a ½m arm, disused since c1934. To the right are glimpses of the small and rather dirty River Trent. Engine Lock (5m 4f) takes its name from a former steam-powered beam engine that pumped water from a nearby mine. Onwards from this point the Potteries are left astern and the countryside becomes progressively more attractive, and it is easy to understand why the local authorities have spent money on developing the canal as a linear park for the inhabitants of congested Stoke-on-Trent. An unnavigable feeder conveys water supplies from Knypersley reservoir, to the north.

*Stockton Brook* (6m 6f)   A closely spaced flight of 5 locks (Waterworks, Fens, Railway, Road and Top) lift the canal 41ft in a pleasant situation near the village of Stockton. Soon a second feeder runs in from Stanley Pool, a substantial sheet of water to the SE used for sailing and canoe training.

*Endon* (7m 5f)   A small basin is now headquarters of the Stoke Boat Club, its entrance marked by a small circular 'island' in the canal on which a light railway bridge originally pivoted. Endon appears to be the only village outside Derbyshire where the custom of 'well dressing' is practised. This 2-day event, held each year in late May, seems to have begun at some time before the middle of the nineteenth century. Intricate designs, generally based on Biblical themes, are worked in thousands of flowers and moss to decorate the village well, erected in 1845.

*Hazlehurst Junction* (9m 4f)   In hilly surroundings the waterway clings to the side of the valley of Endon Brook. Several changes were made to the line of the canal after its initial opening, in order to accommodate the feeder length bringing water supplies from Rudyard Lake via Leek. Endon basin is the surviving stump of the original course. The present layout derives from the opening of the Stoke–Leek railway in 1841. At Hazlehurst the through route to Froghall falls almost 26ft through 3 locks by a notably pretty whitewashed keeper's cottage and cast-iron junction bridge. The Leek route remains at a higher level, continuing along a parallel course for several hundred yards and turning abruptly under a well-proportioned stone bridge to cross first the other canal and then the railway via brick aqueducts. A water flyover is thus formed.

*Leek Branch*   While only 2¾m long, this is a particularly attractive length, passing through dense woods to a broad pool surrounded by rolling fields. The 130yd Leek Tunnel lies at the far side. Beyond this, about ½m of water leads to an aqueduct over the Churnet, the final section to Leek wharves having been filled in and covered with an industrial estate. Three miles of feeder connects with the beautiful Rudyard Lake, an artificial reservoir designed to hold water supplies for the T&M. With wooded shores along its 2m length, the lake is best known as the inspiration for Kipling's Christian name. It is a popular resort among anglers and dinghy sailors. Leek stands at the gateway to the Peak District and was first settled by the Romans. Now it is a centre for silk and textile industries. James Brindley, the celebrated canal engineer, began a millwright's business here in 1742 at the age of 26. Such experience was to prove invaluable when he was asked to survey the route of the T&M Canal in 1758 and his waterways career was launched. His water-driven corn-mill on the Churnet in Leek remained working until 1940 and is now reasonably intact. A trust was formed in 1970 with the object of acquiring and preserving the building.

*Cheddleton* (11m 2f)   The main line of the Caldon embarks on its most memorable stretch after the Hazlehurst Aqueduct, running SW along the Churnet valley for 8m through some of the finest scenery in the Midlands. With little to disturb the peace of this steeply sided, wooded gorge, the boating enthusiast is indeed fortunate that restoration has saved the waterway from dereliction. Cheddleton has a pair of water-driven flint mills, of which one was probably designed by James Brindley. They have been restored by the Cheddleton Flint Mill Preservation Trust since 1967 and are open to the public during summer weekends. The two undershot water wheels, powered by the River Churnet, form part of an exhibit designed to show the preparation of various raw materials used in the ceramic trade. The trust also has a restored Fellows, Morton & Clayton horsedrawn narrow boat of the early twentieth century, decorated in its authentic livery. The waterway descends through 2 locks.

*Consall Forge* (14m 6f)   At Oak Meadow lock (13m 4f) the canal uses the course of the Churnet for nearly 1m as far as Consall Forge, where extensive water-powered ironworks were once established. Within a short distance of the waterway the valley sides rise sharply to a height of 700ft. Near the final lock (Flint Mill, 15m) stands another water-driven works, where sand is still ground as a constituent of pottery glaze.

*Froghall* (17m 4f)  Cherry Eye Bridge (no 53) is a most unusual stone span over the canal, with a pointed arch. Beyond can be seen mill chimneys in Froghall, an industrial settlement dominated by Thomas Bolton's copper works. Shortly before the terminal basin, surrounded by ruined limekilns that were served by a system of plateways that included an inclined plane to overcome part of a 649ft rise, is the 76yd Froghall Tunnel. This is both low and narrow and may prevent larger craft from reaching the extreme end of the canal.

### CAM, RIVER

From a junction with the Great Ouse at Pope's Corner, near Ely, to Cambridge; 14¼m with 3 keeper-operated locks. Maximum craft dimensions are 100ft × 14ft × 4ft draught × 9ft headroom. There are several branches. One is Burwell Lode, leading to Burwell, with side arms to Wicken and Reach, 1 lock and maximum dimensions of 50ft × 13ft 6in × 4ft draught to Burwell, 2ft 6in to Reach, × 9ft headroom. Another, Swaffham Lode, is now navigable for about 2m from the Cam to Slade Farm; it has one lock and admits craft 96ft × 15ft × 2ft draught × 9ft headroom.

Compared with Oxford's river, the Cam is miniature. However, whereas the Thames is allowed to add very little to the visual impact of its university city, the Cam is a central part of Cambridge and the Backs.

*Pope's Corner*  The open windswept character of the lower River Ouse is continued on the Cam as far as Bottisham Lock. The water is wide and deep, and this part of the journey is most appreciated by lovers of Fenland scenery. The Fish & Duck Inn (with restaurant) is a popular mooring at the junction of the two waterways. Maintenance craft derived from old-time Fen lighters may be encountered, drawn in short trains by a tug.

*Wicken Fen* (3m 1f)  The now closed Five-Miles-From-Anywhere Inn at Upware emphasises the isolation of the district. On the right bank is the entrance to Burwell Lode and Upware Lock whose bottom gates are duplicated so as to work craft up or down, depending on prevailing levels of water. The upper guillotine gate is electrically powered. The navigation runs almost straight for 3¾m to Burwell, which has the artonishingly beautiful Perpendicular church of St Mary and vestigial remains of a twelfth-century castle. Two draining mills are now derelict. Beyond Upware Lock one channel bears left to Wicken and another makes straight for Reach, 3m from the Cam. Wicken Fen, owned by the National Trust, must certainly be visited, for it is preserved to display the fauna and flora of East Anglican fenland before so much of it was converted to agricultural land by drainage schemes. Standing above the level of the surrounding country (where shrinkage of the peat has brought about subsidence), the 730-acre fen of reeds, sedge, open water and tree-covered scrub is kept suitably wet by water pumped on it by means of a facsimile windmill similar to those which used to *drain* the land. The swallowtail butterfly has been introduced as one of 5,000 insect species to be found here. There are more than 700 kinds of moth and butterfly, almost 200 sorts of spider, and 300 species of flowering plant.

*Swaffham Lode* (5m 3f)  An entrance lock provides access to this little waterway, whose depth falls below 2ft after the first 2m.

*Bottisham* (6m 6f)  Bottisham Lode is not really navigable, but small boats may make some progress in the direction of the village of Lode. Immediately beyond the entrance is Bottisham, the first of the Cam locks, with large weir and guillotine gate at the upstream end of the chamber. The atmosphere of the river is now much less stark, as it passes through Clayhythe, with sailing club and motor cruisers on moorings (7m 6f).

*Fen Ditton* (10m 7f)  Baitsbite Lock (10m) is situated near the village of Milton, NE and Biggin Abbey, a fourteenth-century summer home of the Bishops of Ely. There is a popular riverside inn, the Plough, in Fen Ditton, and considerable activity in term time with racing eights.

*River Cam. Bottisham Lock and weir with the guillotine head gate*

*Cambridge* (14m 3f)  The waterway is navigable for cruisers through Jesus Lock and past many of the colleges, including the incomparable King's College Chapel, amid lawns and willows known as the Backs. As there are numerous small punts and skiffs hired on this reach, large boats should be wary of proceeding beyond the Town Quay by Magdalene College. Far better to join students and tourists and enjoy this section from a dinghy or similar craft.

There are good central moorings for visiting craft and all facilities, including boatyards and hire craft. To navigate through the heart of Cambridge is an experience unique in England, and parts of the route recall the waterways of Venice, with an added dimension provided by England's native greenery. The pioneering may attempt to travel above Silver Street Bridge in the direction of Grantchester, although the river soon dwindles into a small stream.

### CHELMER & BLACKWATER NAVIGATION

From Chelmsford to the tidal River Blackwater at Heybridge Basin, near Maldon, Essex; 13m 7f, with 13 locks. Maximum craft dimensions are 60ft × 16ft × 2ft draught (one of the shallowest statutory navigations in Britain), with 6ft headroom. After many plans to bring a navigation to Chelmsford, the engineer John Rennie achieved success in June 1797 when a brig arrived in the town laden with coal. Shallow-draught 25-ton barges with curious wedge-shaped bows were horsedrawn until 1960, when they were fitted with diesel-powered outboard engines. The last regular traffic – imported timber – reached Chelmsford in March 1972. A tripping boat is planned by the navigation owners, and their former reluctance to allow pleasure-craft crews to operate the locks on grounds of water shortage has diminished. The scenery of the Chelmer & Blackwater is almost completely pastoral – extremely pleasant rather than exciting.

*Chelmsford*   The flourishing county town of Essex, with several important industrial concerns, including Marconi. Small boats can cruise about 8m upstream of the town on the River Can, connected with the Chelmer by an unusually long set of rollers to bypass a weir in the town centre. The banks of the Can form an agreeable paved walk near the shops. There are several fine mills in Essex weatherboarding.

The waterway has a well-maintained towpath throughout. One small source of extra income for the owners is derived from growing willows in plantations on the banks at many points. There are few road bridges and no villages directly on the navigation between Chelmsford and Heybridge.

*Ulting* (8m)   The little church of All Saints, mainly thirteenth-century, stands quite isolated on the very edge of the Chelmer. Lock cuts are generally very short, showing that the waterway is very largely the improved River Chelmer until it joins the Blackwater below Beeleigh Lock (11m). The course of the Blackwater has been dammed by a weir over which the navigation towpath is carried on a long trestle bridge. Below this point it is tidal and very muddy, as it flows to its estuary through Maldon. The canal continues past a flood lock and through long lines of traditional sailing craft, barges and cruisers.

*Heybridge Basin* (13m 7f)   By the sea lock (107ft × 26ft × 12ft draught) is a pleasing complex of cottages and public house. Moored boats provide a maritime rather than a canal atmosphere. Beyond lie the mudflats and salt creeks of the Blackwater. Nearby is the popular boating town of Maldon, where many rigged and operational Thames sailing barges moor at the quay. Their role is now solely one of pleasure cruising, but the working traditions are perpetuated.

### CHESTERFIELD CANAL

From the tidal Trent at West Stockwith, Nottinghamshire, to Worksop; 26m with 16 locks. Originally running for 46m with 65 locks, the Chesterfield was opened to navigation in 1777. The length above Worksop saw its last commercial traffic in 1908 and the remainder ceased to be commercially used to Stockwith in 1962. Sterling work by members of the Retford & Worksop Boat Club has resulted in a great improvement, and no undue difficulty will be experienced in cruising the lower 26m. Maximum craft dimensions are 72ft × 13ft 6in to Retford and 7ft thereafter × 2ft 6in draught (no more than this can currently be relied on) × 7ft 6in headroom. Advice should be sought on turning craft more than 35ft at Worksop, but a proper winding hole will no doubt be built. The first 6 locks to Retford are wide-beam, and those after are narrow. Barges still carry paper pulp from the Trent to West Stockwith Basin, where the connecting lock admits craft 72ft × 17ft 6in.

Suffering both from its former neglect (a condition that improves yearly) and its isolation from other non-tidal waters, the Chesterfield offers splendid cruising through quiet and almost completely rural terrain.

*West Stockwith* Entry from the fast-flowing Trent is practicable only at certain states of the tide. Advice is best sought in advance from the resident lock-keeper at Misterton 202. Once inside the wide basin, the alarms and difficulties of the river can be forgotten (see p 436).

*Misterton* (1m 1f) Long vistas of richly productive farmland introduce this straggling village, with 2 locks and the first of many waterside pubs. Designed by Brindley (who died before its completion), the Chesterfield winds typically, heading first in one direction and then another. The map reveals that often it is only very vaguely heading for Worksop.

*Gringley-on-the-Hill* (4m 4f) This attractive hilltop village is avoided by the canal but is within easy walking distance from Shaw Lock, Middle Bridge or Gringley Top Lock. Dominating structures are an old windmill and the stone church. The following 9m are lock-free to the outskirts of East Retford.

*Wiseton* (6m 4f) Contortions in the navigation are a fair imitation of those on the Oxford Canal's summit at Wormleighton. In this case a short tunnel, 154yd, was cut at Drakeholes. At its far end is a small basin, a slipway operated by the boat club and the White Swan inn. The canal now passes through the estate of Wiseton Hall.

*Clayworth* (9m 5f) The Retford & Worksop Boat Club has established its headquarters in a former inn from which villagers from the district once set sail to travel by packet boat to Retford market each Saturday.

*Retford* (14m 6f) Wooded country now opens out into meadows. There are canalside pubs in Hayton and Clarborough villages. Just before Retford is reached comes the last wide-beam lock, with the intriguing name of Whitsunday Pie. Reputedly, the canal navvies celebrated its completion with a huge pie baked for them by a farmer's wife. East and West Retford are situated on either side of the River Idle, whose course the canal has closely followed since leaving the Trent. All boating requirements are catered for at Retford Marina, and there are good railway services and plenty of shops. Here is the first narrow lock, shortly succeeded by another. The canal follows an attractive open course through the town and then heads for some of its best reaches between Babworth Park and the 4 Forest Locks.

*Scofton* (22m 2f)   A return to civilisation comes briefly in Ranby village, where the A1 trunk road noisily keeps the canal company for several hundred yards. Then follows a beautiful reach through the centre of the Osberton Hall estate, with a delightfully situated lock in parkland. Manton Colliery has been well grassed and its slagheaps landscaped shortly before Kilton Lock and the final section through Worksop.

*Worksop* (25m 4f)   An interesting but rather gloomy little town built mainly to serve the North Notts coalfields. Pickford's warehouse is a noble three-storey structure in brick, with a broad arch through which the canal passes. There is a wharf with manually operated crane, and a BWB maintenance yard. Craft can proceed as far as Morse Lock (26m), now derelict. The immediate district is full of interest, the surviving parts of Sherwood Forest forming an area of about 50 sq miles known as the Dukeries, with the estates of the Dukes of Portland, Kingston and Newcastle. Welbeck Abbey, now an Army college, is notable for the extraordinary system of underground passages and reception rooms created in the mid-nineteenth century by the fifth Duke of Portland, an eccentric recluse. He had a morbid fear of being seen in public and devised a 1¼m tunnel to enable his carriage to travel to Worksop undetected! This wealth of oddities is unfortunately not at present accessible to the general public.

Constant problems resulting from subsidence caused closure of the 3,102yd Norwood Tunnel (the sixth longest canal tunnel built in Britain) and much of the canal between Worksop and Chesterfield about 1908. Remains of many of the 48 locks in these 20m can be discovered, preferably with the aid of Ordnance Survey maps and a copy of Ronald Russell's *Lost Canals of England & Wales*.

## CHICHESTER CANAL

From Birdham Pool, Chichester Harbour, to Casher Lock; ⅔m with a tidal entrance lock. This is the tiny surviving portion of the grandiose Portsmouth & Arundel Canal, completed in 1823. In conjunction with the Wey & Arun, Arun Navigation and Chichester Harbour, it was designed to reduce the distance for barges between London and Portsmouth by about 100m. A branch of a little over 1m connected the city of Chichester with the line. Never commercially successful, the through route died early, though some trade lingered at the Chichester end until about 1906. This length passed into county council ownership and became used as houseboat and cruiser moorings from 1932. Saltern's Lock, alongside the large Chichester Yacht Basin, admits craft 85ft × 18ft × 7ft draught. Those parts of the canal that have not been filled in or obstructed by low-level road crossings have a certain amenity value, and there are proposals to make fuller use of them. Much of the canal's significance disappears, however, in view of the vast cruising ground offered by Chichester Harbour, one of the most popular sailing centres on the South Coast.

## COLNE, RIVER

From Colne Point, on the Essex coast, to Colchester; 11m and tidal throughout. Maximum craft dimensions are 195ft × 28ft × 9–11ft draught at high water. A long-established estuary navigation that enables small coasters to trade to the Hythe at Colchester. Fishing (especially for oysters) and boatbuilding are traditional local activities. Most of all the Colne is a paradise for small pleasure boats, with creeks to explore near the mouth beyond Mersea Island and Brightlingsea. Above Wivenhoe

(3¾m from Colchester) the waterway narrows to a muddy trickle at low water. Provided the care that is necessary in such tidal waters is exercised, the inland cruising enthusiast could make a most enjoyable exploration of the Colne by trailed boat or inflatable dinghy. Such jaunts offer an exhilarating change from static canal waters.

COVENTRY CANAL

From Coventry to Fradley, near Lichfield, junction with the Trent & Mersey Canal; 38m and 14 locks.

The Coventry Canal, in spite of an exceptionally tangled and difficult period of promotion, was a prosperous concern and was paying a 6 per cent dividend in 1947, the last year of independence. It was designed to carry Bedworth coals to Coventry and also to link with the Oxford and Trent & Mersey Canals as an important section of the route between the north-west and London. Brindley was appointed its engineer but was soon dismissed, probably for devoting too little time to the project. Work continued under various men, with long delays, and it was not until 1790 that the whole line was opened to traffic, 22 years after work had begun. Even then part of the main line from Whittington Brook to Fazeley Junction had been built for financial reasons by the Birmingham Company, resulting in a detached final 5½m of Coventry Canal to Fradley, a situation never remedied. For present purposes the canal is regarded as an entity. The coalmines and consequent industrial development of towns on its banks have certainly left their scars on the Coventry Canal, but quite apart from its present use as a connection with many parts of the Midlands waterways, there are some remarkably pleasant stretches. Maximum craft dimensions are 72ft × 7ft × 3ft draught × 6ft 6in headroom.

*Coventry* In the bright new city that rose from the ruins of the old bombed Coventry the canal's terminal basin, with its slate-roofed warehouses, comes as a welcome contrast. A hotel and offices are likely to surround Bishop Street Basin eventually, but amenity aspects and the canal's character will not be overlooked. Last regular narrow-boat traffic into Coventry ceased soon after World War II, but now, thanks largely to a far-seeing local canal society and growing local-authority support, pleasure boating is increasing considerably and the concept of creating a linear park along the somewhat drab 5¼m to Hawkesbury has become a distinct possibility. Sir Basil Spence's strikingly modern cathedral, close to the medieval tower, spire and ruined nave of war-destroyed St Michael's, is a building of great stature. If the total effect is not to one's personal taste, the fittings and furnishings display the best of twentieth-century art, from John Piper's superb stained glass to Graham Sutherland's 75ft tapestry of Christ and Epstein's exterior bronzes. Shopping is a pleasure in the traffic-free city centre precinct a short distance from the canal. The nearby museum contains important paintings and exhibits reflecting local industry, including a large collection of Stevengraph silk pictures. The first junction with the Oxford Canal was at Longford (4m 4f), the two waterways running parallel for a mile; this ridiculous result of a disagreement between the two companies was rectified in 1785, when a connection was cut at Hawkesbury.

*Hawkesbury Junction* (5m 4f)   A waterways Mecca, although now rather down at heel and dejected. Ingredients include a 6in rise stop lock between the two canals, two fine early nineteenth-century iron bridges, a row of small cottages facing the hair-pin junction, the Greyhound public house and the gaunt ruin of a steam pumping station. It is an area to which boat people retire, feeling at home after years of lying on each side of 'the stop' waiting to load at nearby collieries. Really busy with narrow-boat traffic until the mid-1960s, the turn itself still represents a challenge to the skill of a 70ft motorboat steerer, and still more to the handlers of a pair. Pylons, a sewage works and general-waste heaps cannot hide its magic completely. The quality of Hawkesbury could easily be spoilt by a 'facelift' scheme, which almost inevitably will come; equally, recent removal of some of the simple functional buildings is a great loss. Coalmines, some worked out, others still functioning, have made their own landscape by much of the canal, yet between the towns a wild scrubby countryside keeps suburban expansion at bay.

*Bedworth* (7m 2f)   Just before Bridge 13 comes the short disused Newdigate Colliery arm (left), part of about 5½m of private canals built between 1764 and 1795 through Sir Roger Newdigate's estate. Thirteen locks lifted the various arms 93ft from the Coventry. All navigation had ceased by 1819, except on the first short part that remains. Bedworth is still a mining town, best approached from Bridge 14. Some distance on, past encroaching housing estates, is Charity Dock, an old-established narrow-boat building and repair centre, where (typically for such yards) gloriously decorated narrow boats and conversions rise like phoenixes from the accumulated junk of ages. There is a useful drydock and a fund of expert knowledge and experience. Marston Junction, start of the Ashby Canal, follows on the right (8m 2f), and 1m further on a V-junction is formed with the Griff Colliery arm, in use until 1961.

*Nuneaton* (11m 6f)   Birthplace of the novelist George Eliot (1819), but now an industrial town whose rows of red-brick houses dominate the canal view for a long way. Even in this depressing landscape, where there is none of the interest provided by an area of intense industry, the waterside allotment gardens make a subject for study; culture of runner beans on substantial wooden frames is a speciality. Something like open country follows Bridge 24 (to the right), while on the left are slagheaps with a massive grandeur of their own. In 1971 the Architectural Press published *Civilia: the End of Sub Urban Man*, a thought-provoking blueprint for a new city making full use of the Coventry Canal in this area and transforming the moonscape of spoil-tips into an exciting region for living in by the twenty-first century. The chances of this bold concept materialising are remote, however, and it is more likely that huge tracts of beautiful countryside will disappear under bricks and concrete, as with Buckinghamshire's Milton Keynes. The lack of depth and thick consistency of the canal water here results from quarry washings being poured into the channel. Since the ending of frequent loaded narrow-boat traffic in 1970, the situation has deteriorated, and progress is slow for several miles for all types of craft.

*Hartshill* (14m 2f)   Between Apple Pie Lane Bridge (no 31) and Atherstone Road Bridge (no 32) lies the exquisite maintenance yard of the Coventry Canal Co, in restrained Victorian Gothic. A large brick building surmounted by a fine clocktower and weather-vane covers a drydock. Neatly walled in between the two bridges, the whole site is compact, replete with many satisfying architectural details, and largely original. In a vast quarry nearby apparently toy-sized machines trundle to and fro.

*Atherstone* (16m 4f)  Situated on Watling Street (A5), this small busy market town is located, according to a milestone, exactly 100m from London, Liverpool and Lincoln. The restored parish church is based on an Augustinian friary and nearby (to the left of the canal) is the ruined Merevale Abbey. A flight of 11 locks ('Aristone' to the boat people) falls through 80ft 6in. Coal is still occasionally loaded from lorry into narrow boat at the wharf near the top lock. As craft work through the locks, there is a good opportunity to go shopping. Side ponds to conserve water and large bottom paddles cause the locks to empty quickly, but, without upper gate-paddles, they are unusually slow to fill. They are more widely spaced as the bottom of the flight is approached in open country. On the right the River Anker keeps company with the canal almost to Huddlesford Junction.

*Grendon* (19m 4f)  Shallow yellow sandstone cuttings through pleasant surroundings. A swing bridge (no 50A) marks the start of further industrialism at Polesworth.

*Polesworth* (21m 4f)  Once a centre of boatbuilding and well known for its highly finished traditional decoration. Between Bridges 51 and 52 stand circular pipe-firing kilns. Among dense trees on the left after Bridge 54 is the extensive Pooley Hall, a Tudor brick mansion dating to 1509. There are considerable remains of wharves where traffic moved between canal and railway, in an area dominated by further slagheaps. Mining subsidence has caused some damage to bridges and left flooded flashes throughout the district.

*Tamworth* (25m 4f)  Two locks at Glascote on the outskirts of the town are over-

*Coventry Canal. Fazeley Junction, as cruising narrow boats make a lunchtime halt*

looked by the Reliant car factory and big modern steelworks. An aqueduct carries the canal over the River Tame, which holds the dubious distinction of being one of the most polluted watercourses in England. Tamworth Castle, high above the river, is owned by the local authority and was in continual occupation for 700 years from Norman times. The Tudor banqueting hall and Jacobean state apartments are worth visiting. The Anglo-Saxon King Offa of Mercia had a palace here in AD 757. The parish church of St Editha has a unique double-spiral staircase on one corner of its tower. An elegant town hall was built in 1701 by Thomas Guy, founder of Guy's Hospital in Southwark, London.

*Fazeley* (27m)   Junction with the Birmingham & Fazeley Canal, the 'Bottom Road' approach to Birmingham. The canals provide the best buildings, particularly a red-brick double-fronted junction house and the maintenance yard. Otherwise a cheerless place on the A5.

*Huddlesford* (34m)   The final 11m to Fradley offer the canal's most attractive scenery, mainly through open heathlands and shallow red-sandstone cuttings. The waterway winds considerably, maintaining a height of 200ft. Huddlesford is a tiny village with pub, where a toll island can make negotiation of the junction with the abandoned Wyrley & Essington Canal difficult for a 70ft boat. Several hundred yards of the old canal remain open (left) as moorings terminating in a truly sylvan pool, quite unlike the popular concept of the Birmingham Canal Navigations, part of which system this is. Although equipped with 30 locks in 7m – the Ogley series – its present pleasure-cruising potential would be considerable, for the line passes the outskirts of Lichfield on the way to Brownhills, Walsall and the Black Country. The canal was abandoned as recently as 1954. Lichfield lies about 2½m down the Roman Ryknild Street (A38), briefly touching the canal beyond Huddlesford at Bridge 86.

*Lichfield*   A bustling city, now a centre of light engineering. The famous three-spired cathedral in local red sandstone was built between about 1190 and 1340, but much of the highly ornate exterior decoration of its west front is Victorian restoration. Treasures include the early seventh-century St Chad's Gospels and the Herckenrode windows in the Lady Chapel, brought to England from Belgium in 1802 after their purchase for £200. Birthplace of Dr Samuel Johnson, whose father had a bookshop here, it has a market square statue and a museum of Johnsonian relics.

*Fradley Junction* (38m)   Good open country with wide views for the final 2m past a disused airfield (left) brings the canal to its terminus and junction with the Trent & Mersey (see p 429), with boatmen's Georgian Swan Inn and stabling grouped prettily beyond a swing footbridge.

### CROUCH, RIVER

From Holliwell Point, Foulness, on the east coast, to Battlesbridge; 17½m and tidal throughout. Tidal doors at the head of navigation are disused and prevent further progress. Burnham-on-Crouch is a very busy yachting centre, but otherwise the estuary is remote and unspoiled. It is unlikely to remain so if Maplin Airport and its associated services are ever built on this part of the Essex coast.

## DART, RIVER

From Kingswear and Dartmouth, Devon, to Totnes; 10¼m and tidal throughout. There are no limiting dimensions where pleasure craft are concerned, for coasters up to 750 tons regularly sail with cargoes of timber to Totnes. This is an outstandingly attractive river, with steep-sided tree-covered banks along the upper reaches. Much used by pleasure craft, as it provides good shelter, the chief centres are Dartmouth, with ancient buildings along the quays and the Royal Naval College; Dittisham, offering small craft for hire and a passenger ferry; and Totnes, with the ruins of a thirteenth- and fourteenth-century castle. Passenger cruises are available throughout the summer between Totnes and Dartmouth, providing a trouble-free and agreeable way of enjoying the river's scenery. Trailed craft may be launched at a number of points.

## DEE, RIVER

From Farndon (A534 NE of Wrexham) to Point of Air on the North Wales coast; 35m with no locks. There are no restrictions to craft length and beam. Draught from the estuary to Chester on high-water spring tides is 8ft, Chester to Almere Ferry 3ft, and Almere Ferry to Farndon Bridge normally about 2ft. Headroom is restricted from Connah's Quay to Chester to 10ft, and upstream of Chester to 9ft 6in. The Dee is a river of great contrasts. It rises at Lake Bala, 77m upstream of Chester, and follows an exceptionally steep and dangerous course through rocks and rapids via Llangollen and under the Shropshire Union Canal's Pontcysyllte Aqueduct. Soon it is joined by the River Ceiriog, about 38m from Bala. This part of the waterway should only be attempted by expert whitewater canoeists, as it is extremely hazardous. Slalom championships are regularly staged at Llangollen. For practical purposes the Dee begins to be navigable for light craft drawing about 1ft at Bangor-on-Dee, by which time the spectacular mountain scenery of North Wales has given way to quiet meadows with rather high river banks.

*Farndon* Surprisingly for what is really quite a pleasant river, there are few cruisers in use until the outskirts of Chester are reached. Those that are encountered are mainly small open launches and cabin craft moored alongside weekend shacks and bungalows. Care should be taken to avoid a rocky bottom immediately below the 7-arched bridge, built about 1345. Small craft are hired from a yard, with tearooms, built into a red sandstone cliff. There are many fishermen.

*Aldford* (3m 4f) There are many reminders of the Grosvenor family (Duke of Westminster), whose Eaton Hall estate borders the river near Crook of Dee, an acute U-bend. Several mansions occupied the site from the seventeenth century. The latest was largely demolished in 1961, but numerous relics of the Victorian era remain as important examples of the Gothic revival of the 1870s. One driveway to the Hall crosses the river via a very ornate iron bridge, cast in 1824 by William Stuttle, junior, and designed by John Hazledine. Craft using the river below here must be licensed by Chester Corporation.

*Chester* (12m) Fine houses overlook the river upstream of the city. The boating activity becomes hectic, with tripping launches, sailing dinghies, rowing boats, canoes and cruisers. Spacious gardens, agreeable Victorian houses and open spaces on the left bank combine to create an attractive waterfront. (For more about the city, see p 397.) At Dee Bridge, below a lacy suspension footbridge, a weir spans the navigation. On normal spring tides boats drawing 3ft can cross this barrier, and slightly deeper craft may arrange (by advance notice) to work through a curious water gate that can only be opened once the tide has topped the weir. A wide-beam connection is made between the Shropshire Union Canal and the tidal Dee in Chester. Passage requires prior notice to British Waterways.

*The tidal Dee*   While an ancient navigation, the Dee from Chester to the sea should not be tackled lightly. Local knowledge or the services of a pilot are essential. A tidal bore affects the section between Chester and Connah's Quay at spring tides. It is a muddy fast-flowing river with a good deal of industrial development. Beyond Connah's Quay the Dee can no longer be considered an inland waterway, and precautions appropriate for a sea passage must be taken.

## DERWENT, RIVER

From Malton, Yorkshire, head of navigation, to Barmby-on-the-Marsh, junction with the Yorkshire Ouse; 38m with 5 locks, of which the top 4 are derelict but likely to be restored. A junction is made with the Pocklington Canal (p 375) at Cottingwith.

The $23\frac{1}{2}$m of non-tidal waterway from Sutton Lock to Malton are indisputably one of the most attractive cruising stretches in Britain, although at present only small craft that can be portaged round the sites of the locks between Stamford Bridge and Kirkham Abbey can make the journey. The river dates from 1701 as a navigation. It was extended in 1805 to Yedingham, $11\frac{1}{2}$m upstream of Malton, but this addition has long been unnavigable. The section from Stamford Bridge to Malton ceased to be used in 1935, but a Derwent Trust is pressing for reinstatement of the locks, and in 1972 achieved the reopening of Sutton Lock. There is a good depth of water throughout the river and little trouble from weeds. A number of small cruisers are based on several reaches, the 7m pound from Malton to Kirkham Abbey being the most popular. There is a strong case for the whole river being returned to full navigation.

Maximum craft dimensions (assuming that derelict locks will be rebuilt to their original sizes) are 55ft × 14ft × 4ft 6in draught. Headroom is about 10ft 6in, but varies greatly in the lower reaches with the state of the tide. There is a proposal to construct a tidal barrier with lock near the junction with the Ouse, which should improve conditions considerably below Sutton Lock.

*Malton*   A pleasant old malting town on the congested A64 York to Scarborough road. There was a Roman station here, and some of the excavated remains are on show in a museum in the market place. Fine old houses stand in gardens high above the river. Boats suitable for manhandling can be launched down a steep bank near the railway station. Apart from very occasional small craft and a few anglers, there is nothing to disturb the peace of rolling meadows, patches of woodland and the odd farmhouse.

*Cherry Islands* (2m 5f)   The original navigation channel is easy to miss among a confusing patch of shrubby islands. Best advice is to follow the towpath side, but this is not always simple as it tends to be overgrown.

*Low Hutton* (4m)  Two villages, High and Low Hutton, stand on the right bank, backed with densely wooded cliffs similar to Cliveden Reach on the Thames but on a reduced scale. This is the nearest approach to Vanbrugh's gigantic Castle Howard, built in the early eighteenth century for the Earl of Carlisle. Open to the public, it lies several miles NW, beyond the A64. As if to emphasise the deepness of the river valley, the York–Scarborough railway closely follows the sweeping bends of the Derwent.

*Kirkham Priory* (6m 6f)  A stone bridge with 3 arches of varying width was rebuilt by John Carr in 1806. In a meadow on the left bank are the well-maintained ruins of the Priory (Department of the Environment), founded about 1122. There are substantial remains of an elaborately decorated thirteenth-century gatehouse and enough left of the foundations of the great cruciform church and associated buildings to give an idea of its one-time importance. A popular picnic site by the river. A little downstream, an open weir with modern sluices (left) necessitates the first portage. All signs of the lock chamber have been removed. Boat rollers could be installed with advantage until such time as a new lock has been constructed.

*Howsham Lock* (9m 4f)  Tangled undergrowth on the muddy banks, masses of purple balsam in midsummer and an almost tropical atmosphere provide an impression that this is a real voyage of discovery. Howsham Hall, almost on the river bank (left), is an outstanding Jacobean house, with a south front of about 1619, ornate and completely original. Now a school, it is open to the public in May and June. A weir across the navigation is a rustic affair composed of boulders. From upstream the entrance to the old lock cut is so silted and overgrown that it is difficult to locate. Hidden among trees are the ruins of Howsham watermill, a romantic structure in Strawberry Hill Gothic (late eighteenth-century). The necessary portage is extremely easy, merely 15–20ft along a path of rock slabs and into the weir pool, which tends to be rather overgrown with water crowfoot. The lock soon appears on the left. Voluntary working parties have cleared the chamber and, hopefully, will fit new gates and dredge the short canal cuts. Beyond, a bridge with two wet and two dry arches carries a minor road over the river.

*Buttercrambe* (13m)  Passing the village of Scrayingham (left), where the Victorian railway king George Hudson is buried in the graveyard of the mid-nineteenth-century church of St Peter, there is little else of note on the idyllic reach below Howsham Lock. Until extensive rebuilding works in 1972, Buttercrambe weir was a natural-seeming rocky waterfall. Close to the new sluices, left, the gate-less lock chamber has a charming inhabited cottage nearby.

*Stamford Bridge* (16m)  The reach to Stamford Bridge will be found quite busy with small craft, for Stamford is something of an inland resort, with an extensive waterside caravan site. There are several large forests of conifers in the district, with tangled patches of wild honeysuckle and the echoing calls of many woodland birds. After the extreme lack of commercialism of the upper Derwent, Stamford Bridge may be considered rather tourist-ridden. Conversely, it is good to see so many people deriving enjoyment from an inland waterway. Small boats can be hired. A broad open weir crosses the river, with a cut, right, leading through the caravan park to the lock, which, although fitted with a quite modern guillotine gate at the upper end, is currently out of use. Like the vanished Kirkham Lock, this was built in the most unusual form of a 2-rise staircase (an arrangement seldom seen off canals), with the lower chamber being distinctly banana-shaped. It seems that the lower set of gates were added as an afterthought rather in the manner of a flash lock. Among the inns, shops and fish and chips establishments is a particularly fine 5-storey brick watermill that has been cleverly converted into a pub and restaurant (popular, rather than exclusive) with much of the original corn-grinding machinery displayed and operating. The bridge, designed in 1727 by William Etty, has a large central arch flanked by a pair of semicircular ones. Downstream is an impressive railway viaduct of 1846, with many red-brick arches and an iron span over the river.

*Kexby* (19m 5f)   The old seventeenth-century road bridge has been superseded for vehicles by a new single span of concrete (A1079).

*Sutton Lock* (22m 4f)   Situated nearer to Elvington than Sutton-upon-Derwent. The top end guillotine gate was fitted in 1938, but the lock has been unused since 1960, when the last commercial barge passed through. New gates were installed in 1972 and the river reopened to Stamford Bridge in August. Nearby stands a fine watermill. There is a pretty village green in Elvington with well-maintained rose-covered cottages. Below Sutton Lock the river is tidal (until such time as a barrier is built as planned), with rather high banks and much mud.

*Cottingwith* (26m 4f)   Junction with the Pocklington Canal (see p 375). The tidal Derwent tends to suffer from very high tides and excessive fresh water running from the upper reaches. As the banks are protected by heaps of stone, it can be dangerous to attempt to navigate between low water and half tide, when there is a danger of hitting submerged obstacles. The scenery is not particularly interesting and in any event is largely obscured by the banks.

*Bubwith* (31m 1f)   There is a 3-arched bridge of 1793 and the substantial Norman church of All Saints.

*Wressle* (35m)   Quite impressive remains of Wressle Castle, built for Sir Thomas Percy about 1380, with two squat square towers, one with a tall climbable stair turret.

*Barmby-on-the-Marsh* (38m)   About 2m below Loftsome bridge (A63), where the Derwent meets the fast-flowing tidal River Ouse (p 362). High water is about 1 hour 40 minutes after Hull. The junction is easily located from the distance, as a big modern power station with high concrete chimney stands near the Ouse.

### DRIFFIELD NAVIGATION

From the River Hull at Aike, Yorkshire, to Great Driffield; 11m with 6 locks. This interesting navigation, part river, part canal, was opened in 1770 and extended in 1805, but fell into disuse shortly after World War II. It is included here as efforts are being made to secure restoration, and a Driffield Navigation Amenities Association has been formed. Theoretical maximum dimensions for craft are 61ft × 14ft 6in × 4ft draught × 9ft 6in headroom. As the navigation authority is a body of commissioners whose numbers have fallen to one (and he lives in South Africa), a quorum is impossible, and consequently no maintenance or reconstruction work can be authorised. Efforts are being made to overcome this problem.

At the junction with the tidal River Hull, a 2-rise staircase (Struncheon Hill Lock) has been replaced by a single chamber with steel gates that appears to be operable with difficulty. A 4m pound leads through Brigham, where the waterway is alive with sailing dinghies from two clubs. Snakeholme Locks, 3m below Great Driffield, are in the form of a 2-chambered staircase. Neither these nor the other 3 locks at Wansford, Whin Hill or Driffield are in working order, although new paddle gear and gates where required could easily be fitted, as the chambers are sound.

The general state of the canal is tidy and pleasant, with a landscaped waterside open space in Driffield and terminal basin bordered by agreeable warehouses. Several former swing bridges over the waterway currently restrict headroom for craft. As an exercise in restoration, the physical difficulties could be swiftly overcome, thus providing the East Riding with its only recreational navigation.

## EREWASH CANAL

From the Trent Navigation near Sawley to Langley Mill, junction with the Cromford and Nottingham Canals (both derelict); 12m with 15 locks. Maximum craft dimensions are 72ft × 14ft × 3ft 6in draught × 7ft 4in headroom (Trent to Tamworth Road Bridge) and 6ft (Tamworth Road Bridge to Langley Mill). This is the last survivor of a network that included the Derby, Nutbrook, Cromford and Nottingham Canals. Opened in 1779, it was bought by the Grand Union in 1932. Its last major commercial use was by boats working to the Stanton pipe mill. Under the 1968

*Erewash Canal.
The first lock at the
junction with the
River Trent*

Transport Act most of the Erewash was placed in a Remainder Waterway classification, but Nottingham and Derby county councils in cooperation with the BWB and volunteers have much improved its condition. They have completely restored the derelict Great Northern Basin to create a most attractive terminal point in Langley Mill. It must be admitted that the Erewash ends soon after the point where its scenery starts to become really attractive.

*Trent Lock*   Two public houses stand each side of the lock, overlooking the broad waters of the Trent Navigation, a popular dinghy-sailing reach. The area is much frequented by car trippers at weekends, with good road access from Long Eaton. There are two boatyards on the canal, with drydocks originally for the canal company's own use, and a number of houseboats.

*Long Eaton* (1m 4f)   A small marina is established in a railway transhipment basin. Long Eaton is noted for several tall severe lace-mills fronting the canal and displaying projecting bays.

*Sandiacre* (2m)   At the uphill end of Dock Holme Lock the rubbish-strewn and disused Derby Canal ran via Derby to join the Trent & Mersey at Swarkestone. Its 14½m was abandoned in 1964. This junction is almost rural in a sea of suburbia. Beyond Sandiacre Lock the town centre has been pleasantly landscaped at the canalside. More lace-mills similar to those of Long Eaton.

*Stanton-by-Dale* (5m 5f)   The huge Stanton ironworks are familiar to M1 travellers, as an ugly collection of iron buildings, waste-tips and glimpses of red-hot furnaces. The short Nutbrook Canal, mostly closed in 1895, has completely vanished at its junction with the Erewash.

*Ilkeston* (7m 5f)   An urban area with housing estates. Better things are in store from about Stenson's Lock, although the open country consists in part of grassed slagheaps from the Nottinghamshire collieries. There is a lace-like trestle railway viaduct crossing the River Erewash at Awsworth.

*Shipley* (10m 1f)   A rather low bridge in Cotmanhay village may prevent some craft from reaching the best of the waterway around Shipley. Here is the Boat Inn, a large establishment with a holiday-camp atmosphere and a pretty pair of lockside buildings that were once slaughterhouse and stable. Up the road to the east the weeded Nottingham Canal (closed mainly through mining subsidence) is crossed before one reaches New Eastwood, a drab little coal town noted as the birthplace of D. H. Lawrence.

*Langley Mill* (12m)   Fields at Eastwood Lock are followed by almost river-like windings through woods leading up to Great Northern Basin. As Langley lacks much that is beautiful, the impact of the restored lock, grassed banks, refurbished swing bridge and waterside seating around the basin is all the more noticeable. This work was completed in 1973 and has provided local children with an illicit but much used swimming pool in hot weather. Ahead is the Cromford Canal, a short part of which might be reopened. Further on, an isolated 5m length from Ambergate to Cromford has been restored for unpowered cruising. Since collapse of the Butterley Tunnel in 1900, the Cromford Canal has been split in two halves. Its demise is most unfortunate, as it seeks out splendid countryside in the Derwent Valley. Two outstanding features are the Derwent Aqueduct, by William Jessop, with an 80ft span, and the nearby High Peak Pumping Station.

## EXETER SHIP CANAL

From the Exe estuary at Turf Lock to Exeter; 5m with 3 locks, one being a side chamber into the Exe at Topsham, 3¾m below Exeter. This is the oldest canal in Britain to feature locks, having been opened in 1566 and improved in 1701 and 1830. John Trew was the engineer of the original 1¾m waterway, where the lock gates opened by rising vertically. The maximum capacity of craft was about 16 tons. Following the later improvements and lengthening, it is still used by coasters up to 400 tons.

Maximum craft dimensions are 122ft × 25ft × 10ft 6in draught. As all bridges have swing spans, headroom is unlimited. Topsham Side Lock admits vessels up to 88ft 5in long.

*Exeter*   The terminal basin, alongside the Exe, is preserved in its early nineteenth-century form. Stone-built warehouses are the home of the Exeter Maritime Museum, with a number of fascinating historical craft afloat outside (see p 195). Across the river, served by a small ferry, is the Custom House of 1681, a range of large warehouses dating from 1835 and the fish market. Founded by the Romans in about AD 50, Exeter boasts a magnificent cathedral (mainly thirteenth- and fourteenth-century) and numerous fine buildings from many periods. Its university was established in the 1920s, while the Northcott Theatre, built 1967, has the only full-time professional theatre company in this part of the West Country. A short distance below the basin is a junction with the Exe via Kings Arms flood gates.

*Double Locks* (1m 3f)   The only lock on the actual line of the canal (Turf is a sea lock) with a length of 312ft and sufficiently wide to enable ships to pass each other; ¾m beyond, the A38 Exeter bypass crosses river and canal with a swing span at Countess Wear. It was here that the Countess of Devon had built a weir in about 1285, but it obstructed passage of vessels up the Exe and led eventually to construction of the canal.

*Topsham* (3m 6f)   The river broadens into the upper reaches of its most attractive estuary, providing a popular mooring for pleasure craft. Topsham, on the far (east) bank of the Exe, was the city's port from Roman times until the last century. Dutch-style storehouses and sail lofts have been converted into private residences, and 25 The Strand is a small museum. Topsham Lock provides a connection with the river, which is crossed by a ferry.

*Turf Lock* (5m)   A final length of canal follows the western shore of the estuary to Turf Lock. This extension, completed in 1830, enabled craft drawing 12ft to enter the canal at all states of the tide.

## FOSS, RIVER

From the River Ouse at Blue Bridge, York, to Monk Bridge; 1¼m with 1 lock. A further 7 locks along the original 11½m course to Sheriff Hutton Bridge were abandoned in 1859. Castle Mill Lock is agreeably situated near the city walls and falls into a small basin alongside the Ouse. Maximum craft dimensions are 82ft × 18ft 6in × 6ft 6in draught × 10ft headroom.

### FOSSDYKE CANAL

From the tidal River Trent at Torksey to a junction with the River Witham in Lincoln; 11¼m with 1 lock. This is Britain's oldest man-made canal still in navigable condition, having been dug by the Romans in about AD 120 to provide a link with Lindum Colonia (Lincoln) and the Trent. Improvements were made during the reign of Henry I in 1121 and again in the eighteenth century. The *raison d'être* of the Fossdyke for pleasure cruising is chiefly as a means of visiting the magnificent city of Lincoln. Beyond, via the River Witham (p 444), lies the route to Boston and the Wash. High banks and long straight reaches through flat countryside mean that the Fossdyke has few scenic attractions to offer.

Maximum craft dimensions are 74ft 6in × 15ft 2in × 5ft draught × 12ft headroom (reduced to 9ft 2in at High Bridge, Lincoln).

*Torksey*   Situated on the eastern boundary of Lincolnshire, the little village displays few clues of its one-time importance. In Roman times it was a flourishing port, while in the Middle Ages there was a castle, 3 churches and a pair of religious houses. Entry to the canal is possible from the Trent at virtually any state of the tide. A lock-keeper is on hand to work the elegant iron capstans designed to operate the gates. A safe mooring above the lock is used by dozens of pleasure boats, and, for craft making a passage along the river, the relief of reaching still water at Torksey can be considerable (see also p 435).

*Saxilby* (5m 5f)   The canal is rather dull and featureless until it is joined by the A57 Lincoln road at Drinsey Nook (3m 6f). Saxilby has a long street of nicely varied houses facing the towpath, and must have looked magnificent in former days when square-sailed keels passed through. Ahead, in the far distance, the towers of Lincoln Cathedral pierce a flat skyline.

*Lincoln* (11m 1f)   An isolated but popular inn is the Pyewipe, standing below the canal level and protected by its flood bank. It comes shortly before one reaches the city racecourse and an urban length that leads into Lincoln, past a British Waterways yard by extensive pleasure-craft moorings and a lift bridge that is opened on request. This is the entry to Lincoln's chief aquatic attribute, Brayford Pool, a broad stretch of water no longer used by commercial traffic (grain barges continued to arrive until the 1960s). Fine old warehouses, timber yards and other commercial buildings line the banks of the ancient port where Roman ships floated. To the north are the triple towers of the great cathedral, first erected a few years after the Norman Conquest. The present structure, in the Early English style, overlaps each end of the thirteenth century by a decade. There is a Norman castle, many relics of Roman times and some creditable schemes which have left main shopping streets to pedestrians. Hopefully, the city authorities will eventually make Brayford Pool the visual centre of Lincoln. In its present rather neglected state, landscaping improvements would be appreciated, but not if they were to involve the loss of further waterside buildings. At the eastern end of the Pool the waterway becomes the River Witham (see p 444).

### GLOUCESTER & SHARPNESS CANAL

This waterway is a ship canal constructed as a bypass to the very uncertain navigation of the lower Severn between Gloucester Docks and the estuary at Sharpness. Although work began on the 16m canal in 1794, it was not completed until 1827, with the help of Government finance. There is a considerable trade in ships and coasters to both Sharpness and Gloucester, and pleasure-craft crews require more than the normal degree of alertness. Craft 190ft × 29ft × 10ft draught can reach Gloucester Docks from the Bristol Channel, and headroom is unlimited, as all bridges have opening spans.

*Gloucester*   The Severn locks up into the canal and the busy dockland area is dominated by shipping berths, cranes and many fine nineteenth-century warehouses (see p 385). The Gloucester level is maintained to Sharpness. Oil depots and timber yards extend for a good distance from the city. Concrete mile posts mark progress along the waterway. Traffic is controlled by staff at Gloucester and Sharpness Locks, with telephone contacts between the keepers of the swing bridges. Boats are expected to make the through passage without stopping and bridges will generally be prepared accordingly. If you wish to moor, the nearest keeper should be informed. Local advice should be sought for weekend operation times; at the time of writing, cruising is sometimes possible by arrangement outside commercial hours, on payment of a special fee.

Sims, Rea and Sellars Bridges all have sufficient clearance for normal cruisers when closed, but the traffic-light signals should be obeyed, as commercial craft might be approaching. Rea Bridge has the first of a succession of delightful Regency keeper's houses with classical porticoes. This is a convenient point from which to walk several hundred yards to Stonebench on the Severn, one of the best places from which to view the tidal bore (see p 385).

*Saul Junction* (7m 6f)   A busy 4-way intersection of the canal and the Stroudwater Canal, part of the latter now serving as pleasure-boat moorings. The Stroudwater predates the Gloucester & Sharpness and is locked into the Severn on the right. It was closed in 1954 and is now quite derelict. The Stroudwater Canal Society is attempting to have these 8m restored, together with the Thames & Severn (abandoned in 1927), to create a route from Saul to the Thames upstream of Lechlade, Glos, though there are numerous difficulties in the way.

*Frampton-on-Severn* (8m 7f)   Many fine houses line the village street, with trees and ponds. The Georgian Frampton Court faces the green. The canal is pleasantly wooded in parts.

*Slimbridge* (11m 7f)   After passing the unnavigable Cambridge Arm (left), which brings water supplies to the navigation, one comes to Patch Bridge. This is the mooring for the famous Slimbridge Wild Fowl Trust, established by Sir Peter Scott on the marshes between the canal and the river. At least 160 varieties of captive wildfowl can be seen, together with many migrant birds. The Trust is an important bird research station, and the public are admitted throughout the year. For opening times contact Cambridge (Glos) 333.

*Purton* (14m 2f)   The canal swings close to the banks of the Severn, with extensive views over the wide expanses of river and mudflats. The tidal rise and fall is one of the greatest in Britain. The inland pleasure-boatman can enjoy some of the flavour of the estuary, beyond the canal's towpath wall, without being exposed to its dangers.

*Sharpness* (16m)   Shortly before the docks are reached, a tall stone tower between the canal and the river marks the site of the 22-arched Severn Railway Bridge. A span over the canal was opened for shipping by means of a steam engine. A pair of oil tankers bound for Gloucester in October 1960 missed the entrance to Sharpness Lock in thick fog, continued up the Severn and collided with the bridge, necessitating its subsequent demolition. The original locks into the Severn are disused at the end of an arm (right) now used for moorings overlooking the estuary. The present ship lock lies beyond the extensive docks comprising nearly 30 acres of water. Sharpness is one of the leading sources of revenue for the BWB's Freight Services Division, attracting more than ½ million tons of goods every year. One of the major traffics is imported timber. The lock can only be operated 2–3 hours before high water, for its entrance channel dries out completely. The lower Severn is decidedly a place for experienced navigators and then only in suitable weather. Converted narrow boats have completed the journey from Sharpness to Avonmouth Docks, the Bristol Avon and the K&A Canal, but not without drama. Pilots are used by commercial shipping and are strongly advised for pleasure craft also.

### GRAND UNION CANAL (Main Line)

From the Thames at Brentford, Middlesex, to Birmingham, Salford Junction; 135m 3f with 165 locks. There are also the following branches: (1) Paddington arm, (2) Slough arm, (3) River Chess Branch, Rickmansworth, (4) Wendover arm, (5) Aylesbury arm, (6) Northampton arm, and (7) Saltisford arm, Warwick. The Leicester Section, Erewash Canal, Regent's Canal and Hertford Union, all part of the Grand Union network, are dealt with on pp 301, 279, 375, and 376 respectively. Maximum craft dimensions are 95ft (Thames–Brentford), 77ft (Brentford–Berkhamsted), 72ft (Berkhamsted–Birmingham and all branches), × 14ft beam (Brentford and Paddington–south of Birmingham: Sandy Lane Bridge, Birmingham, to Camp Hill Locks, 12ft 6in), × 3ft 6in draught, × 7ft 6in headroom. Beam on the Aylesbury and Northampton arms is restricted to 7ft, as it is on the section from Camp Hill top lock to Salford Junction.

The Grand Union system, totalling more than 300m, resulted from an amalgamation of several independent waterways in 1929, of which the longest and most important was the Grand Junction and its branches from the Thames to Braunston. The company already controlled the Regent's and Hertford Union, the Warwick canals, and the Leicester line from Norton Junction. Further acquisition of the routes between Leicester and Langley Mill followed after formation of the GUC Co. All these lengths had met with considerable or moderate degrees of commercial success. An improvement scheme mainly directed at converting the northern part of the main line from narrow to wide beam, at a cost of over £1 million, constituted one of the last major modernisation schemes on British canals, 51 wide

*Grand Union Canal. A Brentford tug skipper at work*

locks taking the place of 52 narrow ones between Braunston and Birmingham (a narrow-beam stop lock where the old Grand Junction met the Oxford Canal was also removed, the 5m of Oxford Canal from there to Napton junction becoming common to the Oxford and Grand Union companies). During the same period more than 26m of concrete bank protection were installed on the main line, while a number of bridges were widened or replaced. Considerable dredging was started, but the coming of World War II prevented improvements continuing, so that the full advantages offered by the modernisation were never fully gained. It had been the company's intention to operate 66-ton capacity wide boats on the London–Birmingham route, but these never evolved beyond the experimental stage and pairs of narrow boats remained the normal long-distance craft.

Until nationalisation the Grand Union Canal Company was a formidable traffic concern, serving many towns in the Midlands and SE directly by water or by a fleet of lorries connecting with the boats. A chain of modern storage warehouses played a considerable part in the movement of goods, while ports throughout Northern Europe were regularly visited by the company's associated shipping division, whose coastwise steamers bore canal names such as *Blisworth* to places as far away as Basle, Copenhagen and Antwerp.

The Grand Union Canal Carrying Company had by the late 1930s developed the largest fleet of narrow boats in Britain, amounting to 185 pairs of diesel-engined craft, carrying 72 tons on a 4ft 3in draught at a claimed speed (loaded) of 6 knots. With increased freeboard compared with conventional narrow boats, according to a company statement they were 'able to safely navigate the tidal estuaries'. Considering the large number of smaller operators then at work and the heavy flow of barge traffic in the London area, commercial activity was amazingly heavy compared with the negligible amounts of today. Although both barges near London and narrow boats over the rest of the system are only to be found in very small numbers, the Grand Union retains a very real working atmosphere, one of its greatest attributes as a leading cruising water-way. Another notable feature is the sustained interest of its architecture and the long stretches of outstanding countryside from the Chilterns to Warwickshire (within a short distance of the Birmingham terminus).

*Brentford*  Entry to the canal from the Thames is subject to the state of the tide in the river, pleasure craft being able to work through Thames Locks during the period of 2 hours before until 2 hours after high water at Brentford (1 hour later than at London Bridge). It is advisable to telephone in advance to the BWB's Brentford office to ensure that a keeper will be on hand to operate the hydraulic mechanism. Until 1970 the junction with the river was dominated by warehouse buildings of the former Great Western Railway, whose Brentford Dock was a useful interchange basin between rail and river lighters. It has now been redeveloped as a housing estate, with part of the dock retained as non-tidal pleasure-craft moorings. At high water Thames Locks (duplicated side by side) are opened each end to allow speedy movement of lighters as far as Brentford Gauging Locks. Traffic can be exceptionally busy as dumb lighters are hauled up and down by tugs or sometimes merely allowed to drift after an initial surge from the power capstans at the locks. This is an ideal area to visit to see what a heavily used freight canal looks like.

The western boundary of the canal between the Thames and the High Street is Syon Park, home of the Dukes of Northumberland and dating from 1547. The Tudor mansion was extensively restyled and decorated by Robert Adam during the later eighteenth century and the grounds laid out by Capability Brown. A much newer attraction is the Syon Park Garden Centre, formed around the stable block and huge domed conservatory. It combines a commercial area, where plants and equipment may be bought from a number of leading horticulturists, with show grounds land-scaped and planted in many different styles. There is also an excellent museum of road vehicles at Syon Park.

Brentford, county town of Middlesex (the county no longer officially exists), suf-fered decline for many years, and the new developments that have replaced mouldering brick buildings in the High Street can scarcely be described as an aesthetic improve-ment. But as a shopping centre reached from the Gauging Locks, the town is con-venient. A disused church houses an unusual Piano Museum containing automatic instruments as well as conventional ones. Some excuse should be sought to gain entry to the Victorian canal office alongside Brentford Locks, where a high polished desk with brass rails, gauging rod and other canal paraphernalia is kept. There are good warehouse facilities now served almost as much by road as by water. British Water-ways operate an export barge groupage service from this point. Barge traffic, although declining, remains until Bull's Bridge Junction under tug or tractor tow. A reminder of former extensive narrow-boat activity is provided by the Canal Boatman's Institute, standing back from the canal in an early Victorian square called The Butts, and one of many missions to boat people throughout the canal system.

A £20,000 study to investigate the enlargement of the Grand Union between the Thames at Brentford and a point in the Rickmansworth area where a transhipment depot would be built to serve the M1 motorway was jointly commissioned late in 1973 by the BWB and the Greater London Council. It was estimated that such an improvement could be completed within 5 years of work beginning. LASH 350-ton barges (pp 155–6) would probably be used, resulting in the removal of several million tons of freight every year from the roads of the Metropolis.

*Hanwell* (3m)   Dock Head (Clitheroe's) and Osterley (King's) Locks (nos 99 and 98), and passage beneath the M4 motorway, bring us to the Hanwell flight of 6 locks, all of them manned during normal working hours and equipped with side ponds. They provide an energetic introduction to the almost continuous succession of locks to be negotiated until the Tring summit is reached. The east side of the canal is bordered by a huge mental hospital behind a tall brick wall. Look out for tubular 'hitching posts' by the locks where barge horses would be tied until the last were replaced by tractors about 1961. Beyond the locks, Windmill Lane, Southall, and the railway from Southall to Hanwell make a triple intersection with the canal at a point known as Three Bridges. Norwood locks 91 and 90 mark the start of a 6m level to Cowley Lock. Including the Slough and Paddington arms and Regent's Canal to Camden Town, this section is a 27m lock-free pound. The late sixteenth-century Osterley Park, much decorated by Robert Adam in the 1760s, lies near the canal at Three Bridges, and is open to the public. Many famous manufacturing names are in evidence at waterside works from Brentford to the start of open country on the Buckinghamshire borders, while numerous side docks indicate one-time heavy boat traffic. Coal from the Midlands, raw materials from the London Docks, and completed products were moved in large quantities. In addition there was widespread gravel, ballast and timber movement, and timber barges continue to serve canalside yards.

*Bull's Bridge* (6m)   Junction with the Paddington arm via a blind turn under a humpbacked towpath bridge. Plans were made to widen the junction during the 1930s' improvements, but work was never begun. Opposite are British Waterways drydocks, slipways and boatbuilding facilities, where the GUCCC narrow-boat fleet (later BWB) had its chief depot. In the layby scores of family boats would moor up, waiting for orders or repairs. Bull's Bridge is now primarily a centre for construction and repair of the Board's maintenance craft. Also on the site are the experimental facilities of the British Docks Board Research Centre, where the problems of tidal flow, erosion etc, are examined with the help of huge models.

*Paddington Arm* (13m 6f with no locks)   The arm begins at its junction with the Regent's Canal at Little Venice, London, where there is a picturesque row of houseboats, the floating Argonaut Gallery (embarkation point for *Jason's Trip*) and on the south bank a tree-planted promenade. These elements combine to demonstrate the attractiveness of an urban waterway. Opened to traffic in 1801, the arm quickly prospered, and until the present century experienced heavy goods traffic, especially in sand, gravel and building materials. It contributed greatly to the early growth of NW London and now passes largely through semi-urban surroundings. Rather lacking in navigational or architectural features, the canal is nevertheless a vital link between London and the Midlands waterways system. Little traffic remains, but sites of wharves at waterside factories occur frequently. At Kensal Green (2m 4f), facing the railway tracks out of Paddington and near Wormwood Scrubbs prison, the canal is flanked by the extensive Victorian Kensal Green cemetery. Glimpses through railings reveal a somewhat overgrown collection of monuments, mostly of huge proportions and suited to the hoped-for everlasting stature of the personalities they commemorate. An hour's ramble through the cemetery, designed in 1833, provides a remarkable insight into the last century. About 1m beyond is the Grand Junction Arms, with moorings for passing pleasure boats. It was extensively redecorated in 1969 with a pleasing canals theme. At Alperton (6m) the canal crosses the busy North Circular road via a concrete aqueduct erected in the 1930s. A burst occurred in 1962, resulting in serious flooding. Large factories, including those of Guinness, Heinz and J. Lyons will be noted in the area, all sited to take advantage of canal transport. A mile beyond the aqueduct are the moorings of the West London Cruising Club, with open country at Sudbury Park Golf Course.

*Cowley Peachey Junction* (9m 6f)   Here the 5m Slough arm branches off, crossing the River Colne by a small iron aqueduct, beneath which gravel barges pass between a pit and the screening plant. Halfway to Slough the Iver Boatyard provides a full service in boat hire, sales and repairs, including full-length narrow boats. The terminal basin is surrounded by timber yards and is somewhat unkempt, although there are plans to change all that, ranging from filling in the final mile of the canal to landscaping it and establishing some kind of attraction for boat users. A youth club on the outskirts of Slough makes extensive use of the water. Several interesting schemes for constructing a navigable connection between the arm and the nearby Thames at Windsor have been devised. One such idea suggests using the River Colne, which enters the Thames in Staines. The advantages of creating a circular cruising route would be many, not least the introduction of river boats to this part of the canal network.

Residential houseboats, adding great interest to a pretty section, extend to Cowley lock, where the Fray's River passes under the canal. A double-fronted yellow-brick cottage, the old toll house, stands by the lock, together with a pair of white cottages, while beyond, beside a humpbacked bridge, is the Shovel Inn, one of many boatman's pubs on this route. From this point the waterway rarely becomes very industrial again, and even the lower section through the London suburbs is surprisingly pleasant seen from the water.

*Uxbridge* (11m 6f)   The flourishing Uxbridge Cruising Club has moorings leased from the BWB at the former Fellows, Morton & Clayton yard and boat docks. The drydock here may be used privately on payment of a fee. Good collection of small workshop-type buildings. The shopping centre is a short distance away, and provides a London Underground station. The General Elliott and Swan and Bottle inns stand on the canal bank. Immediately below Uxbridge lock stands a large boatyard on a cut to one side of the navigation. Opposite is a nineteenth-century flour mill that has been considerably enlarged by the addition of a tall and somewhat severe concrete structure. The waterside grounds are landscaped in a commendable manner, providing a lead which other canalside firms could well emulate.

*Denham* (12m 5f)   A straight section crossed by the London–Oxford A40 road leads up to Denham Deep Lock, whose rise of 11ft 1in is the greatest on the canal. Some care is required to avoid opening the upper gate-paddles too early, or the resulting turbulence could swamp a boat. In the village are film studios, the parish church of St Mary with a 500-year-old mural depicting Judgement Day and a number of Tudor half-timbered cottages. A further quite straight length leads to Widewater or Harefield Moor Lock (no 86), with good moorings in a gravel pit alongside the cut.

*Black Jack's Lock* (15m)   After passing some pleasant rolling meadows, one reaches this very pretty lock. The hall of the old Black Jack's Mill, now a private residence, contains a sluice whose operation was the chief preoccupation of a former owner. A well-remembered tale among the narrow-boat people concerns a Negro named Black Jack, employed by a landowner in the canal's early days in order to harass boatmen. He is said to have been murdered by canal folk following his interfering with locks and stealing their windlasses, and haunts the lock to this day. Such stories are so fervently believed that many boatmen would avoid tying up for the night at these locations. No doubt there is more than an element of truth in the legend.

*Rickmansworth* (19m)   Copper Mill Lock (no 84) has a complex of nineteenth-century mills where there was a former asbestos works. Opposite the Fisheries Inn the River Colne runs into the canal, causing a strong flow across the navigation in rainy weather. Above the lock beside the towpath is a row of terraced cottages rather well converted into four houses with new windows, freshly painted front doors and a Victorian street lamp at each end of the block. An excellent example of waterside architecture, which might so easily have been demolished, has in this way been retained to good effect. In the middle of the pound to Springwell Lock (no 83) is a long series of watercress beds using running water pumped from the canal, on the right-hand side. This is a notable feature of the Grand Union, repeated many times to the Cowroast summit. A really rural wooded reach with fields sloping to the water brings us to Stocker's Lock (no 82), where the cottage appears from the canal to be a single-storey building but when viewed from the landward side is seen to have two floors. The pattern is repeated elsewhere as we progress northwards.

Frogmore Wharf, Messrs Walker's timber yard, is situated on the right on the outskirts of Rickmansworth. Until the early 1960s there was a private boat dock here specialising in the building and repair of wooden narrow boats and barges known as 'Ricky' boats. Rickmansworth has two locks side by side; they are Batchworth Locks (nos 81 and 81A). That on the left leads to moorings on the River Chess, with a Grand Union rarity, a wide-beam bascule bridge. Up the arm the filled remains of a lock (built 1903) used until the 1920s to lower boats into a gravel pit can be found now planted with cabbages. Each side of the main line lock is flanked by a broad flight of brick steps.

There is much of interest in the town the boat people know as 'Ricky', and a mile SE lies Moor Park Mansion House, originally built in the fifteenth century for the Archbishop of York; it was subsequently Cardinal Wolsey's country seat and was reconstructed in the early eighteenth century in the baroque style. Both house and gardens are open to the public. For a long distance, almost until Lot Mead Lock (also known as Walker's, Beasley's or Cherry's Lock, after 3 successive canal company overseers), come many residential houseboats, among them plenty of former working craft.

*Croxley* (20m)   Above Croxley or Common Moor Lock (no 79) stands the first of John Dickinson's paper mills. All raw materials used to come in by water, and indeed the firm operated its own craft. Until 1970 considerable quantities of steam coal

K

arrived by narrow boat from the Ashby Canal, the voyage constituting one of the last surviving long-distance runs.

*Watford* (21m)  A new road-crossing at Cassio Bridge, a high level Metropolitan Railway bridge, and heavy lorry traffic bound for the M1 motorway crowd on to the canal for a moment, but soon it reaches the borders of Cassiobury Park and becomes one of the loveliest sections of canal so near a town anywhere in Britain. The 900 acres of the park, formerly the seat of the Earls of Essex, are now a public park and golf course. The house, with ecclesiastical windows and battlements similar to Strawberry Hill Gothic, was demolished about the turn of the century. Pressure from the owners at the time of the canal's construction is obvious even now, for the cut was designed to curve more in the manner of a river than a canal, while many species of mature trees shade the water. Because of the 4 locks within the Park and the towpath and its distinctive bridges, the waterway retains its canal qualities, but as an example of landscaping it could hardly be bettered. Bridge 167 below Lock 77 (Iron Bridge) is a single brick span, in elevation a shallow V. Bridge 165 has brick abutments with a cast-iron railing. Bridge 164 is in honey-coloured stone in the Classical style, with 2 small dry arches either side of the navigation channel and a stone balustrade. It is worth mentioning that the Victorian lattice-windowed cottage in the centre of the Park at Lock 76 had by 1970 been almost completely wrecked by vandals, and that under pressure from the local authority British Waterways were about to commence demolition when the prospective tenant arrived to take possession. With the aid of his Alsatian dog he was able to halt work, and after considerable expenditure has achieved an admirable restoration. Not so fortunate were many dozens, perhaps hundreds, of similar properties throughout the length of the waterways, whose only remains are nettle-infested foundations. An acute bend at Bridge 165 was notoriously difficult to negotiate with a pair of working boats, and the concrete bank bears evidence of wear from passing hulls.

*Hunton Bridge* (24m)  At the northern side of Cassiobury Park by Lady Capel's Lock some real open country seems likely, but shortly the A41 crosses over and stays never very far away until the canal reaches Tring. Just before the bridge itself there is a low brick wall standing by the towpath bearing a stone plaque commemorating the deaths of 2 men engaged in the construction of the Gade Valley Trunk Sewer in 1970. Similar canalside memorials can be found in Ireland and on the French waterways. The River Gade joins the canal at this point to reappear several more times before Hemel Hempstead.

*King's Langley* (25m)  King's Langley station and the main line from Euston appear near Home Park or Five Paddle Lock (no 70), and the line is a frequent sight for a considerable part of the journey to Birmingham. Further Dickinson paper mills at Langley and Apsley introduce an industrial section. A small canal maintenance yard alongside Apsley (or New) Lock is generally the location of dredgers and working boats loaded with new lock gates.

*Boxmoor* (28m 4f)  Rose's limejuice works, to which narrow boats still (1974) bring the raw material in barrels from Brentford, is well known for the Fishery pub, which gives its name to Lock 63. Hemel Hempstead railway station is close by. Then comes ½m of watercress beds between the canal and the railway on a high embankment. Boxmoor House near the canal at Bridge 148 is the site of a Roman villa.

*Winkwell* (29m 4f)  Here the Three Horseshoes Inn, reached down a narrow lane from the A41, is a popular canal centre that is occasionally flooded if the lock above is incorrectly used. A swing bridge (no 147) providing road access to the pub is worked by turning a tediously low-geared wheel, the length of the operation often resulting in a string of cars impatiently waiting for the passage of each boat. Lock 59, one of 3 at Winkwell and known as Irishman's Lock after a former keeper who was drowned here, overlooks Bourne End Mill, badly damaged by fire about 1970 and now extensively remodelled as a motel.

*Berkhamsted* (31m 4f)  One set of watercress beds by Lock 57 is equipped with a narrow gauge railway system along which waggons are manually propelled as the crop is gathered. Lissamer's Lock (no 56) as well as Bourne End (no 57) are alone among locks between the Cowroast summit and Cowley in having side ponds fitted as a means of economising on water in times of drought; although badly silted, they are mostly still quite workable (see p 41). Below this point many rivers feed the canal, so water supply is ample. The southern approach to Berkhamsted is slightly disappointing, for factory development gives little indication of the charm of the old town, with its long and flourishing shopping street. There is an impressive series of early medieval earthworks on the site of the castle, which boasts a unique double moat. Among many later buildings of interest are Berkhamsted Grammar School, founded in the seventeenth century, several churches and 4 important seventeenth- and eighteenth-century coaching inns. Little of this is evident from the canal, which, however, is excellently served by a succession of boatman's pubs, including the Bull, Rising Sun, Boat (at Bridge 142), and the Crystal Palace (near the station). Messrs Horsebarge Hotels have several converted Grand Union and Basingstoke Canal barges here, offering scheduled public trips throughout the summer from various stages between Boxmoor and Bulbourne. The totally silent and seemingly effortless gliding progress of a horse-drawn boat is an experience every canal user should try. Locks 55 and 54, Berkhamsted, are also known as Sweep's after one Eli Oliffe, who kept a general boatman's store at no 55 during the last century and was previously a chimneysweep.

*The Cowroast* (35m)  Progression through Broadwater Lock (no 53), Northchurch (nos 51 and 52) or Old Ned's (Ned Adlum worked on the canal at the time of its building), Awkward Billy or Crooked Billet (no 50), Bush or Barker's (no 49) and the two Dudswell locks (nos 47 and 48), where there is a wharf with several pretty cottages, brings us finally to the first summit level of the Grand Union, the Cowroast, named after a pub on the nearby main road. This is a point at which to take a long breath after the climb from the Thames. From here to Bull's Bridge depot was regarded as a very respectable day's run for working narrow boats, and none but the most ardent canal enthusiasts would try to emulate such progress. The waterway is nearly 400ft above the level of its starting point, a fact easily accepted by anyone who has toiled through the locks from Brentford. The respite lasts but 3m through the deep and wooded Tring Cutting, a place of wild clematis, kingfishers and shade from the hot summer sun. Because of Cowroast's former importance as a staging post, its lock-keeper may well request to see a boat's navigation permit, although he no longer gauges freight craft, or notes their tonnage of cargo in a range of leather-bound volumes containing statistics of individual narrow boats and occupying a broad shelf in the little lockside office.

*Tring* (36m 4f)   The town of Tring lies 1½m west of the canal from Bridge 135, although the station is close to this point. Since the fourteenth century Tring has been a leading market town. The Rothschild family occupied Tring Park, where one of them assembled an excellent zoological museum containing all manner of exhibits, not least a splendid collection of *siphonaptera*, or fleas, of which there are 1,234 known species. The flea institute was started in 1902 by Lord Rothschild's brother Charles and is now the premier source of reference throughout the world. The whole of the Tring museum's collection was bequeathed to the British Museum in 1938 and is open to the public. Unusual among summit levels, Tring receives no water supplies by gravity from natural streams, all water being pumped from the extensive reservoirs beside the Marsworth locks. The channel of the main line is deeper than normal so that considerable quantities can be drawn off in times of drought.

*Bulbourne* (38m)   Alongside Bridge 133 and most satisfying architecturally is the canal company's maintenance depot, very Victorian but functional. It was here that the Grand Junction Company constructed in 1897 a large working model of the Foxton inclined plane, and, having successfully tested the principles of the mechanism, built the full-sized version on the Leicester section. The depot now houses some up-to-date maintenance equipment and is well worth a visit if this can be arranged with the manager. Quite soon, the first of the flight of 7 Marsworth locks comes into sight,

*Grand Union Canal. Within walking distance of Marsworth Junction is Pitstone Mill, built in 1627 and now owned by the National Trust*

falling away from the summit. To the right is a BWB covered drydock, and opposite an unusually large and grand double-fronted lock-keeper's house. Alongside, the Wendover arm leaves the main line. Since shortly before World War I there has been no navigation past Tringford stop lock because of a leaking canal bed. Several low bridges have since been built over the channel between Halton and Wendover, making restoration seem remote. The section that remains is well worth exploring. It passes flour mills at Tring Wharf, where Bushell Bros' boatbuilding yard (birthplace of the experimental wide beamer *Progress* during the mid-1930s) was situated. The remains of Tringford stop lock mark the present terminus alongside a large pumping station. A lead plaque within the building notes that a steam-powered beam engine of 1803 vintage was replaced by the existing electrical machinery in 1927. Although little used for navigation, the Wendover arm continues to fulfil an important function in conveying water to the summit level.

The Marsworth locks constitute one of the most pleasantly situated flights on the Grand Union, set on a wide curve with a keeper's house halfway down. On the west bank lie Tringford, Marsworth and Startopsend reservoirs, while a fourth and larger one, Wilstone, is some ¾m away. Their total capacity is about 500 million gallons and they were built between 1802 and 1839 expressly for canal water supply. The Nature Conservancy has a National Nature Reserve of about 50 acres, while the British Trust for Ornithology has its headquarters nearby. Many rare plants and animals have been found here, including the orange fox-tail, broad-leaved ragwort and round-fruited rush, while the little known glis glis or edible dormouse can still be seen. Of a wide variety of water-birds, both black-necked grebe and little ringed plover have been recorded breeding, while among other visitors are snipe, ringed plover, common sandpiper, dunlin, redshank, greenshank, ruff, spoonbill, osprey and the very rare purple heron. In winter many unusual waterfowl, among them goldeneye, gadwall, smew, red-breasted merganser, and scaup, visit the lakes, and mute, whooper and bewick swans have been sighted.

*Marsworth Junction* (39m 3f)  The canal broadens considerably by the Marsworth Depot, where concrete bank-protection piles are manufactured.

*Aylesbury arm*  This leaves the main line at Marsworth and descends through 16 narrow locks, of which the first 2 are in the form of a staircase. Passing near Wilstone, Puttenham and Aston Clinton, this 6¼m waterway traverses really lovely open country to terminate in Aylesbury's canal basin, where many cruising and residential craft have moorings. Originally there was a plan to continue the arm to join the Thames and Wilts & Berks Canal at Abingdon, but work was never started. The old market town of Aylesbury thrives, although extensive road and office development during the 1960s altered much of its ancient character. The famous ducks are still bred, but in decreasing numbers. At the Mayor's annual Duck Dinner the bird is ceremonially 'danced in' by Morris dancers, the Mayor offering a set of newly minted coins in return for his portion.

Back on the main line, Bridge 132 at Marsworth, by the White Lion Inn, is the first of many lock bridges with a double arch. At these sites duplicate narrow locks were in operation alongside the wide ones from 1839 until their disuse later in the last century. There were 23 examples between Marsworth and Fenny Stratford, with further wide-beam duplicates at Stoke Bruerne.

Locks 37 and 38, Marsworth or Norman's, come shortly after one passes a small thatched village shop, once a pub, on the towpath. The rolling field alongside the upper lock contains a line of ventilation shafts from a railway tunnel beneath the Chilterns. On the skyline the smoking chimneys of a cement factory dominate the scene for several miles. The Dunstable & District Boat Club has moorings on the pound up to Lock 36, one of the Nag's Head Three. Nearby Cheddington became well known in 1963 in connection with the Great Train Robbery. Bridge 125, after a railway crossing, is one of the few Grand Union swing bridges.

Lock 30, Slapton or Neale's, has the easily visible remains of a narrow lock, while Church Lock (no 29) boasts a minute church with belfry, sold in 1973 for conversion into a most unusual private residence.

*Leighton Buzzard* (47m 4f)   Below Grove Lock (no 28) lies a small BWB depot, where maintenance craft are usually to be found. The 200ft spire of Leighton Buzzard's thirteenth-century All Saints church stands high above the meadows of the River Ouse, which divides the twin towns of Leighton and Linslade. There is a substantial pentagonal market cross dating from about 1400, and many old buildings of historical interest around the market place. Thirteen alternative names existed at various times for Leighton Buzzard, of which possibly the most romantic was Lygetune Beaudesert. Beyond the town is the busy headquarters of the Wyvern Shipping Co, whose hire craft include a fascinating variety of converted working boats. The yard was once occupied by Messrs L. B. Faulkener, long-distance carriers. The traditional canal painting of the late Frank Jones, who worked here, is justly famous. Canalside pits owned by George Garside supplied the London area with thousands of tons of waterborne sand and gravel until the late 1940s. Remains of the wharves, with small-gauge railway tracks leading to them, may be seen at four points south of the town. The Leighton Buzzard Narrow Gauge Railway Society was formed in 1967 to take over and operate nearly 4m of 2ft gauge mineral railway in and about Leighton. From their 'station' ½m SE of the town centre they work steam- and diesel-powered trains as a public attraction during summer weekends. One of the locomotives, *Chaloner*, built in 1877, is the only working survivor of a type designed for use in Welsh slate quarries.

After Leighton Lock (no 27) comes the privately owned Globe Inn, whose red tiles and weatherboarding are much photographed from a hilltop on the opposite bank of the canal.

*Three Locks, Soulbury* (51m)   A very popular halt for motorists, whose flight of locks and pub are crowded at weekends and on warm evenings. Woburn Abbey is some 5m NE along the A418. Again the clear remains of a former set of duplicate locks can be seen on the right, while side ponds stand between the towpath and the main road. Talbot's Lock (no 23) has a Victorian pumphouse with semicircular windows in a style not uncommon on this route.

*Fenny Stratford* (55m)   Closely associated with Bletchley. Together with a number of surrounding villages, this is the site of Milton Keynes New Town, whose population between 1990 and 2000 will reach 250,000. Obviously this expansion is making a considerable impact on the once-rural appearance of the waterway, but surroundings of the canal are to be largely preserved as a 'linear park' with points of urban development. Boatyards and tripping boat services are planned. Fenny Lock (no 22) is memorable on several counts. First, its rise of little more than 12in results from difficulties in making the canal banks hold water to the north; by building Fenny Lock in 1802 the problem was overcome. Second, a swing bridge spans the chamber. Third, after a nearly continuous chain of locks since the Thames, there remains only one more lock in the following 16m to Stoke Bruerne, that at Cosgrove some 11m away.

*Simpson* (56m 2f)   Just south of Bridge 91 a footpath leads to the Plough Inn, and at Bridge 83 a sign directs the navigator to the Barge Inn, some 200yd away. The latter establishment is noted for its 'Olde English Country Wines'. Running along the valley of the Great Ouse, the waterway follows a course frequently halfway up a hillside, providing extensive views. Immediately before Bridge 77 stands the Old Wharf Inn, now a private house. Here the Newport Pagnell arm used to branch off to serve marble quarries. It was abandoned in 1863 and converted into a railway.

*Linford* (61m)   On the left, beyond Bridge 77, is a fine agricultural estate partly concealed among mature trees. The Greek temple, light-yellow stone church and stone mansion epitomise the best of the English country village. The Black Horse pub stands by Bridge 76. Linford Lakes on the right are worked-out pits used for sailing.

*Wolverton* (64m)   A rather dreadful town, mainly devoted to railway carriage workshops, but with a convenient station by the canal. A ruined windmill marks its approach from the south. Gaunt buildings showing signs of World War II camouflage rise sheer from the water. By the Galleon pub is a timber yard, once served by the canal, and here a faded sign in elaborate typography announces 'Boats for Hire'. Early twentieth-century postcard views show skiffs and dinghies in use on the straight leading up to Wolverton Aqueduct.

*Cosgrove* (66m)   An 'iron trunk' aqueduct carries the canal over the Great Ouse south of Cosgrove Lock. When the canal had reached this point by 1800, the river was crossed on the level via 4 locks on the southern side and 5 on the northern. But to avoid the delays caused by floods on the Ouse, a three-arch masonry aqueduct was designed by William Jessop. Part of its embankment collapsed in January 1806, followed 2 years later by failure of the aqueduct itself. This was replaced first by a temporary wooden trough and in 1811 by the present structure. Major repairs were undertaken in 1921. In the reed-beds below remains of the original aqueduct can be seen. Above the lock, starting point for the public cruises of narrow-boat *Linda*, the derelict Buckingham arm runs to the SW. It was 10m long with 2 locks and several picturesque drawbridges, and last used by commercial traffic about 1938. Restoration of the first 1½m to Old Stratford was begun in 1973.

Remains of Roman baths were excavated near the junction in 1969, although there is little evidence to be seen. Cosgrove village is a real gem, with a large house in a park extending to the canal, stone cottages and a pedestrian tunnel under the canal. The decorated Gothic stone bridge (no 65) is the most elaborate on the entire waterway. The Barley Mow at Cosgrove itself and the Navigation Inn by Bridge 64 are both worth a visit. Two boat clubs have their moorings here.

*Yardley Gobion* (69m)   A substantial grey stone farm with stables and barns stands near Bridge 61. Like a number of others to be found in the next 20m, its situation offers great scope for restoration, with the full amenities of the waterway at hand. Already several such properties have been bought and renovated as a direct result of the growing popularity of the Grand Union.

*Stoke Bruerne* (72m)   One of the most famous canal villages on the British system, set in glorious countryside and bristling with thatched stone cottages. A flight of 7 locks climbs from the River Tove, the top one beyond a whitewashed twin-arch bridge. Here the village's main street is very definitely the canal, flanked on one side by the Boat Inn and on the other by a row of red-brick and stone cottages, furthest of which is the British Waterways Board Waterways Museum, open throughout the year. Weekend visitors arrive by the coachload at this delightful spot where many an interest in waterways has been born (see pp 109 and 194).

Several hundred yards north is the entrance to Blisworth Tunnel, 3,056yd in length. Seven longer tunnels were once in use on British canals, but of those still regularly navigable, only Dudley, at 3,172yd, exceeds Blisworth. Of all the engineering works on the Grand Union, Blisworth Tunnel presented the greatest problems. Earlier attempts to bore the hill to the east of the present site were abandoned when large quantities of water seeped into the workings. As the canal was carrying traffic on each side of the hill before completion of the tunnel, a double-track horsedrawn railway transferred goods from one end to the other. After the tunnel was opened in 1805 the railway was transferred to Cosgrove to assist with building of the aqueduct. Remains of the tracks, together with a line of brick-topped ventilation shafts, can be seen by following the road between Stoke Bruerne and Blisworth. The tunnel is a 'wet' one, with cascades of water pouring down the shafts on to passing boats. There is no towpath, and until 1871, when the company introduced steam tugs, all boats were 'legged' through. The tugs lasted until 1934, by which time most craft were diesel-powered. There is adequate room for narrow-beam boats to pass when underground, and it is generally just possible to see one end from the other.

*Blisworth* (75m)   A deep tree-covered cutting leads from the north end of the tunnel to the village, with its part thirteenth-century church of St John the Baptist and a number of pleasant Northampton stone houses. On the left of the canal stands a large warehouse of red brick with several courses of blue brick as decoration. Bearing the date 1879, the 5-storey building was one of a series of warehouses operated by the former Grand Union Canal Co. The Sun, Moon and Stars Inn is now a teahouse and art gallery. Some recent residential development on the outskirts of Blisworth does little to improve the appearance of the village from the water.

*Gayton Junction* (76m)   Here, right, is the start of the Northampton arm. In the wide pool maintenance craft are often moored up, for there is a BWB depot with the usual water and refuse-disposal facilities. Although the canal continues through the heart of the country for the next 15m, commercial activities were once numerous at a succession of wharves. Banbury Lane, Bugbrooke, Heyford, Floore Lane, Thornton, Whilton and Buckby, now little different from any other places along the canal bank, were all flourishing loading or unloading points in regular use until World War II. For much of the 16m pound between Stoke Bruerne and Buckby the London Midland railway line keeps company with the canal.

*Northampton arm*   An exceptionally lovely little canal, just under 5m long with 17 narrow locks descending to the valley of the River Nene at Northampton. The first 13 chambers are grouped in a flight near Rothersthorpe, with 4 chunky wooden drawbridges and a soaring concrete arch carrying the M1 motorway over Lock 12. Surroundings change from broad cornfields to railway sidings and industrial premises as the outskirts of Northampton appear at Far Cotton.

*Weedon* (84m 6f)   Heralded by rolling open country. The Narrow Boat Inn, alongside the A5 (Bridge 26), and a small boatyard mark the beginning of a long section of canal embankment with an aqueduct over the River Nene. Several times in the past emergencies have arisen with collapse of sections of canal bank. Weedon, at the junction of the A5 and A45, is well blessed with antique shops, but its chief reason for fame is the extensive military dock and barracks off the canal on the left. Begun in 1803 before the canal was finally completed, this complex of buildings (originally more extensive than now) consisted of 12 powder magazines, accommodation for 2 regiments and what was intended as a Royal Pavilion for George III in the event of a Napoleonic invasion. Weedon was chosen for its central location as far as possible from the coast, coupled with the excellent transport facilities offered by the brand new waterway. A yellow-brick gatehouse protected by a portcullis provides access to the rather severe buildings beside an arm of the canal. Little is available for public inspection. At the nearby (closed) railway station wharves once provided transhipment facilities between rail and water. Fuel and gas for boats are now available at the dock.

*Buckby Locks* (88m)   A thickly wooded Brockhall Spinney partly shields the M1 motorway (right) from the canal, but, on reaching the flight of 7 locks, road, railway and canal run side by side, offering the opportunity to compare 180 years of transport progress. Immediately before the locks comes Whilton Marina, where 125,000 cu ft of carth was excavated in 1971 and the resulting basin flooded. Now that all gate-paddles have been removed from the flight in the interests of maintenance economy, working uphill tends to be slow. Many boatmen's pubs in this area have closed down over the years, leaving only the New Inn, a free house, at the top lock still open. Another casualty of traffic decline was the well-known boatman's shop at the top lock, where the renowned Buckby decorated water cans were sold. Such supporting services generally vanished as recently as the 1930s and 1940s, followed not long after by the majority of the commercial boats themselves.

Soon comes Norton Junction, where the Grand Union's Leicester section branches off to the right (see p 301). A modern pair of cottages dating from the 1930s face a Victorian couple now occupied by the Salvation Army, long established on the canals as friends of the boat people. From beyond Norton, on the main line, look southwards to see the embankment of the Leicester section heading for Watford Gap.

*Braunston* (93m 4f)   The second summit level of the canal is now reached. Here water is supplied by 2 Daventry reservoirs either side of Braunston Tunnel, 2,049yd. As an alternative to travelling underground with the boat, passengers may prefer to follow the old horsepath over the top, which is still clearly defined if a little overgrown at the height of summer. A flight of 6 locks lowers the canal to Braunston village, passing the lockside Admiral Nelson Inn, with a drydock and yard specialising in narrow boats for pleasure alongside the bottom lock. Reservoirs on the left have been

*Grand Union Canal. Lush Warwickshire countryside near Napton Junction*

connected with the canal and converted into one of the largest inland marinas in the country. Part of the Ladyline Group, this yard offers all facilities, an extensive chandlery and boat showroom. But changes have been skilfully carried out to retain much of the earlier character of this Mecca of the canals. A delicate cast-iron towpath bridge from the Horseley Ironworks, and of identical pattern to many on the Northern Oxford Canal dating from its realignment in the 1830s, provides access to the marina along a short remaining section of the original Oxford Canal line. Fellows, Morton & Clayton's covered transhipment depot, where goods were loaded in and out of steamers, 2 narrow-boat drydocks, an early nineteenth-century iron crane, and machinery for steaming planks for boatbuilding remain together with a sophisticated boat sales and moorings complex. Here was the headquarters of the Samuel Barlow Coal Company's narrow-boat fleet, continued by Blue Line Canal Carriers from 1963 to 1970, the last regular long-distance traffic concern on the Grand Union. Many canal people live in retirement aboard narrow boats or in the village, where generations of boatmen are buried in the cemetery of All Saints Church. Set on a hill (right) above the canal, the church, built in 1849, possesses a fine steeple. Nearby the castellated red-brick tower-mill, now without sails and part of a private house, is another landmark (see also p 110).

Until widening of the Warwick–Napton and Warwick–Birmingham Canals, after their acquisition by the Grand Union Canal Co in 1929, a narrow gauge stop lock was situated outside the red-brick toll office at the marina entrance. This was removed during the 1930s. After one passes the A45 road bridge one comes to the Rose and Castle pub (right), a large late-Victorian structure that has extensive moorings to attract pleasure-boat trade. In 1971 a £50,000 restaurant inspired by the design of an

Oxford College Barge was opened as an additional attraction. The canal gave Braunston its original prominence, and the leisure uses of the waterway of today ensure its continuance as one of the busiest boating centres of the Midlands. The Y-shaped Braunston junction, where the Northern Oxford Canal leaves on the right, is equipped with a pair of Horseley iron bridges meeting on a central island. From this point until Napton Junction we follow the line of the Oxford Canal.

*Napton Junction* (98m 4f)   Through the villages of Flecknoe and Lower Shuck-burgh the canal is extremely rural, emphasising that parts of Warwickshire display some of the finest countryside in the Midlands. At the junction the Oxford Canal continues towards the Thames (see p 367), while the Grand Union makes a sharp right-hand turn under a concrete towpath bridge. The next 14m were originally the Warwick & Napton Canal, which had 25 locks with wide-beam concrete chambers and sloping enclosed ground paddle gear. These were all built during the 1930s improvement scheme. In most cases the old narrow locks can be seen alongside, converted into bypass weirs. These new locks are extremely efficient in operation, but the sheer number of them tends to make for tiring cruising. A few gates and paddles to work are not very taxing, but dozens in succession are. Nevertheless, the scenery is rather pleasant and numerous waterside inns will provide necessary refreshment. Three locks at Calcutt lie beyond the junction, with water supply reservoir to the left used by sailing dinghies.

*Stockton* (101m 6f)   Nine locks form a flight a short distance north of Stockton village. Now that commercial traffic has gone, the crumbling concrete surrounds with grass sprouting in crevices, only a few pleasure boats, and an air of isolation combine to create a slightly forbidding atmosphere. Near Lock 12 a disused arm leads to a cement works whose tall chimneys can be seen for several miles.

*Long Itchington* (102m 6f)   Below Itchington Bottom Lock the Two Boats Inn faces the Cuttle Inn on the other side of the waterway. The village has some remark-able half-timbered buildings and a tiny pond at the centre of a shady green.

*Bascote* (104m 4f)   Remote from the village and approached via farm lanes, Bascote locks comprise a 2-rise staircase followed by 2 single chambers. The very pretty cottage and garden is in private occupation.

*Radford Semele* (107m 4f)   Six further locks spaced at regular intervals bring the canal to Radford, now a suburb of Leamington Spa. The Roman Foss Way crosses by Bridge 32.

*Leamington Spa* (109m 1f)   A town that fails to show its best side to the canal traveller. The extensive Sydenham housing estate, left, has been developed with grass extending to the water, but high iron railings seem to indicate that the navigation is something unpleasant, to be shut away. Elsewhere there are backs of factories, refuse in the channel and the railway station with typical terraced houses. The town is best reached from this point, Bridge 41, and within a short walk the grand hotels, formal gardens and other public buildings of the once fashionable spa that grew up in the nineteenth century are revealed.

*Warwick* (112m 4f)  Leamington has expanded almost to meet the outskirts of Warwick, although parts of the canal are green and bordered by trees. Several aqueducts include one over the Warwickshire Avon. Tempting tentative proposals have been advanced to continue river navigation upstream of Stratford with a lock or lift at this point to join the two waterways. If this is eventually achieved, a wide-beam route between the Thames and the Severn would result, without the navigational problems presented by the Severn estuary that will affect the Kennet & Avon when restored. Best approach to Warwick is from the Cape of Good Hope Inn, with its pair of locks. This splendid town is noted for its mainly fourteenth-century castle (open to the public), church of St Mary (more like a cathedral) and sections of wall with two entrance gates. At the short and derelict Saltisford arm, which took the canal boats nearer the town centre, the GU joins the former Warwick & Birmingham Canal.

*Hatton Locks* (113m 5f)  This feature of the northern Grand Union will remain in your memory long after everything else has become vague. Between Napton and Warwick the locks have descended towards the Avon, but now they begin to climb towards the Birmingham plateau. No fewer than 21 at Hatton form a flight with a rise and fall of 146ft 6in. The majority can be seen at once, their dozens of white-painted balance beams and paddle casings striding up Hatton Hill. It is best to share labour and save water by working through in company with another boat. Send a crew member ahead to prepare the next chamber, and resist any temptation to break records unless you are unusually active and healthy. Progress is marked by Middle Lock Bridge (no 53) and the pleasing Victorian maintenance yard buildings 4 locks from the top. A well-deserved rest comes with an 8m level pound after the top lock. The author once took a boat single-handed from below Knowle to Braunston in a nonstop 16-hour bid to complete a journey on time – 29m and 46 locks. He has not since repeated the exercise or is ever likely to try!

*Shrewley* (115m 3f)  Cruising past the very convenient Hatton Station, you shortly reach Shrewley Tunnel, 433yd and without a towpath. Unless you take to the old horsepath over the top, you will miss Shrewley village altogether, for its main street runs over the tunnel centre. A unique feature of the northern portal is that the towpath dives into its own short section of tunnel high above the water. This steeply rising and slimy track emerges in daylight near shops and other useful facilities.

*Lapworth* (118m 2f)  Beyond Rowington, sections of embankment amid the greenest of pastures lead to Lapworth village, where a short arm, left, connects with the narrow beam Stratford-upon-Avon Canal (see p 408). If Birmingham city centre is the objective, an alternative and probably preferable route is via the Northern Stratford to its junction with the Worcester & Birmingham Canal. Otherwise, an interesting circular trip is possible via these waterways and the remaining part of the Grand Union and the Birmingham Canal Navigations.

*Knowle* (122m 1f)  There is a pretty village at Baddesley Clinton (Bridge 66) and a rustic pub called the Black Boy by Bridge 69. Moored craft by a club represent some of the last mass pleasure-cruising activity normally encountered as Birmingham approaches. Five locks at Knowle replace the earlier 6, and their paddles always seem

even harder to lift than those of similar design elsewhere. This can hardly be imagination, for the keeper uses a larger than normal windlass. Knowle lies a little distance
west of the canal, an agreeable and flourishing place with an air that suggests that the
wealthy shop there. (The district is popular with the professional classes of Birmingham.) Two outstanding timber-framed buildings are fifteenth-century Chester House
in the town centre and sixteenth-century Grimshaw Hall in a park near the canal.

*Elmdon Heath* (126m 4f)   Gradually Birmingham's suburbs approach as the waterway follows a generally peaceful course midway between the A41 from Stratford–
Birmingham and the A45 past the city's airport. Near Solihull the West Midlands Gas
Board has landscaped the canalside for its workers with a picnic area, gardens and
swimming pool – an altogether creditable use of the site. But otherwise little development has taken place to capitalise on the canal's potential amenity value.

*Tyseley* (128m 6f)   Deep wooded cuttings, residential districts and rather overgrown towpaths eventually give way to the industrial edges of Birmingham. There is a
complete absence of facilities such as refuse disposal or drinking water points. Near
Bridge 88 stands Tyseley Goods Yard, where the Standard Gauge Steam Trust
displays its collection of railway locomotives during the summer. The BWB wharf
was once the destination for many of the trading narrow-boat pairs.

*Birmingham* (Salford Junction, 135m 5f)   Surroundings become increasingly
urban, with much heavy industry, railway tracks and streets of small houses. After a
time you tend to remark on the beauty of the few individual trees, clumps of flowering
willowherb or waterside bushes of yellow broom. Maximum beam of the waterway
is reduced from 14ft to about 13ft by a single bridge just before Birmingham, but this
matters little, for a flight of 6 narrow locks occurs at Camphill, amid the roar of the
city and the distinctive blend of chemical smells that characterise the waterways of the
district. As on the BCN, a secret quality of the canal, in sharp contrast with the
bustling streets beyond, provides a certain melancholy charm. A short distance left
of Bordesley Junction at the foot of Camphill locks marks the start of the Digbeth
branch, passing via Ashted locks to join the Birmingham & Fazeley Canal (see p 240).
The end of the Warwick & Birmingham Canal is technically ½m beyond Bordesley.
The remainder of the journey along the Grand Union is over the former Birmingham
& Warwick Junction Canal (with 5 locks, the Garrison flight); there is severe difficulty in discovering access from towpath to the outside world and a single shallow
lock (Nechell's) in the shadow of a power station and the motorway maze generally
dubbed Spaghetti Junction. Connections are made with the Birmingham & Fazeley
and Tame Valley Canals.

### GRAND UNION CANAL (LEICESTER SECTION)

From the Main Line of the Grand Union at Norton Junction, near Daventry,
Northants, to the River Trent, near Sawley; 66m with 59 locks. Maximum dimensions
are 72ft × 7ft (Norton–Foxton) and 14ft (Market Harborough–the Trent) × 3ft 6in
draught × 7ft 6in headroom. Locks at Watford, Foxton and Welford are narrow-
beam, and the rest are wide-beam. The Leicester section comprises various navigations
that were acquired by the Grand Union Canal Co to form a through route from their
Main Line to the Trent Navigation. They are the Old Grand Union Canal (Norton–

Foxton), the Leicestershire & Northamptonshire Union Canal (Market Harborough–Leicester), the Leicester Navigation (Leicester–Loughborough), and the River Soar or Loughborough Navigation (Loughborough–the Trent). The 20m summit level between Watford and Foxton Locks is one of the most lonely and beautiful lengths of cruising waterway in Britain. Parts of the River Soar are also particularly attractive.

*Norton Junction*   The route begins near the top of Buckby Locks and follows an embankment before diving into trees.

*Watford* (2m 1f)   The settlement around Bridge 5 has been overshadowed by the Watford Gap M1 service station, accessible from the waterway and a useful source of supplies. There are rather few opportunities for such facilities for many miles afterwards. The Stag's Head Restaurant provides unhurried meals overlooking the waterway. Situated on a curve of the canal are the 7 locks of the Watford Flight, part of them forming a staircase.

*Crick* (4m 5f)   A 1,528yd tunnel pierces a tall grassy hill. Beyond the cutting at the far end a hire-craft yard and tripping boats occupy wharf buildings. Crick village lies a little way to the west, a place of brick and ironstone cottages. The canal now follows an utterly deserted, winding and charming course around the base of Crack's Hill. No villages are in evidence in the rich pastureland.

*Yelvertoft* (7m 1f)   A few wharf buildings by Bridge 19. The village lies to the west. This countryside is deeply rural and perhaps a little forlorn, a region of deserted cattle sheds by bridges, gated roads and depopulated villages. One such is Winwick (Bridge 23), with a sixteenth-century brick manor house.

*Elkington* (10m 3f)   Both wharf and village at Bridge 28 have now vanished. The waterway continues to curve in avoiding a ridge of hills to the east that rise nearly 300ft above the 412ft level of the canal.

*Welford arm* (15m 4f)   Passing Stanford reservoir and South Kilworth, east of Bridge 37, the navigation shortly crosses the Warwickshire Avon on a small aqueduct and enters a wide pool at the junction with the short Welford arm. This 1½m branch serves as a feeder to the summit level, bringing water supplies from Welford and Sulby reservoirs. It lay quite derelict for several decades until its reopening in 1969. Two notable features are a shallow narrow lock at Welford and the gaunt remains of a drawbridge nearby. The terminus lacks any kind of basin, although wharf buildings were doubtless once served by trading craft. There is now a boatyard and restaurant. Situated on the A50, the village straddles the Northants/Leics border.

*Husbands Bosworth* (17m 6f)   Only evidence of North Kilworth on the A427 is the thriving yard and moorings of Hucker Marine by Bridge 43. Then follows a wooded cutting to the mouth of Bosworth Tunnel (1,166yd). At the far end a rustic lane leads from Bridge 46 across a derelict railway line to Husbands Bosworth, a pleasant village with the fourteenth-century spire of All Saints church and the Georgian Hall, parts of which date from the sixteenth century. The whole length of canal towpath within Leicestershire is admirably maintained as a long-distance country walk by the county council.

*Foxton* (23m)   After winding at the foot of the Laughton Hills, to the north, the canal arrives at Foxton Locks, one of the most remarkable staircases in Britain. A local-authority car park and picnic area provided by Bridge 60 indicates the popularity of the area. A change in levels of 75ft is overcome by two sets of risers, each comprising 5 lock chambers with a short pound between. To the right are the overgrown remains of the inclined-plane boat lift that operated between 1900 and 1912 (see p 48). At the lower end of the locks, which are operated by using a series of side ponds, the canal joins the former Leicestershire & Northamptonshire Union Canal, whose original terminus now lies at the end of a 5½m branch leading to Market Harborough.

*Market Harborough arm*   This section passes through the heart of Foxton village, where there is a swing bridge. Thereafter it is agreeable but generally featureless, describing a series of huge loops before reaching Harborough Basin. Heavy hire-craft traffic is ensured by establishment of a leading boatyard in the town basin. A weekly market has been held here since the early thirteenth century. Most memorable aspects are the soaring steeple of the church of St Dionysius, the little grammar school of 1614 and the magnificent wrought-iron sign of the Three Swans Hotel. The very first IWA National Rally of Boats was held here in 1950.

*Saddington* (26m 5f)   From Harborough to the Trent the waterway is equipped with wide-beam locks and bridges, one rather lovely example being the roving bridge at the foot of Foxton Locks. The following countryside is exceptionally attractive, being hilly and wooded, with many old-world villages within walking distance. These include Gumley, Smeeton Westerby and Saddington. The last of the Leicester

*Grand Union Canal, Leicester section. A canalised part of the River Soar at Cossington Lock*

section's tunnels is a ½m bore at Saddington. Beyond its north portal a field path leads from Bridge 76 to Fleckney, a useful source of supplies but otherwise dreary and rather industrial.

*Kibworth* (28m 1f)   Locks now follow at regular intervals – the Kibworth Three, Pywell's and Crane's. Several stand in isolation in fields where cattle and sheep graze alongside the chambers.

*Newton Harcourt* (30m 5f)   Scenery continues to remain very fine, with a wealth of wildflowers (the clusters of waterside dog roses are a memorable feature) and teeming bird and animal life. Three locks at Newton are shaded by trees and much frequented by towpath strollers.

*Kilby Bridge* (32m 7f)   Beyond 4 Wigston locks one reaches the BWB Kilby Bridge maintenance yard, which has been nicely redecorated in cream and chocolate paint. The outskirts of Leicester now increasingly make their presence felt, villages having been swallowed in a suburban sprawl. Nevertheless, the canal retains a typically rural aspect through such places as South Wigston, Blaby and Glen Parva.

*Aylestone* (38m 5f)   The view ahead comprises a vista of electricity pylons converging on Leicester. These are a sadly characteristic feature of much of the Soar Valley and the Trent, where numerous power stations have been sited to benefit from ample supplies of cooling water. A little east of Bridge 105 a fifteenth-century packhorse bridge crosses the Soar.

*Leicester* (42m 4f)   The area of Greater Leicester contains over 250,000 people, the county's major centre of population. Various forms of light industry flourish alongside the older firms specialising in the hosiery trade. The navigation remains one of Leicester's chief assets, forming a wide straight reach beyond Freeman's Meadow Lock. The beautiful Abbey Park is bordered on one side by the canal near Limekiln Lock and on another by a navigable section of the River Soar. Established by the Romans, Leicester can show several important remains from this era. The Industrial Revolution is marked by important collections, including a Museum of Technology and a Railway Museum. From Belgrave Lock the Soar forms the course of the Leicester section for most of the remaining distance to the Trent.

*Thurmaston* (46m)   Rural surroundings return near Birstall Lock. Large unguarded weirs near the head of lock cuts require a degree of vigilance from boat crews. The multiplicity of resulting side streams accounts for many pretty wooden towpath bridges, smartly white-painted. Thurmaston village is best by the river, where lock and adjoining boatyard possess an individuality generally missing in the main street. An extensive Anglo-Saxon pagan cemetery has been discovered here. Various water-based activities are encouraged at a landscaped gravel pit by the navigation at Syston.

*Cossington* (48m)   The Old Junction Boatyard between Syston and Cossington derives its name from a confluence with the quite derelict Melton Mowbray Navigation, which was based on the course of the River Wreake. This fell into disuse in the late 1870s, but originally enabled barges to reach Oakham, via the Oakham Canal, closed in 1846. The two waterways ran for 30m with 31 locks, and are rewarding subjects for land-based exploration. Near Cossington Lock is a splendid watermill, now a restaurant. Some of the Soar's best scenery follows in the reach to Sileby.

*Mountsorrel* (51m 3f)   Overlooked by a lofty granite hill topped by a war memorial, this small town is well known for its quarry, which produces building stone and road chippings. There are two flourishing boatyards above and below the weir pool, a restaurant by the lock and a good deal of traffic along the A6. Spanning the navigation is an exceptionally broad-arched brick railway bridge prominently dated 1860. Being an important river resort, there are caravans in the watermeadows and many moored craft.

*Barrow-on-Soar* (53m 3f)   Perhaps the finest place on the Soar, where the waterway skirts the bottom of a tree-covered cliff. Above is the village centre. By the road bridge is a café whose gardens provide moorings for hired rowing boats. At the end of a reach of almost 2m, the river is left in favour of a long artificial canal cut through Loughborough. Pilling's Lock at the entrance is one of several flood chambers normally open at each end. The Soar is particularly subject to sudden rises in water level.

*Loughborough* (56m 2f)   Seen from the waterway, this is not an attractive town, for the canal seeks out factories, terraced houses and the railway station. Bellmaking is one local industry and there is a municipal carillon tower. A short arm leads to the British Waterways yard. The canal improves once more below Bishop Meadow Lock, where the navigation joins the Soar.

*Normanton* (59m 3f)   This tiny village is dominated by a magnificent waterside thirteenth-century church steeple. There is a public house, delightful thatched post office and, downstream, the headquarters of the Soar Boat Club. At Zouch a long lock cut leads to a splendidly unspoiled reach past Whatton House (gardens open to the public on Sunday afternoons) and Sutton Bonnington. As elsewhere, few buildings are near the river banks because of the flooding risk.

*Kegworth* (63m 2f)   The village is a compact settlement built on a slight hill. Several good Georgian houses stand near the little market square. Kegworth Old Lock is followed after a broad loop by the Flood Lock, usually to be found open at each end. Small craft can avoid this chamber if they wish by navigating a bypass channel.

*Ratcliffe* (65m)   Another lock is situated in open fields close to a large power station that dominates Trent Junction. The final lock is at Red Hill, where the Soar flows into the broad waters of the Trent. Technically the Grand Union continues over this 4-way junction and up the Erewash Canal to Langley Mill (see p 279).

### GRAND WESTERN CANAL

From Lowdwells, Somerset, to Tiverton, Devon; 11m with no locks. Authorised in 1796 to run from Taunton on the River Tone to Topsham, near Exeter, the Grand Western would have provided a navigation from the north to the south coast. In fact only 24m were completed, between Tiverton and Taunton. The 11m Tiverton section was constructed to barge standards, remained in commercial use until about 1924, and was officially abandoned in 1962. The Lowdwells–Taunton length admitted tub-boats measuring up to 26ft × 6ft 6in, and was notable for a series of 7 vertical lifts (6 in association with shallow locks) and 1 inclined plane. Although disused by 1867, some of the masonry of the lifts can still be found, notably at Nynehead, where the levels altered by 24ft.

Devon County Council was given the surviving part of the waterway, together with a substantial sum of money, by British Waterways in 1970. It has since been restored for boating and general amenity. Horsedrawn boat trips begin at Tiverton basin, a good point at which to start exploring the towpath, which constitutes a very pleasant rural walk. It is understood that the county council forbids the use of all motorised craft on the grounds that resulting wash will damage the banks.

Maximum craft dimensions are 7ft beam × 3ft 6in draught × 7ft 3in headroom, and length is unrestricted. As the canal is isolated from other navigable water, all boats must be brought overland.

### HUDDERSFIELD BROAD CANAL

From the Calder & Hebble Navigation at Cooper Bridge to a terminus at Aspley Basin, Huddersfield; 3¼m with 9 locks. Completed in 1776, the Huddersfield Broad, otherwise known as Sir John Ramsden's Canal, formed one of the three trans-Pennine routes, in company with the Huddersfield Narrow from 1811. The Narrow Canal was abandoned in 1944, and its 20m heavily locked course to the Ashton near Manchester is now quite derelict (see pp 224 and 263). Maximum craft dimensions are 57ft 6in × 14ft 2in × about 3ft draught × 9ft 3in headroom.

Scenery along the Huddersfield Broad is a mixture of patches of open space mingled with industrial development, most of which grew up during the nineteenth century. The chief navigational feature is the series of 9 wide-beam locks. Shortly before reaching the terminal Aspley Basin comes the extraordinary Turnbridge vertical lift bridge. Erected in 1865, a system of overhead girders and large pulleys enables the entire deck to rise, parallel with the water. While it is dangerous to describe any aspect of inland waterways as unique, it is probable that, aside from the Barrow Navigation, there are no other examples of this type of structure in the British Isles.

Huddersfield has become something of a boating centre since the establishment of Aspley Marina in recent years. Here all facilities will be found, together with a licensed clubhouse aboard a converted keel. Rowing boats may be hired for short periods. Situated along the River Colne, Huddersfield is surrounded by hills. There is much grand-scale Victorian architecture, with J. P. Pritchett's 1847 Corinthian-style railway station in blackened stone providing one of the best specimens of such buildings in Britain. Well worth visiting are the Art Gallery and Tolson Memorial Museum, where exhibits include machinery connected with the famous Huddersfield worsted trade.

### HULL, RIVER

From Struncheon Hill Lock, junction with the Driffield Navigation, to Hull and the Humber; 20m and tidal throughout. There are no restrictions on the size of craft except for draught, which is 6ft from the Humber to Beverley Beck and 5ft thereafter. The lowest 2m have several connections with Hull docks and the tidal flow is very considerable. The course of the river is a winding one, past rather featureless muddy banks.

## HUMBER, RIVER

From Trent Falls, junction with the Trent and Yorkshire Ouse, to the North Sea off Grimsby; 36m and tidal throughout. The Humber estuary connects with the Rivers Ancholme, Hull, Trent and Ouse, as well as the Market Weighton Navigation. It is a busy commercial piece of water with very fast-flowing tides, and should not be navigated except in suitable craft and with the aid of updated charts.

## IDLE, RIVER

From the River Trent at West Stockwith, Notts, to Bawtry, Yorks; 11m with 1 lock. One of a number of waterways in the NE that appeal to the adventurous cruising enthusiast who must navigate everything, but otherwise a rather dull channel hidden by high banks. The Idle was much improved in the late 1620s by the Dutch engineer Cornelius Vermuyden in connection with his plan for draining the Isle of Axholme. A flourishing commercial trade existed until the opening of the Chesterfield Canal, part of which duplicated its course. Dimensions are beam 18ft, headroom 9ft, and draught (to Idle Stop) 2ft 6in, (to Bawtry) 1ft 6in. Length is unrestricted.

*West Stockwith*  Entry to the river from the tidal Trent is a short distance down river from West Stockwith Basin. At the time of writing the lock consists of a single vertically rising guillotine gate that is only lifted when the 2 rivers make a level. In 1971 the Trent River Authority announced a drainage improvement scheme that envisaged a fixed sluice bypassed by a ramp for trailed boats (see also pp 269 and 436).

*Misterton* (1m)  The site of an eighteenth-century sluice and lock, now removed.

*Bawtry* (11m)  Quiet and exceptionally fertile farmland characterises the course of the river. Bawtry boasts some good Georgian houses, inns and a market place. Nearby villages of Austerfield and Scrooby are well known among Americans as the birthplaces of two leaders of the Pilgrim Fathers, who sailed aboard the *Mayflower* for the New World in 1620.

## KENNET & AVON CANAL

From the Thames at Reading to Hanham Lock on the Bristol Avon; 86½m with 105 locks (roadworks in Bath have necessitated conversion of two of the Widcombe Locks into one single deep chamber). Maximum craft dimensions are 73ft (75ft on the Avon) × 13ft 10in (Avon, 16ft) × 3ft 6in draught × about 8ft 10in headroom. Draught and headroom measurements may in a few cases be rather less than the official sizes. The Kennet was originally fitted with slightly longer locks, but postwar reconstruction has reduced their usable length; thus a 14ft-beam craft would have to be no more than about 67ft long, whereas a 71ft narrow boat on a 7ft beam should be able to pass through.

Based on 3 distinct sections, the navigation comprises the Kennet between Reading and Newbury, opened in 1723, and the Bristol Avon from Hanham to Bath, opened in 1727, plus the canal connecting these two, which saw its first traffic in 1810. Uniting the waters of the Thames with the Bristol Channel by a wide-beam route, the Kennet & Avon should now be one of the most heavily used pleasure-craft waterways. However, following its acquisition by the Great Western Railway Co in 1852 for more than £210,000, commercial traffic was not very actively encouraged. For much of the twentieth century, the K&A has been navigable only with difficulty. The last through passage from end to end was achieved in 1951. Attempts to abandon it were thwarted, and now for a number of years restoration has been in progress, with a strong element of cooperation between BWB and the Kennet & Avon Canal Trust (which began as a section of the IWA).

At the time of writing lengths at the Reading end, at Newbury, along the Wiltshire Pound from Devizes to Crofton Locks and on the Avon downstream of Bath are fully operational. Much of the rest is boatable in canoes and other small craft. In view of the large number of locks that remain to be regated, and the massive backlog of dredging work, it is difficult to estimate when this invaluable waterway will again be open from end to end. At the current rate of progress the breakthrough may not be achieved much before the early 1980s. Throughout, the canal passes through some of the finest scenery in the South of England, and for the scale of its engineering works it deserves to rank with the Grand Union and the Leeds & Liverpool.

*Reading*   The Kennet enters the Thames near the gasworks, giving little promise of the virtually unbroken countryside that continues all the way to Bath. While it proudly maintains a long municipal waterside walk to the Thames, the town seems to ignore its Kennet frontage. Reading is what might be expected of a place whose fortunes are founded on brewing, biscuits and seeds. The first lock, Blake's, is maintained by the Thames Water Authority with characteristic smart paint and a modern keeper's house. The next one, County, is much more in the canal style, with a weir alongside. Originally many Kennet locks (like some of the Wey Navigation) were turf-sided, and several still remain in that form. Pleasant meadows mark the outskirts of Reading, past Fobney and Southcote Locks to Burghfield. Here the lock was

*Kennet & Avon Canal. One of the Wootton Rivers Locks west of Bruce Tunnel, seen during a cruise to celebrate restoration, June 1973*

completely rebuilt in 1968 and the old turf-sided chamber remains nearby. Garston Lock is turf-sided, with iron rails marking the portion to which craft must keep to avoid being stranded on the sides. It has been suggested that a very extensive gravel pit nearby, used for water skiing, could be linked to the canal to provide many boat moorings. A new lock would be necessary, but the resulting marina would be free of the winter flooding problems that affect the Kennet.

*Sulhampstead* (6m 5f)   Near the lock are moorings and an attractive yellow stone keeper's house. Many bridges over the canal are small, manually operated swing spans, and these, it is claimed, would cause severe road congestion if substantial canal traffic again became possible. Tyle Mill Lock, 8½m beyond Reading, is the current (1974) navigation limit from the Thames.

*Newbury* (18m 4f)   Ten locks intervene between Tyle Mill and Newbury, with the villages of Aldermaston, Woolhampton and Midgham. The waterway is easily reached at several points off the A4, a road that has lost much traffic since the opening of the M4. Paper mills are evident at Colthrop, but otherwise the valley of the Kennet is extremely pleasant. From Bull's Lock (no 88) the canal again becomes navigable and may be cruised almost 11m to Hungerford (1974). Newbury is a fine old town, serving the surrounding agricultural areas of Berkshire. Not unusually, its once busy canal basin has been converted into a bus park, although original wharf buildings remain. The town became an important centre of the cloth industry in the time of Henry VIII, and its Perpendicular church of St Nicholas at West Mills also dates from the early sixteenth century. One of the current attractions is the horse-drawn tripping boat *Kennet Valley*, a slightly wider than normal narrow boat previously used on the Grand Union by John Dickinson's Hertfordshire paper mills. Care should be taken when negotiating the temporary wartime bridge near Greenham Lock, whose headroom is about 6ft 6in. Water levels can be lowered by arrangement. Downstream of Newbury Lock is a charming single-arched balustraded stone bridge without towpath. A preserved sign by the lock warns: 'The Captain of every vessel allowing Horses to Haul across the Street will be Fined.' Although fed by the Kennet for a considerable distance, the navigation continues through Guyer's, Higg's and Benham Locks as a mainly artificial canal through meadows. Visible near Benham Lock is the great Benham Park House, built in 1772–5 by Capability Brown.

*Hamstead Marshall* (22m)   Another lovely park borders the waterway, with well-restored watermill near the lock. The stretch from here to Kintbury was reopened in the early summer of 1972.

*Kintbury* (24m 4f)   Well-maintained locks (Copse and Drewett's) lead through mixed pastureland and woods to Kintbury, with a railway station near the canal bridge. The railway follows the waterway for much of the route to Bath. The Dundas Arms stands by the water below a lock.

*Hungerford* (27m 4f)   Beyond Denford the Kennet takes a NW course and leaves the navigation for the last time. The Berkshire Trout Farm, housed in a former mill near Dunn Mill Lock, indicates the fine angling facilities for which the Kennet is well known. Hungerford, current navigable limit, is a good Georgian market town with a broad main street, an old warehouse on the wharf and a curious white-painted iron bridge leading to the front door of a house by the canal. Soon the county boundary with Wiltshire is passed, and a timeless landscape is revealed through the Vale of Pewsey. The Downs of Wiltshire have been settled since ancient times and the county is rich in prehistoric remains.

*Great Bedwyn* (32m 6f)   Ruined locks, swing bridges and villages such as Froxfield and Little Bedwyn make the canal a worthy object of waterside walks. Both Romans and Saxons developed Great Bedwyn, long a place of craftsmanship in stone. The work of 7 generations of masons is preserved in the fascinating Stone Museum, which includes tombstones, statues and the fossilised print of a dinosaur.

*Crofton* (34m)   A series of 9 locks leads to the short summit pound. By Lock 61 restored steam pumps dating from the early years of the nineteenth century may be seen working during certain weekends. They were designed to lift supplies from Wilton Water to the canal immediately above Lock 55. The massive beam engines create an awe-inspiring sound and sight as they methodically rock to and fro, like the heartbeat of a huge animal (p 30). Restoration is now proceeding on the locks with the hope that navigation will be again possible from Newbury to Devizes by 1976.

*Bruce Tunnel* (36m)   A notable feature of the summit level, 502yd long, and passing under a hill on the borders of Savernake Forest. Since the summer of 1973 boats have been able to reach Crofton Top Lock from Devizes, a distance of more than 22m. The tunnel portal in red brick is one of the widest in Britain, and bears at its east end a commemorative stone plaque. As there was no towpath, boats were hauled through by pulling on chains suspended from the wall.

*Wootton Rivers* (38m 4f)   Four locks, now falling towards the Avon, lead to the 15m Wiltshire Pound. The village of Wootton Rivers is exceptionally pretty, being strung out along a street reached from the bridge at Lock 51. Houses display brick, half-timbering and thatch. The church clock was built from bedsteads, prams and other junk by Jack Spratt to mark the Coronation of George V, and its face uses the letters GLORY BE TO GOD in place of numbers.

*Pewsey* (41m 4f)   This little country town lies to the south of Pewsey Wharf, with warehouse, elegant farm buildings and slipway for launching trailed craft. On the Downs several miles south of the canal is a 66ft long white horse cut from the chalk in the eighteenth century and restored in 1937. Ladies Bridge, Wilcot, is an unusually ornamental stone span, believed to have been designed by Rennie and dated 1808. In style it is a good match for the classical aqueducts at Avoncliffe and Limpley Stoke.

*Honey Street* (45m 4f)   The best of several pretty villages near the canal (others are Stanton St Bernard, All Cannings, Allington, Horton and Bishops Cannings). Its Barge Inn near the wharf recalls a former centre of boatbuilding, where many canal craft and sailing trows were constructed. Another white horse may be seen to the north near the wharf, and this dates from 1812. The countryside mainly comprises broad sweeping hills divided into sizeable fields.

*Kennet & Avon Canal. Greatest obstacle to eventually linking the Thames with the Bristol Avon is the flight of 29 Caen Hill Locks at Devizes, here seen quite derelict*

*Devizes* (53m)  Perhaps the most important point on the waterway from a canal viewpoint, for here is a massive congregation of locks whose numbering descends from 50 to 22 within 2m. Seventeen are closely placed at regular intervals down the slope of Caen Hill. Although very overgrown and derelict, the chambers and elongated side ponds present a spectacle that is difficult to equal on any canal elsewhere. Their rehabilitation is likely to be the final task on the waterway and, it will be interesting to see whether they are regated or replaced by some form of inclined-plane boat railway, which would be more economical of labour and water supplies. Since 1950 an annual canoe race from Devizes to Westminster attracting more than 300 entrants has been held at Easter. The record nonstop paddle is about 20½ hours, an astonishing feat of endurance for a 117m course with numerous portages. Devizes is essentially an eighteenth-century market town, and promoters of the K&A are reputed to have held early meetings at the Bear Hotel.

*Seend* (58m 3f)  Beyond Sells Green lie the villages of Seend and Seend Cleave, and the Barge Inn stands by Lock 19. Five locks are set in particularly luxuriant and green countryside.

*Semington* (60m 4f)  This is the junction with the Wilts & Berks Canal, a narrow-beam waterway that had become disused by 1906 and was abandoned in 1914. Its length was 51m, and it connected with the Thames at Abingdon and (via the North Wilts Canal) with the Thames & Severn. A concrete dam and former lock-keeper's cottage are the only signs of its existence at Semington. A fine stone cottage by the lower of 2 locks on the K&A has been completely refurbished, and a drydock and slipway constructed to serve a cruising restaurant boat that was scheduled to ply

between here and Bradford-on-Avon from 1974. Such commercial boating development on the canal is still in its infancy, but very considerable scope exists for the
facilities that will be in demand once the through route is restored. Two small
aqueducts carry the canal over the River Biss and a railway near Staverton (63m 4f).

*Bradford-on-Avon* (65m 4f)   The River Avon approaches the canal near Lady-
down Bridge, Staverton, and reappears again beyond Bradford. The town is situated
on both sides of the steep river valley, with thick woods. Above Bradford Lock lie a
wharf and drydock that are leased to the K&A Canal Trust. Bradford is an ancient
and exciting town, whose church was built about AD 900. There is a medieval Town
Bridge of 9 arches, rebuilt in the seventeenth century and possessing a chapel at its
centre that was for many years used as the local lock-up. Finest buildings are from the
eighteenth century in yellow Bath stone. During that century clothmaking reached its
peak of prosperity, with as many as 32 mills listed by 1800.

*Avoncliffe Aqueduct* (67m)   River and canal leave Bradford side by side through
the dense woods that clothe this beautiful valley. At Bradford Swing Bridge the canal
bed is dry (1974) and remains so for about 3m to Limpley Stoke. Landslips and leaks
are the cause, but a cure will undoubtedly be found. Making an almost right-angled
turn, the waterway crosses the Avon via the 3-arched Avoncliffe Aqueduct, about 110yd
long. Sections of the Bath stone have been crudely repaired with brick and there is a
marked subsidence at the centre. Nonetheless, its classical form is remarkable.

*Dundas Aqueduct* (70m)   Beyond Limpley Stoke the canal is again in water and
continues in close company with river and railway. Once more the Avon is spanned,
this time by Dundas Aqueduct, built in 1804. With its large central arch and upright
side arches, it is a splendidly proportioned structure. Various curious masons' marks
will be found on the beautifully worked stone. Boys from nearby Monkton Combe
School row on the Avon at this point and, horrifically, are reputed to cycle along the
cornice of the aqueduct, which extends less than 4ft from the parapet! The outline
of the first lock of the long-closed Somersetshire Coal Canal will be seen in a private
garden on the west side of the aqueduct. By 1904 this waterway had been sold for
conversion to railway track (part had gone in 1871).

*Claverton* (71m)   Noted for the highly original water-powered pump, now restored
by members of the K&A Canal Trust (see p 30). Access may be gained by following a
lane off the A36 to Claverton Bridge and walking over the railway. An American
museum, housed in nearby Claverton Manor, contains many exhibits of great interest.

*Bath* (75m)   The K&A maintains its level course through the village of Bathamp-
ton, with extensive views of the Georgian city beyond. Two short tunnels, one
supporting the handsome stone Cleveland House, original canal company headquarters, bring the waterway to Sydney Gardens, as good a section of urban navigation
as will be found anywhere. There are dated iron bridges to enhance the scene. The
canal descends to join the Avon via 6 locks in the Widcombe Flight. Until 1974 there
were 7, but nos 8 and 9 were combined to create a rise and fall totalling 19ft 5in as the
result of a road scheme. A pumping station built about 1830 to draw water from the
river was dismantled in the 1850s. A pumphouse can still be found near the Avon, and

a most attractive decorative stone chimney stands halfway up the flight. Bath is a beautiful city that should on no account be missed. One cannot mention more than the briefest selection of attractions, which include the Pump Room by the well-preserved Roman baths, Robert Adam's Pulteney Bridge carrying shops in the style of Old London Bridge, the magnificent curve of the Royal Crescent, and the Abbey, founded in 1499.

*River Avon*   Some commercial traffic remains on the river between Bristol Docks and Bath. Once clear of the inevitable industrial belt that follows the Avon out of Bath, the river becomes pleasantly pastoral. Although provided with a towpath, it has lost some of the former ferry crossings, making a continuous walk difficult. Six locks manned by keepers (Weston, Kelston, Saltford, Swineford, Keynsham and Hanham) follow in the 10m to the boundary with the lower river, under the jurisdiction of Bristol Corporation. The navigation is tidal downstream of Hanham. Fry's chocolate factory dominates the river by a wide bend at Keynsham. (For the continuation of the Avon to Avonmouth and the Severn estuary, see p 225.)

### LAKE DISTRICT

This uniquely beautiful region of lakes and small mountains extends across parts of what used to be called Westmorland, Cumberland and Lancashire. In spite of its fame, it is unlikely to disappoint the visitor. There is a combination of green hills, rocky crags, stone-built villages and farmhouses, and the lakes themselves. Tourists flock to the area for car and coach tours, walking, rock climbing, sailing, powerboating and canoeing, but somehow the Lakes seem to absorb this influx and remain attractive, even at the height of the season.

The lakes are mostly quite natural (several are artificial water-supply reservoirs) without specific navigation works. Apart from the possibility of canoeing from Derwent Water to Lake Bassenthwaite via the River Derwent, there are no connections. An area of 866 sq m was designated a National Park in 1951, and a considerable part belongs to the National Trust.

There are facilities on certain lakes for water-skiing, sailing, motorboat cruising and excursions by tripping craft. Rowing boats are widely available on short-term hire. Perhaps the best method of discovering the Lakes from a boating viewpoint is to take your own trailer craft, spending 1–2 weeks cruising over different sections. Regulations governing the use of boats varies from those waters that are quite private, or where permission must first be obtained, to those that may be navigated at will.

*Windermere*   The largest sheet of water, measuring 10½m by up to 1¼m. It is controlled by the Windermere Urban District Council and is freely open to boats. Most facilities are to be found at Bowness, on the east shore. As well as hired cabin cruisers and chandlery, there is a British Rail pier for 'steamer' trips calling at Lakeside and Ambleside. The first tripping steamers were introduced in 1845. A car ferry operates from near Bowness to the opposite shore. One of the greatest attractions is the Windermere Nautical Trust's remarkable collection of historical boats, which include a 28ft carvel sailing boat of about 1780, several original Victorian steam launches, and an early motorboat built in 1898. Some of them were raised from the bed of the lake after being submerged for upwards of half a century. These craft are expected to go on public view when permanent floating docks have been prepared for them. An official chart and guide to Windermere is published by the UDC, and this provides all practical boating information necessary to enjoy the lake.

*Ullswater*  The second largest lake, $7\frac{1}{2}$m × 2m and available for boating without permission. Arrival of the M6 motorway has put the Lake District within easy reach of the Midlands with the result that unrestricted waters like Windermere and Ullswater can become crowded. There are certain curious local regulations that forbid sleeping on board craft, so if you want a temporary mooring, you are expected to patronise the hotel owning the jetties! The Ullswater Navigation & Transit Co of Kendal operates regular passenger services the length of the lake between Glenridding and Pooley Bridge, calling at Howtown. Points at which to hire small boats include Pooley Bridge and Glenridding. Lakeland rowing craft are particularly attractive, being frequently built in traditional varnished clinker with wrought-iron decoration.

*Derwentwater* (3m × $1\frac{1}{4}$m)  Although private, permission can be obtained locally to launch boats. The main centre is Keswick at the northern end, overlooking wooded islands by the mouth of the River Derwent. As elsewhere in the Lakes, Arthur Ransome's *Swallows and Amazons* and the other books in the series vividly come to life. Craft may be hired in Keswick. Passenger boats make a round trip, calling at 5 other places en route. All islands in the lake are National Trust property.

*Coniston Water*  A long thin sheet of water parallel with Windermere and to the west, about $5\frac{1}{4}$m × $\frac{1}{2}$m. The banks are well wooded, with 2 appealing islands, Peel and Fir, owned by the National Trust. Donald Campbell met his death here in January

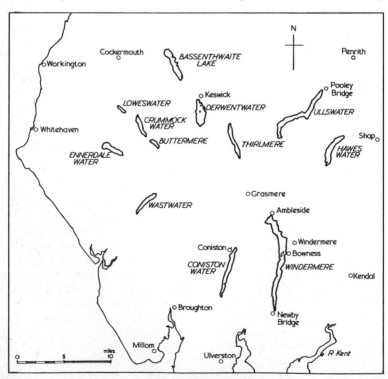

1967 when making his 300 mph water-speed record run in *Bluebird*. There is short-term hire of motorboats and rowing boats.

*Other lakes*   In all there are 16 lakes more than ½m long and many more smaller ones. Those lakes with hired craft and other facilities for day cruising include Bassenthwaite, Crummock Water, Loweswater, Buttermere, Esthwaite and Grasmere. Permission should in all cases be sought before launching private boats. Tourist information is readily obtainable at all large centres or from the Lake District National Park Information Service, Bank House, High Street, Windermere, Westmorland. Good descriptions of this remarkable area will be found in the *Shell Guide to England*. The best map available is the Ordnance Survey *Tourist Map of the Lake District*.

## LANCASTER CANAL

From Ashton Basin, Preston, to the bottom of Tewitfield locks, near Carnforth; 42½m with no locks. There is a branch to Glasson Dock and the estuary of the River Lune; 2m 7f with 7 locks. A further 14½m extended the waterway from Tewitfield locks to Kendal (8 locks) until abandonment in 1955. M6 motorway culverted crossings have since much reduced the prospect of these beautiful northern reaches being re-opened. Maximum craft dimensions are 72ft × 14ft 6in × 3ft draught × 8ft head-room.

Promoted in the main by the rich merchants of Lancaster, this waterway was originally mooted in 1771 when a survey was commissioned for a canal to be built from the Bridgewater at Worsley to Kendal. Plans were changed and by 1799 the section now existing was opened, followed in 1825 by the Glasson Dock branch. Between Preston and Walton Summit a 5m tramroad link connected with what is now the main line of the Leeds & Liverpool Canal at Johnson's Hillock; 10¼m of the L&L to Wigan were originally built by the Lancaster Canal Co. The Lancaster is now quite isolated from the rest of the canal system and remains a beautiful and solitary stretch of water with its own special character in the form of rocky cuttings, embankments, several aqueducts, and countryside that is pleasantly pastoral in the south and wilder as one approaches Tewitfield. It has sea views along the shore of Morecambe Bay. Pleasure boats on the canal are not generally typical canal craft but wide-beam river or small seagoing vessels.

*Preston*   An industrial town originating in Roman times, served by docks on the Ribble and a main line railway. Rows of Victorian terraced houses and cobbled streets are fast disappearing under redevelopment schemes. A northern outpost of the Lancashire cotton belt, it still has a number of impressive mills. One of the best public buildings is the Harris Library and Museum in the Market Place, built 1882–93. The start of the canal is through unspectacular wasteland. Within 200yd is Ashton Basin, recently in decay but now restored. About 1m of the canal was filled in many years ago but its course can be traced through the names of streets and public houses. Preston seems rather to ignore the potential attractions of its waterway. Fortunately the exit from this sordidness is rapid, with pretty Haslam Park on the left and the attractive gardens of bungalows opposite. Here can be seen one of the last complete remaining canal mileposts, a stone pillar with cast-iron plaque reading 'Preston 2 miles, Garstang 15 miles'. The first of many aqueducts takes the canal over the River Savick. They are mostly small but well proportioned, in stone. Near many of them are water-draining devices consisting of a wooden roller mounted on the bank to which a chain is attached to pull out a 'plug' in the canal bed.

Leaving Preston, the waterway takes a westerly direction for 3½m, passing on the left the large atomic works at Salwick. Blackpool lies about 7m to the west. By Salwick Hall the canal enters the first of several impressive rock cuttings. At Bridge 26 is a rare canalside pub, the Clifton Arms.

*Catforth* (7m 4f)   Old stables have been converted into the Jolly Roger Boating Haven, which is also a hire-cruiser fleet base with full range of facilities and slipway. Surroundings are very peaceful and pleasant.

*Bilsborrow* (11m 4f)   Hollowforth swing bridge (no 37) is the first of its type (another lies north of Lancaster). They are unusual in that a chain, which lies on the canal bed, is used to pull the bridge shut. The village of Bilsborrow, a hamlet serving the A6, lies beyond Bridge 44.

*Garstang* (16m 6f)   A pleasing little town beyond the Calder Aqueduct (no 52), where the river passes through a siphon. A magnificent stone and timber tithe barn was restored and opened here as a most unusual restaurant and agricultural museum in 1973. This overlooks a small well-maintained basin. For the entire distance from Preston the hills and fells of the Forest of Bowland have been visible about 5m to the east. They come closest to the canal at Bridge 72.

*Lancaster Canal. Th'owd Tithebarn restaurant and agricultural museum at Garstang Basin*

*Galgate* (24m 2f)  Beyond Garstang the canal passes beneath a strange concrete water duct erected in the 1930s by the Fylde Water Board. Of several large halls, the most interesting is Ellel Grange, whose estate is bisected by the waterway. Bridge 84 is an ornamental structure with balustraded parapet, while no 85 carries 2 roads divided by a wall, one serving the estate and the other for farm use. The junction (left) with the Glasson arm is shortly followed by many pleasure-craft moorings leading to Galgate Wharf, the comprehensive boatyard of Nor'West Holiday Cruises, now part of the Ladyline Group. A new large basin was excavated here during 1972–3. With the M6 motorway just 5 minutes away, it is easy to understand the popularity of the site. Galgate village, with its stone cottages, is somewhat spoiled by the A6 trunk road through its centre.

*Glasson arm*   This is the canal's important link with the sea. Trading craft, drawn by horses, used to travel between the dock and Kendal with sailing gear lowered. The 6 locks are equipped with fixed windlasses that need a key, and this can be obtained from either Galgate Wharf or the first lock-keeper. Chambers are inclined to be slow in filling or emptying, but the detour makes a welcome break from the 42m of level cruising on the main line. Opened in 1825, the branch passes through open and windswept country until it reaches Lock 6; below that is the disused Thurnham mill, which relied for power on water from the River Conder channelled via the canal. Glasson basin is unexpectedly huge, measuring about 500yd × 400yd. It is extensively used for mooring seagoing yachts. Below a swing bridge and sea lock commercial coasters may generally be seen loading and discharging in the tidal dock, for this is a busy and colourful little port.

*Lancaster* (31m 7f)   Bridge 91 is the start of the best cutting on the canal – Burrow Heights – nearly 2m long and with steep sides covered with a multitude of trees and wildflowers. Near the halfway point is Broken Back Bridge (no 93), with its oddly curved stonework. In open country between Bridges 94 and 95 may be seen a castellated boathouse, one of 3 such unusual structures along the canal. Ahead is the first view of Lancaster Castle, with Roman and Norman origins but extensively rebuilt and restored in the eighteenth and nineteenth centuries. It rises high over the River Lune, and much of the structure is now a prison. Preceding the canal, the river provided the city with its port and tree-lined quays, and the Custom House with its Ionic columns that remains. Little can be seen of former wharves on the canal, where commercial traffic (coal from Preston) ceased in 1947. A similar trade to Kendal gasworks terminated during World War II. The old packet-boat house is situated on the right of the waterway, adjoining a public park. Its present roofless and gutted state enables one to appreciate how passenger boats were floated inside to be lifted to the first floor for repairs, a technique that was probably unique. Most of the warehouses surrounding Lancaster basin have been demolished. Old stables that have been renovated are used for sales of refreshments and for small craft hire. Note their stone construction and cast-iron doors. *Lady Fiona* is a converted barge offering trips for 100 passengers.

The waterway passes by mills near the city centre, with a good example of a stone roving bridge. Some landscaping work has been completed. Beyond the new Bulk Road Aqueduct the waterway crosses the Lune via Rennie's magnificent 5-arch stone aqueduct, which is 640ft long, each 116ft elliptical arch rising 60ft from the river bed. During its construction 20 cofferdams were sunk into the Lune, steam pumps being used to clear them of water. At one stage of the construction there were 150 men at work, day and night. Its completion in November 1797 was celebrated with a procession of 6 boats travelling from the city to the aqueduct and back.

*Hest Bank* (34m 4f)   The first glimpses of Morecambe Bay come between Bridges 115 and 116. Hest Bank is a residential area, where the canal comes within ¼m of the coast. For most of the time the mudflats are waterless and the sea must be imagined rather than experienced. A shipping channel led to a stone pier, enabling cargoes to be taken to canal boats for carriage to Kendal and beyond by road, but this became disused about 1831, when the Hest Bank Shipping Co transferred business to Glasson Dock. All services are to be had near Bridge 118.

*Bolton-le-Sands* (35m 6f)   Panorama across Morecambe Bay continues past the last of the swing bridges, Hatlex Swivel (no 120). Morecambe is within easy reach if you need the kind of entertainment offered by this scaled-down version of Blackpool. At low tide it is possible to walk from either Hest Bank or Bolton for 7m across the bay to Grange-over-Sands, though the walker should be accompanied by an experienced guide. To the NW the southern fells of the Lake District can be seen on clear days. The former Preston–Kendal passenger boat service is remembered in the name of the Packet Boat Hotel shortly before Bridge 123.

*Carnforth* (38m 2f)   Beyond Bolton the countryside becomes hillier, with the waterway clinging to the edge of wooded slopes covered by many kinds of wildflowers. Carnforth offers boats for hire by the day or week and moorings are provided in a specially broadened section of the navigation. Steam Town is the name given to a large private collection of locomotives open to the public on certain days and operating over 5m of track. The town's chief industry was its ironworks, now supplemented by many limestone quarries.

*Tewitfield* (42m 2f)   Leaving Carnforth, the canal dives into open country surrounded by limestone hills. Largest is Warton Crag, dominating the remaining 4m and said by geologists to be 280 million years old. Near Bridge 130 the M6 spans the canal, whose bed was redirected, a good example of what was not achieved at the 5 further crossings beyond Tewitfield. The waterway approaches the Skipton–Lancaster railway after Bridge 130, with a high aqueduct over the River Keer at Capernwray. An old mill at the foot of the embankment was built to use river power to pump water up to the canal, and a rusty wheel remains in position. Wooded stone workings and the remnants of boat-loading chutes are now used as a caravan site, with a short arm extending several hundred yards on the right. Navigable with care, this is locally known as Lovers' Creek. Charles II stayed at the Elizabethan manor house of Borwick Hall in 1651. Cruising must come to an abrupt halt at the foot of the flight of 8 Tewitfield locks, for the embankment of a road crossing the M6 has resulted in the canal being culverted. The fine stone lock chambers, with iron bollards, have been weired. The upper 14½m are thus closed to all but portable craft, a most unfortunate situation, as the scenery is better than anything that has been encountered from Preston.

*The northern reaches*   Attempts are being made to secure partial restoration of the upper length through fine Westmorland scenery, if only for walking and local boating. A cruise on the Lancaster Canal might very profitably be combined with a towpath ramble from Tewitfield to Kendal at the southern end of the Lake District. Between Crooklands (49m 3f) and Kendal the canal bed is quite dry. The 377yd Hincaster Tunnel (52m) lacks a towpath but is easily avoided by following the old horsepath through sheep pastures above.

## LEE, RIVER

From Hertford to the River Thames at Limehouse Basin (Regent's Canal); 27½m with 21 locks. Maximum craft dimensions on the main line are 88ft × 15ft 9in beam (18ft from the Thames to Ponders End Lock) × 5ft draught upstream to Enfield Lock, and thereafter 4ft 9in. Headroom is normally 6ft 9in. Junctions are made with the River Stort at Feilde's Weir Lock, and in London with the Hartford Union and Regent's Canals. There are also various sections of tidal water at the lower end, the most important being Bow Creek and the Old River Lee.

The Lee is a river of great contrasts. Upstream to Enfield it is heavily industrial and carries a great deal of commercial traffic. Beyond this point the scenery becomes quite attractive, especially near Broxbourne, Ware and Hertford. In these reaches pleasure cruising is justly popular. The navigation was created and improved under various Acts dating from the thirteenth century until 1824. The valley is noted for market gardening, water-supply reservoirs and gravel pits, and is the subject of an ambitious Lee Valley Regional Park plan where creation of all kinds of open space and sporting amenities is well advanced.

*Hertford*   A pleasant county town, well blessed with pubs and old maltings by the river. Navigation ends abruptly some distance upstream of a small basin. The channel tends to be rather weedy in summer. Important buildings include the eighteenth-century Shire Hall, by the Adam brothers, the remains of a fifteenth-century castle gatehouse in a riverside park, and the seventeenth-century Salisbury Arms Hotel, with projecting upper floor. Beyond Hertford Lock comes open country with woods. Navigation locks are in the charge of keepers, and their Sunday use is at present restricted to boatmen who have passed a proficiency test arranged by the BWB.

*Ware* (2m 7f)   The lock is controlled by the Metropolitan Division of the Thames Water Authority, whose New River accompanies the Lee to London. Not navigable, the New River was constructed by Sir Hugh Myddleton in the time of James I. The town is best by the Lee towpath, with several delightful waterside summer houses (gazebos) and some fine early industrial warehouses.

*Rye House* (6m 5f)   Agreeable scenery with trees is slightly spoiled by the closeness of a railway that follows the river bank from Ware past Hardmead and Stanstead Locks to Rye House Station. Power station cooling-towers and lines of pylons intervene near the junction with the Stort and so establish the character of the rest of the Lee. The Regional Park Authority has completed some landscaping and created various amenity facilities. This is a well-frequented river resort. Small boats may be hired by the Rye House Inn. A gatehouse, now preserved, is all that remains of the building where the Rye House plotters attempted to ambush King Charles II. The charming little River Stort enters beyond Feilde's Weir Lock.

*River Lee. Warehouses in red brick with weatherboarding by the navigation in Ware*

*Broxbourne* (9m)   One of the best-known parts of the Lee, with pollarded willows lining the banks as the river winds through flat meadows. Dobb's Weir and Carthagena Locks are roughly a mile apart, an interval that changes remarkably little on this journey towards the Thames. There are many small waterside bungalows, with a useful boatyard and inn at Broxbourne Bridge. The entire waterway is admirably served by railway stations, making it exceptionally convenient for Londoners.

*Waltham Abbey* (13m 6f)   Downstream of Broxbourne, gravel pits and areas of wasteland predominate. Eventually all will form extensive areas of water space catering for powerboat racing, canoeing, championship rowing and dinghy sailing. Fishing in this part of the Lee has been noted since it was popularised by Isaac Walton's *Compleat Angler*. Waltham was the site of a very early pound lock, built about 1574, 10 years after Britain's first on the Exeter Canal. The Abbey is a magnificently solid Norman building, founded in 1030. Nearby Waltham Cross has one of the thirteenth-century Eleanor Crosses that mark the resting places of the coffin of Edward I's queen during her final journey from Leicestershire to Westminster Abbey.

*Enfield* (14m 6f)   The lock here gives its name to a railway station, and marks the normal upstream limit of commercial barge traffic (a little continues to Ware). Beside it lies a waterway maintenance yard, whose architecture, and that of the lock cottage, is decoratively late Victorian, a legacy of Lee Conservancy days. The first of 13 great reservoirs on the east bank contributes to a rather bleak landscape that is scarcely improved by Brimsdown Power Station and its electricity pylons. There are large BWB warehouses catering for various waterway traffics, of which the most important are timber and copper. Freight is carried in dumb barges drawn in short trains by tugs or singly by towpath tractors. Pleasure craft must remain alert at all times to avoid hampering commercial boats. Moorings must be selected with care and commonsense. By Pickett's Lock stands an extensive indoor-sports centre completed by the LVRPA in 1972. Apart from Pickett's, all locks from Ponders End to the Thames are duplicated, side by side. They were mechanised in the late 1950s and early 1960s to cater for heavy commercial traffic.

*Tottenham* (20m 6f)   The navigation continues somewhat bleakly through Edmonton and Chingford. There are pairs of locks at Stonebridge and Tottenham. Apart from extensive reservoirs at Walthamstow, suburban development now accompanies the river for the rest of the journey to the Thames. Surprisingly rural areas remain in Epping Forest, to the east.

*Clapton* (23m)   Springfield Park, a stretch of municipal grass and trees, slopes down to the towpath on the west bank, opposite Radley's boatyard, a popular mooring for cruising and residential craft. Much of the waterway is canalised into artificial cuts.

*Hackney* (24m)   The Marshes on the east bank are given over to extensive playing fields, in sharp contrast to numerous factories opposite. Steam rises in clouds from many cooling-water outlets. We have now reached the borders of London's East End.

*Old Ford* (25m)   Timber yards mark the area round the junction with the short Hertford Union Canal, or Duckett's Cut, which leads via 3 locks to the Regent's Canal (p 376). At Old Ford Locks is a British Waterways Board freight toll office serving the London area. Access may be gained here to a system of muddy tidal creeks, including the Old River Lee, City Mill River, Waterworks River, Channelsea River and Prescott Channel. These are strictly commercial and not really suitable for pleasure boats.

*Bow* (26m 2f)   During a period of 4 hours before and 2 hours after high water, Bow Locks provide access to the Thames via the winding 2m Bow Creek, which enters the river about 5m downstream of Limehouse. Most inland craft prefer to take the alternative route along the Limehouse Cut.

*Limehouse* (27m 5f)   This is a 'tough' area, once known as London's Chinatown. Canal staff tell stories of the criminal activities associated with the district. Care should be taken to avoid much floating timber and other debris. The Cut had its own barge lock entrance to the Thames alongside Regent's Canal Dock until 1968, when it was closed and a new short canal link opened to connect with the dock itself. No longer used as a transhipment point between coasters and canal craft, the dock is now known as Limehouse Basin. Some lighter traffic remains and its future development to cater more for pleasure cruising is likely and desirable (see also p 376).

### LEEDS & LIVERPOOL CANAL

From the Aire & Calder Navigation at Leeds to Liverpool (via Stanley Dock) and the River Mersey; 127m with 91 locks. The 3 branches are (1) Leigh Branch from Wigan to the Bridgewater Canal at Leigh (7m 2f, 2 locks), (2) Rufford Branch from Burscough to the River Douglas at Tarleton (7m 2f, 8 locks), and (3) Stanley Dock Cut, Liverpool (2f, 4 locks).

L

For the sustained magnificence of its scenery through the moorlands of Yorkshire and Lancashire, the Leeds & Liverpool can justifiably claim to be first choice among cruising enthusiasts. The only remaining trans-Pennine waterway (the heavily locked Rochdale and Huddersfield Narrow Canals are now abandoned), this wide-beam route could have a considerable future as a coast to coast link for seagoing yachts, but so far pleasure-craft traffic has apparently been well below the level of other far less attractive canals of the Midlands and South. The first move to build the canal came with an Act of 1770. While 33½m had been built at the eastern end by 1777 and 28m from Liverpool by 1775, little more was done to link the two sections until Robert Whitworth was appointed engineer in 1790 for the most difficult central portion. The final section between Blackburn and Wigan was the responsibility of James Fletcher, who achieved through traffic in 1816, by which time both the Rochdale and the Huddersfield were already fully operational. James Brindley and John Longbotham were both involved with the early planning of the great canal.

The Leeds & Liverpool possesses a number of distinctive engineering features, most important being the wide-beam locks, which are only long enough to accommodate 62ft craft except on the section from Lock 21 at Wigan to Liverpool. These restrictions gave rise to the 'short boat', a wide-beam vessel loading about 45 tons. The introduction of steam engines (in use until the mid-1950s) allowed a motor and butty system similar to the Midland narrow boats. Later on, diesel engines were installed in many craft, and these or their unpowered butties are the barges to be seen today working on maintenance or occasionally as passenger or camping craft.

Substantial groupings of locks on each side of the Pennines provide a flight of 23 at Wigan, a series of 2-rise and 3-rise staircases, and at Bingley a 5-rise staircase, on the ascent from Leeds. Architecture of locks and bridges is particularly substantial and fine, and, like the wool and cotton mills that grew up by the waterway, they are mainly in Millstone Grit, a hard sandstone which weathers almost black. Lock paddle-gear comes in a number of regional types (all known locally as 'cloughs'), some gate-paddles being worked in an arc with a wooden lever, others being raised via a worm drive wound up with a horizontal bar, and a further type being worked conventionally with a windlass. As a safeguard against vandalism, much of the equipment is kept locked, a special key being provided to crews on entry to the canal. Swing bridges in timber occur in parts at frequent intervals, a reminder that some of the contractors employed in building this waterway preferred the initial lower cost of moving crossings that must since have cost on maintenance and replacement many times the original expense of fixed structures. Maximum dimensions for craft are 62ft × 14ft 3in × 4ft draught × 9ft headroom, although today boats approaching more than one of the upper limits could experience a difficult passage. Generally, the canal is in good condition, with better than average water depth near the banks.

*Leeds*   It is tempting to dismiss this huge city of more than half a million people, for it really adds little to the enjoyment of the waterway. There are good points, of course. The Town Hall and Civic Hall are bold and inspired erections in the classical tradition from the 1850s and 1930s respectively. A town based on the coal, iron and cloth industries, which reached a peak in the nineteenth century, cannot stand still, and Leeds is making strenuous efforts to update itself, with redevelopment schemes and new roads. Creditable experiments have been made to create pedestrian shopping precincts. There are some very fine warehouses near the junction of the canal and the

Aire & Calder Navigation. Behind the City Station stand further warehouses, several locks and associated buildings in chunky blackened stone. Soon the first of a series of multiple-rise locks (Oddy 2-lock staircase) lifts the canal into the hilly surroundings of the city, and the closely confined atmosphere opens out a little; though the area remains predominantly one of factories and mill chimneys. Note the wooden rollers at Armley Mill Bridge (no 225), protecting the abutments from horsedrawn-boat tow-ropes. Leeds has an active Civic Society, which plans far-reaching canal improvements in connection with the NE Region of the IWA.

*Kirkstall* (3m)  Near the water stand the extensive ruins of a twelfth-century Cistercian abbey. Close by is a fine folk museum, which includes 3 complete streets of nineteenth-century shop reconstructions, open to the public throughout the year. With fields of cultivated rhubarb (a major Yorkshire export) the canal has now reached semi-open country that improves all the time as a series of locks makes the climb into the Moors. The River Aire keeps close company with the canal for many miles.

*Rodley* (6m 2f)  A useful canal village, with several swing bridges operated by boat crews. There is a boatyard and the waterside Rodley Barge Inn. Staircase locks are normally a rarity in England, so it is worth noting that Kirkstall Forge (4m), Newlay (4m 4f) and Field Locks (10m 2f) are all 3-rises, with a 2-rise at Dobson Lock, Apperley Bridge (9m). All were built of massive stone blocks with timber gates to match, and their solidity suggests that they were intended to last for ever.

*Shipley* (12m 6f)  A grimy little town, where several buildings among the mills date from the sixteenth and seventeenth centuries. The Bradford Canal, 3m with 10 locks, of which all but the first were 2- or 3-rise, originally connected Bradford with Shipley under the joint ownership of the L&L Co and the Aire & Calder Navigation. Closed to traffic in 1867, reopened in 1873 and shut down for good in 1922, little now remains, and a search for the few traces can be a depressing experience.

*Saltaire* (13m 4f)  A remarkably early 'new town' of the 1850s, Saltaire represents the determination of Sir Titus Salt to remove his mohair and alpaca mills from Brad-ford to the open country. The great mill, opened in 1853, 6 storeys high and 550ft long, is to the design of Sir William Fairbairn, and makes full use of fire-resistant materials such as cast-iron columns and a roof of iron beams. Salt was deeply con-cerned to provide better than normal housing for his workers, and in 20 years had built 820 homes in the town, arranged on a formal grid pattern, each with some Italianate decoration. Public buildings erected by this enterprising man include a school, institute and Congregational church. Four lions, originally considered too small for Trafalgar Square in London, can be seen near the Saltaire grammar school. Streets are named after Sir Titus' children. There are no pawnshops and no pubs. Saltaire Bridge (no 207A), built 1871, crosses railway, canal and river to a park that was described in 1903, 27 years after Salt's death, as 'one of the most beautiful in the world'.

Now comes a really lovely length of canal, which dives into a wooded cutting high above the Aire, soon to cross the river via the 7-arched Dowley Gap Aqueduct (14m 2f).

*Bingley* (15m 3f)   First comes the impressive 3-rise staircase, with a lift of 30ft, though the canal traveller should by now have become used to such feats of engineering. The waterway virtually bisects this bustling market town, which occupies a hollow and sports a number of tall mill chimneys. The canal banks are thickly tree-lined, but from a long way off one can glimpse the famous Five Rise locks, which certainly live up to their nationwide reputation as one of the wonders of the British canal system. The lift is 60ft and is rather daunting to even the most seasoned canal user. The resident lock-keeper will give advice if necessary, and complicated working instructions are displayed, but some hard thinking and commonsense are needed to show you the quickest way to see your boat through.

Beyond the locks begins a 16m pound to Skipton and beyond, which may partly explain why few of the locally based pleasure craft are brave enough to take the difficult eastward passage through the locks. (If any of the boat club members feel maligned by this remark, apologies for the slur are unreservedly tendered.) The Skipton pound is a glorious length of water, nevertheless. At 334ft above sea level the L&L passes through the distinctive Aire Gap, with the wilds of Ilkley Moor stretching away northwards.

*Keighley* (18m 3f)   Less drab and austere than many other towns of Yorkshire's West Riding. East Riddlesden Hall, near Granby swing bridge (no 197A), is a seventeenth-century manor house in stone with tithe barn, owned by the National Trust and on public view every day but Mondays throughout the year (not December). Travel 1m S of the canal to Keighley Station and you can catch one of the scheduled service steam trains using 5m of preserved track to Haworth, home of the Brontës. Some of the locomotives are a century old, and an essential ingredient in this Worth Valley Railway.

*Silsden* (22m 4f)   Swing bridges, fine hilly country and a waterway that boasts a good depth of water (at least by standards that can be expected elsewhere), gives good cruising. Silsden is a place of stone warehouses with canopies over the water. It should be mentioned that the virile commercial traffic of the short boats lasted over the summit of the canal until the mid-1950s, and on shorter, more local runs for another 15 years. Now all has gone except for the occasional 'enthusiast-owned' boat.

*Kildwick* (24m 2f)   The stone cottages both sides of the water, with brightly painted doors and window frames, and the awe-inspiring moorland hills beyond, will long be remembered by visitors to the North. Elements like these tend to make the L&L a favourite among British canals. There are very steep streets and a road under the canal. The river bridge, with 4 arches, is probably fourteenth-century. The A629 follows the canal closely into Skipton. If it is rather noisy, it does provide a bus service for towpath walkers to return to cars; in fact all the E part of the canal to Leeds is well served by public transport. The wide open views continue almost to Skipton.

*Skipton* (29m)   Gateway to the Yorkshire Moors, this small stone-built town combines the atmosphere of a Dales market centre with a typical mill area (mercerised thread is still made). The wide High Street, conveniently near the canal wharf, has excellent shops, some catering for a clientele you would expect in London's Bond Street. The Hole in the Wall, one of several old inns, was until the early nineteenth

*Leeds & Liverpool Canal. Bingley Five Rise Locks*

century a theatre. The canal company's inaugural meeting in 1770 was held at the Black Horse Hotel. Dominating the street at one end is Holy Trinity Church, partly dating from the twelfth century, and the castle, open to the public. Mostly built by the Clifford family between the fourteenth and mid-seventeenth centuries, it has a massive gatehouse and round towers, and, within, cobbled courtyards, one with an ancient yew. An eighteenth-century room lined with pearly shells and the dungeon should be visited. The canal wharf has good warehouses around a cobbled yard, parts bearing the date 1774. It is much to be hoped that mooted redevelopment plans preserve the atmosphere as well as the structures. A hire-craft yard and well-stocked chandlery lie at the entrance to the short but romantic Springs Branch, which runs for ½m under the towering castle walls to terminate by a stone-loading chute, disused since regular commercial boat traffic over the canal's summit ceased in the mid-1950s. About 1m beyond Skipton's centre open country returns, with good views of the surrounding hills. A golf course slopes sharply down to the water (right), and one assumes that the canal bed is littered with balls.

*Gargrave* (33m 6f)   Following the lower slopes of Flasby Fell, with stone-walled fields and few trees along the valley of the River Aire, the canal is perhaps at its scenic best in the 10m from Skipton. Gargrave's 6 locks are individually named from no 30, Holme Bridge, past Eshton Road, Ireland, Anchor, and Scarland to Stegneck. A slipway with good road access and pub stand by Anchor Lock. Bridge 168 (Priestholme Changeline Bridge), a good roving bridge, takes the towpath on to a road for several hundred yards. A faded sign states that 'Boatmen are required to walk along the highway with their horses.' An aqueduct takes the canal over the Aire, whose boulder-strewn course heads northwards and away from the canal for good. Back down the flight, fells over 1,000ft dominate the distance.

*Bank Newton Locks* (35m 2f)   Having passed its most northerly point, the canal turns south, although some amazing contortions send boats along the contours south, east and west within the next 2–3m. Masons' marks incised on the stonework inside the chamber of the first lock of the flight of 6, and noticeable throughout the waterway, no doubt once had a significance, but their exact meaning has been lost. A pretty wharf with cottages is situated beside the first pound. Note the iron hooks at several locks, installed to provide a purchase and guide for horseboat lines.

*Marton Pool* (36m)   Beyond a small waterside beech wood a radio mast appears ahead and to the left. The canal winds so much that although you may be almost within shouting distance of a boat moored up across the fields, you will not arrive alongside it for perhaps 15 minutes of roundabout navigation. Three of the most acute bends are equipped with large vertical wooden rollers to prevent towlines cutting into the towpath wall. This is a wild but friendly countryside, small stone farms and cottages appearing at intervals of about ½m. In spite of the exceptional length of ground covered by the waterway as it clings to the hillsides, some extensive embankment work has been necessary. The towpath provides a magnificent walk into Skipton from East Marton (Bridge 161), where the A59 crosses via a most unusual double arch by the Cross Keys Inn. The excellent system of painting a white band round the arch of each bridge hole, with a vertical stripe at the centre, aids night navigation, and was particularly useful to the working boats whose beam almost filled the available space. This area possesses a number of triangular mile posts, some smaller ones marking ¼m, ½m and ¾m distances, and flat stones carved with the canal company's initials to indicate the boundary of its property.

*Greenberfield Locks* (40m 4f)   An alarmingly sharp bend by Greenberfield Change-line Bridge (no 158) is followed shortly by 3 locks leading to the 6m summit level. Earthworks, a canal bridge crossing a dry depression, and part of an old channel now used as a spillway show how a former 3-lock staircase was replaced in 1820 by the present single locks to help alleviate the severe water shortages from which the highest section of the canal suffered. Even today it is occasionally necessary to close parts of the waterway to traffic if the reservoirs threaten to run dry. A small building dated 1893 by the top lock is the Winterburn Discharge, which brings water to the summit.

*Foulridge* (45m)   Skirting the small town of Barnoldswick, widely known for its Rolls Royce aircraft engine factory, the waterway passes Coates Mill where there is a curious chimney, square in cross-section and well braced, with the upper half cylindrical. Salterforth (43m 4f) is a slightly grimy industrial settlement, but useful for boat's stores. Between Bridges 150 and 149 one crosses the border between Yorkshire and Lancashire and moves from an area of woollen mills into a cotton district extending as far as Manchester. Here water tumbles into the canal from White Moor reservoir, and further supplies come from the extensive Foulridge Upper and Lower reservoirs (worth visiting) and Slipper Hill. Foulridge village is a short distance from the northern portal of the great tunnel, where a photograph in the bar of the Hole in the Wall Inn substantiates the famous story of the cow that swam the tunnel from end to end in 1912 and was revived with quantities of brandy. As there is no towpath, boats were legged through the 1,640yd bore until a steam tug was provided in 1880. Two years later, after a fatal accident to a legger, use of the tug became compulsory. About 1956 a sophisticated system of timed traffic lights was instituted to control the one-way working, but this soon fell into disuse with the end of commercial craft. Times at which boats may now enter are displayed at the entrance.

*Barrowford* (47m 2f)   Seven locks climb steeply down towards the substantial town of Nelson, passing a canal reservoir en route. The top lock cottage does a good trade in sweets and ice cream, supplying quite as much to local families walking by the water as to boat crews. The curving stone retaining walls of the locks are noticeably massive.

*Nelson* (48m 6f)   Not a town that would attract many tourists, it has grown considerably in recent years and supports a thriving textile industry. As in similar places lying on the banks of the Leeds & Liverpool in Lancashire, the hilly countryside is visible on all sides, so that fresh air is nowhere much more than 1m away. The old canal company warehouse, with roof extending over the water, is a good example of its kind, displaying the intricate fretwork on the eaves that was common on Victorian country railway stations.

*Burnley* (54m 5f)   Very sharp bends and an impressive embankment, right, follow with superb views to the north across the Calder Valley, culminating in the distant Pendle Hill. The Hill was a notorious centre for witches and witch hunts, and a number of women found there were tried and executed in 1612. Subsidence from coal-mines has necessitated rebuilding several bridges and raising the level of the canal banks. Pithead winding gear stands by a short arm (left) just before Burnley centre. Coal traffic accounted for 80 per cent of goods moved on the canal in 1955, when about 1 million tons of cargo was recorded. Through the slight mist of a summer morning ranks of mill chimneys possess an austere poetry of their own. A group of sizeable Victorian mansions, one in black stone with a first-floor iron balcony all round, stand on the left bank. A little beyond on the right is the surprisingly pleasant Thompson's Park, with boating lake and trees shading the grassed towpath. Rightly selected as one of the Seven Wonders of the Waterways, Burnley's canal embankment runs quite straight for a mile across the middle of the town at rooftop level, spanning Yorkshire Street by an aqueduct. The claim that many townspeople are unaware of the canal above is surely apocryphal. The sight of rows of slate-roofed streets and hundreds of chimneys from the canal is awe-inspiring. Most convenient moorings are at the maintenance yard (also a pleasure-craft base) at the embankment's far end.

The town has a number of attractions, including Townley Hall Art Gallery and Museum, a huge structure heavily restyled in the nineteenth century and housing an important collection of paintings, with geological, archaeological and natural history exhibits. Local pies, bread, cakes, meat and vegetables are well above average quality in the neighbourhood of small shops close to Finsley Gate moorings. While industrial surroundings approach the canal closely for several miles beyond the embankment, there are always buildings and details to please: the canal warehouses by Bridge 130B, a charming cast-iron factory balcony complete with access ladder moving on counter-weights (just after Bridge 130A), and Slater Terrace (left), a row of period houses with front doors at first-floor level, now dangerously neglected. Further clusters of masons' hieroglyphics appear at the entrance to the 559yd Gannow Tunnel.

*Church* (63m 6f)   A length of derelict and decaying factories, extensive views over the Calder Valley and considerable new housing developments gradually lead to semi-open country, but it wears a worn and worked-out appearance, unlike the Yorkshire landscape passed earlier. Accrington and curiously named Oswaldtwistle scarcely affect the waterway, now slightly bleak. A pleasant golf course intervenes, then once more industry is seen ahead.

*Blackburn* (71m)   On its borders is a power station sited to benefit from water-borne coal supplies and for cooling from the canal. It is sad to see evidence of working boats so recently flourishing but now quite vanished. By Bridge 104B lies the disused sideslip of T. & J. Hodson, where short boats were built and repaired, and at Eanam Bridge (no 103A) stand canal warehouses much extended in 1955 by British Waterways to improve the barge service moving crated machinery to Liverpool Docks. Bales of raw cotton were another major boat traffic, and the mills remain active, displaying a variety of late nineteenth-century design in castellated towers. Looking ahead into Blackburn, it is possible to count the spires of at least 12 churches. The town has been much rebuilt since World War II. The activities leading to its growth and prosperity are demonstrated in the Lewis Textile Museum, where spinning and weaving machines can be seen working. A flight of 6 locks near the town centre marks the end of a 23½m pound from Barrowford. The harsh design of mills and chimneys in Millstone Grit, lock entrances, gates and wooden footbridges combine to show a tough yet somehow pleasing aspect of the canal, far removed from the rural grandeur of the Leeds & Liverpool at Gargrave. The local authority is progressively landscaping the banks of the waterway to create a linear park several miles long, and considerable scope is offered by the elevated embankment section where the Ewood Aqueduct crosses the River Darwen. Gradually the scenery improves again, with woods and open fields at Feniscowles (74m), where there are also a number of stone quarries. Immediately before Bridge 91A one comes across a boatyard (left) with sideways short-boat slip. Hilly fields, woods and patches of sandy heath take the canal through pleasant surroundings.

*Johnson's Hillock Locks* (79m 2f) A popular canal centre where pleasure-craft moorings and all facilities are available. The 7 locks fall from Wheelton in perhaps the most attractively arranged flight on the entire canal. Overflow weirs spanned by tiny timber footbridges are particularly noticeable. About 1967 a small cruiser entered the bottom lock from above, at which point the lower gates collapsed while the top gates were still open. The boat was swept out of the chamber with the alarming rush of water to end up in a reed-bed several hundred yards away. Injuries were fortunately not too serious. Timber framework has been erected at many locks to prevent gates 'blowing' again. A junction at the end of the flight connects with the stump of the Walton Summit Branch, destroyed in 1970 by the M6 motorway, part of which runs down the canal bed. It formerly extended for 3m to a series of basins linked with the Lancaster Canal at Preston via a horse tramway 5m long and closed in 1857.

*Botany Bay* (81m) Hardly touching the industrial town of Chorley, the waterway

*Leeds & Liverpool Canal. Cruising through the Yorkshire Moors between Skipton and Gargrave*

continues southwards to Wigan. Shopping facilities are to be found close by at Adlington (85m). A sizeable black-stone statue of Queen Victoria perches on a building in Chapel Street. The River Douglas flows under the canal at two points, occupying a deep ravine between Bridges 68 and 63A. Remains of worked out collieries have become a naturalised part of the landscape.

*Wigan* (92m 4f)  A lovely 200 acre wooded park by Bridge 61 (88m) surrounds Haigh Hall, acquired in 1947 by Wigan Corporation from the Earl of Crawford and now open to the public. A slagheap planted with pines is the first indication of the utter desolation ahead, where centuries of industrial activity have carved the terrain on each side of the long flight of 23 locks into a weird pattern of hillocks, crags and craters. The canal leads straight ahead to a derelict arm, and sharply to the right to the top lock. The Top Lock, Kirkless Hall and Commercial Inn are pubs standing by each of the first 3 locks, and 2 of them are built in curiously ambitious mock half-timbering. Subsidence from the mines has caused terraces of houses to lean drunkenly, and the canal bank has been raised for the same reason. While short boats still used the flight, strange elderly characters would shuffle out of the pubs offering assistance with the locks for a consideration, and in summer modern counterparts of these 'hufflers' may try to sell their services at rates ranging from upwards of £1. Unless your crew is strong, numerous and very proud, local help is well worth the expense. Anxious to encourage greater use of the Wigan flight, the waterway authority will generally lay on assistance if their Wigan office is notified several hours in advance. In recent years considerable landscaping has been completed, with willow trees and grassy areas by several locks. Eventually Wigan will cease to deserve its reputation, although the view from the top lock to the smoking chimneys almost 250ft below the flight shows that much remains to be done. Bridge 54 (91m) is the first convenient approach to shops. Here the lower gates are operated by using a windlass on a segment gear, as there is insufficient space for conventional balance beams.

An apparent lack of churches of note is compensated for by scores of friendly working men's pubs. Children appear from Canal Terrace and other nearby streets, begging (and offering) sweets and demanding rides on the boat. If approached intelligently, they are invaluable for opening lock gates. Deeply cut Roman numerals show the number of each lock in the stonework of the right-hand walls near the tail. Pride in industrial achievement is evident in iron and stone inscriptions, like the storage tank 'Constructed by Tickle Bros, Engineers of Wigan', and the building marked 'Wigan Corporation Electric Light and Power Station 1900'. There is a concentration of railway bridges at the approach to the large power station to which coal arrived by short boat from the Leigh Branch until 1972. The purposeful barges, decorated with Baroque scrollwork, flowers and birds, have gone, but it is possible to visualise the commercial activity which characterised the canal for many years. Two final locks take the canal past short-boat slips, now a maintenance yard, the regional canal offices and some early warehouses, facing the site of famous Wigan Pier, a raised section of towpath from which a regular service of horsedrawn passenger craft operated to Liverpool until the advent of railways. Towards the end of the nineteenth century, and in the early twentieth, pleasure steamers ran excursions from the Pier in summer.

*Leigh Branch*  Leaving the main line of the canal by Wigan Power Station, between Locks 85 and 86, this 7¼m arm provides a useful link with the Bridgewater Canal (p 248). Severe coalmining subsidence has resulted in the waterway banks being progressively raised, so that the channel is now mainly very deep. Boats thus travel along an embankment offering wide views over a desolate area of waste-tips and extensive 'flashes' (flooded workings). Soon after Wigan junction come the two Poolstock locks, one with a timber-lined chamber, so designed in order to cope more easily with subsidence problems. This region is much used for all forms of recreation, from fishing to unofficial motorcycle scrambling. It recalls the alleged preferences of the working-class Lancashire man for tripe, women and whippets, in that order. Between Ince-in-Makerfield and Abram (3m 5f) some tree planting has softened the starkness of the blackened countryside. Two locks near the Red Lion Inn (Bridge 4) – Dover Top and Dover Low – have long since been removed, as the change in levels rendered them unnecessary. Running close to Bickershaw Colliery (5m 6f), the canal passes an extensive lake on the right where sailing dinghies race. Plank Lane swing bridge (no 8) carries a busy road and is opened mechanically by a keeper. After penetrating the industrial town of Leigh, the branch makes a level junction with the Bridgewater Canal.

As both Wigan and Liverpool canalscapes have a justified reputation of industrial grimness, it is sometimes forgotten that the intervening 35m offers some outstandingly attractive cruising country. The majority of long-distance boaters tend, however, to restrict their travels to the Wigan–Leeds section, which forms a more logical through route via the Leigh Branch and Bridgewater Canal. (Navigation of the Mersey and Manchester Ship Canal from Liverpool Docks is an undertaking to which by no means all canal boats are suited.) From the Leigh Branch junction to Liverpool is the only portion of the Leeds & Liverpool accessible to 70ft narrow boats, for the few locks are both full-length as well as wide-beam. Several of the lock chambers were duplicated side by side, one acting as a side pond to the other. In most instances only one of each pair has been left in working order.

*Appley Bridge* (97m 4f)   The canal leaves Wigan in company with the River Douglas, and the two share a pleasing wooded valley for about 7m. Later transport forms are evident in a railway (Wigan–Southport) with a number of useful stations, and the M6 bridge, immediately before Dean Lock. Appley Bridge is briefly industrial.

*Parbold* (99m 4f)   Here is a notable feature of the River Douglas section in the form of a brick windmill tower alongside Bridge 37. To the north is Ashurst's Beacon, constructed on a hill in Napoleonic times to warn of a possible French invasion. Beyond aqueducts crossing first the Douglas and then the Tawd, the canal's Rufford Branch heads northwards from Burscough Junction.

*Rufford Branch* (begins at 102m 4f)   Completed in 1781, long before the line between Leeds and Liverpool was finally ready, this 7¼m arm provides access to the tidal River Douglas at Tarleton. The 8 locks admit craft 72ft × 14ft. Six are grouped in the first 1¼m (Latham 2, Runnel Brow, Moss, German's and Baldwin's). The Rufford Branch is atmospheric in the extreme. At its upper end the countryside consists of flat but fertile farmland, but at the approach to the village of Rufford (3m) a cluster of ancient trees provides shelter from the wind. Here is situated Rufford Old Hall, a magnificent fifteenth-century timber-framed house containing some of the best decorative work of its period in Britain. The Hall and Folk Museum is open to the public. Nearby Rufford New Hall, built in 1760, has an ice house, an early form of refrigeration, in its grounds. According to local custom, the Old Grey Lady is a phantom that walks from the Old Hall and crosses the canal by a bridge that has long been dismantled. The final miles of the branch follow the original course of the River Douglas, with the remains of an obsolete lock at Sollom. The channel takes on the appearance of a Fenland dyke through tall reeds. There is a useful boatyard at Tarleton, catering mainly for seagoing craft, and beyond is the final lock falling to the tidal Douglas, operable at high water. From 1742 to the late eighteenth century the Douglas provided about 17½m of navigable water between Wigan and the Ribble estuary, with 8 locks. Only 4m now remain in use, from Tarleton to the Ribble, where the body in control is the Port of Preston Authority.

*Scarisbrick* (106m)   Having followed a north-westerly course from Wigan, the canal now turns south to run parallel with the coast, finally making a junction with Liverpool Bay via the city docks. The nearest and most agreeable seaside resort is Southport, about 4m down the A570 from Scarisbrick Bridge (no 27A). The scenery is flat but pleasant, with numerous swing bridges and a wide selection of waterside inns through the villages of Halsall and Haskayne.

*Lydiate* (112m 6f)   Development of Greater Liverpool has much increased the size of Lydiate and Maghull (114m 2f), but the district remains a pretty one. The Scotch Pipers Inn near Lollies Bridge (no 17A) dates from the early fourteenth century, making it reputedly the oldest in Lancashire.

*Aintree* (118m)   The waterway skirts the famous racecourse, with its Canal Turn, and beyond Old Roan Bridge is demoted to 'remainder' canal status, following the 1968 Transport Act. Its future role had not then been decided. Various subsequent proposals have included provision of cruising facilities to encourage use of the direct route between the Mersey and the East Coast. An ill-informed but noisy local lobby continues to press for its elimination because of a number of unfortunate drownings of young unsupervised children. Most likely outcome would involve a compromise plan, with the canal sides 'benched' to reduce water depth without greatly affecting the passage of boats.

*Litherland* (122m 6f)   Here the suburbs end and the thickly industrial length begins. Until 1974 Bridge 2J, Litherland, was a rare vertically rising lift bridge, electrically powered and equipped with lights, bells and barriers, for the road concerned was a busy one. The crossing has sadly been replaced by a high-level motorway, and a distinctive feature of the waterway has thus vanished. Bridges from this point onwards are denoted mainly by letters of the alphabet rather than numbers, as most have presumably been added since the original numeration was devised.

*Liverpool* (127m)   Surroundings through Bootle and the back of the city docks are grim but interesting. Urchins with missiles are one hazard. The canal ends by Tate & Lyle's sugar factory (until postwar times a heavy user of water transport) but originally continued for a further ¼m to Exchange Station. Half a mile before the terminus the Stanley Dock branch descends via 4 locks to provide access to the Mersey through a ship lock. Advance notice to navigate the branch and the dock system is best obtained before arrival. Pleasure craft using this facility will either be seagoing vessels crossing from west coast to east or suitably powered inland cruisers travelling between the L&L and the Manchester Ship Canal, reached at Eastham Locks up the Mersey. The MSC provides connections with the Shropshire Union at Ellesmere Port and the Bridgewater Canal in Manchester (see p 250).

Liverpool is a lively city, with its own seaside resort of New Brighton, reached by regular ferry service from the Pier Head. The docks extend for 7m. Among the most important public buildings are the City Museum and Walker Art Gallery, the huge twentieth-century Gothic Anglican cathedral by Sir Giles Gilbert Scott (still incomplete), and the almost theatrical circular Roman Catholic cathedral, topped by a crown-shaped tower of glass by John Piper. This remarkable church, built in just 5 years, was consecrated in 1967.

## LLANGOLLEN CANAL

From the Shropshire Union at Hurleston, near Nantwich, Cheshire, to Llantysilio near Llangollen; 46m with 21 locks.

This, the surviving part of the Shropshire Union's Welsh section, was constructed by Thomas Telford and William Jessop in an ambitious scheme to link the waterways of the Severn, Dee and Mersey. Originally consisting of the Ellesmere Canal from Hurleston via Welsh Frankton to Carreghofa, and thence the Montgomeryshire Canal to Welshpool and Newtown, with various branches, including the Pontcysyllte Branch between Frankton and Llantysilio, much of the system was closed by Act of Parliament in 1944. Largely because of its importance as a water feeder from the Dee to Hurleston, however, the Llangollen Canal managed to survive, and by the mid-1950s was being actively promoted for pleasure cruising. It now ranks as one of the most popular boating waterways in Britain, passing through utterly remote and unspoilt countryside, with the added attraction of some really spectacular scenery in the final 10m towards Llangollen. Commercial traffic, mainly agricultural goods and slate, ceased before World War II. Craft dimensions are 70ft × 7ft × 2ft 6in draught (2ft only, Trevor to Llangollen) × 7ft 6in headroom).

*Hurleston Junction*   A wide basin on the Shropshire Union main line is bordered by the first of 4 locks in a well-maintained flight lifting the canal on its journey towards Llangollen. A lock-keeper, resident at the top, is available to give advice and help in lock operation. On the right is the embankment of a large reservoir with a capacity of 85 million gallons, which receives supplies, both for drinking water and for the Shropshire Union, brought down from Llantysilio. A fine double-fronted canal house stood opposite the junction until the mid-1960s. The countryside is gently undulating, very rich and green, and supports prosperous Cheshire dairy farming. Upper lock gate-paddles have been removed throughout the canal. The third lock of the flight has a curved 'swan's neck' ground paddle.

*Swanley* (2m 2f)   A huge ash tree towers over the first of 2 locks. A general warning about the fierceness of bypass weirs on the canal is necessary. When there is plenty of water passing down to Hurleston, special care must be taken to avoid boats being slammed against the lock entrances when working uphill. Since the waterway began to be developed for pleasure traffic, much steel and concrete bank protection has been completed. Eventually it is hoped that the entire canal will be treated in this manner, for its already shallow channel is rather liable to silting from the wash against the banks.

*Wrenbury* (6m 2f)   Beyond 3 locks at Baddiley comes Bridge 17 carrying the drive to Wrenbury Hall, now Cheshire County Council hostels and a training centre. The canal passes through a pleasant wood of horse chestnuts, and then Bridge 19 appears, the first of a series of splendid wooden bascules of a design unique to this waterway. While some provide farm access only, others carry minor roads and must be opened and closed for the passage of a boat. Well-maintained in cream and black paint, they contribute much to the photographic potential of this canal. Wrenbury village is best reached from Bridge 20, which has an old corn-mill (now a hire-cruiser base) beside it. The village has a charming green surrounded by Cheshire 'magpie' cottages and a fine church. The Cotton Arms stands between canal and village centre.

*Grindley Brook* (12m 1f)   Quoisley, Willeymoor and Povey's Locks keep up the necessity for gentle exercise until one reaches Grindley Brook, where Bridge 27 carries an abandoned railway line over the canal at a skew. The bridge has beautiful curved courses of blue brick under the navigation arch. Now begins a series of 6 locks, the first 3 well spaced out but the next 3 forming a staircase of nearly 20ft that is preceded by a right-angled turn under the A41 Chester–Whitchurch road. The staircase is a satisfying blend of paddle gear, ribbed brickwork to provide a grip for horses and a remarkably fine bow-fronted cottage by the top chamber. A small general shop and post office offers a range of canal souvenirs. Now begins a 32m cruise to Llantysilio, punctuated by just 2 locks at New Marton, and representing a considerable engineering achievement in terrain reaching into the mountains of North Wales.

*Whitchurch* (13m 5f)   Wilder countryside now follows. Bridge 31, a drawbridge, marks the site of the Whitchurch arm, closed under the 1944 Act and now filled in. The town, about 1½m from Bridges 29 or 32, was a Roman settlement, and relics are on view in the museum. It is now a sizeable market town. The original white church of St Alkmund collapsed in July 1711 and was rebuilt immediately afterwards. In the days of its commercial prosperity, the Welsh canal surfaced its towpath largely with white stone chippings, still visible from time to time where grass and weeds have not yet taken over.

*Platt Lane* (17m 3f)   An old wharf and warehouse in red brick and slate are typical of dozens of small commercial centres that once existed along the canal. A short distance down the road is the Waggoners Inn, completing the former transport picture.

*Whixall Moss* (19m)   Drawbridge 45 marks the start of a strange tract of countryside, quite unlike the rest of Shropshire, where an extensive peat moss stretches into the distance. Bracken and silver birch grow near the canal, now deep and wide, but within 100yd rich black peat is commercially dug, mainly for agricultural use. A packing station lies down the track off Bridge 45. As in Ireland's Grand Canal, the peat it cut in blocks from trenches. A fine wooden roving bridge, its sides composed of X-patterns with chamfered edges, crosses the canal at its junction with the Prees Branch, left, once navigable for nearly 4m to Quina Brook, and partly restored in 1973 to provide access to an extensive marina. Several well-maintained drawbridges of the familiar design cross the branch. Throughout the summer the gaudy flowers of the yellow balsam or musk flourish here, as well as along many other sections of the waterway. Of several canal cottages dotted about near the branch, that by the junction, a square red-brick structure with circular insets on the front elevation, is especially attractive.

*Ellesmere* (25m 5f)   After a brief spell in Flintshire the canal returns to Shropshire, having passed near the village of Bettisfield, and begins to wind considerably. Now comes the little known but beautiful Ellesmere lake district, a series of 9 lakes set mainly in wooded surroundings, several of them popular with dinghy sailors and anglers. Cole Mere, left, may be glimpsed through trees at a rather lower level than the canal, and soon the waterway winds along the banks of Blake Mere. There are many good moorings in this outstanding area. A cutting leads up to the 87yd Ellesmere Tunnel, which is fitted with a towpath jutting over the water on a series of brick arches and a handrail on elegant cast-iron supports. The town itself stands at the end of a short arm with warehouses and an iron and wooden crane. A painted sign across one gable still reads 'Shropshire Union Railways and Canal Company. General Carriers to Chester, Liverpool, Manchester, North and South, Staffordshire and North Wales', although the company's fleet was disposed of in 1921. A large dairy processing works creates steam in the canal from its outfall, and produces a night-long din, although the basin is a convenient mooring for visiting the range of good shops in the town. There is a massive Town Hall, now disused, with exceptionally wide eaves and classical pediment, and several good inns, of which the Black Lion has extensive courtyards and stables. Time has rather passed by this small market town, leaving it largely as it was 50 years ago.

*Llangollen Canal. Pleasing use of timber and stone at the Ellesmere maintenance yard*

*Ellesmere Maintenance Yard*   To a canal enthusiast the yard is a rarity in still preserving the buildings, equipment and atmosphere of a maintenance centre from which waterways over a wide area were serviced. Standing opposite the junction with the Ellesmere arm, there are fine red-brick canal company offices, now 5 private dwellings. Alongside, in stone and timber, are a covered dock, equipment for making lock gates, large blacksmith's and carpenter's shops, and (disused) workmen's 'staff room' fitted with wooden settles and a coal range. Until recent times all power came from a stationary steam engine, now removed, but an internal railway and a system of machine driving belts remain. In addition the yard boasts a rich collection of canal 'antiques', from small oil lanterns marked with the company initials to a complete range of original wooden patterns from which all the ironwork of locks and bridges was cast. Activities of the yard have declined considerably in recent years, but it is vital that in any future reorganisation it should be kept intact as a complete workshop of canal crafts.

*Welsh Frankton* (29m)   Remote and hilly country leads from Ellesmere to the junction with the Montgomeryshire Canal at Frankton, a forlorn and lost little settlement miles from road traffic or passing aircraft, where the atmosphere seems changeless. Four ruined Frankton locks, the first 2 in a staircase crossed by a pretty iron footbridge, fall downhill towards Welshpool. The old towpath is walkable for an idyllic mile with ease through clusters of wildflowers in midsummer.

After years of discussion about the possibility of restoring the canal's 30m, last navigable in 1936, a committee under the chairmanship of the Prince of Wales announced in 1973 that it would promote full reconstruction of 7m and 6 locks between Welshpool and Ardleen. A restoration trust has been set up to coordinate the work. The cost is expected to be in the region of £250,000, with substantial practical help from volunteers. At the same time the Shropshire Union Canal Society is appealing for £300,000, required to resuscitate the remainder of this beautiful waterway. Already the Society has rebuilt a lock in Welshpool and established narrow-boat trips there for the public. Reopening of the Montgomeryshire becomes ever more desirable as the volume of boats increases on the adjoining Llangollen. Problems include 10 lowered road bridges, but the first 14m from Frankton present no major difficulties. There are 2 substantial aqueducts, the Vyrnwy and Berriew, 26 narrow locks and superb Borderland countryside throughout.

*New Marton Locks* (32m 5f)   Bridge numbering starts again at 1 at Frankton Junction, and there follows a peaceful level through farmland. (Many of the farms advertise produce for sale.) No 6 is a curving roving bridge, while no 10, which once carried a railway, has been removed. In all the 46m there is just one working railway left, at Chirk. New Marton locks make an interesting comparison. The lower one is overlooked by a sadly ruined cottage and overgrown garden, while at the upper one the residents serve good meals at short notice and have a plot filled with healthy vegetables. Slots in the stone coping of the locksides are a reminder that this was a point where boats were gauged and tolls collected.

*Chirk* (36m)   Generations of boat people would have bought bread at Usher's canalside bakery (Bridge 13, 33m) established in the mid-nineteenth century and much recommended. After the villages of Rhoswiel and Gledrid (35m 2f) the canal passes

*Montgomeryshire Canal. Peace in decay at Welsh Frankton; parts are now being restored under the auspices of the Prince of Wales' Committee*

into hilly terrain with a sharp drop to the right. Through the trees is the first surprise view of the Welsh Mountains, and the spectacular section that gives the Llangollen its reputation now begins. A mighty stone aqueduct with towpath and grass bank carries the canal at a height of 70ft over the River Ceiriog, passing here through a deep and densely wooded valley, with fine views. The aqueduct is somewhat dwarfed by the taller railway viaduct taking the line from Wolverhampton to Shrewsbury and Chester, but is nevertheless a Telford and Jessop masterpiece and predates Pontcysyllte by several years. Beyond, a small basin provides a good mooring while visiting Chirk – the castle lies about 2m from the canal and is open to the public during the summer. Continuously inhabited since completion in 1310, it contains much interesting furniture of the seventeenth, eighteenth and early nineteenth centuries. Within 100yd of the aqueduct the canal dives into Chirk Tunnel (459yd), a tall bore lined with brick throughout. The overgrown towpath in the cutting at the far end was cleared in 1971 by voluntary labour supplied by unemployed miners. The waterway is by now rather narrower, with shallow edges often making mooring against the bank difficult. Whitehouses Tunnel (191yd) is crossed by the A5 Holyhead road (38m), and is of similar construction to those at Ellesmere and Chirk. All 3, together with the 2 major aqueducts, are for one-way traffic.

*Pontcysyllte* (40m 1f)   At Irish Bridge, no 27, is a signpost to Offa's Dyke, the eighth-century Mercian fortification against the Welsh, which runs 81m along the border; remains can be inspected at several points near the canal. Soon, away across the Dee Valley to the right, comes the first view of the great Pontcysyllte Aqueduct, rising from the river bed into space. It looks unreal from this distance, but is even more unlikely when seen from the deck of a crossing boat! Access for walkers is either via Drawbridge 28 at the foot of a steep winding lane in Vron on the A5 or from Trevor at the far side. Completed in 1805, this amazing structure is 121ft high at its centre and strides 1,007ft over the Dee. It is described in detail on pp 69–71.

The cast-iron trough is carried on a series of finely jointed stone arches. While there is a towpath and handrail down the right side, the other edge offers a sheer drop over the lip of the trough, and those with a tendency to vertigo are advised to stay well within their boat. The trough is drained at intervals of about 8 years for repairs and maintenance by drawing a plug near the centre, having blocked off each end, and the resulting cascade of water is most impressive. In order to continue with a flow of water to Hurleston reservoir during this process, supplies are pumped direct from the Dee to enter the canal at a sluice by Bridge 28. A large tablet commemorating its construction can be seen near the base of a pier at the Vron side, approached by climbing down the river bank. The Dee tumbles and foams over rock slabs with great ferocity but the aqueduct remains as sound as when it was built. There are excellent views up and down river from the trough, vertically down on to a cricket field and across to industrial Ruabon. The works there were originally served by a canal arm with stone-lined banks to its basins, but only a short section remains navigable, leased to a hire-cruiser firm. The drydocks were once used to build working narrow boats. The richness of the scenery has not prevented limited commercial activity, for a flourishing silica works can be found in Trevor village, with kilns glowing bright red.

The final run to Llangollen was built as a navigable feeder and is both shallow, rocky and in places exceedingly narrow, but by running very slowly all except the deepest draught boats can reach the prime objective of this cruise. Clinging to a hillside, the waters of the Dee rushing by beyond the towpath on the left, the canal in its last 6m is probably the loveliest in Britain. Rich pastures roll down on the right, and sections of rocky cliff rise sheer from the water. Little stone bridges, some set at a sharp angle to the water, and the canal itself are made even more insignificant by the towering mountains seen directly ahead from the 2-arched Bridge 41, or to the right of the last drawbridge (no 44), where an extensive range comes into view. The current of water flowing downstream can be quite considerable, so that ascending craft are more easily halted than those coming down.

*Llangollen* (44m)   A late Victorian and Edwardian resort, slate-roofed and slightly severe, with its Dee bridge dating from about 1345, it is an ideal centre for touring the beauties of this part of North Wales. The town crowds into the narrow river valley, overlooked by pine-planted mountains. It suffers rather from souvenir shops and an influx of trippers during the season, while on the confines of the canal, only yards from the main shopping street, overnight moorings can be difficult to find. Since 1947 an annual Llangollen International Musical Eisteddfod has been staged in July. On the thundering waters of the Dee, which falls nearly 120ft in the 6m from Llantysilio to Pontcysyllte, canoe slalom championships are held from time to time by the town bridge. One excellent walk into the hills from the canal wharf leads up to the ancient ruins of Castell Dinas Bran, an important medieval fortress, and in clear weather the heights of Snowdonia are visible from the 1,100ft summit. Another worthwhile ramble is along the canal to its beginnings at the Horseshoe Falls, possible also to small cruisers but involving a trip of 1m in reverse in order to turn round. For large craft the last winding hole is situated shortly above Llangollen wharf, where a small canal museum has been created (see p 194). That is also the embarkation point for horsedrawn cruises, a tradition well over 70 years old. Other excursions include trips to Valle Crucis Abbey near Llantysilio, founded in 1200, and Plas Newydd, 5 minutes from the town centre and home of two celebrated ladies of Llangollen between 1780 and 1831. The 'magpie'-style house has many oak carvings and other relics.

## LYDNEY CANAL

From Lydney, Gloucestershire, to the Severn estuary (northern shore, almost opposite Sharpness); 1m with 1 lock and a pair of tidal doors. The harbour is a pleasant little seaport that recalls the terminal basins of the Crinan Canal. Pleasure craft of any size may enter at an appropriate state of the tide. A terrace of cottages has been adapted as the headquarters of the Lydney Yacht Club, formed in 1962. Here sailing trows were built and repaired in the last century. The canal once connected with Pidcock's Canal, 1½m long to Middle Forge, but this fell into disuse, probably during the first part of the nineteenth century. Lydney is an ideal centre for exploring the woodlands and heaths of the Forest of Dean.

## MACCLESFIELD CANAL

From Marple, Cheshire, junction with the Peak Forest Canal, to Hall Green, beyond the northern end of Harecastle Tunnel on the Trent & Mersey Canal; 26m with 13 locks. Maximum craft dimensions are 70ft × 7ft × 3ft draught × 6ft headroom. Part of the Cheshire Canal Ring (see p 380), this waterway was operated for many years until nationalisation by the Great Central Railway in conjunction with the Peak Forest and Ashton Canals. It has great scenic appeal through rugged countryside in

*Lydney Canal. Timber barges await unloading; cargoes of imported wood are brought from Avonmouth Docks*

east Cheshire, where the 16m Bosley to Marple pound maintains a height of 500ft.

*Marple* The most memorable feature of the Macclesfield is the succession of superb accommodation bridges built of beautifully worked stone blocks. A number have curved ramps, enabling the towpath to be carried from one side of the cut to the other without the need to disconnect a boat horse. Few of the bridges are identical, for the designs were adapted to suit the particular depth of a cutting or some other difference in the situation. Marple is as good as anywhere to admire them. Other places have wooden swing bridges, and these must be opened and closed by boat crews. (For Marple, see p 373.)

*High Lane* (2m 2f) The North Cheshire Cruising Club makes good use of a canal arm. A curious habit in the locality, to be found on few other canals, is to moor cruisers inside strange lock-up boat houses whose utility is greater than their visual appeal. A row of these structures extends along the High Lane arm. The waterway shortly leaves behind these suburban districts (pleasant, but suburban none the less) and passes into a lonely and beautiful stretch through Higher Poynton to Bollington. There are several massive single-arched aqueducts enabling roads (or at Middlewood, a railway) to pass through great embankments. Nowhere is it more evident that canals offer views *down* to surrounding countryside, whereas rivers tend to present a more enclosed prospect. Two miles east of Bridge 15, Higher Poynton, stands the great Palladian mansion and park (9m in circumference) of Lyme, owned by the National Trust and open to the public.

*Bollington* (7m 6f)   The stone-built town lies close to the boundary of the Peak District National Park. It is bisected by the canal on a really high embankment pierced by 2 roads.

*Macclesfield* (10m 7f)   A medieval town, noted since 1743 for its silk mills. Several buildings from soon after this time remain to show with what dignity industrialism came to Cheshire. Macclesfield's eighteenth-century prosperity is clearly shown by fine Georgian houses and the market place. There are 2 boatyards on the canal, offering a range of facilities including hired day boats.

*Bosley Locks* (16m 1f)   The journey continues through exceptionally hilly and broken countryside, with little rocky ravines. There are numerous ideal points at which to moor up for a few hours and explore the terrain on foot. Thomas Telford designed this extraordinary waterway with a boldness that seems virtually to ignore the contours, using a cut and fill technique to maintain a level and seek out the shortest route. The Macclesfield's engineer in charge of construction was William Crosley. Opened in 1831, it was one of the last waterways constructed in England before railway supremacy had gained a hold on inland transport. The series of 12 Bosley locks lowers the canal through 110ft over a mile. Because of the considerable depth of their chambers, double mitre gates are fitted at each end instead of the more normal arrangement of pairs at the bottom and singles at the top. To the east, in a triangle formed by the A54 and the A523, Bosley reservoir supplies the navigation with water.

*Congleton* (21m 6f)   Below the locks the Macclesfield crosses the Dane via an aqueduct, with a wooded hill, rising to more than 1,000ft and known as The Cloud, to the south. From the summit of this National Trust property can be seen the industrial areas of southern Lancashire and the Cheshire Plain towards Nantwich. From the small town of Congleton the countryside becomes more tame and ordered, with rich dairy grazing.

*Mow Cop* (24m 6f)   Another National Trust hill, 1m east of the waterway, whose rugged heights are almost 1,100ft above sea level. The rocky escarpment is crowned by a Gothic tower folly, built in 1750 to enhance the view from the Rode Hall estate. This romantic structure was the setting in 1807 for a 12-hour prayer meeting held by nonconformists. The movement developed into the birth of Primitive Methodism. Rowndes No 2 bridge (no 86) leads via a ¾m track to Little Moreton Hall (National Trust), an exquisite black and white moated sixteenth-century house with a bewildering pattern of exterior wooden beams. There is no other Elizabethan half-timbered building in England to match it. Scholar Green has one of the most charmingly old-fashioned inns on the canal network, the Bird in Hand. The author was once kept waiting a full 20 minutes while the landlord enjoyed his favourite television programme in an inner room. Beer is carried from the cellar in a jug. A shallow stop lock in a cutting at Hall Green leads to a 1½m branch of the Trent & Mersey Canal. The Macclesfield crosses the T&M by means of a flyover aqueduct and then joins it (see p 425).

### MANCHESTER SHIP CANAL
From the tidal River Mersey at Eastham to Manchester; 36m with 5 locks. The

MSC occupies a unique position among British inland waterways for a variety of reasons. Begun in 1887 and completed in 1894, it is both a seaway and a form of linear dock, being lined with deep-water berths and oil-discharge depots. Construction methods were impressive, using plant that had more in common with the very latest machinery now creating new European canals than with the English waterways of a century before. A list of the devices employed during 1891 makes compelling reading: huge steam excavating cranes, French- and German-built land dredgers, floating dredgers, tipping cranes, the massive Ruston & Dunbar 'steam navvy', soil trans- porters, 173 locomotives, 194 steam cranes, 182 steam engines (generally portable), 212 steam pumps, 6,300 waggons, 59 pile engines, and 228m of railway track, much of it laid along the canal section built 'dry', ie between Ellesmere Port and Manchester. In that same year 16,361 men and boys were employed, with 196 horses. About 10,000 tons of coal were used each month to fire the machinery boilers. About 70 million bricks were used during the building of the waterway and almost 750,000 tons of granite. If all the greenheart logs from which timber for the 50 lock gates was prepared had been laid end to end, they would have extended for 29m. In all 48 million cu yd of soil was excavated from the workings.

Although short stretches of the Rivers Mersey and Irwell were canalised for the waterway, most of it consisted of a completely new channel. Problems arose both from a difficulty in raising sufficient funds to complete the job and from serious flooding of the construction sites, the Irlam section being accidentally inundated to a depth of 20ft in 1891. Eventually, all was successfully completed and Queen Victoria officiated at the opening ceremony. Total building costs had been about £14,350,000.

Confidence in this huge investment was destined to be more than justified. The first dividend was paid in 1915, since when the MSC has shown a very healthy profit. Manchester was able to expand to its present industrial greatness directly as the result of being provided with shipping facilities. It is now Britain's third largest seaport, a remarkable achievement for a city that lies 43m inland of Liverpool. More than 5,000 ships navigate the canal each year, handling almost 17 million tons of cargo, nearly half the total transported on all waterways in Britain. Craft of 15,000 tons can navigate from the Mersey to Ellesmere Port and 12,500-tonners (deadweight) between there and Manchester. The MSC is a narrow waterway for such large ships, and at certain points, such as Latchford, a one-way system is operated.

The company tolerates rather than welcomes pleasure boats, imposes stringent (but wise) restrictions, specifies various insurance cover and equipment regulations and tries to shepherd small craft through so that they are unlikely to encounter the problems of wash and suction from ships. Unless you are an experienced cruiser handler and have confidence in your boat, gear and engine, it is best not to run risks by entering the canal.

In addition to connecting with the Mersey at Eastham, the MSC is linked with the Shropshire Union at Ellesmere Port; the Weaver Navigation at Weston Point; the Mersey at Warrington, Runcorn, Old Quay and Weston Mersey; the River Irwell, Upper Reach and thence the Bridgewater Canal via the Hulme Locks branch; and the Runcorn & Latchford Canal at Twenty Steps Lock. Maximum dimensions for the whole canal are 600ft × 65ft × 28ft draught × 70ft headroom. The connections listed above may all be navigated by craft such as wide-beam barges, and consequently will accommodate all pleasure boats normally used on inland waters.

*The Mersey*  Divided for administrative purposes into the Lower and Upper River, the tidal Mersey is navigable for 18¾m from Liverpool to Warrington. The portion of greatest interest to pleasure craft is the 6m upstream of Liverpool to Eastham, start of the MSC. As tidal currents can be dangerous, a journey between the Ship Canal and Stanley Dock, Liverpool, entrance to the Leeds & Liverpool Canal, should only be made in suitable seagoing vessels in the control of experienced navigators. Shifting sandbanks in the upper river make updated charts essential.

*Eastham Locks*  Triplicated locks are situated on the southern shore of the Mersey, opposite Liverpool's Speke airport. The river is over 2m wide at this point. Largest of the locks is 600ft × 80ft. For periods totalling about half the year, tides enter the canal at Eastham, thus affecting levels as far as Latchford locks. Much of the waterway is lined with shipping berths that handle such imports as oil products, grain, chemicals, metals and foodstuffs; and such exports as chemicals, machinery, vehicles and foodstuffs. The sight of ships slowly moving through the landscape or towering above urban streets is both unusual and exciting. On the west side of the canal, ½m above Eastham, is a 'masting crane' that removes funnel-tops, topmasts and other gear from ships which would not otherwise conform with the waterway's 70ft air draught. Vessels regularly making the journey to Manchester are equipped with telescopic masts and specially designed low superstructures.

*Mount Manisty* (1m 6f)  This outcrop of rock and soil between canal and estuary was formed by dumping material during excavation of the waterway. It is named after the engineer responsible.

*Ellesmere Port* (2m 7f)  There are container docks on the right bank, junction with the Shropshire Union Canal and marked by Telford's elegant lighthouse (see p 399). Further along is the huge Stanlow oil refinery complex, where Shell established a works in 1924. They use large quantities of canal water for cooling purposes. Their research centre, designed by Sir Basil Gibberd, dates from 1956. On an inaccessible island site by the river is Stanlow Abbey, but very little remains of the building begun here in 1294. The canal continues across marshes past Helsby and Frodsham to the mouth of the Weaver Navigation at Weston Marsh Lock. The area is known locally as Saltport, on account of the saline water brought down by the river. On the left the Weaver sluices, each about 30ft wide, control flood water.

*Weston Point* (11m)  The Weaver Navigation, MSC and Mersey follow a parallel course to the BWB's Weston Point Docks (p 438). Christ Church, in the heart of the docks, was built by the WN Trustees in 1841 for the benefit of 'watermen, hauliers and others employed upon the river'. Other churches were erected under the same legislative powers at Northwich and Winsford.

*Runcorn* (12m 5f)  The Mersey begins to narrow and is bridged here for the first time. A most useful connection with the Bridgewater Canal via Runcorn locks was destroyed as recently as 1966. (Further details of Runcorn are given on p 251.) The town has a beach on the Mersey somewhat optimistically called Runcorn Sands.

*Latchford* (20m 1f)  The Runcorn & Latchford Canal, a 1¼m navigation connecting the Ship Canal with the Mersey & Irwell Navigation, is entered shortly after Warrington wharf and Walton Lock, on the left bank. With the 2 locks of Twenty Steps near the MSC and Manor off the Mersey, its entrance is marked by the Northwich Road swing bridge, one of a series of opening spans over the upper reaches of the canal, mounted on a gigantic circular roller path. A cutting through rock, up to 30ft deep and sufficiently narrow to necessitate one-way working, leads to Latchford Locks (together with the 3 remaining locks to Manchester, these are duplicated, side by side). Across a mile of pleasant countryside to the right is the town of Lymm, on the banks of the Bridgewater Canal (p 250). The M6 motorway, Birmingham–Preston, soars high above the navigation on a bridge whose long concrete approach viaducts extend far in each direction. Soon afterwards the waterway enters the original but improved course of the Mersey, which it follows for several miles, and near Flixton it joins the Irwell.

*Irlam Locks* (28m 3f)   Craft rise further in their 58ft 8in climb towards Manchester from low-water level below Eastham.

*Barton* (31m 6f)   Beyond Barton Locks (29m 5f) comes the MSC's most celebrated engineering feature – the Barton Swing Aqueduct, conveying the Bridgewater Canal (see p 73). This is generally opened about ½ hour before a ship is due to pass through, as a precaution against possible mechanical failure. It should be appreciated that ocean-going vessels, even if navigating with the assistance of tugs bow and stern, cannot apply brakes and come to a halt at a moment's notice. Wharves and docks line the sides of the Ship Canal for much of its remaining 4¼m. Many are occupied by well-known firms, including Brown & Polson, Proctor & Gamble and Colgate-Palmolive.

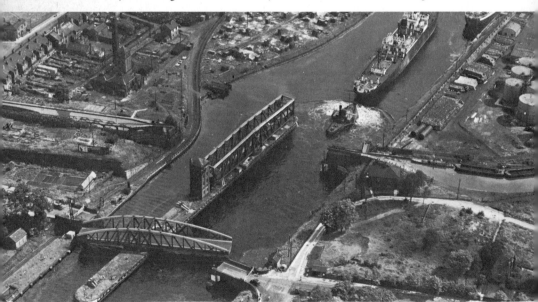

*Manchester Ship Canal. An aerial view of Barton swing road bridge (foreground) and the Bridgewater Canal's Barton swing aqueduct* (Aerofilms)

*Manchester* (36m)   The final locks, Mode Wheel (33m 7f), mark the beginning of the Manchester Docks complex. Immediately to the south lies Trafford Park, the largest industrial estate in Europe. Tripping boat tours of the Docks are available, while several times throughout the summer the local Co-op Travel Service runs day-long public cruises aboard a passenger ship from Manchester to Liverpool or *vice versa*. Beyond Pomona Docks (nos 1, 2, 3 and 4) a junction is made with the River Irwell Upper Reach and the Hulme Locks branch of the Bridgewater Canal (see p 250 for further details about Manchester). This part of the Irwell now runs for just 1¼m to Hunt's Bank, passing the entrances to the Manchester, Bolton & Bury Canal and the Manchester & Salford Junction Canal, both now completely derelict.

## MARKET WEIGHTON NAVIGATION

From the north bank of the River Humber near Trent Falls to Sod House Lock; 6m with 1 sea lock at the entrance. Opened in 1777, the Market Weighton Canal combined transport with drainage duties and originally continued for a further 3½m to Weighton Common, a short distance outside Market Weighton. The northern section, including Sod House, Mill and East Common Locks, was abandoned in 1900. At one time considerable trade in bricks, tiles and agricultural materials was carried on, and the last barge passed through Weighton (or Humber) Lock as recently as 1958.

Weighton Lock has a resident keeper whose duties centre on control of flood water. No fewer than 230 men applied for the job when it was advertised in 1966, and the house, overlooking the Humber, does enjoy an attractive if lonely prospect. Navigation rights along the canal were extinguished in 1971, so use of Weighton Lock is in some doubt. Craft up to 70ft × 14ft 10in × 4ft 6in draught × about 10ft headroom can in theory reach Sod House. In practical terms the future more likely lies in general amenity use with small boats. An active Canal Restoration Committee of the Market Weighton Civic Trust is pressing for development of boating and walking facilities.

## MEDWAY, RIVER

From the Thames estuary at Sheerness to Tonbridge, Kent; 43m with 10 locks. Small cruisers can travel almost 2m beyond Tonbridge, while portable boats should be able to reach Penshurst, 8m above Tonbridge. There are effectively no size restrictions for craft using the tidal river to Allington Lock. Rochester and Aylesford bridges offer a clearance upwards of 10ft. From Allington Lock to Maidstone maximum dimensions are 180ft × 20ft × 6ft 6in draught × 10ft 6in; and from Maidstone to Tonbridge 80ft × 18ft 6in × 5ft 6in draught (to Hampstead Lock, and 4ft to Tonbridge) × 8ft 6in headroom to Tonbridge (6ft 6in under Great Bridge).

The lower parts of the tideway between Sheerness and Chatham are exceptionally busy with shipping movements. Regular visitors are transatlantic LASH ships, whose barges are offloaded near Sheerness for delivery in short trains drawn by tug. There is much industry, including large paper mills and oil refineries. However, the broad expanse of water offers splendid cruising facilities and the area is justly popular with a variety of small craft. The journey to the Medway in a canal or river boat from the Thames or London canals should not be undertaken lightly, though with due care and appropriate safety equipment, the estuaries can be negotiated. The writer has twice travelled from Limehouse Basin to Tonbridge in a 70ft converted narrow boat, but in spite of enjoyable and trouble-free runs, it would be irresponsible to recommend the procedure. The non-tidal Medway is a completely rural and charming navigation, passing for almost 18m through hopfields and orchards that are often called 'The Garden of England'.

*The tidal Medway*   Between Sheerness and the first bridge at Rochester the river is exceptionally broad, though there are numerous mudbanks away from the main channel at low water. It handles an annual goods tonnage of about 30 million. Visiting boats from the main waterway network whose crews prefer to moor to terra firma rather than put down an anchor should continue to Chatham Pier (12m 4f), the first opportunity to bring up in a place of safety and civilisation. Upnor, opposite the naval dockyard, is a much frequented yachting centre. The area provided Charles Dickens with settings for several of his novels. Rochester (13m 4f) is at the centre of the Strood, Rochester, Chatham and Gillingham industrial complex, and offers Roman remains, the waterside keep of a Norman castle and a small cathedral. The M2 motorway bridge at Borstal has a broad prestressed concrete span and offers a magnificent view of the river from its carriageways. Thereafter the Medway narrows somewhat, makes several loops by the paper mills and cement works around Halling and Snodland, and continues to the first low-level bridge at Aylesford (23m 6f). This is a fine stone structure, mainly fourteenth-century, with the addition of a much later central navigation arch. Rows of gabled brick and ragstone cottages make an attractive group with the Norman church of St Peter. The Friars is a Carmelite house, founded in the thirteenth century and reoccupied by the monks from 1949. Much additional building and restoration has been carried out since. The river banks are muddy at low water and lined with willow trees. Kent's most celebrated prehistoric monument, Kits Coty (derived from the Celtic 'tomb in the wood'), is a megalithic burial chamber 1½m NE, comprising three uprights and a massive 13ft capstone. There are a number of similar sites nearby.

*Allington Lock* (25m)   The Medway's first lock is 175ft long and is operated by a keeper from 3 hours before high water until 2 hours afterwards. (HW is 50 minutes later than at Sheerness.) There is a pretty Victorian Gothic cottage. Allington Castle is a well-preserved, largely thirteenth-century stone pile, carefully restored between 1906 and 1932 and now used as a house of retreat by the Carmelites. This is a beautiful reach, with many houseboats in the form of converted Thames sailing barges and other craft, a popular inn, the Malta, and a large marina situated in a tree-fringed basin. One of several hire-cruiser fleets on the upper river is based here. Commercial barge traffic still navigates the Medway to Tovil, just above Maidstone.

*Maidstone* (27m 4f)   The county town, bustling with good shops and inns and various forms of industry, including brewing, flour mills, the Tilling-Stevens commercial vehicle works and Sharp's toffee factory. The stone walls of the Archbishops' palace rise from the river bank beyond Bazalgette's Victorian granite bridge. (Boat crews will welcome the commodious washing facilities offered at an adjacent public convenience.) Public launch trips and rowing boats are available. Beyond the site of Old College Lock, removed in 1899, the river enters a steep-sided wooded valley.

*East Farleigh* (29m 4f)   Here stands one of several exquisite medieval Medway bridges, with pointed arches and massive cutwaters, but providing something of a hazard to navigation. There is a lock with weir sluices immediately below. Several of the locks are provided with keepers, but, following the representations of the local branch of the Inland Waterways Association, restrictions on their use have been lifted and boat crews may work the unattended ones for themselves. Characteristic Kent oasthouses and the first orchards appear at East Farleigh, and a springtime cruise when the blossom is in full flower is much recommended.

*Teston* (31m 2f)   Kettle Bridge at East Barming is a timber structure with piers encased in concrete. The perpendicular needle spire of Barming church rises from a cluster of orchards. A notably attractive reach extends to Teston (pronounced 'Teeson') Bridge, another medieval crossing in ragstone, which has pedestrian refuges above the cutwaters. Teston Lock is set beside a wide weir and ruined linseed mill. Open meadows follow to Wateringbury (rowing boats for hire), a convenient mooring to visit Mereworth Castle, an early eighteenth-century Palladian villa open to the public.

*Hampstead Lock* (34m 4f)   After a broad reach beyond the village of Nettlestead, where dinghy sailing is a popular activity, the channel divides. Take the left fork for Hampstead lock cut, Yalding, or remain on the original river for a pleasant detour of almost 1m to Twyford Bridge, passing the confluence of the River Beult. Beyond the lock the navigation continues via several hundred yards of canal past a river maintenance yard and under a heavy drawbridge by the Anchor Inn. The bridge is lifted by a keeper. The Medway is rejoined near a boatyard facing the River Teise. Several acute bends now demand careful navigation as far as Stoneham Lock, whose gates were removed and a level created during a reconstruction of the waterway that was completed in 1915. In all, 3 locks were completely eliminated.

*Sluice Weir Lock* (36m 6f)   Through Branbridges Bridge and past East Peckham the river banks increase in height and water depth becomes more uncertain, with a possibility of deeper draught boats grounding on shoals in dry seasons. Sluice Weir has the greatest rise and fall of Medway locks.

*Tonbridge* (42m 6f)   The remainder of the journey is through exceptionally rural surroundings, remote from villages. Oak Weir, East, Porter's and Eldridge's Locks are evenly spaced at almost exact mile intervals. For some distance below Eldridge's Lock an astonishing 150ft Gothic folly tower, erected in 1835 at Hadlow Castle, reminds one of the eccentricity of its creator, Walter Barton May, who is alleged to have wanted to obtain views of the sea from his inland estate. One more lock, unique in Britain in that it is crossed by a large wooden drawbridge, marks the arrival in Tonbridge. Warehouses indicate the former importance of the river for trade from its completion as a transport link to the Thames estuary in the mid-eighteenth century. The town has since expanded but still retains a pleasant atmosphere in spite of heavy road traffic. Most memorable building is the ruined Norman castle, floodlit in its public park by the river, immediately above Great Bridge. The IWA has established much needed public moorings for visiting boats. Beyond the castle the channel divides, each route being navigable for craft whose headroom is under 5ft 3in. During 1829–30 one James Christie began work on extending the waterway for 6m beyond Tonbridge to Penshurst. Two locks and various canal cuts were partially built, but the project failed and barges were never to reach their intended destination. At the junction of the River Eden and the Medway stands Penshurst Place, the finest and

most complete fourteenth-century manor house in Britain. It has been in the possession of the Sidney family since the time of Edward VI, and is noted for superb formal
gardens originating from about 1560. Penshurst is open to the public and there are
good transport facilities from Tonbridge.

### MIDDLE LEVEL NAVIGATIONS

A complicated network of navigable drainage channels linking the River Nene at
Stanground Lock, downstream of Peterborough, with the tidal Great Ouse either via
the Old Bedford River or through Well Creek at Salter's Lode, immediately down
river of Denver Sluice. There are basically 2 through routes from which to choose.
Nene to Great Ouse is about 30m. The system has 7 workable locks (locally known
as sluices). Additionally the New Bedford, or Hundred Foot River (tidal) bypasses a
long section of the Ouse between the seaward side of Denver Sluice and upstream of
Hermitage Lock, Earith (see p 358). Maximum dimensions for boats vary to some
extent according to the route selected. Craft travelling via Well Creek must not exceed
46ft × 11ft × 3ft 6in draught × little more than 6ft headroom (legally it should be
8ft). The other way, via the Old Bedford River and Welches Dam, imposes limitations
of 40ft length and 10ft 9in beam. The working boats associated with the Middle
Level were Fen lighters (p 144). For further details of the specification of the MLN,
consult L. A. Edwards' *Inland Waterways of Great Britain*.

The Middle Level is of use more as a connection between Nene and Great Ouse
than as a cruising area in its own right. Fenland villages along Well Creek are pleasing,
and vividly recall smaller canals in Friesland. Elsewhere the MLN passes through an
uncompromisingly flat landscape of great fertility, under the canopy of a vast sky.
Bracing is one apt description. It is not a region for agoraphobiacs.

*Stanground Lock to Salter's Lode Lock*   At the time of the writer's first encounter
with the Middle Level, in 1968, navigation of these waters was a pioneering undertaking. With more boats (many more) and better maintenance, the legendary Middle
Level weed is less troublesome than it used to be. But advance notice to the waterway
authority will help them to prepare for your intended journey. Stanground sluice has
a keeper who can arrange for extra water to fill the ancient Cnut's Dyke, reputedly
cut by the Romans, and allow deeper draughted boats over the lock sill. This leads to
King's Dyke at a junction with the old course of the Nene, where the disused Horsey
Lock prevents a detour past Farcet village and Pig Water to Yaxley. To the north
the smoking chimneys of the London Brick Co's extensive works introduce a not
altogether pleasing odour.

*Whittlesey*   There is a lock at Ashline and then an easy run to Whittlesey, just
within the Isle of Ely. This little town has some pleasant Georgian houses, one of the
best church spires in Cambridgeshire and a useful selection of inns, including the Boat,
Hero of Aliwal, Falcon and the Letter B. The last named was once part of a quartet,
inspiringly named A, B, C and D. The channel is contained within a concrete-banked
cut and can boast the sharpest waterway bend in Britain at an inconsiderately sited
bridge. Any boats much above 40ft in length should have flexible banana-shaped
hulls.

*Middle Level Navigations. Almost certainly the sharpest bend to be found on British inland waterways is at Whittlesey: it can be negotiated by craft up to about 46ft in length*

*Angle Corner*  At a 4-way intersection a left turn leads to the Old Nene along Bevills Leam, but a bridge at Mere Mouth offers little more than 5ft 6in headway. An alternative is to turn right along the Twenty Foot River, rejoining the main route at the head of Popham's Eau, though here again a bridge with about 6ft clearance might cause difficulties. If in doubt, keep straight on in the direction of March.

*Flood's Ferry*  A 3-way junction, where it is necessary to decide whether to continue via the southern, Old Bedford Line, or to reach the Great Ouse along the prettier Well Creek. From mid-1968 until 1974 closure of a lock at Marmount Priory made the Old Bedford route obligatory. Both offer interest.

*March*  On the way towards Well Creek, March is a railway town with extensive marshalling yards. It is also the only proper town on the Middle Level, with boatyard and good waterfront. It is the stronghold of the Middle Level Watermen's Club, whose members are a source of expert and updated information. Beyond March the Twenty Foot enters, left, and navigation continues via Popham's Eau. Splitting yet again, the channel runs through to Marmount Priory Lock or forks right through the Sixteen Foot (utterly straight for $9\frac{1}{2}$m). The latter provides access with the Old Bedford route at Horseway Sluice.

*Well Creek*  From Marmount Priory Lock to the Great Ouse is just 8m. Until the fifteenth century part of this course was the main tidal outfall of the Nene and Ouse and varied in width between 40ft and a mile, depending on flood conditions. Various new channels were cut and drainage greatly improved. Known as the Wellstream, the waterway once left the present course of Well Creek at the village of Outwell and connected with the Nene at Wisbech. (It is reliably recorded that King John lost his jewels in the Wellstream and not the Wash.) The most fascinating part of the Middle Level begins at Upwell, with one bank in Cambridgeshire and the other in Norfolk. Fine old buildings face each other across the navigation in imitation of Dutch villages. There is no noticeable division between Upwell and the next village, Outwell; indeed, during the tenth century, the two were a single community known as Wella. Note several disused draining mills among the houses. Between the late eighteenth century and its abandonment in 1926 the 5¼m Wisbech Canal formed a connection from Outwell. It was failing commercially when the Wisbech & Upwell Steam Tramway was opened in competition along its banks in 1884. Parts of the unsightly and rubbish-filled canal bed can still be seen. During his last voyage through Outwell the writer was introduced to an elderly white South African who had toured the world as a circus act under the name of the Rancho Kid. He then lived in retirement in a council flat over the local Co-op, but could still extinguish a cigarette with a flick of his whip, and did so from time to time at charity functions. Waterway travel results in many such encounters.

Well Creek is closely followed by a road on one or both banks for its entire length, but at the time of writing is weedy and in parts badly silted. Improvements are promised. In 1774 Lord Orford sailed through Upwell and Outwell 'with a fleet of nine ships'. The ships would need to be small ones indeed if a bicentenary re-enactment had been attempted. The last village is Nordelph (North channel), beyond a curious aqueduct carrying the Creek over the Middle Level Main Drain. Entry to the Ouse is through Salter's Lode Lock, operated by a keeper at certain states of the tide and prone to silting. From this point to the safety of non-tidal water above Denver Sluice is a mere few hundred yards, but it is as well to contact the Denver lock-keeper in advance of arrival to ensure that delays on this part of the Ouse are reduced to a minimum.

*Flood's Ferry to Salter's Lode via Horseway Sluice* Following the above route through Whittlesey, turn right at Flood's Ferry. This takes you down the Old River Nene, past fields of strawberries and potatoes reaching almost to the horizon. Benwick village is tiny, grave-quiet and fractionally sinister. A junction at Well's Bridge offers the possibility of a one-way detour along the High Lode to Ramsey. The through route lies along the Forty Foot (Vermuyden's Drain), under a low bridge and past Beezling Fen and the hamlet of Swingbrow. Sixteen Foot Corner marks the entry of the Sixteen Foot from Popham's Eau, which must be chosen by craft with much more than 6ft height above water. Horseway Sluice lies at the end of a mysterious cut fringed by giant reeds (one half expects a primeval swamp inhabitant to appear). In 1968 it took 7 hours to clear rotting weeds from the gates in order to force a passage. Each of the 4 paddles was obstructed by a bird's nest. Conditions have since improved. Should water level in the 3m between Horseway Sluice and Welches Dam be too low, more can be produced by lifting a paddle at the dam and waiting. Allegedly the large nut that works the sluices is moved by applying a tool concealed in the immediate neighbourhood. Rather than rely on this arrangement, arrive armed with a large adjustable spanner.

The Old Bedford runs as straight as an arrow for 12m between Welches Dam and the Ouse, accompanied by the equally straight tidal New Bedford River. It is scarcely a place to linger, but a rousing welcome does await boats at the Three Tuns Inn, Welney, near the halfway mark. Tidal doors within a few yards of Well Creek and Salter's Lode Lock provide egress to the Ouse, but can only be operated by the keeper when a level is made, once every 12 hours.

The Middle Level may not appeal to every taste, but there is nothing quite like it anywhere else in Britain and a visit should be made on those grounds at least. Quite possibly you will actively enjoy the remote lonely quality of these waters and the moments of adventurous navigation.

### NENE, RIVER

From Northampton, junction with a narrow beam branch of the Grand Union Canal (p 297), to the Wash at Crab's Hole; 91½m with 38 locks. In Peterborough there is an important link via the Middle Level Navigations with the Great Ouse and its tributaries.

The Nene is a very English river, winding endlessly through watermeadows, past old mills and skirting numerous attractive villages. Its name is a matter for some dispute, ranging from Nene to Nyne and Nen. The most acceptable pronunciation appears to be 'Neen'. Navigation between Northampton and Peterborough was first promoted under an Act of Queen Anne, when the course from Peterborough to Wisbech was partly over waterways now included in the Middle Level. In common with other rivers of the Eastern Counties, many of the locks were in the form of staunches or navigation weirs, a situation that lasted until the late 1920s. By that time passage was virtually impossible, but an admirable programme of complete reconstruction resulted in a new series of locks being erected. These are all equipped with conventional pairs of mitre gates at the upper ends and steel guillotines at the bottoms. All but 3 guillotines rise and fall vertically; those at Northampton, Rush Mills and Ditchford Locks are of a radial or curved pattern and require 156, 150 and 155 turns of the operating handle respectively to raise or lower them. Normal guillotine gates average about 100 turns. Working of a single lock is not very exhausting, but negotiation of a number in succession can be tiring, so an adequate crew is advisable. Because the locks form an integral part of the Nene's system of flood control, all guillotines must be left in the raised position after use – which results in double operation whether you are cruising up or down river. A special key is issued to boat crews by the navigation authority, enabling the apparatus to be unlocked.

Maximum craft dimensions are 78ft × 13ft × 4ft draught × 7ft headroom (this may be reduced after heavy rain). From Peterborough to Wisbech dimensions are 130ft × 20ft × 7ft draught × up to 13ft headroom (low-water neaps) under Guyhirne Bridge, and from Wisbech to the Wash 260ft × 40ft × 17ft draught. Headroom is not restricted.

*Northampton* A junction is formed with the Grand Union Canal's narrow-beam Northampton Arm a short distance upstream of the South Bridge. Through Northampton River Lock, the town makes magnificent use of its water frontage at Becket's Park. Road-building schemes and considerable recent expansion have changed the character of this essentially industrial town. Northampton's chief attribute is a large and busy open market square where many bargains may be obtained. Most of medieval Northampton was destroyed in a fire of 1675, a loss that has since been rectified by a variety of fine buildings of all ages, including the grandly colonnaded All Saints church and the massive neo-Gothic town hall. The river marks the southern extent of development, so that the countryside is very soon reached at Rush Mills Lock (1m 7f). In addition to the heavy lock gates, another problem of the Nene was until quite recent years heavy weeding in summer. This was often enough to prevent all but the most powerful motorised craft proceeding, but since the late 1960s increased traffic has kept this nuisance in check.

*Billing* (4m 7f)   Delightful countryside is largely quite unspoiled, as the threat of flooding from this rather unpredictable river has always encouraged villages to keep their distance. Locks occur thick and fast at regular intervals, and Abington, Weston Favell, Clifford Hill and Billing Locks are all in sight of each other across the meadows. Beyond Billing is the entrance to a chain of interconnected lakes known as the Aquadrome – something of a Midlands resort, with caravans, funfair and boating facilities. For much of the journey the only living companions will be the occasional crews of boats, and numerous curious cows, which seem to delight in swarming over locksides as you work through.

*Cogenhoe* (6m 2f)   To the right of the lock the village lies up a steeply sloping road. Pronounced locally 'Cooknoe', it possesses some pleasing stone gabled houses and useful shops. After cruising on through Whiston and White Mills Locks (8m 3f), one may step ashore and visit Castle Ashby House, about 2m south of the river and the home of the Marquis of Northampton. The mansion is set in a splendid wooded park, partly landscaped by Capability Brown. The building was begun in the late sixteenth century and is open to the public. Mature gravel workings between White Mills and Barton Locks (9m 1f) are a sanctuary for many varieties of waterfowl.

*Wellingborough* (12m 7f)   Both Doddington and Wollaston Locks are sited by agreeable mill houses. Situated east of a junction formed by the Nene and the Ise, Wellingborough is a centre of shoe and clothing factories, with nearby iron ore works. Its All Hallows church has a lofty stone broach tower. Although begun as recently as 1908, St Mary's church draws freely on the architectural styles of many centuries, and has an elaborate fan-vaulted nave ceiling with fluted pendants. Until 1970 regular cargoes of wheat amounting to around 5,000 tons a year were shipped by narrow boat from Brentford Dock on the Grand Union Canal to the Weetabix mills, and this traffic only ceased with the transfer of grain imports from the London Docks to Tilbury, further down river towards the Thames estuary.

*Higham Ferrers* (16m)   Beyond Upper and Lower Wellingborough Locks, and the third heavy radial example at Ditchford, comes the awkwardly positioned Higham Bridge, lacking in headroom and with timber posts to protect the navigation arch. In flood-time this structure can be a worry to boaters. Higham Ferrers, which lies a short distance due east, is a lovely old Northamptonshire stone town with tall church spire.

*Irthlingborough* (18m 5f)   A pungent tannery and sewage works do not encourage lingering here. The town is in any event rather industrialised, relying on the shoe and iron trades. One of the two road bridges is fourteenth-century. Locks become rather less frequent and some of the Nene's most appealing reaches will be found at Ringstead, Woodford (24m) and Denford.

*Thrapston* (26m 1f)   The A604 Kettering road crosses the river, with Thrapston on the right bank and Islip on the left. The bridge is chiefly medieval, with 9 arches. The Perpendicular church of Islip contains a memorial to Mary Washington, great-great-great aunt of the first American president. Both towns will reward exploration. At Titchmarsh Lock (28m 5f) are the headquarters of the Middle Nene Cruising Club, whose members will be pleased to share their expert local knowledge of the waterway.

*Wadenhoe Lock* (31m 1f)   Thorpe Waterville and Wadenhoe are both tiny but attractive waterside villages, the former noted for a great medieval thatched barn, the only surviving portion of a castle, and the latter for a fine old watermill and church with saddleback tower. The next lock downstream is Lilford (32m 3f), most beautifully situated on the edge of the Lilford Hall park. The present Lord Lilford keeps a narrow boat here, named after his house. Another stately home nearby is Barnwell Castle, a gabled Elizabethan mansion, home of the Duke of Gloucester; it is situated about 1m east of the Nene, upstream of the two Barnwell Locks.

*Oundle* (38m)   The river describes a series of broad loops around this delightful stone-built town, whose tall and slender church spire, towering above the Nene, is one of the finest in Northamptonshire, a county famous for the variety, beauty and number of its steeples. Beyond the lock is the entrance to Oundle Marina, attractively landscaped moorings established in 1963 in former gravel workings. In addition to a full range of boating requisites, hire cruisers are available. Ashton village, near Lock 28, has an old mill house and is the location of the National Conker Championships, held each year under chestnut trees on the second Sunday of October. This is a really serious contest, organised according to a strict code of conduct.

*Fotheringhay* (42m)   Cotterstock and Perio Locks are soon followed by the village of Fotheringhay, where the former castle, scene of the imprisonment and execution of Mary Queen of Scots in 1587, is now a grassy hillock by the river. Richard III was born there. The Collegiate church of St Mary and All Saints, occupying a splendid elevated position above the watermeadows, has a magnificent octagonal lantern above the tower in place of a spire. The fifteenth-century pulpit was a personal gift from Edward IV. There are a number of thatched cottages and several medieval inns. The bridge's central navigation arch is low, and many craft have suffered damage as they shot the hole.

*Wansford-in-England* (49m 5f)   Riverside villages include Warmington, Elton, Nassington and Yarwell. Wansford is rather busier, being at the junction of the A1 and A47 on the borders of Northamptonshire and Huntingdonshire. The river is spanned by a fine ancient stone bridge of 10 arches, each divided by substantial cutwaters. The alleged derivation of Wansford's full name is altogether charming. A seventeenth-century character called Drunken Barnaby is supposed to have collapsed in a stupor on a haycock, and, on waking, discovered with alarm that the Nene had overflowed its banks and carried him to foreign parts. On asking where he was, he was

M

told 'Wansford'. 'Wansford, where?' he questioned. 'Wansford-in-England' came back the reply. The incident is recalled in the name of the Haycock Inn. Having flowed for many miles in a roughly northerly direction, the river now turns to the east and heads for Peterborough. Wooded countryside leads to Sutton and Stibbington villages and on past the site of the Roman town of Durobrivae, where there were once extensive potteries. North of Water Newton Lock (52m 7f) lies a section of the Roman Ermine Street, which forded the river. A long part of the course to the south is now the A1.

*Peterborough* (60m 5f)   Just beyond the Peterborough Cruising Club is Alwalton Lock (54m 7f). One final great loop at Longthorpe leads eventually to Orton Lock and the outskirts of the city of Peterborough. This is the thirty-seventh and last of the crew-operated locks down from Northampton. Peterborough's riverfront is a lesson to every riparian local authority in Britain. There are almost 2m of tidy quays with mooring bollards in park-like surroundings, all provided during the early 1970s for the convenience of visiting boats. Small craft can be hired by the hour, and there is a rowing club and excellent access to the shopping centre. The old Peterborough, with its superb cathedral, seventeenth-century Guildhall and Customs House by the bridge has been rather overshadowed by nineteenth- and twentieth-century industrial expansion. There is a large sugar-beet-processing works, a forest of chimneys belonging to an extensive brickworks towards Whittlesey, and, of our own times, the sprawl of development that has inevitably followed the designation of the area as the site for a New City. The intimacy of the Nene's upper reaches has now been left behind, for the course of the river continues broad and rather windswept along a 5m length to Dog-in-a-Doublet Lock. A useful boatyard catering for inland and coastal craft will be found at Stanground (61m 1f), junction with the Middle Level Navigations (p 348).

*Dog-in-a-Doublet Lock* (65m 5f)   The lowest 26m of the Nene is more of a tidal estuary navigation than an inland waterway, and should be cruised with due caution. The electrically operated Dog-in-a-Doublet Lock (taking its name from a nearby inn) is fitted with massive guillotine gates and is in the charge of a resident keeper. Until it was erected during the 1930s improvements, the tide flowed upstream to Woodstone Staunch, beyond Peterborough. The object, among inland boaters at least, of venturing on to the tidal river is to gain access to the Wash, and thence cruise to the Witham, Welland or Great Ouse. Generally the run is only of interest in terms of successfully guiding your boat on fast-flowing water past muddy banks.

*Wisbech* (80m 4f)   The town combines the functions of market and seaport. Centuries ago it was a mere 4m inland, but changes to the course of the Nene have put the Wash 12m down river now. Stretching along both sides of the waterway, Wisbech posesses a wealth of beautiful Georgian buildings in the pair of waterside streets known as the Brinks. There are old warehouses and active shipping quays where a variety of cargoes are handled. Aesthetically this is one of the finest urban centres in East Anglia. Bulb and fruit growing in the surrounding Fenlands provide a great attraction in spring.

*Sutton Bridge* (87m 3f)   The flow of the river is swelled as it is joined by the North Level Main and South Holland Main Drains at Tydd St Mary (86m 5f). Tides frequently run at 4 knots or even more, while the rise and fall is as much as 25ft. Care must be taken when encountering moored cargo vessels or laden ships, which must keep to the deepest water. The last village is Sutton Bridge, on the A17, offering some prospect of moorings when a voyage into the Wash is contemplated. It was here that an elaborate ship dock, constructed in 1882, promptly collapsed when the water was admitted, and further attempts to create a port were abandoned. The final 4m of waterway run through lonely marshlands to a confluence with the Wash at Crab's Hole. This is a noted area for birdwatching and wildfowling. Sir Peter Scott lived in a lighthouse near the river mouth during 1933-9 at an annual rent of £5. Vast sandbanks are revealed at low water, necessitating employment of an experienced pilot. The region is well known for its seals.

## OUSE, GREAT

From Bedford to the Wash near King's Lynn; 75m with 16 locks. Castle, Willington, Old Mills and Great Barford Locks, in the first 7m below Bedford, are derelict but rebuilding is planned. There are junctions with the New Bedford River, the Cam (p 348), Lark, Brandon River (Little Ouse), Wissey and Middle Level Navigation either via the Old Bedford or Well Creek, both entrances being situated immediately downstream of Denver Sluice. The old course of the navigation between Earith and

*River Great Ouse. Offord Lock, showing a common pattern of gates for the waterway: a guillotine at the head and mitre doors at the tail*

Denver via Ely (the Old West River) is much more attractive than the completely straight and tidal New Bedford, though it adds about 10m to the total distance.

This is one of Britain's finest rivers and was first made navigable from the sea to Bedford in the seventeenth century. Extensive works carried out in the mid-1600s by Cornelius Vermuyden resulted in the creation of great new watercourses and the transformation of huge areas of flood-prone marshes into some of the most fertile farmland in Britain. Since Vermuyden's time the countryside in the Ouse's lower reaches has subsided by as much as 15ft and is still sinking.

The Dukes of Bedford played a prominent part in early development of the waterway. This tradition is continued by the present Duke, who takes a keen interest in the restoration of derelict locks and in promoting the river's amenity potential.

The Great Ouse is admirably suited to all kinds of amenity activity, not least cruising. Especially in its upper reaches, the scenery is varied and attractive. While the river is well used by all kinds of pleasure craft, there is little evidence of congestion. Its condition has not always been exemplary. In common with many other waterways its freight-carrying usefulness declined during the latter years of the last century. Trade to Bedford had died by about 1875 and 20 years later most of the locks were ruined, although some barges managed to struggle to St Neots by carrying their own temporary dam tackle for use where lock gates had collapsed. Navigation rights were acquired by one L. T. Simpson, and he had restored the locks to Bedford by 1895, but 30 years later navigation was no longer possible upstream of St Ives. In 1935 the works were transferred to the Great Ouse Catchment Board, and when war broke out in 1939, locks had been repaired to Tempsford, leaving Bedford isolated by 10m of derelict river with 7 locks and 2 navigation weirs out of action. Following the foundation of the Great Ouse Restoration Society in 1951, pressure was brought to bear for the river authority to start reinstating locks for navigation purposes. The upper 2 at Bedford and Cardington were rebuilt in 1956 and 1963 respectively, followed by Roxton Lock in 1973. Work began on a new Great Barford Lock in 1974. In each case the Society made financial contributions. Meanwhile many of the other working locks have been completely modernised. At the most conservative estimate the water link between Bedford and the Wash will finally be re-established by the end of the 1970s.

Maximum craft dimensions are Great Barford–Brownshill Lock, Earith, 100ft × 10ft 6in × 4ft 6in draught (rather less below St Neots) × 8ft 10in headroom. Rather larger craft can proceed from Earith to the Wash, except at Denver Lock, where the length is restricted to 70ft.

*Bedford*  The Great Ouse rises near Brackley in Northamptonshire, more than 90m above Bedford. It first comes to the notice of waterway enthusiasts at Wolverton, Bucks, where the Grand Union Canal crosses by means of an iron aqueduct (p 295). It was proposed at the end of the last century to cut a lateral canal from Bedford to the Grand Union at Newport Pagnell, but nothing came of the plan. Provided permission is obtained from riparian owners (no easy task), a journey is possible by canoe from Wolverton to Bedford. In spite of its present isolated situation, the Ouse in Bedford is heavily used by tripping launches, rowing boats and other small craft. It is a central feature of the town, with municipally landscaped banks and a notably attractive bow-string suspension footbridge in steel (1888). Duck Mill Lock is nearby, with a guillotine gate at its upper end and conventional mitre gates at the tail. (This is the normal arrangement on the Ouse, a reversal of the policy adopted for otherwise similar structures along the Nene.) The river is the best feature of Bedford, a generally pleasant town that has greatly expanded since Victorian times.

The Ouse is soon clear of its urban surroundings and winds through a surprisingly remote valley to the workable Cardington Lock (2m), before coming to the currently inaccessible reach. Castle, Willington and Old Mills Locks await restoration, but work should be well advanced on the new Great Barford Lock (7m 2f) by the time this book is published.

*Roxton Lock* (9m 5f)   This fine structure in concrete and steel is fitted with mitre gates at each end, but having single gate-paddles is slower to operate than it need have been. Shortly below, the Ouse is joined by the River Ivel, which was canalised under an Act of 1757, although the eventual head of navigation at Shefford, 11m upstream, was not reached until 1823. Commercial traffic had ceased by 1878 and the former locks have since disappeared.

*Tempsford Bridge* (10m 2f)   The bridge has 3 rounded arches and was built during 1815–20. Nearby is the riverside Anchor Hotel, with good moorings. Other features to note are a boatyard and the remains of Tempsford Staunch (flash lock).

*Eaton Socon* (13m 7f)   The waterway stays clear of main roads as it follows a winding course through wooded surroundings to Eaton Socon, with Lock 8. Between river and village are earthworks known as The Hillings, the remains of an eleventh/twelfth-century castle. St Mary's church was burned out in 1930, though the mainly Perpendicular shell was subsequently restored. Close by is a nineteenth-century lock-up, in brick, containing 2 cells.

*St Neots* (15m)   A very agreeable old market town, site of a tenth-century Benedictine priory. The bridge is a new one (1963–5) in concrete with an approach causeway. St Mary's church is one of the largest late medieval buildings in Huntingdonshire. There are boatyards and cruiser-hire facilities. The lock (16m 2f) is followed by a series of shoals, presenting the shallowest section of the whole navigation. The little River Kym offers about a mile of cruising in the direction of Hail Weston. Most attractive scenery accompanies the river through the villages of Offord Darcy and Offord Cluny (20m 1f), with lock and mill. Here also is Buckden Marina, a model development.

*Godmanchester* (24m 3f)   The town is linked across the Ouse with Huntingdon via an early fourteenth-century stone bridge which clearly shows that different authorities were responsible for each half. A bridge chapel dedicated to St Thomas Becket once stood on the Huntingdon side. Now little more than a village, Godmanchester was a Roman station extending over 24 acres, various traces of which, including second-century baths, have been discovered. Among the many pleasing buildings overlooking the weir stream are Queen Elizabeth's Grammar School, founded in 1559, and a gabled Gothicised town hall of 1844. The lock island is connected with the mainland via a charming Chippendale-Chinese wooden footbridge, erected in 1827.

*Huntingdon* (25m 1f)   Another ancient town of Saxon origins. A castle was built in 1068 by order of William the Conqueror. Oliver Cromwell was born and educated here, and the grammar school where Samuel Pepys was also a pupil is now a Cromwell museum. There are numerous Georgian houses and a wide selection of agreeable inns. An island formed by the navigation channel and weir stream, known as Portholme, is noted for several varieties of rare wildflowers. Hartford village (26m 2f) has a marina and sailing club. Interest in the river banks is sustained at a high level during the next few miles, for this part of the Ouse ranks as one of the most pleasant reaches of any river navigation in England.

*Houghton* (27m 7f)   A modern lock, with conventional guillotine upper gate, stands near Houghton Mill. A watermill was established on the site in the tenth century, but the present structure of red brick, weatherboarding and slate roof (in place of the original thatch) dates from the seventeenth–nineteenth centuries. Fitted with 3 water wheels (replaced by sluices), Houghton continued working until 1930. Now National Trust property and used as a youth hostel, it has a lovely setting amid mature trees and overlooking a broad pool.

*Hemingford Grey* (28m 7f)   Hemingford Abbots village is shortly followed by Hemingford Grey, whose waterside church provides one of the most memorable of Ouse views. St James's is perched on the very brink of the river bank and dates chiefly from the twelfth–fourteenth centuries. Constructed in contrasting types of grey stone, its square tower supports the base of a spire, topped with eighteenth-century ball finials. The rest of the steeple was destroyed in a hurricane of 1741. Several notable houses nearby include the twelfth-century Manor House, with a moat on three sides and the river on the fourth; Hemingford Grey House of 1697, whose grounds contain one of Britain's largest plane trees, planted in 1702; and several timber-framed thatched cottages. A recent invasion by modern houses and bungalows has failed to detract from the timelessness of the riverside. Beyond Hemingford Lock lies a busy cruising section of the waterway leading to St Ives.

*St Ives* (30m 6f)   The bridge is a real gem, early fifteenth-century, with a series of 6 stone arches of varying widths. At the centre is a tiny chapel dedicated to St Lawrence. (Similar structures are to be found at Wakefield, Rotherham and Bradford-on-Avon, the last converted into a lock-up.) After 1110 St Ives shared the honour of having one of the 4 busiest fairs in the country with Boston, Northampton and Winchester. All Saints church was built in the mid-fifteenth century, and its unusually slender spire soars above the river. St Ives Lock is ½m downstream of the bridge.

*Holywell* (33m 4f)   A hamlet on the north bank of the Ouse by an old ferry crossing. The Ferry Boat Inn, reputedly established on the same site in 980, is said to be haunted by the spirit of Juliet Tewsley, who committed suicide in 1050. She is said to appear from her tombstone in the inn floor every year on 17 March, the anniversary of her death. The river has now entered true Fenland, with broad skies and flat endless views.

*Earith* (38m 4f)   Brownshill Staunch or lock (36m 2f) lowers craft into a tidal length, an unexpected situation for somewhere so far inland. The most direct route to the Wash is down the tidal New Bedford River (Hundred Foot Drain), which runs for

20m to below Denver Sluice almost in a straight line all the way, passing through Mepal and Welney. In close parallel company, but not directly connected, is the Old Bedford River, which provides one of two through routes between Ouse and Nene via the Middle Level Navigations (see p 348). Although 10m longer, the alternative section of Ouse past Ely is infinitely more interesting. Earith has a useful boatyard and cruiser-hire base.

*Old West River*   Leaving the tidal Ouse at Earith, the Old West is the original course of the Ouse before the cutting of the New Bedford in the mid-seventeenth century. The first 11½m are formed by a curious narrow channel winding between reed-beds. Its entrance is at Hermitage Lock, Earith, which was completely rebuilt during 1967-8. It is so lacking in features by which to gauge cruising progress as to recall Elizabeth Jane Howard's famous canal ghost story *Three Miles Up* (certain inland waterways can provide an alarming sense of utter isolation).

*Stretham* (47m 2f)   Here, on the right bank, is the only surviving steam-powered drainage engine in the Fens, installed in a brick building with tall chimney and keeper's house alongside. It was constructed in 1831 to lift water from Stretham Mere into the Old West River. Two Lancashire boilers powered a beam engine that operated a 37ft diameter scoop wheel. The flywheel is 24ft across. Working at maximum output, the engine could pump 120 tons of water an hour. When a river bank collapsed in 1919, it ran nonstop for 47 days. A diesel engine took over in 1924, but all the old machinery remains intact in the care of the Stretham Engine Preservation Trust, and can be visited by the public.

*Pope's Corner* (50m 1f)   The waterway broadens considerably at the confluence with the River Cam (p 266). The Fish and Duck Inn is a well-known venue for boating parties. Turn left for Ely and the lower Ouse.

*Soham Lode* (51m 3f)   Craft drawing less than 1ft 6in can proceed about 3½m along the Lode, which joins the Ouse near Little Thetford. Beyond Soham this water-course becomes the charmingly named River Snail, rising at Snailwell, several miles north of Newmarket.

*Ely* (53m 4f)   A lovely city, whose first cathedral was begun in 673. The Isle of Ely was indeed an island, 70ft above the surrounding Fenlands. Until the drainage works began in the seventeenth century, access was via causeways or by boat. All is now dominated by the cathedral, most of which is pre-fourteenth century. A great west tower stands at one end and a massive and unique octagonal lantern at the other. On the riverside are extensive boating operations run by Messrs Appleyard Lincoln. Whereas numerous redundant industrial buildings of the last century have been allowed to fall derelict in Britain, with subsequent demolition, Ely can justifiably feel proud of its slate-roofed Maltings. The walls of intricately patterned brick are pierced by 3 rows of small windows, with an additional floor in the roof lit by a series of gabled dormers. Built in 1868, it was expertly converted into a multi-purpose public hall in 1971. Its confident solidity provides a centrepiece for the riverside walk along the towpath from the Cutter Inn to a railway bridge several hundred yards downstream. The Ouse is a wide but bleak navigation for the rest of the journey to Denver Sluice.

*River Lark* (57m 3f)   This tributary was once navigable for 23m to Bury St Edmunds. Craft 88ft × 14ft 6in × 4ft 6in draught to Isleham, and 2ft 6in above × 10ft 3in headroom, may proceed from the Ouse to Judes Ferry, 13m upriver. There is a working lock at Isleham, 6½m above the Ouse and another, still operable but isolated, at Icklingham, 8½m further on. Canoeists will enjoy the upper wooded reaches between Bury and Mildenhall.

*Littleport* (59m 3f)   A former railway dock above Littleport road bridge has been made into a marina. The nearby Black Horse Inn is worth visiting.

*Brandon River (Little Ouse)* (62m 6f)   Leaving the Great Ouse by the Ship Inn, the Brandon River was originally navigable for 22½m to Thetford. Instead of conventional locks, a series of 8 navigation weirs controlled the upper 16½m. These appear to have fallen into complete disrepair by the early years of the present century. Their operation is graphically described in *A New Oarsman's Guide to the Rivers and Canals of Great Britain and Ireland* (1895) as follows:

The staunches consist each of a large 'gallows' erected over the stream. The sluice is raised by a chain wound over a horizontal axle that works just under the top of the gallows. This axle is revolved by a big wooden wheel with spokes projecting some two feet beyond its circumference. To hoist the sluice the orthodox method is to try to walk up the wheel by the projecting spokes, treadmill fashion. As the creek is shallow in summer the local authorities sometimes object to these sluices being opened for pleasure traffic, and insist on portages being made at each staunch. Occasionally a man is sent on horseback to accompany the boat to make sure of these being carried out. This vigilance can generally be successfully evaded so soon as the sun gets high enough to make the river policeman thirsty.

The first upriver obstruction is now Brandon Staunch, 13m above the Ouse and equipped with a guillotine gate that prevents craft progressing further. For craft of any length or beam, a draught of 4ft 6in to Wilton Ferry (2ft 6in to Brandon) and a headroom not exceeding 9ft 9in, the Brandon River offers an enjoyable excursion. As it shares a common source with the River Waveney, 35m east of the Great Ouse, there is a good case to be made for linking the upper reaches of each waterway by a length of canal. In this way the detached Broadland navigations would be joined to those of the Fens and thence, via the Middle Level, to the rest of England's cruising network.

*River Wissey* (68m 4f)   Another navigable tributary, joined a mile above Denver Sluice. It offers 10m of cruising water to the village of Stoke Ferry via Hilgay and a sugar-beet factory at Wissington, where the channel passes through a small lake similar to those in Broadland. As there are no locks, the only limiting factors are 3ft 6in draught and 8ft 2in headroom.

*Denver Sluice* (69m 5f)   The first barrier across the river, just above its junction with the New Bedford from Earith, was erected in the mid-seventeenth century by Vermuyden. The present Denver Lock is fitted with gates facing each direction; thus one locks either up or down into the tideway, depending on the water level. Boats exceeding 70ft can only pass through when levels are equal. There is a keeper on hand who will advise on the best time to lock through if you are planning to enter the Middle Level Navigations at Salter's Lode or the Old Bedford sluice, several hundred yards down river (see p 350). Enforced tide-waiting time can be enjoyably killed in the Jenyns Arms. A widespread flood in March 1947 inundated 37,000 acres of Fenland, and to prevent a recurrence a £10 million protection scheme was carried out during the decade 1954–64. One of the works was the construction of a new relief channel from Denver to a point upstream of King's Lynn. This begins with 3 huge guillotine gates alongside Denver Sluice and terminates in a tail sluice at the outfall.

*Tidal Great Ouse* A stretch of 16m of tideway takes the Ouse to the Wash below King's Lynn Docks. The navigator will see little more than muddy banks during this journey, and the swirling current does not encourage mooring. Downham Market (71m) will best be remembered for its awkward channel, with fierce eddies. Arrive too near low water and you run the risk of grounding, too near high water and there will be insufficient clearance. An unusual form of bank protection in the lower river is the use of plaited mattresses of willow branches to combat constant scouring. There are further bridges at Stowbridge (72m 6f), Wiggenhall St Mary Magdalen (75m 7f) and Wiggenhall St Germans (77m 7f). Beyond, the Middle Level Main Drain enters on the left and King's Lynn appears ahead in the distance, at the confluence of the River Nar and the Ouse. Under an Act of 1751 the Nar was made navigable for 15m from Lynn to Narborough, to the east. Traffic was mainly in coal that arrived by sea from the North East and grain for the Narborough maltings. In common with some other East Anglian waterways, the 10 locks in the upper 5m were navigation weirs or staunches, some with guillotine gates. All had become derelict by 1884, but remains of these devices can still be seen at Narborough, Bonemill Staunch and Abbey Farm Staunch. For those prepared to portage, the Nar is canoeable throughout the length of the former navigation.

King's Lynn is about 2m inland from the Wash at Vinegar Middle Sand. As recently as 1784 it was England's fifth most important port. Vessels of 2,000 tons still trade to the late Victorian docks, whose level is maintained by an entrance lock. Although reduced in size compared with former years, the fishing fleet continues to do a trade in shrimps, cockles and mussels. A marina is planned. The Greenland Fishery Inn is a former whalers' pub built in 1605, while the Custom House on the river bank is a perfectly preserved building of 1683, topped by a lantern tower. Extensive marshlands border the 300 sq m of shallow sandbank-strewn sea that form the Wash. If a passage is contemplated to the Nene, Welland or Witham, the services of a local pilot should be sought.

### OUSE, SUSSEX

From Newhaven Harbour to Hamsey Lock (derelict) above Lewes; 9½m and tidal. Like many other South Coast river navigations, the Sussex Ouse has long been derelict, with the exception of the lower tidal reaches. A length of 22½m of waterway with eighteen 48ft long wide-beam locks upstream of Lewes had been created by about 1812. Its commercial life was short, for it had fallen into disuse by 1861. There is no restriction of craft length to Lewes, to which point maximum beam is 16ft, and 10ft beyond. Boats of 3ft draught can reach Hamsey. Headroom to Lewes is 10ft, and 7ft thereafter. Rowing boats may be hired on an isolated length at Isfield, 7m beyond

Lewes. The upper reaches are in pleasing countryside and are well worth exploring by canoe or similar portable craft.

## OUSE, YORKSHIRE

From Ouse Gill Beck, upstream of which point to Swale Nab the river is known as the Ure, to Trent Falls, junction with the Humber and the Trent; 60¾m from Swale Nab with 2 locks. Maximum craft dimensions on the tidal portion of the waterway from the Humber to Naburn locks are length and beam unlimited, and draught varying with the height of tides, though 8ft 6in is available to Naburn on spring tides with 6ft on neaps. The lower part of the tideway offers even greater draught: from Naburn to York 150ft × 25ft 6in × 8ft 6in draught × 25ft 6in normal headroom under the first fixed bridge at Naburn, and from York to Swale Nab 60ft × 15ft 4in × 4ft draught × 16ft 4in headroom.

The Ouse deserves to be better known among pleasure boaters, although it does have an enthusiastic local following. There is considerable commercial traffic in motor barges to York, but none upstream. Tidal and fast-flowing from the estuary to Naburn locks, the river is decidedly not a suitable place for novices downstream of Selby, where there is a junction with the non-tidal Aire & Calder Navigation. Scenery in the tidal sections is not impressive, but the demands of navigation in company with coasters to Selby normally provide ample interest. Through York and beyond the Ouse is pastoral, undeveloped and frequently most attractive, although the finest reaches will be found above Boroughbridge, part of the Ure.

*Trent Falls*   The lowest part of the river is much more a seaway than an inland waterway, subjected to one of the fiercest tides in Britain. There are sandbanks to avoid, lighthouses and beacons, and winds that whistle across the low-lying marshes. The area is bleak and atmospheric to a degree. Land-based explorers can view the river from several points on north and south banks, notably at Whitgift Ness and Swinefleet. No navigator should enter these waters without the sailing instructions and chart prepared from many years of cruising by Vincent Sissons, proprietor of the *Worksop Guardian*, which deals with the navigation between Trent Falls and York. The 38½m between Trent Falls and Naburn locks can be accomplished on a single tide, though it must be emphasised that the water careers along, reputedly reaching a speed of 9 knots at times at Selby. There are escapes to still moorings at Goole and Selby.

*Goole* (8m)   This nineteenth-century canal town, promoted as the port of the Aire & Calder Navigation, marks the beginning of the tidal Dutch River (see p 387), and immediately beyond is a series of locked entries into the docks (p 216).

*Asselby Island* (13m 4f)   Here the Old River Aire flows into the Ouse on the left. Following completion of the Selby Canal in 1778, most traffic followed the new route, thus avoiding the many acute bends in the lower Aire. This line is still navigable for 16m to its tidal limit at Haddlesey Old Lock, disused since 1937.

*Barmby on the Marsh* (17m 2f)   The Yorkshire Derwent flows into the Ouse on the right bank, leading to the exquisitely beautiful waterway through Stamford Bridge to Malton, and also to the Pocklington Canal.

*Selby* (23m 6f)   A flourishing inland port, with wharves for coasters on the river and additional facilities on the Selby Canal, part of the Aire & Calder system. Until 1792 Selby was provided with a ferry like many other points along the tidal river, but after considerable argument and the promotion of a Bill in Parliament, the remarkable wooden bridge was built, with a swing span to enable sailing keels to pass through. Apart from a modern opening mechanism and various steel braces, the picturesque structure remained much as it had been in the late eighteenth century until it was replaced by a new steel swing bridge in 1971. Consequently boats no longer have to negotiate a navigation channel through giant baulks of timber with a racing current that produces whirlpools locally known as 'boils'. The outstanding feature of Selby is its great Benedictine abbey, founded in 1069, although the present church with white square tower dates from about 1100. Flourishing shops surround the market place. One is an old-style tobacconist's, offering a wide range of home-prepared pipe mixtures sold in paper screws.

*Cawood* (31m 6f)   An outstandingly pleasing village of brick and red tile houses is situated on the left bank by a swing bridge, after 5m of winding river through rich but flat agricultural land. Little more than a gateway remains of a Saxon castle that was converted into a palace for the archbishops of York in the fourteenth century. The Ouse remains tidal but has narrowed considerably, and normally flows less furiously. The tidal River Wharfe, navigable to Tadcaster, enters on the left bank about 1m above Cawood (see p 443).

*Yorkshire Ouse. York remains a flourishing inland port with an outstandingly attractive waterfront*

*Naburn Locks* (38m 2f)   Here the character of the Ouse undergoes a dramatic change. Gone are the muddy banks and the bleak open country. The waterway is now a gracious stream bordered by trees and parkland, with numerous pleasure craft on safe permanent moorings. There are two duplicated locks, 150ft and 90ft long, spanned by a swing bridge and with a resident keeper. The village of Naburn has a fine and extensive marina with all expected services.

*York* (43m 4f)   A mile beyond the Naburn railway bridge stands the superb Bishopthorpe Palace, built for the archbishops of York. The outskirts of the city soon follow, with an almost rural belt of parkland accompanying the river as far as the walls of this ancient Roman settlement. Moorings are generally to be found in a basin still used by commercial barges at the start of the Foss Navigation. This provided a trading route for keels from the late eighteenth century, through 8 locks to Sheriff Hutton Bridge, $11\frac{1}{2}$m to the north. All but the first lock and about $1\frac{1}{4}$m was abandoned in 1859. York's waterfront is one of the best in England, with quays used equally by commercial and pleasure craft. There are few more fascinating cities in Britain and many days could be spent exploring the wonderful heritage of buildings from the substantial wall, $2\frac{3}{4}$m long, following the line of the Roman boundary, to the great Minster with superb stained glass, the castle and prison, city gateways (or bars) and narrow streets such as The Shambles, Stonegate and Goodramgate. The earliest railway station (1840–2) is preserved largely as built, and historic steam locomotives can be inspected in the nearby museum. There are several good river bridges. Foss and Ouse Bridges, both in stone, were designed by Peter Atkinson in the first quarter of the nineteenth century. Lendal and Skeldergate Bridges followed in the 1860s and 1870s, and made agreeable use of Gothic cast iron, heavily decorated. In addition to all these attractions there are many excellent restaurants within yards of the river, ensuring that your visit to York is in every way memorable. Open country follows the modern concrete Clifton Bridge. Boroughbridge is the only town in 24 glorious miles upriver to Ripon, via the Ure.

*Linton Lock* (54m)   Just beyond York, landing stages by the Fox Inn at Nether Poppleton provide a good mooring. The local population makes full use of its river for swimming, dinghy sailing and relaxing on the banks. (Tripping craft and rowing boats are available in York itself, enabling a very pleasant excursion to be made into the countryside upstream.) The unnavigable River Nidd enters the Ouse at Nun Monkton (51m 6f), having followed an astonishingly twisted course from the Pennines. Some miles to the west it passes through dramatic wooded gorges at Knaresborough, where rowing boats may be hired for use on a short but idyllic stretch. Opposite the junction lies an extensive park surrounding Beningbrough Hall, whose trees accompany the river bank almost to the village of Newton-on-Ouse, where a slender church spire is reflected in the water. From this point for several hundred yards to Linton Lock the river suffers from clay 'huts', an almost proverbial hazard of the waterway. These are hard slimy islands caused by clay slipping down the river banks. Many lurk below summer water level and may ground the unwary navigator. An updated chart is available from the Ripon Motor Boat Club. Linton Lock lies beyond, splendidly remote, with a thundering weir on the left. Between 1962 and 1966 it was closed through lack of maintenance, and, being the responsibility of a band of impecunious commissioners, would perhaps have remained so indefinitely had not local boating enthusiasts raised £3,000 for repairs to be carried out by British Waterways. The little brick keeper's cottage is now an unpretentious café, and boat crews must work themselves through the deep chamber. A marina has recently been established and numerous cruisers lie on moorings above. Under the shattering roar of jet planes from Linton airfield, the Ouse continues around broad loops at Aldwark toll-bridge, with a local authority boating centre just downstream.

*Swale Nab* (60m 6f)   The Ouse officially terminates at Ouse Gill Beck, but the authority of the Linton Lock commissioners continues to the confluence of the beautiful but unnavigable River Swale and the Ure. In the late 1760s 28m of the Swale to Morton Bridge were turned into some kind of navigation, but of 5 planned locks only one appears to have been finished and it is doubtful if loaded keels ever completed the journey. Very light craft should be able to proceed for several miles. The voyage towards Ripon is continued via the River Ure (see p 437).

## OXFORD CANAL

From Hawkesbury Junction, where it joins the Coventry Canal, several miles NE of Coventry, to the Thames at Oxford, a short distance upstream of Osney Lock; 78m with 43 locks. In addition there is a short branch, the Duke's Cut, joining the Thames immediately upstream of King's Lock. Other junctions are made with the Grand Union Canal at Napton and with the southern main line of the Grand Union at Braunston. Craft dimensions are 72ft × 7ft × 3ft 6in × 7ft headroom.

This waterway is an important long-distance link, forming part of the original canal 'cross' connecting Thames, Mersey, Trent and Severn. It was designed chiefly to enable coal from the areas served by the Coventry Canal to be brought south to Banbury, Oxford and the Thames. After the first of several Acts of Parliament, in 1769, construction began at the northern end with James Brindley as engineer. But he died in 1772 when the new canal had only been completed as far as Brinklow, 7½m, and consequently credit for the Oxford's design should properly go to other men. Under the control of Brindley's assistant, Samuel Simcock, the line was opened as far as Banbury by 1778. Work then halted for a number of years following disputes with the Coventry Canal Co, whose waterway had not been linked with the Trent & Mersey at Fradley as intended. Finally, with Robert Whitworth as engineer, the Southern Oxford was extended to the Thames by 1790.

The canal lasted only 15 years as a direct route between the Midlands and London, for the Grand Junction (Union) was completed in 1805 and took away much of the traffic previously enjoyed by the Oxford. (Large amounts were paid in compensation, however.) About 1834 the northern portion was shortened by no less than 14m, from Braunston to Hawkesbury, utilising more advanced engineering techniques than were available in Brindley's day. The Northern Oxford retained its coal traffic until very recent times, but commercial carriage had almost ceased on the southern section by the end of World War II.

The Oxford Canal is almost completely rural throughout. South of Napton it is a textbook example of an eighteenth-century contour waterway, with a particularly winding course along the Fenny Compton summit level. Locks now pass more pleasure craft in a summer week than they could ever have seen working boats at the height of the canal's commercial prosperity. This great popularity can lead to water shortages in dry weather, especially at the lock flights either side of the summit. The Oxford is generally unspectacular but very very charming, especially along the Cherwell Valley section and in the villages clustered around the Oxfordshire/Northamptonshire borders, north of Banbury.

*Hawkesbury Junction*   A canal settlement of considerable character, with iron bridges, stop lock, buildings and the little Greyhound Inn. Also, until the early 1960s, a region of hectic narrow-boat activity (see p 271). Just within the Coventry City boundary there is an air of industry, increased by the tall chimneys of Longford power station, sited to take advantage of waterborne coal that now comes by road. A drab but friendly pub, the Elephant and Castle, stands by Tusses Bridge (no 4).

*Wyken Arm* (¾m)   Pleasure-craft moorings are situated in the remains of a colliery branch, expensively bridged by the M6 motorway in 1970-1.

*Ansty* (3m 4f)   This canalside suburb of Coventry retains its village atmosphere and provides useful shopping facilities and other services. Small craft can be launched over a low bank from the road N of Bridge 14. South of here the scenery improves considerably. Between Bridges 19 and 24 comes the first of many loops left by the old course of the canal. These loops are noticeable during a cruise to Braunston because of the occasional gaps in the numbering sequence of bridges. Several of the loops now serve as moorings off the main line. The towpath is generally carried over the junctions by decorative cast-iron bridges from the Horseley Iron Works, dating from the mid-1830s. The M6 spans the canal south of Bridge 24 on a huge concrete bridge supported by rows of cylindrical columns.

*Brinklow* (7m 4f)   The main line railway out of Rugby runs along an embankment down a long straight, left of the canal. This leads to the former toll office at Stretton Stop, where a small swing bridge crosses a narrow channel. The site on each side and up the adjacent Brinklow Arm is occupied by a boatyard offering hire cruisers. There are boat services available here, with shops in the nearby Brinklow village. Several hundred yards S the canal is carried over Smite Brook by a single-arched aqueduct, which replaced an original structure of 12 arches that was removed in the reconstruction programme. Some remains can still be seen.

*Newbold-on-Avon* (11m)   The Avon is the same river that passes through Warwick to become navigable upstream of Stratford. A 250yd tunnel, approached by a conventionally wooded cutting at each end, replaced an earlier bore, one portal of which can be found on the old canal arm near Newbold parish church. Most unusually, the newer tunnel is equipped with a towpath on each side, although only the southern path is now accessible. Two canal inns stand side by side up a lane between the tunnel and Bridge 50 – the Barley Mow and the Boat.

*Rugby* (14m 4f)   This sprawling manufacturing town lies to the S, conveniently close for shopping and the main line railway station, but thankfully divided from the waterway by open spaces and a golf course. The towpath is heavily used by local people seeking the peace of the canal banks. There are several substantial brick aqueducts, including one over the Avon. Willow Wren Hire Cruisers occupies Rugby Wharf, at the end of a short arm. This firm specialises in the hire and building of narrow-boat cruisers and also operates a pair of hotel boats.

*Hillmorton* (16m 4f)  A place that has many of the best ingredients of a typical canal village. There are 3 pairs of widely spaced narrow locks that were duplicated, side by side, in 1840 to relieve traffic congestion. Each pair is linked, chamber to chamber, by a large central paddle, so that one of the two could act as a water-saving side pond for the other. While the practice has been discontinued in recent years, a demand for water economy may well necessitate its reintroduction. There are several pleasant canal cottages in rusty brown brick, with boat docks, workshops and a crane in the little maintenance yard located on a short arm. The BWB southern hire-cruiser fleet is run from here.

*Braunston* (24m)  After passing from Warwickshire into Northamptonshire at Bridge 74, the canal leaves Rugby astern and passes no villages until the tall spire of Braunston church appears ahead. These few miles are quietly pleasant, with large rolling fields. At the 3-way Braunston Junction, where an island in the canal's centre is connected with the towpath by a pair of typical iron bridges, the Grand Union running to London on the left shares a common course with the Oxford, right, for the 5m to Napton Junction. For a description of Braunston and the shared portion of waterway, see pp 297–9.

*Napton-on-the-Hill* (32m)  An extensive marina was excavated from a field by Bridge 109, almost opposite Napton Junction, during 1972–3. The resulting increase in pleasure cruisers using the Southern Oxford, especially its summit level, is quite considerable, taking into account also the large boatyard at Braunston, with smaller developments in 1973 at Fenny Compton and Banbury. Napton (Anglo-Saxon *cnaepp*, hilltop, and *tun*, homestead) is a hill village that has expanded considerably in recent years, many of its residents working in nearby towns like Daventry, Rugby and Leamington Spa. A long-established brickworks has quarried deep into the side of the hill where the canal winds around its base by Bridge 112. The brick company carried out a thorough restoration of the previously very derelict Napton windmill, which has long been a landmark for canal travellers. The first record of a corn-grinding mill on this lofty site dates to 1543. Most convenient approach to the village is from Bridge 113, at the foot of the drawn-out flight of 9 locks that occupies 2m to Marston Doles. Several buildings grouped near the bottom chamber include an old farmhouse that was once a boatman's inn, the Bull and Butcher, and a sizeable cottage for the lock-keeper, who is generally on hand to help craft work up the flight to the summit. Problems of water shortage may entail these locks and the Claydon flight being closed to boats overnight. The surroundings represent the very best of Warwickshire scenery – small green fields divided by hedges with large trees dotted at intervals.

From Lock 14, south of Bridge 116, a footpath leads over a field to Holt Farm, where the Adkins family run a well-stocked provisions and souvenir shop. They also have several hire cruisers and have created moorings along the adjacent Engine House arm, at the end of which a steam pump used to bring water supplies to the navigation.

*Marston Doles* (34m)  This is the last lock before one reaches the 11m summit pound and a minute hamlet (consisting of farmhouse, cottages and mid-Victorian warehouse in bright red local brick with the date of its construction picked out in blue brick). Now follows a classic canal meander for 11m through a lovely and remote tract of countryside, though the straight line distance to Claydon Top Lock is just 5m.

E. Temple Thurston, in his otherwise delightful 1911 travelogue, *The 'Flower of Gloster'*, comments that from Napton through Marston Doles to Wormleighton 'was as though the canal had wilfully sought deserted channels . . . it was scarce worth one's while to travel'. How wrong he was to dismiss this section so lightly, for its very isolation is a quality that most people will relish in this allegedly overcrowded island. Footpaths over the fields left of Bridges 123 and 124 lead to the village of Priors Hardwick, whose population has never managed to recover from its decimation by the Black Death.

*Wormleighton* (39m)   The most astonishing loop occurs between Bridges 129 and 133, where the navigator cruises very nearly in a complete circle around New House Farm, which appears first on the right, then on the left and finally, directly astern. Wormleighton village certainly merits a visit. Use footpaths from the canal either at Bridges 127 or 133, or follow the road from Bridge 134. There is an early sixteenth-century manor house in brick, with a huge stone gatehouse dated 1613, and groups of cottages, some in Victorian Gothic and others, considerably older, whose windows are heavily shaded by overhanging roofs of thatch.

*Fenny Compton* (40m)   The wharf with George and Dragon Inn and useful garage is served by the busy A423 at Bridge 136 and stands a considerable distance from the real Fenny village. A new marina has brought great activity to a former backwater. Soon the canal turns a corner and heads through a shallow, unexpectedly straight cutting, which was built originally in the form of two tunnels of 336yd and 452yd. Because of constant delays to freight boats, the tops were opened out between 1868 and 1870, though the name 'tunnel' persists to this day. The banks of the channel, which is scarcely wide enough for craft to pass in places, are lined with rough stone walls. Bridge 137a, in decorative cast iron, transfers the towpath from one bank to the other. Three large reservoirs supply water to the summit. Wormleighton is alongside the navigation at Bridge 139, and Clattercote and Boddington, connected to the canal by non-navigable feeders, lie SW and NE respectively. The first of the Oxford Canal's distinctive drawbridges, most of them built of great wooden beams, is to be encountered at Bridge 141. All but a few merely provide field access and may well be found raised during the summer, when there are many boats about. Leave them open or closed, depending on their position when you arrive.

*Claydon* (43m)   Five locks begin the long descent to the Thames. The changed pattern of life on the waterways is evident from the deserted range of red-brick stables by the top lock. Here narrow-boat horses, working with the well-known Number One (owner-operator) craft that remained on the Oxford until shortly after World War II, would rest for the night. A lock-keeper's house was inhabited up to 1948, but, like so many others from here to Oxford, is now little more than a grass-grown mound of rubble. Claydon Middle Bridge (no 145) leads to the village, where a single shop and public house make a useful journey of the short walk. But the most memorable feature is the brown stone church of St James, partly Norman, and standing on a raised island where you might expect to see a village green. A little to the S is Clattercote, a private farmhouse containing portions of a Gilbertine priory, founded in 1209.
Elkington's, Varney's and Broadmoor Locks bring the canal to one of its finest villages – Cropredy. (Undoubtedly Messrs Elkington and Varney were lock-keepers.)

*Oxford Canal. One of the delightful little lift bridges characteristic of the waterway south of Banbury; this example is at Nell Bridge*

*Cropredy* (45m 4f)  A Civil War battle was fought over Cropredy Bridge in 1644, but the only subsequent excitement was probably the opening of the canal rather over a century later. Here the River Cherwell introduces itself for the first time, thereafter keeping close company with the navigation all the way to the Thames. Prettiest of the two inns is the Red Lion, overlooking the tombstones in the churchyard of St Mary's. Most of the current commercial initiative of Cropredy seems to belong to the shop and adjacent garage by Bridge 153, and it would be surprising if this concern could not provide all but the most extraordinary needs of any boating party. Cropredy Mill is an ivy-clad ruin astride the Cherwell, guarding a sluice that diverts water into the canal.

*Banbury* (50m)  Three locks about a mile apart herald the approach of this important market town. You cannot help liking the place, even if the actions of local Philistines at various stages in its history have left a number of scars. The original Eleanor Cross of the nursery rhyme was smashed by Puritans in 1602; it was replaced in the last century. In 1792 the Banburians used gunpowder to destroy their beautiful and ancient church rather than pay the expense of maintenance. The present neo-Classical building was completed in 1876. The collection of municipal silver was sold off in the early 1800s, and the superb plaster work, panelling and sixteenth-century mullioned windows from the Globe Room of the Reindeer, one of the two splendid timbered inns that remain, were shipped to the USA in 1912. Our own times are in some ways little different. Nondescript plate-glass shop fronts have replaced centuries-old properties, and the major part of the intimate market square frontages are currently threatened by redevelopment (promises have been made to build mock replicas of the best elevations!). Worst action of all was the conversion in the early 1960s of a well-designed and spacious canal basin by the lock, right in the centre of the town, into a hideous waste of tarmac and wire netting – the Banbury bus station. Less than a decade later an equally spacious pleasure-boat marina was being expensively planned not 200yd from the old basin. While Banbury may not boast a location with the potential of the waterfront at, say, York or Richmond-on-Thames, its utter disregard for the Oxford Canal is alarming. If the situation changes with the passing of years, these words will at least serve as a reminder that the townsfolk of Banbury were slow to appreciate one of their greatest latent assets.

To its credit, Banbury has the largest cattle market in Europe, some excellent shops (including the best of ironmongers and seed merchants), and Banbury cakes, which are still made to a 300-year-old recipe. Herbert Tooley's renowned narrow-boat dock somehow survives in its traditional faded form, clinging to a patch of land above the lock. Neither the bus station nor even a new road bridge and embankment could dislodge Mr Tooley. Patronise him if you can.

To the north of Banbury the scent of coffee wafts from the General Foods works and southwards along the canal is the conveniently close railway station, a belt of new housing and then the open country once more.

*King's Sutton* (53m 4f)   There are no fewer than 10 drawbridges in the 4m from Banbury to King's Sutton, but few road crossings. Villages lie well back from the possibility of flooding from the Cherwell, which is now generally within 200yd of the canal all the way to the Thames. Grant's Lock (52m) has a cottage very close to the chamber, where the overflow weir passes directly under the foundations. Twyford Wharf (53m) is a sleepy group of farm buildings, which once included a boatman's inn and an important brickworks that supplied building materials to the canal company. The old Twyford Mill, a short way to the E, on the Cherwell, is now an important animal feed factory and domestic discount centre. This is a flourishing agricultural area. Ahead, the elegant tall spire of King's Sutton church dominates the landscape, but the village is completely isolated from the canal at its most obvious access point by the unbridged river and a railway. King's Sutton (or Tarver's) Lock retains its original brick and stone cottage, together with some of the buildings that served as a company blacksmith's shop and small maintenance centre. An agreeable uphill walk of 1m westwards over the fields leads from the lock to Adderbury, a substantial settlement of brown stone houses on the busy A423, with shops and public houses.

*Aynho* (55m 4f)   After passing a really good example of a modern house, whose core is an old wharf building on the right bank between Bridges 184 and 185 (both removed), we arrive at Nell Bridge Lock, adjacent to the A41. Road widening has resulted in the original humpbacked bridge at the tail of the lock being buried deep under the new bridge. As no allowance was made for the towpath, boat crews have to cross the road to work the lock, which can present problems for the single-handed navigator, as the rise and fall is almost 9ft. Aynho village, lying a little over 1m SE, is well worth a visit, not only for the many wall-trained peach trees that climb over the cottages, but also to see the classical Aynho House, a large stone mansion remodelled in the late eighteenth century by Sir John Soane and open to the public, May–September, Wednesday and Thursday afternoons.

The Cherwell Valley has changed so little over the years, especially as seen from the canal, that it is depressing to realise that the M40 Oxford–Birmingham motorway is scheduled to run close to the waterway. Meanwhile, enjoy the fact that this solitary part of the Southern Oxford closely resembles a nineteenth-century landscape by B. W. Leader or Henry Parker.

Aynho Weir Lock, ½m downhill of Nell Bridge, is a curiosity of the Oxford in that the chamber is diamond-shaped (broader at the centre than by each gate). Like the similar Shipton Weir Lock, it has a shallow rise and fall, but with its artificially increased capacity it passes downhill an equivalent amount of water to that used by Somerton Deep Lock with a fall of 12ft. Above Aynho Weir the Cherwell crosses the navigation, causing occasional problems with headroom under the bridges on this pound if the level rises. The engineer of the 27½m of canal south of Banbury, Robert Whitworth, had first intended to construct aqueducts over the river at Aynho and Shipton, but level crossings were substituted.

Near Bridge 190 lies Aynho Wharf, where Messrs Morgan Giles have a thoughtfully designed hire-cruiser base that retains a small canopied warehouse by the water's edge. The Great Western Arms Inn nearby is now more a canal pub than its name suggests, for the railway station is closed.

*Somerton Deep Lock* (59m)   A gaunt and somewhat upright cottage stands lonely sentinel by the cavernous chamber of the lock. Few narrow locks in England have a greater rise and fall (Tardebigge Top at 14ft is one). The heavy bottom gates required tend to reach massive proportions. (South of Banbury, both top and bottom gates are single, rather than the lower ones being in pairs.) Somerton village is accessible from Bridge 196, S of the lock.

*Lower Heyford* (62m 6f)   Passing through low-lying meadows, the waterway runs close to several villages, including Steeple Aston, and Upper and Lower Heyford, all of them providing good basic provisions and supplies. A village supermarket in Upper Heyford occupies a converted chapel. From time to time the general tranquillity is shattered by jets from the American Air Force base to the west.

*Shipton-on-Cherwell* (69m 2f)   Through patches of woodland, fields carpeted with brilliant yellow cowslips in late May, and a succession of easily operated locks (Dashwood's, Northbrook and Pigeon's), the canal runs on to Baker's Lock (68m 3f), sited near a large cement factory. There are several long-disused quarries in the immediate district. Here the navigation uses the course of the Cherwell for a mile, providing the luxury of deep, gently flowing water (an exciting trip can be expected when the river is in spate), pollarded willows and a generally Amazonian ambience. Note vertical wooden rollers on the sharpest towpath bends to guide boat towlines. This exquisite reach, recalling the best of Yorkshire's non-tidal River Derwent, ends at Shipton Weir Lock. Almost all traces have gone of the pretty but remote single-storey cottage that was inhabited until about 1966. As an overnight mooring or situation for a swimming party on a hot summer day, it would be difficult to find anywhere so ideal.

From about Shipton village to Thrupp the course of the canal is wider than normal, very much like a river's. A little lane passing the side of Shipton church stops abruptly at the water's edge by Bridge 220, where you would expect to find a ford. These peculiarities are explained by the fact that until the construction of the canal, this length was the bed of the Cherwell, the river having been diverted via a new channel. Blenheim Palace and the Bladon churchyard grave of Sir Winston Churchill are about 2½m W of Shipton. A less tiring but rewarding excursion is to walk through the fields from Shipton Bridge E to the tiny and seemingly forgotten church of Hampton Gay in lush pastures near a ruined manor house. The river is filled in summer with swathes of the white buttercup-like flowers of the water crowfoot, just as in Sir John Millais' *Ophelia* (National Gallery).

*Thrupp* (71m)   Patches of white waterlilies, a wooden liftbridge at a sharp bend marking the end of the old course of the river, and a local BWB maintenance yard in Cotswold stone, are essential ingredients of thos pleasing canal village. A single row of cottages faces the navigation, as in a West Country river port, terminating in the Boat Inn. Around a bend by Bridge 223 is the Jolly Boatman Inn, formerly the Britannia.

*Duke's Cut* (74m 4f)   There is a hint of approaching Oxford suburbs at Kidlington Green Lock, but all is rural again by Shuttleworth's Lock, where the Duke of Marlborough's Canal forks right for the Thames. Fitted with a single shallow lock that can rise or fall according to river levels, the DMC is perhaps the most pleasant approach to the Thames, avoiding the inevitable backyard route into Oxford chosen by the canal. But the last 3m of the Oxford Canal is not without merit or the prospect of interesting encounters.

*Oxford* (78m)   The city has to date done little to enhance its waterfronts either on the canal or on the Thames. The only good view from the water of the 'dreaming spires' is that across Port Meadow on the Godstow–Osney pound of the Thames. Along the canal (inclined to be rather shallow) lie factories, sports fields and housing estates. Beyond an unusual electric liftbridge, operated for boats to pass by Morris Radiators, tall Victorian houses stand at the ends of long narrow gardens where cats sleep among shady ferns in tile-bordered flower beds. Several residents keep cruisers. Near the end of the line the Castle Mill boatyard provides the best mooring for access to shops and the city, coupled with complete security. Alternatively, press on to the Thames and tie up near Folly Bridge. Oxford's sights demand attention from all visitors, but it is not appropriate to attempt to describe them here.

The Oxford Canal wharves and original basin were obliterated after their sale to Nuffield College in 1937, so the waterway now lacks any very satisfactory terminal. Through a good iron roving bridge with long sweeping brick approach ramps is Louse (or, more politely, Isis) Lock, built wide-beam to enable Thames barges to reach canal quays, but remodelled in the middle of the nineteenth century when Thames trade had declined. Below the lock the navigation bends sharply to the right and is crossed by a railway swing bridge carrying a lesser line from Oxford Station. Normally this bridge is now left open for boats to pass through to the Thames, but, if closed, application to the signalman or station staff will result in the appearance of a gang of spanner-men whose function is to unbolt the tracks prior to winding the span aside.

### PARRETT, RIVER

From Thorney Mills to the Bristol Channel at Bridgwater Bar, near Burnham-on-Sea; 34¼m with 1 lock (now derelict) at Langport.

The coast at Bridgwater Bay is a huge nature reserve comprising over 6,000 acres of mudflats that attract large numbers of wildfowl. Small coasters still navigate the Parrett to Bridgwater (19m), although the port's trade has much declined in comparison with that carried on during the last century (see p 111). A tidal bore, largest at spring tides, is formed below Combwich and travels upriver beyond Bridgwater. The height rarely exceeds 4ft. The River Brue can be entered above Burnham-on-Sea and is navigable for about 1½m. Access to the Bridgwater & Taunton Canal and Bridgwater Dock is most regrettably impossible, following the sealing of the entrance lock with a concrete barrier. A junction 6½m upstream of Bridgwater with the River Tone offers almost 6m of cruising water to Knapp Bridge. Langport (30m 4f) has lost all its former river trade, though its one-time importance is suggested by the many Georgian houses. As the lock here is derelict, further progress upriver is practicable only by portable craft. These can normally reach Ilchester, 7m up the River Yeo (31m 2f), or travel 2m along the River Isle, which lead to the Westport Canal, abandoned in 1878.

This system of rivers offers rewarding cruising of a slightly adventurous sort, and care must be taken when encountering strong tides in the Parrett below Bridgwater.

### PEAK FOREST CANAL

From Dukinfield Junction on the Ashton Canal at Ashton, to Buxworth Basin; 14½m with 16 locks. There is a ½m branch to Whaley Bridge, near Buxworth. Maximum craft dimensions are 70ft × 7ft × 3ft draught × 6ft headroom. Historically this waterway has long been coupled with the Ashton and Macclesfield Canals, the 3 being in common ownership for many years before nationalisation. The section between Marple and Dukinfield forms part of the Cheshire Canal Ring (see p 380) and was restored after a period of dereliction, being reopened with the Ashton Canal in 1974.

The most scenic length is from the foot of the splendid flight of 16 Marple locks and Marple Aqueduct to Whaley Bridge.

*Dukinfield*  The Peak Forest Canal Society and other voluntary organisations must take much of the credit for the opening of the lower 8m of the waterway to Marple for cruising. Unusable throughout the 1960s and early 1970s, it was the subject of constant pressure. Before the official decision to undertake restoration, many working parties were held, notably around Marple locks, where much rubbish was removed from chambers and new balance beams fitted to gates. Leaving the Ashton Canal, the Peak Forest crosses the murky waters of the River Tame via a small aqueduct. Surroundings comprise mainly waste tips with a sewage farm. Matters improve near Hyde (2m 4f). Captain Clarke's Bridge (no 6) is a classic among stone roving bridges, with broad and assured walls sweeping up from the towpath on one side of the canal and round to the bridge hole on the other.

*Marple* (7m to bottom lock)  Residential suburbs of Manchester follow, with 176yd Butterhouse Green Tunnel at Woodley, complete with towpath, and another, Hyde Bank, running for 308yd near Romiley. This time the horsepath runs over the top of the hill. Until it was opened out into a cutting in 1820, a 100yd third tunnel called Rose Hill immediately preceded Marple Aqueduct. Attractions now arrive in plenty. First is the most handsome aqueduct, taking the canal over the River Goyt at a height of more than 100ft. The structure consists of 3 arches of about 8,000 cu yd of masonry, each pierced with a pair of circular 'windows' under the puddled and brick-lined water trough. It was jointly designed by Benjamin Outram and Thomas Brown of Disley and opened in 1800. Now come the locks, 16 of them connecting the wild tree-clad valley of the Goyt with Marple town centre. Notable features include stone warehouses, a very pretty cottage at Lock 9 and a landscaped and paved area below Posset Bridge. Here the towpath divides, offering one tunnel under the road for boat horses, another for pedestrians and a third opening for the canal itself. Marple derives considerable visual benefit from its canal, and the lock flight is one of the most agree-able to be found in England. Immediately beyond Lock 16 comes the junction with the Macclesfield Canal. Jinks' boatyard built and repaired narrow boats here from about 1840 until the 1930s, and the old drydock has been converted into a sunken garden in the grounds of Top Lock House. Having risen 210ft beyond the aqueduct, the Peak Forest Canal remains at 500ft above sea level, the highest navigation still operating in Britain.

From Marple to Whaley Bridge the waterway clings to a heavily embanked hillside, providing splendid views over the Goyt valley. A serious breach occurred at Strines in the 1940s, followed by an equally disastrous one in the same area in July 1973, when prolonged torrential rain caused the canal bank to collapse. Several moored cruisers (fortunately unoccupied) were swept into the chasm. Repairs were in progress for many months.

*Whaley Bridge* (14m 4f)   There are 6 swing bridges, some with overhead footways also, between Marple and the terminus. Buildings connected with brief touches of industry at Disley and New Mills do not really detract from the continuing pleasure offered by stone farm walls and views across the moors. A small basin at Whaley Bridge marks the end of the waterway journey and the start of the former Cromford & High Peak Railway, connecting the Peak Forest with the Cromford Canal and so to the Trent. The railway had a summit level 1,200ft above the sea, and at one point a gradient of 1 in 7. The last portion closed in 1967. The local council has said it will demolish a superb stone-built warehouse by the canal basin and construct a swimming pool in its place.

*Buxworth Basin*   Originally the terminus of the canal, with Whaley Bridge at the end of a branch. These positions are now virtually reversed. Bugsworth was the name until inhabitants sought a change. It is now a fascinating complex of limestone loading points. The Peak Forest Tramway, opened in 1799, ran for 6½m between the basin and Doveholes quarries. Traction for the waggons was supplied by horses, and engineer-ing features included tunnels and an inclined plane. Buxworth handled up to 600 tons of limestone and lime (30–40 narrow-boat loads) daily during the 1880s, and the operation continued until 1926. After many years of dereliction, members of the Inland Waterways Protection Society have reclaimed large portions of the basins and approach canal, with emphasis on rebuilding the waterway to its original depth and specification.

### POCKLINGTON CANAL
From the tidal River Derwent at Cottingwith, Yorkshire, to Pocklington; 9½m with 9 locks. Maximum craft dimensions are 57ft × 14ft 3in × 4ft draught × 9ft

headroom (until full restoration, these last two figures are perhaps optimistic). An endearing little waterway, mild and unremarkable, but not without charm. Its recent history is a textbook example of the decline and revival of a canal through changing attitudes to environmental worth and the influence of volunteer groups on central and local government policy. The last commercial barge arrived in 1932, and 2 years later 10 motor cruisers came to Melbourne for Easter – the last pleasure traffic. The 1959 report of the Inland Waterways Redevelopment Advisory Committee objected to a scheme that the canal's bed should be used for tipping sludge, but failed to advocate restoration. Swing bridges were replaced by fixed spans in 1962. Under the 1968 Transport Act the Pocklington was dubbed a 'remainder waterway' (to be dealt with as economically as possible, consistent with public health, amenity and safety). In the following year the Pocklington Canal Amenity Society was formed. The first lock at Cottingwith was restored and reopened in mid-1971. An announcement in August 1973 revealed that complete restoration was to be started, with the cost of the first phase, £27,000, being shared by British Waterways and the county council. It is therefore probable that the waterway will be completely navigable again soon after the mid-1970s. The course of the canal is completely rural, passing through agreeable farmland.

*East Cottingwith*   From the tidal River Derwent (which may soon be improved by construction of a weir and lock near its mouth) the first lock lies near this little village, with its delightful Georgian church in red brick. Navigation is currently possible for 1½m to Storwood. Small villages at Melbourne and Thornton (5m 2f) add interest. Four of the road bridges are of an unusual design, with rounded pillars in brick at each corner and pleasing curves. Another notable feature is the distinctive lock paddle gear, displaying substantial iron balance wheels. Is it too much to hope that these will be preserved instead of being replaced by standard equipment?

*Pocklington* (9m 4f)   The waterway terminates in a small basin at Canal Head by the A1079 York to Market Weighton road, with mellow brick warehouses. Pocklington, a small market town, lies 1m to the north. The finest collection of waterlilies in Europe (about 2,000 of them) can be visited at Burnby Hall Gardens, open every afternoon from May to September.

## REGENT'S CANAL

From the Thames at Limehouse, London, to Paddington; 8m 5f with 12 locks and a ship lock into the Thames.

London's own canal is one of the secret delights of the capital. For much of its route from the East End to Camden Town, occasional glimpses of boats and water from the top decks of buses are all that the average Londoner is likely to know of it. Its banks range from sordid to sylvan, presenting a unique view of London's back door seen from the deck of a boat. Completed in 1820 to link the Grand Union's Paddington arm with the Docks, the canal was responsible for much of the commercial development that grew up alongside during the nineteenth century. Until the early 1960s traffic was quite brisk, both with horse- or tractor-drawn dumb lighters and long-distance family narrow boats bound for the Midlands. Almost throughout its length, wharves and factories, a few still served by the canal, bear witness to its former trading position.

The architect John Nash played a large part in the promotion and construction of the waterway, and although subsequent building development drastically altered the original rural character of its route, his conception of 'barges moving through an urban landscape' remains a notable feature of the canal at its western end. Built too close to the coming of the railways to produce the hoped-for financial success, the Regent's Canal nevertheless carried vast quantities of coal, timber, building materials and food produce. Today, while trade is negligible, pleasure-craft traffic grows all the time. As an amenity waterway, parts of the Regent's Canal rank with the most important in Britain. Craft dimensions: 78ft × 14ft 6in × 4ft 6in × 9ft.

*Regent's Canal Dock*   These 11 acres under water formed the London terminus of the Grand Union Canal Co, where ships of up to 3,000 tons could interchange cargoes. After declining prosperity, the Dock was finally closed to shipping in 1970, but the 350ft × 60ft entrance lock from the Thames remains available for lighters and pleasure craft. Its future role is undecided, but amenity facilities must surely be provided side by side with any commercial development. The connection with the Thames is available from 2 hours before high water, 6.00am–10.00pm, every day of the year. Advance notification to the BWB's Limehouse office is desirable. On the eastern side of the basin a connection with the Limehouse Cut (see River Lee, p 321) was opened in 1968. To the north, beneath a railway viaduct, lies the first pair of locks (Commercial Road), each manned by a keeper generally living in a cottage on site. Immediately you are transported from the wide open reaches of the Thames and the Dock to the confines of the canal, frequently protected for security reasons by high brick walls.

All locks on the Regent's Canal were constructed in duplicate, in order to handle heavy barge traffic. At the end of 1973, when most freight movement had finished, the BWB began a 3-year programme of converting one chamber of each pair into an overflow weir for the remaining lock alongside. When finished, this system will enable pleasure craft crews to operate locks without the supervision of keepers. Hitherto this was not possible because of a danger of serious flooding resulting from incorrect use of the paddles.

For the first few miles there is little greenery or trees, although the occasional wild-flower has managed to secure a foothold on the towpath. At present this section of towpath is only available to the public on payment of a fee for a walking permit, although there are hopes that eventually the whole route may be opened for the free use of everyone.

*Hertford Union Canal* (1m 6f)   Reached at a junction after passing through Salmon's Lane, Johnson's and Mile End Locks. Known also as Duckett's Cut, it was acquired from Sir George Duckett by the Regent's Canal Co in 1855. Little more than 1m in length, it provides a connection with the Lee via 3 locks officially known as Upper, Middle and Lower. Notice (24 hours) to British Waterways at Paddington is advised before a passage is attempted.

*Hackney* (1m 4f)   Bordering both the Hertford Union and the Regent's is the extensive Victoria Park, laid out for East Enders in a romantic landscape style by Sir James Pennethorne in 1842. A small BWB engineering depot is situated by Old Ford Locks in a building that originally housed a steam pump to bring water up the canal.

*Islington* (4m)   Several large basins, with Acton's and Sturt's Locks (Sturt was a local landowner when the canal was built), bring the waterway to City Road Basin, a huge area of water housing a children's boat club in a converted lighter, and the premises of the London Hydraulic Power Company, whose system of pipes spread throughout the capital in order to operate lifts, cranes and similar machinery. Almost opposite the basin end is the Narrow Boat Inn, with direct access to the towpath. Modernised in 1970 from a Victorian pub called the Star, its trendy canal-inspired interior reflects a growing tendency for once drab waterways to be considered fashionable. Local authority cooperation with the BWB has resulted in planting of several groups of trees about City Road locks, together with the opening of part of the towpath. A delightful leafy cutting leads up to the portal of 960yd Islington Tunnel. On the right bank of the approach stand the early Victorian houses of Noel Road, one of a select number of residential streets that overlook the water. Again the social acceptability of canals is mirrored in the price such properties now fetch.

The tunnel, passing beneath the Angel, has no towpath. Diesel tugs haul the remaining barge traffic, and pleasure craft should ensure that the way is clear, for the wide-beam lighters are an exact fit (see pp 79–80).

*St Pancras* (5m 4f)   Unaccustomed views of St Pancras and King's Cross Stations and the delicate tracery of Victorian ironwork on the huge gasholders near the canalside are among the architectural pleasures of this area. The former coal basin was converted into a pleasure-craft basin in 1958, but is now a little down at heel. The lock-keeper's garden supports a good crop of vegetables, surprisingly for the location, and access is possible to the outside world via gates, alleyways and railway siding arches.

*Regent's Canal. The end of the Paddington Level at Camden Town*

*Camden Town* (6m 4f)   A group of 3 locks – Kentish Town, Hawley and Hampstead Road – lift the canal to the Long Level, extending as a lock-free pound 21m to Cowley and Norwood Top Lock on the Grand Union main line. Just before Kentish Town Lock and the white concrete building of the Aerated Bread Company stands the Regent's Canal's sole waterside garage, a modern structure with a pleasing footbridge over the water. A good shopping centre at Camden Town is easily reached from Hampstead Road Lock, where the keeper's cottage is a castellated Regency fantasy, probably dating from the opening of the canal. Cruises aboard narrow boat *Jenny Wren* to Paddington and return start at the exciting Camden Lock Crafts Centre (see p 177). Above the lock is a fine angled-iron towpath bridge spanning the canal and a now-silted side arm diving beneath dark arches under a warehouse. Attempts were made to install a hydro-pneumatic lock (designed in 1813 by Colonel Congreve) consisting of caissons to transfer craft from one level to the other without loss of water, but the company proprietors grew impatient with its failure to perform according to the claims of the inventor, and conventional locks were built instead. The towpath is open from here to Regent's Park.

*Regent's Park* (7m)   Now begins one of the best sections of urban canal landscape on the British system, as the waterway leaves for a short time the industrial development that has characterised its banks since the Thames. St Mark's Crescent, a street of Victorian houses whose owners (many of them, at least) use their canal frontages for boat moorings, and a modern terrace development opposite illustrate again the popularity of waterside town houses. Viscount St Davids established a children's boat club here in 1967. A sharp bend takes the canal into the Park itself. To the left is the truncated remains of the Cumberland Arm, filled with bomb-damage rubble during World War II. Originally it ran for ¾m to the Cumberland Market, a few yards from Euston Station. The stub is fully used for private boat moorings and a flourishing floating restaurant. Now follows the famous Zoological Gardens on each bank, providing glimpses of exotic birds and animals, some adventurous architecture (including Lord Snowdon's spiky aviary) and a truly rural stretch of trees in a deep cutting. Several bridges are worthy of mention, especially Macclesfield Bridge, a three-arched structure in yellow stock brick on Coalbrookdale cast-iron columns, scene of the renowned explosion of October 1874, when *Tilbury*, one of three barges drawn by steam tug *Ready* and loaded with gunpowder, blew up, causing widespread damage, demolishing the bridge and killing the barge crew. The iron columns of the bridge were salvaged from the wreck and re-erected facing the 'wrong' way, so that today towline abrasions can be seen in the metal where no ropes could ever have cut it. The structure is often known as 'Blow Up Bridge'.

The reach between Camden Town and Paddington is busy with pleasure craft in summer, including private cruisers, boat-club youngsters, and passenger vessels *Jason* (with butty *Serpens*), *Jenny Wren* and the BWB zoo buses. The towpath between Lisson Grove and Primrose Hill (Regent's Park) has been made available as a public walk maintained by Westminster City Council. Numerous schemes for further canal improvements have been suggested by local authorities and several energetic civic societies. Further private moorings at Lisson Grove – Broadwater – overlook a large municipal housing estate on the old Marylebone goods yard site. Just beyond, where a canal building spans the waterway at Lisson Grove, boats appear to pass through a basement. A deep chasm between tall buildings terminates abruptly at Maida Hill Tunnel (272yd), passing under the busy Edgware Road.

*Little Venice* (8m 5f)  Formerly known as Paddington Stop, the junction of the Regent's Canal and Paddington Arm is a most attractive area, where a wide stretch of water is now generally referred to as Little Venice. Robert Browning, who lived here in a house on the south side (now demolished), is said to have provided the new name. His own name is normally given to willow-clad Rat Island at the centre of the pool. A small public garden, fine Victorian stucco mansions and some thoughtfully blending council flats, combine to enhance the area. Further boat moorings line the approach to the tunnel, and a pair of satisfying canal cottages, one a toll-house, stand at each entrance to the pool. On the south bank the tall white Victorian pile of Beauchamp Lodge houses a wide range of community services, including a thriving children's boat club in a barge. Alongside, the vast and virtually deserted Paddington Basin, spanned by a motorway and subjected for years to a range of redevelopment pressures, may in part be used to solve an acute shortage of cruiser moorings in the capital.

### RIPON CANAL

From the River Ure at Oxclose Lock to Ripon; 2m 2f with 3 locks, of which the upper 2 are derelict. Maximum dimensions are 57ft × 14ft 3in × 2ft 6in draught with 8ft 6in headroom.

Historically the canal is really a continuation of the Ure, which becomes rocky and impracticable for boats larger than canoes upstream of Oxclose Lock. The short canal and Ure Navigation were opened to traffic in 1773, having been surveyed by William Jessop with guidance from John Smeaton. It was reported in 1906 that boats could no longer reach Ripon, and the upper part of the canal was officially abandoned in 1955 under an arrangement granting certain rights over the lower 1¼m to Ripon Motor Boat Club. The 2 locks were converted into cascades. In 1973 there were plans to reopen them, restore the route to Ripon basin and build a marina.

*Ripon*  This is the northernmost point on the connected waterways network of England and Wales. A small stone-walled basin, silted but still in water, marks the terminus of the canal near the cathedral, which dates mainly from the twelfth and thirteenth centuries. (A church founded by Scottish monks about AD 660 occupied the site until its destruction in 950; the present crypt, built about 670, has remained as one of the earliest Christian survivals in England.) At the centre of the city is the rectangular market place, with a 90ft obelisk erected in 1781 to William Aislabie, MP for 60 years. One tradition, over 1,000 years old, is for the Hornblower, in his three-cornered hat, to blow a blast in the market square each night. While in Ripon, a visit can conveniently be made to the superb Fountains Abbey, about 4m SW on the River Skell.

Passing Ripon and Littlethorpe Locks (derelict), one reaches the present head of navigation near the city's racecourse. The Ripon Motor Boat Club has its headquarters here, with moorings and a slipway.

*Oxclose Lock* (2m 2f)  The lock has a rise of about 10ft 6in from the Ure, which is joined at the tail of a short cut whose entrance from the river is easily missed among trees on the W bank. (For continuation of the navigation via the River Ure, see p 437.)

### ROCHDALE CANAL

From Castlefield, junction with the Bridgewater Canal, Manchester, to Dale Street, junction with the Ashton Canal; 2m with 9 locks. One of three trans-Pennine water-ways, the Rochdale Canal was finished in 1804, its original 33m course linking the Bridgewater and Calder & Hebble Navigations. It boasted no fewer than 92 locks, each capable of passing one barge or a pair of narrow boats. The last working boat to trade over its complete length made the passage in 1937. Escaping nationalisation in 1948, all but the 2m in Manchester was abandoned by Act of Parliament in 1952. During the early 1970s lengths of the derelict section in Manchester were expensively reduced in depth to a few inches and locks replaced by cascades. One obvious result of this arrangement is that the rubbish attracted by disused urban waterways is more obvious and offensive. Surveyed by John Rennie, but mainly engineered by William Jessop, the Rochdale retains much of its grandeur as it climbs to a summit between Rochdale and Todmorden. The entire length provides an interesting towpath walk. Maximum craft dimensions are 74ft × 14ft 2in × 4ft draught × 9ft headroom.

The navigable section through Manchester consists largely of a succession of wide locks, hidden for the most part behind high walls. One lock is situated in a dark cavern created by erecting a tower office block above it. Dale Street Basin, by the junction with the Ashton, is a car park, but original warehouses and a grand stone gateway survive. There is also a popular floating restaurant housed aboard a pair of converted barges. The condition of this part of the Rochdale was indifferent for much of the time that the Ashton and Lower Peak Forest Canals were closed (1961–74). Forming a vital section of the 105m Cheshire Waterways Ring, this fragment of Rochdale Canal can now anticipate ever-increasing use by pleasure craft.

### ROTHER, RIVER

From the South Coast at Rye Harbour to Bodiam Castle; 16½m with 1 lock. This is the Eastern Rother, in no way connected with the Western Rother, which joins the Arun at Stopham (p 221). While the chief function of the river is one of land drainage, an agreeable cruise may be made from Rye to Bodiam. The upper 12½m beyond Scot's Float Lock is subject to reduced draught at times. The sluice-keeper must be consulted before a journey is begun. Maximum craft dimensions are 56ft × 13ft 9in × 3ft draught × 9ft 9in headroom.

*Rye Harbour* (1m)   The entrance from the South Coast is along a channel through the dunes of Camber Sands. A Martello tower, one of a series erected during the Napoleonic Wars as military defence works to combat a threatened French invasion, stands on the west shore. A little inland is Camber Castle, built in Tudor times and originally on the seashore (parts of the estuary have since been reclaimed). Coasters regularly dock at the Harbour.

*Rye* (2m 3f)   Sturdy fishing craft moor at landing stages below the fascinating hill town of Rye, one of 2 additions to the 5 Cinque Ports. At low water the navigation dries out to a muddy trickle. Narrow cobbled streets are noted for their half-timbered buildings, such as the Mermaid Inn of about 1500 erected over a vaulted thirteenth-century cellar. Seen from a distance across Romney Marshes, Rye resembles a cone surmounted by the squat tower of St Mary's Norman church. Wooden warehouses and inns with smuggling traditions preserve the atmosphere of the eighteenth-century port along the river quay. The thirteenth-century Ypres Tower was built as a castle and used later as a prison. The fourteenth-century Landgate, once with portcullis and drawbridge, and parts of contemporary town wall in flint emphasise Rye's former strategic importance. A junction is made with the River Brede (p 248). On the river bank on the edge of the town is a brick and weatherboarded smock windmill.

*Scot's Float Lock* (4m 7f)   Fitted with doors that open either way, depending on water levels, one of the lock gates must be forced open with a wooden pole, a task assumed by the keeper. Iden Lock (5m 7f), situated at the start of the Royal Military Canal (below), is closed to boats. The Rother's non-tidal reaches are characterised by high grassy banks on which dredgings are deposited.

*Newenden* (13m 2f)   Here is a fine stone bridge with rounded arches. Quite soon the river becomes very narrow and fast-flowing, making a safe arrival at Bodiam (16m 3f) something of an achievement. Bodiam Castle is a remarkably well preserved structure of the late fourteenth century, with a series of massive stone towers rising sheer from the waters of its lily-pond moat.

### ROYAL MILITARY CANAL
From West Hythe Sluice to Iden Lock (not available for navigation), junction with the River Rother, near Rye, Sussex; 19m. A unique waterway, opened in 1806 as a defence barrier against a possible Napoleonic invasion of the South Coast. After 1807 it was made suitable for commercial traffic, but was disused a century later. The original length, including sections of the Rivers Brede and Rother, was 30m; 8½m of the surviving portion as it skirts Romney Marsh is now owned by the National Trust. Boating activity is restricted to rowing dinghies and other light craft. A full account of the history of this unusual waterway is contained in *The Royal Military Canal* by P. A. L. Vine (David & Charles).

### SALCOMBE, RIVER
From the South Devon coast at Salcombe to Kingsbridge; 6m and tidal throughout. The only limitation on craft bound for Kingsbridge is a draught of about 10ft at high water.

The river takes the form of an extensive sheltered harbour, with sandy beaches and a full range of boating facilities, including launching points, rowing and motorised craft for hire and public tripping launches. During the last century Salcombe was known for its building and running of schooners engaged in a fruit trade with the Iberian Peninsula. Tennyson's poem 'Crossing the Bar' was inspired while he was anchored aboard his yacht *Sunbeam* at the sea entrance, where tides flow furiously. The region is extremely popular with sailing enthusiasts still. Apart from the main line of the river, there are several adjoining creeks to explore. The market town of Kingsbridge was a port for the export of wool in the fourteenth century. The quays are now converted to car parks, a stationary paddle steamer has become a café and small craft can be hired.

SEVERN, RIVER

From Stourport, Worcestershire, junction with the Staffs & Worcs Canal to Gloucester, junction with the Gloucester & Sharpness Canal; 42m 1f with 6 locks.

The Severn is one of those river navigations whose useful length has contracted alarmingly over the years. During the early nineteenth century barges could reach Welshpool, 128m upstream of Gloucester, but by 1895 much of this stretch was navigable only by light pleasure craft. Today the upper limit is best said to be Stourport, although with care small boats may be able to travel several more miles past Bewdley towards Arley. Compared with the Thames, the Severn is wild and relatively undeveloped. It is a river on a grand scale, and scenically frequently quite fine, although high banks often obscure the view of the surrounding countryside from the deck of a boat. In winter it is liable to flood seriously (hence the high banks), and one tends to find mooring points only at infrequent intervals. In some respects the Severn is best regarded as a pleasant waterway, providing a navigable link with some even more worthwhile navigations – the Staffs & Worcs, Worcester & Birmingham, Warwickshire Avon, and Gloucester & Sharpness Canal. Still of some importance as a commercial route, the river has lost much tanker and large motor barge traffic upstream of Gloucester, although some will be encountered between there and Worcester. Maximum dimensions for craft to Stourport are 89ft × 18ft 11in × 5ft 9in draught. Headroom is about 17ft.

*Stourport*   From the river the 6 chimneys of a massive red-brick and stone power station tend to dominate the scene, and the town is better viewed at closer range by the Staffs & Worcs Canal (see p 399). A pleasing cream-painted iron bridge of 1870 spans the river. Former boat-unloading facilities can be seen alongside a liquid-fuel store and the power station, whose outflow causes considerable currents. The River Stour enters the Severn shortly below. All Severn locks are of a size and complexity to necessitate keepers. The first, Lincomb (2m), is situated just below Redstone Rock, a section of riverside cliff interlaced with caves, and another heavily wooded rocky cliff stands below the lock. A Bulmer's cider house, the Hempstall, stands about 1m downstream of Lincomb on the right bank. A number of similar bargemen's inns remain on the river, most with mooring facilities. Some badly sited waterside bungalows and caravans contrive to spoil the scene for a short distance, but, as these do at least encourage recreational use of the river, it would be wrong to condemn them completely. Fishing is extremely popular, and salmon can be seen leaping from the water both here and lower down towards the estuary.

*Holt Lock* (5m 5f)   Below the lock and the popular resort of Holt Fleet on the A4133 stands Holt Castle (right bank), with a fourteenth-century keep, and turrets and additions largely from about 1690. The Droitwich Barge Canal at Hawford (8m 5f), whose entrance is on the left, has become ruinous and silted since its closure about 1938, but full restoration has been in progress since 1973 under the aegis of the Droitwich Canals Trust. When completed, the DBC will make a useful short cut to the Worcester & Birmingham Canal at Hanbury. At one time there was much salt traffic in sailing trows, but now the junction is almost jungle-like, though the private lock cottage is well maintained.

*Bevere Lock* (9m 1f)   Here one finds a colourful garden with caged rabbits and a charmingly chunky circular iron distance plate to Stourport on the bank below the chamber. The river now begins to broaden, although further rock cliffs restrict its width before Gloucester.

*Worcester* (12m 4f)   The high banks continue through meadows lined with willows and alders. As the outskirts of the city are reached, large Victorian houses with gardens overlooking the river and a yard where rowing boats may be hired combine to make some use of the amenity potential of the river, but in no sense does Worcester complement the Severn in the same way as Windsor, Henley or Abingdon complement the Thames. There is some industrial development, including a printing works and power station. The bridge, in light brown sandstone, is a masterpiece by John Gwynn, built between 1771 and 1780 and subsequently widened. The magnificent cathedral, dating from the eleventh, twelfth and thirteenth centuries, dominates the area, but is best viewed from the opposite bank of the Severn, which forms a fortunate barrier to the continued expansion of the city. Recent road building has been responsible for the loss of a good deal of architecture and character, although much of historical interest remains. The Queen Anne Guildhall, timber-framed fifteenth- and sixteenth-century houses in Friary Street (several owned by the National Trust), and the early eighteenth-century Berkeley Hospital are among the city's highlights. Long-established industries include glove-making, the famed Royal Worcester Porcelain Works and, of course, Worcester Sauce. The Worcester & Birmingham Canal enters the river in the centre of the city, via Diglis Basin. Passenger craft ply on the Severn from this point. A little downstream, extensive storage depots, an oil basin, and the navigation maintenance yards, where a variety of tugs, barges and dredgers are usually to be seen, contrive to give the river the appearance of a flourishing commercial waterway, although barge traffic is now light. Diglis Locks are duplicated, side by side. From time to time large shiny white seagoing motor yachts are to be found grouped together on moorings with tall piles that allow for a sharp rise and fall of the water.

*Kempsey* (16m 1f)   Abandoned on the left bank is the skeleton of a Severn trow, now filled with mud and young willows but still displaying the essentials of construction of this type of sailing barge. Distant views of hills include Bredon to the SE. Further red sandstone cliffs rise sheer from the water. A wharf at Severn Stoke is used for loading lumps of stone into barges, this material being used for bank protection. Several imposing houses in their own grounds stand high above the water.

*Upton-upon-Severn* (23m)   Situated on the right bank alongside a graceful 1940 concrete and steel road bridge, this is a charming little town offering all services for boats. There are good moorings below the bridge, and many lovely Georgian houses, several attractive public houses on the river bank, and, in the High Street, the early seventeenth-century Anchor Inn and impressive stuccoed White Lion. Upton old church is notable for its extraordinary Germanic green copper cupola standing on a dome that in turn surmounts the red stone tower. The tower is thirteenth-century, but the dome was designed in 1769 by Anthony Keck. The main body of the church was abandoned in 1879 and demolished in 1937. Wharf buildings, inns, a chandlery, private houses and a hire-cruiser yard combine to create a memorable waterfront. When there were few bridges over the Severn, this ancient crossing place would have been a busy commercial centre. At Ripple (25m) a pretty Victorian cottage with dormer windows originally housed a ferryman, but regular Severn ferries have largely disappeared with a growth in road transport and the high running costs. A high-level modern bridge carrying the M50 motorway over the Severn is approached by a long viaduct on each side.

*Tewkesbury* (29m)  First indication of the town from upstream is its splendid iron Mythe Bridge, with a single arch of 176ft. Designed by Thomas Telford, its cream-painted lattice work is ornate without being fussy. Each side of the span bears the date 1825. There is a pretty little toll-house at the eastern approach. Then follows a view across the fields to the magnificent Norman Abbey. Standing near the confluence of the Severn and Avon, Tewkesbury belongs more to the Avon (see p 226). Beyond the Avon junction, Tewkesbury Lock on the right bank of the Severn is well provided with mooring piles for waiting craft. Here, as well as at other Severn locks, care should be exercised near the weirs, which are largely unprotected and could present a hazard in times of heavy rain or flood. There is a blue-brick Victorian double-fronted lock house, with decorative work round the gable, bearing the date 1858. At some time the lock chamber has been increased in length by the erection of an additional set of gates at the bottom end, where it widens considerably. A useful waterside inn is to be found about a mile downstream at Lower Lode, site of an old-established ferry. A look upriver gives another view of the Abbey, with Bredon Hill rising beyond.

*Haw Bridge* (34m 6f)  A modern structure with 2 wet arches and a public house on each bank. Mooring could be difficult here, as the banks are high and muddy. Driftwood caught in the branches of willow trees indicates the level of the winter's floods.

*River Severn. A broad loop of the waterway seen from the top of Wainlode Hill, seven miles upstream of Gloucester*

Speed limit notices displayed at intervals on the river dictate 6mph upstream and 8mph down, while the occasional patrol launches keep an eye open for offenders, and even water-skiers, who can constitute a great hazard to other river users.

*Wainlode Hill* (35m 1f)   The disused lock entrance to the derelict Coombe Hill Canal can be seen on the left bank a little upstream of the River Chelt. Built about 1796 to facilitate carriage of coal in 70-ton barges to Cheltenham, it ran only for 2¾m of the required distance through 2 locks. After suffering falling traffic and flood damage, it was closed in 1876. The riverfront at Wainlode Hill is extremely popular, within easy reach of both Gloucester and Cheltenham, and with a long stretch of 'beach' below the sheer cliff of Keuper marl. Erosion has been increased by the considerable wash of passing motor barges. At one end of the cliff stands the Red Lion Inn, with launching facilities for small craft. The view over the Severn from the top of the cliff is quite fine. In this area a number of small wooden punts with upswept swim ends will be noticed; these are traditional Severn fishing boats of the type used for netting salmon in the lower reaches of the river, especially below Gloucester.

*Gloucester* (42m 1f)   The waterway divides about 2m above Gloucester. On the left the Maisemore Channel leads via a disused lock to the old Severn Navigation, the former route to the estuary before the Gloucester & Sharpness Canal was opened to traffic. High tides run over this weir, sometimes affecting the river as far as Tewkesbury. The top of Maisemore Channel is known as the Upper Parting. Another connection with the old Severn from the present navigation at Lower Parting is via Llanthony Lock, also disused, just above Gloucester Lock and the Docks. Provided great care is exercised, and preferably with expert local knowledge, it is possible to take a motor cruiser over these weirs (at a suitable state of the tide) and navigate the original course of the river all the way to Sharpness, about 17m below Lower Parting. The journey constitutes one of the most adventurous inland boat trips available in Britain, especially if the Severn bore (or tidal wave) is scheduled to reach maximum proportions. With ever-shifting sandbanks, a huge rise and fall of the tide, ripping currents and the broad unsheltered expanses of the river, widening as the Bristol Channel is approached, it must be emphasised that this cruise should not be lightly undertaken. To ride the bore it is essential to meet it head on and then turn into it, trying to surf along. Riding the bore on surfboards is becoming a local sport, but it is an activity recommended only to knowledgeable and strong swimmers. The most spectacular of Britain's natural phenomena, the Severn bore begins as an Atlantic tide; the shallowing water of the Continental Shelf reduces its speed, and the funnel shape of the Severn estuary builds up a series of about 7 waves of decreasing height but reaching a maximum of about 9ft. The noise of rushing water, spray on the banks and sheer force behind the bore, which instantly reverses the effect of an ebb tide, give one a memorable experience. It occurs about 260 times each year, and is at its best with the spring and autumn equinoctial tides. One of the best viewing points is Stonebench, a short distance from the Gloucester & Sharpness Canal at Quedgeley. Much useful information is contained in F. R. Rowbotham's *The Severn Bore* (David & Charles).

Craft lock up into Gloucester Docks from the navigation channel to find good moorings in the extensive basins, which are still heavily used by motor barges and sizeable ships, and it comes as something of a surprise to discover this flourishing

N

port so far inland. There are some magnificent red-brick Victorian warehouses, maltings, oil docks, timber yards and even a mariners' church inside the complex. All shopping facilities are within 10 minutes' walk from the main dock gates. With substantial beginnings in Roman times – the site of a complete forum covering about 2 acres has been excavated – Gloucester was also an important Anglo-Saxon and Norman centre. Both the city museum and the folk museum in a sixteenth-century timber-framed house in Westgate Street should be visited. Exhibits in the latter show traditional salmon- and eel-fishing techniques, activities still pursued on the lower Severn. The New Inn in Northgate Street is one of several ancient hostelries and features a well-preserved fifteenth-century courtyard and timber balconies. The great Norman cathedral dating from 1089 is rich in architecture from the eleventh to fifteenth centuries. Stained glass in the great east window is unequalled anywhere in Britain.

Shipping movements to Gloucester docks have declined somewhat in recent years.

### SHEFFIELD & SOUTH YORKSHIRE NAVIGATION

From the River Trent at Keadby, Lincolnshire, to Sheffield; 43m with 29 locks. The whole waterway admits craft 61ft 6in × 15ft 6in × 6ft draught × 10ft headroom. Substantially larger craft can at present reach Doncaster, and important improvements planned for the later 1970s will considerably upgrade the commercial capacity of the waterway. The S&SY was formed in 1895 with the amalgamation of a number of individual waterways. These were the Stainforth & Keadby, from the Trent to the River Don at Stainforth, completed in 1802; the Don (or Dun) Navigation, between Stainforth and Tinsley, which was fully operational by 1751; and the Sheffield Canal, from Tinsley to Sheffield Basin, completed in 1819. In addition to several short branches, the S&SY Co had joint control (with the Undertakers of the Aire & Calder Navigation) of the New Junction Canal (otherwise known as the A&C&S&SY Junction Canal), linking the Don at Bramwith with the main line of the A&C. This section was opened as recently as 1905, enabling the well-known Tom Pudding compartment coal-boat trains to reach the Sheffield & South Yorkshire. One further waterway operated by the S&SY was the 9½m Dearne & Dove Canal, running between the Don at Swinton and the A&C's Barnsley Canal. All but ½m of the D&D, with 4 locks at Swinton, was abandoned in 1961, while the Barnsley had been totally closed by 1953. In spite of the apparent complexity of the S&SY, the through route between Keadby and Sheffield is, in fact, a logical entity and is most easily regarded as one single waterway.

South Yorkshire is undeniably industrial, and the navigation is no stranger to coal traffic and many outbreaks of manufacturing squalor. The true horror of the area is alarmingly evident to anyone making the short train journey from Doncaster to Sheffield, past great steelworks, factories, coalmines and slagheaps. Coal, of course, was a major factor in the development of the waterway, which in turn allowed such natural resources to be exploited. In spite of this background, parts of the S&SY are extremely pleasant, notably near Conisbrough. Elsewhere the interest of a journey is kept alive by the procession of commercial boats and the honest but sometimes grim face of a waterway that still contributes to the national transport pattern. Late in 1974 the BWB was authorised to upgrade the navigation between Doncaster and Rotherham at a cost of some £2·4 million, though finance had not then been provided. Thus, old keel-sized locks are to be replaced and awkwardly placed bridge holes and bends removed. Already the Board's own BACAT barges trade on the S&SY between the Humber ports and Rotherham, the 3 units and pusher tug requiring operation of each lock beyond Doncaster 4 times, since the train has to be broken down into its component units each time. When the enlargement has been completed, large motor barges and BACAT craft direct from the Continent will be able to use this, one of Britain's most flourishing freight waterways. An additional plan envisages remote surveillance and operation of locks and swing bridges from one of 3 Yorkshire control points at Swinton.

At present the number of visiting pleasure craft to the S&SY is few, although a growing interest in boating has resulted in sizeable moorings at Thorne, Doncaster and Sheffield. Anyone who reacts to the atmosphere generated by a commercial freight waterway should certainly cruise this route.

*Keadby* Normal entry to the S&SY for craft from other areas will be via the tidal Trent (see p 436). Pleasure boats can generally work through the lock at all states of the tide, but it is best to give notice of intended arrival by telephone, to ensure that the keeper, who also operates an adjacent swing bridge, is on duty. The village, dominated by a power station, is a centre of commercial activity, with wharves on the canal as well as on both banks of the Trent. The great steelworks of Scunthorpe lies several miles to the east. The majority of bridges along the Stainforth & Keadby section are swing spans worked by keepers (check opening times locally). The railway bridge by the power station is most unusual in that it slides sideways.

*Crowle* (3m 2f) Scenery is rather dull, over very flat but fertile fields. A busy railway hugs the canal bank as far as Thorne. Crowle Station is beside the waterway, but the little town lies a mile to the north. Most facilities are available. The former Regal cinema now contains a small but interesting car museum. Minor road swing bridges, each bearing intriguing names, are mainly worked manually by keepers living in isolated cottages.

*Thorne* (9m 7f) A busy town with many activities centred on the canal, it has a waterway maintenance yard, colourfully planted lock and 3 boatyards. One builds quite substantial commercial vessels – seagoing tugs and barges. Another specialises in the larger type of pleasure cruiser. The third is within the Ladyline Group and offers the usual range of grp canal craft, with well-stocked chandlery. Beyond the M18 high-level bridge is Fishlake village (12m 4f), with the fine medieval church of St Cuthbert, notable for its intricately carved late Norman doorway.

*Stainforth* (12m 7f) The remains of a side lock, closed in 1939, can be seen on the right. This originally provided access with the tidal River Don through Fishlake to Goole, a distance of 11m. The section from Newbridge beyond Fishlake to the Yorkshire Ouse, known as the Dutch River, was constructed in 1625 by the Dutch engineer Vermuyden. It is navigable between Goole and Bramwith Aqueduct, but is not an attractive proposition for pleasure craft, being dull, often very fast-flowing and indeed dangerous when there is plenty of 'fresh', following heavy rain. Stainforth offers little of interest.

*Bramwith Junction* (14m 7f) Having now joined the Don Navigation from the

Stainforth & Keadby, the route passes by the pleasing little village of Kirk Bramwith, situated between the canal, the Don and the New Junction. Ahead are the great towers of Thorpe Marsh power station, relying on the river for cooling water supplies. Beyond Bramwith swing bridge and lock the New Junction runs absolutely straight NE to connect with the Aire & Calder near Pollington.

*New Junction Canal*   This newcomer among British canals (completed in 1905) is considerably more interesting than its unswerving course might suggest. The country-side is still flat, but rural, and all bridges carry very minor roads. Care should be exer-cised when passing long trains of Tom Puddings, whose steering tends to be erratic in windy conditions. There are 3 navigation features in the 5½m – Sykehouse Lock and swing bridge, 3½m from Bramwith, and a pair of really impressive aqueducts taking the canal over the Don at Bramwith and the River Went just before the A&C junction. Each is equipped with a towering pair of guillotine gates that can be lowered either to isolate the structure from the canal if repairs are needed, or to prevent flood waters from the rivers increasing the canal level and thus causing a breach.

*Doncaster* (21m 2f)   The village of Barnby Dun (16m 2f) is now virtually a suburb of Doncaster, in the shadow of Thorpe Marsh power station. Its small church of St Peter and Paul is mostly early fourteenth-century. Navigation channel and natural river lie close together, but do not finally unite until the other side of Doncaster. Long Sandall Lock, with a rise and fall of 1ft 9in, was rebuilt with a 215ft chamber next to the old 63ft lock in 1959, enabling Tom Pudding trains and motorised barges to use the waterway with greater convenience. It is mechanised. Good pleasure-craft moor-ings may be arranged with the BWB. Industrial works and wasteland characterise the waterway until one reaches the city centre, with, by way of a complete and welcome contrast, the tree-shaded moorings of the energetic Strawberry Island Boat Club established in a backwater leading to the long-disused Milethorne Lock. Visitors are always given a rousing welcome. Doncaster is the centre of the South Yorkshire coalfield and has a famous racecourse. An instructive and enjoyable outing should be made to Cusworth Hall Museum, NW of the town near the M1. One room of this remarkable collection of documents and objects relating to the industrial history of the county is concerned with navigable waterways (see p 198). Doncaster's lock lurks beneath bridges and has a friendly lock-keeper with suitably aggressive-looking guard dog. (Fierce dogs are a feature of the navigation, but seem to be able to distinguish between genuine boaters and potential vandals.) At present this is the last of the large locks and is capable of accommodating a 3-unit BACAT train and pusher tug in one working.

*Conisbrough* (27m 1f)   The 5m between Doncaster and Conisbrough offer delight-ful cruising through a steeply banked wooded gorge. This begins near a tall M1 viaduct at Sprotborough (23m 5f), with a lock and short cut. Vast limestone quarries, however, cast a white dust on the trees, and the water is black and uninviting; 90-ton barges thunder along the deep navigation, their bluff bows either pushing a wall of water when loaded, or towering up if unladen. Until the autumn of 1972 there was a shallow lock at Conisbrough, but this is now removed and the first weir downstream has been raised to compensate for the change in levels. Conisbrough is industrial, hilly and rather impressive, with a magnificent twelfth-century castle whose keep is

66ft in diameter at the base and 90ft tall. Castle and grounds are open to the public.

*Mexborough* (28m 5f)   Once more the surroundings degenerate and remain urban, on and off, right through to Sheffield. There are coalmines and slagheaps all around this drab little mining town. The public houses are lively in a down to earth fashion. There are 2 locks.

*Swinton Junction* (30m 2f)   Little remains of the well-known pottery, which produced Rockingham china between 1745 and 1842. Beyond Swinton Lock is the junction with the Dearne & Dove Canal, derelict except for 4 locks and a short length still occasionally used by barges travelling to a glassworks. Messrs E. V. Waddington, a canal carrying firm founded about 1770, operate a fleet of more than 70 90-ton steel barges from their repair yard and drydock here. They provide the S&SY with the major part of its traffic. The Swinton yard is a splendid place of assorted buildings, discarded boat engines, hatch covers and propellers, presided over by Victor Wadding-ton, who believes that waterway transport in Yorkshire will inevitably make a big comeback. In 1973 he began construction of a large drydock at the entrance of the D&D, where 400-ton barges will be built and maintained in readiness for the enlarge-ment of the adjoining navigation. Three canal inns keep close company at the head of the locks. The main navigation channel continues along the Mexborough cut, through Ford's flood lock and Kilnhurst flood lock, where it rejoins the exceptionally twisting course of the Don.

*Rotherham* (35m 6f)   Patches of scrubby country are mixed with waste tips and collieries at the approach to Rotherham, where locks increase in frequency. There is one at Aldwarke, 2 at Eastwood and a further (flood) lock in the town itself. Gruff but friendly keepers give willing help to pleasure craft. Rotherham has important water-side warehousing facilities to which the BACAT barges trade, and much heavy industry, of which steel production, in common with Sheffield, is the leading activity. The fifteenth-century All Saints church provides a memorable feature of the town centre. A fifteenth-century bridge over the Don boasts a little chapel that after the Reformation was used as prison, almshouse and tobacconist's until its restoration in 1924. The unnavigable River Rother, running from the upper reaches of the Chester-field Canal, feeds the waterway, and the Don also flows in and out until it is finally left shortly below the first of the locks on the Sheffield Canal.

*Tinsley* (Bottom Lock, 39m)   Three more locks (Ickles, Holmes and Jordan) lead to a long, curved and completely unprotected weir (left). Now begins the Sheffield Canal, classed as a 'remainder' waterway under the 1968 Transport Act; there are no plans to enlarge its locks to enable 400-ton barges to reach the heart of the city. A massive steel viaduct on 2 levels carries the M1 and another road across the valley. Nearby a small brick building originally housed a steam pump to lift water to the canal's top pound, but the pump was replaced in 1918 by a pair of 125hp diesel engines that are still at work, one at a time, shifting almost 3,500 gallons a minute. The outlet can be seen immediately above the top lock. Tinsley locks are numbered 1 to 12 from the top, but since 1959 there have only been 11 for 7 and 8 were combined in a new concrete chamber with a rise and fall of about 12ft. This enabled construction of a low railway bridge, but with sufficient clearance for boats beneath. Another lock is of interest in that it bears a painted sign commemorating the fact that it was blitzed by enemy action in December 1940. Tinsley locks are impressive, with their monumental stonework, heavy paddle gear and enlarged intervening pounds.

*Sheffield* (43m)   The run-in to Sheffield basin is characterised by many bridges (one, partly dismantled, was a bascule), and a single-arched stone aqueduct over the Worksop road. At one stage there is a 40ft cutting, with rubbish spilling down the slopes from terraced houses along the brink. The canal saves its *pièce de résistance* until it finally turns into Sheffield basin, when a magnificent group of warehouses may be seen, some projecting over the water so that goods could be hauled from barges direct to the storage floors. All is now derelict and decaying, in spite of a Department of the Environment preservation order. Some use is made of this splendid haven by pleasure-craft moorings, but the potential is virtually untapped. Sheffield could have the most exciting canal basin in Britain (in other ways, the city has displayed commendable originality in its new municipal buildings and soaring blocks of flats). That the basin is dangerously unkempt is not entirely unconnected with its value as a prime development site. One hopes for the best, but is fearful for the future. Sheffield has much to offer the water traveller, from many beautiful parks to the City Museum and Art Gallery – the museum has an excellent collection recording the history of cutlery and Sheffield plate manufacture. Several miles to the south is the Abbeydale Industrial Hamlet, preserved as a completely original and intact eighteenth-century water-powered scythe factory. The whole process from start to finish is shown in delightful stone buildings clustered around a courtyard. This survival is quite remarkable, and Abbeydale is without doubt one of the most important and fascinating industrial museums in Britain.

### SHROPSHIRE UNION CANAL

From the Staffs & Worcs Canal at Autherley, near Wolverhampton, to Ellesmere Port, Cheshire, junction with the Manchester Ship Canal; 66½m with 46 locks. There is a branch of 10m from Barbridge, near Nantwich to Middlewich, junction with the Trent Mersey Canal, on which there are 4 locks.

Part of the extensive system of the Shropshire Union Railways & Canal Company's empire, the Shropshire Union Main Line is composed of 3 distinct sections. First is the line between Nantwich Basin and Chester, opened in 1774. Second comes the Wirral line (1796), northwards from Chester to the banks of the Mersey at Whitby, which later assumed the name of Ellesmere Port on account of the connection thus made with Ellesmere, Shropshire, via the Llangollen Canal. The third is the line southwards from Nantwich to Autherley, with Thomas Telford as engineer and not completed until 1835. The 3 waterways are quite noticeably different, reflecting the advances of engineering techniques over rather more than half a century. The SU Canal Company was formed in 1846, by the amalgamation of several older canal companies. Except at its extreme northern end, the waterway runs largely through rural areas, having been built rather late to attract the kind of industry that came to the banks of the earlier and parallel Trent & Mersey. Commercial traffic remained heavy until after World War II, including oil products and metals, and continued well into the 1960s. Craft dimensions are 71ft 6in × 7ft × 3ft 3in draught, Autherley–Nantwich and on the Middlewich Branch; 74ft 5in × 13ft 3in × 3ft 3in draught, Nantwich–Chester; and 74ft × 14ft 6in × 3ft 3in, Chester to Ellesmere Port.

*Autherley Junction*   A fine curving brick towpath bridge spans the T-junction with the Staffs & Worcs Canal near Wolverhampton. Beyond is a shallow stop lock with toll office manned by the legendary Sam Lomas until shortly before his death in 1970. Ahead, the canal stretches quite straight for a considerable distance, a characteristic of this, one of the last cross-country routes to be completed. Built to provide the shortest journey times between its terminal points, the Shropshire Union is noted for long straight cuts, deep cuttings and dramatically high embankments with a minimum of locks. Where locks do occur, they are mainly grouped in convenient flights as far as Nantwich. Large numbers of pleasure craft lie on moorings at each side of the canal beyond the junction, showing rather clearly that marinas are visually preferable if kept off the main navigation; this policy has now been officially recognised, and one may hope for a decrease in linear moorings in future. Of 2 original red- and blue-brick boat-horse stables remaining, one has been well converted into the premises of the Autherley Boat Club. Facilities include a well-stocked shop and chemical WC disposal point. Many of the bridges of this canal are in the best traditions of the Telford era, being built of finely dressed stone and showing good proportions. No 3 is a roving bridge, beyond which are the moorings of the Wolverhampton Boat Club. The hint of Wolverhampton lingers until one reaches Pendeford Bridge (no 4), where real country begins, to last almost all the way to Chester, more than 50m off. Through Staffordshire and Shropshire into Cheshire the SU traverses some of the best scenery in the West Midlands, especially attractive where wide views are obtainable from the embankments.

*Brewood* (5m)   The first rocky cutting appears between Bridges 4 and 5, narrow and tree-lined in contrast to other sections of the waterway, which are quite wide. Some magnificent larches introduce another cutting, spanned by Avenue Bridge (no 10), the open classical balustrade of which was designed in deference to the Giffard family whose drive to Chillington Hall, dating from the reign of Henry II, crosses here. Nearest approach to Brewood (pronounced 'Brood') is at Bridge 12, an unexpected brick arch. There are some very deep towline abrasions under these bridges. Shops and a pub are about ¼m distant. The church stands on the right, its red sandstone square tower surmounted by a spire with tiny turrets at each corner. A small basin beyond Bridge 14 has been delightfully landscaped, and a cottage restored as a base for Countrywide Cruisers. The stump of an old crane is a reminder that here was once a bustling wharf. Soon afterwards one approaches the substantial single-arched Stretton Aqueduct carrying Telford's canal over his A5 Holyhead Road. Both stonework and cast-iron railings are examples of good design.

*Wheaton Aston* (7m 6f)   A wide range of flowers may be seen in the approaches to Lapley Wood Cutting during summer, with an equally interesting selection of elm, sycamore, hawthorn, and ash. Wheaton Aston Lock, beyond Bridge 18, is the only change in level in about 25m. Its original cottage is now sadly ruined. The Hartley Arms Inn stands by Bridge 19. Further cuttings at Rye Hill and High Onn (9m 6f) are followed by a beautiful tract of open farmland, with a small wharf and warehouse by Bridge 25.

*Gnosall* (13m)   Telford's original plan had been to construct a tunnel at Cowley (690yd), and the engineer in charge, William Provis, began work in the summer of

1830 at the northern end. Dangerously crumbling rock, however, demanded that pro-gressively more and more tunnel be opened out, with the result that only 81yd of the initial bore remained. It is wide and impressive, being of unlined rock with a towpath. The cutting leading to the tunnel is deep and narrow, its cliff-like sides draped with young trees, moss and ferns that create an almost tropical gloom when there is summer foliage. Gnosall village has two canal pubs in the Boat Inn (Bridge 34) and the Navigation Inn (Bridge 35). In fact, the Shropshire Union is amply provided with pubs.

*Norbury Junction* (15m 4f)   A high, long and partly wooded embankment, with several places where stop planks can be inserted in the event of a burst, is pierced twice (Bridges 37A and 37B) by tunnel-like roads, both of them blind corners. The embank-ment leads into Norbury, a busy little canal centre from which 28m of the Shrewsbury Canal were formerly navigable past Newport (with a branch to the Donnington Wood tub-boat canal). The main section was closed under the notorious 1944 LNWR Act, and enthusiastic efforts to secure its restoration during the mid-1960s were refused official support to the extent that a section of canal bed was deliberately removed at Norbury as if to deter future recovery work. Boat moorings in the short pound leading to the first of the Newport locks culminate in the lock chamber, now used as a con-venient drydock. Interesting relics of these Shropshire canals are gradually becoming more difficult to find, as remains of locks and aqueducts are removed. Between Wap-penshall Junction and Trench the narrow locks were the narrowest in England, admit-ting a boat of only 6ft 2in beam. A 123yd inclined plane on the Donnington Wood Canal at Lilleshall last worked under steam power in 1879, whereas that at Trench continued in use until 1921. Telford was concerned with the building of the first iron aqueduct in Britain at Longdon-on-Tern (to be preserved on a new site at the Iron-bridge Museum), and the relics of unusual guillotine lock gates can be found on the Shrewsbury section. A good guide to exploration of this and other derelict canals is Ronald Russell's *Lost Canals of England and Wales* (David & Charles).

Canal company workshops at Norbury have been largely taken over by a pleasure-boat firm, but the low single-storey buildings are substantially unchanged from their original design. The same cannot be said of the Junction Inn, an old pub's modern replacement, whose amenity value is only part compensation for its ugly and anony-mous exterior. Norbury has a wide basin and flourishes in a new affluence brought by pleasure craft.

*Shebdon* (19m 4f)   The grand scale of the Shropshire Union cannot be taken to imply that its construction was any easy matter. Some of the problems encountered delayed completion for several years, while the company directors almost despaired of boats ever getting through. The final troubles almost certainly contributed to the death of Telford in September 1834, the year before work was finished. Just beyond Nor-bury the 80ft-deep Grub Street cutting, extending for rather over a mile, was subject to constant rock falls during construction. One of the most dramatic points is at High Bridge (no 39), where one arch is stacked on top of another, with a telegraph pole set on the central support. Such poles follow many miles of the waterway, which, under one ownership, was a convenient track along which to erect them. In much the same way the railway companies granted wayleaves for telephone lines. Spoil from these cuttings was transported by tramway and in some cases by boat to build up the great embankments further along the route. Just before Bridge 42, near High Offley, stands the Anchor Inn, one of the most charming and unspoilt canal pubs on the British network. The inn was a typical mooring for horseboats, which was bypassed as commercial craft became motorised. Nevertheless it retained both its licence and its unpretentious character, with oak settles and (almost) sawdust on the floor. For many decades the landlady was the late Mrs Lily Pascall, who carried beer from the cellar glass by glass until the end of the 1960s, although then at a very advanced age. It is to be hoped that the Anchor can resist the modern trend for revamping canal pubs. It opens on Friday nights, Saturdays and Sundays only.

Shebdon Great Bank, 1m in length and 60ft high, was the cause of Telford failing to live to see his last canal completed. Construction began on the embankment in 1829 but was not finished for 6 years, as the structure constantly shifted, partly collapsed and consistently failed to hold water. Planting of grasses helped to make it stable, and today you cruise on a level with the top branches of trees growing on its lower slopes.

*Knighton* (21m)   Cadbury's waterside factory here was once supplied by narrow boats working to Bournville, and before World War II churns of milk by the dozen were conveyed to Knighton by narrow boat from the Cheshire dairy farms to the north. A feeder from Knighton reservoir enters on the right.

*Woodseaves Cutting* (24m)   Beyond Bridge 51 there are magnificent open views to the left of hilly fields dotted with trees. The canal is here 341ft above sea level, but soon begins the long descent towards the Mersey. By Bridge 55 stands the Wharf Tavern. From the next bridge onwards Woodseaves Cutting extends for nearly 2m

*Shropshire Union Canal. One of the five locks at Tyrley near Market Drayton*

reaching a depth of 90ft. It is carved through dangerously friable rock that is now hung with ferns thriving in the damp habitat. The towpath frequently becomes a quagmire, a condition not helped by dredgings from the channel being piled on this bank. The cutting is spanned by a memorable and exceptionally tall bridge (no 57), whose sides appear to slope inwards down to water level. Trees arch over the canal, sometimes blocking out the sky and producing an atmosphere that can be slightly menacing at night. It is easy here to believe in the boat people's ghost stories.

*Tyrley Locks* (25m 2f)   The long pound extending from Wheaton Aston comes to an end in a very pretty flight of 5 locks, falling through 33ft. A wharf at the top possesses an outstanding group of buildings with stone-mullioned windows that mix local stone with red brick. They are dated 1837. Between Locks 1 and 2 is a typical Shropshire Union keeper's single-storey cottage. As the flight nears the bottom, another rocky cutting begins. The ground then falls away, with a single-arched aqueduct taking the canal over the River Tern shortly before it reaches the border between Staffordshire and Shropshire. Here, for the second time, the waterway passes into the county giving it its name.

*Market Drayton* (26m 5f)   The full use of the waterway made by pleasure-boating firms has made it necessary to create a major cruiser centre. In the basin between Bridges 62 and 63 the former commercial wharves are utilised by Holidays Afloat Ltd. There is a fine warehouse at Market Drayton Wharf. Beyond the bridge is the main base of the Ladyline Group, where large purpose-built boat showrooms and a chandlery complement a specially excavated marina accommodating many cruisers moored at right-angles to the canal. The fullest possible boating facilities and services are available. Market Drayton lies ½m to the left, an attractive old town with many seventeenth- and eighteenth-century black and white half-timbered houses. The market, founded almost 700 years ago, is held each Wednesday. The annual fair, in the autumn, was formerly an important gathering of horse dealers, who would gather from the Welsh hills and surrounding area. While a pupil at the sixteenth-century Grammar School, Robert Clive (Clive of India) climbed the tower of St Mary's Church and perched on one of the gargoyles. Mainly fourteenth-century, St Mary's also has a fine Norman doorway. Coaching inns include the Corbet Arms, and for those who prefer to get wet outside there is a large Shropshire Lido, whose swimming bath is a popular attraction with families taking holidays on the canal.

Just beyond Bridge 64, Lord's Bridge, a 3-leaved cast-iron mile post marks the distance to Nantwich (12m), Autherley (27m) and Norbury. Dating from the 1830s, similar posts can be seen elsewhere on the Shropshire Union, on the Trent & Mersey Canal, and also on the A5 Holyhead Road, suggesting that the design was widely available about that time.

A well-proportioned roving bridge (no 67) at Betton Coppice marks the area where a shrieking ghost is said to haunt a wooded cutting. The dark deed that gives rise to this superstition is forgotten, but doubtless there is some basis in fact for the rigid refusal of narrow-boat families ever to lie there for the night.

*Adderley Locks* (29m 7f)   A flight of 5 closely placed locks is pleasantly rural, with the village about ½m to the left. The Cheshire/Shropshire border follows between Bridges 73 and 74, where a beautiful deep valley may be seen from an embankment.

*Audlem* (31m 4f)  A flight of 15 locks spread over 1½m marks one of the most pleasant sections on a narrow canal. Well spaced out at the top, they move nearer together as the series descends. The design of lock bypass weirs varies from open cascades to standard culverts, and care should be taken when cruising past the fast-flowing outfalls. A pretty keeper's bungalow in brick and slate stands by the top lock, as does a similar one near Kingbur Mill at Bridge 78, most convenient access point for Audlem village, a short distance to the right. The Gothic twelfth-century church of St James the Great possesses a well-preserved oak ceiling, and a number of timber-framed houses can be seen nearby. The variety of lock-keepers' huts is considerable, those contemporary with the canals themselves displaying early industrial architecture in miniature. For instance, the one by the bottom lock has red-brick walls and chimneystack under a slate roof. A new housing development dominates the lower end of the flight, which provides their occupiers with a panorama of cruisers moving up and down. A lovely old stable block by Bridge 79 (now a private residence) bears a painted sign warning that the stables are for the use of the Shropshire Union Company's own animals only.

The character of the waterway now changes with the advance into the green Cheshire meadows, where cuttings become things of the past, although embankments, like that leading to Moss Hall Aqueduct over the River Weaver, retain the proportions of earlier counterparts. From here the Weaver flows through Nantwich, becoming navigable above Winsford.

*Nantwich* (38m 7f)  The last pair of narrow locks on the Shropshire Union are Hack Green, each side of Bridge 86, where another stable has 2 wooden ventilators running along the apex of the roof. A long curving embankment carries the waterway over a single-arched cast-iron aqueduct spanning the A51 Chester Road. But for the objections of the owner of Dorfold Park, this ½m Nantwich Bank would have been unnecessary; during construction there were constant problems in making it stable and to this day its condition must be frequently checked to avoid serious flooding on the outskirts of the town. A large basin lying off the main canal is the original terminus of the Chester Canal. It is set among several quality warehouses and associated buildings sympathetically restored and painted in tertiary colours – olive, ochre, grey, black and white – and forms a base for the BWB northern hire-cruiser fleet. Starting here and extending a long distance northwards are the private moorings of the Nantwich & Border Counties Yacht Club, with a collection of mainly good-looking and well-cared-for boats. Situated about ½m to the SE, Nantwich is an old salt-producing centre. (*Wych* means a brine spring, and similar uses of the word occur in place names in Worcestershire and other parts of Cheshire.) Among a number of fine timber-framed houses is the magnificent Churche's Mansion, an Elizabethan merchant's dwelling dating from 1577, painstakingly restored by E. C. Myott after a threat to transport it to the United States. The mansion is open to the public every day and it contains an excellent restaurant. The red sandstone church of St Mary's has a central octagonal tower, some fine stone carving and fascinating carved choirstalls with grotesque oak misericords depicting a strange collection of beasts, knights, dragons and monks. Near the rather neglected River Weaver in the town centre stands an elaborate Victorian Gothic savings bank. Several miles to the NE the conurbation of Crewe provides excellent transport services to the area by rail, with frequent buses into Nantwich.

*Barbridge Junction* (42m 1f)   The flight of locks at the start of the Llangollen Canal bears away to the left at Hurleston Junction (40m 6f), to be immediately followed by the tall grassed bank of Hurleston reservoir. The surrounding countryside is pleasantly open. An embankment enables boat crews to look down on the village of Barbridge, with its terraced cottages, along the A51 Chester road. Here is a T-junction with the Shropshire Union's Middlewich Branch (see below), where a long low building once acted as a boatmen's mission church. A wooden cross still stands at one end. The canal alongside there was once bridged by a wide slated roof and footbridge protecting a gauging point underneath; it looked rather like another roof over Etruria Lock on the Trent & Mersey, also now removed. Near the water a charming canal pub, the Jolly Tar, has been replaced by a no doubt more profitable but characterless roadhouse of the same name. Barbridge is a popular boating area, with extensive moorings and facilities at the junction, developed in part because of the closeness of the Llangollen Canal.

*Middlewich arm*   A quiet 10m link between the main line at Barbridge and the Trent & Mersey Canal in Middlewich, this narrow-beam canal was a latecomer, not being opened until 1833. Once clear of the double line of moorings past Ladyline's Barbridge marina, the canal passes through characteristic rolling Cheshire meadows. Cholmondeston Lock (1m 3f) precedes a large marina development and caravan park operated by Venetian Marine. The deep Minshull Lock, with a rise and fall of 11ft 6in (3m), is followed by an embankment and high aqueduct over the River Weaver. Church Minshull (4m 7f) is a pretty village near Bridge 14 containing several exquisite timber-framed houses. From Bridge 22 there are excellent views down to the Top Flash of the Weaver, upstream of its navigable limit near Winsford (p 440). Stanthorne Lock (9m 1f) marks the outskirts of Middlewich (10m). It is succeeded by a pair of aqueducts, one over the River Wheelock and the other spanning a road. The final lock, Wardle, and a few yards to the junction with the Trent & Mersey Canal are technically a branch of the T&M.

*Bunbury* (44m 7f)   The character of the old Chester Canal north of Nantwich is quite different from the later Birmingham & Liverpool Junction. Gone are the narrow locks, deep cuttings, embankments and long straights. Instead the waterway now wanders more, and pleasure-boat movement, reduced beyond Barbridge, is quite insignificant north of Chester. A twin staircase of locks lies NE of Bunbury village, a collection of well-cared-for cottages around the fourteenth- and fifteenth-century church of St Boniface. Left of the locks stands a most satisfying group of canal buildings in red brick and slate, including a very long stable block now used for constructing new steel narrow boats. Apart from the removal of stalls, it remains in substantially original condition. A section nearest the bridge was set aside for veterinary purposes. The gable end of a warehouse still advertises in faded lettering 'Shropshire Union Rys and Canal Co Carriers', more than half a century after these activities have ceased. The side weir bypassing the 15ft 7in rise locks terminates at its lower end in a broad pool.

*Tilstone Lock* (45m 5f)   One of the prettiest pounds on this upper length of the canal follows Bunbury Locks, with hilly broken ground, well wooded. A charming small watermill by Tilstone Mill Bridge is now used by local Scouts. Alongside the lock is one of several circular lengthsmen's huts, solidly built in brick and stone with fireplace and chimney, and, an intriguing feature, the bowed wooden door maintaining the line of the walls. Others can be found at Beeston Stone Lock (containing a water point) and at Tarvin Road Lock, Chester.

*Beeston* (46m 5f)   The Stone Lock is so called to distinguish it from Beeston Iron Lock, which follows a short distance beyond. The chamber is formed of massive iron plates joined diagonally in much the same style as at Longdon-upon-Tern and Pontcysyllte Aqueducts, and is dated 1828. An original lock had caused much trouble as a result of unstable sand at the site, and had collapsed in November 1787. But it was not until the building of the 2 new Beeston locks, with a short section of realigned canal, 40 years later that the problem was permanently overcome.

Nearest approach (under 1m) to the ruins of thirteenth-century Beeston Castle is south from the canal at Wharton's Bridge (no 108). The Castle occupies a virtually impregnable 740ft hilltop offering wide views of the Cheshire Plain. Built about 1220 by an Earl of Chester, it was reduced to ruins at the time of the Civil War. Its 370ft deep well is reputed to conceal the treasure of Richard II in passages near the base, but attempts to recover this wealth in recent times have failed. Administered by the Ministry of Public Buildings and Works, the Castle is open for a small charge throughout the year. Its immediate surroundings of rocks, bracken and pines present a challengingly steep walk to the summit. A neighbouring structure to the S is nineteenth-century Peckforton Castle, designed by Anthony Salvin.

*Waverton* (53m 6f)   Several miles of pleasant countryside follow. There is an aqueduct over the diminutive River Gowy between Bridges 111 and 112, and beyond that a shallow cutting. Overlooking Egg Bridge (no 119) is the magnificent Waverton Mill in red brick, which has been converted into the offices of a boat and caravan company. To the left lies Rowton Moor, scene of the final sizeable battle of the Civil War in 1645, after which the defeated Charles I retreated to nearby Chester. Christleton (55m 3f), although close to Chester, keeps its individuality and character. A boatyard at Rowton Bridge (no 120) generates most of the activity in the area.

*Chester* (57m)   The approach by canal is rather typical of most canals in large towns, and the city is seen to better advantage when cruising down the River Dee. From Christleton, urban development closes in, but there are many notable features on the waterway, among them a nineteenth-century warehouse with projecting unloading canopy by Quarry Bridge (no 121). Between Christleton and Greenfield Locks an aqueduct carries the canal over the railway to Crewe. The Shropshire Union descends rapidly to the Dee via 11 locks in less than 3m, each lock with a fall of 8–9ft. The area is memorable for the number of well-kept lock cottages remaining, particularly that at Chemistry Lock, whose small but defiantly magnificent garden is bisected by the open bypass weir. There are terraced houses on the right and facing them water-supply filter beds, with a flamboyant brick and iron Victorian water tower. Access to the canal is good, and although the immediate surroundings are given over to light engineering and warehouses, the industrial development is tidy.

Best mooring for city centre and shops is on the towpath south of Cow Lane Bridge (no 123E). Chester retains virtually all its surrounding walls, providing a delightful traffic-free 2m walk, often at rooftop level. Portions of Roman stonework remain, but most date from the Middle Ages, with Tudor and Civil War additions. At the race-course – the Roodee – a large section of harbour wall constructed by the Romans is visible. East of Newgate lies Britain's largest Roman amphitheatre, the city streets follow their Roman pattern, and many fascinating remains of this period characterise Chester. A massively decorative clock spanning the road at Eastgate commemorates Victoria's diamond jubilee of 1897. There is much black and white timbered architecture, both ancient and nineteenth-century. One most unusual feature is the access to many shops at first-floor level along covered pedestrian walkways known collectively as 'The Rows'.

Passing the city walls, which rise sheer from the canal towpath, the Shropshire Union enters a deep rocky cutting. King Charles' Tower stands directly above, housing a Civil War exhibition on two floors. Three lock chambers gouged from the solid sandstone form the impressive Northgate Staircase, with a total fall of 33ft. There are landscaped banks at the top where the new ringroad (opened 1966) spans the waterway and then plunges through the city wall. A well-designed free-standing plaque of slate and granite marks the bicentenary of the Chester Canal in 1972. A stone model of Grosvenor Bridge spanning the Dee lies half concealed in undergrowth at the bottom of the staircase. The sheer size and weight of the Northgate lock gates call for greater efforts when working through than is normal. Diving under a railway bridge below the locks, the canal takes a sharp turn to the right to enter the broad reach by Tower Wharf, originally the company headquarters, and still a waterways maintenance centre. There is a fine red-brick Georgian office building, small warehouses and manual crane (right), while ahead a pretty cast-iron roving bridge takes the towpath from left to right. Alongside the towpath a short branch connects with the tidal Dee via 3 wide locks, the lowest rebuilt in 1970 during roadworks. This branch leaves the main line at an acute hairpin junction. An elegant slate-roofed drydock, fitted with a single 14ft wide gate, stands between the canal and the branch. There are good safe moorings in the area, which, although pleasant, would benefit from controlled tree-planting, landscaping and encouragement as a public amenity. Taylor's old-established boatyard, specialising in the building and repair of pleasure craft, was sold to new owners in 1974.

*Ellesmere Port* (66m 4f)   The remaining waterway from Chester is rather deserted and slightly forlorn, pretty in sections but generally unremarkable. There is little evidence of boating activity and fewer facilities offered than hitherto. Bridge 132 at Mollington, which carries the Chester–Birkenhead railway, is approached via a splendid red stone viaduct dated 1839 and is thus representative of the earliest years of British railway architecture. Caughall Bridge (no 134) is within easy walking distance of Chester Zoo, where the most natural environment possible for wild animals has been adopted. The well-cultivated grounds include a small canal with boat trips. From Stanney (64m 3f) the ever-growing and vast Stanlow oil refineries and storage depots dominate the scene, with views northwards over the wide Mersey and east to the National Trust's Helsby Hill, 462ft above marshland on the river bank. Heavy industry crowds into the canal's surroundings, lit at night by the flaming torches of the refineries.

Ellesmere Port dates only from the opening of the system now known as the Shropshire Union. Until the late 1960s the old canal town around the junction of the Shropshire Union and the Manchester Ship Canal was perhaps the premier survival of an early nineteenth-century British waterway centre. A flight of neglected narrow locks runs parallel with broad ones past a complex of unloading basins to enter the Ship Canal via a 'sea lock' which, until the building of the Ship Canal, connected directly with the Mersey. A charming little lighthouse dating from 1795 marks the entrance. The Whitby Locks, and acres of canal warehousing providing dozens of covered barge berths, were leased to the MSC Co in 1922. Until after World War II, the Port was alive with constant boat movement, functional yet picturesque, with its massive arched warehouses over the water, gas lamps, and steam engines supplying power to cranes and other plant. Gradually commercial use declined. Vandalism at various levels, coupled with apparent complete disinterest in the buildings by the owners, encouraged a national campaign to secure their restoration and preservation, culminated in the destruction by fire of the General Warehouse in April 1970. Since then much demolition, infilling of basins and accelerated decay have reduced the grandeur of Ellesmere Port to insignificance. But at least the water route from the Shropshire Union to the Ship Canal and Mersey remains tenuously open. What has happened here is a waterways equivalent of the destruction of Euston Station's Doric arch, underlining the lack of official respect granted to our industrial monuments. Passing vessels on the Ship Canal may be glimpsed through decayed buildings at Whitby Locks. A sea breeze blows off the mudflats of the Mersey beyond. Pleasure craft are permitted only to enter the Ship Canal if prior notification is made and certain stringent conditions of insurance and equipment guaranteed. In view of the size and frequent movement of commercial ships, these regulations are scarcely unreasonable.

### STAFFORDSHIRE & WORCESTERSHIRE CANAL

From the River Severn at Stourport, Worcestershire, to the Trent & Mersey Canal at Great Haywood, near Stafford; 46m 1f with 43 narrow locks.

Designed by James Brindley as part of the Grand Cross system linking Thames, Trent, Severn and Mersey, the canal was opened throughout in 1772, and became a very considerable commercial success. Last regular traffic was the carriage of Cannock Chase coal to Stourport power station, on which 70 pairs of narrow boats were employed, but this ceased abruptly during the 1950s. The Staffs & Worcs is a remarkably attractive waterway to navigate, with its deep narrow cuttings through red sandstone, small-scale locks and bridges, and a mellow timeless atmosphere. In spite of the proximity of much of its route to the industrial centres of the West Midlands, the canal remains largely rural. Few other waterways so well convey the spirit of the early canals.

While the channel tends to be shallow in parts and the locks rather narrower than is normal, maximum dimensions of craft are 70ft × 7ft × 3ft draught × 7ft 6in headroom.

*Stourport-on-Severn*　Originally known as Lower Mitton, the town owes its existence entirely to the arrival of the canal. In spite of some ill-conceived destruction of its eighteenth-century character and buildings, Stourport is a substantial survival of a canal town. A series of connected basins overlooking the Severn are equipped with sets of both broad and narrow gauge locks. The narrow flight nearest the Severn bridge is that now normally used unless craft are too beamy. Once busy with narrow boats and local sailing barges (Severn trows), the basins now provide extensive pleasure-craft moorings, especially for river and seagoing craft. There are drydocks, boatyards and a good chandlery. Some lovely Georgian red-brick warehouses remain, one surmounted by a small clock tower and now headquarters of the Stourport Yacht Club. Two vast Georgian red-brick inns dominate the area by the canal basins: the first is the Angel, and the second the Tontine, opened in 1788 and named after the Italian Lorenzo Tonti's species of annuity whereby a certain number of persons placed money in a fund that eventually became the property of the survivor. Today Stourport manufactures carpets and boasts the largest chain-works in Europe. Shopping facilities are good. Remaining curiosities include a roller set on the parapet of a bridge spanning the narrow locks to take the wear from horseboat lines, a pretty cast-iron footbridge over the lower chamber of the narrow 2-rise locks by the river, and a splendid Victorian Gothic cottage, dated 1854, by York Street Lock. Canal souvenirs can be obtained from the former toll office. A few yards up the canal are the canal company's old workshops, which were turned into a hire-cruiser base in 1950. Best building is a blue- and red-brick warehouse with an overhanging roof supported on cast-iron columns.

A large number of the Staffs & Worcs bridges bear oval cast-iron plates bearing the bridge number and (more unusual) its name also. The River Stour follows the line of the canal on the right, and shortly after Oldington Bridge (no 10) one may see the remains of a disused canal arm and Pratt's Bridge Lock, which enabled coal and iron to be carried via the Stour to the Wilden Ironworks until about 1949. Soon after comes Falling Sands Lock, whose name commemorates the instability of the red sandstone through which so much of the canal is carved. It has a pretty iron footbridge below the bottom gates which is made in 6 sections bolted together but leaving a gap at the centre through which towlines could be passed. Similar structures can be found on the Stratford, Caldon, and Trent & Mersey Canals. A superb Victorian cottage here was allowed (like so many others throughout the country) to fall into decay and was demolished about 1961. Similarly, one at the next lock (Caldwall) built into the face of a cliff disappeared in the late 1960s. Both were unique examples of domestic architecture and added much to their surroundings.

*Kidderminster* (4m 3f)   Some good wooded surroundings, with the Stour remaining close by, are replaced gradually by somewhat decayed buildings and a really tumbledown group at the tunnel-like entrance to Kidderminster Lock. The town's carpet-making industry was established in the eighteenth century, and exhibits illustrating its history can be seen in a museum in Exchange Street. Apart from a late-medieval red sandstone church, with many interesting monuments, there is little of note in the town, lately subjected to extensive redevelopment. Creditable attempts have been made to landscape the surroundings of the lock, beyond which the canal soon crosses the dirty waters of the Stour on a small aqueduct. There are convenient moorings for the town above the lock.

Stourvale Ironworks on the left bank shortly before Wolverley Court Lock marks the end of Kidderminster's industrial surroundings. The Lock Inn by Wolverley Lock boasts a fine collection of horse gear and harness. A few hundred yards to the left on the top of a hill is an unusual open-roofed sandstone cavern with an iron gate which used to be a pound for strayed animals and, because of its form, is believed to be unique.

Now comes an excitingly narrow, wooded and rocky section of canal, the banks sometimes rising 20ft sheer from the water. Most of the original canal bridges are of

*Staffordshire & Worcestershire Canal. An early tunnel through red sandstone and complete with towpath at Cookley*

red brick with stone round the arch and along the parapets. Few are identical. Massive twisted oaks and other deciduous trees must date from after the cutting of the waterway, although many look much more than 200 years old. Alongside Debdale (or Cookley) Lock, a substantial cave in the sandstone by the lock chamber doubtless acted as a canal company store and keeper's shelter. The 65yd Cookley tunnel, complete with towpath, passes through sandstone, its roof lined with brick. A massive slab of rock considerably overhangs the canal just before Austcliff Bridge (no 24), the top covered with a thick cluster of oaks. Passing now from Worcestershire to Staffordshire, the canal comes to Whittington Lock, where the attractive well-maintained cottage is privately occupied.

Whittington Horse Bridge (no 28) provides best access to the ancient oak-timbered Whittington Inn, originally a manor house built in 1300 and once belonging to Dick Whittington's family. Lady Jane Grey's ghost, a 300yd secret tunnel and priests' hiding holes are some of its attractions. Queen Anne stayed here in 1711.

*Kinver* (10m 3f)   This small town lies a short distance to the west of Kinver Lock and is renowned for Kinver Edge, a long wooded cliff providing excellent views over Staffordshire. The Edge is National Trust property and the site of an early Iron Age fort; some ancient cave houses, several still occupied, can be seen. All boat services are available at the lock from Messrs Dawncraft, and day trips aboard narrow boat *Bellatrix* begin nearby at Hyde Bridge Lock (bridge no 30).

A deep rocky section leads to the 25yd Dunsley Tunnel, which would undoubtedly have been engineered as an open cutting if the canal had been built later.

*Stewponey* (12m)   Beside the Stourbridge–Bridgnorth A458 road, Stewponey takes its name from Estepona, and can be assumed to date from the Peninsular War. A very large public roadhouse dating from the 1930s replaced an earlier inn, the first Stewponey. Steaks are advertised. A pleasure-boat works (Dawncraft), and one of those circular lock weirs mainly but not exclusively associated with the Staffs & Worcs, are to be seen here. Thick undergrowth and swamps by the waterside give little indication that the Black Country is very close. Stourbridge, Tipton and Wolverhampton all lie in turn to the east, but the waterway seems to have effectively halted development to the west. At Stourton Junction sylvan surroundings give the Stourbridge Canal (see p 406) a good start on its journey into the fastnesses of the Birmingham Canal Navigations. Another aqueduct carries the canal over the River Stour. By the towpath just beyond Prestwood Bridge one may see the ruins of a canal roundhouse, whose purpose, like that of a similar complete example further on at Gailey, was to provide a lookout for toll collectors. Very isolated, it was inhabited until World War II.

*Hockley Lock* (14m 3f)   Here is a true circular weir, unlike that at Gothersley Lock, shortly before, which is more bottle-shaped. A cave by the lockside (the lock is also known as Rocky Lock) bears a sadly necessary notice: 'This cave is of historic interest. Do not deposit rubbish.' The former NCB-owned Ashwood Basin beyond Flatheridge Bridge (no 36) now provides a good mooring for cruisers. Beyond Bridge 38 comes Hinksford waterworks pumping station, in Victorian red brick but not unlike a castle in design. A steelworks run by Richard Thomas & Baldwins occupies most of the left bank between Swindon and Marsh Locks (16m 7f), operating at much reduced capacity. A range of services and pubs lie within easy reach of the canal at Bridge 40. Marsh Bridge (no 41) is a fine roving bridge, taking the towpath from the right to the left bank with long approach parapets. Botterham locks are 2-rise, with a bridge over the central gates. They have a total fall of 20ft, and working them single-handed necessitates climbing from the boat up the gates. For the first time since leaving Stourport the waterway is beginning to rise above the surrounding countryside, which, however, is becoming slightly urbanised as Wolverhampton draws near.

*The Bratch* (18m 7f)   This flight of 3 locks with a total fall of 30ft is not quite a riser, since there is a pound of only a few feet between each chamber. Operation must be attended to with care to avoid flooding, but a keeper is generally on hand. The whitewashed bridges, parapets and delightful octagonal toll-house comprise one of the most satisfying architectural complexes on a narrow canal. There is an extensive view from the top down on to the conical slate towers of Bilston waterworks. There is good fishing in a pair of reservoirs alongside the canal at Dimmingsdale Bridge (no 53). Permits are available locally.

*Compton Lock* (23m 2f)   Here James Brindley began construction of the canal, and beyond is a 10m summit pound to Gailey. The quality of the water is now similar to that of the Birmingham Canal Navigations, which locks down the Wolverhampton Flight at Aldersley Junction (25m 1f). The outfall from a nearby Wolverhampton sewage works does little to improve matters.

*Autherley Junction* (25m 5f)   Here the Shropshire Union enters on the left (see p 390). The slightly urbanised surroundings improve towards Coven village (28m 3f).

*Hatherton Junction* (31m)  The level of the canal's summit is maintained by a twisting course beyond Bridge 72, mainly through open heathland. Calf Heath Marina is established at Hatherton Junction, where the 3½m Hatherton branch of the S&W provided a link with the BCN's Churchbridge branch, leading in turn to the disused northern portion of the Cannock Extension Canal. This most useful connection survived until about 1954, when problems of mining subsidence near Cannock presented severe maintenance difficulties.

*Gailey* (33m 3f)  Here is the first of the locks that drop the canal towards the Trent & Mersey. The keeper's cottage includes a pretty circular tower in brick, from the top of which a view of approaching traffic could be obtained. Watling Street (A5) crosses at the tail of the lock, and ½m E are Gailey and Calf Heath reservoirs, situated either side of the M6 motorway and providing the navigation with water supplies. Six further locks lead the way to Penkridge. For several miles the peace of the canal is to some extent affected by the M6 motorway linking the Midlands with the NW.

*Penkridge* (36m 1f)  This is a bustling little town, with a good boatyard at the wharf, which takes its name from the River Penk. Longford Lock (36m 5f) is shortly followed by an M6 bridge and then by another lock, Park Gate, location of the Teddesley Boating Centre. Teddesley Park, right, is the agreeable wooded estate of a large mansion, now demolished. The motorway ends its association with the canal at Acton Trussell (38m 6f), and tranquillity returns for the remainder of the journey.

*Stafford* (42m)  This ancient county town, containing a number of fine buildings and a small museum and art gallery, was formerly connected with the main line of the S&W by a mile-long branch entered via Baswich Lock near Weeping Cross Bridge (no 101). This branch consisted of a canalised section of the River Sow and became derelict during the early 1920s. The best approach to the town is from Radford Bridge, no 98 (41m 2f).

*Milford* (43m 6f)  The S&W continues through agreeable open country extending for many miles to the south over Cannock Chase. This is the valley of the River Sow, which is spanned by a low canal aqueduct of brick arches in Milford.

*Tixall* (44m 6f)  The final lock (no 43), Tixall, introduces the strange and appealing Tixall Wide, a long broad reach more like a lake than an artificial narrow-beam canal. It seems likely that this was created to enhance the view from the Elizabethan Tixall Hall, which formerly stood in its park to the north but is now represented only by a huge and derelict stone gatehouse.

*Great Haywood Junction* (46m 1f)  This lovely eighteenth-century waterway completes its course at a junction with the Trent & Mersey Canal (p 428), beyond a wide but slender towpath bridge. Great Haywood wharf, with a collection of mellow red-brick warehouses, is one of several hire-cruiser bases operated by Anglo-Welsh Narrowboats. Other features are an aqueduct over the River Trent and a small brick lengthsmen's hut with iron lattice window frames.

## STORT, RIVER

From Bishop's Stortford to the River Lee near Rye House; 13¾m with 15 locks. Maximum craft dimensions are 88ft × 13ft 4in × 4ft draught and 6ft 3in headroom (after heavy rain this may be reduced, especially at Roydon railway bridge). The Stort is easily one of the prettiest navigations in Southern England, again and again recalling a Constable landscape. There are a number of fine weatherboarded mills typical of the Eastern Counties. All is quietly pastoral.

The river was made navigable between 1766 and 1769 by Sir George Duckett. Trade was mainly in agricultural produce. It was acquired by the Lee Conservancy in 1911 and the locks completely rebuilt during the next decade. A most useful and appealing plan to link the upper Stort with the Cam and other Fenland waterways less than 30m away was unfortunately never carried out.

*Bishop's Stortford*  Still an agricultural town serving the surrounding farming community. Just above the navigation limit are the foundations of Waytemore Castle, surrounded by public gardens. There are several fine timber-framed inns of the sixteenth and seventeenth centuries. Cecil Rhodes was born here, the Old Vicarage being a museum devoted to him. At South Mill Lock the river becomes rural and remains so for most of its course.

*Little Hallingbury* (3m 2f)  Twyford Mill is a charming Georgian building near the lock. A backwater above Tednambury Lock leads to Little Hallingbury Mill (brick and weatherboarding) and a boatyard. The village can boast a small pond, some timber-framed houses and a partly Norman church.

*Sawbridgeworth* (5m)  There is a derelict mill by the lock and operational maltings in the town, situated to benefit from barge traffic. (Commercial trade ceased in the 1940s.) Pishiobury Park, below Feakes Lock, was remodelled by James Wyatt from an earlier mansion, and the grounds were landscaped by Capability Brown. It is now a school.

*Harlow* (7m)  The original village lies near Harlow Lock. The New Town is situated by Burnt Mill Lock and Harlow Station. With an intended population of 80,000, the town was planned in 1947 as one of 8 overspill settlements around London. One of its notable features is the traffic-free pedestrian shopping area. Parndon Mill, by the lock of that name, is an arts and crafts centre, making and selling various products.

*Roydon* (12m)  After passing through some delightful countryside with further watermills, the canal reaches the village of Roydon, which has a waterside caravan site and a pretty eighteenth-century Gothic lock cottage bearing the Duckett arms (there is another similar but single-storey cottage at Brick Lock, just downstream). As on the Lee, railway stations serve many points. A curious shanty town exists near Lower Lock, last on the navigation. A short distance beyond, the river joins the Lee, which is here both wider and more exposed than the Stort.

## STOUR, RIVER (ESSEX AND SUFFOLK)

From Harwich, junction with the estuary of the River Orwell, to Sudbury; 35½m with 15 locks, of which some have vanished and none are at present workable. Large craft may navigate the tidal reaches upstream to a barrier at Cattawade Bridge. Thence to Sudbury the waterway is now suitable only for light craft that can be lifted round the lock sites and similar obstacles.

This is the world-famous river of John Constable, who immortalised the English landscape around his home at Dedham. With more than 24m of non-tidal water downstream of Sudbury, one would expect it to be in excellent order, preserved, perhaps as a national monument to the memory of Constable. The Government has been known to provide a grant of several hundred thousand pounds to keep a single painting in Britain, so why not a similar amount to secure the original living source of inspiration?

The 4 lower locks – Brantham, Flatford, Dedham, and Stratford St Mary – were rebuilt in 1933 to an original design incorporating unusual wooden lintel beams overhead. But they were little used and are not now available for craft. Passage from the sea has been prevented by the construction of the barrier at Cattawade in connection with water-supply works. The associated boat rollers are inefficient and inconvenient.

For all its drawbacks, the Stour is supreme among smaller English rivers, and navigating the full length from Sudbury really is like seeing the waterways through the eyes of Constable. While small craft appear to have every right to pass, objections may be raised both by landowners and anglers. The River Stour Trust will be pleased to advise. There are launching sites at Sudbury, Henny Street, Nayland, Dedham and from the Flatford towpath. Boats may be hired for local use in Sudbury, Dedham and Flatford. The river can show a number of fine watermills, a pipe-like tunnel under a road at Nayland, and many pleasant villages. One of Britain's largest gatherings of swans collects at Mistley in the tidal estuary. Commercial shipping docks at the quays and pleasure craft make full use of the broad sailing reaches here and on the adjoining Orwell. The area is a good one to see preserved Thames sailing barges. The River Stour Trust has recovered one of some 14 wooden horsedrawn barges abandoned in silt at Sudbury in 1918, and is working towards a complete restoration. It is an exact replica of the vessels depicted in Constable's pictures. His masterpiece 'The Leaping Horse' recalls the curious necessity for barge horses to jump stiles erected across the towpath.

## STOUR, RIVER (KENT)

From the coast at Pegwell Bay to Fordwich; 19¼m and tidal. An ancient navigation, the Stour has experienced many changes. In Roman times the Isle of Thanet (bounded by Margate, Broadstairs, Ramsgate and Minster) was an island indeed, divided from the mainland by the wide Wantsum Channel. Fordwich had become a flourishing port for Canterbury by the time of the Norman Conquest. Between about 1594 and about 1877 navigation continued to Fordwich via a pair of flash locks. Coasters continue to trade with timber to Sandwich. Maximum dimensions for craft upstream are 4ft draught and 20ft headroom.

The lower reaches of the waterway across the mudflats of Pegwell Bay to Richborough and Sandwich are subject to strong tidal currents. Richborough's waterside castle of the first–fourth centuries AD still can show extensive remains of flint walling. A little downstream are the 3 gigantic cooling towers of a power station, completed in 1963 and dominating the view for miles around. Sandwich, one of the Cinque Ports, was a leading harbour for the wool trade in the thirteenth century when the Wantsum was still a seaway. The toll-bridge over the Stour has an opening section and a mid-sixteenth-century gatehouse. Until 1893 a drawbridge stood here.

The 15m of navigation between Sandwich and Fordwich are pretty, and Fordwich has a tiny half-timbered fifteenth-century Town Hall. Canterbury is accessible to boats that can be portaged round 3 mill weirs.

## STOURBRIDGE CANAL

From the Staffs & Worcs Canal at Stourton Junction to a junction with the Dudley Canal (BCN) at Black Delph; 5¼m with 20 locks. A branch leads to the centre of Stourbridge, where the upper section has lately been amputated. Maximum craft dimensions are 70ft × 7ft × 3ft draught × 8ft 6in headroom. Opened in 1779, this important link carried heavy traffic until after World War II. Its subsequent history is a tale of decline to a state of near dereliction and then complete restoration. In 1962 the Inland Waterways Association held its National Rally in Stourbridge in the face of attempts by British Transport Waterways (illegally) to prevent the event taking place. A grand total of 118 boats was accommodated where weeks before a dinghy could scarcely have floated. Many of them descended the famous flight of 16 locks, taking a complete day over the passage, such was the locks' condition. Full restoration, with volunteers organised by the Staffs & Worcs Canal Society working alongside BWB staff, was achieved by May 1967.

*Stourton Junction*  The lower end of the canal through 4 locks is through pretty woods in company with the River Stour.

*Stourbridge* (2m)  The Stourbridge Branch leaves the main line at Wordsley Junction, to run for about 1m to the centre of this busy town, whose fortunes were based on a thriving glass-making industry, established in the seventeenth century.

*Sixteen Locks*  Spread over 1¼m, the flight runs through semi-urban surroundings at Wordsley and Amblecote to the outskirts of Brierley Hill. Most memorable feature is the bottle-shaped glass kiln in brick between Locks 12 and 13, at the Stuart Crystal factory. There are examples of 'split' bridges, with central slot for horseboat towlines, and two lock chambers built within feet of each other almost (but not quite) to form a 2-rise staircase. Beyond Lock 1, head of the flight, lies Brockmoor Junction, where the unnavigable Fens Branch brings water supplies from reservoirs on Pensnett Chase.

*Brierley Hill* (5m 2f)  After a winding course around Brierley Hill the canal ends at the foot of the Dudley Canal's Delph Locks, having provided more than a foretaste of the heavy industry and tracts of derelict land characteristic of this part of the Black Country. Local glassware produced during 4 centuries is exhibited in a museum at the Branch Library in Moor Street.

## STRATFORD-UPON-AVON CANAL

From the Worcester & Birmingham Canal at King's Norton to the Warwickshire Avon at Stratford; 25½m with 56 locks. There is a short branch at Lapworth, connecting with the Grand Union Canal. Maximum craft dimensions are 71ft 8in × 7ft × 3ft draught × 6ft headroom. The northern section (King's Norton–Lapworth) was completed in 1802, but Stratford was not reached until 14 years later. Early intentions to construct wide-beam locks were changed when it was seen that the Warwick canals and Worcester & Birmingham were to be narrow-beam. The Stratford passed into railway ownership in 1856, early commercial prosperity declined, and in the last years of GWR control the southern part was quite derelict below Lapworth. One of the Inland Waterways Association's earliest successful campaigns was to secure replacement at Lifford Lane, King's Norton, of a swing bridge that had been permanently fixed by the canal owners. Protest cruises were made by Sir Peter Scott and L. T. C. Rolt in their narrow boats *Beatrice* and *Cressy* respectively, with several hundred supporters on rooftops, lining the banks and hanging from trees. The Southern Stratford mouldered in decay until 1958, when the British Transport Commission and Warwickshire County Council announced their intention of lowering a bridge at Wilmcote, thus precluding any restoration attempt. The BTC published a figure of £119,000 as the estimated cost of efficiently closing the waterway (but not eliminating it). Instead, the Southern Stratford was transferred to the National Trust, and, under the direction of David Hutchings, restored to navigation in 3 years at a cost of £56,000. Volunteer, Services and prison labour was used in this exercise, proving that it was cheaper to reopen a derelict canal than to destroy it. The Stratford Canal was navigable again by February 1964 and was officially opened by the Queen Mother on 11 July. This canal restoration experiment was to be a blueprint for many similar schemes elsewhere.

The waterway is pleasantly rural in its northern reaches, in spite of the proximity of Birmingham. The countryside from Lapworth to Stratford is superb, with pleasing villages in the Forest of Arden, several aqueducts and many locks.

*King's Norton Junction* (northern section)  The waterway leaves the Worcester &

*Stratford-upon-Avon Canal. The guillotine stop lock at King's Norton where the Worcester & Birmingham Canal is joined*

Birmingham Canal (see p 447) and passes through a most unusual guillotine stop lock designed to prevent water supplies being taken from one canal to the other. Since nationalisation the gates have been left raised at each end, and some of the original cast-iron machinery is missing. There is a heavy swing bridge shortly afterwards, scene of the protest cruises of 1947. The area is one of suburban development but, as with so many canals, is tree-lined and consequently almost rural. Brandwood, or King's Norton, Tunnel is 16ft wide, with the remains of an iron handrail by which boats were hauled through. The west portal of this 352yd bore is decorated with twin niches in the brickwork, seemingly intended for a pair of statues, and a stone plaque of William Shakespeare, repeating the design of the canal company's official seal. A wooded cutting follows.

*Yardley Wood* (3m)   Between Bridges 7 and 8 comes the Cole Aqueduct, a single arch spanning the river and a road. Bridge 8 is a massive steel and timber bascule, windlass-operated, alongside the Boatman's Rest Inn. Less developed countryside now accompanies the waterway.

*Earlswood* (5m 6f)   Brick accommodation bridges along this earlier portion of the canal are much wider than the narrow boat-sized crossings on the later southern section. A canal feeder enters, right, near Bridge 16 and the Earlswood Marine Services boatyard. This feeder leads from three Earlswood reservoirs, $\frac{1}{2}$m to the south and covering 40, 30 and 15 acres respectively. Holding about 14,000 lockfuls of water, some fed by gravity but most intended to be pumped, they now supply water only in times of emergency. The original steam-powered beam engine, erected in 1823, was superseded in 1936 by a pair of electric pumps. The lakes are widely used for sailing and angling.

*Waring's Green* (7m 6f)   The Blue Bell Inn at Bridge 19 is attached to a complex of farm buildings. Home-brewed beer was served until the late 1960s, when it was acquired by a cider firm.

*Hockley Heath* (9m 6f)   A short arm by the Wharf Inn is occupied by a boatyard at Bridge 25. The canal now begins to converge on the Grand Union from Birmingham, to the east. Bridges 26 and 28 are both bascules, wound open with a lock windlass.

*Lapworth* (11m 4f)   Locks 2–20 lower the waterway to the Grand Union at Kingswood Junction. They are well spaced to begin with, but occur more frequently as the village centre is reached. Those in the middle of the flight have widened intervening pounds extending alongside the chambers themselves and pretty, vertical overflow weirs. There are pleasing lock cottages and several of the 'split' bridges characteristic of the Stratford, comprising iron decks cantilevered in two halves from brick abutments. A slot at the centre enabled horseboat lines to be dropped through without the need to detach them. Nearby Packwood Hall is a sixteenth- and seventeenth-century timber-framed house owned by the National Trust and open throughout the year. A feature of the grounds is the yew topiary, representing the Sermon on the Mount. The canal enters a broad lagoon above the short branch to the Grand Union. Lock 21 lies ahead, the first of 36 on the National Trust's southern section. Note another 'split' bridge at the junction, the NT canal office and a boatyard specialising in the building and repair of narrow boats. Facing the yard is one of 6 delightful barrel-roof cottages, unique to the Southern Stratford, and, like other structures, in a good state of repair. Their curved roofs were constructed in exactly the same way as bridges and tunnels. Originally the Grand Union connection was from the short pound between Locks 21 and 22, but there is now no trace of the arm or its guillotine stop lock.

As the waterway is maintained by a small staff working to a very modest budget, extra care is required to avoid failure of lock gear or loss of water. Boat crews are particularly requested to close all lock paddles and gates after use. During the 3-year restoration of these 13m and 36 locks about 200,000 cu yd of mud were dredged from the channel, at a maximum rate of 2½m a month, 70 of the 75 lock gates were replaced completely, and some lock chambers had to be virtually rebuilt. Average time for demolition and construction of each of the Wilmcote locks was 16 days.

*Lowsonford* (14m 4f)  Locks continue with great regularity through fields and woods, with occasional half-timbered cottages. All signs of the great heaps of mud that followed restoration have now disappeared, and it is difficult to believe that the canal has not always kept its tranquil appearance. The Fleur de Lys Inn near Lock 31 has a large waterside garden.

*Preston Bagot* (16m 2f)  At Yarningale Common, uphill of Lock 34, a small cast-iron aqueduct carries the canal over a stream. One suspects that little has changed since E. Temple Thurston passed this way by narrow boat in the early years of this century and recorded his impressions of the Warwickshire countryside in *The 'Flower of Gloster'*. Preston Bagot features a number of fine houses and cottages and a late sixteenth-century manor of brick and timber frames. There is a respite from locks, with only one in the 4m to Wilmcote.

*Wootton Wawen* (18m 4f)  An iron trough aqueduct takes the canal over the A34 Stratford–Birmingham road. It was completed in 1813. Anglo-Welsh Narrow Boats have a Civic Trust award-winning cruiser base in the small basin next to the Navigation Inn. Nearby is a well-maintained watermill on the River Alne.

*Bearley* (19m 5f)  Aptly named Odd Lock (no 39) stands alone shortly before the waterway's major engineering feature – Bearley (or Edstone) Aqueduct. Spanning a road, railway track and stream, it is very similar in design to one on the Shrewsbury Canal at Longdon-on-Tern. The waterway is contained in an iron tank 475ft long, and has a towpath alongside at the level of the canal bottom.

*Wilmcote* (21m 7f)  The village is best known for Mary Arden's cottage, an early sixteenth-century timber and stone farmhouse, reputedly the home of Shakespeare's mother. Locks 40–51 form the impressive Wilmcote flight, which was virtually rebuilt in concrete during 7 months of 1963.

*Stratford* (25m 4f)  Beyond the village of Bishopton the worst face of Stratford is revealed, with gasholders and industrial premises. Several more locks continue the secret course of this route to one of Britain's leading tourist towns. Before the final (rather low and tunnel-like) bridge, the towpath comes to an end. A boatyard specialising in the hire and building of traditional craft, and also supplying replica steam engines and boilers, is situated near Lock 52. Compared with its shy progress through the fields of Warwickshire, the Stratford Canal completes its course in a blaze of glory as it enters a large basin surrounded by lawns and flowers, a short distance from the Shakespeare Memorial Theatre. Before this stretch could be used by boats in 1964, about 10,000 tons of mud had to be removed with draglines, fleets of lorries and prison labour. Prim Stratford had never seen anything like the chaos! A wide-beam lock (no 56), with neat steel footbridge built at Wormwood Scrubbs Gaol, provides access with the Avon, another of David Hutchings' remarkable restoration successes (p 232). The attractions of Stratford are too numerous to record here, but quite the best method of making a pilgrimage to the town is to cruise slowly down the canal from Lapworth.

## TAMAR, RIVER

From Weir Head, Morwellham, to Plymouth on the south Devon coast; 19m and tidal throughout. This is an exceptionally attractive waterway, providing fine cruising facilities. Former connections with the Tamar Manure Canal (an extension of the river) and the Tavistock Canal from Morwellham have long been closed. At high water craft drawing up to 5ft can reach Weir Head, while maximum headroom is 100ft. Length and beam are not restricted.

*Plymouth*    An important naval base (since 1691) which suffered from intense bombing during World War II and has since been much rebuilt. The Hoe, a grassy hillside overlooking Plymouth Sound, is best known for Sir Francis Drake's game of bowls before the harrying of the Spanish Armada in 1588. Drake's Island is a youth adventure centre.

*St Germans River* (1m 4f)    Also known as the Lynher, this tidal river is navigable for over 6m to Tideford.

*Saltash* (4m 3f)    At a narrowing of the estuary, Brunel's magnificent Royal Albert railway bridge has linked Devon with Cornwall since 1859. It is partly arched and partly suspension, soaring high above the narrow streets of this fishing port. Alongside is the Tamar suspension road bridge, opened in 1962. There are launching facilities for small craft and embarkation quays for tripping boats that travel upriver to Calstock.

*River Tavy* (5m 7f)    At high tides this tributary is navigable for about 5m to beyond Maristow Quay.

*Calstock* (14m 5f)    Although still a sizeable waterway, the Tamar gradually narrows above the Tavy junction. Its banks are at times steep and thickly wooded. Throughout the nineteenth century the valley was the centre of intense industrial activity, with sailing ships and barges trading with numerous quays built to serve limekilns and mines producing large quantities of iron ore, copper, tin, lead, granite and arsenic. These activities have left many remains, which are recorded in Frank Booker's comprehensive *Industrial Archaeology of the Tamar Valley* (David & Charles). One of the most attractive reaches is at Cotehele Quay, on the Cornish bank (13m). Here stands

Cotehele House, a medieval and Tudor mansion in grey granite with a timber-ceilinged great hall. It is owned by the National Trust. A 12-arch railway viaduct spans the Tamar at Calstock, a boom town of the mid-nineteenth century and port for 17 mines within 5m of Tavistock by 1865. There were then steam-powered inclined planes and many mineral railways running into the hills, but 20 years later a depression had set in and mining declined. Other activities included shipbuilding at yards such as that of the Goss Brothers.

*Morwellham* (17m 5f)   Deserted for more than 70 years, the town and its quays were the scene of hectic industrial activity throughout the last century. Between 1796 and 1929 navigation continued via the Tamar Manure Canal for 2¾m to Newbridge, with a lock at Weir Head (19m). Sections of the 4m Tavistock Canal (1817–73), with its 2m branch, tunnel and inclined planes, have been preserved as part of an open-air industrial museum complex since 1971 (see p 197). A ship dock built in 1858 for 6 300-tonners, with massive granite bollards sprouting from the quays, is now heavily silted and covered in thick vegetation.

### TEES, RIVER

From the North Sea at Hartlepool Bay to Fardean Side Ford, via Middlesbrough and Stockton-on-Tees; 24m and tidal throughout. The lower part of the river, known as Teesside, is one massive industrial complex, concentrating on steel and chemicals. Busy with shipping and barges, the Tees is not normally associated with pleasure cruising.

### THAMES, RIVER

From its estuary off Shoeburyness, Essex, to Inglesham, Gloucestershire; 190m with 44 locks. Maximum dimensions for pleasure craft from the sea to Teddington are unrestricted. Draught and headroom under bridges varies with the state of the tide, the lowest bridge over this section being Hammersmith, with about 14ft clearance at high-water spring tides. Dimensions from Teddington to Windsor are 132ft × 17ft 6in × 5ft 6in draught × 13ft 2in headroom; from Windsor to Reading 130ft × 17ft 6in × 4ft 6in draught × 12ft 6in headroom; from Reading to Oxford 120ft × 17ft 3in × 4ft draught × 11ft 8in headroom; and from Oxford to Inglesham 109ft × 14ft × 3ft draught × 7ft 7in headroom.

The Thames is easily Britain's best-known waterway, and a journey from London to Gloucestershire is like travelling through the pages of English history. With Britain's capital city, Hampton Court, Windsor and Oxford situated on its banks, the river is an essential cruising ground for everyone who wishes to be reasonably well versed in inland waterways. Navigable since ancient times (prehistoric craft have been recovered from the bed of the upper river), there were about 70 flash locks or navigation weirs in use in the time of Elizabeth I. Pound locks made their appearance during the first half of the seventeenth century, but barges were subjected to long delays through flood or drought until well into the nineteenth. The last flash lock was not removed until the late 1920s. As the chief water route across Southern England, the Thames provided connections with the Thames & Severn, Oxford, Wilts & Berks, Kennet & Avon, Wey, Grand Union, Lee and Medway. Sadly there is now virtually no commercial trade upstream of Teddington, and even in the London reaches lighterage traffic is sharply declining.

There is a long tradition of pleasure boating, extending well back into the last century. Facilities are widespread and efficient, although the demise of small traditional boatyards in favour of large marinas will be regretted by many lovers of the Thames. There are about 15,000 powered craft registered annually with the Thames Water Authority for the waterway above Teddington, with a steady yearly increase. Pressure on locks has resulted in the conversion of all downstream of Oxford to mechanical operation since the late 1950s. Even so, queues of boats form at the more popular locks during some summer weekends. But in midweek and for 9 months of the year the Thames is far from being crowded, and much of its Victorian and Edwardian charm remains. The river is easily the best maintained waterway in Britain, elegant and spruce. Lock equipment, towpath bridges and weirs are painted in black, white and grey, in strict contrast to the magnificent flower gardens that many keepers tend in their own time. At one extreme the Thames is bordered by the immaculate houses and gardens of the wealthy, but elsewhere, especially in the almost medieval reaches above Oxford, its valley is a place of willows, watermeadows and unpretentious villages.

More books have been published on the Thames than on any other waterway in Britain, perhaps in the world. The description that follows can only attempt to select personal highlights and convey some indication of what awaits discovery. For historical background refer to Fred Thacker's *The Thames Highway*, republished in two volumes by David & Charles. Eric de Maré's *Time on the Thames* of 1952 contains a sympathetic text and admirable photographs, some of them already historical. Lifelong devotee Sir Alan Herbert (A.P.H.) produced a study in 1966 called *The Thames*, and for really evocative descriptions of the tidal waterway about Hammersmith the same author's novels *The Water Gipsies* and *The House by the River* are unequalled. The best cruising guide, *Nicholson's*, contains quantities of potted information from source to sea, maps and many illustrations.

There are numerous ways to enjoy the river – in private or hired cruisers, hotel boats, long-distance passenger vessels, self-drive motor launches, rowing boats and punts, or walking the towpath. Much of the river is easily accessible by car, and most places are well served by either bus or train.

The tideway down river of Limehouse is rather beyond the scope of this book; there are no particular navigational problems, but the area is better regarded as a seaway than a river. Boats making such a passage (to travel, for example, from the Upper Thames or London canals to the River Medway at Sheerness) should make the preparations necessary for any craft venturing into fast-flowing tidal waters where there are busy commercial shipping activities.

*London Tideway*   Plans have been agreed in principle to build a flood barrier across the river, possibly in the Woolwich area. Should this eventually materialise, it is likely to take the form of a movable series of gates rather than a fixed weir with ship locks, but it would keep the river above constantly near its high-water point, with consequent amenity and visual advantages. Meanwhile the tide flows with considerable strength, and a combination of commercial traffic, wind, police launches and tripping boats can create substantial wash. Due care should therefore be taken when navigating small craft. One hazard is driftwood. Chief connection in Dockland is via Limehouse basin with the Regent's Canal and the River Lee. As the lock can only operate at favourable states of the tide, advance notice of arrival will avoid delays. There are numerous river attractions in the capital, from HMS *Belfast* moored above Tower Bridge to floating restaurants and historical waterside buildings.

London can no longer claim to be 'the Greatest Port in the World', and its docks have declined greatly since World War II. Some, like St Katherine's, laid out by Telford below Tower Bridge, are serving a new role as housing developments, with a marina. On the south bank the Surrey Commercial Docks and 2½m Surrey Canal were closed in the early 1970s. Traffic has moved further down river, but new barge-carrying ship systems (LASH and BACAT, see p 155) could result in a revival. Small coasters make regular passages as far upstream as Isleworth, 14m above London Bridge.

The bridges of London's river display an extraordinary variety of styles. The best known include Tower Bridge, built in 1894, with bascules raised by hydraulic pressure supplied by steam engines; Waterloo Bridge, a modern streamlined structure in concrete, designed by Sir Giles Gilbert Scott and opened in 1945; and the suspension Albert, Hammersmith and Chelsea Bridges, dating from 1873, 1887 and 1934, respectively.

Wharves, cranes and power stations give way to more open surroundings at Putney, starting point for the Oxford and Cambridge boat race. Instituted in 1845, it has long been rowed upriver to Mortlake. There are many rowing clubs on these reaches, together with sailing dinghy facilities. An unexpectedly rural stretch lies upstream of Kew Bridge and the entrance to the Grand Union Canal at Brentford. The Surrey shore is devoted to the world-famous Royal Botanical Gardens (containing many architectural delights as well as the plants, trees and flowers), while opposite is Syon Park, a mainly sixteenth-century mansion owned by the Duke of Northumberland and open to the public. The interior was decorated by Robert Adam, and the grounds contain a commercial Garden Centre, a collection of historical road vehicles and the London Transport Museum. Beyond Syon is one of the surviving Middlesex riverside villages, Isleworth, with a really good row of Georgian houses, the substantial London Apprentice Inn and the church of All Saints. All but the fifteenth-century tower and early eighteenth-century walls of the nave were destroyed by fire in World War II, but a new church has been built inside the ruin, providing an interesting combination of traditional and ultra-modern styles.

Past houseboats and cruisers, the river approaches Richmond Half Tide Lock and sluices. This barrier, with decorative iron footbridge, was erected in 1894. Three gates are lowered to the river bed at certain states of the tide, resulting in the reach above to Teddington being semi-tidal. With the barriers dropped, boats may pass through the adjoining lock, maintained by the Port of London Authority, which is responsible for the river up to a point downstream of Teddington. The thriving and elegant town of Richmond now follows on the Surrey side, East Twickenham lying opposite across the lovely classical white stone arches of Richmond Bridge. The view from the top of Richmond Hill down to the wooded banks of the Thames is really memorable. A number of boatyards offer small craft on hire. The area, especially Twickenham, was a fashionable district during the eighteenth and early nineteenth centuries. Residents included Alexander Pope (nothing remains of his house except a rocky grotto in the grounds of St Catherine's convent school) and Horace Walpole, whose Gothic Revival Strawberry Hill is a training college for teachers. Houses open to the public include Marble Hill, built about 1720 for a mistress of George II, and the 1730 Octagon of Orleans House, now an art gallery. Across the river lies Ham House, an exquisite Jacobean mansion in red brick, now owned by the National Trust. Public gardens surrounding York House, c1700 and now council offices, contain magnificent flower borders, and, by the river, a rose garden with an extraordinary group of classical statues rising from the slime of a small pool. The Twickenham riverside and embankment show the best of this former Thames village, which elsewhere is almost totally twentieth-century suburbia.

*Teddington* (following distances are measured from this point)   An obelisk among willows on the Surrey bank marks the boundary between PLA and Thames Conservancy (Thames Water Authority since 1974) waters. Three locks in parallel are the Barge, 650ft long; Old Lock, 178ft; and the Skiff Lock, just 49ft 6in × 5ft 10in and believed to be the smallest working chamber in Britain. As at Richmond, there are boat rollers in addition. Keepers are on duty 24 hours a day and direct traffic from below with light signals. All locks to Godstow, above Oxford, are mechanised. Apart from the 24-hour service at Teddington and Molesey, keepers are available between 9 am and sunset (earlier in winter). Above Teddington Locks the navigation channel is spanned by a footbridge that continues as a suspension bridge over the weir stream.

*Kingston* (2m)   A flourishing shopping centre with many large stores, a colourful open-air market, and a large waterside power station designed to receive coal supplies by water. There are several boatyards and a very well stocked chandlery, The Boat Shop, at the Middlesex bank approach to the bridge.

*Hampton Court* (4m 6f)   Hampton Court Park borders the Thames between King-

*River Thames. Competitors in a Thames Barge sailing match recall the once familiar sight of tan sails on London's waterway; this scene is at Greenwich*

ston Bridge and Molesey Lock, opposite the suburbs of Surbiton. Much of the waterway is lined by houses and summer bungalows up to Staines, with further outbreaks thereafter. Although individually pleasant, collectively they can become overpowering. Cardinal Wolsey's great palace, seized by Henry VIII in 1529, ranks as the finest Tudor building in Britain. Wren made various additions, but subsequently few changes have been carried out. The buildings, deer park, gardens and maze are open to the public throughout the year.

*Hampton* (5m 6f)   Further elegant houses include Garrick's mansion and waterside temple and a genuine Swiss chalet at Huck's boatyard. A car ferry used to operate between Hampton and Hurst Park racecourse, but houses have now taken over from horses. The village is dominated by its Gothic church of 1831. Metropolitan Water Board (now TWA) pumphouses and filtration beds are a feature of the district.

*Sunbury* (8m)   A broad and quite pleasant stretch of suburban river extends to Sunbury weir stream, where good houses are gathered around the mid-Victorian church, with unusual Georgian tower. The local authority pursues a vigorous policy of buying waterside land as it becomes vacant to create public open spaces. A large lock island is reached by ferry from the Middlesex bank or via a footbridge over the lock cut from the Surrey side. Twin locks are accompanied by boat rollers. One keeper's cottage is a gem of mock Georgian styling and, like many others on the river, looks 200 years older than its real age. Another cottage alongside the cut and former site of a lock is genuine Regency, dated 1812, and a match with one at Penton Hook.

*Walton* (9m 4f)   The town is hardly evident from the water, and, instead, you see many boats in a lagoon marina near the ugly temporary bridge. Gravel pits on the Shepperton side were connected with the navigation to form another marina in 1974. Above the bridge at Cowey Sale is the site of a ford reputed to have been used by Julius Caesar. Beyond, the navigation divides. Shortest route lies up the Desborough Channel, cut during the early 1930s to relieve flooding. A more attractive course lies along the original river, past Halliford Bend.

*Shepperton* (10m 2f)   A very pretty riverside group of houses, church and several well-known inns and hotels. The early Victorian Manor House boasted the longest lawn on the Thames until part of the estate was sold as a public park. This is a lovely and tranquil reach used by members of the Desborough Sailing Club. A long-established traditional boatyard at the mouth of a backwater known as the Secret Pool was closed in 1971 and the site developed as an hotel extension. At the head of the Desborough Channel lies D'Oyly Carte Island, with Sir Arthur Sullivan's former house, Ladye Place, on the Middlesex bank. A long weir stream curves away from the lock to a wide pool, with the Wey Navigation and, further up, the little River Bourne flowing into the Thames.

*Chertsey* (12m 7f)   Broad meads accompany the Surrey bank to Chertsey Bridge, with the wooded slopes of Woburn Hill beyond the River Bourne. The bridge is a steeply sloping late eighteenth-century structure in grey stone. Beyond the lock with weir that closely follows the navigation channel stands a new concrete bridge carrying the M3 motorway. Then comes a sailing reach at Laleham, with well-patronised public park.

*Staines* (16m 6f)  A U-shaped loop of the river, now a weir stream, gives its name to Penton Hook Lock. This backwater leads to the largest inland marina in England, occupying a corner of Thorpe gravel pits. Numerous bungalows and houses line the banks through Staines, where the London Stone marks the former limit of the jurisdiction of the City of London over the waterway. Beyond Rennie's stone bridge lies Bell Weir Lock, completely rebuilt during the winter of 1973-4. The famous meadows of Runnymede, where Magna Carta was sealed in 1215, lie on the Surrey bank, with woods opposite. On the top of Cooper's Hill is the Commonwealth Air Forces Memorial and at its foot the simple stone slab commemorating President John Kennedy.

*Windsor* (24m 1f)  Old Windsor Lock, with narrow canal cut above and winding weir stream, precedes a lovely reach past the fringes of Windsor Great Park and the village of Datchet on the facing (Buckinghamshire) bank. There are distant views of Windsor Castle. At Romney Lock a backwater runs past the playing fields of Eton College and the lock cut emerges almost beneath the castle walls. As a much-frequented tourist centre, Windsor is well supplied with tripping boats and small hire craft. At last some real open country is evident in the run past Boveney Lock, Queen's Eyot (belonging to Eton College), Monkey Island, an M4 bridge and Bray village. For many years Bray Lock and Sonning, near Reading, have taken prizes in the annual lock garden competition.

*Maidenhead* (30m 5f)  A fashionable Edwardian boating centre, recalling steam launches and skiffs packed like sardines into Boulter's Lock, especially during Ascot Week. Skindles Hotel is still exclusive (and expensive). Notable structures are Brunel's GWR span, whose twin arches are the largest pure brick spans in the world (123ft each), and Sir Robert Taylor's road bridge of the 1770s. The river tends to become congested on midsummer weekends.

*Cliveden* (33m)  In complete contrast, the reach to Cookham Lock is perhaps the finest section of the Thames. Great beechwoods rising on the right bank are topped by Cliveden House, designed in 1850 by Sir Charles Barry in an Italianate style for the Astor family. Scene of the Profumo scandal in 1963, it is now National Trust property. Magnificent wooded islands provide idyllic moorings that are distinctly Amazonian. Best time is as a white mist rises from the water early on a summer morning and wood-pigeons call in the trees. If Cliveden is all you see of the Thames, your journey will have been more than worth while.

*Cookham* (33m 7f)  With a backdrop of Cliveden Woods, Cookham Lock is the first on the Thames that was mechanised in the late 1950s. The village, with its elegant cast-iron bridge, is consciously attractive, each house in immaculate order. Sir Stanley Spencer lived here most of his life, and there is a permanent exhibition of his religious paintings, which draw heavily on the river for inspiration. The Queen's Swan Keeper, F. J. Turk, has a boatyard here. Each summer, swans along the middle reaches of the Thames are sought out by a colourful waterborne company of 'uppers'.

Those swans belonging to the Crown are unmarked, birds of the Vintners' Company are given two small nicks on each side of the mandible, and those of the Dyers' Company one nick on the right side. The number of these graceful creatures, which are synonymous with the Thames, is maintained at about 610. Beyond Cookham comes one of the river's best sailing reaches, Bourne End. A railway branch line on the Buckinghamshire bank is known locally as the Marlow Donkey.

*Marlow* (37m 7f)  A beautifully situated town, with broad weir curving above the lock to the splendid suspension bridge of 1831-6, restored in 1966. Left is the Compleat Angler Hotel and opposite the tall spire of All Saints church. The following reach is notable for the little Norman waterside church at Bisham and Bisham Abbey, now a sports centre. The pound from Temple Lock to Hurley Lock is the shortest on the river at ⅝m (the longest is at Wallingford, between Cleeve and Benson Locks, 6½m).

*Medmenham* (41m 5f)  An abbey (Buckinghamshire bank) based on a Cistercian building of the thirteenth century is mostly Elizabethan, Georgian Gothic and *fin de siècle* Victorian. Now a private house with fine topiary, it was the headquarters of Sir Francis Dashwood's notorious Hell Fire Club and formerly displayed various pornographic architectural details. Early earthworks nearby include an Iron Age hill fort. Overlooking the reedy weir pool at Hambledon Lock is a really attractive white-painted weatherboarded mill.

*Henley* (46m)  A classic Thames-side town, just within the county of Oxford. The regatta, held on 4 days in early July, was established in 1839. It is very British, attracting entries from the best world oarsmen to a course that is non-standard under international regulations. Racing is upriver from Temple Island to below the bridge, where keystone masks representing Thames and Isis face London and the river's source respectively. The town contains many good buildings along its wide main street. Marsh Lock, with pleasing long wooden footbridge over the weir, precedes an elegant reach through Wargrave, with tree-covered islands and grand waterside houses. Light craft may bypass a section of the main channel via the secretive Hennerton backwater below Wargrave village. Another exciting passage for canoes and similar small boats completely avoids Shiplake Lock. Head up the River Loddon below the lock and turn into St Patrick's Stream to rejoin the Thames midway between Shiplake and Sonning; the current is strong, so a downstream trip is easier. There are a number of first-rate hotels in the area, with restaurants overlooking the water.

*Reading* (55m 2f)  Sonning Bridge is a good-looking many-arched structure in red brick. The village seems to know how pretty it is, and consequently loses some of its charm. Reading, although not all bad, is generally a blot on the river, with prominent gasholders, railways tracks, terraced houses and 3 leading industries – biscuits, beer and seeds. The Kennet & Avon Navigation starts in particularly depressing surroundings (see p 308). Salter's 'steamers' (alas now diesel-powered!) make their overnight halt by Caversham Bridge, the midway point on the 2-day journey from Kingston to Oxford. Upstream, the Berkshire (Caversham) bank is tamed as a municipal grassy promenade, while the Oxfordshire shore is devoted to substantial houses at the foot of a wooded slope. One, called 'Isomer', is an astonishing expression of late Victorian extravagance, with integral boathouse. Fine country, with islands and a

o

sheer-sided railway embankment wall at Tilehurst, lead to Mapledurham Lock and mill, and to an Elizabethan mansion open to the public.

*Pangbourne* (61m 5f)   An agreeable residential town connected with Whitchurch by a toll-bridge. The Swan Hotel overlooks the weir and lock. Kenneth Grahame was born here and captured the spirit of the Upper Thames in *The Wind in the Willows* more faithfully than any other writer. On the left bank large houses are squeezed between a chalk cliff, the main road and the river bank, with meadows opposite and islands marking the site of vanished Hart's Lock, which seems to have become disused in the early nineteenth century. The grounds of Basildon Park, a fine Georgian mansion beyond the railway on the Berkshire bank, are open to the public and display a collection of riverside statuary. Further on is an attractive thirteenth-century church.

*Goring* (65m 6f)   The Goring Gap is a deep wooded gorge with lock, weir and bridge. There are splendid views of the river valley from Streatley Hill (National Trust). A short pound leads to Cleeve Lock.

*Wallingford* (71m 5f)   This long level reach can show another Brunel railway bridge at Moulsford, with pretty islands beyond. Like almost all similar crossings, the ferry from Cholsey to Littlestoke no longer operates, much reducing the potential value of the Thames towpath as a long-distance footway. A grim Victorian mental hospital adds a depressing note at Cholsey. Wallingford is an ancient town with notable 17-arched bridge (5 span the river) whose origins are medieval but was remodelled in 1809. Nearby is the open pierced spire of St Peter's church, built in the 1770s rather in the style of Wren's city steeples. There are fragmented remains of a castle, demolished in the Civil War. Near Benson Lock (72m 7f) the old coaching village on the Henley–Oxford road now caters for a large RAF station.

*Shillingford* (74m 1f)   By the pleasing brick and stone bridge of 1827 stands the Shillingford Bridge Hotel, with small swimming pool and Oxford College barge ashore on the lawns. The view upriver is dominated by the twin hills at Sinodun, topped by trees and known as Wittenham Clumps. Earthworks probably predate the Roman settlement of the area. The view over Day's Lock to Dorchester is very good.

*Dorchester* (76m)   A village of antique shops around a bridge on the River Thame. The Abbey, in the Decorated style, is notable for its Jesse window. Small craft that can clear the towpath bridge over its entrance can navigate several hundred yards of the Thame to reach Dorchester. Traditionally the main river is the Isis above this point, and Thames below, though this distinction is rarely made in practice.

*Clifton Hampden* (79m 3f)   Delightful scenery here, as in many other reaches of the Oxfordshire/Berkshire section. The red-brick Victorian Gothic bridge (1864) and little church on a mound above make a picturesque group with several thatched cottages. Clifton Lock, just beyond, is followed by a long cut.

*Sutton Courtenay* (82m 5f)   Sutton Pools, lying in the weir stream by Culham Lock, constitute one of the prettiest Thames backwaters. There are several medieval domestic buildings.

*Abingdon* (84m 6f)   A side stream midway between Culham and Abingdon Bridge, on the Oxfordshire bank, was originally the navigation channel, bypassing the town. Known as the Swift Ditch, it was provided with early pound locks in 1624 by the Oxford-Burcot Commission. They remained in use until about 1790, when the present route through Abingdon Bridge was opened. Small boats can penetrate the Swift Ditch, through the lovely fifteenth-century Culham Bridge, almost as far as a weir above Abingdon Lock. Remains of an old lock chamber are clearly visible. On the Berkshire bank, the River Ock enters, and, close by, a stone warehouse reminds us of the Wilts & Berks Canal, abandoned in 1914. Abingdon is a good-looking place, mostly eighteenth-century but with ruins of a seventh-century abbey (open to the public). There is a fortress-like stone prison of 1805-11, and a memorable bridge with many arches of varying height and width. Although substantially rebuilt in 1927, the bridge still looks much like its real date of 1416. Beyond the lock a beautiful reach runs past the parkland of Nuneham (Oxford bank), with its eighteenth-century mansion, which is owned by Oxford University. Wooded islands mark the site of a former lock.

*Oxford* (92m 7f)   Sandford Lock (89m 6f) is the deepest on the Thames, with a fall of almost 12ft. A nineteenth-century mill and inn stand on the site of one erected in the thirteenth century. Here also was one of the 3 early Oxford-Burcot Commission locks; the present chamber was completely rebuilt and enlarged in 1972-3. From Iffley Lock (91m 4f) the City of Oxford dominates, and on the riverside is often far less attractive than might be expected. Iffley has a set of boat rollers spanned by an agreeable balustraded footbridge. The Norman church is a real gem, with typical rounded arches and zigzag decorative patterns. Upstream lie many college boathouses, ranging from severe structures of the 1930s to elegant modern ones with exterior spiral staircases. The elaborate college barges, of which the earliest were discarded City Livery Companies' vessels (see p 202), have nearly all gone. The navigation channel divides at Folly Bridge (the 'folly' was a tower demolished in 1799) by the headquarters of Messrs Salter's, a long-established boatyard whose large passenger steamers (now diesel-powered), camping craft and launches have been an essential feature of river life since Victorian times. Below the bridge, Christ Church Meadow is bordered by the River Cherwell, famous punting water but obstructed by weirs which occur on its course through the county, as it flows into and alongside the Oxford Canal.

It is quite impossible to catalogue the attractions of the city here. A university town since the thirteenth century, it is now also a thriving industrial centre and home of the British Leyland Corporation. Gasworks, backs of terraced houses and a railway bridge all indicate the desperate need for environmental improvement. Things improve at Osney Lock (93m 6f), with Thames Water Authority workshops. Osney Bridge, with its average headroom of just 7ft 7in, effectively bars larger boats from the upper reaches of the waterway. Until the mid-1960s the remaining 30m of river were wonderfully quiet, undeveloped and almost medieval, but an increase in the numbers of craft has somewhat shattered the calm during peak season, though for many people this section is the most beautiful. Above Osney Bridge lies one of the two entrances to the altogether different world of the narrow-beam Oxford Canal, route for the Midlands. In spite of modern building and electricity pylons, the 'dreaming spires of Oxford' are still memorable when seen from the water at Port Meadow. Godstow Lock is the last of the mechanised chambers; after this, paddles are lifted by spiked wheels and the gates opened by leaning on balance beams. The ruins of a twelfth-century nunnery lie close to the Berkshire bank by the bridge (with only 1ft more headroom than Osney). Beyond the Oxford bypass bridge come meadows, with an enchanting mooring to a grassy bank at Pixey Mead. King's Lock, one of the last Thames flash locks until converted in the late 1920s, is another point at which to turn off for the Oxford Canal, reached via the little Duke's Cut. The manoeuvre can be tricky if the river is in spate as you cruise across the top of King's weir. (This remark is occasioned by a worrying personal experience!)

*Eynsham* (100m 1f)    From the Oxford border the Thames changes its character and becomes a more intimate and sharply winding stream. Some distance below Eynsham Lock the River Evenlode, and later the long-derelict Cassington Canal, may be seen on the left bank. The canal once passed through a lock to join the Evenlode about 3m up. Swinford Bridge, Eynsham, is late eighteenth-century, classical, with 3 wet arches and a little toll-house. From now on there are very few river-bank villages until one reaches Lechlade, but just occasional farms and inns near bridges. Beyond Pinkhill Lock (101m 4f) comes Bablock Hythe, where a car ferry operated until about 1967. Caravans tend to intrude. A pleasant walk can be made to Stanton Harcourt, a lovely grey stone village, where remains of the fifteenth-century manor include Pope's Tower and the Great Kitchen.

*Newbridge* (107m 4f)    Northmoor Lock is really remote, with difficult road access. The bridge of Newbridge is, predictably, one of the oldest over the Thames, with wide cutwaters and pointed arches from the thirteenth century. On one bank stands the Rose Revived Inn and on the other the Maybush. The River Windrush enters on the Oxon shore.

*Shifford* (110m 1f)    Numerous flash locks obstructed the navigation above Oxford, some lasting into the present century, and compared with the canals, the Upper Thames was a rather inefficient and time-wasting commercial highway. This situation undoubtedly contributed to the death of the Thames & Severn Canal. As late as 1898 the newest of all Thames locks was built at Shifford, Duxford village being bypassed by a long new willow-shaded cut. A hamlet attractively named Chimney and steep wooden footbridge (Tenfoot Bridge) lead to Tadpole Bridge and the Trout Inn.

*Radcot* (117m 6f)    Beyond Rushey and Radcot Locks comes what is generally believed to be the oldest Thames bridge, Radcot, with pointed arches flanking a central rounded one. An improved channel and new single-arched bridge were provided in 1787. With the help of Thacker's *The Thames Highway* it is possible to locate the sites of many navigation weirs.

*Kelmscott* (120m)    Grafton Lock (118m 7f) has a pretty late-nineteenth-century stone keeper's cottage. As one approaches the Cotswolds, most village buildings tend to come in yellow/grey stone. An Elizabethan and Jacobean manor house at Kelmscott was the home of William Morris, and has associations with the Pre-Raphaelites. The house is open to the public by advance application only.

*River Thames. Lechlade church seen across the meadows from St John's Lock in Gloucestershire*

*Lechlade* (124m) Another lock, Buscot, is soon followed by the final one, St John's. Here is a statue of Father Thames. Beyond, across low-lying fields, is Lechlade, a cluster of stone buildings situated around the spire of St Lawrence's church, a Perpendicular structure and one of the Gloucestershire 'wool' churches. (The town lies just inside the county and within a short distance of Oxfordshire, Berkshire and Wiltshire.) There are many fine eighteenth- and early nineteenth-century stone houses, for this was a prosperous market town. Today it offers the only comprehensive shopping facilities on the river since Oxford. Halfpenny Bridge, built in 1792, takes its name from the pedestrian toll, removed in 1839. Boats of a moderate size can continue past Lechlade wharf for a further ½m to the junction with the Thames & Severn Canal, abandoned in 1927 and 1933. A charming circular keeper's house stands by the overgrown Inglesham Lock, one of several such houses along the 28¾m line to Stroud, some with a conical roof, others with an inverted cone. There are tentative moves to reopen the waterway and the Stroudwater Canal, which would once more link the Thames with the Gloucester & Sharpness Canal at Saul Junction. The prospect of this plan succeeding must sadly remain somewhat remote. A major feature of the T&S is 3,808yd Sapperton Tunnel, with Doric columns and niches at its east portal, and an embattled parapet at the west end. Laden barges were once able to reach Waterhay Bridge, 16m above Lechlade, but this part of the river ceased to be used with the opening of the T&S in 1789. The source of the Thames is generally agreed to be Thames Head, where a stone slab marks the site. Water runs from this point after heavy winter rain, but the Thames is normally evident only downstream of Thames Head Bridge.

## TRENT & MERSEY CANAL

From the Bridgewater Canal at Preston Brook to the Trent Navigation at Shardlow; 93m and 76 locks, of which a number between Middlewich and the Harecastle summit level are duplicated, side by side. There are 3 branches: (1) Caldon Branch, from Etruria, Stoke-on-Trent, to Froghall, (2) Leek Branch, from the Caldon at Hazlehurst Junction to Leek (both listed under Caldon Canal, p 263), and (3) Hall Green Branch, from Hardingswood Junction, at the northern end of the Harecastle Tunnel, to Hall Green, junction with the Macclesfield Canal (1m 4f).

The Trent & Mersey is a waterway of very considerable character and charm, and although its route remains largely rural, its atmosphere vividly recalls its commercial origins. It is James Brindley's most ambitious work (he died while construction was still in progress in 1772), and although designed as a single unit, it is one of the most diverse waterways in appearance and construction from one end to the other. Between Preston Brook and Middlewich it was engineered wide-beam, allowing salt barges to reach the town, though reconstruction of Croxton Aqueduct some distance north of Middlewich has restricted the length of broad canal now available. Between Middlewich and Horninglow Wharf, Burton-on-Trent, the locks, bridges and tunnels are designed only to accommodate narrow boats, and from Horninglow to the Trent, maximum beam is 13ft 6in. Designed headroom is 7ft (now reduced at Harecastle to a little under 6ft) and normal draught is about 3ft 4in.

The waterway was popularly known as the Grand Trunk Canal, reflecting its promoters' hope that many branches would extend from the main line. Josiah Wedgwood, the Burslem pottery owner, provided finance and encouragement to the scheme. Parliament finally gave its consent in June 1766 and construction began the following month at Burslem. Within 4 years there was a direct water link between there and the Trent, but difficulties with tunnelling under Harecastle Hill and completion of a length by the River Dane at Middlewich delayed opening of the entire 93m until 1777. The canal was a great commercial success and was entirely responsible for the growth and development of the Potteries. Narrow boat traffic remained heavy, especially from the Potteries northwards, until after World War II. It was only in the late 1960s that regular freight movement virtually ceased.

In spite of the industrial activities originally generated by the Trent & Mersey, the countryside through which it passes is now mostly very pleasant (though rarely spectacular). A voyage through the Potteries is a fascinating or alarming experience, depending on your view of a long-established urban landscape; but, at worst, the passage through Stoke from open country to open country need take less than half a day.

*Preston Brook*    The Trent & Mersey begins not at the junction with the Bridgewater Canal's Runcorn Branch, in Preston Brook, as might be expected, but at the northern portal of Preston Brook Tunnel, ½m south. The tunnel, 1,239yd long, has no towpath, but like Saltersford and Barnton, both to follow within 6m, possesses a still walkable horsepath over the top. These were among the earliest navigation tunnels completed in Britain and suffer in varying degrees from crookedness.

*Dutton* (6f)    Here a wide-beam stop lock with a rise and fall of about 6in prevented loss of water from or to the Bridgewater. An attractive cottage (former toll office) stands alongside, and nearby is a drydock with roof and decorated wooden bargeboards along the gable, all supported on simple cast-iron columns. The upper half of the sides is enclosed by ornate planking. The surroundings of the canal to Anderton and beyond are especially beautiful, consisting in part of wooded cuttings along the side of the River Weaver. Several times good views of the river appear on the right, and from Bridge 211 (3m 2f) Dutton Locks and weir are visible 50ft below. Most of the original cast-iron mile posts (c1819) remain, looking like pairs of pages in an open book. Near the fourth post is a small lake surrounded by mature trees lying beside the canal on the left, and this could easily be converted into boat moorings by digging a short cut. In spring the area is thick with bluebells and red campion.

*Barnton* (6m)   Saltersford Tunnel, 424yd, is followed by a pleasant tree-lined basin, enclosed at the southern end by Barnton Tunnel, 572yd. View to the right of the Weaver's Saltersford Locks. The next bridge, 201, has been rebuilt and is awkwardly placed over the navigation, making for difficult handling where craft are more than 40ft long. The nearby village provides all services.

*Anderton* (6m 6f)   The vast ICI chemical works, seagoing ships on the Weaver and distant sightings of the now unique (in Britain) Anderton vertical boat lift now appear, for 1m before the lift is reached. The approach to a small basin, right, lies under a wide concrete towpath bridge. This basin in turn leads to the pair of cast-iron aqueducts connecting the Trent & Mersey with the caissons of the lift, which since 1875 has transferred craft between the canal and the river. (For a full description of the lift, see pp 49–51.) A comprehensive rebuilding scheme was completed in time for the centenary, decayed portions of ironwork being made good.

Until recent years the Anderton Lift was operated on two shifts from 6.00 am to 10.00 pm, but is now available to craft from 8.00 am to 5.00 pm Mondays–Fridays, and 8.00 am to 11.00 am on Saturdays. A charge for its use has been introduced – £2 single and £3 return.

*Marston* (8m 4f)   The village is famous for its old salt mines, covering about 35 acres and extending to a depth of 360ft. The Tsar of Russia dined in the workings with members of the Royal Society during a visit in 1844. The caves were specially illuminated by thousands of lights. Severe subsidence from centuries of brine pumping has left a legacy of crooked buildings, and many water-filled flashes. In 1958 the canal was diverted for ½m via the Marston New Cut, and 6 months later the old line collapsed into a crater. At the time of its opening the new cut was thought to have been the first such length of canal to be built in Britain in half a century. Messrs Ingram's Lion Salt Works buildings themselves have suffered considerable distortion. As on sections further south, where coalmining has caused sinking, raising the canal banks with concrete goes on constantly.

*Broken Cross* (11m 6f)   Extensive factories threaten brown brick farmhouses. Shortly after, beyond Bridge 181, the canal joins a wide flash containing the rotting hulks of many wooden narrow boats, reputedly stacked one on top of another and dumped by the then canal authority amid great protest during the late 1950s. Drowned trees stand in the water with bare black branches. Whatcroft Hall, a large Georgian mansion surmounted by a massive copper cupola, stands on the canal's left near Bridge 178. Beyond, the Roman-built King Street runs quite straight towards Middlewich. The winding River Dane accompanies the waterway as far as the town, and is bridged by Croxton Aqueduct (16m 4f). The aqueduct has been converted from wide to narrow beam, and it is possible to see the old piers supporting the original trough. Nearby a small heronry is established in a canalside flash.

*Middlewich* (17m 6f)  Good country extends as far as the outskirts of the town at Big Lock, sufficiently wide for barges that can no longer reach it. Several interesting features include a drum and chain to close the lower gates, which are made of steel. A Victorian public house beside the lock displays a liberal use of ornamental red sandstone and its name, 'The Big Lock', is inscribed on a scroll over the towpath door. Middlewich has recently lost a good deal of interest and character as old salt works have closed down, and the trading narrow boats, such as those of Messrs Seddon's Salt and Cerebos, have disappeared. Never a pretty place, its aspect has not been improved by razing whole sites and streets of small houses. It is a traditional home of retired narrow boatmen who will appear as if by magic on the locksides while pleasure craft work through. Little encouragement is needed to have them recall the days of working boats. Three narrow locks, with a total rise of nearly 33ft, lift the canal into the centre of the town. At the top, a waterways office and depot complex (right) is notable for brown brick and slate, much fretted woodwork and an almost Chinese bay window.

The Shropshire Union's Middlewich Arm branches off to the right (see p 396); technically the first few yards are the Wardle Lock Branch of the T&M, from the junction to the head of Wardle Lock. A stone plaque in the bridge parapet is inscribed in Gothic Script 'Wardle Canal, 1829'. Shortly beyond the junction on the main line is King's Lock, with boatyard and pub, and an attractive small manual crane on the point between the lock island and the weir-stream backwater. This is the most convenient place to moor while visiting the town, the second oldest of the Cheshire salt centres; origins of the industry date back to Roman times. The parish church is largely Perpendicular. Just beyond Rump's Lock (18m 6f), the extensive premises of British Salt Ltd, left, are followed by another works bearing household names like Cerebos, Saxa and Stag. In his classic *Narrow Boat* of 1944, L. T. C. Rolt savagely condemns the 'dreary industrial hinterland' of the Cheshire locks, as the canal ascends to the Harecastle Summit by 32 steps in 12m. Even today this criticism is unjustified, for in spite of commercial operations there is much of beauty in the slow climb. Three widely spaced Booth Lane Locks are equipped with characteristic split bridges over the tail; these bridges are of the simplest pattern, consisting of cast-iron brackets supporting a wooden decking. Many more examples will be encountered.

*Wheelock* (23m 6f)  Further subsidence and a water-filled flash with progressively built up canal banks lead to Bridge 154, Wheelock Wharf, with several pleasant brick warehouses and boat services. The town's shops are close by. Sandbach, 1¼m, left, an ancient small market town, has black and white timbered buildings and a pair of 1,300-year-old Anglo-Saxon crosses, one 16ft and the other almost 11ft high, believed to commemorate the conversion to Christianity of Paeda, son of Penda, King of Mercia. Having been broken up after the Reformation and used as building material, they were restored and placed in their present position in the cobbled square in 1816. Silk and salt are two local industries that continue to thrive. A small aqueduct carries the canal over the River Wheelock, when come the 8 locks of the Wheelock Flight, all duplicated, side by side. Since the late 1950s a number of the alternative chambers have fallen derelict, and several of them have been completely filled in. A red and white disc system indicates which are to be used. The village of Hassall Green (25m) comes after the M6 crossing by Lock 60. Basic supplies are available a short distance to the left of Bridge 147.

*Thurlwood* (27m 2f)  Chellshill Aqueduct, a single arch, carries the navigation over a minor road (Bridge 143), and the lower Thurlwood Locks are soon followed by upper Thurlwood Locks, where the right-hand chamber is the unique steel lock. This was built at considerable expense in 1958 to combat subsidence that necessitated removal of the brick twin-arched road bridge. The new structure was fitted with guillotine gates, obviating the need for conventional paddles, and is similar to a steel aqueduct 106ft long and 26ft high, supported every 8ft on concrete piers. In the event of further subsidence hydraulic jacks can be used to lift the lock to its required level. Ironically, in 1972 the conventional chamber was able to function normally while the steel lock was out of service. Its operation is certainly complicated to the extent that working boatmen with a pair of craft have been noted working through the regular lock, one boat at a time, rather than trying to follow the instructions displayed on a noticeboard by the steel structure. Some charming brick cottages contrast with modern bungalows, while a short distance south is a nineteenth-century warehouse with boat-loading dock beneath.

*Lawton Flight* (28m 2f)  This is a curious mixture of open countryside and new housing development round the 6 locks, with hilly fields, stone walls and pleasing lock features such as stone-sided bypass weirs. The grey pinnacled tower of Church Lawton's Norman church on a rocky outcrop, left, contrasts with the red brick nave (1803), which is more like an industrial pumping house than part of a church. Beyond, among trees, stands the rather Gothic Lawton Hall, whose seventeenth-century origins would not be suspected from the exterior.

*Red Bull Flight* (29m 6f)  Beyond 3 locks in a series of 6 leading to the 408ft Harecastle Summit, before Bridge 134, the A34 Newcastle–Macclesfield road, lies Kidsgrove maintenance yard, where a variety of workboats are generally tied up alongside a severe 3-storeyed building with small crane on the towpath. Beyond Lock 43 the Macclesfield Canal crosses the waterway via Red Bull Aqueduct, which explains why the Macclesfield appears to leave the T&M on the 'wrong' right-hand side at Hardingswood Junction (30m). It is said that much time has been wasted in looking for an entry on the other and obvious side. There is nothing novel about the motorway flyovers of the later twentieth century, for similar canal features occur on the Caldon and Birmingham Canals. Two further T&M locks raise the canal to Hardingswood, thus providing the necessary clearance under the aqueduct.

*Harecastle Tunnel* (30m 2f)  To inland navigators the 2,897yd passage beneath Harecastle Hill possesses only a partially justified element of menace. One prominent hire-cruiser operator forbids customers to pass through. Certainly long-standing subsidence has reduced headroom to fractionally less than 6ft, but remedial work involving removal of the dangerously sunken towpath has much improved matters. Brindley's tunnel, running parallel on the right and built without towpath, has been disused for about half a century. Height gauges at each end of the present route indicate clearance. Ventilation in the tunnel is achieved by a powerful fan at the south end. As the tunnel is worked on a one-way system, craft must enter only in accordance with the scheduled timings or telephone the keeper at the south end for instructions. For a full description of Harecastle, see pp 77, 80. The influence of the Potteries is strongly felt after leaving Harecastle and true country does not return for about 9m. A plaque at the southern portal was erected in 1966 to commemorate Josiah Wedgwood's association with the canal 200 years before.

*Stoke-on-Trent* (37m 1f)   Those familiar with the writings of Arnold Bennett will know that the Potteries consist of 5 towns. In fact Stoke was combined in 1910 with Tunstall, Burslem, Hanley, Fenton and Longton, which have their counterparts in the fictional names invented by Bennett. Pottery was produced from Roman times, although the earliest origins of the craft date from about 1700 BC. Completion of the canal, providing cheap reliable transport ideally suited to breakable wares and bringing supplies of coal and Cornish china clay, encouraged the industry to blossom. In 1760 the population of the area was about 7,000, but by 1800 it had reached 25,000 and in 1861 some 120,000. Postwar modernisation has seen the demolition of most bottle-shaped kilns, traditional symbols of the region, although some remain at the Gladstone Pottery Museum, Longton. Excellent museums include the City (Broad Street, Hanley), containing one of the best ceramic collections anywhere; Messrs Spode's museum (Church Street, Stoke), open by appointment only; the Wedgwood Museum, Barlaston, appointment only; and the Arnold Bennett Museum (205 Waterloo Road, Cobridge), devoted to personal relics and drawings. Also, one of the City's few ancient buildings, the beautiful little Ford Green Hall at Smallthorne, is a sixteenth-century timber-framed manor house, open to the public.

North of Bridge 128 a lake, right, is used for dinghy sailing amid newly landscaped surroundings. Elsewhere there is much dereliction, with shabby buildings fronting the canal. At a wharf near Bridge 125, Burslem, are stacks of grey and white china clay, with the finished product visible within the works. (There are good industrial buildings, with manual cranes formerly used for unloading boats.) The short Burslem Branch runs northwards from the main line. Then follows a gigantic complex – the Shelton Steel Works on both sides of the waterway, with overhead gantries. The din, heat and brightness of the furnaces are intense. Cheerful acknowledgements from the workers may be expected by boat crews. To be able to navigate through the centre of such a hive of heavy industry is indeed an experience to remember. (The works is reportedly threatened by closure proposals.) This is the setting for H. G. Wells' macabre story *The Cone*.

The summit level ends at Etruria (35m 6f), as prosaic as its name is poetic. The beautiful Caldon Canal curves to the NE above the lock through surroundings that provide little clue to the delights of the Churnet Valley soon to come. A standard design mile-plate records 'Uttoxeter 30 miles' well over a century after the line to that town was abandoned for conversion to a railway in 1847. The charming wooden roof over Etruria gauging lock was regrettably removed in 1971, largely because of subsidence problems. Below there is an impressive vista of blue-brick chimneys and buildings as the centre of Stoke comes nearer. Smoke rising from the tallest chimney, attached to a works alongside the second lock in a flight of 5, indicates that the 'Etruscan Bone and Flint Mill Erected A.D. 1857' (to quote the plaque on a gable end) is operating under steam power. The beam engine dates from about 1850, although the beam itself was renewed in 1917. The diameter of the flywheel is about 15ft, with a 15in cylinder bore and roughly a 5ft stroke. Running speed is 20–30 rpm. One of the boilermen in charge should be approached for a conducted tour of the fascinating machinery.

A temporary respite from industrialisation is provided by a canalside cemetery by Locks 36 and 37. Best mooring for the shops and city centre is beyond Stoke Bottom Lock, by the Bridge Inn. The area near Bridge 113 is scheduled for road improvements affecting both canal and one of the locks. Unlike some canal towns, access to civilisation from the towpath is generally good. By the Doulton Sanitary Potteries, Bridge 110, are a convenient public house and several shops. The Trent has been crossed for the first time between Bridges 112 and 113. Here it is a dirty, polluted little stream, and although it accompanies the canal for much of the remaining distance, it does not join the navigation until it reaches Alrewas, towards Burton. Properly speaking it is not navigable today until beyond Shardlow, more than 50m away.

*Trentham* (40m 3f)   Services and fuel are available on the B5038 road at Bridge 106. Trentham is a not unattractive suburb of Stoke and marks the start of open country again. The new Wedgwood factory, with its own railway station, stands beyond Trentham Lock, right. Many of the single-arched accommodation bridges bear original carved stone number plaques, but these no longer correspond with current numeration.

*Meaford* (43m 2f)   Three tall chimneys and a group of vast cooling towers mark the position of the power station, which relies on the Trent for water supplies. As recently as 1970 the internal railway system was worked with steam locomotives. Four locks are pleasantly situated in a flight amid open and hilly country.

*Stone* (44m 7f)   Four locks take the waterway through this ancient town, whose appearance from the water is somewhat run down. Road Bridge 95, below the second lock, comprises one narrow arch for boats and another, even smaller, for the towpath. Hire cruisers, a wide range of chandlery and new craft are available from the Stone Boat Building Co in new and depressingly functional premises. Above the third lock another yard uses a system of 3 long established drydocks with canopies on cast-iron columns. Easiest access to the convenient shopping street is from this lock and through the courtyard of the Crown Inn, designed in 1779 by Henry Holland to serve the Mail and other well-known coaches. The High Street is a prosperous collection of mainly eighteenth- and nineteenth-century shops. The town is said to take its name from the cairns erected over the bodies of two Mercian princes whose pagan father, King Wulfhere, killed them for practising Christianity in the seventh century. An aqueduct by the bottom lock crosses a stream shortly before it joins the Trent. Here also is an unpretentious canal pub called the Star, whose only entrance is on the towpath. It is one of many in the district owned by the Stone brewery.

*Sandon* (49m 1f)   A pleasant stretch now follows past Aston and Sandon Locks. In the grounds of Sandon Hall, the nineteenth-century home of the Earl of Harrowby, stands a 75ft column surmounted by a statue of William Pitt the younger, and a Gothic shrine to Spencer Perceval, who was assassinated in the House of Commons. Both house and its 50 acre gardens are opened to the public. The thirteenth-century parish church contains a mural in the form of an elaborate decorative genealogical tree to the Erdeswicke family, painted in 1603.

*Great Haywood Junction* (54m 5f)   The canal continues through rolling open country, always close to the Trent. The Earl of Shrewsbury's Ingestre Hall, right, ¾m from Bridge 78, was a Jacobean building destroyed by fire in 1882 whose skilful restoration is now an Arts Centre. The park was landscaped by Capability Brown. St Mary's church in Ingestre village was erected in 1676 to a design by Sir Christopher Wren. Like many canal junctions, Great Haywood, although widely known among waterway addicts, consists merely of a group of mellow red-brick warehouses, mill and cottages, where the Staffs & Worcs Canal branches away towards Wolverhampton and Stourport, to the right. The site was developed as a hire-cruiser base in 1972. Notable is the unusually wide brick arch of the towpath bridge spanning the junction. Near Haywood Lock, Essex Bridge spans the Trent (see p 54). This leads to Shug-borough Park, family home of the Earl of Lichfield, which is owned by the National Trust and run by Staffordshire Council, whose county museum is established there. The house contains features from the seventeenth to nineteenth centuries, is magni-ficently furnished and decorated within, and has a fine collection of garden monu-ments in the Greek Revival style.

High above the river the canal enters a wood of beech, pine and rhododendron. The hills to the right are the edges of Cannock Chase.

*Colwich Lock* (56m 1f)   A charming Victorian lock cottage, with church tower in the village visible behind, and farmyard beyond a tunnel-like bridge at the lock's tail, are all rather dominated by the noise and wirescape of the electrified main line railway between Stafford and Lichfield.

*Rugeley* (59m 5f)   The outskirts of this small town are reached just beyond an aqueduct over the Trent, which by this distance from Stoke *looks* wide enough to be navigable, although it is not. There are numbers of new houses, many making attrac-tive use of their water frontages, with landing stages for small cruisers. But the canal is for the most part unkempt, while Rugeley offers no attractions visible from a boat. Its claim to notoriety rests on 31-year-old Dr William Palmer, publicly executed in Stafford in 1855 as a multiple poisoner. A massive stone railway bridge partly col-lapsed into the canal in the 1920s. Lea Hall Colliery, left of Bridge 64, is a modern plant of glass, brick and concrete, standing over a reputed reserve of 200 million tons of coal in this part of the Trent Valley. A nearby power station is just one of a chain down the length of the Trent.

*Armitage Tunnel* (61m 5f)   Since 1972 the 130yd bore through red sandstone has been more of a deep cutting, for the roof was progressively removed and a new road built over the top on account of unstable rock. The effect recalls sections of the Corinth Canal, on a much reduced scale. Near the east end the Plum Pudding Inn supports a thriving boat club on the busy A513. A large sanitary-ware factory by Bridge 59 takes its name from the village, to reappear on countless sinks, WCs and baths throughout Britain.

*Fradley Junction* (67m 3f)  After passing the housing estates of Rugeley and Handsacre, it is something of a relief to return to unspoilt Staffordshire, and travel through heathland and Ravenshaw Wood to Woodend Lock. Conifers, silver birch and rhododendrons are massed with bracken. Fradley is a small group of warehouses, cottages and the Swan Inn (almost too popular at weekends), facing the end of the Coventry Canal. Built entirely to serve trading craft, it is now busy with hire cruisers and private boats. Lichfield lies several miles SW. Locks occur quite frequently as the canal is lowered to the Trent.

*Alrewas* (69m 1f)  Pronounced as it is spelt, the village contains many charming black and white thatched buildings and a mainly thirteenth- and fourteenth-century church of dark honey-coloured stone with pinnacles on the corners of its square tower. Below Alrewas Lock the Trent enters the canal on the left, where the towpath is raised on a long iron footbridge. River flow affects the navigation for several hundred yards, and although protective wooden fendering has been erected, it can be dangerous to use this section in times of flood. A series of 6 normally dry streams, left, necessitate further towpath bridges on wooden piles with iron handrails.

*Wychnor* (70m 5f)  A pretty little church of mixed brick and local brown stone stands on the left of Bridge 45. Beyond are the grounds of Wychnor Hall, where a 'flitch' (cured side of bacon) is kept to be awarded to any couple who can prove their marriage to be completely harmonious. The cut leading from the Trent to Wychnor Lock is prone to partial obstruction by driftwood deposited by the river. Immediately alongside, right, the A38 Lichfield–Derby road is the Roman Ryknild Street. An

*Trent & Mersey Canal. Near Colwich Lock, close to Great Haywood Junction*

impressive red-brick Georgian farmhouse on the roadside was once an important coaching inn named the Old Flitch of Bacon. Further red-brick buildings by Barton Lock (72m 1f) include the Vine Inn, but the closeness of the main road and the approach of Burton-on-Trent have spoilt some of the rural character of the area. One may see cooling towers in the distance, a gravel screening plant by the narrow arch of Bridge 36 and unkempt canal banks. To the left, 2m, a line of hilly wooded country marks Sinai Ridge on the edge of the Needwood Forest.

*Burton-on-Trent* (76m 6f)   Bridge 33 is the nearest point to Burton (¾m, right). Here Marston's brewery is served by a disused side arm crossed by a towpath bridge bearing number plate 1. Dallow Lane Lock is the last narrow one before the Trent, and in 1974 gates dated 1915 were still in use. Paddle posts bear deep towline cuts. Still an important brewing town, Burton is bisected by the Trent, with a fine Victorian Anglesey suspension bridge in iron. Its industrial atmosphere holds few attractions. Extensive new roadworks have swallowed up most of the former Horninglow Basin (77m 1f), although a small boatyard occupies what remains. Three aqueducts carry the canal between Bridges 28 and 25, including a remarkable one of nine arches over the River Dove. Nearby, Ryknild Street also crosses the river via a pleasant old stone bridge with three wet arches and one dry; beyond, a new concrete span now carries the A38. Throughout the eighteenth century the Trent was navigable to Burton, but once the T&M was open on a parallel route with broad-beam locks, the difficulties of floods and occasional shallows led to its commercial disuse upstream from Derwent Mouth from about 1805.

*Findern* (82m 5f)   A small village on the outskirts of Derby, ¾m left of Bridge 21, with some of the few permanent signs of pleasure boat activity to be seen since Fradley and a useful pub called the Greyhound. Stenson Lock, 1m further on, has a rise and fall of 12ft 4in. A pleasing small community of buildings includes the keeper's cottage, and a big Georgian stone house. A large new marina was excavated in 1974–5. Left of Bridge 18, Arleston House is a charming eighteenth-century farmhouse, the lower part of stone and the rest of brick.

*Swarkestone Junction* (86m 5f)   Just above Swarkestone Lock, a toll-house in dark red brick and slate, right, stands by a narrows in the canal. This was required to deal with traffic entering the T&M from the Derby Canal, left, which, until its closure by Act of Parliament in 1964, ran to Little Eaton and to join the Erewash Canal at Sandiacre. The Swarkestone Boat Club, formed in 1951 when the Derby was already derelict, can provide moorings at the junction. The Derby Canal Co's toll cottage was due for demolition, but club members saved it for use as a HQ. Unusually for this section of the T&M in the Trent Valley, the canal passes through a shallow rocky cutting, near Bridge 11, bearing the date 1770.

*Shardlow* (92m 3f)   Pleasant open country on the Derbyshire/Leicestershire border accompanies the canal in its final stages to Shardlow, a textbook example of an original canal village, in contrast to a newer ugly extension of the same place along the A6. Shardlow Hall is a Georgian house in grey stone, left, before the lock, flanked on each side by red-brick waterways cottages. Below, left, is an excellent large-scale brick building bearing the sign 'Trent Corn Mills. No 2 Mill 1780', under which an arm, now choked with weed and silt, runs via an arch where boats unloaded. Beyond the A6 bridge (no 3) Dobson's old-established boatyard is a busy centre for building and selling pleasure craft. Formerly working boats were launched and repaired in the village. There is a wealth of exquisite late eighteenth-century detail in the brick and stonework of many warehouses, including a fascinating and elegant upper storey built to project progressively beyond the ground floor. There are two convenient pubs.

*Derwent Mouth* (93m 3f)   The last mile of the T&M lacks features of particular note. The canal enters the Trent at a 4-way intersection, with the Derbyshire Derwent coming in on the left. This was a navigation, like the Upper Trent, until about 1795 and provided water transport over 10m into Derby. The opening of the Derby Canal resulted in a more advantageous route.

## TRENT, RIVER

From Wilden Ferry, Shardlow, near the junction with the Trent & Mersey Canal, to Trent Falls, junction with the Yorkshire Ouse and River Humber; 94¾m with 13 locks (including the 2 on the Nottingham Canal forming part of the through route). Maximum dimensions for craft are 190ft × 19ft 6in × 7ft 3in × about 12ft headroom (where beam is under 15ft). The Trent is a mighty waterway and still supports considerable commercial traffic to Nottingham. As a cruising route it is obviously important in that it connects the navigations of the East Midlands with Yorkshire waterways. Connections are made with the Trent & Mersey, Erewash, River Soar, Grantham, Fossdyke, Chesterfield and Stainforth & Keadby. While there is no great difficulty for pleasure craft navigating the non-tidal reaches, except in times of flood, the tidal sections between Cromwell Lock and the Humber should be treated with great respect. Adequate and reliable engine power is needed. Craft that habitually use the Trent fall more into the river/seagoing than the narrow-beam canal-boat classification. Scenery is much what would be expected of the Eastern Counties, tending towards flatness and high river banks obscuring a good deal of the view in parts. To most people, therefore, this river is more a transit waterway than a place to linger. Surprisingly large distances can be covered within a short period of time. Excellent navigation charts of the tidal part are published by Vincent Sissons of the *Worksop Guardian*.

An ancient navigation, the Trent was improved over a long period, beginning with a Parliamentary Act in 1699. Originally navigable for nearly 19 additional miles to Burton, this section had become virtually disused by 1805 and traffic had transferred to the adjacent Trent & Mersey Canal. Further locks have been added during the present century (the last, at Newark in 1952) and they are now mostly mechanised below Nottingham. Cargo craft of old were Humber keels and barges drawn by horses and steam tugs. Present-day boats are motorised barges.

*Derwent Mouth* (1m 3f)   This is the point at which craft join the River from the Trent & Mersey Canal below Shardlow. The contrast between the narrow waters of the canal (a wide-beam one, nevertheless) and the river is startling. To the right the Trent enters the navigation under a very wide concrete towpath bridge bearing the initials of the Trent Navigation Co and the date 1932. Opposite is the outfall of the River Derwent (not to be confused with the Lake District and Yorkshire rivers of the same name); this carried barge traffic 10m to Derby between 1721 and about 1795, when a more reliable route was offered by the Derby Canal. Below the junction, 200yd, a pipeline crosses the river via a bow-shaped steel bridge dating from the early 1930s. An M1 motorway bridge follows that.

*Sawley* (2m)   After passing a broad unguarded weir on the left, the navigation channel moves via Sawley flood lock into a short canal section. Extensive moorings and marina facilities belonging to Messrs Davison's and the Derby Motor Yacht Club lead one to the end of the reach at Sawley Locks, where chambers are duplicated. The first of many groups of cooling towers belonging to riverside power stations rears up ahead. Associated electricity cables and pylons are a typical feature of the Trent.

*Cranfleet Cut* (3m 3f)   A broad and complicated 4-way junction is formed upstream of Thrumpton weir by the Erewash Canal entering, left; downstream below a wooded cliff on the right, is the River Soar, and ahead on the left bank, the Cranfleet Cut. This continues through navigation of the Trent, so bypassing the weir. The area is noted for dinghy sailing and small summer bungalows. A set of flood gates keeps Trent water out of the cut, which is extensively used for moorings. Beyond Cranfleet Lock (resident keeper as at all Trent locks) the river is rejoined, and pleasant but unremarkable meadows and trees are mingled with waterside shacks – one even has willows growing through its roof.

*Beeston* (8m 3f)   Now nearing the outskirts of Nottingham, the route passes through Beeston Lock and follows the Beeston cut. This deviation from the river itself continues via the remaining portion of the Nottingham Canal, which is reached at Lenton Chain (11m). Surroundings are occasionally rather squalid, with houses and factories. Trevithick's boatyard, Lenton, has a sizeable drydock and a number of former steam tripping launches. The yard hires out small craft on the Trent at Victoria Embankment, above Trent Bridge. The factories of Boot's (the chemists) and John Player's are prominent. Left, at Lenton, one may see the disused section of the Nottingham Canal whose total length was almost 15m between the Trent and Langley Mill, junction with the Erewash and Cromford Canals. All but the 2m from here to the river, however, were abandoned in 1937.

*Nottingham* (12m)   Castle Lock is in the town centre. The castle was first built by William the Conqueror and is best known through its connections with Robin Hood. The present structure is mostly a Victorian rebuild on a towering rock, and houses a museum and art gallery. A cunningly devised traffic maze keeps much of the shopping area free from cars and lorries. Nottingham Goose Fair is held each year on an 11-acre site (first Thursday of October and following 2 days). Wollaton Hall is a truly vast and impressive Elizabethan mansion now maintained by the local corporation. Several canal docks include one formerly owned by the narrow-boat operators Fellows, Morton & Clayton. Although in reasonable order, no attempt has been made to land-scape the Nottingham Canal or otherwise enable it to contribute to the town's attrac-tion. Soon after a right-angled turn, admirers of Victorian cast-iron architecture will be rewarded by a magnificent public urinal standing on a great stone pedestal above the water. Meadow Lane Lock marks the junction with the river, with commercial BWB warehousing and wharf facilities. It is possible to turn up the Trent, past Victoria Embankment, but the river eventually ceases to be navigable, for the old Beeston Lock has long been out of commission. Opposite Meadow Lane Depot, the 33m Grantham Canal enters the river; it is a wide canal running through pleasing countryside and 18 locks to Grantham. All but the first lock were abandoned in 1936, but there are now efforts being made to restore the line throughout.

*Holme Pierrepont* (15m 6f)   Disused gravel workings on the right of the river were converted in 1972 into an international rowing course and water sports centre. Above the duplicated Holme locks, a weir stream leads to a large 4-arched sluice on the left. One lock is mechanised, the other worked manually.

*Radcliffe-on-Trent* (18m)   Here is a Victorian iron railway bridge with 3 brick and stone arches to the right. Extensive sidings may be seen on the left riverbank. A 70ft high red-sandstone cliff, right, is topped by trees and houses. Residential caravans fill a meadow beyond.

*Stoke Bardolph* (18m 6f)   A single chamber lock lies below the continuation of The Cliffs. Near the village a little riverbank settlement is clustered around the Ferry Boat Inn (left). The area is popular with fishermen and picnickers. Generally the Trent is not pretty, but it is a virile waterway, still reasonably busy with barge traffic, though this is a shadow of what it was once. The barge men and tug skippers are the current members of a race that have worked here for generations, acquiring skills in using the tides and currents, and collecting a wealth of information about the ever-changing channel of the tidal reaches. Unlike many Trent ferries, that at Stoke still operates with a rowing dinghy.

*Gunthorpe* (23m 4f)   The river makes a broad curve at Burton Joyce and arrives at Gunthorpe Bridge, a 3-arched structure in reinforced concrete. The site of Roman Margidunum, protecting the convenient ford, lies 1½m SE. This was one of the very few points where the Trent was easily crossed. Trippers pack the banks on summer afternoons. The Anchor and the Unicorn Inns standing by the water were established at the ferry crossing, which was superseded by the first bridge in 1875. In a cut on the left is Gunthorpe Lock, with large weir alongside; clouds of foam indicate pollution from detergents. Old Hill, right, rises from the waterside.

*Hoveringham* (25m 4f)   A small village on the left bank which gives its name to a large gravel concern. Gravel and ballast were originally scooped from the river bed and carried by barge, but work has now been transferred to pits alongside and there are many loading staithes on the waterway. The demand for this material in making concrete ensures a steady flow of barge traffic. Bank protection over much of the water-way takes the form of loose piles of rock, making mooring difficult and uncertain. The Elm Tree Inn is a Georgian building with Victorian additions near a ferry.

*Hazleford Lock* (28m 2f)   Situated downstream of Hazleford Ferry, with its Star & Garter Hotel, the lock is on the right, with weir very close. It is manually operated, with a wheel to work each gate.

*Fiskerton* (30m)   A very pleasing little village on the left bank close to the water, with cranes, wharves and red-brick Georgian houses.

*East Stoke* (31m 3f)   Nearby is the site of the Roman station Ad Pontem. In 1487 the final battle of the Wars of the Roses was fought here. Stoke Hall stands in a fine park overlooking a loop of the Trent.

*Farndon* (33m 1f)   A village on the right bank whose chief interest to river users is the very extensive marina formed in old gravel pits connected with the navigation via a short channel spanned by a lifting towpath bridge. Within, willow-clad islands and enough space to moor perhaps several thousand boats illustrates that commercial marinas need not necessarily look ugly.

*Newark* (36m 5f)   At Upper Water Mouth the navigation leaves the Trent by a weir and follows a course partly formed by the River Devon. The junction is marked by Staythorpe power station. After the brick stump of an old windmill, right, the town can be seen ahead, with maltings. Among warehouses is a fine old steam crane, and beyond it the BWB Newark repair yard, generally busy with barges and maintenance boats. Newark Town Lock is powered, and stands alongside an older chamber now partly roofed to form a useful drydock. Newark is famous for its cathedral-sized parish church and castle, the latter looking most impressive from the water, its grey stone walls rising sheer from the river bank. It probably dates from the late twelfth century and only the north gateway and part of the west wall and towers now remain. The grounds are laid out as a municipal park. St Mary Magdalen ('among the two or three dozen grandest parish churches in England' in the estimation of Nikolaus Pevsner in *The Buildings of England*) raises its 252ft spire by the impressive and busy cobbled market place, where there is an excellent range of shops, a Palladian Town Hall and the superb fourteenth-century timber-framed White Hart Inn. Once equal in size to Nottingham, Newark has stayed small, with a population of 25,000. There are narrow alleyways with antique shops, a really notable baker's, a flourishing cattle market on the other (left) bank of the river across the 5-arched bridge, and sufficient fine buildings to make a stay of several hours both imperative and enjoyable. In 1787 John Wesley described the town as 'one of the most elegant in England', and his judgement would doubtless be much the same today. Beyond a narrow railway bridge (slightly widened in 1972 to enable 350-ton barges to reach Nottingham) lies Newark Nether Lock. The acute blind turn upstream is controlled by traffic lights.

*Winthorpe* (38m)   A pretty riverside village on the right bank, dominated by the late nineteenth-century spire of All Saints church.

*Cromwell Lock* (42m 1f)   After passing North Muskham, left, and Holme, right, neither with easy landing points, we arrive at Cromwell Lock, a huge chamber with equally large unguarded weir on its right. There was a Roman bridge at this point. Here the tidal river begins – a roaring, exhilarating and at times dangerous waterway with a flow often reaching 5 knots. Most pleasure craft will be heading for tide-free connections such as the Fossdyke, Chesterfield or Stainforth & Keadby. Advice should be sought from the lock-keeper on the best time to set out, bearing in mind that it is always preferable to travel with the current rather than to punch against it and that mooring up anywhere on the tidal Trent is to court disaster. Suitable navigation lights, anchor and chain and other equipment should be carried. Commercial traffic tends to be heavy and creates a considerable wash. Another factor to add to the general excitement is that the ægre, or tidal wave (similar to the Severn bore), affects the navigation upstream to around Gainsborough. At one moment there is a steady ebb which, on the arrival of the ægre, is immediately altered to a strong flow headed by a breaking wave up to 4ft high. Often it is accompanied by a procession of barges. Take the fullest advice before starting, and obtain charts from Vincent Sissons of the *Worksop Guardian*. From now on the towns and villages of the Trent hold little interest for the navigator, as stopping to investigate is ill-advised. Further, the view is severely restricted by high banks. In spite of these necessary warnings, this river is a most rewarding one to cruise, its size and power being more akin to the Lower Rhine or Ijssel in Holland than to the typical peaceful English navigation. The banks are of sand and piles of rock.

*Carlton-on-Trent* (45m 2f)   The tower of an old windmill stands by a large double-S bend. Surroundings are generally little developed and there are few bridge crossings. Marker posts indicate the river channel limits when banks are awash in times of flood.

*High Marnham* (51m 2f)   On the left bank a huge power station stands with 5 cooling towers. Beyond is the Fledborough railway viaduct, with suspension footbridge alongside. This is the first bridge since the A1 crossing at Newark, about 12m upriver.

*Dunham* (54m 1f)   A steel toll-bridge carries the A57, with wooded cliffs nearby.

*Laneham* (56m)   A pleasing village with a Norman church. Two willow-covered islands follow in the wide navigation near Cottam power station.

*Torksey* (58m 2f)   After a horseshoe loop, the Fossdyke Navigation enters, right. Mooring to barges is often possible below the first lock, or better still in the tideless waters above. A convenient point at which to break the journey. Good meals (in an area not over endowed in this respect) may be had at the Hume Arms. The Trent from about this point marks the boundary between Nottinghamshire (left bank) and Lincolnshire. In meadows at the junction of the 2 waterways stands the impressive remains of Torksey Castle, an Elizabethan mansion.

*Littleborough* (61m 6f)   At the site of a Roman ford, the village features a floating jetty offering the possibility of temporary moorings. Astonishing bends and twists reveal muddy banks near low water. At Knaith (63m 4f) there are attractive wooded hills to be appreciated if the problems of navigation, chart reading and avoidance of commercial traffic allow time.

*Gainsborough* (68m 4f)   BWB jurisdiction ends here and the British Transport Docks Board takes over. Mooring for short periods is possible at the wharves. Ask permission first. The town grew considerably in the last century as an inland port and is the original of St Ogg's in George Eliot's *The Mill on the Floss*. Trent Bridge, by William Weston, has 3 handsome arches and was completed in 1791. There are castle remains from the mid-twelfth century and a fifteenth-century manor house known as Old Hall.

*River Trent. Throughout its length, power station cooling towers dominate the riverscape: these are at Sawley*

*West Stockwith* (73m)  A large keel lock leads to a delightful basin at the terminus of the Chesterfield Canal. Once a place noted for river freight and boatbuilding, the village is now slightly decayed, but several good canal buildings remain, such as the lock-keeper's cottage, warehouse and inn. Winches on the river bank were used to haul sailing keels into the lock. Facilities include a boatyard, clubhouse and moorings. The area is windswept and bleak, with long vistas over highly productive agricultural land. The village extends along a single street, crowded with extraordinarily Dutch-seeming houses in red brick. A little down river of the basin is the outfall of the River Idle (see p 307). Until the early 1950s a ferry connected West Stockwith with its neighbour East Stockwith across the Trent, but the two villages are now many road miles apart via Gainsborough Bridge. Narrow roads hug each bank of the river for a long way, with concrete flood walls rising to conceal the waterway from cars.

*Owston Ferry* (76m 3f)  A short distance below Gunthorpe and also on the left bank. Like Stockwith, it is Dutch in appearance, farm buildings mingling with cottages in the village centre.

*East and West Butterwick* (81m 6f)  The twin villages face each other across the river. To the east lies the Isle of Axholme, 80,000 acres of fertile fenland that were drained by Vermuyden in the seventeenth century.

*Keadby* (85m 6f)  A busy little port lying to the east of steel-producing Scunthorpe.

For all but the most powerfully engined seagoing pleasure craft, this is effectively the end of the Trent. Some distance below George V road and rail bridge (built in 1916 with a 4,000-ton bascule span that has been closed since the 1950s) lies Keadby Lock and the entrance to the Sheffield & South Yorkshire Navigation, Stainforth & Keadby section. As barge traffic is often quite heavy, pleasure boats may have to wait for some time before they can enter the lock, a manoeuvre best accomplished by stemming the tide, which can have the effect of slamming a boat hard against the entrance. Once inside the chamber, the safety of non-tidal waters is regained, generally with a sense of relief! But the undoubted difficulties of the lower Trent should not be allowed to detract from its attributes. There is no better account of the river life and barge traffic that constitutes the major appeal of the river than that in John Seymour's *Sailing Through England*, published in 1956. This fascinating book chronicles a journey made by a Dutch barge through waterways of the NE and across the Leeds & Liverpool Canal to the Mersey.

*Trent Falls* (94m 6f)  The junction of the Trent with the Yorkshire Ouse and Humber is a wide and wild reach of angry water, with a savage tide flow. Much more a seaway with large ships than an inland waterway, it is not the recommended route for small craft bound for Goole and the Yorkshire Ouse. The canal system from Keadby provides a safer alternative.

### TYNE, RIVER

From Hedwin Streams to Tynemouth on the north-east coast; 19m and tidal throughout. The river forms the boundary between Durham and Northumberland. There are no limits for pleasure craft, except for a clearance of 21ft under Newburn Bridge, 1½m from the head of navigation. The lower reaches of the waterway through Newcastle, Jarrow, and North and South Shields are noted for heavy industry. Rather more than 30m of river above the tidal limit offers sport for canoeists, in wild and wooded scenery.

### URE, RIVER

From the Swale junction at Swale Nab to a junction with the Ripon Canal at Oxclose Lock; 7½m with 2 locks. Maximum craft dimensions are 57ft × 14ft 6in × 5ft draught × 8ft 6in headroom. The Ure is an outstandingly beautiful river navigation, made suitable for craft, together with the Ripon Canal, in 1772. A large enclave of pleasure boats is based near Ripon, but surprisingly few visitors bring cruisers from further afield.

*Boroughbridge* (2m 7f)  Having changed its identity from the Ouse to the Ure at Ouse Gill Beck, 2m above Linton Lock, and its navigation authority at Swale Nab (see p 365), the navigation enters a long canal cut, with Milby Lock near its lower end. (Locks are worked by boat crews.) This navigation rejoins the river in the town centre, beyond the former A1 road bridge. Boroughbridge is a small market town, well endowed with former coaching inns – at one stage there were 22. It was established in Roman times, when the first bridge was built, and in the later eighteenth century developed as a port for the linen trade of Knaresborough, several miles to the SW. A gaunt brick warehouse and mill stand on the river bank near the broad unguarded weir. To the SW, on the road to Roecliffe, are the Devil's Arrows, 3 prehistoric standing stones weighing about 36 tons each. According to legend, they were bolts shot by the Devil to destroy ancient cities. Upstream of the town the modern A1 bypass bridge spans the waterway. Beyond, on the right bank, is a public slipway. Sandy banks, thick woods and fields combine to create a very pleasant riverscape.

*Westwick Lock* (5m 1f)  A sharp bend precedes the approach to Westwick Lock, which is equipped with fixed windlasses to operate the paddles. A shady cut with alders leads to an exquisite reach through the parkland of Newby Hall. This Queen Anne mansion was remodelled in the 1760s by Robert Adam. Open to the public, it is noted for its tapestries and collection of classical statuary. The gardens, covering 25 acres, may be reached via a landing stage from which a tripping cruiser operates. Another attraction is the miniature railway. The beginning of the Ripon Canal (7½m) lies through a short and easily missed cut on the left side of the river (see p 379). Beyond this point the Ure is obstructed by rocky shallows and weirs, although the determined canoeist, prepared to make portages, can enjoy 48m of beautiful scenery, beginning near Askrigg in Wensleydale.

### WEAVER, RIVER

From Winsford Bridge, Cheshire, to Weston Point Docks, junction with the Manchester Ship Canal; 20m with 5 locks. There is a connection with the Trent & Mersey Canal at Anderton, via the vertical lift. Maximum dimensions are 150ft (Weston Point to Northwich) and 130ft (Northwich to Winsford) × 35ft beam × 10ft draught × 60ft headroom to Hartford and 30ft to Winsford. Limitations for use of the Anderton Lift are 72ft × 14ft 6in × 5ft draught × 9ft headroom.

This is a fine modern commercial waterway (one of all too few in Britain), which has seen constant reconstruction and improvement since flats (sailing barges) first navigated from the Mersey to Winsford in 1732 to load salt from the Cheshire mines. Other chemicals now form the greater part of the goods carried between the Northwich area and the Manchester Ship Canal, with substantial 500-ton coasters working far inland. A proposal has been made to establish an inland shipping port near the head of the waterway, thus enabling materials to be distributed by road to towns throughout the north-west.

*Weston Point Docks*  Linked with the MSC, the docks handle an annual tonnage of over 460,000. They are one of the two most important centres of such activity under the control of the BWB (Sharpness on the Severn estuary is the other). There are 2 exits to the Ship Canal, via Weston Mersey or Weston Marsh locks. A junction with the Runcorn & Weston Canal (leading to the Bridgewater Canal) has been closed since 1966. Loss of this link was unnecessary and unfortunate, for even at the time of abandonment its value to pleasure craft was widely appreciated. Many inland craft are not suitably equipped to travel on the Ship Canal and in any event are scarcely encouraged to do so by a range of regulations specifying safety equipment to be carried and extra insurance – and with good reason. But in 1966, the Bridgewater Department of the MSC Co seemed to have very little appreciation of the amenity potential of canals like the R&W and were notorious for issuing threatening letters to anyone who dared criticise their actions or motives.

The first 4m of navigation towards Winsford lie along the Weston Canal section, with the tidal Weaver running close by. This is crossed by the M56 motorway at

Frodsham. All bridges are either swing spans or high level with ample clearance for small ships. Remains of a former flood lock can be seen near the A56 at Sutton (3m 4f). An old line of navigation, now disused, passed through a lock at Frodsham to join the tidal Weaver.

*Dutton Locks* (7m 5f)   From Frodsham the wide river valley narrows through a green and wooded cutting. A Victorian gabled lock-keeper's house and one wall of the chamber are reminders of the vanished Pickering's Lock (7m), up to which point the navigation was long ago tidal. Dutton Locks are duplicated, with chambers of different widths and intermediate sets of gates, enabling the length used to be varied according to the size of boat. A short distance to the north the Trent & Mersey Canal can be seen, high above the river and shaded by tall trees. The two waterways remain in close company for the next 5m.

*Saltersford Locks* (10m 6f)   Another duplicated pair, right alongside the T&M Canal tunnel of Barnton.

*Anderton* (13m)   There is a huge industrial complex at Winnington (left bank), where ships load soda ash, potassium and caustic soda at the ICI works. Opposite, and suffering from the rotting effects of the chemical pollution, is the extraordinary Anderton vertical boat lift, making a connection with the Trent & Mersey Canal (see pp 49–51 and 423). At the time of writing the lift is undergoing extensive repairs and rebuilding, so that it can emerge resplendent and entire in time for its centenary in 1975. A charge is made for use of the lift, an experience not to be missed.

*River Ure. Westwick Lock between Boroughbridge and Ripon*

*Northwich* (15m 6f) The town is based on the long-established salt trade, and grew as an administrative centre for the Weaver Navigation. Here are boat repair and building yards, the BWB offices and depot, and signs of much former small-ship and barge construction work (see p 113). Hunt's Locks lie beyond the town, manned by keepers (like all Weaver locks) and possessing interesting patterns of paddle gear, and other distinctive 'furniture', such as lamp posts to assist night-time operation and traffic signals of a type more normally associated with railways. A small and flourishing shipyard builds tugs and similar craft on sideslips midway between Hunt's Locks and the high level Hartford Bridge.

*Vale Royal Lock* (18m 2f) This is a really pleasing riverscape, secluded from any kind of development and offering most attractive pleasure cruising. The lock stands alongside a fine Victorian steel and stone weir structure with single guillotine sluice. A series of swing bridges span the lock and weir stream. Beyond lie the remains of Vale Royal Abbey, founded by Edward I for the Cistercians, whose site is now occupied by a mainly seventeenth-century mansion built by the Cholmondeley family, which is used as an industrial firm's summer school.

*Winsford* (20m) The approach to the town is spoiled by towering waste tips, derelict salt works and loading staithes. In the early 1970s a new terminal for 400-ton barges was established here. Beyond Winsford Bridge (headroom 10ft 8in) further progress is possible into a magnificent lake, 1m × ½m. This is not owned by the BWB but has been expertly landscaped by the local authority. Numerous sailing dinghies race between the wooded slopes surrounding Winsford Bottom Flash, formed as the result of salt-mining subsidence. The river continues through a smaller flash (this can be entered only by light draught boats such as rowing dinghies, available on hire) and ahead, at a higher level, is the Middlewich branch of the Shropshire Union Canal. It is temptingly close, but there is no navigable link and boats must travel about 25m by way of Anderton and the Trent & Mersey Canal through Middlewich to appreciate the view from the opposite direction.

## WELLAND, RIVER

From Deeping St James, Lincolnshire, to the Wash below Fosdyke Bridge; 24¼m with 1 lock. Until the late nineteenth century the river was navigable for a further 8m to Stamford, but the upper locks have long been derelict. A connection is made with the River Glen (p 441). A strong tide affects the 9m from the Wash to Fulney Lock, and at spring tides a small bore or tidal wave may be experienced. The Welland traverses completely flat Fenlands that are intersected by many drainage channels. There is considerable interest in the highly productive bulb fields around Spalding.

Between Spalding and the Wash, maximum craft dimensions are 110ft × 30ft × 8ft draught (on the most favourable tides); headroom is unrestricted. From Spalding to Deeping St James the river is much smaller, but will pass craft about 35ft × 3ft draught × 6ft headroom.

*Deeping St James* This is a large village with a derelict lock. Boats that can be portaged can continue for 1½m upriver to Market Deeping, a pleasing little town with a wide street of stone houses and the church of St Guthlac, partly twelfth-century.

There is another disused lock by the mill. South of Deeping St James and the Maxey Cut (drainage channel) are sections of the Roman Car Dyke, built to connect nearby Peterborough with Lincoln.

*Crowland* (5m 4f)   A small town clustered around an abbey founded in the eighth century to commemorate the island in the Fen where St Guthlac had created a solitary habitation for himself. Like modern travellers by water, the saint had to disembark from his vessel on the Welland a mile from the site of Crowland. In the town a remarkable fourteenth-century triangular bridge of stone, with 3 arches connected to each other at 120 degrees, originally spanned 3 streams leading into the Welland.

*Spalding* (14m 4f)   This pleasing town of brick buildings is intersected by the river in a style that feels Dutch and no doubt owes something to a former trade with Holland. Much pleasure will be derived from inspection of the architectural detail of eighteenth- and nineteenth-century houses. A mile downstream of Spalding Bridge is Fulney Lock (15m 4f), beginning of the tideway and the start of glistening banks of mud such as characterise the lower reaches of other rivers flowing into the Wash.

*River Glen* (18m 2f)   Of similar character to the Welland, the Glen is navigable from its junction midway between Spalding and Fosdyke to Tongue End, $11\frac{1}{2}$m upstream. The only lock is a pair of tidal gates at the entrance, which can be passed when a level is made by either an incoming or an ebb tide. The best time to make an exploration is in spring, when the bulbs are in flower. The only villages en route are Surfleet, whose church spire leans 6ft from the vertical, and Pinchbeck.

*Fosdyke* (22m 2f)   An opening bridge will be operated if a signal flag is flown at the masthead and 3 blasts given on the boat's horn. A final 2 miles of broadening estuary through extensive marshlands acts as a prelude to the Wash. Provided the correct state of tide is selected, it is an easy run of about 4m northwards along the coast to The Haven, entrance to the River Witham (p 444).

## WEY NAVIGATION

From the River Thames at Weybridge to Guildford, and continuing via the Godalming Navigation to a terminus at Godalming, Surrey; $19\frac{1}{2}$m with 16 locks. One of the earliest river navigations to be equipped with pound locks, the Wey was opened to Guildford in 1653 and extended to Godalming 80 years later. Maximum dimensions for craft are 73ft 6in × 13ft $10\frac{1}{2}$in × 4ft draught (to Coxes Lock, Weybridge), 3ft 3in to Guildford and 2ft 6in to Godalming. Headroom is 7ft to Guildford and 6ft to Godalming, the lowest bridge being at Shalford.

In view of its closeness to the London suburbs, the Wey retains a remarkable rural quality, and in many ways has changed little in 2 centuries or more. The navigation to Guildford was owned for many years by the Stevens family. The late Harry Stevens presented it to the National Trust in 1964, while the Godalming Navigation followed shortly afterwards. Some of the more rustic and antique facets of the waterway have disappeared during the Trust's modernisation programme, which has been made necessary by a huge growth of pleasure boats in the 1960s and 1970s. Several examples of partially turf-sided river locks remain. Commercial traffic in Stevens barges between the London Docks and Coxes Lock grain mill continued until 1969. The Wey makes

junctions with the (currently) semi-derelict Basingstoke Canal at West Byfleet and
with the Wey & Arun Junction Canal near Guildford. The latter has been closed since
1871, but work in progress hopefully could result in the Wey once more forming part
of a Thames–South Coast route through Surrey and Sussex.

*Weybridge*   The entrance to the Wey lies on the south side of the Thames, where
a series of backwaters and weir streams converge at Shepperton Lock. The first lock,
Thames, is unusual in that it is equipped with a single wide gate some distance below
the chamber, virtually forming a flash lock for use when the Thames is low or if craft
of more than anout 2ft 6in draught are to float over the bottom lock cill. The original
keeper's cottage was due for replacement in 1975, and above the lock a mill was
served by barges until the early 1960s. Wooded gardens hint at the closeness of the
sprawling residential town of Weybridge, parts of which are among the most exclusive
areas of Surrey. A long canal section begins at Town Lock, between the two Weybridge road bridges. This is the most convenient mooring for the excellent shopping
centre. The museum sometimes features various aspects of local boating. A pretty
backwater of several miles is formed by the natural river, and this stretch can be navigated as far as the remains of Brooklands Race Track (now owned by British Aircraft
Corporation).

*Addlestone* (1m)   Not a very likeable town, which introduces a rare touch of
industry to the Wey between Black Boy Bridge and Coxes Lock. The grain mill at
Coxes comprises brooding but rather magnificent brick buildings surprisingly dating
from as recently as 1901 and 1906. Their scale has been altered by concrete additions
of the late 1960s. Wildfowl congregate on the large mill pond.

*New Haw* (2m 2f)   Almost an extension of Addlestone, but providing convenient
shops near the lock, which is partly turf-sided. A pretty red-brick keeper's cottage is
perched on the edge of a rushing weir. Many pleasure craft moor along the long (rather
shallow) straight leading to the West Byfleet junction with the Basingstoke Canal.

*Pyrford* (4m 7f)   A popular canal resort by the Anchor Inn and lock. The Royal
Horticultural Society's Wisley Gardens lie 2m SE.

*Newark* (6m)   The long canal cut ends at Walsham Gates, a flood lock normally
open each end. Here the real Wey is rejoined, with expansive watermeadows and a
number of backwaters. (Small boats should be able to penetrate to Old Woking.)
A walk over the fields from Walsham reintroduces civilisation at Ripley, a busy former
coaching village on the A3. Newark Priory is a picturesque flint ruin alongside the
Newark Lock weir stream. It was founded in the late twelfth century. Beyond the lock
stood a magnificent weatherboarded mill until it was destroyed by fire in 1966. Then
follow more open meadows, intersected by the winding course of the river to Paper
Court Lock (keeper resident).

*Send* (8m 5f)   A 1½m stretch of canal ends with the shallow Worsfold Gates Lock,
whose paddle gear, of a type once common on the Wey and other rivers, could now be
unique. Formerly a handspike used as a lever was carried by boat crews in addition
to a conventional windlass. Trigg's Lock (keeper) comes shortly before the extensive

estate of Sutton Place, an early sixteenth-century brick mansion built by Sir Richard Weston, promoter of the Wey Navigation. It is now the home of Paul Getty and his renowned art treasures. A very lovely part of the waterway. A right-angled turn leads to Bower's Lock, where the late nineteenth-century mill is an attractive private house.

*Guildford* (15m 1f)  Pollarded willows and a trestle wooden towpath bridge lead to Stoke Lock, still very rural on the outskirts of this expanding town. Treatment of the waterfront in Guildford varies from the bus park, and exceptionally hard modern concrete architecture of the latest shopping and commercial centre, to the grassed areas around Millmead Lock, where the curved walls of the 1965 Yvonne Arnaud Theatre are partly concealed by weeping willows. The steeply sloping cobbled High Street and seventeenth-century Guildhall, with contemporary decorated clock suspended over the roadway, are worth seeing. Near its original site on Guildford Wharf, and fully restored (1972) but lost amid impersonal slabs of concrete, is a man-powered treadmill crane in a timber-framed 'shed'. The wheel is 18ft in diameter and was last used to unload barges in 1908. Close by were the nineteenth-century offices of the navigation company, which looked positively Dickensian until their wholesale demolition in the late 1960s. The town crowds both sides of the steep valley through chalk and sand. Small boats may be hired by the hour and there are trips in an unusual electric launch as well as a diesel-powered wide boat. High over watermeadows stands the ruined St Catherine's Chapel, known to have existed in the very early fourteenth century.

*Shalford* (16m 6f)  A fine brick and weatherboarded watermill on the River Tilling-bourne is owned by the National Trust. This lies near St Catherine's Lock. These final reaches of the Wey are perhaps its most unspoilt and delightful. Boats on moorings beyond Broadford Bridge mark the remains of the Wey & Arun Junction Canal, on which restoration attempts are in progress (see p 222).

*Godalming* (19m 4f)  After Unstead Lock comes the final lock, Catteshall. Here an exceptionally large fleet of punts and skiffs, tea-room and narrow boats on weekly hire ensure that the river is enjoyed by many. There are good temporary moorings at Godalming Wharf, close to the centre of this busy and pleasant town, once a centre of cloth manufacture. Navigation for all but the smallest craft ends at the brick-arched bridge, though the Wey continues to one of several sources near Alton, Hants.

## WHARFE, RIVER

From the Yorkshire Ouse about 1m above Cawood (p 363) to Tadcaster; 9¼m and tidal throughout. This is one of Britain's most beautiful rivers, flowing through the Yorkshire Dales. The adventurous canoeist should be able to cruise downstream from Kettlewell, about 72m above the Ouse (there are doubts about the legality of this, however, as a court case involving angling interests has shown). For the purposes of normal motorised craft, Tadcaster weir is the upstream limit and some difficulty may be experienced in reaching as far as that after a dry spell. One hazard is a series of clay 'huts' (shallows) in the river bed at Ulleskelf, 4m below Tadcaster. The scenery of the tidal section is not particularly inspiring, being characterised by willow-fringed muddy banks. Tadcaster is best known for John Smith's brewery. Its early eighteenth-century river bridge has 7 arches and was built with stone removed from the castle.

Maximum craft dimensions are length and beam, unlimited; draught about 5ft 6in on spring tides to Ulleskelf and about 3ft 6in to Tadcaster, when there is a reasonable amount of 'fresh' flowing down from the Dales; and headroom unrestricted to Ulleskelf but 8ft beyond.

### WITHAM NAVIGABLE DRAINS

From the River Witham at Anton's Gowt Lock (p 446) to various points in an area bounded on one side by the Wash and on the other by the river. The total navigable mileage is about 59. Three locks remain of a former larger number, and, of these, East Fen Lock linking the Maud Foster Drain and the Cowbridge Drain is at present out of order. This is an extraordinary system of waterways whose prime function is to assist drainage of the surrounding Fenlands. Once used for carriage of agricultural cargoes, they are now occasionally frequented by pleasure craft alone. As advice on prevailing conditions can be difficult to obtain, even locally, exploration tends to be somewhat pioneering in spirit. During the winter months (October–March inclusive) water levels may be lowered without warning, with the possibility of boats being stranded.

The most useful section is between Anton's Gowt and the centre of Boston via Frith Bank and Maud Foster Drain, negotiating Cowbridge Lock. Undoubtedly the absence of other boats does spur a certain type of waterway enthusiast to 'go down the Drains', but as they mostly lie below the level of the surrounding flat landscape they are unlikely ever to develop into a major cruising area.

Maximum craft dimensions are 72ft (through Anton's Gowt Lock and along much of the system, but 60ft is a safer guide) × 11ft (18ft through Anton's Gowt) × 3ft 6in draught × 8ft headroom. Certain unofficial low bridges may have to be dismantled to enable boats to pass.

### WITHAM, RIVER

From a junction with the Fossdyke Canal at Lincoln to the Wash; 36½m with 3 locks. At Anton's Gowt, 29m below Lincoln, there is a connection with the extensive Witham Navigable Drains (above). An integral part of the drainage system of much of Lincolnshire, the Witham was navigable in Roman times and, after centuries of decline, was much improved under Parliamentary powers obtained in the eighteenth and early nineteenth centuries. No commercial traffic now remains. The Witham runs largely through low-lying fenland, bracing rather than beautiful in any immediately obvious sense.

Maximum craft dimensions are 78ft × 15ft 2in × 5ft draught × 9ft 2in headroom. Boats exceeding 59ft in length can only pass through Boston Sluice when the tide makes a level.

*Lincoln* (see also p 282)  At the eastern end of Brayford Pool in the city centre a narrow channel leads past a mellow warehouse with exterior iron spiral staircase to High Bridge. This splendid structure features a row of sixteenth-century shops and houses in timber framing with characteristic overhanging sections. At one time there was also a chapel dedicated to Thomas Becket. Although much restored, what we now see is substantially original. High Bridge is unique in England. Footpaths allow one to take a pleasant waterside walk. Numerous swans are evident, appropriately, for this is the bird traditionally associated with St Hugh, who founded the great cathedral

*River Witham.*
*The Glory Hole,*
*Lincoln*

in the late twelfth century, several years after the first church was demolished by an earthquake. Stamp End Lock (4f) is equipped with a guillotine top gate (a device commonly used in the Eastern Counties to assist with rapid dispersal of flood water). There is an electric liftbridge with keeper by an industrial complex that includes a power station, and soon afterwards the navigation enters open country. For almost the entire distance to Boston a railway line, closed for passenger traffic, accompanies the river.

*Bardney* (9m 4f)   Waterside villages or any kind of development are rare. Washingborough (2m 5f) lies well back from the waterway on the south bank, displaying many pleasing stone cottages amid trees. Fiskerton (4m 7f) was originally a small fishing port served by boats sailing up the Witham on the tide before the construction of Boston Sluice. East Anglian landscape painter Peter de Wint (1784–1849) was one of many water colourists who frequented the village and surrounding district, famous for its huge expanses of sky and the distant towers of Lincoln and Boston. Branston Island is formed by the present navigation channel and an old section of the Witham (8m 4f). There is Bardney Lock at the lower end, immediately followed by a junction with Barling's Eau, accessible for a little over a mile to an inn. Next comes Bardney village, with fifteenth-century church and green. A sugar-beet factory dominates the area. A mile to the north may be seen the overgrown remains of a Saxon abbey, once covering 25 acres. The body of St Oswald, King of Northumbria, was conveyed here for reburial.

*Kirkstead* (15m 7f)   A series of straight drainage channels flowing into the river take their names from their villages of origin – Nocton, Metheringham and Timberland Delphs. These connect with the course of the Roman Car Dyke, a canal that appears to have provided navigation facilities between the Nene at Peterborough and Lincoln. To the east of Kirkstead Bridge (B1191) are the fragmented remains of a great Cistercian monastery founded in 1139. St Leonard's church, near Kirkstead Bridge, was built in the mid-thirteenth century as a chapel connected with the monastery, and contains a rare wooden screen of the same age.

*Horncastle Canal* (19m 3f)   Shortly before Tattershall Bridge (A153) a flood bank has been thrown up over the entrance to the 11m Horncastle Canal, constructed between 1792 and 1802. Fed by the River Bain, it had 7 locks and carried agricultural produce until it was closed to traffic in 1885. Several weired lock chambers can be found; various sections are still watered and one of a pair of terminal basins in Horncastle can be seen surrounded by warehouses. Back on the Witham, the keep of a fifteenth-century castle (National Trust and open to the public) can be visited from Tattershall Bridge.

*Kyme Eau* (21m 7f)   A useful inn stands on one side of the river, with a restaurant on the other, connected by a ferry at Dogdyke (20m 7f). A mile further downstream at the village of Chapel Hill, automatic flood-gates mark the confluence of Kyme Eau, otherwise known as the Sleaford Navigation. Although abandoned in 1878 and the former locks replaced by fixed sluices, small portageable craft should be able to cruise for $12\frac{1}{4}$m to Sleaford. Boats 70ft × 14ft × 3ft draught can penetrate the first $1\frac{1}{2}$m from Chapel Hill.

*Boston* (31m 6f)   The remainder of the Witham consists of long featureless straights, with just one single road bridge at Langrick (27m 2f). At Anton's Gowt the river makes its only navigable connection with the extensive Witham Drains, offering a non-tidal route to the centre of Boston (see p 444). By the Witham, the middle of the fine seaport of Boston lies on tidal water through the Grand Sluice, beyond which mooring on the tideway is not recommended. The Grand Sluice was built in 1766, primarily to improve drainage and to control flooding. At high water the level of the North Sea rises above that of the river; the lock may be used for several hours either side of high water. Navigation beyond Boston should only be attempted in suitable seagoing craft and with adequate knowledge of the Wash and its sandbanks, where seals congregate in sizeable colonies. The route does provide a connection with the Rivers Welland, Nene and Great Ouse. Above the Sluice are various facilities, including a boatyard and two clubs. Boston is an ancient market town, which received its first charter from King John in 1204; its volume of trade then was eclipsed only by London. There are many links with the New World, for it was from this port that the *Mayflower* sailed in 1620, and 4 July is celebrated each year with clusters of American flags. Most notable feature is the great Perpendicular tower of St Botolph's church – 'Boston Stump' – standing 272ft above the surrounding fenlands. Those who brave the tiring climb are rewarded by a magnificent view. The waterfronts are filled with eighteenth- and nineteenth-century warehouses. Among a wealth of delightful buildings is a 5-sailed working windmill on the Maud Foster Drain, which is spanned by 3 elegant bridges designed by Thomas Telford (his Witham bridge was rebuilt in 1913). To arrive in Boston by water is an experience that makes up for having to endure a sometimes tedious run down from Lincoln.

## WORCESTER & BIRMINGHAM CANAL

One of the most heavily locked canals in Britain, connecting the Birmingham Canal Navigations at Gas Street Basin, Birmingham, with the Severn at Diglis Basin, Worcester. There are junctions with the Northern Stratford Canal at Kingswood and with the Droitwich Junction Canal at Hanbury. In addition to the interest provided by the 58 locks, there are 5 tunnels and some especially fine countryside. The canal is 30m in length.

The W&B was opened to traffic in 1815, acquired by the Sharpness New Docks Co in 1874 and nationalised in 1948. Maximum dimensions are 71ft 6in × 7ft × 3ft 3in draught × 6ft headroom. Craft up to 76ft × 18ft 6in may enter Diglis Basin from the Severn.

*Birmingham* From the city centre at Gas Street or Worcester Bar, where a physical barrier necessitated transhipping of goods until the construction of a stop lock between the W&B and the BCN in 1815, the canal's surroundings are urban for its first 5m. A right-angled turn several hundred yards beyond the junction is overlooked by a 3-storey canal stable block, where the boat horses were led to the upper levels via ramps. Although passing through the outskirts and suburbs of Birmingham, the canal occupies a wooded cutting (shared with a railway) for several miles, providing a totally unexpected illusion of countryside.

*Edgbaston* (1m 1f) A wide-beam tunnel (105yd) is equipped with a towpath. On the left bank are the Victorian and modern buildings of Birmingham University, set in parkland. A careful watch should be kept for stop gates, designed to be closed by the abnormal water flow that would result from a bank burst, for sometimes these are partly shut and awash and might not be noticed if navigating in twilight.

*Selly Oak* (3m) Streets of houses seen from the canal embankment are considerably below the level of passing boats. A junction with the Dudley Canal No 2 Line through Lappal and Gosty Hill Tunnels to Netherton has been closed since the collapse of Lappal in 1917.

*Bournville* (3m 5f) In 1879 Richard and George Cadbury moved their chocolate factory from the centre of Birmingham to what was then a rural site by the canal, where they established their garden factory, a pioneering concept of providing pleasant surroundings for the workers instead of cramped slum conditions. The garden city now comprises over 3,500 Cadbury houses. Cadbury's made considerable use of canal transport until the mid-1960s. Note the railway trucks marked 'Cadbury's Chocolate. For internal use only'!

*King's Norton* (5m 4f) Now within the Birmingham City limits, it retains its original village character. Opposite the junction with the Stratford Canal, left, is a fine double-fronted brick canal house. Beyond is the magnificent medieval church of St Nicholas, with fifteenth-century tower and octagonal spire. A cutting leads to West (or Wast) Hill Tunnel, 2,726yd long, wide-beam but lacking a towpath like the other

3 tunnels yet to come. West Hill is lined throughout in red brick, and is slightly kinked and rather wet, with cascades of water pouring from the ventilation shafts. The far end emerges in good countryside.

*Bittell* (9m 6f)  Two sizeable reservoirs bring water supplies to the canal between Bridges 65 and 66. They are popular with birdwatchers and anglers. In spite of the very hilly terrain, the canal retains its level with a small aqueduct over the River Arrow.

*Alvechurch* (10m)  Another pleasing village, around which the waterway winds. The Bishops of Worcester had a house here, demolished in 1780. St Laurence's church is an ancient structure with mid-Victorian additions by the prolific William Butterfield. There is a useful boatyard at the wharf.

*Tardebigge* (14m)  Shortwood Tunnel, 613yd, is followed by the first of the Worcestershire orchards. In spring masses of bluebells coat the canal banks. The cutting leading up to the 580yd Tardebigge Tunnel runs through red sandstone, a material that mainly lines the bore. A boatyard, BWB yard and drydocks, and full boating facilities will be found at Tardebigge New Wharf. Here the Birmingham Level ceases and the first of 58 locks in 16m begins the descent to the Severn. With a rise and fall of 14ft, the top lock is the deepest narrow-beam example in Britain; it was originally constructed as a vertical boat lift, but proved unsatisfactory, and was given its present form in 1815. In spite of their great number, the locks are quick and efficient. Including those at Stoke Prior, there are 36 in less than 3m, with a lift of 259ft. To the E of the top lock the spire of St Bartholomew's (1777) shows up as a magnificently slender construction. Above Lock 57 is a ruined ivy-clad brick pump-house. One of the best views of the locks may be obtained by climbing to the edge of Tardebigge reservoir, immediately uphill of Bridge 54.

*Stoke Prior* (17m 2f)  A classic canal hamlet, with warehouses, inn and boatyard. The Avoncroft Museum of Buildings, lying 1m N, has exhibits that include a recon-structed Iron Age hut, timber-framed houses, a nail and chain works and an eighteenth-century post mill. The public are admitted from mid-March to mid-October from 11.00 am to 6.00 pm (closed on Mondays). A salt-producing factory between Bridges 42 and 43 once brought considerable trade to the canal, but it now does little to enhance the surroundings. Brine was pumped here from 1828. Good scenery returns for the Astwood Flight of 6 locks.

*Hanbury* (20m 6f)  The Ladyline Group's Hanbury Marina occupies a triangle of land formed by the canal, a short arm and the B4090 Salt Way, leading to Droitwich. The 1¾m Droitwich Junction Canal, with 7 deep and narrow locks, branches off here to connect with the Droitwich Barge Canal, which follows a 6¾m course through 8 wide locks to join the Severn at Hawford. The Barge Canal was opened in 1771 to enable trows loaded with salt to reach the Severn, and the Junction followed in 1853. Both were legally abandoned in 1939 but are currently being restored by the Droitwich Canals Trust with the help of Droitwich New Town Development Committee. A volunteer working party of 500 cleared almost a mile of canal bed at Ladywood in October 1973; a further mile had by then been restored in Droitwich itself, and it was hoped that the route between Hanbury and the Severn might be again navigable by 1976–7. The National Trust's Hanbury Hall is a fine red-brick mansion in the Wren style, built in 1701 and open to the public on Wednesday and Saturday afternoons, April–September. Best approach from the canal is via a footpath leading from Lock 17. Droitwich is famous for its brine baths, 40 per cent more salty than the Dead Sea.

*Dunhampstead Tunnel* (22m 2f)  The only feature worthy of mention in several miles, the 230yd tunnel, with stone portals, is more square in cross-section than is normal.

*Tibberton* (24m 1f)  Beyond an M5 motorway bridge come the 6 Offerton Locks, with distant views of hills beyond the Severn.

*Worcester* (30m)  The city is visible from Blackpole Lock (no 9). Here open countryside gives way to industry and the general condition of the canal deteriorates somewhat as it passes by terraced houses, playing fields and allotment gardens. Lowesmoor Basin (right bank between Bridges 9 and 10) is a potentially useful mooring site, now surrounded by scrapped cars. Worcester does not yet seem to have considered the amenity value of its canal, whose banks contrast vividly with those of the nearby Severn. But the Worcester & Birmingham does revive considerably as it enters Diglis Basin, where the world of narrow-beam cruisers meets that of seagoing craft. Boatbuilding and repair facilities, a drydock and an altogether marine atmosphere mark these moorings, safe from possible Severn flooding. Two wide locks, operated by keepers, lead to the river (see also p 383).

## WYE, RIVER

A classic example of how a British river navigation declined. In the early eighteenth century barges could reach Hereford from the Severn, a distance of almost 70m. Later the Wye was opened up to Hay, 97m from the estuary. After about 1860, however, all but the lower 37m fell into disuse. Now craft can only reach Tintern, 4¾m from the Severn, over tidal water. This is particularly to be regretted, as the river valley is without doubt one of the finest in Britain. For canoeists, long journeys are possible over rapids, but experience should first be obtained on less adventurous waters. Some local boating is possible without danger, for example, at Hereford. The finest reaches of the Wye lie between Ross and Chepstow.

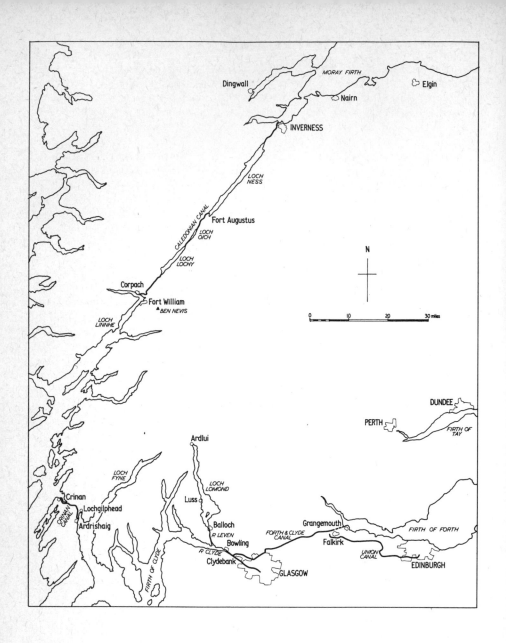

# *Scotland*

## CALEDONIAN CANAL

FROM the Beauly Firth near Inverness to Corpach; 60m 5f with 29 locks. Artificial cuts connecting Lochs Lochy, Oich, Ness and Dochfour comprise 22m of the route.

The canal was constructed under the supervision of Thomas Telford to enable sailing ships and naval vessels to avoid the often hazardous passage round Cape Wrath and through the Pentland Firth. After numerous delays, it was finally opened to navigation in 1847.

The canal was never commercially successful, largely because the introduction of steamships soon after its completion made the Cape Wrath passage less difficult and, subsequently, because the size of the new steamships rapidly outgrew the dimensions of the canal's locks. Nevertheless, the Caledonian Canal today is moderately busy with small coastal craft, fishing vessels and, in the summer months, numerous yachts and motor cruisers.

The Caledonian is one of 2 small ship canals in Scotland which are administered by the British Waterways Board. It is capable of being navigated by craft of up to 150ft long by 35ft beam by 13ft 6in draught. Its 29 locks lift vessels up to the summit level at Loch Oich – 106ft above sea level, 15 locks being situated on the west of the summit and 14 to the east. The recent mechanisation of the locks has speeded up the time taken to pass through the canal and, although it still incurs an annual loss, the Caledonian Canal plays an important part in the Highland economy, particularly to the Scottish inshore fishing industry, whose boats make regular use of this maritime short cut throughout the year.

The Caledonian cannot be compared with any other canal in Britain. Its nearest contemporary is that Swedish cross-cut, the Gota Canal, which is part lake and part canal and was also engineered by Thomas Telford. The Caledonian passes through some of the most dramatic and impressive terrain in Britain. Its entire route lies through hill and mountain country rising steeply from the water's edge, including, within sight from the canal, the highest mountain in the British Isles – Ben Nevis, 4,418ft – which overshadows Fort William. Some of the waterside slopes have been planted with coniferous forests designed to feed the large paper mill constructed in recent years at Corpach. Much of the mountainside, however, is still bare moorland dotted with free-ranging sheep and, sometimes, long-haired Scottish cattle.

By contrast, the waters of Loch Ness are over 700ft deep, deeper than any part of the North Sea and the reputed haunt of the elusive Loch Ness Monster.

One of the most striking things about the Great Glen, particularly to those used to living in urban areas, is its quietness. At night the silence is broken only by the distant bleating of sheep on the mountains and the murmur of streams falling down the hillsides into the lochs.

At any time of the year it is inspiring territory, and efforts are now being made to publicise the Caledonian Canal as a tourist attraction. Day trips are once again being operated in the summer months and hire cruisers are now available for holidays afloat in the heart of the Highlands. The Caledonian has an interesting future.

*Clachnaharry* The eastern entrance to the canal lies on the Beauly Firth at Clachnaharry, a suburb of Inverness and administrative HQ of the waterway. One wall of the canal offices bears a plaque on which the poet Robert Southey praises in verse Thomas Telford's great and nationwide engineering works.

> Telford it was by whose presiding mind
> The whole great work was planned and perfected . . .
> Telford who o'er the vale of Cambrian Dee
> Aloft in air at giddy height upborne
> Carried with navigable road; and hung
> High o'er Menai's Strait the bending bridge:
> Nor hath he for his native land performed
> Less in this proud design: and where his piers
> Around her coast from many a fisher's creek
> Unsheltered else, and many an ample port
> Repel the assailing storm: and where his roads
> In beautiful and sinuous line far seen
> Wind with the vale and win the long ascent
> Now o'er the deep morass sustained, and now
> Across ravine, or glen or estuary
> Opening a passage through the wilds subdued.

At the western end of the village stands a monument commemorating a battle between the Clans Mackintosh and Munroe in 1454. The railway from Inverness to Wick and Thurso crosses the canal here by a swing bridge.

*Inverness* (1m) The canal passes round the northern outskirts of Inverness and climbs an impressive staircase of 4 locks at Muirtown. From May to October passenger excursions are operated to Loch Ness from the top of the locks aboard the motor vessel *Scot II*, owned by the British Waterways Board.

Inverness is rightly known as the capital of the Highlands. For centuries it has been the centre of Highland trade and activity, though, curiously, its coat of arms is supported by a dromedary on one side and an elephant on the other, neither of which can be described as Highland beasts. The city has much of interest. It is a good shopping centre and an important business, marketing and administrative entrepôt for the Highlands. Delightfully situated at the eastern end of the Great Glen (Glen More), Inverness offers many opportunities for recreational pursuits and excursions, one of the most popular of the latter being that to the memorial cairn on Culloden Moor, the scene of the bloody defeat of Charles Stuart's Jacobite army on 16 April 1746 in the last battle fought in the United Kingdom. The battlefield is now the property of the National Trust for Scotland.

Among the places of interest in Inverness are St Andrew's Cathedral beside the sparkling River Ness; the Castle (an early Victorian structure built on the site of more ancient fortifications) whence there are extensive panoramic views and a statue of Flora Macdonald looking SW towards the hiding place of Bonnie Prince Charlie; the Museum; and the Gothic-styled Town House which has an interesting collection of paintings, stained-glass windows depicting clan arms, and a framed document bearing the signatures of 16 ministers (including David Lloyd George, Stanley

Baldwin and Winston Churchill) who attended the first Cabinet meeting ever to be held outside London – at Inverness on 7 September 1921. The riverside offers pleasant walks with fine views of the city's numerous church spires and the towers of the castle.

Tomnahurich on the outskirts of Inverness has a wooded cemetery of intriguing beauty where tombstones stand like sentinels in terraces up the tree-shaded hillside overlooking the canal.

*Loch Dochfour* (6m)   At the end of the 6m eastern canal section boats pass through the single lock at Dochgarroch and enter the smallest of the 4 natural lochs in the Caledonian waterway – Loch Dochfour. A spillway weir carries water from the loch into the River Ness down to Inverness and the Inverness Firth. The hulks of an old ferry and some fishing craft are beached in the loch and serve a new purpose as vantage points for fish-seeking herons and other diving birds.

*Loch Ness* (8m)   Loch Ness is world-famous for the rugged grandeur of its mountainous surroundings and for its fearsome Monster. The loch is 23m long and about 1m wide over most of its length, and over 700ft deep. The route of the canal passes down the length of the loch, lighthouses indicating the entrances to the canal sections at each end. Although completely landlocked, Loch Ness can become quite rough when strong SW or NE winds are blowing through the Great Glen, but it maintains a remarkably constant temperature throughout the year and has never been known to freeze.

Contrary to popular belief, the elusive Loch Ness Monster is not a twentieth-century newspaper story, for St Adamnan, Abbot of Iona, wrote of the beast in the seventh century and the legend has persisted. Certainly, in the evening light when the sun has sunk behind Mealfourvounie and the glen is filled with pink-tinged mist, the loch has an air of mystery and intrigue. However, despite numerous scientific investigations in recent years, the loch guards its secret well. In view of the great depth of Loch Ness it is not unlikely that some creature may have survived from before the Ice Age.

Urquhart Castle stands in a commanding position on the west side of Loch Ness guarding the entrance to Urquhart Bay, one of the few safe anchorages in the loch. Today the castle is a picturesque ruin and a favourite picnicking place but it has a war-battered history. It was a ruin even before the 1715 Jacobite rising and most of the present structure is pre-sixteenth century.

At Foyers, on the eastern shore of the loch, stands a new hydro-electric station. Water from Loch Ness is pumped to the top of the mountain behind Foyers and electricity is generated from turbines powered by the falling torrent.

A memorial cairn stands on the western shore between Drumnadrochit and Invermoriston in memory of John Cobb, who was killed on Loch Ness in 1952 when his boat *Crusader* exploded during an attempt to break the world water speed record.

*Fort Augustus* (31m)   The staircase of 5 locks that lifts the Caledonian Canal up from Loch Ness towards its summit level is the focal point of the little town of Fort Augustus. Originally known as Kilcummin, the town was garrisoned by the Government after the Jacobite rising of 1715 and the fort named after William Augustus, Duke of Cumberland. In 1867 the Government sold the fort to Lord Lovat, who presented it to the Catholic Benedictine order for the erection of the present St

Benedict's Abbey and School. The School and the clocktower were designed by Joseph Hansom, better known for his Hansom Cab. Now only part of the fort remains, but conducted tours of the Abbey are undertaken by the monks.

Also of interest in Fort Augustus are the castellated masonry piers of the bridge which formerly carried the railway line over the River Oich to a loch-side landing near Inchnacardon Bay. Beside the swing bridge at the bottom of the locks is a well stocked Highland Industries shop, and the post box of the typical Highland post office, in the row of shops beside the locks, warrants a closer look.

A 5m canal section starts at Fort Augustus, linking Loch Ness with Loch Oich. There are two locks at remote Kytra and one at Cullochy, closely followed by a road swing bridge at Aberchalder, beyond which boats enter the summit level at Loch Oich.

*Loch Oich* (36m)   Loch Oich, 106ft above sea level, is the shallowest of the 4 lochs in the Caledonian Canal, and Telford employed the earliest type of steam-driven continuous bucket dredger in making the navigable channel through it. The deep water is indicated by buoys and beacons and the helmsman needs to exercise care in navigating this section.

The loch is surrounded by the finest of Highland scenery. The ruins of Invergarry Castle, for centuries the home of the Macdonnels of Glengarry, lies on its western shore. The castle has been a ruin since it was burnt by the Duke of Cumberland during the harrying of the Highlands that followed the Battle of Culloden. Invergarry House, now a hotel, stands in pleasant loch-side grounds near the castle.

To the north of Glengarry, beside the waters of the loch, stands an unusual monument in the form of a pyramid surmounted by 7 severed heads and inscribed on 4 sides in Gaelic, Latin, French and English. Erected in 1812 by Macdonnel of Glengarry, the monument commemorates the murder of the two sons of the eleventh Chief Macdonnel by 7 of his brothers. The murderers were subsequently slain and their heads washed in the spring that continues to rise below the site of the memorial.

After leaving Loch Oich through the Oich swing bridge, the canal passes through the long tree-lined Laggan Cutting, which pierces the watershed between the east and west coasts. The cutting is one of Telford's most impressive but least known engineering works. At its western end two locks lower vessels into Loch Lochy.

*Loch Lochy* (42m)   The shores of Loch Lochy are thickly forested with conifers planted in recent years by the Forestry Commission to supply timber to the pulp mill at Corpach. Steep mountains, including Ben Tigh, otherwise called 'Glengarry's Bowling Green' (2,956ft), surround Loch Lochy, which is 450ft deep. On the eastern shore the route of the former railway to Fort Augustus can be seen hugging the mountainside.

A lighthouse marks the entrance to the 8m canal section linking Loch Lochy with the sea at Corpach. The two locks at Gairlochy are followed by an attractive two-leaf iron swing bridge (the only one of its type on the canal), which carries a farm track over the waterway at Moy. The most interesting feature of this section is, however, the spectacular staircase flight of 8 locks at Banavie (58m), with a change in level of 64ft. It is probably the most remarkable lock flight in the whole of Britain and is appropriately known as Neptune's Staircase. When not shrouded in mist, there is a fine view of Ben Nevis from Banavie.

The A830 crosses the canal at the foot of the locks by a modern, electrically operated swing bridge. In contrast, the signalman from the adjacent attractive wooden signal-box must manually wind open the swing bridge carrying the Fort William to Mallaig railway over the canal – the second of two railway swing bridges on the Caledonian. Close by is Banavie Station, a charming West Highland structure fortunately untouched by modernisation, although the trains that serve it are now diesel-hauled. The line to Mallaig has been described as one of the most beautiful railway routes in Britain, and it is certainly well worth making the trip for the views, which are superb on a clear day.

*Fort William*  Canal voyagers can travel into Fort William from Banavie Station. The town cowers beneath the bulk of Ben Nevis, although some of its more recent housing estates seem intent on climbing the mountain's lower slopes. The fort, named after William III, was demolished to make way for the railway in 1864 and the town as a result developed considerably. Today it caters for a thriving holiday and tourist traffic and many different accents may be heard in its streets.

The sharp-eyed will notice some delightful decorative ironwork on some of the main street shop fronts. There is an informative Information Bureau in Cameron Square opposite the West Highland Museum. By far the most interesting exhibit here is a remarkable 'Secret Portrait' of Prince Charles Stuart. This is painted on a wooden tray and resembles an abstract impression of a plate of bacon and eggs rather than a prince. It is only when the 'portrait' is reflected in a strategically placed, polished cylinder that it becomes alive and in proportion. Visitors should notice also in the museum the hilarious photograph of a Model T Ford and attendant company, driven

*Caledonian Canal. Fishing boats lie on the waterway at the foot of Ben Nevis*

to the summit of Ben Nevis in 1911 – a feat that well equipped expeditions failed to emulate until over 40 years later.

*Corpach* (60m)   The Caledonian Canal meets the sea at Corpach. Small coasters, locally known as 'puffers' (although the true steam-driven 'puffer' is now a rare sight), load and discharge material for the Western Isles in the terminal basin. The sea lock has been enlarged to accommodate vessels serving the large wood-pulp mill recently constructed beside Loch Eil.

## CRINAN CANAL

From Ardrishaig, Loch Gilp, to Crinan, Sound of Jura; 9m with 15 locks. The waterway is used by seagoing pleasure and commercial vessels wishing to avoid a 132m passage round the Mull of Kintyre on the west coast. Maximum craft dimensions are 88ft (sea locks leading to non-tidal basins at each end permit a length of 199ft) × 20ft (23ft in the sea locks) × 9ft 6in draught (up to 11ft 10in at the sea locks) × about 100ft headroom. All bridges are opening spans, the only restrictions being overhead power lines. This exceptionally beautiful waterway was opened, after constructional difficulties, in 1809. Apart from its convenience for seagoing craft, the towpath makes a superb walk for canal enthusiasts.

*Ardrishaig*   This collection of buildings on the shores of Loch Gilp has grown up around the southern end of the waterway. The entrance is marked by a lighthouse situated on the end of a stone harbour wall that provides protection for craft waiting to enter the sea lock. Keepers are normally in attendance at the entry locks, but may not be available for other locks and swing bridges, a situation greeted with alarm by habitual users when announced in 1972 but one which is quite normal on the majority of nationalised smaller waterways. While gate, paddle and bridge gear is suitably massive, it presents no problems for manual operation. A further 3 locks lift the canal to its longest level section, a distance of almost 4m.

*Lochgilphead* (2m 2f)   Hugging the shores of Loch Gilp, the canal passes above this, the county town of Argyll. It is a bustling place of whitewashed houses and shops, which grew to its present size largely because of canal traffic. From here the waterway heads inland, taking the shortest possible route across the peninsula through rocky hills clothed in bracken and firs. Wild cats have been seen here, while in winter deer come down from the mountains to seek food.

*Summit Level* (4m 1f)   Beyond the fashionable Cairnbaan Hotel Locks 5–8 climb to the short summit, from which Locks 9–13 descend through the village of Dunardry. A minor road accompanies much of the waterway.

*Bellanoch Lagoon* (7m)   A dramatically narrow section carved from rock cliffs winds along the shore of the SE corner of Loch Crinan near the confluence with the River Add. Sleek offshore yachts are generally to be found on moorings in the broad lagoon.

*Crinan* (9m)   An enchanting little place, where the canal basin stands between the open waters of Loch Crinan and a towering cliff. There is an hotel, boatyard, further

*Crinan Canal. Sleek ocean sailers, a cluster of cottages around the locks, a tiny lighthouse and an hotel: this is Crinan, one of the best situated villages in Britain, with magnificent views towards the Western Isles and the Sound of Jura*

luxury sailing-craft and a lighthouse by the sea lock. The silence, far from aircraft routes and main roads, is something that must be experienced to be believed. Across the loch, well known for its vivid sunsets, is Duntroon Castle. Canal dues are payable at the Ardrishaig office. The through passage normally takes between 4½ and 6 hours.

### FORTH & CLYDE CANAL

From the Clyde at Bowling Harbour to Grangemouth on the east coast of the Scottish Midlands; 35¼m with 39 locks. Perhaps the greatest postwar scandal on our waterways was the closure of the Forth & Clyde Canal in 1962. This incredibly stupid and short-sighted move was made by British Transport Waterways just before the creation of the present British Waterways Board. Anyone remotely interested in either inland or seagoing craft is unfailingly angered at the sight of its derelict locks and increasingly numerous culverted road crossings. As late as 1956 139 pleasure boats, 98 powered fishing craft and 14 cargo vessels passed through the canal, but figures such as these were deemed insufficient to justify the expense of keeping it open. That was the official reason. Needless to say, the real excuse was to avoid construction of a £160,000 lifting bridge for the Denny bypass on the Glasgow to Stirling road. Unless the waterway can be restored to navigation within the reasonably near future, it will continue to be an increasingly expensive and disagreeable liability. Already the expenditure of huge sums of money has been proposed to eliminate a section in Glasgow, where, predictably, its derelict state has resulted in children being drowned.

With no fixed bridges over its entire length, the F&C enabled masted vessels to travel from one coast to the other within a single day. Maximum dimensions were 68ft 6in × 19ft 8in × 8ft 6in draught. Lock chambers are intact but weired, with some of the paddle gear removed. The channel remains deep, with clear water and few weeds, and is continuous except for a length of about 1m uphill from Grangemouth Docks, now filled in. This would not present an insuperable problem if restoration were to be undertaken, for a link could quite easily be created with the River Carron and thence to the Firth of Forth. At present much of the canal is well suited to cruising in canoes and similar small boats that can negotiate fixed bridges or culverts or be portaged round these obstructions. The value of the waterway for this type of activity was well demonstrated in the summer of 1973, when 54 two-man outboard powered inflatables competed in a trans-Scotland marathon from near Edinburgh on the Union Canal to Glasgow, via the F&C from Falkirk.

The western terminus of the canal at Bowling Harbour, overlooking the wide waters of the Clyde, is kept in good condition as a non-tidal mooring for seagoing pleasure craft. After passing through Clydebank and near the famous shipyards, the F&C enters Glasgow in attractive surroundings by Maryhill Locks. The masonry, iron mooring hooks in place of bollards, heavy paddle gear operated by handspikes, and remaining manually worked two-leaved bascule bridges carrying minor roads are all features of particular interest. An outstanding aqueduct carries the waterway over the River Kelvin (see p 71). A short branch in the city leads to Glasgow Basin, which has impressive warehouses and canal offices.

A 16m summit level passes through very pleasant countryside (not as dramatic as the Highlands terrain of the Caledonian Canal) with stone-built bridge-keepers' houses. At Falkirk a flight of locks dropping the canal towards the Forth has been admirably landscaped by the local authority, which tends to emphasise the locks' regrettable state of disuse. Port Downie, Falkirk, was the junction with the Union Canal until its closure in 1933, when the Union's flight of locks was filled in. The well painted Union Inn now looks over a grassed and tarmac square, where barges once passed, and the hillside that locks used to climb is a landscaped park through a housing estate.

The Scottish Inland Waterways Association has met with considerable success in promoting small-boat cruising on the F&C, and holds a long-term and ambitious aim of seeing the waterway reopened for sizeable craft throughout.

### LOCH LOMOND AND RIVER LEVEN

Generally claimed as Britain's second largest lake, Loch Lomond is 24m long and up to 5m wide. Lying north of the Clyde and within easy reach of Glasgow, its waters are justly famous as one of Scotland's leading tourist attractions. Exploration can be undertaken by driving along the A82, which follows the west shore, aboard one of the tripping craft that operate on scheduled runs, or by private sailing or motor cruiser. There are safe and convenient moorings at several points. The loch contains about 30 wooded islands, some inhabited, and lies in rugged mountainous country, the greatest peak being Ben Lomond (3,192ft).

*Balloch*   A rather tripper-ridden resort with bed and breakfast establishments, small hotels and restaurants, Balloch is situated each side of a bridge over the River Leven, which flows from the loch to the Clyde at Dumbarton, 7¾m S. Craft drawing up to 3ft can sometimes reach Lomond from the Clyde, although the journey can be hazardous, depending on the height of tides in the Clyde and the amount of 'fresh' running down from the loch. A recent river barrier connected with an undertaking

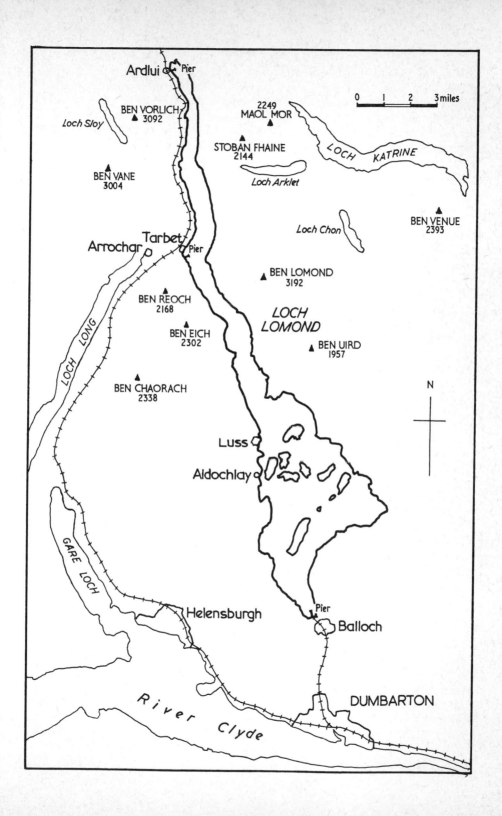

supplying 100 million gallons of water daily can be navigated under the right conditions. Advice should be sought from watermen in Balloch. Connected by direct rail links with both Edinburgh and Glasgow, a short branch-line extends to Balloch Pier, where the paddle-steamer *Maid of the Loch* (Caledonian Steam Packet Co Ltd) sails to various points throughout the length of Loch Lomond between late May and early September. There are overland connections with other services on Lochs Long, Goil and Katrine. *Maid of the Loch*, 193ft overall and 555 tons, was built as recently as 1953, and offers the facilities of a dining-saloon and bar in the manner of many similar craft that plied the Scottish lochs and West Coast at the turn of the century. There is a public Bear Park near the pier.

*Luss* A charming village, with cottages, pier, hotel and moorings. Fine views of Ben Lomond to the NE.

*Balmaha* A small sailing centre surrounded by pines on the SE corner of the loch. It lies opposite Inchcailleoch, 'the island of old women', which was the burial place of the MacGregors.

*Rowardennan* A popular resort for canoeing, water-skiing and fishing, with hotel and youth hostel. Starting point for the 2–3 hour climb of Ben Lomond, where the vista from the summit sometimes extends as far as Ben Nevis at the western end of the Caledonian Canal.

*Tarbet* At a junction of the Glasgow–Fort William A82, it has a hotel and steamer pier. A 2m isthmus separates Lomond from Loch Long at Arrochar, where passenger boats sail for the Clyde.

*Inversnaid* On the E shore, with a good hotel. Rob Roy's Cave is to be found nearby.

*Ardlui* The head of the loch.

There are rowing, sailing and powered craft on hire for short or long periods, and launching facilities for trailed craft at Balmaha, Cluan, Rowardennan, and Balloch. Portable boats can be manhandled into the water at Luss and from several beaches along the A82 near Tarbet.

### UNION CANAL

This canal is otherwise known as the Edinburgh & Glasgow Union Canal, from Port Hopetoun, Edinburgh, to Falkirk; 30m with no locks. Opened in 1822, the Union was linked with the Forth & Clyde at Falkirk via a flight of 11 locks that was closed in 1933. All traces of the flight have now gone (see p 458). The rest of the waterway remains largely intact, although it was officially abandoned in 1965 by the BWB, several years after its predecessors, British Transport Waterways, had put a number of small hire cruisers into service as an experiment. That act alone is an indication of the scenic qualities of the canal. Apart from several culverted road crossings and variable amounts of weed, the Union is an attractive cruising proposition for small craft that can be carried round obstructions.

The main features are 3 unusually massive aqueducts, crossing the Rivers Almond, Avon and the Water of Leith (see p 71). Near the Falkirk terminus is a 696yd tunnel with walkable towpath (the whole line of the Union is well suited for ramblers). Carved masks on the keystones of the nearby lofty bridge arch at Glen display laughing and aggrieved faces traditionally said to represent the feelings of two contractors involved in the canal's construction. One made a profit and the other went bankrupt!

*Loch Lomond. An ideal way of seeing Lomond is to take a trip aboard steam paddle wheeler* Maid of the Loch, *moored here at her pier by Balloch station*

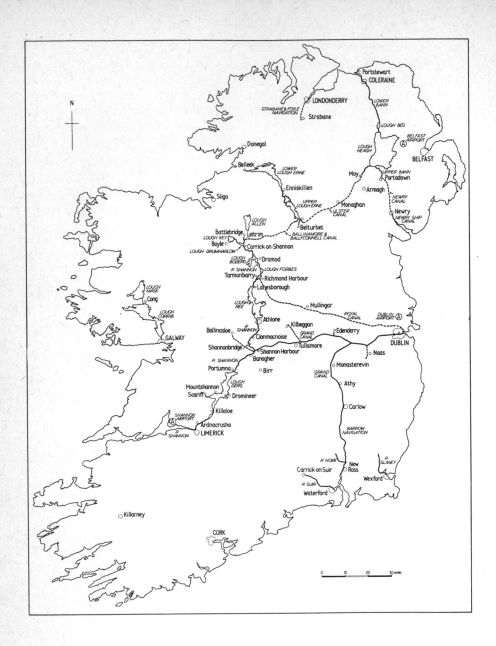

# Ireland

FROM Lowtown, junction with the Grand Canal Main Line, to St Mullins Sea Lock, entry to the Barrow estuary; 69m 7f with 32 locks, of which 3 are 2-rise.

Formed by a canal, opened in 1791, from the main line of the Grand to Athy, and by a river navigation making extensive use of long canal cuts from Athy to the sea and opened to traffic in 1790, parts of the Barrow, especially in its lower reaches, rank as among the most beautiful of waterways in these islands. Minimum dimensions of the locks are the same as for the Grand Canal (p 473), although during dry weather levels downstream of Carlow provide a draught of only 2ft 6in. Commercial traffic on the waterway below Carlow was withdrawn in 1950 and sugar barges working from Carlow refinery to the Grand Canal ceased in 1959. Maintenance over most of the route has been minimal since that time, although improvements are slowly being made. Little navigational difficulty will be experienced between Lowtown and Carlow, with the possible exception of weeding in high summer. Conditions below Carlow improved in 1970 with the start of a programme to dredge silted lock cuts, but a tendency to flood in wet weather or become very shallow in times of drought, coupled with a distinct lack of navigation markers and a series of completely unguarded weirs, makes the Barrow rather hazardous for novices. The Carlow Branch of the Inland Waterways Association of Ireland, which has done much to improve conditions, will always offer advice and encouragement to intending navigators. Some indication of the keenness of Irish waterways enthusiasts to see more craft using the Barrow is provided by the Harp Lager Award. At the time of writing all visiting boats reaching the Shannon via the Barrow are presented with a Golden Harp and a case of beer, and their lock fees are refunded by the Irish Tourist Board. Similar inducements were offered for a complete passage of the Grand Canal, which, being less adventurous, merited a Silver Harp! Full details may be obtained from the Hon Secretary of the Dublin Branch of the IWAI.

Having thus given warning of the hazards, it is only fair for us to emphasise that this is an outstandingly lovely, remote and nearly deserted navigation. The author managed to explore most of the Barrow in a substantial Shannon hire cruiser in May 1970 without undue difficulty. Conditions are likely to have improved since that time.

*Lowtown*    Perversely, this canal junction now consists of a single cottage standing rather above the level of the surrounding country. Once an important centre of barge activity, together with nearby Robertstown, it now sees few boats on its deep waters, which, from this point to the outskirts of Athy, are as transparent as on any canal in the British Isles. Thousands of sizeable fish can be seen from the bows of a cruiser. While there are keepers to help work craft through the locks, their presence cannot be relied upon in the same way as on the Grand. The further down the Barrow one navigates, the fewer there are, some having responsibility for as many as 4 locks at widely spaced intervals. Until 1971 the man in charge of Locks 20 and 21 at Lowtown was Murt Murphy, a genial character with a fund of stories of the time when he skippered first horseboats and later diesel Bolinder-powered barges throughout the system. He graphically recalled the fate of Barge 45M, which was lost in the Shannon off Lough Derg's Holy Island 3 days before Christmas 1946. Four men were drowned, and the 50 tons of porter comprising the cargo was lost. One of the lost crew was 27-year-old McGrath who 'lived in the cottage with the red roof a mile down the canal. As you pass, you can see him there still' – according to Mr Murphy. Due south, 4m distant, stands the Hill of Allen, 676ft high and surmounted by a tower, and still extensively quarried. To the NW the giant cooling towers of Allenwood Power Station dominate the landscape for many miles. This station is one of a series of turf-fired plants, supplying the national grid, which will be noticed during the passage of the Grand Canal across the Bog of Allen to the Shannon.

On the right bank ancient Ballyteige Castle, unlike so many similar structures seen from the Irish waterways, is still occupied, as is evidenced by the television mast sprouting from its roof. Remains of the original Lock 21 at Ballyteige, where the dry chamber is carpeted with flowers, can be seen on the left, a short distance from the canal's present route. Subsidence of bogland made the rerouting necessary at a lower level in 1803.

*Rathangan* (7m 6f)   The tall white spire of the church can be seen across the bogland, which becomes progressively greener and more wooded as the canal nears the Barrow valley. Here there are quays providing good moorings close to shops and a garage. Fuel supplies for boats have not yet been catered for on the Barrow Line;

*Barrow Navigation. The weir at Carlow* (Irish Tourist Board)

petrol can be obtained in the small waterside towns and carried back to the canal in cans, but the problem of refuelling a diesel-powered cruiser without paying the heavy road fuel tax can be extremely difficult. Local enquiry should pinpoint canalside supplies on the Grand Canal, where tanks should be filled for an expedition down the Barrow. If, as is likely, additional diesel is required en route, one tax-free and legitimate source is private agricultural supply tanks. A satisfactory bargain can generally be struck with the farmer.

A short distance beyond the town lies the double-chambered Lock 23, which is nameless, although the grey stone accommodation bridge at its lower end bears a carved plaque with the name Spencer Bridge and the date 1784 in beautifully incised capitals. This well preserved example of masonic typography is in sharp contrast to the twin-faced stone distance pillar on the left below the lock, on which in crude lettering we are told that Dublin is 27m and Monasterevan 4. Presumably the distances are quoted in Irish miles, for the actual figures are 34 and 6 respectively: in addition the spelling is curious, for all the letters N and the figure 4 have been laboriously engraved backwards! Progress through locks about here is more than usually slow, so interesting and informative are their keepers.

*Monasterevan* (14m 3f)   This large prosperous village is a good centre for basic supplies. South of it stands Moore Abbey, on the site of the seventh-century St Evin's monastery, from which the place derives its name. Built in 1607 and altered in 1846, the Abbey was the property of the tenor John McCormack until 1946 and is now a home for epileptics run by the Sisters of Charity. A cross in the market place commemorates a Father Prendergast, hanged for his activities in the 1798 insurrection. One local legend concerns *Beurnan Eimhin* (St Evin's Bell), on which it was customary for local warriors to swear to keep the peace in future. When, however, one individual swore a false oath on the bell, it spontaneously rolled out of the church and tumbled into a deep hole in the Barrow, never to be seen again. The site of its disappearance is known as the Bell Pool.

A nineteenth-century Catholic church, with huge rose window in the elevation facing the canal, overlooks one of the most curious navigation liftbridges in Britain and Ireland. A huge rectangular metal frame, counterbalancing the road platform, is supported on the most slender upright columns, cross-braced with wires in all directions. The whole structure is surmounted by a great grooved winding wheel. The honour of operating the bridge for boats lies with the keeper of Lock 25, several hundred yards down the canal. He will arrive after an appropriate Irish delay with a small gang of stalwarts to apply their energies to the windlasses. First, clanking barriers of outsize chainmail are stretched across the roadway on each side of the canal to warn the not inconsiderable traffic, during which time a sizeable crowd of onlookers will have gathered to witness the operation. Monasterevan's bridge was erected in 1826, the same year as the fine stone aqueduct that immediately afterwards carries the navigation over the River Barrow. There are 3 arches, each with a 40ft span. Formerly the navigation descended to river level, with barges being worked from one bank to the other. Both liftbridge and aqueduct were constructed in connection with a plan to build a branch line linking the Castlecomer collieries in County Kilkenny with the Barrow line, but that plan was never carried out, although an 11½m section running east from Monasterevan to Portarlington and Mountmellick, with 3 locks, was opened in 1830. It was last used by a powered pleasure boat in the late 1950s and is now ruinous. From this point to Athy the canal closely follows the River Barrow on a 14m level pound.

Shallow cuttings lined by hawthorn hedges, and at times a narrow channel on which tall reeds encroach, combine to provide a sense of complete isolation.

*Vicarstown* (21m 6f)   This little village on the L126 road is reached after crossing Grattan Aqueduct over a Barrow tributary. Here a game reserve borders on the waterway, with rows of straw baskets and adapted oil drums on the right bank to encourage waterfowl to nest. There is a fine group of grey stone warehouses, now derelict, by the canal in the village. A little under 4m SW lies Stradbally, where the steam museum is well worth a visit. Considerable quantities of malt for brewing used to be brought from here by Grand Canal Company and other lorries to Vicarstown, where it was transhipped into barges. Dunrally Bridge, less than 1m NE along the L126 from Vicarstown, crosses the Barrow, flanked on the east bank by one of the many ancient castles in this valley. A short distance upstream is the great ring fort of Dunrally.

*Athy* (28m 2f)   An ancient and now flourishing market and manufacturing town, Athy is situated at the junction of the canal and the Barrow. The fifteenth-century remains of Woodstock Castle and the sixteenth-century White's Castle, now a national monument, are indications of Athy's former strategic importance. A startling Dominican Church, built here 1963–5 and pentagon-shaped with a hyperbolic paraboloid roof, dominates the view upriver from the junction. A narrow stone bridge known as the Horse Bridge crosses the Barrow at the junction and carries the towpath from the canal to the eastern bank of the river. At the Quay, above Lock 27, lies an extensive wharf, with canopy, warehouses and a small crane, though its drydock is now gone. Chief canal traffic was carrying malt to Dublin. Extensive maltings still operate, traditional methods being used in the nineteenth-century buildings on the waterfront, while behind is the largest and most modern malting plant in Ireland, completed late in 1969. Huge vats of fermenting barley used in the manufacture of Guinness lager are controlled by a single operator facing a battery of buttons and dials. A conducted tour of the works is recommended. Between Locks 27 and 28 a most attractive row of low white-painted stone cottages with pastel-coloured doors stretch out along the canal. It is most unfortunate that a place of the antiquity and interest of Athy should blatantly discharge raw sewage into the canal, producing a foul stench in warm weather and contaminating the River Barrow for many miles downstream. Additional treatment facilities are, however, being planned.

The first of the many unguarded weirs is found below a concrete bridge, one of whose piers is placed in the navigation channel, making it rather tricky to manoeuvre into Ardreigh lock cut on the east bank. Of the 41m of river navigation between Athy and St Mullins, 11m are composed of artificial channels. It is not always clear where these channels leave the river, so a sharp watch should be kept on the towpath. The deepest water is generally about 10ft from the path. Ardreigh cut is spanned by a spindly drawbridge that is generally found open.

*Levitstown Lock* (32m 6f)   The lock cut is 2m long and care is necessary in passing the open weir at its upstream end. The countryside is now well wooded and fertile compared with the boglands at the top of the Barrow Line. The scenery is at its best from this point as far as the estuary. Just above Levitstown Lock is a most unusual, vertically rising liftbridge whose counterbalance weights descend to ground level to act as road blocks. It is easily operated by the boat's crew, and served as a most useful impromptu crane to lift a cruiser's badly choked propeller clear of the water on one occasion. On the right side of the lock is a huge ruined crenellated mill, one of many such mills on the Barrow. It was burnt out in 1942.

*Carlow* (40m) The river approach to this county town is most attractive as the waterway broadens out. First sign of civilisation is the large sugar-beet factory on the left bank, served by its own canal arm off the river. Government-owned and the largest in Ireland, it was established in 1923. The boot and shoe factory in the centre of the town near the bridge is a fine example of industrial architecture, dating from 1903. Below Waterloo Bridge (1815) the navigation channel crosses to the right bank above a broad curved weir, before entering Carlow Lock. The view upstream from this point is superb, with the low skyline of the town dominated by the keep of an ancient castle, all that remains of a once extensive structure. In 1814 a medical practitioner started to convert it into a lunatic asylum, but his over-zealous use of gunpowder to reduce the thickness of the walls and to enlarge windows resulted in destruction of much of the building. The lock-keeper issues navigation permits, and the officials of the Carlow Branch of the Inland Waterways Association of Ireland will be pleased to offer advice on prevailing conditions on the river downstream of the town. The stone warehouses formerly used by the Grand Canal Company, above the bridge, are now the headquarters of one of Ireland's leading rowing clubs. An annual regatta is staged in early summer.

*Milford* (44m) Beyond Clongrennan Lock and near a castle that is now the gateway to Clongrennan House, the river proceeds to Milford, where there is an 850yd lock cut. Once an area of great commercial activity, Milford is now a peaceful spot with a famous and well maintained horse stud owned by the Alexander family. Another 2 great castellated mills stand on the banks of the navigation where the river divides into several channels, with weirs. One of these weirs was repaired during the 1950s by the expedient of sinking a steel barge across a breach, an unsatisfactory action, resulting in a general lowering of the levels. The upper mill of the 2, which are both eighteenth-century and owned by the Alexanders, has had different functions at different times: it has ground wheat, and until the late 1950s was a sawmill, but from 1896 or even earlier it generated electricity, providing Carlow with the first electrically lit streets of any town in Ireland. The Middlesbrough-made turbines can still be seen, substantially complete though derelict. Further down the lock cut a chain-operated drawbridge across the navigation provides access to the seemingly fortified gateway of the second mill, which worked as a tannery until 1970. A 'tombstone' at the roadside by the upper mill commemorates an itinerant woman, Mary Cash, who threw herself into the river in December 1968.

*Leighlinbridge* (47m 6f) This small Barrow village comes after Rathvindon, where there is a lock. Here is the oldest bridge spanning the waterway, built in 1320 by Canon Jakis, the engineering priest from Kildare. Its weathered stonework is hung between May and September with bunches of the crimson spur valerian, and there are patches of the rarer white variety of this noble wall plant. Black Castle at the eastern end of the bridge dates from 1181, when it was erected by John de Claville.

*Barrow Navigation. Certain river navigations feature completely unguarded weirs like this example on Southern Ireland's River Barrow near Goresbridge*

*Muine Bheag* (50m 4f)   Known as Bagenalstown until 1924, it was founded towards the close of the eighteenth century by Walter Bagenal, who determined that its architectural delights should rival Versailles. While a pleasant little town, the only building with a hint of grandeur is the courthouse, with its Doric portico. Re-routing of a coach road resulted in Bagenalstown becoming rather a backwater, but it was once an important centre of barge trading, with a brewery and two mills, one of them alongside the lock.

The lock, which in 1970 had suffered from a broken cill for over 15 years, can be difficult to negotiate, and mechanical assistance may be required to open the top gates against a head of water. The drawbridge above it is both heavy and badly balanced but responds to force of numbers. Waterside features of the town include a massive complex of barred windowed maltings, an open-air swimming pool and a diving board on the river immediately upstream of an unguarded weir! 

Winding gear was once common on the river to assist the motorised barges upstream against the current. Men operating these craft were known as the Barrow Boys and their boat-handling skills were superior to those of the crews who normally stayed on the canal system.

*Goresbridge* (56m)   Through Fenniscourt, Slyguff and Upper Ballyellen Locks, the canal's route finds more fertile surroundings all the time, with cultivated fields and pastureland for cattle and sheep. Little green hills reach down to the river, where solitary anglers fish for eels (and reputedly grander catches of salmon) from clearings in the reeds or aboard ubiquitous clinker-built open skiffs, generally outboard-powered, which are almost the only boats one can expect to encounter. In these reaches of the Barrow it is very important to keep strictly to the navigation channel close to the towpath. Sizeable rocks are visible when the river is running at normal or low level. If a cruiser should ground, the safest means of regaining deep water will be for one of the crew to wade in the river bed, easing the boat over the obstructions to avoid damage to stern gear. There was formerly a heavy malt traffic by barge from Barraghcore, a little way upstream from Goresbridge, although nothing remains to indicate this former industry. The left-hand arch of Goresbridge is the course of navigation. Mountains on each side now begin to close in on the river, at times producing an effect not unlike that of the Rhine. To the east the Blackstone Mountains extend from Goresbridge to New Ross, the highest peak being Mount Leinster at 2,610ft. On the west a range including Brandon Hill forces the Barrow to make many sharp bends.

*Graiguenamanagh* (65m 7f) Beyond the pleasant Georgian village of Borris, the most convenient base from which to explore Mount Leinster, the Barrow plunges into a deep gorge with thickly timbered slopes. Ballykeenan Lock consists of an upper and lower chamber, a great rarity for a river navigation. Graiguenamanagh is a small market and woollen manufacturing town that once provided varied canal boat cargoes. The parish church is a crudely restored Cistercian abbey dating from the thirteenth century. A small rock castle stands in ruins at Tinnahinch, ½m downstream of the bridge on the east bank. The summit of Brandon Hill to the SW provides good views down the Barrow valley, and there is a prehistoric cairn and a stone circle to see.

*St Mullins* (69m 7f) Here the sea lock marks the start of the tidal Barrow. Care was always required by canal barges in navigating these reaches, and the same applies to pleasure craft today. It is most desirable to take advantage of the stream, which can run at 2 knots. At low water there is insufficient draught to cross the cill of St Mullins Lock and, in addition, a shoal known as The Scars runs out into the river ½m below. Tidal constant for Waterford Bridge or New Ross is −4 hr 53 min high water at Dover with about an additional ½ hr for St Mullins and Inistioge. (Inistioge is the present limit of navigation of the River Nore, joining the Barrow between St Mullins and New Ross.) Inland craft in experienced hands can reach Waterford, 5m 4f up the River Suir from Cheekpoint, and beyond to Carrick-on-Suir, 24m 6f distant. The appropriate Admiralty Chart is No 2046.

### CORRIB, LOUGH

This superb cruising ground is situated near the west coast of Ireland, north of Galway Bay. Comprising two connected lakes, the upper and lower loughs, the original navigation from Galway and the coast to Maam was 34m long, but the short Eglinton Canal at Galway with 2 locks was closed in 1955 and the way to the sea is consequently barred. The lakes had been made suitable for steamers by 1859, but much of the traffic had gone to the railways by 1905, when there were 3 steamers still in operation. The 68 sq m of water is maintained in good condition by the Lough Corrib Navigation Trustees, with markers to indicate the channels.

There are 145 islands, creating a vista generally far superior to any of the Shannon lakes. Apart from many open fishing skiffs, a handful of private cruisers and a modern passenger waterbus based at Galway and called the *Maid of Coleraine* (it was originally on the River Bann), the pleasure boating potential of Corrib is quite untapped. There are no cabin craft for hire, few sheltered quays – those for the former steamers are rather exposed, and fishing-boat harbours admit shallow draught craft only – and an absence of lakeside water and fuelling points. In spite of these limitations, Corrib can provide ample scope for a week's holiday aboard a trailed cabin cruiser and should appeal to the adventurous lover of lonely places. Riding on Connemara ponies and excellent fishing are further attractions.

Useful additional information is contained in Hugh Malet's *In the Wake of the Gods* and P. J. G. Ransom's *Holiday Cruising in Ireland.*

The upper lough was intended to be connected with Lough Mask by the 3m Cong Canal, built during 5 years in the 1850s. Sadly, when water was admitted to the channel and 4 locks, it all drained away through the carboniferous limestone. Navigation works that could never be used can be seen between Lislaughera and Cong, surely the most unfortunate lock chambers to be found anywhere! Another curiosity is a 24ft high stone lighthouse with outside spiral stairway, which was built to mark the shoals of the Ballycurran peninsula opposite Oughterard.

## ERNE NAVIGATION

One writes about the Erne hesitantly, for this is one of the few really wild and deserted navigations in Britain, perhaps in Europe. Any publicity will result in more people, more boats, and this inevitably means some loss of the magical (yet slightly melancholic) atmosphere. The waterway is known as 'Ulster's Lakeland' and is largely in Fermanagh, westernmost of the 6 counties of Northern Ireland. Fermanagh is no small county, yet one-third consists of water, mostly available to pleasure craft. The border with Southern Ireland is never far away, and indeed the Erne lies partly in the Republic. This magnificent cruising ground consists of 2 distinct halves – Upper Lough Erne and Lower Lough Erne – joined by a narrowing at Enniskillen, where the sole remaining lock on the system is normally open at each end.

Maximum dimensions for craft are 112ft × 20ft beam. To explore everywhere, draught should not much exceed 3ft or headroom about 9ft, although these may be increased to 8ft and 15ft respectively and not greatly restrict the cruising possibilities.

The navigation was created between 1876 and 1890 and was briefly connected with the Shannon via the Ballinamore & Ballyconnell Canal (closed about 1869). Another link was between the River Finn at Wattle Bridge and the River Blackwater by means of the 45m Ulster Canal, disused by 1929. The Erne is thus now landlocked in relation to other rivers and canals.

The 2 loughs cover about 300 sq m, approximately equal to the combined water areas of the English Lake District, Loch Lomond and the Broads. There are 154 mostly wooded islands, chiefly concentrated in the eastern part of the Lower lough and throughout the Upper one. With the encouragement of the Northern Ireland Tourist Board, several good hire-cruiser firms have operated since the 1960s and facilities such as an excellent series of marker posts and mooring quays have been added. In spite of the political troubles of the region during the 1970s, tourist growth has been surprisingly steady. It should be remembered that Fermanagh is remote from the problems associated with Belfast. Useful aids are the Admiralty charts 5082 and 5083, originally prepared in 1836 and still applicable except that water levels were reduced in the 1950s by a hydro-electric scheme with power station below Belleek. A simplified coloured chart was published by Geoffrey Dibb Ltd in 1970. Mary Rogers' excellent study of the history, folklore and wild life of the region

*Prospect of Erne*, was published by the Fermanagh Field Club in 1967. Easily the most evocative and helpful cruising material, resulting from a week's holiday journey, is John Liley's series of 3 articles in *Motor Boat & Yachting*, dated 1, 15 and 29 December 1967.

The most direct route between Belleek and Belturbet, involving navigation of both loughs, is about 53m. There are, however, so very many detours or alternatives that the true length of navigation offered by the Erne is considerably more. The following description presents some of the highlights, travelling upstream in a south-easterly direction.

*Belleek*   The village lies partly in Ulster, partly in the Republic, about 4m down the River Erne from the lower lough. There are two quays and good access, following dredging that was done in connection with the power station, and because of a dam that prevents progress downstream to the coast. A pottery (open to the public) makes a well-known lustre-finish chinaware.

*Murkinish Island*   Near the junction of river and lough, this island, like many others, is inhabited by wild and rather savage goats. This end of the lough offers fewer islands and an immense expanse of open water, reaching 9m in width and up to 5m from north to south. The cliffs of Magho, otherwise the Poola Fookas Range, extend along the southern shore, reaching a height of 1,018ft. Beyond lies the Lough Navar Forest, intersected by a road to a lookout point (cars are charged an admission fee). The whole of the Lower lough is encircled by a road, while many parts of the Upper lough are similarly accessible to the motorist.

*Tully Castle*   A ruin on the southern shore. A little south of here, where islands are thickly clustered, lies Inish Macsaint, with jetty, ruined church and unique Celtic cross, dating from very early Christian times.

*Lakeland Marina*   A useful, newly built harbour on the northern side of the lough, near the village of Kesh. Beyond Gubbaroe Point, to the south, is White Island, where 8 carved figures of doubtful origin possibly date back to the eighth century.

*Castle Archdale*   Shelter is provided by a harbour between Rossbeg Point and Davy's Island. One of the few large-scale holiday developments in the area is the caravan camping park, whose range of facilities are available to boat crews. A wartime base for Sunderland flying boats remains in the form of jetties and slipway.

*Devenish Island*   As the lough narrows near the approach to Enniskillen, Devenish or Ox Island has a useful jetty at which to moor when visiting the ecclesiastical monuments. These include parts of a monastery founded in the sixth century by St Mo-Laisse, an 81ft high round tower of the twelfth century and a museum. Other islands in the lough present an almost Amazonian jungle to the voyager. The county has been alarmingly depopulated during the last 100 years and all railways have been torn up, so it is quite likely that you will cruise for hours without seeing another person or boat. The fishing is described as among the best anywhere in Europe.

*Enniskillen* The island town of Kathleen, although the county capital, has a population of little more than 7,000. There are strong military connections; a riverside castle in the Scottish baronial style, partly fourteenth-century and housing local and regimental museums; and Portora Royal School, where Oscar Wilde and Samuel Beckett were educated. Eastwards 1½m stands the finest classical mansion in Ireland – Castlecoole. Built for the first Earl of Belmore between 1789 and 1798 and now administered by the National Trust, it contains fine stucco work and furniture and is well worth visiting. The Portora barrage and lock normally provide a level passage, unless the water is low, in which event a keeper is on hand to operate the gates. The Upper lough is a quite astonishing complex of channels and islands for which the word 'maze' seems hopelessly inadequate. But for the numbered marker posts one could easily become hopelessly lost. The lake shores are hilly and, like the many islands, tend to be well wooded. Islands bear names like Lusty More, Lusty Beg, Creaghancreasty and Bleanish; the alternative Bilberry, Jubilee, Turkey and Rabbit were inventions selected by the early nineteenth-century naval hydrographers.

*Crom Castle* In fact there are two castles by the lake 4m from Newtown Butler. The earliest, built in 1611, was acquired by the Crichton family. After surviving Jacobite sieges, it was accidentally burned in 1764. The newer castle, erected on a nearby site, was the home of the Earls of Erne. Until the creation of the Republic a number of wealthy families acted out a fashionable existence in the district, with racing yachts on the lough. Crom, being in Ulster, is still occupied by the Crichtons, but Lanesborough Lodge and Castle Saunderson, both just over the border, are now boarded up and forgotten (the Lodge suffered a fire during the Troubles). Derryvore

*Lough Erne. Boating on the upper lough by Enniskillen castle* (Northern Ireland Tourist Board)

has a British Customs Post, where boats are requested to call, although regulations are quite relaxed for holidaymakers.

*Belturbet*  At the southernmost point on the Erne system and lying within the Republic, Belturbet is best approached via the Folias cut, the only section of artificial navigation on the river. It is a very quiet market town with wide range of shops and boating facilities. The current of the River Erne flows quite strongly and shoals shortly below the bridge prevent navigation further upstream.

*Woodford River*  Joining the Erne west of the Folias cut, this formed part of the sadly under used Ballinamore & Ballyconnell Canal link with the Shannon. About 6m can be cruised, as far as the first gate-less lock chamber at Corraquill. The water is deep, if coloured almost black by the turf, and the twisting and mysterious journey is one that every true waterways enthusiast will be compelled to make if only to dream of some day being able to continue through the rebuilt locks and loughs of the B&B, and so down the centre of Ireland to Dublin or Limerick (see also p 483).

*River Finn*  At the eastern extremity of Upper Lough Erne, this was the way to the now ruined Ulster Canal and Lough Neagh. The canal is virtually dry. Wattlebridge may be reached and a shore expedition mounted to find the abandoned Castle Saunderson, which, in true Sleeping Beauty tradition, is intact but deserted, with half a century of weeds gradually eliminating all traces of the fine gardens. Castle Saunderson eloquently symbolises the entire Erne – a place from which the people have mostly vanished, leaving behind them a waterway paradise in muted greens and soft silver.

### GRAND CANAL

From the Shannon Navigation at Shannon Harbour to James' Street Harbour, Dublin; 79m 3f with 36 locks, of which 5 are staircase pairs. Branches comprise (1) The Circular line or Ringsend branch, connecting the main line near James' Street Harbour with the tidal River Liffey and thence Dublin Bay (3m 6f, 8 locks); (2) Barrow line (see p 463); (3) Edenderry branch (1m, no locks); (4) the derelict Ballinasloe branch, from the west bank of the Shannon, via Clonfert and Kylemore (13m 7f, 2 locks); (5) Kilbeggan branch (8m, no locks), which is derelict but with a chance of reopening; (6) the derelict Naas and Corbally branch (8m, 5 locks), whose first 2½m might be restored to Naas; and (7) Milltown Feeder (7m), a water supply line from Robertstown, of which about 2m is still navigable from the main line.

The only surviving waterway between the east coast and the Shannon, the Grand Canal was opened between Dublin and Shannon Harbour in 1805. Work started at the eastern end, reaching Lowtown in 1780, Daingean in 1798, and Tullamore in 1799. Maximum dimensions for craft are 61ft × 13ft × 4ft 6in draught × 9ft headroom. Although traffic figures for the waterway never reached equivalent proportions to similar canal systems in Britain, the Grand was by Irish standards a prosperous concern. Reaching an annual peak of 380,000 tons in 1875, the figure was about 100,000 tons in the mid-1950s. The canal was nationalised in 1950, and commercial craft withdrawn by May 1960, amid the protests of waterway enthusiasts. Even today there is a strong case for economic carriage of goods on the Grand, although after a break in continuity there is little chance of a return of working boats. As with most other waterways throughout the British Isles, the future must lie very definitely in development for amenity use.

A passage of the Grand Canal provides a slow-moving panorama of rural Ireland that can probably not be appreciated in any other way. The grandeur of the Shannon and its vast expanses of open water lack the intimacy of the canal which comes into close contact with the farming, architecture and history of the country. Elevated above bogland for a large part of its course, the Grand Canal is Ireland at its most basic and tourist-unfrequented self. Moreover, although now lacking the clamour of its commercial traffic, this is one waterway where one strongly feels that the boats and boat people left only yesterday and that the original reason for its construction remains alive in the deserted locks, bridges and warehouses. The British canal enthusiast cannot fail to respond to the atmosphere of the Grand.

*Shannon Harbour*  About 2m upstream of Banagher on the Shannon, the Grand Canal crosses from one side of the river to the other. On the west bank can be seen the decayed remains of the first lock on the 14m Ballinasloe branch, last used in 1959. As it lacks features of any great interest, restoration of the line for pleasure craft use seems unlikely at the present time. A late nineteenth-century cruising guide mentions the attractions of Ballinasloe's great October cattle fair, and indeed transport of cattle by water from this town was for many years a feature of trade on the branch, with special boats operated by the Grand Canal Company reserved for this purpose. There are a harbour and warehouses at the terminus, where canal passengers once transferred to Bianconi coaches on their journey from Dublin to Galway.

Locks 35 and 36 were constructed larger than the remainder between the Shannon and Dublin to accommodate Shannon steamers entering Shannon Harbour, where there was a transfer of goods and earlier passengers between the smaller canal boats. The Harbour is now a sleepy village, like so many decayed inland ports whose commercial activity has vanished. Lining the southern bank of the canal, grey stone warehouses, two of them with rounded gables, neat Georgian houses for company officials and the huge ruined Canal Hotel, together comprise an elegant complex. Like its 4 counterparts on the Grand, the hotel's days in that capacity were short-lived. During the late 1940s it had descended to a tenement block, and now its ivy-clad walls and ruined interior are a refuge for scores of wild birds. But Shannon Harbour is far from being a depressing place, for there is an active boat repair yard, with canopy extending over the water, and a drydock. The village street boasts the usual Irish bar and general store and an antiquated post office. Full services are available in Banagher, about 3m to the SW.

Compared with their counterparts on English canals, the Irish canal locks are quick to fill or empty, with a good supply of paddles (or racks, as they are known here). Keepers are generally familiar with the care required in regulating the water when a pleasure boat is working uphill, but it is strongly recommended that lines are firmly made fast fore and aft.

*Belmont* (4m 1f)  Here is the first double lock – two chambers, one leading directly into the next via an intermediate set of gates. The lower chamber is spanned by an accommodation bridge, which, like others at locks, includes no towpath under the arch, making for difficulties in working a boat through. The village stands on the River Brosna, crossed by a fine bridge with weir and mill. The Brosna flows into the Shannon at Shannon Harbour and accompanies the canal for 13m to Pollagh, its place alongside then being taken first by the Clodiagh River and then by the Tullamore River into Tullamore.

*Ferbane* (7m)   Shallow wooded cuttings and quite fertile farmland now begin to give way to great tracts of bogland. With few home-based coal supplies, Ireland relies on dried turf (peat in England) as a fuel. Throughout much of the journey to Dublin one may see turf workings. Until quite recent times carriage of this fuel by canal boat was a regular sight, and during World War II huge stacks of turf could be seen in Phoenix Park, Dublin, where the material was stockpiled. Both the traditional workings can be seen in operation on the bogs as well as the great Governmental mechanical plants, where supplies for the power stations and domestic consumption (briquettes) are produced. A frequent term in the sale of property in Ireland is 'rights of turbary', ie rights to cut fuel from the bog. Small gangs of country people using long spades known as slanes, barrows and donkey carts are to be seen from the canal working at the face of dark brown cliffs of a treacly consistency, cutting supplies of turf for the winter. Cutting generally takes place in May. Excellent descriptions of this and many other facets of Irish rural life can be found in *Irish Folk Ways* by E. Estyn Evans (Routledge & Kegan Paul, 1967).

On the southern bank rise the towers of Ferbane generating station, although the village of Ferbane lies about 1m to the north from Armstrong Bridge. All supplies can be obtained in Ferbane, where a Georgian cement-rendered house bears the name Gallen Priory, from a fifth-century monastery situated between the house and the Brosna of which few traces survive. Part of the shaft of an intricately carved early stone

*Grand Canal. Cutting turf for fuel on the navigation's banks*

cross and fragments of a number of eighth- to eleventh-century gravestones are displayed in the ruins of a fifteenth-century parish church (national monument).

McCartney Aqueduct, an inscribed stone arch carrying the canal over the Silver River, is followed in about 4m by the little waterside village of Pollagh.

*Rahan* (16m 4f)  This is the end of the bog for the present. Here are the remains of the ancient monastery of Rahan together with 3 small churches (2 in ruins). Just beyond Corcoran's Bridge there is a jetty on the south bank serving the Thatch Inn, one of surprisingly few public houses that appear to have been built especially to serve the canal. Charleville and Huband Aqueducts now in turn carry the waterway over the Clodiagh River. Standing next to the river and the canal by the eastern aqueduct is the battered but substantial ruin of Ballycowan Castle. There was a structure here in medieval times, but what now remains is largely the fortified house built by Sir Jasper Herbert in 1626. Like many Irish ruins, no attempt is apparent to save the castle from further decay and parts serve as a shelter for cattle from the adjoining farm buildings.

*Tullamore* (22m 4f)  Beyond Lock 29, on the north bank, stands the ruined Shra Castle, built in 1588 by John Briscoe. In complete contrast is Charleville Castle in the Georgian Baronial style, about 1m to the south. This mock fortification, the work of Francis Johnston in 1801, stands in a deer park with magnificent oaks.

Tullamore is a very fine town, with prosperous, brightly painted shops and a pleasant square, a welcome change after the rather poor countryside and desolate boglands. It is of comparatively recent origin, for in 1785, when still a village, it was destroyed in an accident to a great balloon. After rebuilding, it replaced Daingean as the county town of Offaly. There is a concentration of locks here, starting with 2 on the western approaches, followed in turn by another 6 to the east. There can be few safer places to leave an unattended boat than on a rural reach of Irish waterway, but town youngsters in the Republic are notoriously unable to control their curiosity, and mooring should not be attempted until the safety of the harbour is reached. Passing the stone waterside buildings of the whiskey distillery, one of Tullamore's best-known industries and one providing a considerable traffic for the canal boats in the past, the canal reaches the harbour entrance 2 bridges after Lock 27 on the south bank. Proceed down the 200yd arm until the very end and you will be surprised to find an opening on the right leading into a large concealed basin surrounded by warehouses. This has become one of the chief maintenance centres for repair work to the canal, so that generally several of the Grand Canal Company fleet of barges retained for maintenance can be found equipped with their 15hp Bolinder semi-diesels. There is a good stone-lined drydock and facilities for fuelling and repair of cruisers. Another of the chain of canal hotels, the Presbytery, stands by the harbour.

Tullamore lies at the crossroads of several important routes from Birr, Mountmellick, Portarlington and Clara and is consequently a convenient place to change boat crews. About 10m due S and SW is the Slieve Bloom mountain range, with peaks over 1,500ft.

After passing through the 6 locks eat of Tullamore, one may see (left) the abandoned Kilbeggan branch, which was last used about 1940. It has no locks and could well be restored if pressure of pleasure traffic on the main line ever reaches the proportions of some English canals. There is a harbour at the terminus, just outside Kilbeggan.

*Daingean* (31m)   From the Tullamore locks there is a 25m level pound with the exception of single locks at Ticknevin and Lowtown. Situated in the Bog of Allen, through which the canal passes, Daingean takes its name from the medieval island fortress of O Conor Faly. Mary Tudor named the place Philipstown after her husband, Philip II of Spain, and until 1833 it was the seat of King's County. With the formation of the Republic, both town and county name were changed. Now Daingean is of little importance, with buildings affected by subsidence as the level of the bog has altered. An interesting local industry is the manufacture of turf briquettes, clean and shiny blocks of compressed peat, at a factory near the waterway on the south bank outside the town centre. At a number of places between here and Robertstown massive mounds of drying turf covered with polythene sheeting are noticeable. The plant life of these damp but springy bogs is of considerable interest, for, apart from masses of yellow gorse, bracken and common heather, drifts of white-tufted bog cotton flourish, with several varieties of wild orchid and insect-eating sundew plants.

Preparation of turf is a large state industry, with its own railway system connecting the bogs being worked and the processing plants. The railway crosses the canal several times, the track being carried over vertical-rising liftbridges, or – between Killeen and Toberdaly Bridges – a cantilever. Bridge-keepers are in attendance to open these crossings for pleasure craft, and they seem invariably to do so the moment the boat comes into view. Trains are hauled by little diesel locomotives, the wagons carrying milled peat for the generating stations consisting of flat bogies with wire mesh sides.

Croghan Hill, about 1m to the NW, stands 769ft above the bog and provides good views. On the hill are several holy wells, the remains of Croghan Castle, and two churches in ruins.

*Rhode* (36m 4f)   This small village, providing basic services, is situated about 1m north of Rhode Bridge, from which it can be reached. The nearby generating station, with its twin cooling towers, has brought a new prosperity to what was once a depressed area.

*Edenderry* (43m)   Any canalside town that has made the effort to welcome visitors arriving by water surely deserves a visit. Quite apart from its most attractive water-front, the facilities offered by this little town must rate as high as any on the Grand Canal. It stands at the terminus of a wide well-cared-for arm 1m off the main line and to the N. A wide sweep is necessary to navigate a sizeable boat beneath the pretty stone junction bridge. Standing on a high embankment well above the level of the bog and the town itself, the banks of the branch are rather prone to breaching. Bursts occurred in 1849 and again in 1916. A convenient water tap (key held by the chemist's shop, opposite) stands beside the terminal warehouse. Every advantage should be taken of such facilities, which are generally less common than on the British water-ways. Edenderry possesses a lively and flourishing main street of considerable width and length, and is on the main T41, almost equidistant from Enfield and Daingean. The local curate has himself landscaped the banks of the harbour with flowers, shrubs, trees and grass, producing an unselfconscious amenity that many more important canalside local authorities should take note of. The local children appear to have gained a reputation for interfering with boats. In 1970 the author's cruiser was molested, no doubt by the offspring of an earlier generation who bothered L. T. C. Rolt shortly after World War II.

A market and shoe-making town, Edenderry, stands near the edge of the English Pale, with the result that there are many border castles nearby. To the east of the canal harbour stands Blundell's Castle, in ruins on a hilltop.

Back on the main line, Blundell Aqueduct carries the canal over a road from whose level the structure is locally known as 'the tunnel'. Out once more on to the Bog of Allen, another peat briquette factory and two opening rail bridges follow Ticknevin Lock. For a number of miles there is no human habitation as the peat bogs extend to the horizon, but, especially to a visitor from outside Ireland, this fairly typical Midland scenery is far from boring.

*Lowtown* (54m)   Within sight of the great Allenwood generating station cooling towers, north of the canal, is the junction of the main line and the Barrow line (see p 463). Apart from Lowtown Lock, the final one before the summit level, there is little to see. One of the longest established cruiser-hire firms has a base here, and the water is of a notable clarity – so clear, in fact, that the lock-keeper, if asked for drinking water, will trundle a diesel pump on a hand cart to the lockside and proceed to fill the boat's tanks from the canal. Set into one wall of the lock is a canal authority diesel supply line, but this is now used for their own maintenance craft only, and there seems to be no way, official or otherwise, of buying some, in spite of its great scarcity along the canal. At the upper end of the lock the Milltown Feeder branches off to the SE in line with the Barrow Navigation. While officially described as unnavigable, it can be used by sizeable craft for about 2m, until further progress is halted by a crude footbridge nearly at water level. Supplied by St James' Wells on the northern edge of the Curragh, the Milltown is the main feeder to the Grand Canal. The same water is used by Messrs Guinness' Dublin brewery, not the waters of the River Liffey, as is popularly supposed. A convenient bar is situated by a canal bridge at Kilmeagh about 1m 4f from Lowtown.

About 8m due S is the Curragh, 5,000 acres of unfenced arable country, famous for its army camp and the headquarters of Irish horse racing. About 12m from Lowtown on the L180 road, lies Kildare, the county town, with a cathedral and many other attractions worth visiting.

*Robertstown* (55m)   The approach to this once important staging point on the packet-boat run between Dublin and the Shannon, with the Canal Hotel framed in the arch of Binn's Bridge, might well give one the impression of a still important canal town. But Robertstown is a sleepy little village whose past activity briefly returns for a short while during the annual canal 'festa', staged each summer. The exterior of the fine hotel (1801) is well preserved, though it never flourished in its intended role. After a chequered career it is now a canal museum whose interior, for most of the year, is slightly decayed and musty, and whose range of exhibits is very limited. An interesting survival at Robertstown is the oldest boat on the canal, a wooden horsedrawn barge named *Pomeroy*, used for passenger trips during the festa. Stone and whitewashed buildings, including garda (police) station and pub, stand alongside the wide quay. Across the water another very pretty group of thatched cabins lies slightly below canal level. The waterway curves round the dominating hotel, with its backdrop of tall trees. It is an enchanting place to linger, and, less decayed than similar Shannon Harbour, must rate as the most evocative settlement of the Irish canal age.

*Landenstown* (59m 7f)   The summit is supplied by the Black Wood feeder, entering the canal near Haeley's Bridge. Some of the finest scenery on the waterway now follows as the route starts to descend towards Dublin through Locks 18–16. Near Lock 17 stands the beautiful Landenstown House, a Queen Anne mansion in a wooded park. The 4-arched stone Leinster aqueduct carries the canal over the River Liffey, where there is a small pumping station to draw river water into the navigation when required.

*Sallins* (63m)   An 8m branch to Naas (61m 4f) to the south is disused and weedy, but restoration has been proposed and could quite easily be accomplished. Sallins is a useful village for supplies, followed within 3m by Locks 15 and 14 and the Morell feeder.

*Lyons Lock* (69m 1f)   Lyons House and estate by the side of the canal is now an agricultural college. Lock 13 is 2-rise, and as with Lock 12 at Lucan Bridge, the chambers widen at the centre. It is likely that this was an experimental design intended to prevent the walls caving inwards. A tree-lined reach follows Lock 13 before arriving at an embankment from which there are magnificent views of the Dublin mountains to the south. The approach to Lock 12 is through a rock cutting.

*Clondalkin* (76m 1f)   The waterway has now reached the outskirts of Dublin, with 12 locks in the final 7m. No 9, by Clondalkin Bridge, is notable for a double chamber. Beyond are filter beds where water is taken from the canal for the manufacture of Guinness.

*Dublin* (79m 3f)   The main line is normally taken to end at Suir Road Bridge. James' Street Harbour at the end of a branch is partly filled in and choked with rubbish. For several miles before the city centre the canal becomes unkempt, passing through drab surroundings. Dublin children are notorious for their interference with boats. If at all possible, it is best to cruise this length during school term time. (The problem is in no way exaggerated!) The Circular Line of the canal (Ringsend Branch) connects the main line with the River Liffey, with 8 locks in 3¾m. The former passenger boat terminal harbour at Portobello has been filled in, but the canal hotel remains in the same style as those at Shannon Harbour and Robertstown. The waterway passes through the city streets, shaded by trees and overlooked by gracious Georgian terraces. Two huge basins at Ringsend are virtually deserted by traffic, but beyond the Sea Lock can be seen ships on the Liffey. It is only a short distance to Dublin Bay. This is the gateway to Ireland's inland waterways for pleasure craft able to brave the sea passage from England.

No attempt can be made here to describe Dublin, except for the passing remark that it is a beautiful and lively city and the centre of commercial and cultural activities in the Republic. An excellent account will be found in *The Shell Guide to Ireland*.

### NEAGH, LOUGH, AND RIVER BANN

From The Barmouth, 2½m west of Portstewart on the north coast of Ulster to Portadown, via Lough Neagh; 65½m with 5 locks. This is a little known but most interesting cruising area, equally suited to craft that enter from the sea or are brought overland and launched off trailers. The navigation is composed of the Lower Bann (tidal from the coast to Cuts Lock, Coleraine) which enters Lough Neagh at Toome. The waterway then continues through the huge inland sea of Lough Neagh, 17m long and 11m wide, the largest freshwater lake in the British Isles. At its southern end the navigation joins the Upper Bann, providing a link with Portadown, 8½m away (the unnavigable Bann continues to its source in the Mountains of Mourne, east of Newry). In addition to the mileage total, above, the River Blackwater is navigable from the south-west corner of Neagh to Moy, 7½m.

Maximum dimensions for craft are 100ft × 18ft × 6ft draught (this is sometimes reduced to 4ft 6in when levels fall on the Lower Bann) × about 13ft headroom (the limiting factor is Coleraine road bridge; other bridges have swing spans, opened by advance arrangement if necessary, but clearance under the spans when closed varies, and at times is reduced to as little as 7ft).

Lough Neagh lay at the heart of Ulster's decimated waterways network. Lost connections include the Tyrone Navigation from Coalisland to the River Blackwater, where work began as early as 1729 (open 1787–1954); the 25m Lagan Canal between Belfast and Neagh (open 1794–1954 and 1958); the Newry Canal, 18½m from Newry to Portadown on the Upper Bann (open 1742–1959); and the 45m Ulster Canal, connecting Charlemont on the River Blackwater with the River Finn on Upper Lough Erne (open 1841–1931).

*Coleraine* (7m)   The tidal estuary is one of the prettiest parts of the Bann, with fine bathing beaches and sandy golf courses. This is not a difficult section even for small inland craft. Comprehensive cruising directions are contained in a guide to the system published by the River Bann Association at Coleraine. Gradually the channel

*River Bann. One of Ulster's largest marinas at Ballysally near Coleraine* (Northern Ireland Tourist Board)

narrows to 200yd wide, with steeply sloping banks. Commercial coasters trade as far as Coleraine Bridge. St Patrick is reputed to have built a church here in the fifth century, and the Danes rowed up the Bann 500 years later to burn the priory and set up a fleet on Lough Neagh. The present town dates from 1613, when it was established as one of the leading Plantation towns and colonised by settlers from the British mainland. From Cutts Lock (9m) to Neagh (39m) the river climbs to 50ft above sea level, passing through lush yet isolated countryside, meadows alternating with forestry plantations. In times of flood considerable quantities of surplus water pass through the navigation's weirs, forced towards the sea by the vast lough and its tributaries.

*The Cutts* (9m)   Former rapids and a waterfall were blasted away in the seventeenth century to enable timber bound for England to be floated through in rafts, hence the name. All locks are manned and must only be worked by keepers. Width of the navigation varies from 50 to 150yd and a certain degree of care is necessary to avoid shoals.

*Kilrea* (17m)   Beyond Carnroe Lock (19m) and Movanagher Lock (20m) is the pleasant little linen and fishing town of Kilrea. The river is so prolific a source of fish that servants used to stipulate in their terms of employment that they would not be fed on salmon more than thrice weekly!

*Portna Double Lock* (23m)   Situated in fine rolling country, this is a real waterways curiosity, for immediately upstream of the 2-rise staircase chamber the whole width of the channel is occupied by a drydock. It is advisable to ascertain in advance if this is being used and the way ahead consequently barred.

*Lough Beg* (34m)   Beyond a wide river reach through Portglenone (30m) the Bann passes into Lough Beg, a shallow lake with reedy sides, about 3m × 1m. There are several islands, including Church, site of an early monastery and now with a tall eighteenth-century spire. Wildfowl abound, among them the rare ruffs and godwits.

*Toome* (37m)   A small town on the Belfast–Derry road, with range of facilities close to the short canal that links Beg with Neagh. The lock here is unusually busy with commercial traffic, a rarity in Ireland, and up to 15 sand barges every day pass through after dredging operations in the lough.

*Lough Neagh*   Covering 153 sq m of mainly open water with a small number of islands at the southern fringes, the lake provides excellent sailing. Commercially it is navigated by sand barges (the shores are frequently of fine sand), and open fishing craft used to catch pollen, a type of freshwater herring found only in Neagh. As would be expected, conditions can become quite rough in adverse weather. Surrounding land is generally quite low. An up-to-date chart does not appear to be available at the time of writing, but navigation is not difficult, especially if boats travel about ½m from the shore, thus avoiding rocky points known as 'rigs' that often terminate in a bushy island or underwater shallow known as a 'flat'. There are numerous small fishing-boat jetties where you can normally moor by arrangement. The chief town is Antrim, in a bay at the NE corner, with public cruises aboard the *Maid of Antrim* and facilities in the town about 1m away. South of Antrim Bay is Moore's Quay boatyard, while beyond that Ram's Island, once inhabited, has a good anchorage near the south shore.

R

Small boats can penetrate a short distance up the Crumlin River. Kinnegoe Bay, from which the derelict Lagan Navigation leads, has a sheltered marina and yacht club.

*Upper Bann*    The entrance is at the south-west corner of Neagh, marked by posts. Care must be taken to avoid the wires of the Bannfoot 'chain' ferry near the mouth. A bridge carrying the M1 motorway lies 5m up. Portadown, head of navigation, is a small linen and manufacturing town, also well known for fruit and rose nurseries. Scenery on the river is not particularly interesting, for dredging has created rather high banks in places.

*River Blackwater*    The river flows into the lough a short distance west of the Upper Bann at Maghery, where the short canal is navigable. As on the Upper Bann, banks are high until one reaches the disused Coalisland Canal. The remainder of the route past low green hills and meadows is very agreeable. Shortly before Moy comes the first lock of the closed Ulster Canal, formerly the way through to the Erne. Boating facilities are planned at Moy, a pleasing village, with tree-lined square, laid out after the plan of Marengo in Lombardy.

### NEWRY SHIP CANAL

From Victoria Lock in Carlingford Lough to Albert Basin, Newry; $3\frac{1}{2}$m with 1 lock. Until its abandonment in 1949, navigation was continued for another $18\frac{1}{2}$m by the Newry Canal, leading to the Upper Bann. This waterway was constructed by 1742, considerably in advance of the first 'modern' canal in England. Maximum dimensions for the Newry Ship Canal are 220ft × 50ft 9in × 14ft 6in draught with unlimited headroom. In commercial use up to 1974, the Ship Canal is too short to have much pleasure cruising interest.

### SHANNON, RIVER

From Battlebridge, County Leitrim, to Limerick; 128m with 7 locks. There are several navigable branches and a selection of routes across the various loughs that produce a total mileage not far short of 150. Maximum craft dimensions for the whole river are 96ft × 19ft × 4ft 6in draught × 16ft 6in headroom above Killaloe and 13ft below (clearance to the sea via Ardnacrusha Lock is reduced to about 9ft 6in). The Shannon is a wonderful river, wild, amazingly spacious and in parts very beautiful. A considerable hire-cruiser industry has been encouraged by Government support during the 1960s and 1970s, but any hint of overcrowding must lie many decades away. Quite unlike any other river in these islands (it is incorrect to consider the Republic of Ireland as a part of Great Britain), the Shannon is like the backbone of Ireland, consisting in part of a series of 2 large lakes (loughs) and 11 smaller ones. One of these, Lough Ree, contains 39 sq m of island-dotted water and is about 18m in length. The other major lough, Derg, is even longer at 24m. Due caution should be exercised in navigating these inland seas, which demand skills rather different from those required to pass through a conventional canal or river.

While parts of the river and its loughs have been navigable since ancient times, it was not opened throughout as a continuous route for barges until the 1760s. Substantial improvements were made in the mid-nineteenth century as part of a scheme to alleviate famine.

*Battlebridge* Now the upstream limit of the river, it was possible to continue a further 4¼m via the Lough Allen Canal, which was closed about 1930 when levels were altered under a hydro-electric scheme. Battlebridge Lock is derelict, but consideration may be given to its restoration.

*Leitrim* (1m) A village situated off the Shannon on what remains of the Ballinamore & Ballyconnell Canal. It is now possible to navigate only as far as the bridge. The 38m canal with 16 locks was opened in 1859 to connect with Upper Lough Erne over the Ulster border, but it was derelict 10 years later and never saw the passage of more than a handful of craft. Not surprisingly, much discussion has been noted since World War II with the hope that some day the B&B will be restored, so uniting the wonderful cruising grounds of the Erne with the waters of the Shannon. Technically this would seem feasible, and tourist authorities both sides of the border are keen, but little is likely to happen until a more stable political situation prevails. The Shannon continues downstream to a junction with the Boyle River, near Tumna.

*Boyle River* This provides almost 10m of navigable water between the Shannon and the beautiful tree-fringed Lough Key. As on other lakes of the network, navigation markers indicate the correct course to take through Lough Drumharlow. It is essential for boats to carry good binoculars, large-scale charts and other equipment, such as a suitable anchor and preferably an echo-sounder. The Boyle reverts to a winding channel, where the bottom is rocky in places. A small lough below Cootehall (hire-cruiser station) precedes Oakport Lough, reed-fringed and leading to Knockvicar Quay. The keeper for Clarendon Lock, some 800yd upstream, will be located here. The lock is situated in leafy lush surroundings at the eastern side of Lough Key. This is without doubt one of the most splendid of all the Shannon lakes, with some 32 wooded islands and views of the Curlew Mountains to the west. Most craft head for a small sheltered harbour on the south shore at Rockingham, now developed as the Lough Key Forest Park. Since it was burnt out in 1957, Rockingham House, designed by John Nash, has been a gaunt but romantic ruin standing high above the lake in an exquisite park. It has now, regrettably, been demolished. Ruins will be seen on Castle Island, Trinity Island (an abbey) and Hog's Island (remains of a church). One can navigate to Drum Bridge, SW corner of the lake, to about 1¼m from Boyle, with its impressive twelfth- and thirteenth-century Cistercian abbey ruins, or to a superb sandy beach called Doon on the west shore.

*Carrick-on-Shannon* (5m 3f) Since the late 1960s Government aid has assisted development of extensive hire-cruiser facilities, for the town is well situated as a holiday base. One firm, Emerald Star Line, is a subsidiary of Messrs Guinness. This is a busy little town, deriving much of its prosperity from summer tourists. Navigation passes through Lough Corry, midway between Carrick and Jamestown.

*Jamestown* (10m 6f) The river is navigable for a short distance to Jamestown Quay, by the bridge. A weir lies beyond. The route for downstream craft is via the Jamestown Canal and Albert Lock, a curiously British combination of names that persists. Remains of fortifications in Jamestown, a former royal borough, include a gateway over the main street. As with so many other Irish towns, it is a tiny place, for outside of Dublin depopulation has long been the trend. The countryside is positively littered with abandoned castles and derelict mansions, telling their own story of the nation's troubled history.

*Drumsna* (12m 4f)　This was the navigable limit of the Shannon until opening of Jamestown Cut. A small harbour is reached by turning upriver below the tail of Albert Lock. The loop of river between Drumsna and Jamestown is very attractive, fast-flowing and rocky.

*Lough Tap* (13m)　This small lake is crossed at its northern end by a bridge carrying the Mullingar–Sligo railway.

*Lough Boderg* (14m)　A large sheet of water, with rocky shores. The through route lies towards its eastern side.

*Carnadoe Lakes*　A fine cruising ground, offering a choice of ways through reed-bordered loughs. The entrance is near the SW corner of Lough Boderg. After passing through extensive reed-beds, along a marked channel in Carnadoe Lough, one can either cruise the length of Grange Lake to moor at a quay, or take the Kilglass Cut, run through Kilglass Lough and discover the little Mountain River, navigable for about 1m.

*Lough Bofin* (16m)　Another large lake with a highly irregular outline. At certain times a severe chop can build up and, as on other Shannon lakes, it is possibly wise not to trust an anchorage in mid-channel. Overnight moorings are best found on the river sections (provided the banks are not rocky) or in one of the little harbours. One of these, Dromod, has been restored in recent years for pleasure cruisers. Situated on the east side of Bofin, its entrance is concealed and one must place complete trust in the accuracy of the chart if approaching in an onshore wind. A pair of markers indicate the opening, leading to a sheltered quay. It is satisfying indeed to reach this haven and to see white-topped waves breaking on the shore of the lough outside.

*Rooskey* (19m 3f)　A lifting span in the road bridge increases headroom from 11ft to 18ft. Elsewhere, lower bridges require opening for even the smallest cruisers to pass. It is amazing to realise that during the 1950s there were proposals to replace these structures by low-level fixed bridges! The Shannon is the most important feature of the village, situated at the borders of Leitrim, Roscommon and Longford counties. The bars are lively places on summer evenings. Below Rooskey Lock the river broadens to 300yd in width.

*Lough Forbes* (23m)　A medium-sized, elongated lake with reeds at the edges.

*Camlin River* (25m)　At the southern end of Lough Forbes, a narrow river enters from the east. This leads eventually to Richmond Harbour (Cloondara), beginning of the disused Royal Canal that followed a route through Longford and Mullingar to Dublin, roughly parallel with the Grand Canal. Never commercially very successful, it was abandoned as recently as 1961 (just too early to be saved by the growth of pleasure cruising). The line is generally more interesting than that of the Grand, possessing several fine aqueducts and being in water throughout, though heavily

*River Shannon. Dromod, a tiny, but sheltered harbour on the shores of Lough Bofin*

weeded and with decaying locks. There is a classic description of a journey through the Royal just after the last war in L. T. C. Rolt's *Green and Silver*, still the best book on the waterways of the Republic. Richmond Harbour has been reopened to boats (1970) and is reached by working up through a single lock. There is a restored drydock and a row of stone cottages overlooking the broad basin. The Shannon may be rejoined via Cloondara Lock (also repaired in 1970), the Camlin River detour having bypassed a lock on the main channel of the Shannon at Termonbarry.

*Termonbarry* (27m)  Here is another opening span bridge (see the lock-keeper if your headroom exceeds 9ft). The village is named after St Barry, who died in AD 595. One of dozens of legends associated with the river concerns the boat of St Barry, a stone of several tons preserved in the church at Whitehall. It is said that the saint, wishing to cross the Shannon, stepped on to this rock, which was conveniently transformed into a boat. A long open reach extends through dredged cuttings to Lanesborough. Midway lies a light railway bridge carrying trains loaded with turf (peat), the fuel of power stations such as that by the waterway upstream of Lanesborough Bridge.

*Lanesborough* (34m 7f)  At the head of Lough Ree on the east bank of the river. On the other side of a 9-arched bridge is Ballyleague. A small harbour above the bridge provides good moorings.

*Lough Ree*  The Shannon above this point may be cruised without great difficulty by inexperienced boaters, but the expansive inland sea formed by Lough Ree and extending almost to Athlone is not really a place for complete novices, especially as there are few safe moorings at which to break the journey should the weather turn bad. It is recommended that, where possible, craft strange to the area should cross in company. Although hire boats are equipped with flares for use in the event of trouble, whether anyone will be within reach to render help in this isolated district is another matter! If the weather is uncertain, the journey is often best begun at daybreak, before the wind has risen. For all the warnings, Ree is a magnificent stretch of water, containing numerous islands. It is best to use the appropriate Admiralty chart, remembering that binoculars are required to follow the sequence of marker buoys. Safe moorings include a quay at Lecarrow, head of a short canal on the west shore; Barley Harbour, opposite; a jetty in Hodson Bay at the southern end; and the Porteena boatyard, part of the area known as the Inner Lakes, to the south-east. There are extensive religious ruins on a number of islands, chief of which is Inchcleraun, where St Diarmaid founded a monastery in the sixth century.

*Athlone* (54m)   The only town of any real size on the Shannon apart from Limerick. Nevertheless, it is small by British standards, with a population under 10,000. Almost midway between Dublin and Galway, Athlone has long had a strategic importance. A castle dating from 1210 overlooks the river. Quays were served by both pleasure steamers and (more recently) barges working between points on the Shannon, Grand Canal and Barrow. Beyond Athlone Lock the river follows a winding course mainly through flat countryside, passing a number of islands.

*Clonmacnoise* (64m)   One of Ireland's most important ecclesiastical settlements, this monastic city was founded by St Ciaran in AD 548. The various raids by Norsemen, Normans and Irish over the next 1,000 years were nothing compared with the destruction wrought by the English in 1552. The ruins, overlooking the bogs of the Shannon, include 8 churches, 3 high crosses, 2 distinctive round towers and more than 400 early tombstones bearing intricate Celtic designs. A jetty enables boats to moor and crew members to visit this remarkable site.

*Shannon Bridge* (69m)   Here is a river crossing with 16 arches to the bridge, a small harbour and useful village set back from the water. Beyond the confluence of the River Suck, entering from the west, the landscape is dominated by a power station.

*Shannon Harbour* (75m)   There is little of specific interest (but as always much wild and lovely countryside) until a 4-way junction with the Grand Canal at Shannon Harbour. Running quite straight across the bogs to the west, the 14m Ballinasloe Branch has been closed since 1961. Opposite, a short cut leads to the first lock of the Grand Canal main line, navigable to the coast via Dublin and, via the Barrow, to Waterford (see p 474).

*Banagher* (77m)   A long village, with fortified bridgehead (early nineteenth century). The framework of a derelict barge projects from the water like the skeleton of a stranded whale. Nearby will be seen a disused lock cut and keeper's house, although there is no longer any change in water levels on the navigation.

*Meelick Cut* (82m)   A multiplicity of small channels forming several large islands eventually lead to a fast-flowing weir bypassed by a cut ending at Victoria Lock. Note the heavy, manually operated winding machinery for the gates and the large paddle gear. Friar's Island and Big Island are passed on the starboard side. These are followed in turn by Ballymacegan, Long and Portland Islands, the channel in each case being clearly indicated.

*Portumna* (90m)   The busy road bridge must be opened for cruisers to pass, but, as this is Ireland, both boats and cars are generally content to wait a while. A short length of canal leads to the harbour upstream of the bridge, a convenient place to await a suitable time and favourable weather conditions before setting off into Lough Derg.

*Lough Derg*   A wonderful lake, with wooded shores, many safe ports of call and enough variety to provide different cruises every day during a fortnight's holiday. (At the other extreme, all the Shannon and its branches, together with much of the Grand Canal and Barrow *can* be cruised in a 2–3 week trip, but such a pace is the antithesis of the Irish way of life.) Warnings expressed about the dangers of Lough Ree equally apply to Derg. From the northern end of the' lough there are quays at Rossmore and Kilgarvan, and further south safety from a sudden squall may be found at the tiny Williamstown Harbour (west shore), though permission to land should be sought. Traditional open wooden fishing-craft in clinker are built here. Opposite, at Dromineer, there are a marina and a flourishing sailing club, which are located by homing in on the ruined castle. The broad section of lake around here can become quite rough off Parker Point, a rocky promontory. West of Youghal Bay, another safe harbour with a ruined tower is Garrykennedy, with a yard that builds pleasure craft. One of the most interesting places at which to moor is Mountshannon, on the western shore. Apart from facilities in the village, an excursion can be made by dinghy (there is insufficient water for most cruisers) to Inis Cealtra (Holy Island), about 1m SW. Get ashore by the rowing boat landing stage and investigate a number of early Christian ruins, including a round tower. Sheep and wild birds are the only permanent inhabitants. A welcome addition is a small enclosed summerhouse bearing an invitation to shelter there as long as it is left as found. In this part of rural Ireland any question of vandalism may be safely overlooked. At the western extremity of Derg navigation is possible through Scarriff Bay and up the twisting and reed-fringed river to Scarriff Quay, just under 2m from the lough. The journey is well worth making, although the village is an ugly, slightly industrialised place. At the southern tip of Derg a broad reach leads to Killaloe.

*Killaloe* (114m)   This is effectively the lowest point on the Shannon for hired craft. Following construction of Ardnacrusha Lock and Power Station down river, the lock and cut at Killaloe have become redundant, except when a strong flow passes under the town bridge. There are good boating facilities, public trips into Lough Derg and several good hotels. One of the town's chief features is St Flannan's Cathedral (Church of Ireland), dating from the twelfth century. Killaloe is well known as an angling resort, and Shannon fishing is better than perhaps any other river's in Europe. Killaloe is also a dinghy-sailing centre.

*Ardnacrusha* (125m)   A large artificial lake formed by the hydro-electric scheme comes south of Killaloe, and navigation is continued via a 7m Head Race canal, entered under a guillotine gate at Parteen. Telephone in advance to ensure that this is open. Ardnacrusha Lock comprises 2 chambers, the upper one actually within the power station complex. There can be very strong currents when the turbines are in use. The locks have a combined rise and fall amounting to an amazing 110ft, easily a record within these islands. The only method of getting ashore at the lower end is by means of a 60ft vertical ladder!

*Limerick* (128m)   The tidal navigation leaves the Shannon above the city, following instead the Abbey River. Ball's Bridge can only be passed at a favourable state of the tide. This is a dangerous area, and should only be cruised after expert advice has been obtained. Limerick is the fourth largest city in Ireland and originated as a Norse settlement in the early tenth century. Among its many attractions are St Mary's Cathedral (twelfth-century) and the remains of King John's Castle. There are commercial shipping docks with pleasure-craft berths. The upper part of the estuary is littered with markers, shoals and mudbanks, and the appropriate Admiralty charts are needed if a passage is to be made to or from the sea.

*River Shannon. A midsummer sunrise over the broad expanse of Lough Derg at Williamstown*

# Index